T0332776

Research Anthology on Artificial Neural Network Applications

Information Resources Management Association
USA

Volume I

Published in the United States of America by
  IGI Global
  Engineering Science Reference (an imprint of IGI Global)
  701 E. Chocolate Avenue
  Hershey PA, USA 17033
  Tel: 717-533-8845
  Fax: 717-533-8661
  E-mail: cust@igi-global.com
  Web site: http://www.igi-global.com

Library of Congress Cataloging-in-Publication Data

Names: Information Resources Management Association, editor.
Title: Research anthology on artificial neural network applications /
  Information Resources Management Association, editor.
Description: Hershey, PA : Engineering Science Reference an imprint of IGI
  Global, [2022] | Includes bibliographical references and index. |
  Summary: "This book covers critical topics related to artificial neural
  networks and their multitude of applications in a number of diverse
  areas including medicine, finance, operations research, business, social
  media, security, and more, covering everything from the applications and
  uses of artificial neural networks to deep learning and non-linear
  problems,"-- Provided by publisher.
Identifiers: LCCN 2021034008 (print) | LCCN 2021034009 (ebook) | ISBN
  9781668424087 (hardcover) | ISBN 9781668424094 (ebook)
Subjects: LCSH: Neural networks (Computer science)
Classification: LCC QA76.87 .R47 2022 (print) | LCC QA76.87 (ebook) | DDC
  006.3/2--dc23
LC record available at https://lccn.loc.gov/2021034008
LC ebook record available at https://lccn.loc.gov/2021034009

British Cataloguing in Publication Data
A Cataloguing in Publication record for this book is available from the British Library.

The views expressed in this book are those of the authors, but not necessarily of the publisher.

For electronic access to this publication, please contact: eresources@igi-global.com.

List of Contributors

Table of Contents

Section 2
Development and Design Methodologies

Section 3
Tools and Technologies

Section 4
Utilization and Applications

Section 5
Organizational and Social Implications

Section 6
Emerging Trends

Preface

Intelligent technologies such as artificial neural networks have played an incredible role in their ability to predict, analyze, and navigate different circumstances in a variety of industries ranging from medicine to education, banking, and engineering. Artificial neural networks are a growing phenomenon as research continues to develop about the applications, benefits, challenges, and impacts they have. These statistical modeling tools are capable of processing nonlinear data with strong accuracy and are an effective and efficient problem-solving method. Helping to solve real-world issues, the advantages of artificial neural networks are difficult to ignore, as more and more businesses begin to implement them into their strategies.

Staying informed of the most up-to-date research trends and findings is of the utmost importance. That is why IGI Global is pleased to offer this three-volume reference collection of reprinted IGI Global book chapters and journal articles that have been handpicked by senior editorial staff. This collection will shed light on critical issues related to the trends, techniques, and uses of various applications by providing both broad and detailed perspectives on cutting-edge theories and developments. This collection is designed to act as a single reference source on conceptual, methodological, technical, and managerial issues, as well as provide insight into emerging trends and future opportunities within the field.

The *Research Anthology on Artificial Neural Network Applications* is organized into six distinct sections that provide comprehensive coverage of important topics. The sections are:

1. Fundamental Concepts and Theories;
2. Development and Design Methodologies;
3. Tools and Technologies;
4. Utilization and Applications;
5. Organizational and Social Implications; and
6. Emerging Trends.

The following paragraphs provide a summary of what to expect from this invaluable reference tool.

Section 1, "Fundamental Concepts and Theories," serves as a foundation for this extensive reference tool by addressing crucial theories essential to understanding the concepts and uses of artificial neural network applications. Opening this reference book is the chapter "Fundamental Categories of Artificial Neural Networks" by Profs. Arunaben Prahladbhai Gurjar and Shitalben Bhagubhai Patel of Ganpat University, India, which provides an overview on the various types of neural networks like feed forward, recurrent, feedback, classification-predication. This first section ends with the chapter "A Journey From Neural Networks to Deep Networks: Comprehensive Understanding for Deep Learning" by Profs. Priyanka P. Patel and Amit R. Thakkar of Chandubhai S. Patel Institute of Technology, CHARUSAT University,

India, which discusses deep learning fundamentals and the recent trends and mentions many advanced applications, deep learning models, and networks to easily solve those applications in a very smart way.

Section 2, "Development and Design Methodologies," presents in-depth coverage of the design and development of artificial neural networks for their use in different applications. This section starts with "Artificial Neural Network Models for Large-Scale Data" by Prof. Vo Ngoc Phu of Duy Tan University, Vietnam and Prof. Vo Thi Ngoc Tran from Ho Chi Minh City University of Technology, Vietnam, which proposes algorthims to process and store big data sets succesfully. The section ends with "Artificial Neural Network (ANN) Modeling of Odor Threshold Property of Diverse Chemical Constituents of Black Tea and Coffee" by Prof. Jillella Gopala Krishna of NIPER Kolkata, India and Prof. Probir Kumar Ojha from Jadavpur University, India, which develops an artificial neural network model using odor threshold (OT) property data for diverse odorant components present in black tea (76 components) and coffee (46 components).

Section 3, "Tools and Technologies," explores the various tools and technologies used in the implementation of artificial neural networks for various uses. The section starts with "Tool Condition Monitoring Using Artificial Neural Network Models" by Prof. Srinivasa P. Pai of NMAM Institute of Technology, India and Prof. Nagabhushana T. N. from S. J. College of Engineering, India, which deals with the application of artificial neural network (ANN) models for tool condition monitoring (TCM) in milling operations in order to develop an optimal ANN model, in terms of compact architecture, least training time, and its ability to generalize well on unseen (test) data. The section ends with "A Novel Prediction Perspective to the Bending Over Sheave Fatigue Lifetime of Steel Wire Ropes by Means of Artificial Neural Networks" by Profs. Tuğba Özge Onur and Yusuf Aytaç Onur of Zonguldak Bulent Ecevit University, Turkey, which focuses on a novel prediction perspective to the bending over sheave fatigue lifetime of steel wire ropes by means of artificial neural networks.

Section 4, "Utilization and Applications," describes how artificial neural networks are used and applied in diverse industries for various technologies and applications. The section begins with "Literature Survey for Applications of Artificial Neural Networks" by Profs. Pooja Deepakbhai Pancholi and Sonal Jayantilal Patel of Ganpat University, India, which discusses the major applications of artificial neural networks and the importance of the e-learning application and presents an investigation into the explosive developments of many artificial neural network related applications. It ends with "Forecasting and Technical Comparison of Inflation in Turkey With Box-Jenkins (ARIMA) Models and the Artificial Neural Network" by Prof. Erkan Işığıçok of Bursa Uludağ University, Turkey and Profs. Ramazan Öz and Savaş Tarkun from Uludağ University, Turkey, which predicts inflation in the next period based on the consumer price index (CPI) data with two alternative techniques and examines the predictive performance of these two techniques comparatively.

Section 5, "Organizational and Social Implications," includes chapters discussing the impact of artificial neural networks on society and shows the ways in which artificial neural networks are used in different industries and how this impacts business. The section opens with "Comparative Analysis of Proposed Artificial Neural Network (ANN) Algorithm With Other Techniques" by Profs. Deepak Chatha, Alankrita Aggarwal, and Prof. Rajender Kumar of Panipat Institute of Engineering and Technology, India, which develops robust edge detection techniques that work optimally on mammogram images to segment tumor area and presents output results of proposed techniques on different mammogram images of MIAS database. It ends with "Forecasting Automobile Sales in Turkey with Artificial Neural Networks" by Profs. Aycan Kaya, Gizem Kaya, and Ferhan Çebi of Istanbul Technical University, Turkey, which aims to reveal significant factors which affect automobile sales and estimates the automobile sales in Turkey by using artificial neural network (ANN), ARIMA, and time series decomposition techniques.

Section 6, "Emerging Trends," highlights areas for future research within this field. The final section opens with "Artificial Neural Networks in Medicine: Recent Advances" by Prof. Steven Walczak of the University of South Florida, USA, which examines recent trends and advances in ANNs and provides references to a large portion of recent research, as well as looks at the future direction of research for ANN in medicine. The last section ends with the chapter "Convolutional Neural Network" by Prof. Mário Pereira Véstias of INESC-ID, Instituto Superior de Engenharia de Lisboa, Instituto Politécnico de Lisboa, Portugal, which focuses on convolutional neural networks with a description of the model, the training and inference processes, and its applicability and provides an overview of the most used CNN models and what to expect from the next generation of CNN models.

Although the primary organization of the contents in this multi-volume work is based on its six sections, offering a progression of coverage of the important concepts, methodologies, technologies, applications, social issues, and emerging trends, the reader can also identify specific contents by utilizing the extensive indexing system listed at the end of each volume. As a comprehensive collection of research on the latest findings related to artificial neural networks, the *Research Anthology on Artificial Neural Network Applications* provides researchers, computer scientists, engineers, practitioners, educators, strategists, policymakers, scientists, academicians, and students with a complete understanding of the applications and impacts of artificial neural networks. Given the vast number of issues concerning usage, failure, success, strategies, and applications of artificial neural networks in modern technologies and processes, the *Research Anthology on Artificial Neural Network Applications* encompasses the most pertinent research on the applications, impacts, uses, and development of artificial neural networks.

Section 1
Fundamental Concepts and Theories

Chapter 1
Fundamental Categories of Artificial Neural Networks

Arunaben Prahladbhai Gurjar
Ganpat University, India

Shitalben Bhagubhai Patel
Ganpat University, India

ABSTRACT

The new era of the world uses artificial intelligence (AI) and machine learning. The combination of AI and machine learning is called artificial neural network (ANN). Artificial neural network can be used as hardware or software-based components. Different topology and learning algorithms are used in artificial neural networks. Artificial neural network works similarly to the functionality of the human nervous system. ANN is working as a nonlinear computing model based on activities performed by human brain such as classification, prediction, decision making, visualization just by considering previous experience. ANN is used to solve complex, hard-to-manage problems by accruing knowledge about the environment. There are different types of artificial neural networks available in machine learning. All types of artificial neural networks work based of mathematical operation and require a set of parameters to get results. This chapter gives overview on the various types of neural networks like feed forward, recurrent, feedback, classification-predication.

CONVOLUTIONAL NEURAL NETWORKS

A CNN architecture consists of different ConvNet stages. For each degree winding of the following comparison module / Sub sampling order module. While the traditional clustering ConvNet modules conceal the average or most of the groups, this grouping uses LP. Ordinance and that, unless it is to become a parameter, as opposed to subtractive. Subtractive is not division, that is, on the average of the value of each of its immediate surroundings; own extended withdrawn(Lawrence,1997). Finally, as is known, also multi-stage the functions that are used in place of the same rank.

DOI: 10.4018/978-1-6684-2408-7.ch001

One-dimensional convolution is an operation between a vector of weight m 2 Rm and vector entries seen as a series of s 2 Rs. The carrier m is the convolution filter. In particular, we think of it as an insertion phrase and yes 2 R is a unique function value associated with the ith word of the phrase. The idea behind the one-dimensional convolution is to take the point product of the vector m with every m-gram in the sentence s another series c:

$$c_j = m|\ s_j - m + 1 : j \tag{1}$$

Equation 1 gives rise to two types of convolutions according to the scope of the J. Lo strait index the type of convolution requires that s ³ give me a series c 2 Rs-m + 1 with j going from m one s. The broad type of convolution does not have this requirements for s or m and give a series of c 2 Rs + m-1 where the index j varies from 1 to s +m - 1. Enter out of range values where i <1 where i> s are considered zero. The result of the narrow convolution is a partial sequence of the result of wide convolution (Cireşan,2011). Two types of one dimensional convolution are illustrated in Fig. 1.

Figure 1. Narrow and wide types of CNN
m=5

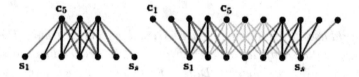

Figure 2. A classic convolutional network

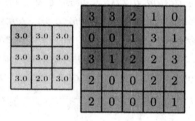

Why ConvNets Over Feed-Forward Neural Nets?

An image is just a matrix of values in pixels, isn't it? So why not paste the image (for example a description of 3x3 images into a 9x1 vector) and send it to a multi-part Perceptron for processing?

In the case of high quality imagery(Kalchbrenner,2014), the method may show sufficient scale during class imaging, but is low or poorly organized for complex images with pixel dependencies.

ConvNet is able to efficiently capture spatial and model dependencies in the image through the use of appropriate filters. The architecture is more efficient for the data structure due to the reduced number of parameters involved and the overload of the load. In other words, the network can be formed to better understand image stability.

Figure 3. Flattening of a 3x3 image matrix into a 9x1 vector

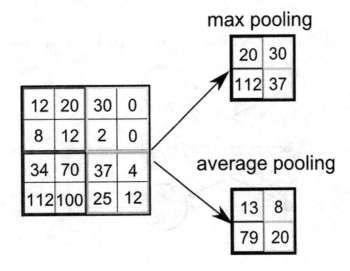

Input Image

In the figure we have a separate RGB image of the three color areas: red, green and blue. There are many color spaces that contain images: grayscale, RGB, HSV, CMYK, and so on.

You can imagine the intensity of the calculation when the images are the desired size, for example 8K (7680 × 4320). The role of ConvNet is to shrink the images into a simpler form to process, without losing the essential functions to get a good prediction. This is important when designing an architecture that is not only powerful for learning functions, but also scalable for large data sets.

Figure 4. 4x4x3 RGB Image

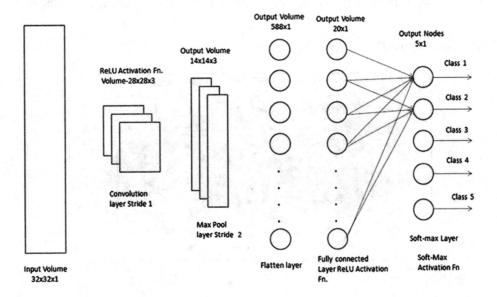

Convolution Layer — The Kernel

Figure 5. Convoluting a 5x5x1 image with a 3x3x1 kernel to get a 3x3x1 convolved feature

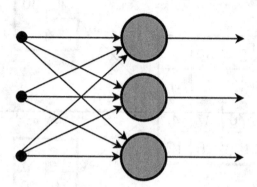

Image Dimensions = 5 (Height) x 5 (Breadth) x 1 (Number of channels, e.g. RGB)

In the above image, the green part looks like the image 5x5x1, Me. The factor involved in performing the phase operation in the first phase of the called phase is called the value, K, is shown by the radius. We have chosen K as the 3x3x1 matrix.

Core / Filter, K = 1 0 1

0 1 0

1 0 1

The kernel moves 4 or 9 times because of the length of the process = 1 (unsigned), each time or matrix multiplication process is performed between the K and P part of the image on which the kernel falls.

Figure 6. Movement of the Kernel

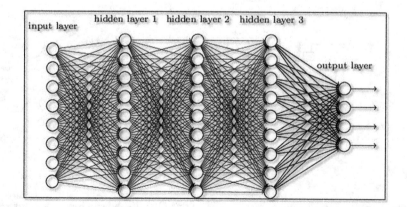

The filter moves to the right with the column type until it fills the width. As you progress, it moves down to the start (left) of the image as well as melting the value and adjusting the function so that the whole image is in good shape.

Figure 7. Convolution operation on a MxNx3 image matrix with a 3x3x3 Kernel

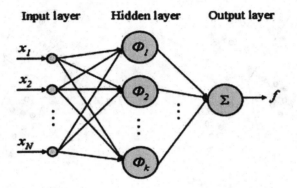

For multichannel (ie RGB) images, the kernel has a depth similar to that of the input image. Matrix multiplication is performed between Kn and In ([K1, I1], [K2, I2], [K3, I3]) and the total output is added along the ring to obtain an entity output joining a single-depth channel.

Figure 8. Convolution Operation with Stride Length = 2

Linear separability

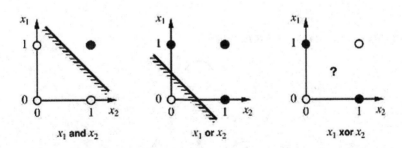

The purpose of the design is to remove high-step tasks, as a process, from a low-level image. ConvNets doesn't just need to be locked on one platform. In fact, the first ConvLayer was responsible for capturing small-scale events such as location, color, grid path, and so on. With the addition of a wall, design is like high-performance, so finding a network that is good at integrating images into a store is the way to go.

There are two types of service costs: one is that the link is decreasing relative to participation, the other is increasing in size or similarity. This is done by applying for an Undergraduate Degree in either a Secondary agreement or a Secondary degree.

Figure 9. 5x5x1 image is padded with 0s to create a 6x6x1 image

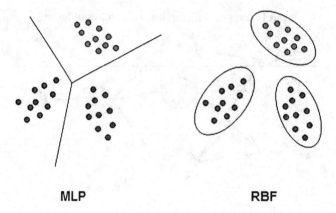

MLP   RBF

Same Padding (Boureau, 2010)

If we add the 5x5x1 image to the 6x6x1 image, write the 3x3x1 graph above and see that the only gene shown is the size of 5x5x1. That is why the name - paragraph is paper. On the other hand, if we perform the same operation without a table, we get a square with the same kernel components (3x3x1) - Advanced Manufacturing.

The following functions include various functions such as GIF files to help you better understand why we need to work with People and virtualization to deliver the best results for us.

Figure 10. 3x3 pooling over 5x5 convolved features

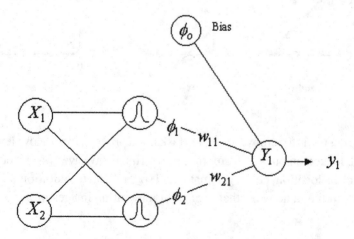

Pooling Layer

Like the bonding layer, the polar layer is responsible for reducing the size of the bonding process. This will reduce the processing power required to process the data by reducing the size. In addition, it is advisable to take in the main features of the visitors of rotation and positioning, thus keeping them in good working position of the model.

There are two types of pooling: max pooling and average pooling. Max Pooling returns the maximum value of the image segment covered by the kernel. On the other hand, drawing compression returns an average of the total value of the part of the image that contains the kernel.

Noise suppressant is also done by Max pooling. Generally it helps to remove noisy activations and do de-noising with region decrement. At next end Average pooling operate for dimensionality reduction as a noise suppressing system. The output is Average pooling is less effective than Max Pooling.

Figure 11. Types of pooling

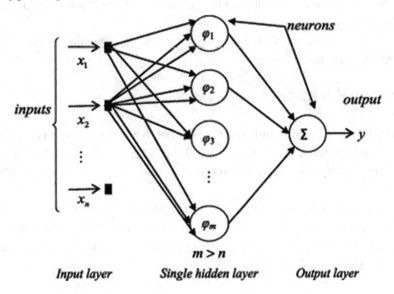

The broad layer and the cluster layer form an i-th tool of convolutional neuron networks. Depending on the complexity of the images, the number of components may be greater, but depending on the severity of the stress.

After following the above, we conducted a mod to understand the behavior. Moving forward, we will move on to the final version and feed the neural network for treatment.

The development of a real layer is a (usually) economical way to study non-linear relationships of layer (Baroni,2010). Layers as a method characterized by the flow of the extraction layer. The whole point of the fabric collection may not be a linear design at that point.

Figure 12. Classification — fully connected layer (FC Layer)

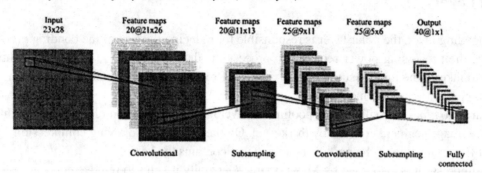

While our space has revolutionized image placement in the form that is appropriate for our multiple Perceptron, we respect the image in a combination of colors. Aviation information is provided in the neural network and in the progress, and latency is used for each level of training. For the most part, the feature can distinguish between high resolution images and other low resolution images and is analyzed using Softmax classification method.

There are many CNN platforms available that are become key to develop algorithms that are powerful and powerful for all AI anticipated future.

Feed Forward Neural Network

This neural network is one of the simplest simple networks, while data or inputs work in the same way. The data passes through the input and output fields at the output. This network of neurons may not be secret. In simple terms, it has an avant-garde interface and does not extend using standard classification functions.

Below are the networking and networking sites. Here, the price of a product or a product is calculated and the output is given. The result can be seen if it is higher than the price, ie the initial neuron (usually 0) as well as the active neuron with a positive output (usually 1) if it does not burn and eliminating the potential value (usually -1).

The anticipated neural network is an artificial neural network to which the connections between the nodes do not form a cycle. (Sermanet,2012) As such, it differs from recurrent neural networks.

The direct-acting neural network was the first and simplest type of artificial neural network designed. On this network, the information is only moved one way forward, from the input nodes to the hidden nodes (if any) and to the output nodes. No cycles or loops on the net.

One of the output nodes; tickets are fed directly to departures via a series of pesos. The sum of the products of weights and inputs is calculated in each node, and if the value is above the threshold (usually 0), the neurons are turned on and the value takes activation (usually 1); otherwise, the value is removed (usually -1). Neurons with this kind of activation function are also called artificial neurons or linear threshold units. In literature, the term perceptron often refers to networks that consist only of one of these units.

You can create a perctron using any value for enabled and disabled states whenever the threshold value is between the two.

Figure 13. A classic feed forward neural network

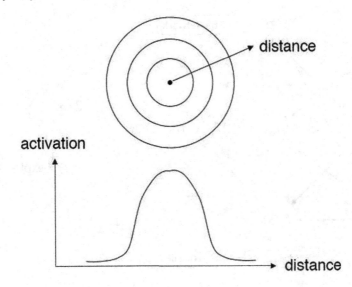

The tax collectors can be trained by a simple learning algorithm commonly called delta rule. Calculate the errors between the calculated output data and the output samples and use this option to create a weight adjustment, thus implementing a gradient descent form.

Single-layer perceptors can only study linearly separable patterns; in 1969, in a well-known monograph called Perceptrons, Marvin Minsky and Seymour Paper showed that it was impossible to study the XOR function of a single-layer drum network (however, it was known that multilayer perktrons were capable of producing any possible Boolean function.).

Although one threshold unit has rather limited processing power, it has been shown that parallel threshold units of the network can approximate any continuous function from a compact range of real numbers in the interval. This result can be found in Peter Auer, Harald Burgsteiner and Wolfgang Maass "The Rule of Learning for very simple universal approximators consisting of one layer of percetron" (Cireşan,2011).

A single layer neural network can calculate a continuous output instead of a passage function. A common choice is the so-called logistic function:

With this choice, a monolayer network is identical to the logistic regression model widely used in statistical modeling. The logistics function is also called sigmoid function. It has a continuous derivative, which allows its use in posterior propagation. This function is also preferable because its derivative is easily computable:

$$f'\left(x\right) = f\left(x\right)\left(1 - f\left(x\right)\right)\} f\left(x\right) = 1$$

(The fact that f satisfies the differential equation above can easily be shown by applying the Chain Rule)

A feed-forward neural network is classification algorithm galvanize by biological concept. There are number of simple neuron like refine unit formulated in layers and every entity in layer coherent with all other entity in preceding layer. There is no equality in all connections, every connection might have various potency or density. The knowledge of network are encode by weights on these connections.

Figure 14. The architecture of feed forward neural network

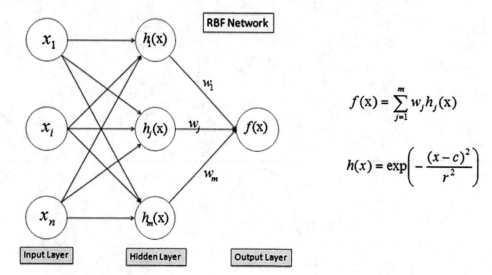

$$f(x) = \sum_{j=1}^{m} w_j h_j(x)$$

$$h(x) = \exp\left(-\frac{(x-c)^2}{r^2}\right)$$

The cost of training for the training sessions reflects the difference between the estimate made by our model and the exact target value that we are trying to achieve, which is a one-time price, he says the network is reviewing everything. Similar to machine learning cycles, manual control networks have also been created using slower learning. In this teaching method, an algorithm is used, such as the gradient.

To choose an exercise that I think increasingly worth taking another example of traditional models.

In cases where we compare the distribution model $p(j|i, \Sigma)$, and we use this for us in terms of information transfer between the train and the model is an affordable price. You can also choose to add to this number for x and y not modify in any part, in a way, in order to predict differs of distribution.

The distribution and use of the process is to be turned again because they are in the best of the two Properties. As it is written, the average cost function should be possible.

From the output of the activation depends on the price of the same is not part of the investors.

A particular form of cost function 100 (W, B, S Onan Sela), where W is the weight of the neural network, the network is destroyed R, S has entered the exercise is one of ideal is the desired exit from training him cf.

Some functions can be taken:

Quadratic Cost Function

$$C_{MST}\left(W, B, S^r, E^r\right) = 0.5 \sum_j \left(a_j^L - E_j^r\right)^2$$

This function is also namely like squared error, maximum likelihood, and sum squared error.

Cross-Entropy Cost Function

$$C_{CE}\left(W, E, S^R, E^R\right) = -\sum_{J}\left[E_j^r \ln a_j^L + \left(1 - E_j^r\right)\ln\left(1 - a_j^L\right)\right]$$

Exponential Cost Function

$$C_{EXP}\left(W, B, S^r, E^r\right) = \Gamma \exp\left[\frac{1}{\Gamma}\sum_{j}\left(a_j^L - E_j^r\right)^2\right]$$

Hellinger Distance Cost Function

$$C_{HD}\left(W, B, S^r, E^r\right) = \frac{1}{\sqrt{2}}\sum_{j}\left(\sqrt{a_j^L} - \sqrt{E_j^r}\right)^2$$

This is a function is also referred to as the statistical distance.

The output of those units that output layer. Their job is to get us the desired output or forecast to complete the operation so that the neural network to run. The output will be close to the selection function is taken. Nothing can be hidden from drive to drive the neural network can also be as a monitor.

The output is equally chosen;

The Linear Units

The proportions of the output unit used for an output of linear Gaussian output distributions, these are connected, according to a transformation that does not propose the compatible output level. Given the functions h, a linear vector layer of output of the generator:

$$\hat{Y} = W^T h + b$$

Linear Function Unit

This is tantamount to maximizing the linear minimize the superposition of bars with ignorance of the average, and the propaganda street makes it easier for most likely to support the Gaussian covariance distribution(Blunsom,2006).

The usefulness of these units is to say, that the lines do not become saturated, that is to say, what is the same as He is always, and does not come: there is not them. These units can therefore be a problem because according to their algorithms.

Sigmoid Unit Function

$$S\left(x\right) = \frac{1}{1 + e^x} = \frac{e^x}{e^x + 1}$$

To solve the above question of a binary kind, as we combine the top and the bottom of the output units have no probability. The Gulf components of the output unit 2, which uses a linear layer consists of calculating z = w * h B uses the activation function and then transformed into z are opposite. When at any time the loss of all rights and without hesitation others, such as the level of a square at the same time a little bit of error, it may be useful to saturate the experience of loss. Therefore, the most desirable.

Softmax Unit

The units are used for softmax output distributions multitudinali, because of the probability distribution of a discrete variable with n possible values, this function can also be considered as a bay associated with it, general manager of the probability distribution of the binary variable. Softmax. The function is defined as follows:

$$soft \max \left(z\right)_i = \frac{\exp\left(z_i\right)}{\sum_j \exp\left(z_i\right)}$$

When Sigmoid is running, the Softmax feature may also be weak, which means it can reduce obstacles to learning. In the case of Softmax, the outputs being larger, the units can always be filled when the entered values change.

These groups are dominated by the stock market because they are generally at Level 1 and not so much, and its value for one, is clear that other units of production are closer to value 0.

Hidden Units

Searching for the hidden unit type is also a powerful finding that no unit can ensure that everything is in order for every problem, but we still have units with a clear choice in the beginning. For example, the line numbers are changed or called Relu. It is widely used, because of this knowledge, rather than test cases, which, on the other hand, cannot be predefined before they work. Selecting the hidden option option will include trial and error, which requires a specific type of corrector to be properly managed and tested.

Possible options for hidden options are:

ReLU(Rectified Linear Units)

These functions use the activation function defined by $g(z)$

$$g(z) = \max\{0, z\}$$

Optimize similar to the linear rails are easy, and only 0. Since their role is always the case with a hearty side in unison. The direction of development of learning useful for the activation features that characterize the effects of second order.

Relu is able to have the disadvantage that they do not know the method of gradient is activated, in which there is none.

Radial Basis Function Neural Network

Typically, an RBFN is composed of three layers: the input layer, the RBF layer (masked layer), and the output layer. The masked layer inputs are the linear combinations of scalar weights and the input vector x=[ ] x1, x2, L, xn T, where the scalar weights are usually assigned. Thus, the complete input vector appears for each neuron of the hidden layer. Inbound vectors are mapped by radial base functions on each hidden node. The output layer produces a vector y = [ ] y1, y2, L, ym for m outputs by linearly combining the outputs of the hidden nodes to produce the final output. Figure 1 shows the structure of a single output RBF network; the network output can be obtained via

$$y = f\left(x\right) = \sum_{i=1}^{k} w_i \varphi_i\left(x\right)$$

where f (x) is the final output,)(i). denotes the radial basis function of the i-th hidden node, w_i denotes the hidden weight at the output corresponding to the hidden i-node, and k is the number total hidden nodes (Sun et al.,2009)

Figure 15. A typical radial basis function neural network

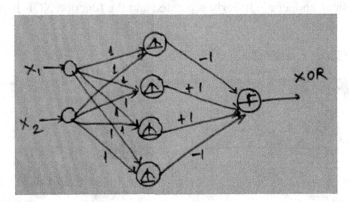

Ligament function, which describes the distance function between the center and the passenger multidimensional approach and a predefined vector. There are other types of radial basic functions. Q1 "RBFNN general education is divided into two stages

1. Determine the parameters of the radius functions, namely the Gaussian center and the propagation width. In general, the grouping method k-means, as a rule, here.
2. In real time, determine the way out of the weight management training process. Usually shorter mean square (LM) or recursive (RLS) squares are smaller.
3. Everything, the scene, first of all, is very important, and the place where, under the passage above, and from the moment of the number of centers, the performance of RBFNN itself.

One of the great benefits of RBF networks is learning (Zaremba,2014) The algorithm involves solving a linear problem and is therefore faster. Because of the linearity of the basic function, the network can do it. Create complex non-linear mappings. Theoretical learning strategies Can be created with changes of place and form Radial basic functions. The advantages of the linear learning algorithm it will always be lost. It is possible to choose from a variety of centers and functions Way. The natural option is to take Yi as the input vector Creating data, or XP time of its traffic. The number of hidden areas is less than the number of study areas.

If the network is used as a grouping model, the base number usually the operations are considered to be larger in size.

Inclusion criteria. Then, the hidden units plan the input vectors instead of the line.
The size of the quantity. Work can be divided into tasks
This is an upward trajectory even if it does not divide the root
Especially In this case, a layer of weight differs between the hidden values
And the output components are good at giving accurate signals
[Improving the Generalization Properties of Radial Basis Function Neural Networks]

In a single perceptron / multi-layer perceptron (MLP), we have only linear segmentation because it contains input and output levels (multiple layers hidden in MLP).

For example, functions and, or are linearly separated and the function XOR is not linearly different.

Figure 16. Chart for Linear separability.

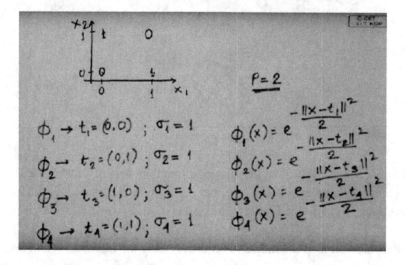

To separate non-linearities, at least one hidden layer is required.

What R RBNN does is convert the input signal to another format and feed it into the network to achieve linear separation.

B RBNN is structurally similar to perceptron (MLP)

Figure 17. Distinction between MLP and RBF

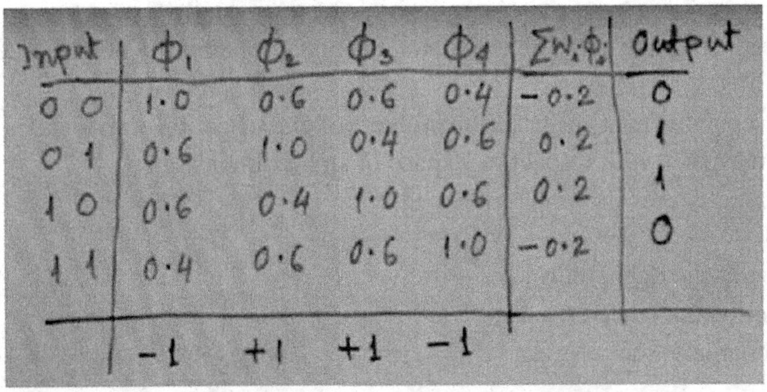

Input	ϕ_1	ϕ_2	ϕ_3	ϕ_4	$\Sigma w_i \phi_i$	output
0 0	1·0	0·6	0·6	0·4	−0·2	0
0 1	0·6	1·0	0·4	0·6	0·2	1
1 0	0·6	0·4	1·0	0·6	0·2	1
1 1	0·4	0·6	0·6	1·0	−0·2	0
	−1	+1	+1	−1		

RBNN is temperate of input, hidden, and output layer. RBNN is strictly limited to have exactly one hidden layer. We call this hidden layer as feature vector.

Figure 18. RBNN increases extents of feature vector.

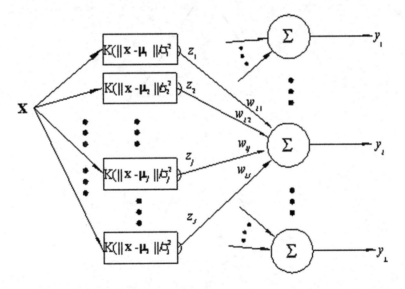

Figure 19. Simplest diagram shows the architecture of RBNN

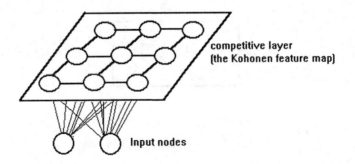

Before starting the classification problem, we apply a nonlinear transfer function to the function vector.

- When we increase the size of the object vector, the linear separability of the object vector increases.

The problem of separable non-linearity (the problem of classification of models) is strongly separable in a multidimensional space with respect to a space of small dimension.

[Cover's Theorem]
What is the function of the radial base?
In the middle we define the receiver $= T$
We map the conflict around the receiver.

Radian Basis Function(confront mapping) conventionally used by Gaussian Functions . So we define the radial distance $r = \|x- t\|$.

Figure 20. Radial distance and Radial Basis function with confrontal map

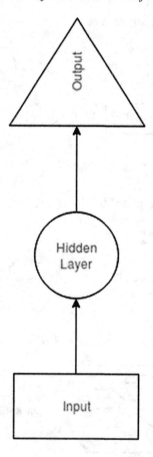

Gaussian Radial Function:= $\phi(r) = \exp(-r^2/2\sigma^2)$

where $\sigma > 0$

$$f(x) = \sum_{j=1}^{m} w_j h_j(x)$$

$$h(x) = \exp\left(-\frac{(x-c)^2}{r^2}\right)$$

Figure 21. Formula of RBF network

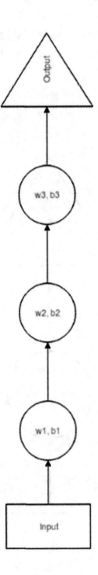

This is not only a division in the period when the linear combination of functions leads to the hidden output layer.

Example. XOR function:-

- I have 4 inputs and I will not increase dimension at the feature vector here. So I will select 2 receptors here. For each transformation function $\phi(x)$, we will have each receptors t.

Now consider the RBNN architecture,

- P:= # of input features/ values.
- M = # of transformed vector dimensions (hidden layer width). So M ^{3} P usually be.
- Each node in the hidden layer, performs a set of non-linear radian basis function.
- Now consider the RBNN architecture,
    - •:= # of input features/ values.
- M = # of transformed vector dimensions (hidden layer width). So M ^{3} P usually be.
- Each node in the hidden layer, performs a set of non-linear radian basis function.

Figure 22. Architecture of XOR RBNN

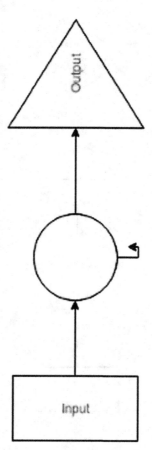

Output C will remain the same as for classification problems (a number of predefined class tags).
Only the nodes of the masked level perform the basic radiant transformation function.

The output level performs the linear combination of the outputs of the hidden level to give a final probabilistic value to the output level.

Figure 23. Transformation function with receptors and variances

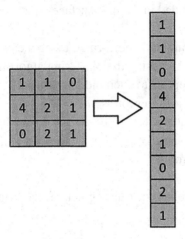

Figure 24. Output → linear combination of transformation function is tabulated

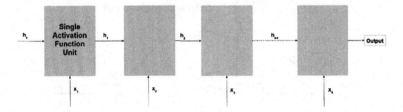

So the classification is performed only @ (masked level ® output level)

Training the RBNN:-

First, we must form the hidden level using the subsequent propagation.

Training Neural network training (subsequent propagation) is a method of adapting the curve. It adapts to a non-linear curve during the training phase. This involves the stochastic approach, which we call later propagation.

- For each of the nodes of the hidden layer, it is necessary to find t (receivers) and variance (σ) [variance - the diffusion of the radial basic function]

On the second phase of the training, we need to update the weighting vectors between the hidden layers and the output layers.

Layers In hidden layers, each node represents each basic function of the transformation. Any of the functions could satisfy the non-linear separability OR even the combination of a set of functions could satisfy the non-linear separability.

- Then, in our hidden layer transformation, all nonlinearity terms are included. Let's say that x^2+y^2+5xy; Everything is included in a hyper-surface equation (X and Y are inputs).

Therefore, the first step of the training is performed using a classification algorithm. We define the number of cluster centers we need. And using the clustering algorithm, we calculate the clustering centers, which are then assigned as receptors to each hidden neuron.

Do group N samples or observations in groups $M(N>M)$.

Therefore, the "groups" of output are the "receivers".

For each receiver, I can find the variance as "the square sum of the distances between the respective receiver and each nearest cluster sample": $=1/N*\|x–t\|^2$

- The interpretation of the first phase of training is that the "characteristic vector is projected onto the transformed space".

Figure 25. Complex diagram depicting the RBNN

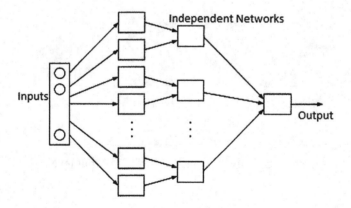

Training with RBNN is much faster than the multilayer Perceptron (MLP) ® requires many interactions with MLP.

We can define what is the function / function of each node in the RBNN encryption layer. This is very difficult in MLP.

(what should be the number of hidden positions and the number of hidden points) is this parameterization difficult in MLP. But this was not found on RBNN.

The configuration will take longer in RBNN than in MLP.

Kohonen Self Organizing Networks

Among various network Kohonen's networks is one of diverse of self-organizing neural networks. The strength of self-organize offers new possibilities - adaptation to previously unknown input data. It look like the way of natural learning and that is used in our brains, where patterns are not defined. These patterns take shape during the learning process associated with normal work(Kiang,2001). Kohonen's networks are synonymous with a whole group of networks that use self-organizing, competitive learning methods. We set up signals at the entrances of the network and then select the winning neuron, the one that best matches the input vector. There are many rivalry-based subtypes that differ in precise self-organizing algorithms.

Architecture of the Kohonen Network

The Kohonen network consists of an input layer, which distributes the inputs to each node in a second layer, so it is called competitive layer.

Each of the nodes at this level acts as an output node.

Each neuron in the competitive layer is connected to other neurons in its neighborhood and feedback is restricted to neighbors through these lateral connections. Figure 26 show the Architecture of the kohonen network.

Figure 26. Architecture of the Kohonen Network

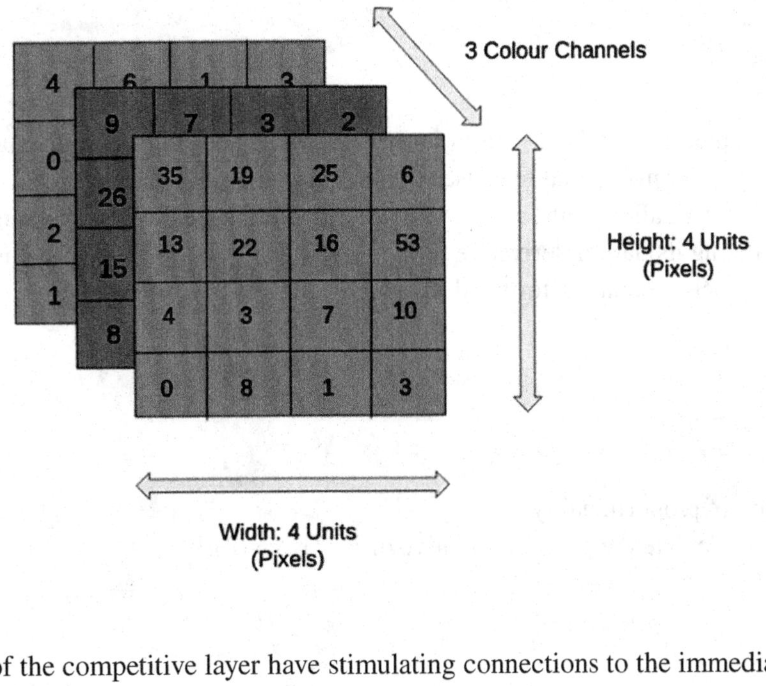

The neurons of the competitive layer have stimulating connections to the immediate neighbors and inhibitory connections to more distant neurons.

All neurons in the competitive layer receive a mixture of stimulating and inhibitory signals from the neurons of the input layer and other neurons of the competitive layer.

The Kohonen Network in Operation

When an input model is presented, some of the neurons are sufficiently enabled to produce outputs that are returned to other neurons in their vicinity.

The node whose weighting vector is closest to the input pattern vector (called the "winning node") produces the largest output. During training, the input weights of the winning neuron and its neighbors are adjusted to make them look even more like the input model.

At the end of training, the weighting vector of the winning node is aligned with the input pattern and produces the strongest output when presenting that particular pattern.

The weighting of the nodes in the neighborhood of the winning node has also been changed to give an average representation of that pattern class. As a result, even invisible patterns belonging to this class are correctly classified (generalization).

The m neighborhoods corresponding to the m possible pattern classes are to form a topological map representing the patterns(Kohonen,2007).

At above we mentioned the initiative size of neighbourhood and the fixed values of excitatory (positive) and inhibitory (negative) weights to neurons in the neighbourhood are among the design decisions to be made.

Learning Rule for the Kohonen Network

The square sum error for pattern p for all neurons in the output layer can be written as (Gregor,2015)

$$E_p = \frac{1}{2} \sum_j \left(w_{ij} - x_j^p \right)^2 \tag{2}$$

where x_j^p is the ith component of the p pattern for neuron j. The addition is made on all neurons j. Any Δw_{ij} change in weight is conventional to cause a reduction in the error E_p.

Now E_p is a function of all weights, so its exchange rate with respect to any w_{ij} weight value must be measured by calculating its partial derivative with respect to w_{ij}. (For that we have use the small delta δ, instead of d in the below equation for the derivative)

$$\Delta_p w_{ij} = -\eta \frac{\delta E_p}{\partial w_{ij}} \tag{3}$$

whereη is a constant of proportionality.

Now we have to calculate the partial derivative of E_p. Using (2):

$$\frac{\delta E_p}{\partial w_{ij}} = w_{ij} - x_j^p \tag{4}$$

Combining (3) and (4), we get

$$\Delta_p w_{ij} = -\eta \frac{\delta E_p}{\partial w_{ij}} = -\eta(w_{ij} - x_j^p) = \eta(x_j^p - w_{ij})$$

The Kohonen Algorithm

1. Initialiseweights: Each node's weights are initialized.
2. Present new input: A vector is chosen at the random from the set of data and presented to the network.
3. Compute distances to all nodes:

To calculate distances d_j between input and every output node j by using

$$d_j = \sum_i^{n-1} \left(x_i(t) - w_{ij}(t) \right)^2$$

where $x_i(t)$ is the input to node i at time t and $w_{ij}(t)$ is the weight from input node i to output node j at time t.

4. Select output node with minimum distance:

   Select output node j* as the output node with minimum d_j.

5. Update weights to node j* and neighbours

   Weights updated for node j* and all nodes in the neighbourhood defined by $N_j*(t)$. New weights are

$$w_{ij(t+1)} = w_{ij}(t) + \eta(t)\left(x_i^{(t)} - w_{ij}^{(t)} \right)$$

for j in N_j*, $0 \leq i \leq N\text{-}1$
   The term$\eta(t)$is a gain term $0 \leq \eta \leq 1$. Both η and $N_j*(t)$ decrease with time.

6. Repeat by going to step 2

   Issue in Kohonen Neural Nets Algorithm

- **Vector normalization:** In order to compare the vectors independently of the scales and depend only on the orientation, the vectors are normalized by their scaling. It also helps to reduce exercise time.
- **Weight initialization:** A random distribution of the initial weights may not be optimal, resulting in sparsely populated trainable nodes and poor classification performance. Possible assistance:

a. Initialization of weights at the same value and grouping of input vectors to a similar orientation. This increases the probability that all nodes are closer to the pattern vector. Entries slowly returned to the original orientation with training.
b. Adding random noise to the inputs to distribute vectors in a larger pattern space.
c. Using a large initial neighborhood slowly changing.

Decreasing the Size of Neighbourhood

The shape of the neighborhood may vary by application. For example, circular or hexagonal instead of rectangular.

Applications of the Kohonen Network

The Kohonen network is used in speech and image processing and has potential for statistical and database applications.

Speech Processing - Kohonen's Phonetic Typewriter

Unlimited, speaker-independent vocabulary, continuous speech recognition has not yet been achieved using conventional techniques. The problem is made difficult by the fact that the same word is pronounced with different pronunciations, volume levels, accent and background noise. In addition to analyzing individual sound units (phonemes), the human brain uses stored speech patterns, context, and other clues to effectively recognize speech (Campos,2009).

Kohonen Phonetic Typewriter Combines Digital Signal Processing Techniques and Using a Rule Base with a Kohonen Network to Achieve 92-97% Accuracy with Unlimited Vocabulary for Multiple Speakers in Finnish and Japanese.

RECURRENT NEURAL NETWORK (RNN)

Today, different Machine Learning techniques are used to handle different types of data. One of the most difficult types of data to handle and forecast is sequential data. Sequential data is different from other types of data in the sense that, although it can be assumed that all the characteristics of a typical data set are independent of order, this cannot be assumed for a sequential data set. To handle this type of data, the concept of recurrent neural networks was conceived. It is different from other artificial neural networks in its structure. While other networks "travel" in a linear direction during the feedback process or the backward propagation process, the recurring network follows a recurrence relationship instead of a feedback pass and uses backward propagation over time to learn.

The recurrent neural network (RNN) is a type of neural network in which the outputs of the previous step are fed into the input of the current step. In traditional neural networks, all inputs and outputs are independent of each other, but in cases such as when it is required to predict the next word in a sentence, the previous words are required and, therefore, it is necessary to remember the previous words(Mikolov,2010).

The recurrent neural network consists of multiple units of fixed activation function, one for each time step. Each unit has an internal state that is called the hidden state of the unit.

Thus, RNN came into existence, which solved this problem with the help of a hidden layer. The main and most important feature of RNN is the hidden state show in Figure 27, in which remembers certain information about a sequence.

Figure 27. Hidden layer in RNN

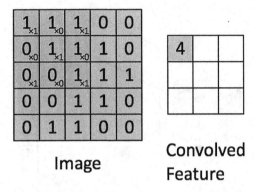

Image

Convolved
Feature

RNN has a "memory" that remembers all the information about what has been calculated. Use the same parameters for each entry as it performs the same task on all hidden inputs or layers to produce the output. This reduces the complexity of the parameters, unlike other neural networks.

How RNN Work

The working of a RNN can be understood with the help of below example:

Suppose there is a deeper network, with its have one input layer, three hidden layers and one output layer. In each hidden layer will have its own set of weights and biases. In first hidden layer weights and biases are (w1,b1), second layer consists (w2,b2) and third layer consists (w3,b3). This means that each of these layers are independent of each other, i.e. they do not memorize the previous outputs. The below Figure 28 shows work of RNN.

Now the RNN will do the following:

RNN converts independent activations into dependent activations by providing the same weights and biases to all layers, thus reducing the complexity of increasing the parameters and memorizing each previous output by giving each output as input to the next hidden layer.Hence, these three layers can be joined together such that the weights and bias of all the hidden layers is the same, into a single recurrent layer.

This hidden state means the past knowledge that the network currently has in a given time step. This hidden state is updated at each step to indicate the change in network knowledge about the past. The hidden state is updated using the following recurrence relationship: -

$$h_t = fw(x_t - h_t - 1)$$

Where

h_t -> current state

h_t–1 -> previous state
x_t -> input state
fw -> The fixed function with trainable weights

Figure 28. Example of RNN work

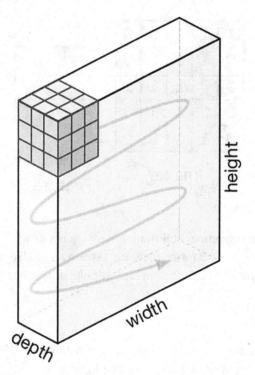

At each time step, the new hidden state is calculated using the recurrence relation as given above. This new generated hidden state is used to generate indeed a new hidden state and so on(Sreekanth,2010).

The basic work-flow of a Recurrent Neural Network is as follows in Figure 30.

Training Through RNN

1. A single time step of the input is provided to the network.
2. Then calculate its current state using set of current input and the previous state.
3. The current ht becomes ht-1 for the next time step.
4. One can go as many time steps according to the problem and join the information from all the previous states.
5. Once all the time steps are completed the final current state is used to calculate the output.
6. The output is then compared to the actual output i.e the target output and the error is generated.
7. The error is then back-propagated to the network to update the weights and hence the network (RNN) is trained.

Figure 29. Joined three layer into hidden layer

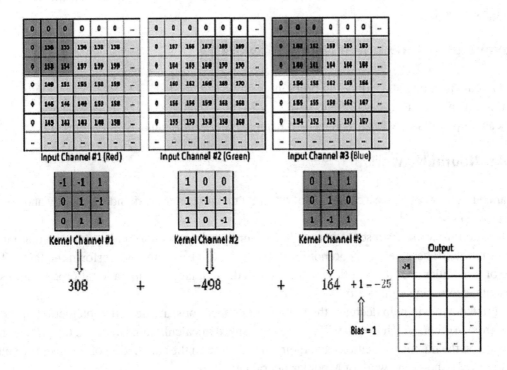

Figure 30. The basic work-flow of a RNN

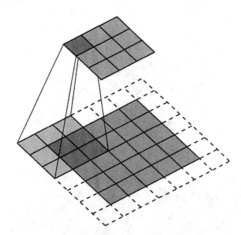

Advantages of Recurrent Neural Network

- An RNN remembers each and every information through time. It is useful in time series prediction only because of the feature to remember previous inputs as well. This is called Long Short Term Memory.

- Recurrent neural network are even used with convolutional layers to extend the effective pixel neighborhood.

Disadvantages of Recurrent Neural Network

- Gradient vanishing and exploding problems.
- Training an RNN is a very difficult task.
- It cannot process very long sequences if using tanh or relu as an activation function.

Modular Neural Network

Modular neural networks have a collection of different networks that work independently and contribute to the output (Devin, 2017).

Each neural network has a set of inputs that are unique compared to other networks that build and perform subtasks. These networks do not interact or point to each other to perform the tasks. The advantage of a modular neural network is that it breaks down a large computational process into smaller components, decreasing complexity.

This breakdown will help decrease the number of connections and deny the interaction of these networks with each other, which in turn will increase the speed of calculation. However, the processing time will depend on the number of neurons and their participation in the calculation of the results (Kourakos, 2009). Figure 31 shows the work of Modular neural networks.

Figure 31. The work of MNN

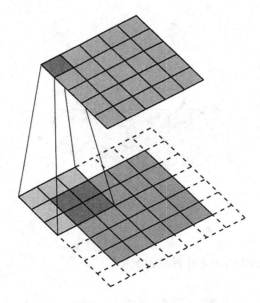

REFERENCES

Baroni, M., & Zamparelli, R. (2010, October). Nouns are vectors, adjectives are matrices: Representing adjective-noun constructions in semantic space. In *Proceedings of the 2010 conference on empirical methods in natural language processing* (pp. 1183-1193). Academic Press.

Blunsom, P., Kocik, K., & Curran, J. R. (2006, August). Question classification with log-linear models. In *Proceedings of the 29th annual international ACM SIGIR conference on Research and development in information retrieval* (pp. 615-616). ACM.

Boureau, Y. L., Ponce, J., & LeCun, Y. (2010). A theoretical analysis of feature pooling in visual recognition. In *Proceedings of the 27th international conference on machine learning (ICML-10)* (pp. 111-118). Academic Press.

Campos, B. R. (2009). *Character recognition in natural images*. VISAPP.

Cireşan, D., Meier, U., Masci, J., & Schmidhuber, J. (2011, July). A committee of neural networks for traffic sign classification. In *The 2011 international joint conference on neural networks* (pp. 1918–1921). IEEE. doi:10.1109/IJCNN.2011.6033458

Danisman, K., Dalkiran, I., & Celebi, F. V. (2006). Design of a high precision temperature measurement system based on artificial neural network for different thermocouple types. *Measurement*, *39*(8), 695–700. doi:10.1016/j.measurement.2006.03.015

Devin, C., Gupta, A., Darrell, T., Abbeel, P., & Levine, S. (2017, May). Learning modular neural network policies for multi-task and multi-robot transfer. In *2017 IEEE International Conference on Robotics and Automation (ICRA)* (pp. 2169-2176). IEEE. 10.1109/ICRA.2017.7989250

Gregor, K., Danihelka, I., Graves, A., Rezende, D. J., & Wierstra, D. (2015). *Draw: A recurrent neural network for image generation*. arXiv preprint arXiv:1502.04623

Kalchbrenner, N., Grefenstette, E., & Blunsom, P. (2014). *A convolutional neural network for modelling sentences*. arXiv preprint arXiv:1404.2188

Kangas, J. A., Kohonen, T. K., & Laaksonen, J. T. (1990). Variants of self-organizing maps. *IEEE Transactions on Neural Networks*, *1*(1), 93–99. doi:10.1109/72.80208 PMID:18282826

Kiang, M. Y. (2001). Extending the Kohonen self-organizing map networks for clustering analysis. *Computational Statistics & Data Analysis*, *38*(2), 161–180. doi:10.1016/S0167-9473(01)00040-8

Kohonen, T., & Honkela, T. (2007). Kohonen network. *Scholarpedia*, *2*(1), 1568. doi:10.4249cholarpedia.1568

Kourakos, G., & Mantoglou, A. (2009). Pumping optimization of coastal aquifers based on evolutionary algorithms and surrogate modular neural network models. *Advances in Water Resources*, *32*(4), 507–521. doi:10.1016/j.advwatres.2009.01.001

Lawrence, S., Giles, C. L., Tsoi, A. C., & Back, A. D. (1997). Face recognition: A convolutional neural-network approach. *IEEE Transactions on Neural Networks*, *8*(1), 98–113. doi:10.1109/72.554195 PMID:18255614

Mikolov, T., Karafiát, M., Burget, L., Černocký, J., & Khudanpur, S. (2010). Recurrent neural network based language model. In *Eleventh annual conference of the international speech communication association*. Academic Press.

Sermanet, P., Chintala, S., & LeCun, Y. (2012). *Convolutional neural networks applied to house numbers digit classification.* arXiv preprint arXiv:1204.3968

Sreekanth, J., & Datta, B. (2010). Multi-objective management of saltwater intrusion in coastal aquifers using genetic programming and modular neural network based surrogate models. *Journal of Hydrology (Amsterdam)*, *393*(3-4), 245–256. doi:10.1016/j.jhydrol.2010.08.023

Sun, T. Y., Liu, C. C., Lin, C. L., Hsieh, S. T., & Huang, C. S. (2009). A radial basis function neural network with adaptive structure via particle swarm optimization. In *Particle Swarm Optimization*. IntechOpen. doi:10.5772/6763

Zaremba, W., Sutskever, I., & Vinyals, O. (2014). *Recurrent neural network regularization.* arXiv preprint arXiv:1409.2329

This research was previously published in Applications of Artificial Neural Networks for Nonlinear Data; pages 30-64, copyright year 2021 by Engineering Science Reference (an imprint of IGI Global).

Chapter 2
Comprehensive Modelling of ANN

Meghna Babubhai Patel
Ganpat University, India

Jagruti N. Patel
Ganpat University, India

Upasana M. Bhilota
Ganpat University, India

ABSTRACT

An artificial neural network (ANN) is an information processing modelling of the human brain inspired by the way biological nervous systems behave. There are about 100 billion neurons in the human brain. Each neuron has a connection point between 1,000 and 100,000. The key element of this paradigm is the novel structure of the information processing system. In the human brain, information is stored in such a way as to be distributed, and we can extract more than one piece of this information when necessary from our memory in parallel. We are not mistaken when we say that a human brain is made up of thousands of very powerful parallel processors. It is composed of a large number of highly interconnected processing elements (neurons) working in union to solve specific problems. ANN, like people, learns by example. The chapter includes characteristics of artificial neural networks, structure of ANN, elements of artificial neural networks, pros and cons of ANN.

INTRODUCTION

Features of Artificial Neural Network

- It's an impartially applied scientific model.
- Its contains vast figure of interrelated handling components named neurons to do all operations.
- Information put in storage in the neurons are basically the weighted linkage of neurons.

DOI: 10.4018/978-1-6684-2408-7.ch002

- The input signals reach at the processing components through associates and attaching masses.
- It has the capability to study, remember and simplify from the given data by suitable assignment and adjustment of weights.
- The mutual activities of the neurons define its computational power, and no single neuron transmits explicit data.

Structure of ANN

An ANN is recognized as a Neural Network, it is mainly based on mathematical model based on the arrangement and roles of natural neural networks. This is almost a non-natural human nervous system to receive, process and transmit information in Computer Science (Mehrotra et al., 1997) (Agatonovic-Kustrin & Beresford, 2000).

The ANN idea is created on the certainty of the functioning of the People mind in creation the accurate influences can be copied for use of silicon and cables like neurons and active a short branched extension of a nerve cell.

The People mind is ready up of 86 billion nerve cells is known as neurons. neurons connected to a multiple other cells by Axons. A short branched extension of a nerve cell accepts the provocations of the outside atmosphere or the assistances of the physical structures.

The inputs generate electrical compulsions, which are transmit through the neural network. A neuron cannot send any message to some other neuron to solve the any difficulties. (Mehrotra et al., 1997)[2].

ANNs are made up of multiple nodes that mimic the genetic neurons of the People mind. Neurons associated with bonds and interrelate to each other.

The intersection is takings contribution information and do basic Process on the information. The outcome of these processes is spread to next neurons. The productivity on individually intersection applies to the beginning or importance of the node.

Separately connection is connected to a weight. ANNs are skilled of learning and altering weight values.

The structure of an ANN contains of artificial neurons in a clustered layer. The ANN structure contains three layer like: an input layers, hidden layers, and an output layers (Agatonovic-Kustrin & Beresford, 2000; Artificial Neural Networks in Data Mining, n.d.; Maind & Wankar, 2014; Mehrotra et al., 1997; Papantonopoulos, 2016; Sharma et al., 2012; Xenon Stack, n.d.).

Details of layers in a neural network see in below Figure 1.

1. **Input Layer:** Every input is sent to the prototypical through this layer.
2. **Hidden Layer**: There are many masked layers used to procedure the input acknowledged from the input layers.
3. **Output Layer:** Post-processing data is accessible at the output layer.

- **Input Layer:** Input layer is the starting layer of the neural network. The layer links to the outside atmosphere that offerings a strategy of the neural network. This layer handles only input. Gets the input and transfers it to hidden layers and detailed in the Hidden layer. The input layers have to signify the form for working in the neural network. Each inputs neuron has to mean approximately autonomous variable that influences the outcome of the neural network. It does not calculations on the given values like no weight and preference value connected. In figure there are four input

Figure 1. Structure of ANN

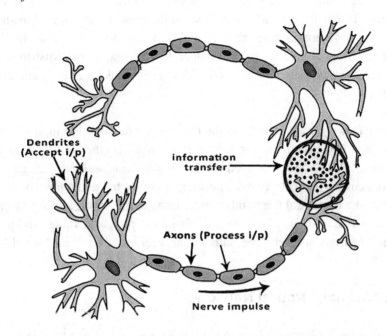

signals x1, x2, x3, x4 (Agatonovic-Kustrin & Beresford, 2000; Artificial Neural Networks in Data Mining, n.d.; Maind & Wankar, 2014; Mehrotra et al., 1997).

- **Hidden Layers:** It is one type bridge layer that lies of the input layers and the output layers. That is why the layer is answerable for extract the essential features from the input data. The layer works on to get the input value from the previous layer. The hidden layer of the group of neurons that have the startup function applied. This layer has devices that put on altered transformations in the given data. A hidden layer is a group of straight up arranged neurons (Rendering) (Agatonovic-Kustrin & Beresford, 2000; Artificial Neural Networks in Data Mining, n.d.; Maind & Wankar, 2014; Mehrotra et al., 1997; Papantonopoulos, 2016; Sharma et al., 2012; Xenon Stack, n.d.).

Given figure shows 5 hidden layers. In that, the layer contains 4, 5 and 6 devices respectively first, second and third, the 4th consumes 4, and the 5th consumes 3 devices. In the last layer passes the values to the output layer. All devices in middle layer are linked to every device in the last layer. Finally, the hidden layers were completely connected (Maind & Wankar, 2014)[5].

Much research has been done to assess the quantity of neurons in the hidden layer, but none of them has managed to find the exact outcome. on that they define how the problem arise in middle layer. Assume that the information is in linearly separated, without use of middle layer the trigger function can be applied on the input layer, for solve the problem.

When complex decisions create for some problems, we can access 3, 4 and 5 middle layer dependent on the notch of difficulty of the problematic or the notch of accuracy essential. It certainly does not mean that if we continue to increase the number of layers, the neural network will provide great accuracy! A phase occurs when the accuracy matures constant or cuts when we enhance a further layer! In adding, we also necessity to compute the amount of neurons in the network.

If the problem is bigger than the neurons, In the hidden layer there are less neurons to identify signals in a complex database. If they have avoidable neurons in the network, an over-adjustment can occur. So far, various procedures have not provided the particular method for computing the amount of hidden layers, as well as the number of neurons in each hidden layer. (Agatonovic-Kustrin & Beresford, 2000; Artificial Neural Networks in Data Mining, n.d.; Maind & Wankar, 2014; Papantonopoulos, 2016; Xenon Stack, n.d.).

- **Output Layer:** This layer is last layer in the linkage and receives the inputs from the last hidden layer. The last layer of the neural network gathers and transfers the data consequently, in the method it was planned for. The design offered by the last layer can be drawn straight to the input layer. The number of neurons in this layer must be straight connected to the form of effort performed by the neural network. To control the number of neurons in this layer, initial reflect the planned use of the neural network. With this layer we can obtain the preferred values and preferred series. In last, we given 3 neurons and get three outputs like y1,y2,y3 (Artificial Neural Networks in Data Mining, n.d.)[5-7].

Components of Artificial Neural Networks

Posture in mind the discussed features, we can gather the basic components of any non-natural neural network as follows (Agatonovic-Kustrin & Beresford, 2000; Artificial Neural Networks in Data Mining, n.d.; Maind & Wankar, 2014; Mehrotra et al., 1997; Xenon Stack, n.d.):

- Handling Components
- Topology
- Learning Algorithm

Handling Components

The Ribonucleic Acid (RNA) is a basic computer prototypical of a biotic neuron network, an RNA contains of simple treatment parts or components like to neurons in the mind.

The Figure 2 displays the general configuration of processing elements

In common, a processing unit is composed of a summation part trailed by a productivity part see in Figure 3. The basic purpose is to summation of takings n input and weight for every input then compute the weighted sum of these inputs.

On the basis of the symbol of the weight of every entry, it is resolute whether the entrance has an +ve or -ve weight. The weighted amount of the summation entity is called the initiation worth and, depending on the sign after the beginning value, the outcome is generated.

Entry and exit may be continuous or discrete, as well as deterministic or uncertain.

Topology

The ANN will develop suitable only when all the processing elements are appropriately prepared, so that the pattern recognition task can be performed.

Figure 2. Processing elements

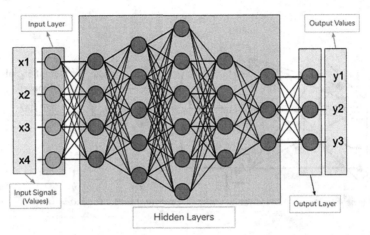

Figure 3. Composed of a summation unit

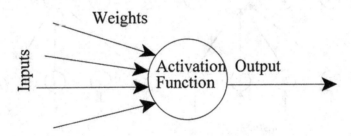

This association or organization of the handling components, their mutual connections, inputs and outputs, is called a topology.

Typically, in an ANN, handling parts are layered and entirely elements in a specific level have the similar beginning and amount produced values. The assembly between the layers can be made in some ways, for example, a part to procedure a layer associated to a part to alternative layer, a part to procedure a layer associated to a part to the similar layer, etc.

Nearly of the topologies normally used in ANN:

- Instar
- Outstar
- Group of Instars
- Group of Outstar
- Bidirectional Associative Memory
- Autoassociative Memory

The below figure displays an procedure of two layers F1 and F2 with an M and N number of handling parts, each in the Instar and Outstar topologies.

Figure 4.

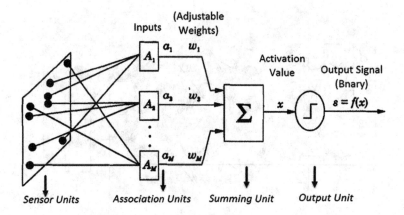

Figure 5.

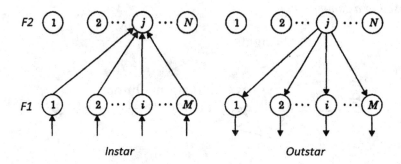

Learning Algorithm

The last main components of any ANN are learning algorithms or laws. The functioning of any neural network is ruled by neural subtleties, which includes both the subtleties of the activation state and the dynamics of synaptic weight.

The procedures or learning rules are executions of synaptic subtleties and are defined in terms of primary derived weights. The learning rules can be managed, unverified or a mixture of the two.

Approximately the top recognized learning processes are:

- Hebb's Law
- Perception Learning Law
- Delta Learning Law
- Wildrow & Hoff LMS Learning Law
- Correlation Learning Law
- Instar Learning Law
- Outstar Learning Law

Pros and Cons of ANN

ANN have marched in the world of 20th era is developing fast. Today, in present day examine the ANN advantages and disadvantages means problems encountered during the use of ANN. It is not forgeable that day by day problems in ANN is going to reduce and advantages of ANN is increasing. So, now a days ANN become incredible part of live. The following section discuss the advantages and drawbacks of ANN (Kohli et al., 2014; Mijwel, 2018; Mohamed, 2016).

Advantages of ANN

ANN has benefits that best suitable based on particular problems and situations:

Storage of Information

Like traditional programming, the information is stored in the network instead of the database. Losing little information from one location does not prevent the network from connecting.

Capability of Working with Lack Knowledge

The ANN is established on adaptive learning. In ANN the output is generated even with partial knowledge after ANN training. The performance depends on significance of missing data. The ANN has ability to learn itself so it doesn't need to be reprogrammed.

Having Superior Fault Tolerance

Compare to traditional network, ANN provide superior potential for fault tolerance because the network is capable for regenerating a failure of any component, without loss of stored information. It means the ANN able to found missing information or nodes or servers which cannot communicate in the case when the network proportion done on multiple server and machines.

Easy Implementation

ANN can be easily implemented without any complications. It is adaptable and flexible because neural networks are robust for cracking difficulties. Neural networks are efficient in their software design and experts agree that the benefits of using ANN balance the possibilities.

Distributed Memory ANN

In order for the ANN to learn, it is essential to define the examples and teach the network based on the desired result, showing the cases to the network. The success of the network is directly relational to the instances selected and, if the experience cannot be exposed to the network in all its facets, the network may generate an incorrect outcome.

Corruption Progressive

A network decreases over time and undertakes relation poverty. The network problem is not corrected instantly.

Capability to do Machine Learning

ANN study procedures and do choices by remarking on comparable procedures. ANN are flexible and take the ability to learn, generalize and adapt to situations based on its results.

ANNs Can Generalize

ANN can learn organically. This means that the outputs of an ANN are not entirely limited by the inputs and that the results are initially provided by a proficient method. Artificial neural networks have the capability to simplify their inputs. This capability is invaluable for automation and pattern recognition systems.

Later knowledge the original contributions and their relations, it can also conclude unseen relations from unseen information, allowing the prototypical to simplify and guess unseen information. Generalize knowledge to produce appropriate responses to unknown situations.

Parallel Processing Capability

ANN have the capability to absorb and prototypical non-linear and difficult relations, which is actually main as in actual lifecycle, various relations among contributions and productions are non-linear and complex.

Non-Linearity

A neural network can do duties that a linear program cannot do. This functionality permits the network to obtain information efficiently while learning. This is a different benefit above a usually linear network, which is insufficient for showing non-linear information. ANN have a numerical power proficient of deed many jobs in same time. When a part of the neural network breakdowns down, it can continue smoothly due to its parallel nature. Nonlinear systems have the ability to find shortcuts to get exclusive resolutions in computation. The systems can also derive associates between statistics facts, rather than waiting for records from a data source to be clearly associated. This nonlinear shortcut tool is used in artificial neural networks, which kinds it valued for profitable analysis of large information.

Self-Repair

Artificial neural networks can do more than route around parts of the network that no longer work. If they are asked to find specific data that no longer communicate, these artificial neural networks can regenerate large amounts of data by inference and help determine which node is not working. This attribute is useful for networks that require their users to be aware of the current state of the network and result in self-debugging and network diagnostics.

Scientists are now trying to understand the capabilities, assumptions, and applicability of various approaches that can dramatically improve the performance of artificial neural network systems.

Disadvantages of ANN

Dependency on Hardware

ANN require processor accordingly its structure. The processor must contain the power of parallel processing. That's why, the recognition of the tackle is dependent.

Inexplicable Network Performance

The main vital disadvantage of ANN because when ANN generate an exploratory solution then it doesn't give hint for how and why it's generated like this. That's why it degrades the trust factor on network.

Define Appropriate Network Structure

The rules are not defined for ANN structure. So, based on trial and error and with experience, proper network structure is generating.

Trouble to Showing Problems to the Network

The problems should be translated in numerical value before presented to ANN because ANN can purely work with numeric standards. Network performance is directly influenced by the display mechanism which is confirmed and depends on the capacity of the user.

The Unknown Time Duration

The training will be considered as completed because the system compacts to assured importance of a fault on samples and because of this value cannot obtain finest result. So, for large network ANN requires high processing time.

REFERENCES

Agatonovic-Kustrin, S., & Beresford, R. (2000). Basic concepts of artificial neural network (ANN) modeling and its application in pharmaceutical research. *Journal of Pharmaceutical and Biomedical Analysis, 22*(5), 717–727. doi:10.1016/S0731-7085(99)00272-1 PMID:10815714

Artificial Neural Networks in Data Mining. (n.d.). Computer & Information System, Sadat Academy for Management Sciences.

Kohli, S., Miglani, S., & Rapariya, R. (2014). Basics of Artificial Neural Network. *International Journal of Computing Science and Mobile Computing, 3*(9), 745-751.

Maind, S. B., & Wankar, P. (2014). Research paper on basic of artificial neural network. *International Journal on Recent and Innovation Trends in Computing and Communication*, 2(1), 96–100.

Mehrotra, K., Mohan, C. K., & Ranka, S. (1997). *Elements of artificial neural nets*. Academic Press.

Mijwel, M. (2018). *Artificial neural networks advantages and disadvantages*. Academic Press.

Mohamed, N. E. (2016). Artificial Neural Networks in Data Mining. *IOSR J Comput Eng*, *18*(6), 55–59.

Papantonopoulos, G. (2016). *On the use of complexity methods in*. Personalized Periodontology and Implant Dentistry.

Sharma, V., Rai, S., & Dev, A. (2012). A comprehensive study of artificial neural networks. *International Journal of Advanced Research in Computer Science and Software Engineering*, *2*(10).

Xenon Stack. (n.d.). https://www.xenonstack.com/blog/artificial-neural-network-applications/

This research was previously published in Applications of Artificial Neural Networks for Nonlinear Data; pages 18-29, copyright year 2021 by Engineering Science Reference (an imprint of IGI Global).

Chapter 3
Neural Network for Big Data Sets

Vo Ngoc Phu
Duy Tan University, Vietnam

Vo Thi Ngoc Tran
Ho Chi Minh City University of Technology, Vietnam

ABSTRACT

Machine learning (ML), neural network (NN), evolutionary algorithm (EA), fuzzy systems (FSs), as well as computer science have been very famous and very significant for many years. They have been applied to many different areas. They have contributed much to developments of many large-scale corporations, massive organizations, etc. Lots of information and massive data sets (MDSs) have been generated from these big corporations, organizations, etc. These big data sets (BDSs) have been the challenges of many commercial applications, researches, etc. Therefore, there have been many algorithms of the ML, the NN, the EA, the FSs, as well as computer science which have been developed to handle these massive data sets successfully. To support for this process, the authors have displayed all the possible algorithms of the NN for the large-scale data sets (LSDSs) successfully in this chapter. Finally, they have presented a novel model of the NN for the BDS in a sequential environment (SE) and a distributed network environment (DNE).

INTRODUCTION

We have already considered where many big data sets (BDSs) have been generated from. We have already found that: Many large-scale corporations, big organizations, and etc. have been created, built and developed more and more for many years in the world from that lots of economies of countries in the world have been developed in the strongest way for the recent years. Each massive corporation (each large-scale organization, and etc.) has had thousands of branches in the countries in the world. Each branch has had thousands of employee certainly. Therefore, the big corporation could have had millions of the employees in the countries in the world. From its business process, many massive data sets (MDSs) have

DOI: 10.4018/978-1-6684-2408-7.ch003

already been generated from the millions of the employees, and etc. certainly. Many hard problems and challenges have been generated and grown from which a lot. For example, these negative problems have been as follows: What are the problems? How to store the MDSs? How to handle the large-scale data sets (LSDSs)? How to extract many helpful values from the BDSs? Whether to necessarily save them or not? Where to store them? Whether to save them for a long time or not? Whether to necessarily store them for a long time or not? Whether to necessarily process them or not? Whether to successfully handle them or not? How long time to process them? How long time to handle them successfully? Whether to extract their significant values? Whether to get successfully their helpful values? And etc.

Besides, many different fields of the computer science have already been developed in the strongest way in the world. These fields such as machine learning (ML), neural network (NN), evolutionary algorithm (EA), fuzzy systems (FSs), and etc. have been very useful for many fields of everyone's life. Their algorithms, methods, models, and etc. have successfully been built, and in addition, they have also been applied to the BDSs. Thus, we have presented many simple concepts of the ML, the NN, the EA, the FSs, and etc. in this book chapter. In addition, we have also displayed a novel model of the NN for handling the LSDSs successfully.

According to our opinion, ML is a sub-area of the AI of the computer science which uses many statistical techniques to allow computers to be the ability to learn with data sets. The ML is also a method of data analysis which automates analytical model building. It is based on the idea which computer systems can learn from many data sets, identify many patterns, and make many decisions with minimal human intervention

NN based on our opinion is a computing system which is similar to the biological neural networks which constitute human brains. It comprises a set of connected units or nodes (called neural network) which look like the neurons in a biological brain. One connection looks like the synapses in a biological brain which can transmit a signal from one neuron to another. Then, one neuron can receive a signal which can process it and in addition, signal additional neurons connected to it.

According to our opinion, EA is a subset of evolutionary computation which is a type of meta-heuristic optimization algorithm. Many mechanisms inspired by biological evolution can be used by the EA as follows: reproduction, mutation, recombination, and selection. Many approximating solutions to all types of problems are often implemented well by the EAs

FS based on our opinion is a control system according to a fuzzy logic (a math system) which can analyze analog input values in terms of logical variables which take many values between 0 and 1.

We have found why these problems and challenges are important.

1. According to our opinion and the reviews which we have already referenced, these large-scale data sets have been needed to store certainly and successfully. Moreover, they must be saved in a time-saving way. Many reasons for these are as follows:

    a. The big data sets of the massive corporations, large-scale organizations, and etc. have been protected surely. If the massive data do not store surely, they are stolen. Thus, the secrets of the corporations, organizations, and etc. can be exploited for many bad purposes. In addition, the corporations, organizations, and etc. can be crashed.

    b. They must be stored regularly and fully: When there have any incidents, they can be rehabilitated surely.

    c. They must be backed up regularly and fully: When there have any incidents, they can be rehabilitated surely.

    d.   They can be saved in the most economical way: They are very large and are increased every day. Thus, costs of computer hardware of the storing are very expensive.

    e.   Human resources of the storing also need to be saved costs.

    f.   We have also asserted that this stage has been performed with so much cost and time surely.

    g.   …

2.   We have also confirmed that those massive data sets have needed to be handled carefully, effectively, fully, successfully, and etc. because of the below reasons as follows:

    a.   The above items of (A) must be performed firstly.

    b.   Processing them to store them as following above reasons in (A).

    c.   Handling them as quick as possible, effectively, and etc. for aims of extracting them in a valuable way to get, save, and use many helpful values.

    d.   Processing them to demonstrate professional levels of the corporations, organizations, and etc.

    e.   Based on our opinion, we have also found that it has taken lots of cost and time to this stage clearly.

    f.   At the present time, there have been many problems and challenges to perform this stage certainly and successfully because of the below reasons as follows:

        i.   There have not been a lot of awareness fully and clearly yet about the massive data sets.

        ii.   There have not been many tools, software, hardware, algorithms, methods, models, and etc. of the large-scale data to implement this stage yet.

        iii.   Because of so much cost and time, the corporations, the organizations, and etc. still do not want to make this stage fully, and etc.

        iv.   …

    g.   …

3.   We have also asserted that those large-scale data have been very necessary for being extracted automatically the significant values from them:

    a.   The above items of (A) and the above items of (B) must be implemented firstly.

    b.   If this stage is not performed, the stage of (A) and the stage of (B) should not be implemented: The reason is as follows: In addition to the values of (A) and (B) presented in more details, this stage is performed for complementing to the previous two phases (A and B). If the stages of (A) and (B) are only implemented and this stage is not performed, lots of cost and time are spent in a wasteful way.

    c.   This stage brings core values to the massive corporations, the large-scale organizations, and etc.

    d.   We have also confirmed that we have already extracted automatically the crucial positive values from the large-scale data sets with a lot of cost and time certainly.

    e.   Based on our opinion, this stage is also a most expensive duration for the corporations, the organizations, and etc., and this stage also takes a lot of time for them.

    f.   …

According to our opinion, a big data set is a set of many records (many samples) which has a large of quantity comprising over 500,000 data samples – 1,000,000 data samples or this data set has a large of size about over millions of GB. Sometimes, a big data set has a large of quantity including over 500,000 data samples – 1,000,000 data samples and this data set also has a large of size about over millions of GB

The problem has been done so far by others as follows:

1. Some algorithms, methods, models, and etc. have been studied, developed, and deployed for the BDS but there is not a lot.
2. There have been not enough many algorithms, methods, models, and etc. for the LSDSs yet to be applied to many different areas for the economies, countries, societies, corporations, organizations, and etc.
3. There have been not a lot of those algorithms, methods, models, and etc. of the MDSs which have been implemented in sequential environments (SEs) – sequential systems (SSs)
4. Those algorithms, methods, models, and etc. of the LSDS in the SSs have already been developed with small samples.
5. There have also been not lots of those algorithms, methods, models, and etc. of the big data sets which have been performed in distributed network systems (DNSs) – parallel network environments (PNEs)
6. Those algorithms, methods, models, and etc. of the LSDS in the DNS have also already been performed with small samples.
7. …

The main contributions of this chapter to the problem from many studies related to lots of new computational models (related to the NN) for the massive data sets are as follows:

1. This chapter helps the readers have information and knowledge about the MDSs.
2. The chapter also helps the reader understand most of all novel computational models (related to the NN) of the LSDS certainly.
3. Most of those computational models (related to the NN) of the BDSs in many different fields are shown in both the SEs and the DNSs in more details in the below sections.
4. From lots of the information and knowledge above of (1), (2), (3), and (4), the readers (comprising scientists, researchers, CEO, managers, and etc.) can build, develop and deploy many commercial applications, studies, and etc. so much.
5. Many different technologies of those models have already been displayed carefully.
6. We also show that a novel computational model (related to the NN) of us for the LSDSs have successfully been built with over 500,000 data samples - 1,000,000 data samples in the SS and the PNE
7. …

The contribution original of this chapter is as follows:

1. This chapter helps the readers understand many simple concepts of the big data sets clearly.
2. This chapter also helps the readers know many novel models of the MDSs fully in the SEs and the DNSs
3. A novel model, which we have built and developed in the SE and the DNS successfully, is presented in this chapter.
4. Many techniques, algorithms, methods, models, and etc. to handle the large-scale data in the SE and the DNS are fully shown in this chapter.

5.   Based on all the things displayed in this chapter, many commercial applications, researches, and etc. can be developed and deployed successfully.

6.   ...

The contribution non-trivial is as follows: In this book chapter, we have proposed a new model for the MDS sentiment classification (SECL) in the parallel network environment – a Cloudera system (CPNS) with Hadoop Map (M) and Hadoop Reduce (R). Our new model has used an Artificial Neural Network Algorithm (ANN) with multi-dimensional vector (MDV) and 2,000,000 documents of our training data set (TRADS) for document-level sentiment classification in English. We have tested the novel model in both a SE and a PNS. Our novel model can classify sentiments (positive, negative, or neutral) of millions of documents based on many documents in the parallel network environment in English. However, we tested our new model on our testing data set (TESDS) including 1,000,000 reviews (500,000 positive and 500,000 negative) and achieved 84.25% accuracy.

BACKGROUND

In this section, we describe summaries of many studies related to an Artificial Neural Network Algorithm (ANN), vector space model (VSM), Hadoop, Cloudera, etc.

There are many works related to vector space modeling in [(Vaibhav Kant Singh, & Vinay Kumar Singh, 2015), (Víctor Carrera-Trejo, & et al, 2015), and (Pascal Soucy, & Guy W. Mineau, 2015)]. First, we have transferred all English sentences into many vectors, which have been used in the VSM algorithm. In this research (Vaibhav Kant Singh, & Vinay Kumar Singh, 2015), the authors examined the vector space model, an information retrieval technique, and its variation. The rapid growth of the Internet and the abundance of documents and different forms of information available underscored the need for good information retrieval technique. The vector space model was an algebraic model used for information retrieval. It represented natural language documents in a formal manner using of vectors in a multi-dimensional space and allowed decisions to be made as to which documents are similar to each other and to the queries fired. This research attempted to examine the vector space model, an information retrieval technique that was widely used today. It also explained the existing variations of VSM and proposes the new variation that should be considered. In text classification tasks, one of the main problems (Víctor Carrera-Trejo, & et al, 2015) was to choose which features give the best results. Various features could be used like words, n-grams, syntactic n-grams of various types (POS tags, dependency relations, mixed, etc.); or a combination of these features could be considered. Also, algorithms for dimensionality reduction of these sets of features could be applied, such as latent Dirichlet allocation (LDA). In this research, the authors considered multi-label text classification tasks and apply various feature sets. The authors considered a subset of multi-labeled files of the Reuters-21578 corpus. The authors used traditional TF-IDF values of the features and tried both considering and ignoring stop words. The authors also tried several combinations of features, like bi-grams and uni-grams. The authors also experimented with adding LDA results into vector space models as new features. These last experiments obtained the best results. KNN and SVM (Pascal Soucy, & Guy W. Mineau, 2015) were two machine learning approaches to text categorization (TC) based on the vector space model. In this model, borrowed from information retrieval, documents were represented as a vector where each component was associated with a particular word from the vocabulary. Traditionally, each component value was assigned using the information retrieval TFIDF measure. While this weighting method seemed very appropriate for IR, it was not clear that it was the best choice for TC problems. Actually, this weighting method did not leverage the information implicitly contained in the categorization task to represent documents. In this research, the authors introduced a new weighting method based on statistical estimation of the importance of a word for a specific categorization problem. This method also had the benefit to make feature selection implicit, since useless features of the categorization problem considered get a very small weight. Extensive experiments reported in the research showed that this new weighting method improved significantly the classification accuracy as measured on many categorization tasks.

Many research projects related to implementing algorithms, applications, studies in parallel network environment in [(Hadoop, 2017), (Apache, 2017), and (Cloudera, 2017)]. In (Hadoop, 2017) and (Apache, 2017), Hadoop is an Apache-based framework used to handle large data sets on clusters consisting of multiple computers, using the Map and Reduce programming model. The two main projects of the Hadoop are Hadoop Distributed File System (HDFS) and Hadoop M/R (Hadoop Map /Reduce). Hadoop M/R allows engineers to program for writing applications for parallel processing of large data sets on clusters consisting of multiple computers. A M/R task has two main components: (1) Map and (2) Reduce. This framework splits inputting data into chunks which multiple Map tasks can handle with a separate data partition in parallel. The outputs of the map tasks are gathered and processed by the Reduce task ordered. The input and output of each M/R task are stored in HDFS because the Map tasks and the Reduce tasks perform on the pair (key, value), and formatted input and output formats will be the pair (key, value). Cloudera (Cloudera, 2017), the global provider of the fastest, easiest, and most secure data management and analytics platform built on Apache™ Hadoop® and the latest open source technologies, announced today that it will submit proposals for Impala and Kudu to join the Apache Software Foundation (ASF). By donating its leading analytic database and columnar storage projects to the ASF, Cloudera aims to accelerate the growth and diversity of their respective developer communities. Cloudera delivers the modern data management and analytics platform built on Apache Hadoop and the latest open source technologies. The world's leading organizations trust Cloudera to help solve their most challenging business problems with Cloudera Enterprise, the fastest, easiest and most secure data platform available to the modern world. Cloudera's customers efficiently capture, store, process, and analyze vast amounts of data, empowering them to use advanced analytics to drive business decisions quickly, flexibly, and at lower cost than has been possible before. To ensure Cloudera's customers are successful, it offers comprehensive support, training and professional services.

There are the works related to the Artificial Neural Network Algorithm (ANN) in [(R.J. Kuo, & et al, 2001), (K. P. Sudheer, & et al, 2002), (Carsten Peterson, & et al, 1994), (D.C. Park, & et al, 1991), (Kuo-lin Hsu, & et al, 1995), (Xin Yao, 1999), (B. Samanta, & K.R. Al-Balushi, 2003), (V Brusic, & et al, 1998), (Muriel Gevrey, & et al, 2003), (C. Charalambous, 1992), (K. P. Sudheer, & et al, 2002), (Zhi-Hua Zhou, & et al, 2002), (Laurent Magnier, & Fariborz Haghighat, 2010), (Sovan Lek, & J.F. Guégan, 1999), and (Kyoung-jae Kim, & Ingoo Han, 2000)]. The authors in (R.J. Kuo, & et al, 2001) developed a genetic algorithm based fuzzy neural network (GFNN) to formulate the knowledge base of fuzzy inference rules which could measure the qualitative effect on the stock market. The research in (K. P. Sudheer, & et al, 2002) investigated the prediction of Class A pan evaporation using the artificial neural network (ANN) technique, etc.

The latest researches of the sentiment classification are [(Basant Agarwal, & Namita Mittal, 2016a), (Basant Agarwal, & Namita Mittal, 2016b), (Sérgio Canuto, & et al, 2016), (Shoiab Ahmed, & Ajit Danti, 2016), (Vo Ngoc Phu, & Phan Thi Tuoi, 2014), (Vo Thi Ngoc Tran, & et al, 2014), (Vo Ngoc

Phu, & et al, 2017a), (Nguyen Duy Dat, & et al, 2017), (Vo Ngoc Phu, & et al, 2016), (Vo Ngoc Phu, & et al, 2017b), (Vo Ngoc Phu, & et al, 2017c), (Vo Ngoc Phu, & et al, 2017d), (Vo Ngoc Phu, & et al, 2017e), (Vo Ngoc Phu, & et al, 2017f), (Vo Ngoc Phu, & et al, 2017g), (Vo Ngoc Phu, & et al, 2017h), (Vo Ngoc Phu, & Vo Thi Ngoc Tran, 2017a), and (Vo Ngoc Phu, & Vo Thi Ngoc Tran, 2017b)]. In the research (Basant Agarwal, & Namita Mittal, 2016a), the authors presented their machine learning experiments with regard to sentiment analysis in blog, review and forum texts found on the World Wide Web and written in English, Dutch and French. The survey in (Basant Agarwal, & Namita Mittal, 2016b) discussed an approach where an exposed stream of tweets from the Twitter micro blogging site were preprocessed and classified based on their sentiments. In sentiment classification system the concept of opinion subjectivity has been accounted. In the study, the authors presented opinion detection and organization subsystem, which have already been integrated into our larger question-answering system, etc.

In Figure 1, our training data set includes 2,000,000 documents in the movie field, which contains 1,000,000 positive documents and 1,000,000 negative documents in English. All the documents in our English training data set are automatically extracted from English Facebook, English websites and social networks; then we labeled positive and negative for them.

Figure 1. Our English training data set

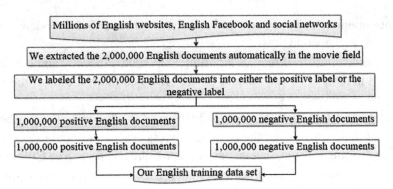

In Figure 2, our testing data set comprises 1,000,000 documents in the movie field, which have 500,000 positive documents and 500,000 negative documents in English. All the documents in our testing data set are automatically extracted from English Facebook, English websites and social networks; then we labeled positive and negative for them.

The accuracy of this novel model is dependent on many different factors. One of the factors is our data sets including a the TESDS and the TRADS

To improve the accuracy of our model, we can reform many aspects of the TESDS and the TRADS as follows:

1. The TESDS must be similar to the TRADS
2. The documents of the TESDS must be standardized carefully.
3. The documents (or the sentences) of the TRADS must be standardized carefully.
4. The documents of the TESDS must be similar to the documents of the TRADS.
5. The sentences of the TRADS must be similar to the sentences of the TESDS

Figure 2. Our English testing data set

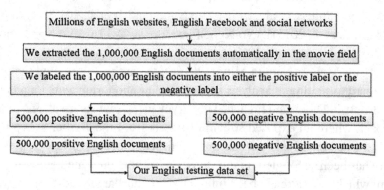

MAIN FOCUS OF THE CHAPTER

Issues, Controversies, Problems

In this part, we have presented many algorithms, methods, models, and etc. of the NN for the LSDSs in the SE and the DNS.

According to our opinion, we have not found any algorithms, methods, models, and etc. of the NN in the SS for the BDSs in the world.

This section, we have confirmed that all algorithms, methods, models, and etc. of the NN, which have been performed in the DNSs, can process for the BDSs certainly although their data sets can be many small data sets

The authors in (P. Chanthini, & K. Shyamala, 2016) used a NN which the distributed execution of the NN was achieved up to the level of the training process. This work could work well on hardware implementations, a software package, special purpose hardware and multicore CPUs through MPI. The authors used each neuron and full neural network to duplicate to multiple threads for achieving parallelism and speeding up the training process.

The authors displayed a technique to parallelize the training of NNs in (George Dahl, & et al, 2008). They designed this technique for parallelization on a cluster of workstations. Pattern Parallel Training was their solution to duplicate the full neural network et each cluster node. Each cooperating process in the cluster trained the neural network on a subset of the training set each epoch. The authors implemented and tested an MPI version of Pattern Parallel Training for the eight bit parity problem. The communication costs of our technique was analyzed and the authors discussed which types of common neural network problems would benefit most from their approach.

In (Dr. K. Usha Rani, 2010), the authors have proposed a parallel approach by using neural network technique to help in the diagnosis of breast cancer. The neural network was trained with breast cancer data base by using feed forward neural network model and back-propagation learning algorithm with momentum and variable learning rate. The performance of the network was evaluated.

A theoretical basis for a Hadoop - based neural network for parallel and distributed feature selection in BDSs was introduced in (Victoria J.Hodge, & et al, 2016). The implementation details of five feature selection algorithms was constructed using the authors' artificial neural network framework embedded in Hadoop YARN.

The authors of (Cristian Mihai BARCA, & Claudiu Dan BARCA, 2017) used the two main methods to distribute the patterns which were used for training – training set level parallelism or to distribute the computation performed by the neural network – neural network level parallelism. The first method was focused a lot in this research.

There have been many surveys of the NN for the BDSs which have not been displayed yet in this book chapter. However, there have not been enough researches of the NN for the LSDSs yet for many years.

In the below sub-section "Solutions and Recommendations", we have shown a novel model using a ANN algorithm and many MDVs of SECL for a MDS in a SE and a DNE in English.

Solutions and Recommendations

Many different algorithms of data mining, machine learning, and etc. have already been applied to sentiment analysis certainly. We have developed our models including the algorithms for the semantic classification.

To implement our new model, we have proposed the following basic principles:

1. Assuming that each English sentence has m English words (or English phrases).
2. Assuming that the maximum number of one English sentence is m_max; it means that m is less than m_max or m is equal to m_max.
3. Assuming that each English document has n English sentences.
4. Assuming that the maximum number of one English document is n_max; it means that n is less than n_max or n is equal to n_max.
5. Each English sentence is transferred into one one-dimensional vector (ODV). Thus, the length of the vector is m. If m is less than m_max then each element of the vector from m to m_max-1 is 0 (zero).
6. Each English document is transferred into one multi-dimensional vector (MDV). Therefore, the MDV has n rows and m columns. If n is less than n_max then each element of the MDV from n to n_max-1 is 0 (zero vector).
7. All the documents of the TRADS are transferred into the MDVs in English. The positive documents of the TRADS are transferred into the positive MDVs, called a positive vector group (PVP). The negative documents of the TRADS are transferred into the negative MDVs, called a negative vector group (NVP).
8. All the documents of the TESDS are transferred into the MDVs in English
9. One MDV (corresponding to one document in the TESDS in English) is the positive polarity if the vector is clustered into the PVP. One MDV (corresponding to one document in the TESDS) is the negative polarity if the vector is clustered into the NVP. One MDV (corresponding to one English document in the TESDS) is the neutral polarity if the vector is not clustered into either the PVP or the NVP

In this study, we have developed a new model by using the ANN to classify emotions (positive, negative, neutral) of the documents in the DNE. A study of semantic classification – SECL (emotional analysis - EMA) using the ANN does not currently exist in the world.

Our model has had many significant applications to many areas of research as well as commercial applications:

1. The ANN is applicable to the SECL of natural language processing.
2. This study also proves that different fields of scientific research can be related in many ways.
3. Millions of English documents are successfully processed for emotional analysis.
4. Many studies and commercial applications can use the results of this survey.
5. The semantic classification is implemented in the parallel network environment.
6. The principles are proposed in the research.
7. The opinion classification of English documents is performed on English documents.
8. The proposed model can be applied to other languages easily.
9. The Cloudera distributed environment is used in this study.
10. The proposed work can be applied to other distributed systems.
11. This survey uses Hadoop Map (M) and Hadoop Reduce (R).
12. Our proposed model can be applied to many different parallel network environments such as a Cloudera system
13. This study can be applied to many different distributed functions such as Hadoop Map (M) and Hadoop Reduce (R).
14. The ANN - related algorithms are proposed in this work.

This section has two parts: semantic classification for the documents of the testing in the SS is presented in the first part. In the second part, sentiment classification for the reviews of the testing in the DNE is displayed.

With the TRADS, there were two groups. The first group included the positive documents of the TRADS and the second group was the negative documents of the TRADS. The first group was called a positive cluster (POSC). The second group was called a negative cluster (NEGC). All the documents in both the first group and the second group went through the segmentation of words and stop-words removal; then, they were transferred into the MDVs (vector representation). The positive documents of the POSC were transferred into the positive MDVs which were called the PVP (or positive vector cluster). The negative documents of the NEGC were transferred into the negative MDVs which were called the NVP (or negative vector cluster). Therefore, the TRADS included the PVP (or positive vector cluster) and the NVP (or negative vector cluster).

In [(Vaibhav Kant Singh, & Vinay Kumar Singh, 2015), (Víctor Carrera-Trejo, & et al, 2015), and (Pascal Soucy, & Guy W. Mineau, 2015)], the VSM has been an algebraic model used for information retrieval. It has represented a natural language document in a formal manner by the use of vectors in a multidimensional space. The VSM has been a way of representing documents through the words they contain. The concepts behind vector space modeling has been that by placing terms, documents, and queries in a term-document space, it has been possible to compute the similarities between queries and the terms or documents and allow the results of the computation to be ranked according to the similarity measure between them. The VSM has allowed decisions to be made about which documents are similar to each other and to queries.

We have transferred all English sentences into one-dimensional vectors similar to VSM [(Vaibhav Kant Singh, & Vinay Kumar Singh, 2015), (Víctor Carrera-Trejo, & et al, 2015), and (Pascal Soucy, & Guy W. Mineau, 2015)].

1. An Artificial Neural Network Algorithm (ANN) in a Sequential Environment

In Figure 3, in the SE, the documents of the TESDS were transferred to the MDVs: each document of the TESDS was transferred to each MDV (each sentence of one document in the TESDS was transferred to the ODV similar to VSM [(Vaibhav Kant Singh, & Vinay Kumar Singh, 2015), (Víctor Carrera-Trejo, & et al, 2015), and (Pascal Soucy, & Guy W. Mineau, 2015)]). The positive documents in the TRADS were transferred to the positive MDVs, called the PVP in the SS: each document of the positive documents was transferred to each MDV (each sentence of one document in the positive documents was transferred to the ODV similar to VSM [(Vaibhav Kant Singh, & Vinay Kumar Singh, 2015), (Víctor Carrera-Trejo, & et al, 2015), and (Pascal Soucy, & Guy W. Mineau, 2015)] in the SE). The negative documents in the TRADS were transferred to the negative MDVs, called the NVP in the SE: each document of the negative documents was transferred to each MDV (each sentence of one document in the negative documents was transferred to the ODV similar to VSM [(Vaibhav Kant Singh, & Vinay Kumar Singh, 2015), (Víctor Carrera-Trejo, & et al, 2015), and (Pascal Soucy, & Guy W. Mineau, 2015)] in the SE).

Figure 3. Overview of transferring all English documents into the multi-dimensional vectors

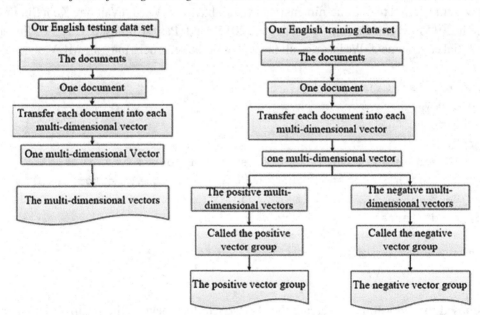

We have performed this part in Figure 4. In the SS, the ANN was implemented to cluster one MDV (called A) of the English TESDS to the PVP or the NVP. The document (corresponding to A) was the positive polarity if A was clustered to the PVP. The document (corresponding to A) was the negative polarity if A was clustered to the NVP. The document (corresponding to A) was the neutral polarity if A was not clustered to both the PVP and the NVP.

Figure 4. An artificial neural network algorithm (ANN) in the Sequential Environment

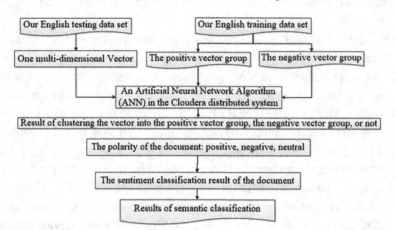

We built many algorithms to perform the ANN in the SE. We built the algorithm 1 to transfer one English document into one MDV. Each document was split into many sentences. Each sentence in each document was transferred to one one-dimensional vector based on VSM [(Vaibhav Kant Singh, & Vinay Kumar Singh, 2015), (Víctor Carrera-Trejo, & et al, 2015), and (Pascal Soucy, & Guy W. Mineau, 2015)] in the sequential environment. We inserted all the ODVs of the sentences into one MDV of one document

```
Input: one English document
Output: one MDV
Step 1: Split the English document into many separate sentences based on "."
Or "!" or "?";
Step 2: Each sentence in the n sentences of this document, do repeat:
Step 3: Transfer this sentence into one one-dimensional vector based on VSM
[(Vaibhav Kant Singh, & Vinay Kumar Singh, 2015), (Víctor Carrera-Trejo, & et
al, 2015), and (Pascal Soucy, & Guy W. Mineau, 2015)];
Step 4: Add the transferred vector into one MDV
Step 5: End Repeat - End Step 2
Step 6: Return one MDV;
```

We proposed the algorithm 2 to create the PVP. Each document in the positive documents in the English TRADS was split into many sentences. Each sentence of the document was transferred to one ODV based on VSM [(Vaibhav Kant Singh, & Vinay Kumar Singh, 2015), (Víctor Carrera-Trejo, & et al, 2015), and (Pascal Soucy, & Guy W. Mineau, 2015)] in the SE. We inserted all the ODVs of the sentences of the document into one MDV of the document. Then, the positive documents in the TRADS were transferred to the positive MDVs.

```
Input: the positive English documents of the TRADS.
Output: the positive vector group - PositiveVectorGroup
Step 1: Each document in the positive documents of the TRADS, do repeat:
Step 2: OneMultiDimensionalVector:= Call Algorithm 1 with the positive English
```

```
document  in the TRADS;
Step 3: Add OneMultiDimensionalVector into PositiveVectorGroup;
Step 4: End Repeat - End Step 1
Step 5: Return PositiveVectorGroup;
```

We developed the algorithm 3 to create the NVP. Each document in the negative documents in the English TRADS was split into many sentences. Each sentence of the document was transferred to one ODV based on VSM [(Vaibhav Kant Singh, & Vinay Kumar Singh, 2015), (Víctor Carrera-Trejo, & et al, 2015), and (Pascal Soucy, & Guy W. Mineau, 2015)] in the SE. We inserted all the ODVs of the sentences of the document into one MDV of the document. Then, the negative documents in the TRADS were transferred to the negative MDVs.

```
Input: the negative English documents of the TRADS.
Output: the negative vector group - PositiveVectorGroup
Step 1: Each document in the negative documents of the TRADS, do repeat:
Step 2: OneMultiDimensionalVector:= Call Algorithm 1 with the negative English
document  in the TRADS;
Step 3: Add OneMultiDimensionalVector into NegativeVectorGroup;
Step 4: End Repeat - End Step 1
Step 5: Return Negative VectorGroup;
```

We built the algorithm 4 to cluster one MDV (corresponding to one document of the TESDS) into the positive vector group - PositiveVectorGroup, the negative vector group - NegativeVectorGroup, or not.

```
Input: one MDV A (corresponding to one English document of the TESDS), the
positive vector group - PositiveVectorGroup, the negative vector group - Nega-
tiveVectorGroup;
Output: positive, negative, neutral;
Step 1: Implement the ANN based on the ANN in [(R.J. Kuo, & et al, 2001), (K.
P. Sudheer, & et al, 2002), (Carsten Peterson,  & et al, 1994), (D.C. Park, &
et al, 1991), (Kuo-lin Hsu, & et al, 1995), (Xin Yao, 1999), (B. Samanta, &
K.R. Al-Balushi, 2003), (V Brusic, & et al, 1998), (Muriel Gevrey, & et al,
2003), (C. Charalambous, 1992), (K. P. Sudheer, & et al, 2002), (Zhi-Hua Zhou,
& et al, 2002), (Laurent Magnier, & Fariborz Haghighat, 2010), (Sovan Lek, &
J.F. Guégan, 1999), and (Kyoung-jae Kim, & Ingoo Han, 2000)] with input is one
MDV (corresponding to one English document of the TESDS), the positive vector
group - PositiveVectorGroup, the negative vector group - NegativeVectorGroup;
Step 2: With the results of Step 1, If the vector is clustered into the PVP
Then Return positive;
Step 3: Else If the vector is clustered into the negative vector group Then
Return negative; End If - End Step 2
Step 4: Return neutral;
```

The ANN uses Euclidean distance to calculate the distance between two vectors

2. An Artificial Neural Network Algorithm (ANN) in a Parallel Network Environment

In Figure 5, all documents of both the TESDS and the TRADS were transferred into all the MDVs in the CPNS. With the documents of the TRADS, we transferred them into the MDVs by using the M/R in the CPNS with the purpose of shortening the execution time of this task. The positive documents of the TRADS were transferred into the positive vectors in the CPNS and were called the PVP. The negative documents of the TRADS were transferred into the negative vectors in the CPNS and were called the NVP. Besides, the documents of the TESDS were transferred to the MDVs by using the M/R in the CPNS with the purpose of shortening the execution time of this task.

Figure 5. Overview of transferring all English documents into the multi-dimensional vectors in the Cloudera distributed system

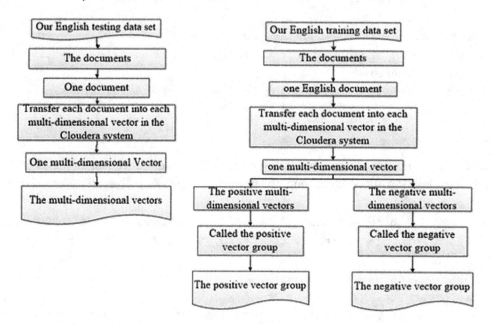

We have implemented this part in Figure 6. In the CPNS, by using the ANN, one MDV (called A) of one document in the TESDS was clustered into the PVP or the NVP. The document (corresponding to A) was the positive polarity if A was clustered into the PVP. The document (corresponding to A) was the negative polarity if A was clustered into the NVP. The document (corresponding to A) was the neutral polarity if A was not clustered into both the PVP and the NVP.

An overview of transferring each sentence into one vector in the CPNS has been presented in Figure 7.

In Figure 7, transferring each English document into one vector in the CPNS included two phases: the M phase and the R phase. The input of the M was one document and the output of the M was many components of a vector which corresponded to the document. One document which was input into the M, was split into many sentences. Each sentence in the document was transferred into one ODV based on VSM [(Vaibhav Kant Singh, & Vinay Kumar Singh, 2015), (Víctor Carrera-Trejo, & et al, 2015), and (Pascal Soucy, & Guy W. Mineau, 2015)]. This was repeated for all the sentences of the document until all the sentences were transferred into all the ODVs of the document. After finishing to transfer each sentence of the document into one ODV, the M of the CPNS automatically transferred the ODV into the R.

Figure 6. An artificial neural network algorithm (ANN) in the parallel network environment

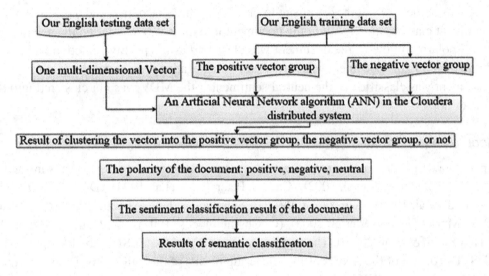

In Figure 7, the input of the R was the output of the Map phase, and this input comprised many components (many ODVs) of a MDV. The output of the R was a MDV which corresponded to the document. In the R of the CPNS, those components of the vector were built into one MDV. The documents of the TESDS were transferred into the MDVs based on Figure 7.

Figure 7. Overview of transforming each English sentence into one vector in Cloudera

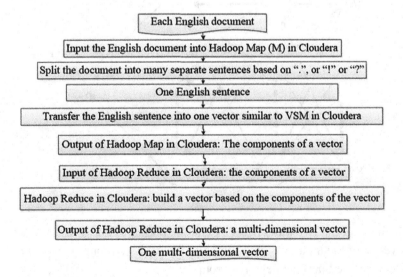

The ANN in the CPNS had two main phases: the first main phase was the M phase in the CPNS and the second main phase was the R phase in the CPNS. In the M of the CPNS, the input of the phase was the MDV of one English document (which was classified), the PVP, the NVP; and the output of the phase was the clustering results of the MDV of the document to the PVP or the NVP, or not. With the R of the CPNS, the input of the phase was the output of the M of the CPNS and this input was the clustering results of the MDV of the document to the PVP or the NVP or not; and the output of the phase was the sentiment classification result of the document into the positive polarity, the negative polarity, or the neutral polarity. In the R, the document was classified as the positive emotion if the MDV was clustered into the PVP; the document was classified as the negative semantic if the MDV into the NVP; and the document was classified as the neutral sentiment if the MDV was not clustered into the PVP, or the NVP, or not.

2.1 Hadoop Map (M) Stage

We have performed this stage in Figure 8. The ANN in the CPNS was based on the ANN in [(R.J. Kuo, & et al, 2001), (K. P. Sudheer, & et al, 2002), (Carsten Peterson, & et al, 1994), (D.C. Park, & et al, 1991), (Kuo-lin Hsu, & et al, 1995), (Xin Yao, 1999), (B. Samanta, & K.R. Al-Balushi, 2003), (V Brusic, & et al, 1998), (Muriel Gevrey, & et al, 2003), (C. Charalambous, 1992), (K. P. Sudheer, & et al, 2002), and (Zhi-Hua Zhou, & et al, 2002)]. The input was one MDV in the TESDS, the PVP and the NVP of the TRADS. The output of the ANN was the clustering results of the multi-dimensional vector into the positive vector group or the NVP, or not.

The NN in our model included the learning stage and the testing stage. An overview of our neural network was displayed in Figure 8.

Figure 8. Overview of neural network

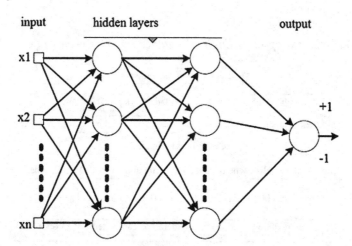

In Figure 8, the input of the NN was a MDV X and the output of network was +1 or -1. If the output was +1 then this vector of the input was classified into the positive group. If the output was -1 then this vector of input was classified into the negative group.

Our learning stage: in this stage, we used the positive vectors of the PVP and the negative vectors of the NVP to identify the parameters of our neural network, such as weights, outputs, etc.

Our testing stage: with the parameters of our neural network, each vector of the TESDS was the input of our neural network.

Algorithm 1. The basic algorithm of the supervised learning of our neural network

```
Supervised learning can be considered as mapping approximately: X ® Y, where
X is the set of problems and Y is the corresponding set of solutions to that
problem. The samples (x, y) with x = (x1, x2,..., Xn) Î X, y = (y1, y2,...,
Ym) Î Y be given.
Input: x = (x1, x2,..., Xn) Î X,
Output: y = (y1, y2,..., Ym) Î Y
begin
1. Build the appropriate structure for neural network, for example with (n+1)
neurons input (n neurons for input variables and 1 neuron for threshold x0), m
output neurons, and initialize the weights of the network links.
2.  Input one vector x in the X TRADS input into network
3.  Calculate the output vector o of network.
4.  Compare the expected output vector y (is the given result of TRADS) with
the output vector o which network generated; if can be then identify error
5.  Adjust the weights in some way so that in the next time, when inputs vec-
tor x to the network, the output vector o will resemble y more.
6.  Can repeat step 2 to step 5 if want, until converging. The evaluation of
error can perform in many different ways, using the most used instant error:
Err = (o - y), or Err = | o - y |; mean squared error (MSE: mean-square er-
ror): Err = (o- y) 2/2;
end;
```

There were two types of errors in the evaluation of a neural network. Firstly, called as clear error, assess approximately the training samples of a network have been trained. Second, called as test error, assess the ability of a total process of a network has been trained, the ability to react with the new input vector.

In this study, we used back-propagation algorithm of neural network for our new model.

The main ideal of the back-propagation algorithm: we wanted to train a multi-layer feed-forward network by gradient descent to approximate an unknown function, based on some training data consisting of pairs (x,t). The vector x represented a pattern of input to the network, and the vector t the corresponding target (desired output). As we have seen before, the overall gradient with respect to the entire training set was just the sum of the gradients for each pattern; in what follows we would therefore described how to compute the gradient for just a single training pattern. As before, we would number the units, and denoted the weight from unit j to unit i by w_{ij}.

1.   **Definitions:**

  a. The error signal for unit j: $\delta j_= -\P E/\P netj$
  b. The (negative) gradient for weight w$_{ij}$: $\Delta w_{ij}= -\P E/\P w_{ij}$
  c. The set of nodes anterior to unit i: $A_i= \{j: \exists w_{ij}\}$
  d. The set of nodes posterior to unit j: $P_j= \{i: \exists w_{ij}\}$

2. **The Gradient:** As we did for linear networks before, we expanded the gradient into two factors by use of the chain rule:

$$\Delta w_{ij} = -\frac{\partial E}{\partial net_i}\frac{\partial net_i}{\partial w_{ij}}$$

The first factor is the error of unit i. The second is

$$\frac{\partial net_i}{\partial w_{ij}} = \frac{\partial}{\partial w_{ij}}\sum_{k\in A_i} w_{ik}y_k = y_j$$

Putting the two together, we get

$$\Delta w_{ij} = \delta i_y j$$

To compute this gradient, we thus needed to know the activity and the error for all relevant nodes in the network.

3. **Forward Activation:** The activity of the input units was determined by the network's external input x. For all other units, the activity was propagated forward:

$$y_i = f_i\left(\sum_{j\in A_i} w_{ij}y_j\right)$$

before the activity of unit i could be calculated, the activity of all its anterior nodes (forming the set Ai) must be known. Since feedforward networks did not contain cycles, there was an ordering of nodes from input to output that respects this condition.

4. **Calculating Output Error:** Assuming that we were using the sum-squared loss

$$E = \frac{1}{2}\sum_o (t_o - y_o)^2$$

the error for output unit o was simply

$$\delta o = to - yo$$

5. **Error Backpropagation:** For hidden units, we must propagate the error back from the output nodes (hence the name of the algorithm). Again using the chain rule, we could expand the error of a hidden unit in terms of its posterior nodes:

$$\delta_j = \sum_{i \in P_j} \frac{\partial E}{\partial net_i} \frac{\partial net_i}{\partial y_j} \frac{\partial y_j}{\partial net_j}$$

Of the three factors inside the sum, the first is just the error of node i. The second was

$$\frac{\partial net_i}{\partial y_j} = \frac{\partial}{\partial y_j} \sum_{k \in A_i} w_{ik} y_k = w_{ij}$$

while the third was the derivative of node j's activation function:

$$\frac{\partial y_j}{\partial net_j} = \frac{\partial f_j(net_j)}{\partial net_j} = f_j'(net_j)$$

For hidden units h that used the tanh activation function, we could make use of the special identity

$$f_h'(net_h) = 1 - y_h^2$$

Putting all the pieces together we got

$$\delta_j = f_j'(net_j) \sum_{i \in P_j} \delta_i w_{ij}$$

In order to calculate the error for unit j, we must first know the error of all its posterior nodes (forming the set Pj). Again, as long as there were no cycles in the network, there was an ordering of nodes from the output back to the input that respects this condition. For example, we could simply use the reverse of the order in which activity was propagated forward.

After finishing to cluster the MDV into the PVP, or the NVP, or not, the M transferred this results into the R in the CPNS.

2.2 Hadoop Reduce (R) Stage

We have performed this stage in Figure 9. After receiving the clustering result of the M, the R identified the semantics polarity for the MDV which was classified. Then, the output of the R would return the semantics polarity of one document (corresponding to the MDV) in the TESDS. One document was the positive polarity if the MDV was clustered into the PVP. One document was the negative polarity if the MDV was clustered into the NVP. One document was the neutral polarity if the multi-dimensional vector was not clustered into both the PVP and the NVP.

Figure 9. Overview of the Hadoop Reduce (R) in the Cloudera

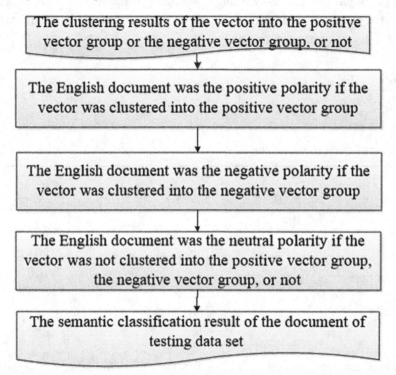

We have used an Accuracy (A) measure to calculate the accuracy of the results of emotion classification. Java programming language (JAPL) have been used for programming to save data sets, implementing our proposed model to classify the documents of the TESDS. To implement the proposed model, we have already used the JAPL to save the TRADS, the TESDS, and to save the results of emotion classification.

The SE in this research included 1 node (1 server). The JAPL has been used in programming the ANN. The configuration of the server in the SE has been: Intel® Server Board S1200V3RPS, Intel® Pentium® Processor G3220 (3M Cache, 3.00 GHz), 2GB PC3-10600 ECC 1333 MHz LP Unbuffered DIMMs. The operating system of the server has been: Cloudera. We have performed the ANN in the Cloudera parallel network environment; this Cloudera system included 9 nodes (9 servers). The JAPL has been used in programming the application of the ANN in the Cloudera. The configuration of each server in the Cloudera system has been: Intel® Server Board S1200V3RPS, Intel® Pentium® Processor G3220 (3M Cache, 3.00 GHz), 2GB PC3-10600 ECC 1333 MHz LP Unbuffered DIMMs. The operating system of each server in the 6 servers has been: Cloudera. All six nodes had the same configuration information.

The results of the opinion mining of the documents of the TESDS are presented in Table 1.

Table 1. The results of the 1,000,000 English documents in the TESDS

	Testing Dataset	**Correct Classification**	**Incorrect Classification**
Negative	500,000	420,259	79,741
Positive	500,000	422,241	77,759
Summary	1,000,000	842,500	157,500

The accuracy of the emotional classification of the documents of the TESDS is shown in Table 2.

Table 2. The accuracy of our new model for the documents of the TESDS

Proposed Model	Class	Accuracy
Our new model	Negative	84.25%
	Positive	

In Table 3, the average times of the classification of our new model for the documents in TESDS are displayed

Table 3. The average times of the classification of our new model for the documents of the TESDS

	Average time of the classification /1,000,000 English documents
The Artificial Neural Network Algorithm (ANN) in the sequential environment	5,461,091 seconds
The Artificial Neural Network Algorithm (ANN) in the Cloudera distributed system – 3 nodes	1,738,739 seconds
The Artificial Neural Network Algorithm (ANN) in the Cloudera distributed system – 6 nodes	874,378 seconds
The Artificial Neural Network Algorithm (ANN) in the Cloudera distributed system – 9 nodes	631,084 seconds

Although our new model has been tested on our English data set, it can be applied to many other languages. In this paper, our model has been tested on the 1,000,000 English documents of the TESDS in which the data sets are small. However, our model can be applied to larger data sets with millions of documents in the shortest time.

In this work, we have proposed a new model to classify the sentiments (position, negative, or neutral) of the documents using the ANN with the M and the R in the CPNS. With our proposed new model, we have achieved 84.25% accuracy of the TESDS in Table 2.

In Table 3, the average time of the EMA of the ANN algorithm in the SE is 5,461,091 seconds /1,000,000 English documents and it is greater than the average time of the SECL of the ANN in the CPNS – 3 nodes which is 1,738,739 seconds /1,000,000 English documents. The average time of the SECL of the ANN in the CPNS – 9 nodes, which is 631,084 seconds /1,000,000 English documents, is the shortest time. Besides, the average time of the SECL of the ANN in the CPNS – 6 nodes is 874,378 seconds /1,000,000 English documents

The execution time of the ANN in the CPNS is dependent on the performance of the CPNS and also dependent on the performance of each server on the CPNS.

The proposed model has many advantages and disadvantages. Its positives are as follows: It uses the ANN algorithm to classify the semantics of the documents based on the documents. The proposed model can process millions of documents in the shortest time. This study can be performed in distributed systems. It can be applied to other languages. Its negatives are as follows: It has a low rate of accuracy. It costs too much and takes too much time to implement this proposed model.

The accuracy of this novel model is dependent on many different factors as follows:

1.   The algorithms
2.   The data sets including the TESDS and the TRADS.

To improve the accuracy of our model, we can reform many aspects of the algorithms, the TESDS and the TRADS as follows:

1.   We can improve the algorithms related to the ANN
2.   We can combine the algorithms of the machine learning, the data mining, and etc.
3.   The TESDS must be similar to the TRADS.
4.   The documents of the TESDS must be standardized carefully.
5.   The documents (or the sentences) of the TRADS must be standardized carefully.
6.   The documents of the TESDS must be similar to the documents of the TRADS.
7.   The sentences of the TRADS must be similar to the sentences of the TESDS.

The execution times of this model are dependent on several factors as follows:

1.   The algorithms related to the ANN: we can improve them to get better execution times.
2.   The performance of a parallel network system such as Cloudera, Hadoop and Hadoop Reduce
3.   A number of nodes (servers) in the distributed environment: We can increase the number of nodes in the parallel system to get faster execution times
4.   The performance of a server: We can increase the performance of a server to get better execution times

FUTURE RESEARCH DIRECTIONS

From those results of this novel model and according to the above proofs, we are going to study this model for applying to billions of English documents in both the SE and the PNE. In addition, we are also going to research this approach for being performed in the PNE with over 50 nodes. Furthermore, the accuracy of this new computational model can be studied to improve certainly.

From the results of this chapter, many algorithms, methods, models, and etc. are going to be developed more and more for handling the massive data sets fully in the near future.

CONCLUSION

In this chapter, we have displayed the simple concepts of the ML, the NN, the EA, the FSs, and etc. We have shown the possible novel computational models of the NN for the BDSs successfully in more details.

We have also shown a novel model using the ANN and the MDVs of the SECL for the LSDS in the SS and the PNE successfully.

These models can be performed in the SS or the DNS fully.

There can be many models of the NN for the LSDSs, which have not been presented in this chapter yet.

In the near future, many novel computational models are going to be developed more and more for the MDSs. This is very significant for many organizations, economies, governments, countries, commercial applications, researches, and etc. in the world.

REFERENCES

Agarwal, B., & Mittal, N. (2016a). Machine Learning Approach for Sentiment Analysis. In Prominent Feature Extraction for Sentiment Analysis (pp. 21–45). Academic Press. doi:10.1007/978-3-319-25343-5_3

Agarwal, B., & Mittal, N. (2016b). Semantic Orientation-Based Approach for Sentiment Analysis. In Prominent Feature Extraction for Sentiment Analysis (pp. 77–88). Academic Press. doi:10.1007/978-3-319-25343-5_6

Ahmed, S., & Danti, A. (2016). Effective Sentimental Analysis and Opinion Mining of Web Reviews Using Rule Based Classifiers. In Computational Intelligence in Data Mining (Vol. 1, pp. 171–179). Academic Press. doi:10.1007/978-81-322-2734-2_18

Apache. (2017). Retrieved from http://apache.org

Brusic, V., Rudy, G., Honeyman, G., Hammer, J., & Harrison, L. (1998). Prediction of MHC class II-binding peptides using an evolutionary algorithm and artificial neural network. *Bioinformatics (Oxford, England)*, *14*(2), 121–130. doi:10.1093/bioinformatics/14.2.121 PMID:9545443

Canuto, Gonçalves, & Benevenuto. (2016). Exploiting New Sentiment-Based Meta-level Features for Effective Sentiment Analysis. *Proceedings of the Ninth ACM International Conference on Web Search and Data Mining (WSDM '16)*, 53-62 10.1145/2835776.2835821

Carrera-Trejo, V., Sidorov, G., Miranda-Jiménez, S., Ibarra, M. M., & Martínez, R. C. (2015). Latent Dirichlet Allocation complement in the vector space model for Multi-Label Text Classification. *International Journal of Combinatorial Optimization Problems and Informatics*, *6*(1), 7–19.

Chanthini, P., & Shyamala, K. (2016). A Survey on Parallelization of Neural Network using MPI and Open MP. *Indian Journal of Science and Technology*, *9*(19). doi:10.17485/ijst/2016/v9i19/93835

Charalambous, C. (1992). Conjugate gradient algorithm for efficient training of artificial neural networks. *IEE Proceedings. Part G. Circuits, Devices and Systems*, *139*(3), 301–310. doi:10.1049/ip-g-2.1992.0050

Cloudera. (2017). Retrieved from http://www.cloudera.com

Cristian Mihai, B. A. R. C. A., & Claudiu Dan, B. A. R. C. A. (2017). Distributed algorithm to train neural networks using the Map Reduce paradigm. *Database Systems Journal*, *8*(1), 3–11.

Dahl, G., McAvinney, A., & Newhall, T. (2008). Parallelizing neural network training for cluster systems. *PDCN '08 Proceedings of the IASTED International Conference on Parallel and Distributed Computing and Networks*, 220-225.

Dat, N. D., Phu, V. N., Vo, T. N. T., & Vo, T. N. C. (2017). STING Algorithm used English Sentiment Classification in A Parallel Environment. *International Journal of Pattern Recognition and Artificial Intelligence*, *31*(07), 1750021. doi:10.1142/S0218001417500215

Gevrey, M., Dimopoulos, I., & Lek, S. (2003). Review and comparison of methods to study the contribution of variables in artificial neural network models. *Ecological Modelling*, *160*(3), 249–264. doi:10.1016/S0304-3800(02)00257-0

Hadoop. (2017). Retrieved from http://hadoop.apache.org

Hodge, V. J., O'Keefe, S., & Austin, J. (2016). Hadoop neural network for parallel and distributed feature selection. *Neural Networks*, *78*, 24–35. doi:10.1016/j.neunet.2015.08.011 PMID:26403824

Hsu, K., Gupta, H. V., & Sorooshian, S. (1995). Artificial Neural Network Modeling of the Rainfall-Runoff Process. *Water Resources Research*, *31*(10), 2517–2530. doi:10.1029/95WR01955

Kuo, R. J., Chen, C. H., & Hwang, Y. C. (2001). An intelligent stock trading decision support system through integration of genetic algorithm based fuzzy neural network and artificial neural network. *Fuzzy Sets and Systems*, *118*(1), 21–45. doi:10.1016/S0165-0114(98)00399-6

Kyoung-jae, K., & Han, I. (2000). Genetic algorithms approach to feature discretization in artificial neural networks for the prediction of stock price index. *Expert Systems with Applications*, *19*(2), 125–132. doi:10.1016/S0957-4174(00)00027-0

Lek, S., & Guégan, J. F. (1999). Artificial neural networks as a tool in ecological modelling, an introduction. *Ecological Modelling*, *120*(2–3), 65–73. doi:10.1016/S0304-3800(99)00092-7

Magnier, L., & Haghighat, F. (2010). Multiobjective optimization of building design using TRNSYS simulations, genetic algorithm, and Artificial Neural Network. *Building and Environment*, *45*(3), 739–746. doi:10.1016/j.buildenv.2009.08.016

Park, D. C., El-Sharkawi, M. A., Marks, R. J., Atlas, L. E., & Damborg, M. J. (1991). Electric load forecasting using an artificial neural network. *IEEE Transactions on Power Systems, Volume*, *6*(2). doi:10.1109/59.76685

Peterson, C., Rögnvaldsson, T., & Lönnblad, L. (1994). JETNET 3.0—A versatile artificial neural network package. *Computer Physics Communications*, *81*(1–2), 185–220. doi:10.1016/0010-4655(94)90120-1

Phu, Vo, Vo, Duy, & Duy. (2017g). Semantic lexicons of English nouns for classification. *Evolving Systems*. doi:. doi:10.100712530-017-9188-6

Phu, Ngoc, Ngoc, & Duy. (2017b). A C4.5 algorithm for english emotional classification. *Evolving Systems*, 1-27. doi:10.100712530-017-9180-1

Phu, V. N., Dat, N. D., Vo, T. N. T., & Vo, T. N. T. (2016). Fuzzy C-Means for English Sentiment Classification in a Distributed System. In International Journal of Applied Intelligence (pp. 1–22). APIN. doi:10.100710489-016-0858-z

Phu, V. N., & Tuoi, P. T. (2014). Sentiment classification using Enhanced Contextual Valence Shifters. *International Conference on Asian Language Processing (IALP)*, 224-229. 10.1109/IALP.2014.6973485

Phu, V. N., Vo, T. N. C., Dat, N. D., Vo, T. N. T., & Nguyen, T. A. (2017c). A Valences-Totaling Model for English Sentiment Classification. Knowledge and Information Systems. doi:10.100710115-017-1054-0

Phu, V. N., Vo, T. N. C., & Vo, T. N. T. (2017d). Shifting Semantic Values of English Phrases for Classification. International Journal of Speech Technology. doi:10.100710772-017-9420-6

Phu, V. N., Vo, T. N. C., & Vo, T. N. T. (2017e). SVM for English Semantic Classification in Parallel Environment. International Journal of Speech Technology. doi:10.100710772-017-9421-5

Phu, V. N., Vo, T. N. C., Vo, T. N. T., & Dat, N. D. (2017a). A Vietnamese adjective emotion dictionary based on exploitation of Vietnamese language characteristics. *Artificial Intelligence Review*, 1–69. doi:10.100710462-017-9538-6

Phu, V. N., Vo, T. N. C., Vo, T. N. T., Dat, N. D., & Khanh, L. D. D. (2017f). *A Valence-Totaling Model for Vietnamese Sentiment Classification. International Journal of Evolving Systems*. doi:10.100712530-017-9187-7

Phu, V. N., & Vo, T. N. T. (2017a). A STING Algorithm and Multi-dimensional Vectors Used for English Sentiment Classification in a Distributed System. American Journal of Engineering and Applied Sciences. doi:10.3844/ajeassp.2017

Phu, V. N., & Vo, T. N. T. (2017b). English Sentiment Classification using Only the Sentiment Lexicons with a JOHNSON Coefficient in a Parallel Network Environment. American Journal of Engineering and Applied Sciences. doi:10.3844/ajeassp.2017

Phu, V. N., & Vo, T. N. T. (2018a). English Sentiment Classification using A Gower-2 Coefficient and A Genetic Algorithm with A Fitness-proportionate Selection in a Parallel Network Environment. *Journal of Theoretical and Applied Information Technology, 96*(4), 1-50.

Phu, V. N., & Vo, T. N. T. (2018b). English sentiment classification using a Fager & MacGowan coefficient and a genetic algorithm with a rank selection in a parallel network environment. *International Journal of Computer Modelling and New Technologies, 22*(1), 57-112.

Phu, V. N., & Vo, T. N. T. (2018c). Latent Semantic Analysis using A Dennis Coefficient for English Sentiment Classification in A Parallel System. *International Journal of Computers, Communications and Control, 13*(3), 390-410.

Phu, V. N., & Vo, T. N. T. (2018e). English Sentiment Classification using A BIRCH Algorithm and The Sentiment Lexicons-Based One-dimensional Vectors in a Parallel Network Environment. *International Journal of Computer Modelling and New Technologies, 22*(1).

Phu, V. N., & Vo, T. N. T. (2018f). A Fuzzy C-Means Algorithm and Sentiment-Lexicons-based Multi-dimensional Vectors Of A SOKAL & SNEATH-IV Coefficient Used For English Sentiment Classification. *International Journal of Theoretical and Applied Information Technology*, *96*(10).

Phu, V. N., & Vo, T. N. T. (2018g). A Self-Training - Based Model using A K-NN Algorithm and The Sentiment Lexicons - Based Multi-dimensional Vectors of A S6 coefficient for Sentiment Classification. *International Journal of Theoretical and Applied Information Technology*, *96*(10).

Phu, V. N., & Vo, T. N. T. (2018h). The Multi-dimensional Vectors and An Yule-II Measure Used for A Self-Organizing Map Algorithm of English Sentiment Classification in A Distributed Environment. *Journal of Theoretical and Applied Information Technology*, *96*(10).

Phu, V. N., & Vo, T. N. T. (2018i). Sentiment Classification using The Sentiment Scores Of Lexicons Based on A Kuhns-II Coefficient in English. International Journal of Tomography & Simulation, 31(3).

Phu, V. N., & Vo, T. N. T. (2018j). K-Medoids algorithm used for English sentiment classification in a distributed system. *Computer Modelling and New Technologies*, *22*(1), 20-39.

Phu, V. N., & Vo, T. N. T. (2018k). A Reformed K-Nearest Neighbors Algorithm for Big Data Sets. *Journal of Computer Science*. Retrieved from http://thescipub.com/abstract/10.3844/ofsp.11819

Phu, V. N., Vo, T. N. T., & Max, J. (2018d). A CURE Algorithm for Vietnamese Sentiment Classification in a Parallel Environment. *International Journal of Computer Science*. Retrieved from http://thescipub.com/abstract/10.3844/ofsp.11906

Phu, V. N., Vo, T. N. T., Vo, T. N. C., Dat, N. D., & Khanh, L. D. D. (2017h). A Decision Tree using ID3 Algorithm for English Semantic Analysis. International Journal of Speech Technology. doi:10.100710772-017-9429-x

Rani. (2010). Parallel Approach for Diagnosis of Breast Cancer using Neural Network Technique. *International Journal of Computer Applications, 10*(3), 1-5.

Samanta, B., & Al-Balushi, K. R. (2003). Artificial Neural Network Based Fault Diagnostics Of Rolling Element Bearings Using Time-Domain Features. *Mechanical Systems and Signal Processing*, *17*(2), 317–328. doi:10.1006/mssp.2001.1462

Singh & Singh. (2015). Vector Space Model: An Information Retrieval System. *Int. J. Adv. Engg. Res. Studies*, *4*(2), 141-143.

Soucy, P., & Mineau, G. W. (2015). Beyond TFIDF Weighting for Text Categorization in the Vector Space Model. *Proceedings of the 19th International Joint Conference on Artificial Intelligence*, 1130-1135.

Sudheer, K. P., Gosain, A. K., Mohana Rangan, D., & Saheb, S. M. (2002). Modelling evaporation using an artificial neural network algorithm. *Hydrological Processes*, *16*(16), 3189–3202. doi:10.1002/hyp.1096

Sudheer, K. P., Gosain, A. K., & Ramasastri, K. S. (2002). A data-driven algorithm for constructing artificial neural network rainfall-runoff models. *Hydrological Processes*. doi:10.1002/hyp.554

Vo, T. N. T., Phu, V. N., & Tuoi, P. T. (2014). Learning More Chi Square Feature Selection to Improve the Fastest and Most Accurate Sentiment Classification. *The Third Asian Conference on Information Systems (ACIS 2014)*.

Yao, X. (1999). Evolving artificial neural networks. *Proceedings of the IEEE*, *87*(9). DOI: 10.1109/5.784219

Zhou, Z.-H., Wu, J., & Tang, W. (2002). Ensembling neural networks: Many could be better than all. *Artificial Intelligence*, *137*(1–2), 239–263. doi:10.1016/S0004-3702(02)00190-X

This research was previously published in Computational Intelligence in the Internet of Things; pages 271-303, copyright year 2019 by Engineering Science Reference (an imprint of IGI Global).

Chapter 4
Artificial Neural Network Research in Online Social Networks

Steven Walczak

(iD) https://orcid.org/0000-0002-0449-6272

University of South Florida, Tampa, USA

ABSTRACT

Artificial neural networks are a machine learning method ideal for solving classification and prediction problems using Big Data. Online social networks and virtual communities provide a plethora of data. Artificial neural networks have been used to determine the emotional meaning of virtual community posts, determine age and sex of users, classify types of messages, and make recommendations for additional content. This article reviews and examines the utilization of artificial neural networks in online social network and virtual community research. An artificial neural network to predict the maintenance of online social network "friends" is developed to demonstrate the applicability of artificial neural networks for virtual community research.

INTRODUCTION

The origins of computer-based (online) social networking go back to the 1970's when communities of users interested in a specific topic would gather on a Bulletin Board System (BBS) (Rafaeli, 1984), but these systems were limited by the ability to access computer systems at that time. Modern electronic social network sites began in 1997 and generated numerous specialized as well as general communities (boyd & Ellison, 2008). Social networking sites continued to gain in popularity and expanded rapidly in the early 21st century (Thelwall, 2009).

Online social networks have become the new norm for communication between individuals and also between individuals and organizations (Cheung et al., 2011; Culnan et al., 2010; Dijkmans et al., 2015; Loader et al., 2014). Gen Z and millennials prefer to perform research online and communicate through online social networks (Hampton & Keys, 2016; Riordan et al., 2018). Prior research has found that in

DOI: 10.4018/978-1-6684-2408-7.ch004

2011, 70% of teens used social media at least once per day and 25% of these did it at least 10 times daily (Ali & Senan, 2016). Not only do millennials prefer to perform research through online social networks, but they are more engaged as participants and more likely to respond to research survey requests when approached via Twitter (Guillory et al., 2016) or other online social networks.

It is estimated that over one third of the world's population will be social network users, with a projected 2.62 billion users, by the end of 2018, and a growth rate of 6.5-7.9% annually (Statista.com, 2018). Online social networking applications produce enormous quantities of data. Mayer-Schönberger and Cukier (2013) claim that Facebook, LinkedIn, Twitter, and other online social network applications have datafied our experiences as humans, including both personal and business information. As an example, Facebook generates over 3 billion pieces of data content every day (Chen & Zhang, 2014). These big data resources from online social networks provide a vast resource for performing research, which includes: academic, customer relationship management, marketing, medical, and political research, to name a few.

Machine learning provides a solution for performing research with big data (Landset et al., 2015; Wu et al., 2014), including data generated from online social networks. Artificial neural networks (ANNs) is a subfield of machine learning, sometimes referred to as soft computing methods that also includes genetic algorithms. ANNs are a popular solution method in numerous domains including: business (Tkáč & Verner, 2016; Wong et al., 2000), engineering (Ali et al., 2015; Bansal, 2006), and medicine (Reggia, 1993; Yardimci, 2009). Research and development with ANNs continues to be highly productive with the quantity of articles published in this subfield increasing annually (Walczak, 2017). ANNs are already being applied in online social network research.

Using the compound search query of the term "neural network" combined with one of the following social network terms: "facebook" or "twitter" or "snapchat" or "instagram" or "youtube", on a university article database to search for academic articles produced 134,000 hits. The actual number is somewhat smaller than this, since authors' Facebook or Twitter accounts (if published in the contact information for an article) would cause the search engine to accept that for the second part of the combined search terms. The term "social network" was excluded from the original query terms to eliminate the large number of false positives associated with the use of the research methodology social network analysis in combination with ANNs but not focused on an online social network or virtual community topic or problem. However, at a reviewer's recommendation, a search was also performed on Google Scholar for the phrases "artificial neural network" and "social network" both appearing in the title of an article, which produced 13 new articles, though only 7 of these actually had the term "social network" in the title and only 4 (31%) utilized both online social network data and ANNs in their research methodology.

The purpose of this article is three-fold. Familiarizing online social network and virtual community researchers with the capabilities of ANNs and how to develop ANNs for performing online social network research is the first goal. Next, will be a brief review of current research in online social networks that already utilizes ANNs, utilizing the search terms given previously. These first two goals may be interpreted as a review of previous research. The research question for the review analysis is: what are the types of research for which an ANN methodology has either been used with online social network data or to analyze online social networks and virtual communities. Finally, the efficacy of utilizing ANNs for performing online social network research is demonstrated by developing an ANN to predict the maintaining, unfollowing, or unfriending of friends on Facebook.

BACKGROUND

ANNs are a viable research methodology in the social and behavioral sciences, including for online social network and virtual community research. Previous research has demonstrated that ANNs are capable of approximating arbitrary functions and solution surfaces (Hornik et al., 1989, 1990; White, 1990). While traditional statistical methods, such as regression, are commonly used in social and behavioral science research, ANNs have been widely compared to various statistical techniques and may be thought of as nonlinear and nonparametric equivalents of most statistical methods, but with better performance than standard statistical methods for nonlinear problems (Cheng & Titterington, 1994; Detienne et al., 2003; Kumar, 2005; Warner & Misra, 1996; White 1989). The nonparametric machine learning approach to model development means that ANNs are not subject to most of the constraints of parametric statistical methods. Research has shown that ANNs are a valid and useful tool for evaluating decision making heuristics of various types of businesses (Walczak, 2008).

Care must be taken to not abuse the machine learning nature by giving the ANN model a very large number of variables and hoping that the ANN will figure out which ones to use (Zhang, 2007). Independent variables must not be correlated (Smith, 1993) and must be selected carefully to minimize noise in the resulting classification or prediction model (Tahai et al., 1998).

Once non-correlated independent variables are identified, the machine learning method and algorithm must be selected and then the optimal ANN architecture developed (Walczak & Cerpa, 1999). ANNs are able to produce complex models of nonlinear solution surfaces through machine learning. Learning in ANNs is performed through adjustment of the connection weights associated with the connections between each processing element or neurode within the ANN. Learning algorithms for ANNs are commonly classified as being either unsupervised learning or supervised learning methods or may be a hybrid of both types of learning. Unsupervised learning is commonly used for pattern recognition in images and image classification (Ghosh & Pal, 1992; Lippmann, 1989). Online social network users may post images, memes, videos, or emojis, which could be a focus for ANN unsupervised learning classification. Examples of unsupervised learning algorithms are the self-organizing map (SOM) sometimes called Kohonen networks (Kohonen, 1990) and adaptive resonance theory (ART) (Carpenter & Grossberg, 1987).

Supervised learning requires that a known value for the dependent variable be known for training the ANN. A sample supervised learning ANN is shown in Figure 1. ANNs trained with a supervised learning algorithm are used for classification and also prediction research problems. The backpropagation algorithm, created in 1974 (Werbos, 1974), is the most widely used supervised learning method (Kotsiantis, 2007; Walczak & Cerpa, 1999). The name backpropagation implies how this learning algorithm works by propagating errors in training examples back through the ANN architecture to adjust the weights on the neurode connections to minimize the output error. Weight adjustment may occur through any algorithm, such as gradient descent learning (Baldi, 1995). Other supervised learning algorithms include: radial basis functions (Lowe & Broomhead, 1988), probabilistic learning (Specht, 1990), general regression-based learning (Specht, 1991), and fuzzy ARTMAP (Carpenter et al., 1992). Each learning rule attempts to address a perceived shortcoming of the original backpropagation algorithm under specific conditions, such as radial basis function trained ANNs being more resilient when only small or incomplete training examples are available (Barnard & Wessels, 1992) and general regression ANNs converging faster when a very large number of training examples are available (Specht, 1991).

The architecture of supervised learning systems, as shown in Figure 1, is made up of processing elements or neurodes arranged in interconnected layers. The quantity of neurodes per layer and the number of layers is the design of the ANN architecture. The number of hidden layers is directly related to the degree of nonlinearity achievable in the subsequent ANN model (Walczak & Cerpa, 1999). The input layer size or independent variables and output layer size or dependent variable are defined by the research problem. The goal is to have as few neurodes as possible in each of the hidden layers to inhibit overlearning, while providing sufficient neurodes to limit underlearning (Walczak & Cerpa, 1999; Zhang, 2007). This may require evaluating a large number of possible architectures to achieve optimal results.

Various alterations to the architecture shown in Figure 1 have been proposed. Recurrent ANNs or RNNs have connections from hidden layers to previous layers to enable time-based learning for problems such as time series predictions (Kamijo & Tanigawa, 1990) or classification and prediction of audio-based input (Mikolov et al., 2011). Other variations in architecture involve the combining of ANNs into a more complex system. Ensemble ANNs utilize a collection of ANNs running in parallel, with a decision algorithm to coalesce all the ANN outputs into a single value (Hansen & Salamon, 1990). More recently the idea of Deep Learning has become popular. Deep learning with ANNs is a technique for stacking different ANNs or ANN ensembles in layers, where the first layer serves as input to the second layer and so forth (Yosinski et al., 2014). An advantage of deep ANNs is the use of multiple types of data and data representations to gain a better understanding of classes (Schmidhuber, 2015), such as using text Twitter messages or Facebook messenger text messages along with images, audio and video from the same or related online social network posts.

Figure 1. Sample supervised learning ANN architecture elements ($w_{i,j}$ indicates a weight associated with a connection between neurodes, not all weights shown to make the figure more readable)

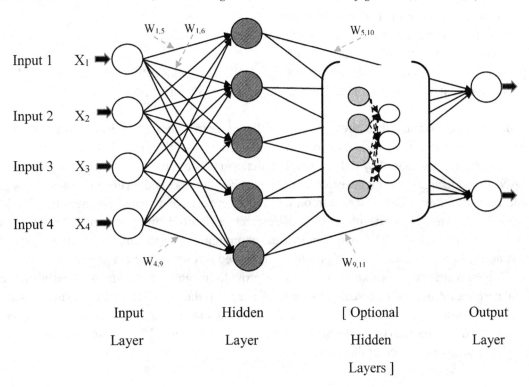

Numerous tutorials and guidelines for developing ANNs have been published (Goldberg, 2016; Jain et al., 1996; Rodvold et al., 2001; Walczak & Cerpa, 1999) to help researchers working in the field of online social networks and virtual communities develop ANNs. Due to their nonlinear and nonparametric machine learning approach to model development, ANNs should be a tool in every online social network and virtual community researcher's toolbox.

ANN RESEARCH IN ONLINE SOCIAL NETWORKS

ANNs are appropriate as a research design method for studying a variety of online social network and virtual community research questions. Due to ANN capabilities to perform complex nonlinear classifications and predictions, some research topics of interest to online social network and virtual community researchers based on the definition of a social network (Borgatti, 1998) include:

- classification of the members (of an online social network or virtual community into subgroups, based on different posting behaviors or posting types)
  - activity frequency
  - centrality
  - connectivity
  - perceived expertise, being a go to member
  - perceived relationships (friends)
- classification of content:
  - sentiment within posts
  - post accuracy or validity
- predicting changes to the network structure:
  - shift in centrality, connectivity, dominance
  - other structural affects to the network
- predicting effectiveness or substantive outcome of online social network interactions and consequent emergent actions precipitated by the online social network's posts.

Existing research has already addressed some of these research questions pertaining to online social networks. Some of the individual factors may measure influence of the individual on the group and be tied to emergent actions caused by online social media posts. The remainder indicate needed areas for future ANN and machine learning research in online social networks and virtual communities.

Table 1 shows current ANN research in online social networks and virtual communities. Table 1 is not exhaustive, but representative of the type of research currently being performed. The strategy for analyzing ANNs in online social network and virtual community research emphasizes the source of the data first and then the specific types of problems addressed through ANN classification or prediction models. The emphasis on data sources is meant to provide insights on commonly used virtual communities, perhaps influenced by researchers' ease-of-access to the very large data amounts produced.

Research has also shown that in addition to using ANNs to classify and predict online social network values, data from online social networks may be used as input values to ANNs created for other purposes. Table 2 shows sample research of this type.

As demonstrated by the research shown in Table 1 and Table 2, use of ANNs in online social network and virtual community research has already begun and should continue to grow rapidly over the coming years. This pattern of growth in use of ANNs in domain specific research has been repeatedly demonstrated in other areas of research including: business and finance (Vellido et al., 1999; Widrow et al., 1994; Wong et al., 1997; Wong & Selvi, 1998), engineering(Adeli, 2001; Zhang & Huang, 1995), medicine(Amato et al., 2013; Lisboa, 2002; Papik et al., 1998; Walczak, 2018), and the sciences (Hussain, 1999, Widrow et al., 1994), and a similar increase in ANN research development for online social networks and virtual communities research is expected to follow the precedents from these other disciplines.

Table 1. Representative ANN research in online social networks and virtual communities

Online Social Network(s)	Research Topic	Reference
Facebook	Classifying states of emergency	(Pogrebnyakov & Maldonado, 2017)
Flickr	Image recommendations	(Niu et al., 2018)
Twitter	Classify age (50%) and gender (72%) of poster	(Bayot & Gonçalves, 2017)
	Sentiment classification	(Dong et al., 2014)
		(Kalchbrenner et al., 2014)
		(Ren et al., 2016)
		(Severyn & Moschitti, 2015)
	Behavior classification	(Kumar et al., 2013)
	Brand sentiment	(Ghiassi et al., 2013, 2016)
	Detecting emotions in images	(Islam & Zhang, 2016)
Microblogs (including Twitter)	Detecting sentiment in/from images	(You et al., 2015)
Yelp	Predict ratings using sentiments	(Tang et al., 2015)
YouTube	Classify videos for violence	(Ali & Senan, 2016)
	Calculate ratings and make recommendations	(Covington et al., 2016)
	Transcribe videos	(Liao et al., 2013)
Multiple (Facebook, WhatsApp, Twitter)	Tagging parts of speech in mixed language messages	(Patel et al., 2016)
	Encryption of social media messages	(Yayik & Kutlu, 2014)
VKontakte	Detecting bot accounts	(Zegzhda et al., 2017)
Multiple/ not specified	Indexing and retrieval of multimedia data	(Liu & Zhang, 2016)

The ANN learning method most frequently used in online social network and virtual community research is the supervised learning method of backpropagation. Interestingly, an example research that utilizes unsupervised learning SOM ANN is the work by Le et al. (2016), which utilizes input values from Twitter to try and predict demand for hotel reservations in Philadelphia.

A factor that is implied form Tables 1 and 2 is that Twitter is the most commonly used online social network as either a research domain or to gain data for non-social media-based predictions, followed by Facebook, other microblogs similar to Twitter, and YouTube. With respect to the problem types for which ANNs are applied in virtual communities, as may be seen from Table 1, sentiment analysis of online social network posts is a popular current research topic. Sentiments may be used to help determine veracity of statements and the likelihood that a poster is impassioned about the topic and also likely to act on it.

Table 2. Online social network and virtual community data used in ANNs for solving other problems

Online social network data source	Research Topic	Reference
Twitter	Stock market time-series Hotel reservation predictions Power demand forecasting	(Bollen et al., 2011) (Le et al., 2016) (Luna et al., 2016)
Blogs and microblogs	Customer persona classification Product recommendations	(Priya et al., 2017) (Zhao et al., 2016)

ANN FOR PREDICTING FACEBOOK UNFRIENDING

The previous section indicates that ANNs are a method with small, but growing popularity among virtual community researchers. This section provides an example of how to utilize ANNs as a research methodology for utilizing online social network data to make a prediction relevant to the online social network virtual community.

Online social network sites are typically defined by their social relationships or connections (e.g., friends in Facebook and followers on Twitter) (Wu et al., 2014). Sibona and Walczak (2014) define posting behaviors and characteristics that lead to social relationship termination or unfriending on Facebook. Based on these and other defined Facebook behaviors (Ellison et al., 2014; Ross et al., 2009; Walther et al., 2008) a simulation was created to simulate posting behavior of individuals on Facebook. An ANN model is created, called the VC-ANN (Virtual Community ANN) to predict relationship maintenance and/or termination in online social networks. The frequency of posting, along with the posting behavior in 14 topics and their alignment with the simulated user, and the real-world relationship between the poster and the simulated user are used as independent variables to the VC-ANN, which is trained using the supervised learning method of backpropagation. The real-world relationship is treated as a categorical variable, producing 18 input variables to the VC-ANN model. Unlike the binary classification of friendship in the Sibona-Walczak model of social capital from online social networks (Sibona & Walczak, 2014), the output of the VC-ANN model is a ternary prediction of the maintenance of a friend relationship, or unfollowing the friend to keep the relationship but no longer see their posts, or unfriend to terminate the relationship that uses three output variables (one for each class of prediction). To simulate the dynamic and noisy nature of online social networks, a 20% noise ratio biasing user action toward maintaining friendships is inserted into the friend maintenance decision. The predicted action is determined by the VC-ANN output variable that has the maximum value.

A two hidden layer architecture with 16 neurodes in the first layer and 6 neurodes in the second layer is used to evaluate the efficacy of the VC-ANN model for predicting Facebook relationship management. The VC-ANN architecture is displayed in Figure 2, minus many of the connections between layers for purposes of readability. Two-fold cross validation is used so that all simulated posting behaviors and frequencies could be predicted. Random chance would produce an overall accuracy of 33.3% for this 3 class problem. The ANN architecture described produced an overall prediction accuracy of 70% ($p < 0.001$), with 67.7% friend maintenance accuracy, 70.8% unfollowing accuracy, and 71.1% unfriending accuracy. Results for 100 simulated posting friend relationship management decisions based on corresponding behaviors are given in Table 3. As may be seen from Table 3, the feature-relationship samples (Wu et al., 2014) created in the simulation were 45% unfriend behavior samples, 31% friend behaviors samples, and 24% unfollow behavior samples. This distribution is biased towards unfriending behaviors to better simulate the Sibona-Walczak model of social capital from online social networks (Sibona & Walczak, 2014).

Figure 2. ANN architecture to predict Facebook friend management

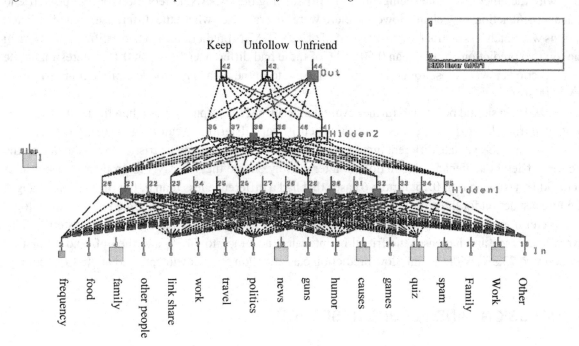

Table 3. ANN Facebook friend maintenance prediction performance

Simulated Real-World Decision	ANN predicts keep Friend	ANN predicts Unfollow	ANN predicts Unfriend
Maintain friendship	21	6	4
Unfollow	4	17	3
Unfriend	6	7	32

Even with a 20% noise ratio causing unfriend and unfollow posting actions to be interpreted as maintaining the friend status, the ANN adapts well and only has an overall rate of 10% false maintain the friend status predictions. This indicates that even with a relatively high noise ratio, which is expected due to the highly subjective nature of individual decisions for online social networking relationships, the VC-ANN model still produces a reliable prediction of relationship actions based on posting behaviors. Different types of ANN machine learning algorithms may also better handle noisy data, such as radial basis function-based training, which has been proven to be slightly more resilient when training data sets are more limited in number and when noisy data is present (Walczak & Cerpa, 1999).

Prior research indicates that ANN performance can be improved when the ANN is combined with other machine learning or statistical methods using methodological triangulation (Walczak, 2012). Examples include: using statistics like Pearson's correlation matrix or factor analysis or genetic algorithms to determine the optimal and non-correlated set of input variables; using genetic algorithms to determine the optimally performing ANN hidden layer and node architecture; and using fuzzy reasoning or other methods to interpret ANN output values. The majority of the VC-ANN outputs had a single value close to 1, with the other two values being close to zero, making the VC-ANN prediction for Facebook friend management action very clear. However, there were several cases where the difference in the predicted actions was much less distinct. There was a total of 22 VC-ANN predictions that had a difference between the top two predictions of less than 0.50 and 6 of these had differences less than 0.15. Interestingly, the 22 predictions is very close to the 20 percent noise rate in the data. The smallest prediction difference was 0.0096.

Fuzzy logic should be used to further evaluate the VC-ANN output values when the highest value is separated from the next value by less than some heuristically determined cutoff, alpha (α). The fuzzy system could then re-evaluate different input values and use additional fuzzy heuristics to try and determine a correct friend maintenance prediction, or alternatively enable the VC-ANN to produce a response of undecided. Using an α of 0.15, for the 6 cases that had a difference less than α, the fuzzy logic changes the forecast action for three of these cases. The new VC-ANN predictions combined with a fuzzy logic interpreter improves the overall accuracy of the VC-ANN friend maintenance prediction system to 73% overall accuracy and increases the friend maintenance accuracy to 74.2% and the unfriend prediction accuracy to 73.3%, with the unfollow prediction classification accuracy unchanged at 70.8% accuracy.

CONCLUSIONS AND FUTURE RESEARCH

ANN research using data from virtual communities is progressing. The increasing reliance of current generations on electronic social media for daily communication and information gathering as well as the plethora of data being generated by these virtual communities, indicates a need for ongoing research using machine learning techniques to effectively handle the very large amount of data generated by these online social network and virtual community domains. Unsupervised learning ANNs have already been shown to work well with audio and image data, but advances in deep learning ANNs will enable even more accurate classifications of this type of data in online social networks and virtual communities. Additional research applying ANNs to online social networks and virtual communities is needed to further validate ANNs as an appropriate and preferred research methodology for the social sciences, particularly with respect to virtual communities.

Several promising areas for ANN research questions in the online social networks and virtual community domains were listed in the ANN Research in Online Social Networks section. Future research is needed to expand ANN research to better cover these questions, including the impact of communications through online social networks and validation of message veracity, and to expand into novel areas of classification and prediction enabled by online social network data. For example, one such future research topic could be determining the predictive performance of ANNs for forecasting election outcomes, based on online social network data.

This article has provided a brief overview of ANN development for online social network and virtual community researchers, as well as providing pointers to other published tutorials to assist virtual community researchers in developing ANN research models. Next, a review of research from 2013-2018 on how ANNs are currently being used in online social network research was presented. Finally, an ANN application using a backpropagation trained ANN to predict user actions for management of Facebook friends based on simulated posting behavior was developed. The Facebook friend management prediction ANN achieved a 70% overall prediction accuracy for the three possible actions of maintaining the friendship, unfollowing the friend, or defriending. These results demonstrate the efficacy of using ANNs as a research method in online social networks and virtual communities.

Combining the VC-ANN using methodological triangulation (Walczak, 2012) with a fuzzy logic back end, improved the overall prediction accuracy to 73%. These results indicate that triangulating ANNs with other machine learning and statistical methods such as fuzzy logic heuristics could serve to further improve ANN outcomes in online social network and virtual community research. Utilizing ANNs in combination with other machine learning and statistical methods is an area for future research. This article only discussed the machine learning paradigm of ANNs to the exclusion of other machine learning methods, such as: Bayesian learning, support vector machines, and random forests to name a few. Future research should compare ANN performance for specific virtual community classification and prediction problems against other machine learning techniques as well as combined techniques to determine under what circumstances ANNs will perform better than other machine learning methods.

The implications of this research are that ANNs provide a versatile machine learning method for working with online social network big data. The nonparametric nature of ANNs means that researchers can freely utilize this method without the need for significant amounts of statistical testing on population data to make sure that the data is appropriate for use with other machine learning and statistical methods. Additionally the nonlinear modeling capabilities indicate that ANNs are appropriate for solving virtual community modeling problems that are both complex and imprecise in nature. Investigators are cautioned to make sure that the independent variables selected are meaningful and also not highly correlated (Smith, 1993; Zhang, 2007).

REFERENCES

Adeli, H. (2001). Neural Networks in Civil Engineering: 1989–2000. *Computer-Aided Civil and Infrastructure Engineering*, *16*(2), 126–142. doi:10.1111/0885-9507.00219

Ali, A., & Senan, N. (2016). A Review on Violence Video Classification Using Convolutional Neural Networks. *Proceedings of the International Conference on Soft Computing and Data Mining* (pp. 130-140). Cham: Springer.

Ali, J. M., Hussain, M. A., Tade, M. O., & Zhang, J. (2015). Artificial Intelligence techniques applied as estimator in chemical process systems–A literature survey. *Expert Systems with Applications*, *42*(14), 5915–5931. doi:10.1016/j.eswa.2015.03.023

Amato, F., López, A., Peña-Méndez, E. M., Vaňhara, P., Hampl, A., & Havel, J. (2013). Artificial neural networks in medical diagnosis. *Journal of Applied Biomedicine*, *11*(2), 47–58. doi:10.2478/v10136-012-0031-x

Baldi, P. (1995). Gradient descent learning algorithm overview: A general dynamical systems perspective. *IEEE Transactions on Neural Networks*, *6*(1), 182–195. doi:10.1109/72.363438 PMID:18263297

Bansal, R. C. (2006). Overview and literature survey of artificial neural networks applications to power systems (1992-2004). *Journal of the Institution of Engineers (India) Part EL*, *86*(1), 282–296.

Barnard, E., & Wessels, L. F. A. (1992). Extrapolation and interpolation in neural network classifiers. *IEEE Control Systems*, *12*(5), 50–53. doi:10.1109/37.158898

Bayot, R. K., & Gonçalves, T. (2017). Age and Gender Classification of Tweets Using Convolutional Neural Networks. *Proceedings of the International Workshop on Machine Learning, Optimization, and Big Data* (pp. 337-348). Cham: Springer.

Bollen, J., Mao, H., & Zeng, X. (2011). Twitter mood predicts the stock market. *Journal of Computational Science*, *2*(1), 1–8. doi:10.1016/j.jocs.2010.12.007

Borgatti, S. (1998). What is Social Network Analysis? Analytictech. Retrieved from http://www.analytictech.com/networks/whatis.htm

boyd, d.m., & Ellison, N. B. (2008). Social Network Sites: Definition, History, and Scholarship. *Journal of Computer-Mediated Communication, 13*(1), 210-230.

Carpenter, G. A., Grossberg, S., Markuzon, N., Reynolds, J. H., & Rosen, A. B. (1992). Fuzzy ART-MAP: A neural network architecture for incremental supervised learning of analog multidimensional maps. *IEEE Transactions on Neural Networks*, *3*(5), 698–713. doi:10.1109/72.159059 PMID:18276469

Chen, C. P., & Zhang, C. Y. (2014). Data-intensive applications, challenges, techniques and technologies: A survey on Big Data. *Information Sciences*, *275*, 314–347. doi:10.1016/j.ins.2014.01.015

Cheng, B., & Titterington, D. M. (1994). Neural Networks: A Review from a Statistical Perspective. *Statistical Science*, *9*(1), 2–30. doi:10.1214s/1177010638

Cheung, C. M., Chiu, P. Y., & Lee, M. K. (2011). Online social networks: Why do students use Facebook? *Computers in Human Behavior*, *27*(4), 1337–1343. doi:10.1016/j.chb.2010.07.028

Covington, P., Adams, J., & Sargin, E. (2016). Deep Neural Networks for Youtube Recommendations. *Proceedings of the 10th ACM Conference on Recommender Systems* (pp. 191-198). ACM. 10.1145/2959100.2959190

Culnan, M. J., McHugh, P. J., & Zubillaga, J. I. (2010). How large US companies can use Twitter and other social media to gain business value. *MIS Quarterly Executive*, *9*(4), 243–259.

Detienne, K. B., Detienne, D. H., & Joshi, S. A. (2003). Neural networks as statistical tools for business researchers. *Organizational Research Methods*, *6*(2), 236–265. doi:10.1177/1094428103251907

Dijkmans, C., Kerkhof, P., & Beukeboom, C. J. (2015). A stage to engage: Social media use and corporate reputation. *Tourism Management*, *47*, 58–67. doi:10.1016/j.tourman.2014.09.005

Dong, L., Wei, F., Tan, C., Tang, D., Zhou, M., & Xu, K. (2014). Adaptive Recursive Neural Network for Target-Dependent Twitter Sentiment Classification. *Proceedings of the 52nd Annual Meeting of the Association for Computational Linguistics* (*Vol. 2*, pp. 49-54). Academic Press. 10.3115/v1/P14-2009

Ellison, N. B., Vitak, J., Gray, R., & Lampe, C. (2014). Cultivating Social Resources on Social Network Sites: Facebook Relationship Maintenance Behaviors and Their Role in Social Capital Processes. *Journal of Computer-Mediated Communication, 19*(4), 855–870. doi:10.1111/jcc4.12078

Ghiassi, M., Skinner, J., & Zimbra, D. (2013). Twitter brand sentiment analysis: A hybrid system using n-gram analysis and dynamic artificial neural network. *Expert Systems with Applications, 40*(16), 6266–6282. doi:10.1016/j.eswa.2013.05.057

Ghiassi, M., Zimbra, D., & Lee, S. (2016). Targeted twitter sentiment analysis for brands using supervised feature engineering and the dynamic architecture for artificial neural networks. *Journal of Management Information Systems, 33*(4), 1034–1058. doi:10.1080/07421222.2016.1267526

Ghosh, A., & Pal, S. K. (1992). Neural network, self-organization and object extraction. *Pattern Recognition Letters, 13*(5), 387–397. doi:10.1016/0167-8655(92)90036-Y

Goldberg, Y. (2016). A Primer on Neural Network Models for Natural Language Processing. *Journal of Artificial Intelligence Research, 57,* 345–420. doi:10.1613/jair.4992

Guillory, J., Kim, A., Murphy, J., Bradfield, B., Nonnemaker, J., & Hsieh, Y. (2016). Comparing Twitter and Online Panels for Survey Recruitment of E-Cigarette Users and Smokers. *Journal of Medical Internet Research, 18*(11), e288. doi:10.2196/jmir.6326 PMID:27847353

Hampton, D. C., & Keys, Y. (2016). Generation Z students: Will they change our nursing classrooms? *Journal of Nursing Education and Practice, 7*(4), 111–115. doi:10.5430/jnep.v7n4p111

Hansen, L. K., & Salamon, P. (1990). Neural network ensembles. *IEEE Transactions on Pattern Analysis and Machine Intelligence, 12*(10), 993–1001. doi:10.1109/34.58871

Hornik, K., Stinchcombe, M., & White, H. (1989). Multilayer Feedforward Networks Are Universal Approximators. *Neural Networks, 2*(5), 359–366. doi:10.1016/0893-6080(89)90020-8

Hornik, K., Stinchcombe, M., & White, H. (1990). Universal Approximation of an Unknown Mapping and Its Derivatives Using Multilayer Feedforward Networks. *Neural Networks, 3*(5), 551–560. doi:10.1016/0893-6080(90)90005-6

Hussain, M. A. (1999). Review of the applications of neural networks in chemical process control—simulation and online implementation. *Artificial Intelligence in Engineering, 13*(1), 55–68. doi:10.1016/S0954-1810(98)00011-9

Islam, J., & Zhang, Y. (2016). Visual sentiment analysis for social images using transfer learning approach. *Proceedings of the 2016 IEEE International Conferences on Big Data and Cloud Computing, Social Computing and Networking, Sustainable Computing and Communications* (pp. 124-130). IEEE. 10.1109/BDCloud-SocialCom-SustainCom.2016.29

Jain, A. K., Mao, J., & Mohiuddin, K. M. (1996). Artificial neural networks: A tutorial. *IEEE Computer, 29*(3), 31–44. doi:10.1109/2.485891

Kalchbrenner, N., Grefenstette, E., & Blunsom, P. (2014). A Convolutional Neural Network for Modelling Sentences. *Proceedings of the 52nd Annual Meeting of the Association for Computational Linguistics* (Vol. 1, pp. 655-665). 10.3115/v1/P14-1062

Kamijo, K. I., & Tanigawa, T. (1990). Stock price pattern recognition-a recurrent neural network approach. *Proceedings of the 1990 IJCNN International Joint Conference on Neural Networks* (pp. 215-221). IEEE. 10.1109/IJCNN.1990.137572

Kotsiantis, S. B. (2007). Supervised Machine Learning: A Review of Classification Techniques. *Informatica*, *31*, 249–268.

Kumar, H., Arya, A., Divyalakshmi, V., & Nishanth, H. S. (2013). Artificial Neural Network in Prognosticating Human Personality from Social Networks. *International Journal of Modern Education and Computer Science*, *5*(8), 51–57. doi:10.5815/ijmecs.2013.08.06

Kumar, U. A. (2005). Comparison of neural networks and regression analysis: A new insight. *Expert Systems with Applications*, *29*(2), 424–430. doi:10.1016/j.eswa.2005.04.034

Landset, S., Khoshgoftaar, T. M., Richter, A. N., & Hasanin, T. (2015). A survey of open source tools for machine learning with big data in the Hadoop ecosystem. *Journal of Big Data*, *2*(1), 24. doi:10.118640537-015-0032-1

Liao, H., McDermott, E., & Senior, A. (2013). Large Scale Deep Neural Network Acoustic Modeling with Semi-Supervised Training Data for Youtube Video Transcription. *Proceedings of the 2013 IEEE Workshop on Automatic Speech Recognition and Understanding* (pp. 368-373). IEEE. 10.1109/ASRU.2013.6707758

Lippmann, R. P. (1989). Pattern Classification Using Neural Networks. *IEEE Communications Magazine*, *27*(11), 47–50. doi:10.1109/35.41401

Lisboa, P. J. (2002). A review of evidence of health benefit from artificial neural networks in medical intervention. *Neural Networks*, *15*(1), 11–39. doi:10.1016/S0893-6080(01)00111-3 PMID:11958484

Liu, W., & Zhang, T. (2016). Multimedia hashing and networking. *IEEE MultiMedia*, *23*(3), 75–79. doi:10.1109/MMUL.2016.39

Loader, B. D., Vromen, A., & Xenos, M. A. (2014). The networked young citizen: Social media, political participation and civic engagement. *Information Communication and Society*, *17*(2), 143–150. doi:10.1080/1369118X.2013.871571

Lowe, D. S., & Broomhead, D. (1988). Multivariable functional interpolation and adaptive networks. *Complex Systems*, *2*(3), 321–355.

Luna, A., Nunez-del-Prado, M., Talavera, A., & Holguín, E. S. (2016). Power demand forecasting through social network activity and artificial neural networks. Proceedings of the 2016 IEEE ANDESCON (pp. 1-4). IEEE. doi:10.1109/ANDESCON.2016.7836248

Mayer-Schönberger, V., & Cukier, K. (2013). *Big Data: A Revolution That Will Transform How We Live, Work, and Think*. Boston: Houghton Mifflin Harcourt.

Mikolov, T., Kombrink, S., Burget, L., Černocký, J., & Khudanpur, S. (2011). Extensions of recurrent neural network language model. *Proceedings of the 2011 IEEE International Conference on Acoustics, Speech and Signal Processing*, (pp. 5528-5531). IEEE. 10.1109/ICASSP.2011.5947611

Niu, W., Caverlee, J., & Lu, H. (2018). Neural Personalized Ranking for Image Recommendation. *Proceedings of 11th ACM International Conf. on Web Search and Data Mining* (pp. 423-431). New York: ACM.

Papik, K., Molnar, B., Schaefer, R., Dombovari, Z., Tulassay, Z., & Feher, J. (1998). Application of neural networks in medicine-a review. *Medical Science Monitor*, *4*(3), 538–546.

Patel, R. N., KBCS, C., Pimpale, P. B., & Sasikumar, M. (2016). Recurrent Neural Network based Part-of-Speech Tagger for Code-Mixed Social Media Text. *Proceedings of the Tool Contest on POS Tagging for Indian Social Media Text, ICON 2016*. Academic Press.

Pogrebnyakov, N., & Maldonado, E. (2017). Identifying emergency stages in Facebook posts of police departments with convolutional and recurrent neural networks and support vector machines. *Proceedings of the 2017 IEEE International Conference on Big Data*, (pp. 4343-4352). IEEE. 10.1109/BigData.2017.8258464

Priya, M. S. V., Gokhila, B., Santhiya, T., & Saranya, K. (2017). Connecting Social Media to Ecommerce Using Microblogging and Artificial Neural Network. *International Journal of Recent Trends in Engineering and Research*, *3*(3), 337–343. doi:10.23883/IJRTER.2017.3087.4IJNP

Rafaeli, S. (1984). The electronic bulletin board: A computer-driven mass medium. *Social Science Micro Review*, *2*(3), 123–136. doi:10.1177/089443938600200302

Reggia, J. A. (1993). Neural computation in medicine. *Artificial Intelligence in Medicine*, *5*(2), 143–157. doi:10.1016/0933-3657(93)90014-T PMID:8358491

Ren, Y., Zhang, Y., Zhang, M., & Ji, D. (2016). Context-Sensitive Twitter Sentiment Classification Using Neural Network. *Proceedings of AAAI* (pp. 215-221). AAAI.

Riordan, M. A., Kreuz, R. J., & Blair, A. N. (2018). The digital divide: Conveying subtlety in online communication. *Journal of Computers in Education*, *5*(1), 49–66. doi:10.100740692-018-0100-6

Rodvold, D. M., McLeod, D. G., Brandt, J. M., Snow, P. B., & Murphy, G. P. (2001). Introduction to artificial neural networks for physicians: Taking the lid off the black box. *The Prostate*, *46*(1), 39–44. doi:10.1002/1097-0045(200101)46:1<39::AID-PROS1006>3.0.CO;2-M PMID:11170130

Ross, C., Orr, E. S., Sisic, M., Arseneault, J. M., Simmering, M. G., & Orr, R. R. (2009). Personality and motivations associated with Facebook use. *Computers in Human Behavior*, *25*(2), 578–586. doi:10.1016/j.chb.2008.12.024

Schmidhuber, J. (2015). Deep learning in neural networks: An overview. *Neural Networks*, *61*, 85–117. doi:10.1016/j.neunet.2014.09.003 PMID:25462637

Severyn, A., & Moschitti, A. (2015). Unitn: Training Deep Convolutional Neural Network for Twitter Sentiment Classification. *Proceedings of the 9th International Workshop on Semantic Evaluation* (pp. 464-469). Academic Press. 10.18653/v1/S15-2079

Shahin, M. A., Jaksa, M. B., & Maier, H. R. (2001). Artificial Neural Network Applications in Geotechnical Engineering. *Australian Geomechanics*, *36*(1), 49–62.

Sibona, C., & Walczak, S. (2014). Unfriending on Facebook: Factors affecting online relationship termination in social networks and its impact on business. *International Journal of Business Environment*, 6(2), 199–221. doi:10.1504/IJBE.2014.060237

Smith, M. (1993). *Neural Networks for Statistical Modeling*. New York: Van Nostrand Reinhold.

Specht, D. F. (1990). Probabilistic neural networks. *Neural Networks*, 3(1), 109–118. doi:10.1016/0893-6080(90)90049-Q PMID:18282828

Specht, D. F. (1991). A general regression neural network. *IEEE Transactions on Neural Networks*, 2(6), 568–576. doi:10.1109/72.97934 PMID:18282872

Statista.com. (2018). Number of social network users worldwide from 2010 to 2021 (in billions). Retrieved from https://www.statista.com/statistics/278414/number-of-worldwide-social-network-users/

Tahai, A., Walczak, S., & Rigsby, J. T. (1998). Improving Artificial Neural Network Performance Through Input Variable Selection. In P. Siegel, K. Omer, A. deKorvin, & A. Zebda (Eds.), *Applications of Fuzzy Sets and The Theory of Evidence to Accounting II* (pp. 277–292). Stamford, CT: JAI Press.

Tang, D., Qin, B., Liu, T., & Yang, Y. (2015). User Modeling with Neural Network for Review Rating Prediction. In IJCAI (pp. 1340-1346). AAAI Press.

Thelwall, M. (2009). Social network sites: Users and uses. In M. Zelkowitz (Ed.), *Advances in Computers 76* (pp. 19–73). Amsterdam: Elsevier.

Tkáč, M., & Verner, R. (2016). Artificial neural networks in business: Two decades of research. *Applied Soft Computing*, 38, 788–804. doi:10.1016/j.asoc.2015.09.040

Vellido, A., Lisboa, P. J., & Vaughan, J. (1999). Neural networks in business: A survey of applications (1992–1998). *Expert Systems with Applications*, 17(1), 51–70. doi:10.1016/S0957-4174(99)00016-0

Walczak, S. (2008). Evaluating medical decision making heuristics and other business heuristics with neural networks. In G. Phillips-Wren, N. Ichalkaranje, & L. C. Jain (Eds.), *Intelligent Decision Making: An AI-Based Approach* (pp. 259–287). Berlin: Springer. doi:10.1007/978-3-540-76829-6_10

Walczak, S. (2012). Methodological Triangulation Using Neural Networks for Business Research. *Advances in Artificial Neural Systems*, (517234), 1–12. doi:10.1155/2012/517234

Walczak, S. (2016). Artificial Neural Networks and Other AI Applications for Business Management Decision Support. *International Journal of Sociotechnology and Knowledge Development*, 8(4), 1–20. doi:10.4018/IJSKD.2016100101

Walczak, S. (2017). Artificial Neural Networks. In M. Khosrow-Pour (Ed.), *Encyclopedia of Information Science and Technology* - (4th ed., pp. 120–131). Hershey, PA: IGI Global.

Walczak, S. (2018). The Role of Artificial Intelligence in Clinical Decision Support Systems & Classification Framework. *International Journal of Computers in Clinical Practice*, 3(2), 31–47. doi:10.4018/IJCCP.2018070103

Walczak, S., & Cerpa, N. (1999). Heuristic Principles for the Design of Artificial Neural Networks. *Information and Software Technology*, 41(2), 107–117. doi:10.1016/S0950-5849(98)00116-5

Walther, J. B., Van Der Heide, B., Kim, S. Y., Westerman, D., & Tong, S. T. (2008). The Role of Friends' Appearance and Behavior on Evaluations of Individuals on Facebook: Are We Known by the Company We Keep? *Human Communication Research*, *34*(1), 28–49. doi:10.1111/j.1468-2958.2007.00312.x

Warner, B., & Misra, M. (1996). Understanding Neural Networks as Statistical Tools. *The American Statistician*, *50*(4), 284–293.

Werbos, P. J. (1974). *Beyond Regression: New Tools for Prediction and Analysis in the Behavioral Sciences* [Doctoral Dissertation]. Harvard University, Boston, MA.

White, H. (1989). Learning in Artificial Neural Networks: A Statistical Perspective. *Neural Computation*, *1*(4), 425–464. doi:10.1162/neco.1989.1.4.425

White, H. (1990). Connectionist nonparametric regression: Multilayer feedforward networks can learn arbitrary mappings. *Neural Networks*, *3*(5), 535–549. doi:10.1016/0893-6080(90)90004-5

Widrow, B., Rumelhart, D. E., & Lehr, M. A. (1994). Neural Networks: Applications in Industry, Business and Science. *Communications of the ACM*, *37*(3), 93–106. doi:10.1145/175247.175257

Wong, B. K., Bodnovich, T. A., & Selvi, Y. (1997). Neural network applications in business: A review and analysis of the literature (1988–1995). *Decision Support Systems*, *19*(4), 301–320. doi:10.1016/S0167-9236(96)00070-X

Wong, B. K., Lai, V. S., & Lam, J. (2000). A bibliography of neural network business applications research: 1994–1998. *Computers & Operations Research*, *27*(11–12), 1045–1076. doi:10.1016/S0305-0548(99)00142-2

Wong, B. K., & Selvi, Y. (1998). Neural network applications in finance: A review and analysis of literature (1990–1996). *Information & Management*, *34*(3), 129–139. doi:10.1016/S0378-7206(98)00050-0

Wu, X., Zhu, X., Wu, G. Q., & Ding, W. (2014). Data mining with big data. *IEEE Transactions on Knowledge and Data Engineering*, *26*(1), 97–107. doi:10.1109/TKDE.2013.109

Yardimci, A. (2009). Soft computing in medicine. *Applied Soft Computing*, *9*(3), 1029–1043. doi:10.1016/j.asoc.2009.02.003

Yayik, A., & Kutlu, Y. (2014). Neural network based cryptography. *Neural Network World*, *24*(2), 177–192. doi:10.14311/NNW.2014.24.011

Yosinski, J., Clune, J., Bengio, Y., & Lipson, H. (2014). How transferable are features in deep neural networks? *Proceedings of the Twenty Eighth Advances in Neural Information Processing Systems Conference* (pp. 3320-3328). Academic Press.

You, Q., Luo, J., Jin, H., & Yang, J. (2015). Joint visual-textual sentiment analysis with deep neural networks. In *Proceedings of the 23rd ACM international conference on Multimedia* (pp. 1071-1074). ACM. 10.1145/2733373.2806284

Zegzhda, P. D., Malyshev, E. V., & Pavlenko, E. Y. (2017). The use of an artificial neural network to detect automatically managed accounts in social networks. *Automatic Control and Computer Sciences*, *51*(8), 874–880. doi:10.3103/S0146411617080296

Zhang, G. P. (2007). Avoiding pitfalls in neural network research. *IEEE Transactions on Systems, Man and Cybernetics. Part C, Applications and Reviews*, *37*(1), 3–16. doi:10.1109/TSMCC.2006.876059

Zhang, H. C., & Huang, S. H. (1995). Applications of neural networks in manufacturing: A state-of-the-art survey. *International Journal of Production Research*, *33*(3), 705–728. doi:10.1080/00207549508930175

Zhao, W. X., Li, S., He, Y., Chang, E. Y., Wen, J. R., & Li, X. (2016). Connecting social media to e-commerce: Cold-start product recommendation using microblogging information. *IEEE Transactions on Knowledge and Data Engineering*, *28*(5), 1147–1159. doi:10.1109/TKDE.2015.2508816

This research was previously published in the International Journal of Virtual Communities and Social Networking (IJVCSN), 10(4); pages 1-15, copyright year 2018 by IGI Publishing (an imprint of IGI Global).

Chapter 5
A Journey From Neural Networks to Deep Networks:
Comprehensive Understanding for Deep Learning

Priyanka P. Patel

(iD) https://orcid.org/0000-0002-2618-072X

Chandubhai S. Patel Institute of Technology, CHARUSAT University, India

Amit R. Thakkar

Chandubhai S. Patel Institute of Technology, CHARUSAT University, India

ABSTRACT

The chapter is about deep learning fundaments and its recent trends. The chapter mentions many advanced applications and deep learning models and networks to easily solve those applications in a very smart way. Discussion of some techniques for computer vision problem and how to solve with deep learning approach are included. After taking fundamental knowledge of the background theory, one can create or solve applications. The current state-of-the-art of deep learning for education, healthcare, agriculture, industrial, organizations, and research and development applications are very fast growing. The chapter is about types of learning in a deep learning approach, what kind of data set one can be required, and what kind of hardware facility is required for the particular complex problem. For unsupervised learning problems, Deep learning algorithms have been designed, but in the same way Deep learning is also solving the supervised learning problems for a wide variety of tasks.

INTRODUCTION

DL is a subclass of ML and ML is a sub-branch of AI. Capabilities of deep learning diverge in many key respects from ancient machine learning. Deep learning acquiesces to computers to resolve a number of complex, advanced and novel issues that have been not somewhat be tackled by Ancient machine

DOI: 10.4018/978-1-6684-2408-7.ch005

learning approaches (Arel, I. et al, 2010; LeCun et al, 2015; Schmidhuber, J., 2015). These issues are that swathes of issues in the real world are not a good fit for such simple models means some advanced and high configuration models, techniques, and approach is required. A handwritten number recognizing is one of the examples of these complex real- world problem. To resolve such problem one needs to gather a huge dataset related to handwritten numbers also the computer system should handle such data. Every digit between 0 and 9 can be written in numerous ways also the size and exact shape of each handwritten digit can be very different depending on whose writing and in what circumstance. So to manage the diversity of these multiple feature set and to further communication between them is where deep learning and deep neural networks become very beneficial as compare to Ancient learning. Neural networks are mathematical models whose construction of the network is broadly inspired by the human brain. Each neuron of the network is a mathematical function which receives data through an input layer and, transforms that input data into a more responsible form, and then it will spit it out through an output layer. You can think of neurons in a neural network as being arranged in layers, as shown below (Adamczak et al, 2004; Buduma et al, 2017; Goodfellow et al,2016; LeCun et al, 2015). The terms like Deep Belief Nets, Convolutional Nets, Backpropagation, non-linearity, Image recognition, and so on or maybe across the big Deep Learning researchers like Geoff Hinton, Andrew Ng, Yann LeCun, Andrej Karpathy, Yoshua Bengio.If we follow and see the news of technology we may have even heard about Deep Learning in big companies NVidia and its GPUs, Apple and its self-driving Car, Google buying DeepMind for 400 million dollars, and Toyota's billion dollars AI research investment(Arel et al, 2010).

Deep Learning is About Neural Networks

The neural system's structures and any other simple network's structures are the same structure. Nodes of webs are interconnected with each other. Nodes are called neurons and we called edges to those joints which are used to join node to node. The main function of neural networks is to collect or receive a set of inputs, do some complex and progressively calculate some process and end up with some useful information called the output of the problem (Adamczak et al, 2004; Buduma et al, 2017; LeCun et al, 2015Schmidhuber et al, 2015).

Figure 1. Neural Network

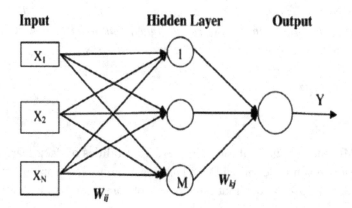

Figure 2. Deep Neural Network

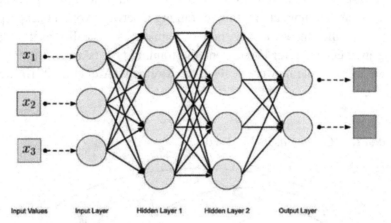

Figure 3. Cheat sheet on Neural Networks and deep networks topologies (Fjodor van Veen)

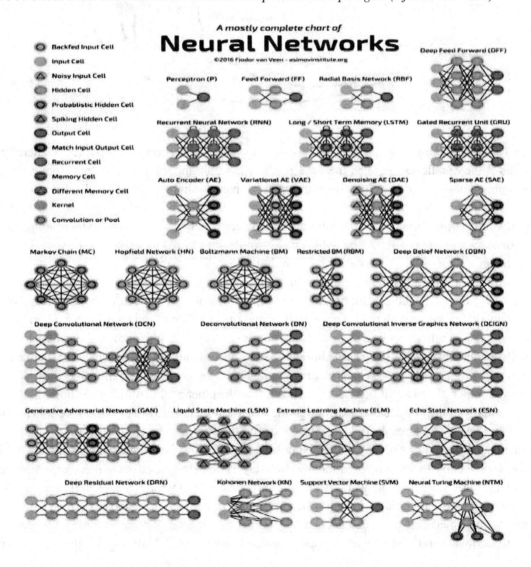

The current state-of-the-art in deep learning is to recognition pattern through deep learning which is worth noting. In ancient learning, attempting to training a network with a backpropagation method, we fall into a basic error called the vanishing gradient, sometimes it is called as the exploding gradient. Once the vanishing gradient the error encounters, the training task takes an extremely long time and consequently, the accuracy of the network will suffer extremely (Arel et al, 2010; LeCun et al, 2015; Patterson et al, 2017).

Figure 4. AI, ML, and DL (Copeland, B. M., 2016)

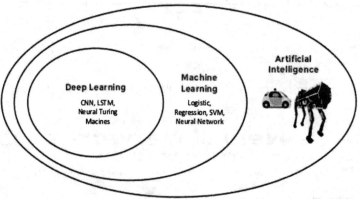

When we are training a neural network, we are constantly computing a cost-value. Generally, the cost-value is the excellence between the net's predicted output and the actual output from a group of labeled training data. The cost value is then dropped by making slight changes or adjusts to the weights and biases over and over throughout the training method until the lower possible value are obtained. Here is that forward propagation again; and here are the instance weights and biases. The training process utilizes one factor spoken as a gradient, which measures the rate at that the cost will change with respect to a change in weight or bias (Brownlee, J., 2016; LeCun et al, 2015).

For complex machine learning problems such as facial recognition, the deep architectures are the best and sometimes only choice. But up until 2006, there was no way to accurately train deep nets due to a fundamental problem with the training process and the problem of the vanishing gradient. For example, think that Gradient is like a slope and the training process like a rock rolling down that slope. A rock will roll quickly down a steep slope but will barely move at all on a flat surface. The same is true with the gradient of a deep net. When the gradient is larger, the network will train speedily. When the gradient is smaller, the net will train slowly. Here's that deep net again. And here is how the gradient could potentially vanish or decay back through the net. As we can see, the gradients are much smaller in the earlier layers. As a result, the early layers of the network are the slowest to train. But this is a fundamental problem! The early layers are responsible for detecting the simple patterns and the building blocks – when it came to facial recognition, the early layers detected the edges which were combined to form facial features later in the network. And if the early layers get it wrong, the result built up by the net will be wrong as well. It could mean that instead of a face like this, our net looks for this. The method used for training a neural net is called back- propagation or back-prop. We saw before that forward prop starts with the inputs and works forward; back-prop does the reverse, calculating the gradient from right to left. For example, here are 5 gradients, 4 weight, and 1 bias. It starts with the left and works back through the layers, like so. Each time it computes a gradient, it usages all the previous gradients up to thereto purpose (Brownlee, 2016; Copeland, B. M., 2016; LeCun et al, 2015).

LEARNING TYPES

Two types of learning terminology are described here: supervised and unsupervised learning. In unsupervised learning – it extracts patterns from a set of unlabelled data – then it will utilize either a Restricted Boltzmann Machine or an auto-encoder (Adamczak et al, 2004; Goodfellow et al, 2016; LeCun et al, 2015; Zhang, G. P., 2000). In Supervised Learning: Labelled data for supervised learning and it will build a classifier, there are several different options depending on our application. For text processing tasks like sentiment analysis, parsing, and named entity recognition – use a Recurrent Net or a Recursive Neural Tensor Network, which we'll refer to as an RNTN (Adamczak et al, 2004; Goodfellow et al, 2016; LeCun et al, 2015).

CLASSIFICATION

Neural systems are utilized for heaps of various distinctive applications here they have examined about classification problem (Kotsiantis et al, 2007). Classification is the way toward sorting or categorizing a group of objects while just utilizing some fundamental information or feature of that objects includes that portray them with the help of those highlighted features (Adamczak et al, 2004; Kotsiantis et al, 2007). There are lots of classifiers available today like Logistic Regression, Naive Bayes, Support Vector Machines, Neural networks (Goodfellow et al, 2016; Zhang, G. P., 2000).

The Activation or output of a classifier is generally known as the score. For example, to predict that the patient is sick or healthy? The data required for prediction are the patient's height, weight, and body temperature. The classifier would receive these patient data and, process the data with complex calculations, and finally, it will catch out a confidence-score. The patient is sick if the confidence score is high, and a low score would indicate that the patient is fit. For the classification task, neural nets are used where an object can dive into one of at least two different categories of classification Not at all like different networks sort of a social network and the NN is extremely organized, structured plus NN comes in the layer by layers. The input layer is the first year of the network also called primary layer. The last layer is the output Layer or classification layer and all the layers in between input and the output layers are declared as hidden layers (Brownlee, J., 2016; Yu, F. R., & He, Y.). As a result of every node within the hidden and output layers have its own classifier, the neural internet is viewed because of the results of spinning classifiers along in an exceedingly layered net (Brownlee, J., 2016; Buduma et al, 2017; Deng, L., 2014; Nielsen et al, 2015; Zhang, G. P., 2000).

Take that node for example - it gets its inputs from the input layer, and activates. Its score is then passed on as input to the next hidden layer for further activation. The principal neural nets were conceived out of the need to address the error of an early classifier, the perception. It was demonstrated that by utilizing a layered web of perceptron's predictions accuracy could be made progress. Subsequently, this new type of neural nets was known as a Multi- Layer Perceptron or MLP. Since then, the nodes within neural nets have replaced perceptron's with a lot of powerful classifiers, however, the name MLP has stuck. Take that node for instance — it gets its inputs from the input layer, and activates. Its score is then passed on as input to succeeding hidden layer for advanced activation.

The principal neural nets were planned out of the necessity to handle the error of associate early classifier, the perception. It absolutely was incontestable that by utilizing a superimposed net of perceptron's predictions accuracy may well be created progress. Afterward, this new style of neural nets was called a Multi-Layer Perceptron or MLP. Since then, the nodes within neural nets have replaced perceptron's with additional powerful classifiers, however, the name MLP has stuck (LeCun et al, 2015).

Forward propagation: every node has a similar classifier, associated none of them fire randomly; if we repeat an input, we get a similar output. Thus, if each node within the hidden layer received a similar input, why didn't all of them fireplace out a similar value? The explanation is that every set of inputs is changed and modified by distinctive weights and biases. As an example, for that node, the primary input is changed by a weight of 10 the second by 5, the third by 6 then a bias of 9 is added on top. Every edge incorporates a distinctive weight, and every node incorporates a distinctive bias. This implies that the combination used for every activation is also distinctive that explains why the nodes fire otherwise (LeCun et al, 2015).

NEURAL NETWORK ACCURACY IS PREDICTED BASED ON WEIGHTS AND BIASES

What we want from the neural net is the net to predict a value that is as close to the actual output as possible every single time. In other words, we want that accuracy to be high. The process of improving accuracy of a neural networks is called training, much the same as with other machine learning techniques. Here's that forward propagation again - to prepare the network, the yield from forward propagation is contrasted with the yield that is known to be right and the cost is the distinction of the two. The purpose of training is to make that cost as little as would be prudent, crosswise over a huge number of training cases. To do this, the net changes the weights and biases step by step in well-ordered until the point when the prediction intently coordinates the right yield. Once prepared well, a neural net can possibly set aside a few minutes. This is a neural net more or less (Adamczak et al, 2004; Bengio, Y., 2009; Géron, A., 2018; Schmidhuber et al, 2015). Figure-1 Shows the Deep learning techniques.

Figure 5. Bias and Weights

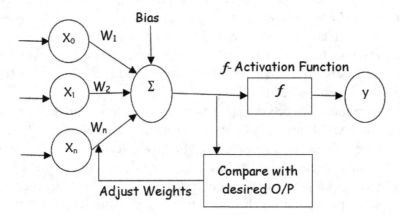

Figure 6. Deep Learning Techniques

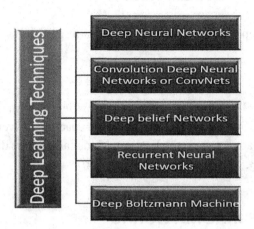

- Deep Belief Network or a Convolutional Net, and Recurrent Net are used for image recognition.
- Convolutional Net or an RNTN uses for object recognition
- Recurrent Net use for speech recognition

In general, Deep Belief Networks and Multilayer Perceptron's with rectified linear units – also known as RELU – are both good choices for classification. For time series analysis it's best to use a Recurrent Net (Adamczak et al, 2004; Goodfellow et al, 2016; LeCun et al, 2015).

DEEP LEARNING DRAWBACKS

One of the biggest disadvantages of deep learning training phase required huge data. Before some time ago Facebook announced that they had used one billion images for their image-recognition system to accomplish record-breaking compliance. So, in deep learning always large datasets are required to train systems and it can take vast amounts of time, it also required distributed computing power or GPU to access it.

Another drawback is the training cost of the network. Because of the large datasets and a huge number of training cycles it requires high computing -powered GPU and GPU array (Copeland, B. M., 2016. To train Deep network is also challenging, because of the vanishing gradient problem, but there are solutions in deep learning to solve it. When more layers are added to the network the vanishing gradient error will occur and it will result in the unfeasible mode and also compromise the accuracy. The problem doesn't trouble every network, but it will affect those which use gradient-based learning methods. so, these kinds of problems can be addressed by choosing a suitable activation function means instead of using sigmoid function use ReLu function or Leaky ReLu function or there are many other variations of ReLu Functions are also available (Arel et al, 2010; Shi, S. et al, 2016).

Deep learning does not have a strong theoretical foundation. It is like a black box because when the network generates features no one can figure out how it will be calculated. There's no fundamental mathematics for that. This leads to the next disadvantage. To decide the topology and hyper-parameters for deep learning is a black art with no theory to guide you.

HARDWARE REQUIRED FOR LEARNING

Hardware requirement for deep learning network to the training process is GPU, for that two options are here:

- Build own deep learning ring
- Hire the Hardware from GPU clouds from a cloud provider like Amazon, NVIDIA, IBM, Google, and Azure. The advantage of using Cloud is they offer machine driven systems that streamline the training process another advantage is the learning Model also offers drag- and-drop tools to setting parameters (Copeland, B. M., 2016; Shi, S. et al, 2016).

TRAINING OF DEEP NEURAL NETWORKS

As covers about deep neural networks. Due to large numbers of layers and the link between each neuron to the neuron in the middle layer deep neural networks are difficult to train. During the training time, the calculation and the adjustment of the parameter are too difficult for the very wide network. Also refer Drawback of Deep learning section. Below figure-3 process shows the distribution of large dataset for training and validation set. It quite changes is the distribution of data as compared to ancient learning. During training time fine tune the hyper parameters to achieve desired accuracy from the network.

Figure 7. Training and validating a Network

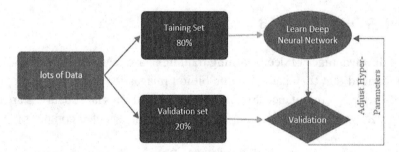

RESENT RESEARCH GOING ON DEEP LEARNING

Some leading organizations are work on it. Names are NVIDIA researchers making super- slow motion videos using deep learning, Google's making electronic health records, LG to NVIDIA and ARM doing IoT projects using deep learning (Copeland, B. M., 2016).

DEEP LEARNING MODELS

1. Restricted Boltzmann Machine

- The first researchers to devise a breakthrough idea for training deep nets and it was by Geoff Hinton at the University of Toronto. The researcher's approach directed to the creation of the Restricted Boltzmann Machine, also known as the RBM. Because of his pioneering work he declared to as one of the father of deep learning. A RBM is thin and one layered network. Mainly two layers:
  - The first layer- Visible layer
  - Second layer- Hidden layer
- That is why it also known as a shallow network. Visible layer's every node is connected with each node of the hidden layer.
- A RBM is well-thought-out "restricted" since in a same layer there is a no connection between two nodes.
- A mathematical analogy of a two-way translation of the RBM is mentioned below,
  - **Way -1:** The forward propagation, an RBM will take the inputs and translates them into an encrypted set of numbers.
  - **Way-2:** The backward-propagation- it will take above encrypted set of numbers and translates them back to re-establish inputs.
- A well-trained net will be able to execute the backward translation with a high degree of accuracy.
- In each steps, the weights and biases have a really vital role. They permit the RBM to decode, the interrelationships among the input features plus they additionally facilitate the RBM to decide that input features are the foremost vital once when detecting patterns.
- Through many forward and backward passes, associate RBM is trained to recreate the input data.
- Mention steps are repeated over and over through the training process:
  - **Step-1:** With a forward propagation, each input information is pooled with one general bias and different weights, and subsequently, the outcome is passed to the activated or not activate the hidden layer.
  - **Step-2:** Next in a backward propagation, every activation is pooled with a specific weight and a total bias, and subsequently, the outcome will be transferred to the input layer for rebuilding.
  - **Step-3:** At input layer, the rebuilding is compared against the original input which decided the quality of the outcome.
- For step 1, 2 and 3, RBM is using KL Divergence measure. Until the input and the re- construction are as close as possible the weights and biases are changing repetitive.
- A motivating aspect of an RBM is that the data does not need to be labelled. This turns out to be very important for real-world data sets like photos, videos, voices, and sensor data – all of which tend to be unlabeled.
- Rather than having people manually label the data and introduce errors, an RBM automatically sorts through the data, and by properly regulating the weights and biases, an RBM is able to extract the important features and reconstruct the input.

- An imperative and necessary annotation is that an RBM is essentially generated conclusions of which input features are significant and how those input features should be combined to form patterns.
- In other words, an RBM belongs to feature extractor neural network family, which are altogether intended to identify natural patterns in dataset. These nets are likewise known as"Auto-encoders" in light of the fact that, they need to encode their own structure (Deng et al, 2013).

2. Deep Belief Nets (DBN)

- RBM can extract features and reconstruct inputs plus help to out of the vanishing gradient problem? By combining RBMs together and introducing an adroit training method, it obtain a powerful new model that finally solves the vanishing gradient problem. Now take a look at a Deep Belief Network. Just like the RBM, DBN were also conceived by Geoff Hinton as an alternative to backpropagation. Because of his accomplishments, he was hired for image recognition work at Google, where a large- scale DBN project is currently believed to be in development. In terms of network structure, a DBN is identical to an MLP (multi-layer perceptron). But when it comes to training, they are entirely different. In fact, the key factor is the difference in training methods which enables DBNs to outpace their shallow equivalents. DBN, the hidden layer of one RBM is the visible layer of the one "above" it. It can be viewed as a stack of RBMs.
- Training of DBN is as follows:
  a. Earliest RBMs were trained to re-build input as correctly as it promising.
  b. Earliest RBM- The hidden layer is salted as the visible layer for the second and also the second RBM is trained using the outputs from the first RBM (Glauner et al, 2015)
  c. The whole above process is repeated until each layer within the network is trained. An important note about a DBN is that every RBM layer learns the whole input (Glauner et al, 2015).
- In other kinds of models – alike convolutional networks, primary layers detect simple edges patterns and later layers recombine them to follow abstract feature from the layers to layers. For example in facial recognition application, the early layers would detect edges from the entire face image, next layers would detect more abstract feature and later layers would use these results to form facial features. On the other hand, A Deep Belief Networks generally, the model slowly improves, when fine-tune the complete input in progression– it's like a camera lens slowly focusing a picture. The reason that a DBN is highly technical and it works so well. A stack of RBMs will outperform a single unit – just like a Multilayer perceptron was able to outperform a single perceptron working alone. After this primary training, the RAM creates a model that can detect natural patterns in the data, but we still don't know exactly what the patterns are called. Now, labels the all patterns and fine-tune the network with supervised learning to finish training, to complete training, one need tiny set of labelled dataset so that the features and patterns can be associated with a name. The biases and weights are adjusted slightly, due to this small change the net's perception of the patterns are also change, and sometime the over-all accuracy also increase slightly. Fortunately, the set of labelled data can be slight relative to the original data set, which as we've discussed, is extremely helpful in real-world applications. So, Deep Belief Nets is provided the solution of problem vanishing gradient (Glauner et al, 2015; Hinton et al, 2009).

3. Convolution Neural Network

- Convolution Neural Network also referred to as CNN or ConvNets. CNNs have wide range of applications in all the space some of them are Image Detection and Image Recognition, Detection in Video data, Recommender Systems, Video Recognition, and Natural Language Processing (Dehghan et al, 2017; Lan, S. et al, 2018). ConvNets are very similar to regular Neural Net's. Convolutional Neural networks enable computers to see and visualize, means CNN are used to recognize images by transmuting the original image through layers by layers to a class scores. The network was inspired by the visual cortex on every occasion that can see something by our eyes, a series of layers of neurons gets activated, and every layer will detect a group of features such as lines, edges. The initial layers of network will detect more complex features in order to recognize what layers are detects edges and finally the last layer of the network will decide the result or outcome of the problem based on score value. So, the process is like, the networks are made up of neurons and each neurons have weights and biases. Each weight and biases are learnable. So every neuron receives inputs, accomplishes with a dot product and optionally follows it with a nonlinearity (Lan, S. et al, 2018). So, how are Convolutional Neural Networks different than Neural Networks? Figure 8 shows the architecture of a regular 3-layer Neural Network (Kumar et al, 2017).

Figure 8. A regular 3-layer Neural Network (Johnson et al, 2015)

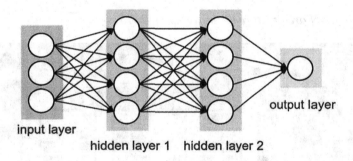

- A CNN gathers neurons in over-all three dimensions which are the depth, height, and width, as visualized in one of the layers. Each layer of a CNN's transforms the 3D input volume to a 3D output volume of neuron activations. In figure 9 example of architecture, the input holds the image red bar, so its dimensions are width and height of the image, and also the depth would be 3 channels Red, Green, Blue.
- A CNNs is a sequence of layers, every layer of a ConvNet transforms one volume of activations to different through a differentiable function. ConvNet has two parts:
  - Feature learning and
  - Classification.
- Convolution, Relu, Poolings are the used to generate and craft the feature of the Image and to classify the Image fully connected layer and the softmax are used.

For an instance we can make a flow like;

- There are three main kinds of layers to make Convolution Neural network architectures: Convolutional Layer, we'll stack these layers to create a full ConvNet design.
  ○ Conv Layer,

Figure 9. A ConvNet with 3channeks (Johnson et al, 2015)

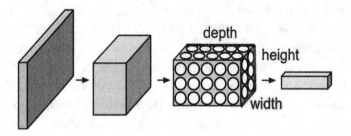

- Pool Layer,
- Fully-Connected Layer
  ○ Typical architecture of CNN is shown below.

Figure 10. Example of CNN architecture (Johnson et al, 2015)

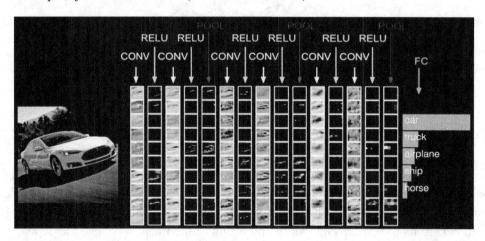

Step-1 The Training of Input Data

- The input volume or input layer is an image that has the sequel dimensions: It is a matrix of pixel values.

Example: In input, here The depth, represents R, G, B channels.

Figure 11.

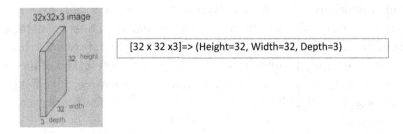

Step-2 CONV Layer

- A convolution is an operation that changes a function into something else. Means to get more information out of it.
- The whole input image is associated with progressive Conv layer in this manner, if all the pixels of the input layer is associated with the Conv layer, it will be exceptionally expensive in terms computation. So to apply dot products between a receptive field and a filter on all the dimensions. The final product of this task operation is a single integer of the output volume which is also referred as a feature map. Then after the filter over the successive receptive field of the same input image by a Stride and compute again the dot products between the new receptive field and the same filter. Repeat this process until go through the entire input image. The next layer input would be the output of the previous layer.

Figure 12. Conv layer with K = 2 filters, with a spatial extent F = 3, stride S = 2, and input padding P = 1 (Johnson et al, 2015)

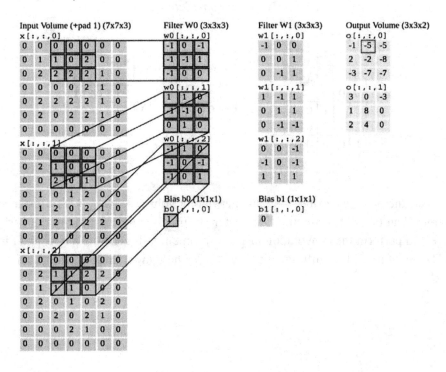

- The whole input image is associated with progressive Conv layer in this manner, if all the pixels of the input layer is associated with the Conv layer, it will be exceptionally expensive in terms computation. So to apply dot products between a receptive field and a filter on all the dimensions. The final product of this task operation is a single integer of the output volume which is also referred as a feature map. Then after the filter over the successive receptive field of the same input image by a Stride and compute again the dot products between the new receptive field and the same filter. Repeat this process until go through the entire input image. The next layer input would be the output of the previous layer.

Need to Know

- **What is Feature detector or the Filter or the Kernel:** Convolutions aren't a new notion. They have been used in image and signal processing for quite a while. Be that as it may, convolutions in machine learning are unique in relation to those in picture handling. Numerous filters are available like sobel, horizontal, vertical filter. It is an odd number small matrix used for features detection. A typical filter on the primary layer of a ConvNet might have a size [5x5x3]. The filter is also known as convolutional matrix.
- **Feature Map:**
  ◦ It is the output volume formed by sliding the filter over the image and computing the dot product.
  ◦ It is also referred as Convolved Feature, conv feature, Activation Map.
- **Receptive field:** It is a local region of the input volume that has the equivalent size as the filter.
- **Depth column:** It is the set of neurons that are all pointing to the same receptive field.
- **Depth:** the amount of filters.

Figure 13. Input Image matrix, Filter matrix, result convoluted feature matrix

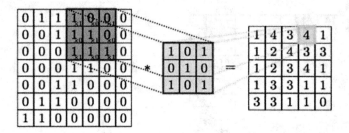

- **Stride:** it has the objective of building smaller output volumes spatially. For instance, if the image is larger than the size of the filter, the filter shifting one unit at time to the various parts of the image and perform the convolution task. Each time it will generate a new pixel in the output image. The amount of filter shifting unit to unite on whole input image k with kernel is known as the stride.

Figure 14. Convolution matrix or, filter computation with layer (Johnson et al, 2015)

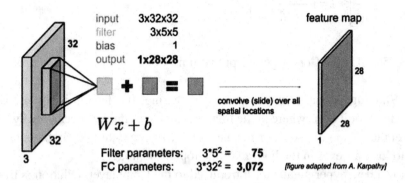

- **Zero-padding:** it includes zeros around the outside of the input volume so that the convolutions end up with the same number of outputs as inputs. . In the event that we don't utilize padding the information at the borders will be lost after each Conv layer, which will reduce the size of the volumes as well as the performance.

$$ZeroPadding = \frac{K-1}{2},.\ \text{Where K Filter size,}$$

The formula for calculating the output size for any given conv layer is,

$$Output = \frac{(W-K+2P)}{S}+1$$

→ So, [W2xH2xD2] compute the Output value:

$$\mathcal{W}2 = \left[\frac{w1-F+2P}{S}\right]+1,\ H2 = \left[\frac{H1-F+2P}{S}\right]+1,\ \text{D2=K1, where:}$$

[W1xH1xD1]: input volume size
F: receptive field size
S: stride
P: amount of zero padding used on the border.
K: depth

  ◦ The first Convolutional Layer output volume with given input size is: [227x227x3], W=227, F=11, S=4, P=0, and K=96.

$$\mathcal{W}2 = \left[\frac{227-11+2(0)}{4}\right]+1 = \left[\frac{227-11}{4}\right]+1 = \frac{216}{4}+1 = 55$$

$$H2 = \left[\frac{227-11+2(0)}{4}\right]+1 = \left[\frac{227-11}{4}\right]+1 = \frac{216}{4}+1 = 55$$

D2= 96, So, [55x55x96] is the Conv layer output volume.

- **Parameter Sharing:** it is also known as weight sharing. If a feature is beneficial it will also be beneficial to look for it everywhere in the image. . Be that as it may,, occasionally, it is odd to share the same weights in some cases. For instance, in a training data that contains faces centered, we don't have to look for eyes in the bottom or the top of the image.
- **Dilation:** It is a new hyper-parameter introduced to the Conv layer. Dilation is filters with spaces between its cells. for instance, we have one dimension filter W of size 3 and an input X:

Dilation of 0: w[0]*x[0] + w[1]*x[1] + w[2]*x[2].
Dilation of 1: w[0]*x[0] + w[1]*x[2] + w[2]*x[4].

- *ReLU layer: ReLU Layer applies an elementwise initiation function max(0,x), which turns negative values to zeros means thresholding at zero. This layer does not change the size of the volume and there are no hyperparameters.*
- **POOL layer:** Pool Layer completes a function to reduce the spatial dimensions of the input, and the computational complexity of our model. And it also controls overfitting. It operates independently on every depth slice of the input. There are different functions such as Max pooling, average pooling, or L2-norm pooling. However, Max pooling is the most used type of pooling which only takes the most important part (the value of the brightest pixel) of the input volume. Example of a Max pooling with 2x2 filter and stride = 2. So, for each of the windows, max pooling takes the max value of the 4 pixels.
- Pool layer doesn't have parameters, and no zero padding, but it has two hyperparameters: Filter (F) and Stride (S).All the more generally, having the input W1×H1×D1, the pooling layer produces a volume of size W2×H2×D2 where:
  - W2= {(W1−F)/S}+1
  - H2={(H1−F)/S}+1
  - D2=D1
- A typical type of a Max pooling is filters of size 2x2 applied with a stride of 2. The Pooling sizes with larger filters are too destructive and they usually lead to worse performance.
- Numerous individuals do not likes using a pooling layer since it throws away information and they replace it with a Conv layer with increased stride once in a while.

Step-3 Fully Connected Layer (FC):

- Fully connected layers connect each neuron in one layer to each neuron in another layer. The last fully-connected layer usages a softmax activation function for classifying the generated features of the input image into numerous classes on the training dataset. Example, Classification Of a ConvNet architecture:
- [INPUT—CONV—RELU—POOL—FC]

Figure 15. Max pooling with 2x2 filter and stride = 2

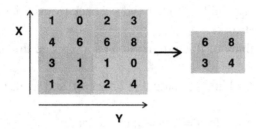

Figure 16. Operation upon the pixel space

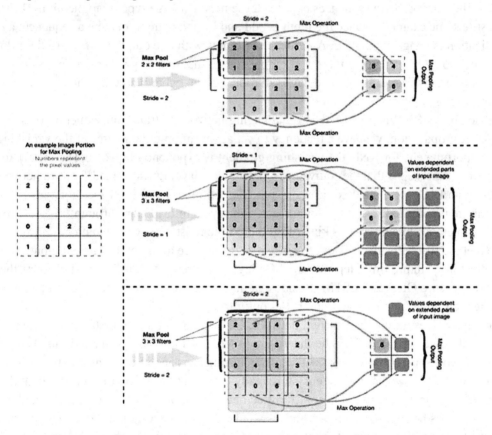

4. Recurrent Nets

- Recurrent neural networks is also a deep learning model and it also has a simple structure with a fundamental feedback loop, permitting it to perform as a predicting machine.
- Recurrent nets, or rnns, have a long history, but their recent popularity is mostly due to the works of Juergen Schmidhuber, Sepp Hochreiter, and Alex Graves. Their applications are extremely versatile – ranging from speech recognition to driverless cars.
- All the nets we've seen up to the present purpose are feedforward neural networks. During a feed-forward neural network, the flow of signals is in one single direction from the input layer to the

output layer solely and one layer at a time. During a recurrent network, succeeding input is that the output of a previous layer and it'll other and fed back to a similar layer, that is usually the sole layer within the whole network.

- For illustration, we can think of this progression as a passage through time – shown here are 4 such time steps.
  - At t = 1, the network takings the output of time t = 0 and sends it back into the network along with the next input.
  - The network repeats this for t = 2, t = 3, and so on.
- Unlike feedforward networks, a recurrent networks input is a sequence of, and it may turn out a sequence of values as output.
- The ability to work with sequences exposes these nets to a large type of applications. Here square measure some examples. Once the input is odd and also the output may be a sequence, a possible application is image captioning. A sequence of inputs with one output is often used for document classification. Once each the input and output square measure sequences, these nets will classify videos frame by frame. If a time delay is introduced, the cyber web will statistically forecast the demand in provide chain designing.
- Classically, an RNN is a particularly challenging network to train. Subsequently these networks use back propagation, we have a tendency to yet again run into the matter of the vanishing gradient. Unfortunately, for RNN the vanishing gradient is exponentially worse The reason for this is that every time step is that the equivalent of a complete layer during a feed-forward network. Thus training an RNN for a hundred time steps are like training a 100-layer feed forward net — these end up in exponentially small gradients and a decay of information through time. There are numerous methods to address this kind of problem - the most popular of which is Gating.
- The method that helps the network to make a decision once to forget the current input, and once to recollect it for future time steps is called Gating. The foremost well-liked gating sorts these days square measure GRU and LSTM. Besides gating, there are a couple of different techniques like gradient clipping, steeper gates, and better optimizers.
- When it involves training a recurrent network, GPUs area unit an understandable alternative over a normal processor like CPU. The investigation team of Indico has validated this. Which usages these networks on text process tasks like sentiment analysis and effectiveness extraction. The team initiate that GPUs we have a tendency tore ready to train the nets 250 times faster than the CPUs! That's the distinction between in some unspecified time or one day time of training and over eight months! Thus beneath what circumstances would we use a recurrent net over a feedforward net? We all know that an output of feedforward networks is one value, that in several cases it was a category or a prediction.
  - When it includes preparing a repetitive system, GPUs region unit a reasonable option over an ordinary processor like CPU. This was approved by an examination group at Indico, which utilizes these nets on content process assignments like feeling investigation and supportiveness extraction.
- A recurrent network is appropriate for statistic knowledge, time series data, wherever the output is following value during a sequence or following next several values. Thus the answer depends on whether or not the application calls for classification, regression, or forecasting.

5. Autoencoders

- There are times when it's extremely useful to figure out the underlying structure of a data set. Having access to the most important data features gives us a lot of flexibility when we start applying labels. Autoencoders are an important family of neural networks that are well-suited for this task.

- In a previous model we looked at the Restricted Boltzmann Machine, which is a very popular example of an autoencoder. But there are other types of Autoencoders like DE noising and contractive, just to name a few. Just like an RBM, an autoencoder is a neural net that takings a set of typically unlabeled inputs, and after encoding them, tries to reconstruct them as accurately as possible. Subsequently, as an outcome of this, the net must choose which of the data features are the most vital, essentially acting as a feature extraction engine.

- Autoencoders are typically very shallow, and are usually encompassed of an input layer, a hidden layer and the output layer. An RBM is an example of an autoencoder with only two layers. Here is a forward pass that ends with a reconstruction of the input. There are two steps - the encoding and the decoding. Typically, the same weights that are used to encode a feature in the hidden layer are used to reconstruct an image in the output layer.

- Autoencoders are trained with backpropagation, using a metric called "loss". As opposed to "cost", loss measures the amount of information that was lost when the net tried to reconstruct the input. A net with a small loss value will produce reconstructions that look very similar to the originals.

- Not all of these nets are shallow. In fact, deep Autoencoders are extremely useful tools for dimensionality reduction. Consider an image containing a 28x28 grid of pixels.

- A neural net would need to process over 750 input values just for one image – doing this across millions of images would waste significant amounts of memory and processing time.

- A deep autoencoder could encode this image into an impressive 30 numbers, and still maintain information about the key image features. When decoding the output, the net acts like a two-way translator. In this example, a well-trained net could translate these 30 encoded numbers back into a reconstruction that looks similar to the original image. Certain types of nets also introduce random noise to the encoding-decoding process, which has been shown to improve the robustness of the resulting patterns.

- Deep Autoencoders perform better at dimensionality reduction than their predecessor, principal component analysis, or PCA. Below is a comparison of two letter codes for news stories of different topics – generated by both a deep autoencoder and a PCA. Labels were added to the picture for illustrative purposes.

6. Deep learning Platforms

- A platform may be a set of tools that others will devolve on from top to bottom of. As an example, consider the applications which will be designed off of the tools provided by Windows, Android, iOS, MacOS, and IBM Websphere, and even Oracle BEA. Thus a Deep Learning platform provides a collection of tools associated an interface for building custom.

Figure 17. Platform and set of tools

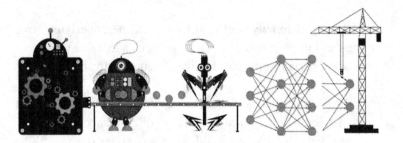

- Deep Learning platform provides a collection of tools asssociated an interface for building custom deep networks. Typically, they provide a user with a spread of deep nets to determine on from DBN/MLP, RBM, Convo Net, Autoencoder, RNN, and RNTN. Beside the ability of knowledge-mining to integrate data from extremely different sources, manipulate information, and manage models through a UI. Some platforms collectively facilitate with performance if a net should be trained with huge data set.

Figure 18. Deep learning tools and Techniques

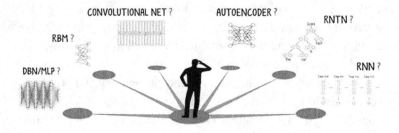

- There are some benefits and downsides of employing a platform vs. employing a software code library. A platform is associate out-of-the-box application that enables us to put together a deep net's hyper-parameters through associate intuitive UI; with a platform, we don't have to be compelled to grasp something concerning about coding so as to use the tools. The drawback is that we constrained by the platform's selection of deep nets and also the configuration choices. Except for anyone trying to quickly deploy a deep web, a platform is that the best approach to go.

Figure 19. Platform

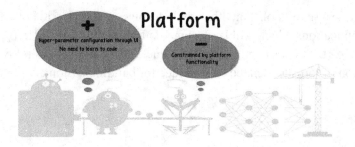

- A software library is a set of functions and modules that we can call through our own code in order to perform certain tasks. Deep net libraries give us a lot of extra flexibility with net selection and hyper-parameter configuration. For example, there aren't many platforms that let we build a Recursive Neural Tensor Net, but we can code our own with the right deep net library! The obvious downside to libraries is the coding experience required to use them, but if we need the flexibility, they really are a great resource.

Figure 20. Libraries

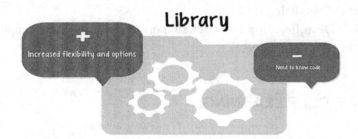

- Ersatz Labs - a dedicated Deep Learning platform that handles all the technical issues like code, deployments, and performance – and allows the user to go straight to modelling. Two machine learning software system platforms referred to as H2O, and GraphLab produce, each of which supply Deep Learning tools.
- Set of functions and modules that we can call through our own programs. Libraries are typically created by highly-qualified software teams, and popular libraries are regularly maintained. Many libraries are open-source, and are surrounded by big communities that provide support and contribute to the codebase.
- Deep Learning has plenty of great libraries available like,
  - deeplearning4j
  - Torch
  - Caffe
  - Theano
  - Deepmat
- Google's TensorFlow library may be a great alternative for building commercial-grade deep learning applications with Python. There is a lot of popularity and hype encompassing TensorFlow.
- TensorFlow grew out of Associate in earlier Google library referred to as "DistBelief", that may be a proprietary deep web library developed as a part of the Google Brain project.
- Much like the Theano library, Tensor Flow is predicated on the conception of a computational graph.
- In a computational graph, nodes represent either persistent data or a math operation and edges represent the flow of data between nodes. The data that flows through these edges is a multi-dimensional array known as a tensor, hence the library's name, "TensorFlow".
- The output from one operation or set of operations is then fed as an input into the next. Even though TensorFlow was designed to support neural networks, it can support any domain where

computation can be modelled as a data flow graph. TensorFlow also adopts several useful features from Theano such as auto differentiation, shared and symbolic variables, and common sub-expression elimination. And for an open source library, it has comprehensive and informative.

- TensorFlow users have to work with an additional library called Keras if this flexibility is required. Right now TensorFlow has a "no-nonsense" interface for C++, and the team hopes that the community will develop more language interfaces through SWIG, an open-source tool for connecting programs and libraries. Recently, Jason Toy of Somatic announced the release of a SWIG interface to Ruby for the summer of 2016. TensorFlow performed reasonably well in the ImageNet category, with no Theano-based libraries listed in the analysis. Another improvement over Theano comes in the form of parallelism.
- Even though most Deep Learning Libraries support CUDA, very few support OpenCL, a fast-rising standard for GPU computing.

GPU ACCELERATE DEEP LEARNING:

- To train a complex model with a large dataset.
- Deep learning networks need a lot of computational power for building a model. In deep learning pipeline, the training phase of the modelling is the most intensive task, and the most time consuming one.
- Deep learning is an iterative process. When we train a deep learning model, two main operations are performed:
  - Forward Pass and
  - Backward Pass.

Figure 21. Deep learning Need for Acceleration

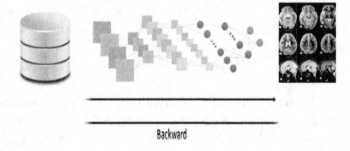

Backward

- In the forward pass, after processing the input which is passed through the neural network, the output is generated (Shaikh, F., 2017).
- In the backward pass, first, on the basis of the error(s) which received from forward pass, update the weights of the neural network. Second, deep learning involves heavy computations.
- For Example: in below Convolutional Neural Network figure 16 has each pixel within a single image becomes a feature point after being multiplied by the colour channel. We can consider the first array as the input to the neural network, and the second array can be considered as weights

or a filter of the network. The size of these matrices are usually very big, that is, the data is high-dimensional here. So, considering that training is an iterative process, and Neural Networks have usually many weights, which should get updated with each iteration, it involves expensive computations that are mostly matrix multiplication. Therefore, Deep Learning requires much computing power (Shaikh, F., 2017).

Figure 22. Deep learning Need for Acceleration

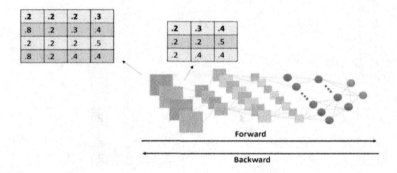

Figure 23. Matrix Multiplication in CNN

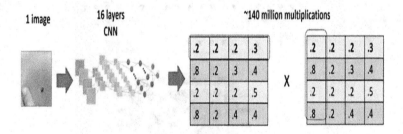

- Multiplication done as we seen in CNN, but the thing is where the data is going to instruct and process and store. We know that The CPU is responsible for executing a sequence of stored instructions, which in our case are multiplications. We need to fetch data and instructions from main memory to be run by the CPU. CPU is good at fetching small amounts of memory quickly, but not very well for big chunks of data, like big matrices, which are needed for deep learning. CPUs run tasks sequentially, rather than in parallel, even though they have 2 or 4 cores.
- Some companies used to build multiple clusters of CPUs to have a powerful system to do their processing in parallel, for example, built for training huge nets.These systems are usually very expensive and as such, most businesses can't afford them. So, we can conclude that CPUs are not fast enough for operations on big chunks of data and they're not the proper use for high parallelism, as they are very slow for these kinds of tasks (Shaikh, F., 2017).

Figure 24. Multiplication on CPU

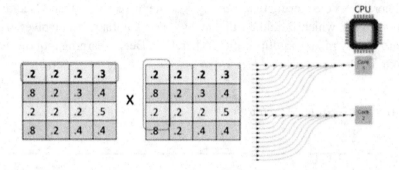

Figure 25. Multiplication on GPU

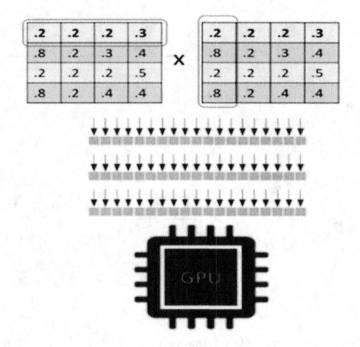

DISTRIBUTED DEEP LEARNING

• Distributed Deep Learning is a bunch of software systems, packages and algorithms that automatize and optimize the parallelization of huge and complex computing task across hundreds of GPU accelerators attached to dozens of servers. Most popular deep learning frameworks configure with a single server along with multiple GPUs, but, not configured with multiple servers along with GPUs. To reduce training times for large models with large datasets here distributed Deep Learning is introduced. It solves major-challenge scaling issue by distributing deep learning training across large numbers of servers and GPUs.

REFERENCES

Adamczak, R., Porollo, A., & Meller, J. (2004). Accurate prediction of solvent accessibility using neural networks–based regression. *Proteins, 56*(4), 753–767. doi:10.1002/prot.20176 PMID:15281128

Arel, I., Rose, D. C., & Karnowski, T. P. (2010). Deep machine learning-a new frontier in artificial intelligence research. *IEEE Computational Intelligence Magazine, 5*(4), 13–18. doi:10.1109/MCI.2010.938364

Bengio, Y. (2009). Learning deep architectures for AI. Foundations and trends® in Machine Learning, 2(1), 1-127.

Brownlee, J. (2016). *Master machine learning algorithms: Discover how they work and implement them from scratch*. Jason Brownlee.

Buduma, N., & Locascio, N. (2017). *Fundamentals of deep learning: Designing next-generation machine intelligence algorithms*. O'Reilly Media.

Copeland, B. M. (2016). The difference between AI, machine learning, and deep learning?. The Official NVIDIA Blog. Np, 29.

Dehghan, A., Masood, S. Z., Shu, G., & Ortiz, E. (2017). View independent vehicle make, model and color recognition using convolutional neural network. arXiv preprint arXiv:1702.01721.

Deng, L. (2014). A tutorial survey of architectures, algorithms, and applications for deep learning. APSIPA Transactions on Signal and Information Processing, 3.

Deng, L., Hinton, G., & Kingsbury, B. (2013, May). New types of deep neural network learning for speech recognition and related applications: An overview. In *Proceedings 2013 IEEE International Conference on Acoustics, Speech, and Signal Processing (ICASSP),* (pp. 8599-8603). IEEE.

Fjodor van Veen from Asimov Institute compiled a wonderful cheatsheet on NN topologies.

Géron, A. (2018). Neural networks and deep learning.

Glauner, P. O. (2015). Comparison of training methods for deep neural networks. arXiv preprint arXiv:1504.06825.

Goodfellow, I., Bengio, Y., Courville, A., & Bengio, Y. (2016). *Deep learning* (Vol. 1). Cambridge, MA: MIT Press.

Hinton, G. E. (2009). Deep belief networks. *Scholarpedia, 4*(5), 5947. doi:10.4249cholarpedia.5947

Johnson, J., & Karpathy, A. (2015). *Convolutional neural networks for visual recognition. Convolutional neural networks for visual recognition* (p. 94305). Stanford, CA: Stanford University.

Kotsiantis, S. B., Zaharakis, I., & Pintelas, P. (2007). Supervised machine learning: A review of classification techniques. Emerging artificial intelligence applications in computer engineering, 160, 3-24.

Kumar, V., & Garg, M. L. (2017, November). Deep learning in predictive analytics: A survey. In *Proceedings International Conference on Emerging Trends in Computing and Communication Technologies (ICETCCT),* (pp. 1-6). IEEE. 10.1109/ICETCCT.2017.8280331

Lan, S., He, Z., Chen, W., & Chen, L. (2018, July). Hand gesture recognition using convolutional neural networks. In *2018 USNC-URSI Radio Science Meeting (Joint with AP-S Symposium)* (pp. 147-148). IEEE. 10.1109/USNC-URSI.2018.8602809

LeCun, Y., Bengio, Y., & Hinton, G. (2015). Deep learning. *Nature, 521*(7553), 436.

Nielsen, M. A. (2015). *Neural networks and deep learning* (Vol. 25). USA: Determination Press.

Patterson, J., & Gibson, A. (2017). *Deep learning: A practitioner's approach*. O'Reilly Media.

Schmidhuber, J. (2015). Deep learning in neural networks: An overview. *Neural Networks, 61*, 85–117. doi:10.1016/j.neunet.2014.09.003 PMID:25462637

Shaikh, F. (2017). *Why are GPUs necessary for training deep learning models?* Analytics Vidhya.

Shi, S., Wang, Q., Xu, P., & Chu, X. (2016, November). Benchmarking state-of-the-art deep learning software tools. In *2016 7th International Conference on Cloud Computing and Big Data (CCBD)*, (pp. 99-104). IEEE. 10.1109/CCBD.2016.029

Yu, F. R., & He, Y. (n.d.). Deep reinforcement learning for wireless networks.

Zhang, G. P. (2000). Neural networks for classification: A survey. *IEEE Transactions on Systems, Man and Cybernetics. Part C, Applications and Reviews, 30*(4), 451–462. doi:10.1109/5326.897072

This research was previously published in Neural Networks for Natural Language Processing; pages 31-62, copyright year 2020 by Engineering Science Reference (an imprint of IGI Global).

Section 2
Development and Design Methodologies

Chapter 6
Artificial Neural Network Models for Large-Scale Data

Vo Ngoc Phu
Duy Tan University, Vietnam

Vo Thi Ngoc Tran
Ho Chi Minh City University of Technology, Vietnam

ABSTRACT

Artificial intelligence (ARTINT) and information have been famous fields for many years. A reason has been that many different areas have been promoted quickly based on the ARTINT and information, and they have created many significant values for many years. These crucial values have certainly been used more and more for many economies of the countries in the world, other sciences, companies, organizations, etc. Many massive corporations, big organizations, etc. have been established rapidly because these economies have been developed in the strongest way. Unsurprisingly, lots of information and large-scale data sets have been created clearly from these corporations, organizations, etc. This has been the major challenges for many commercial applications, studies, etc. to process and store them successfully. To handle this problem, many algorithms have been proposed for processing these big data sets.

INTRODUCTION

We have displayed the surveys of the massive data sets (MASSDSs) related to the Artificial Neural Network (ARTNEURNET) in this book chapter.

These above problems and challenges of the ARTNEURNET for the big data sets (BIGDSs) are very crucial as follows:

1. The large-scale data sets (LARSCDSs) have certainly been the massive advantages for the big corporations, the large-scale organizations, the economies of the countries in the world, etc.
2. There have been the massive positives of the MASSDSs for the different fields in the world.

DOI: 10.4018/978-1-6684-2408-7.ch006

3. People have spent too much time and cost of storing, handling the BIGDSs, and furthermore, of extracting the significant values from the LARSCDSs
4. People have considered how to reduce time and cost of (3) fully.
5. …etc.

We have also given an example of a novel model of the ARTNEURNET for the MASSDSs using the ARTNEURNET, and the multi-dimensional vectors (MULTDIMVECTs) of the opinion lexicons of the RUSSELL & RAO coefficient (RUSRAOC) through an international search engine – Google (GOOGSE) with the And and Or operator (ANDOROPs) in a sequential system (SEQSYS) and a parallel network system (PANETSYS).

We have implemented the problem so far by others as follows:

1. There have not been enough the algorithms, methods, models, and etc. of the ARTNEURNET for the MASSDSs yet to be applied to the different areas for the economies, countries, societies, corporations, organizations, and etc.
2. There have not been the algorithms, methods, models, and etc. of the ARTNEURNET for the LARSCDSs, which have been implemented in the SEQSYS and the PANETSYS.
3. The algorithms, methods, models, and etc. of the ARTNEURNET for the BIGDSs have already been developed with the small samples in the SEQSYS and the PANETSYS.
4. …etc.

We have given a novel model of an example of the ARTNEURNET of the semantic analysis (SEMANAL) for the MASSDSs in the SEQSYS and the PANETSYS.

We have been the main contributions of this book chapter to the problem from the surveys related to a lot of novel models of the ARTNEURNET for the MASSDSs as follows:

1. This book chapter has helped the readers have the information and knowledge about the ARTNEURNET for the BIGDSs certainly.
2. Most of the models of the LARSCDSs of the ARTNEURNET in the different areas have been displayed in both the SEQSYS and the PANETSYS on more details in the below sections.
3. According to the above information and knowledge, the readers (including scientists, researchers, CEO, managers, and etc.) can build, develop, and deploy the commercial applications, studies, and etc. so much.
4. The different techniques of the models have already been presented carefully.
5. We have also shown that a novel model of us for the MASSDS have been proposed successfully.
6. …etc.

We have already presented the contribution non-trivial as follows: A proposed model of the SEMANAL for the BIGDS has been developed in the SEQUENTS and the PANETSYS – the Cloudera environment with Hadoop Map (M) and Hadoop Reduce (R). This model has used the ARTNEURNET with the MULTDIMVECTs of the opinion lexicons (OPINLEXs) to classify the sentiments (positive, negative, or neutral) for the documents (1,000,000) of the testing data set (TESTDSET) based on the documents (2,000,000) of the training data set (TRAINDSET) in English. We have calculated the semantic values of the terms (verbs, nouns, adjectives, adverbs, and etc.) in English by using the RUSSELL & RAO coefficient (RUSRAOC) through the GOOGSE with the ANDOROPs. In addition, we have already achieved 87.03% accuracy on the TESTDSET of this novel model.

We have already displayed the simple concepts in this book chapter:

1. Based on our opinion, Artificial Intelligence (people have called it as machine intelligence sometimes) has been machines, programs, and etc. which can perform many intelligent tasks such as learning from experience, adjusting to new inputs, implementing human-like tasks, etc.
2. According to our opinion, the ARTNEURNET has comprised a set of small units (or small nodes) which they have been called the artificial neurons (ARTNEURs) similar to the neurons in a biological brain of the Human. The ARTNEURs have been connected together, called the connections which have been like the synapses of the biological brain. They can transmit a signal from one ARTNEUR to another easily and quickly. Furthermore, one ARTNEUR can also receive a signal and it can also handle it fully, etc.
3. Based on our opinion, a big data set has been a set of records (or samples) which have been thousands of records and a large size. In addition, a massive data set has been a set of records (or samples) which have been millions of records, etc.
4. According to our opinion, a sequential environment has been an environment of the computer science which has only been a computer (or a node).
5. A parallel network environment has been an environment of the computer science which has been many computers (or a nodes) and at least a server (or many servers). Furthermore, they have been connected together. They have transmitted many signals to each other easily, quickly, fully, and etc. In addition, they can handle the signals in a parallel way at the same time.
6. …etc.

BACKGROUND

In this section, we have briefly shown the surveys related to our novel model, and in addition, we have also presented the TESTDSET and the TRAINDSET of this proposed model.

Based on the studies presented in this part, we have proved that calculating a valence and identifying a polarity of one word/phrase in English have also been used by the RRC.

We have been the studies related to the Point-wise Mutual Information measure (PMIMEA) in [(Aleksander Bai, & Hugo Hammer, 2014), (P.D.Turney, & M.L.Littman, 2002), (Robert Malouf, & Tony Mullen, 2017), (Christian Scheible, 2010), (Dame Jovanoski, & et al, 2015), (Amal Htait, & et al, 2016), (Xiaojun Wan, 2009), (Julian Brooke, & et al, 2009), (Tao Jiang, & et al, 2015), (Tan, S.; & Zhang, J.; 2007), (Weifu Du, & et al, 2010), (Ziqing Zhang, & et al, 2010), and (Guangwei Wang, & Kenji Araki, 2007)].

The authors have already presented the PMIMEA and the Jaccard coefficient (JACCCO) in the studies (Shi Feng, & et al, 2013) and (Nguyen Thi Thu An, & Masafumi Hagiwara, 2014).

The JACCCO was used in the surveys [(Nihalahmad R. Shikalgar, & Arati M. Dixit, 2014), (Xiang Ji, & et al, 2015), (Nazlia Omar, & et al, 2013), (Huina Mao, & et al, 2014), (Yong REN, & et al, 2014), (Oded Netzer, & et al, 2012), and (Yong Ren, & et al, 2011)].

The similarity measures have been presented to identify the opinion scores of the words in the works [(Vo Ngoc Phu, & et al, 2017a), (Vo Ngoc Phu, & et al, 2017b), (Vo Ngoc Phu, & et al, 2017c), (Vo Ngoc Phu, & et al, 2017d), and (Vo Ngoc Phu, & et al, 2017e)].

The surveys have presented the dictionaries in English in the studies [(English Dictionary of Lingoes, 2017), (Oxford English Dictionary, 2017), (Cambridge English Dictionary, 2017), (Longman English Dictionary, 2017), (Collins English Dictionary, 2017), and (MacMillan English Dictionary, 2017)]. In addition, they have been more than the 55,000 words (nouns, adjectives, verbs, and etc.) in English.

The RRC has been displayed in the surveys [(Seung-Seok Choi, & et al, 2010), (Donald A. Jackson, & et al, 1989), (Andréia da Silva Meyer, & et al, 2004), (S. M. Shafer, & D. F. Rogers, 2007), (S. C. Beer, & et al, 1992), (Daniel P. Faith, 1983), (Khan Md. Saiful Islam, & Bhaba R. Sarker, 2000), and (Eviatar Nevo, & et al, 2013)].

The authors have shown the vector space modeling (VSM) in the surveys [(Vaibhav Kant Singh, & Vinay Kumar Singh, 2015), (Víctor Carrera-Trejo, & et al, 2015), and (Pascal Soucy, & Guy W. Mineau, 2015)].

The works have presented the algorithms, applications, studies, and etc. to perform in a distributed way in a parallel network environment in [(Hadoop, 2017), (Apache, 2017), and (Cloudera, 2017)].

The ARTNEURNET has been displayed in the works [(R.J. Kuo, & et al, 2001), (K. P. Sudheer, & et al, 2002), (Carsten Peterson, & et al, 1994), (D.C. Park, & et al, 1991), (Kuo-lin Hsu, & et al, 1995), (Xin Yao, 1999), (B. Samanta, & K.R. Al-Balushi, 2003), (V Brusic, G Rudy, & et al, 1998), (Muriel Gevrey, & et al, 2003), (C. Charalambous, 1992), (K. P. Sudheer, & et al, 2002), (Zhi-Hua Zhou, & et al, 2002), (Laurent Magnier, & Fariborz Haghighat, 2010), (Sovan Lek, & J.F. Guégan, 1999), and (Kyoung-jae Kim, & Ingoo Han, 2000)].

There have been a lot of the surveys related to the SEMANAL for the MASSDSs in the SEQSYS and the PARNETSYS as follows: (Vo Ngoc Phu, & Phan Thi Tuoi, 2014), (Vo Ngoc Phu, & et al, 2017f), (Vo Ngoc Phu, & Vo Thi Ngoc Tran, 2017a), (Vo Ngoc Phu, & et al, 2017g), (Vo Ngoc Phu, & et al, 2017h), (Nguyen Duy Dat, & et al, 2017), (Vo Ngoc Phu, & et al, 2017i), (Vo Ngoc Phu, & Vo Thi Ngoc Tran, 2017b), (Vo Ngoc Phu, & Vo Thi Ngoc Tran, 2018a), (Vo Ngoc Phu, & Vo Thi Ngoc Tran, 2018b), (Vo Ngoc Phu, & Vo Thi Ngoc Tran, 2018c), (Vo Ngoc Phu, & et al, 2018), (Vo Ngoc Phu, & Vo Thi Ngoc Tran, 2018d), (Vo Ngoc Phu, & Vo Thi Ngoc Tran, 2018e), (Vo Ngoc Phu, & Vo Thi Ngoc Tran, 2018f), (Vo Ngoc Phu, & Vo Thi Ngoc Tran, 2018g), (Vo Ngoc Phu, & Vo Thi Ngoc Tran, 2018h), (Vo Ngoc Phu, & Vo Thi Ngoc Tran, 2018i), (Vo Ngoc Phu, & Vo Thi Ngoc Tran, 2018j)]

All the documents of the TESTDSET and the TRAINDSET have automatically been extracted from Facebook, websites, and social networks in English. Then, we have labeled positive and negative for them fully.

The TRAINDSET has been the 2,000,000 documents of the movie area including the 1,000,000 positive and the 1,000,000 negative in English.

The TESTDSET has been the 1,000,000 documents of the movie field comprising the 500,000 positive and the 500,000 negative.

MAIN FOCUS OF THE CHAPTER

Issues, Controversies, Problems

We have displayed all the possible novel approaches of the ARTNEURNET for the MASSDSs in the different fields.

We have considered that if a model successfully processes its data set over 500,000 samples - 1,000,000 records in a SEQSYS, this model can be used for the MASSDSs.

We have also considered that if a model is successfully implemented in a PARNETSYS, this model can be used for the LARSCDSs. The reason here has been that the PARNETSYSs have been used for the MASSDSs fully.

The novel models in this book chapter have been divided into the two environments: the SEQSYSs and the PARNETSYSs

There have not been a lot of the studies of the ARTNEURNET for the MASSDSs in the SEQSYS. We have displayed the ARTNEURNET surveys of the BIGDSs in the SEQSYS firstly as follows:

The authors used context-dependent pre-trained deep neural networks in the survey (George E. Dahl, & et al, 2012) for large-vocabulary speech recognition in using deep belief networks for phone recognition, etc.

A novel model was described how to train neural network for the LARSCDSs effectively in the study (Tomas Mikolov, & et al, 2011). The hash-based implementation of a maximum entropy model was introduced can be trained as a part of the neural network model, etc.

The authors displayed a proposed model related to deep neural networks to automate large-scale statistical analysis for the massive data applications in the work (Rongrong Zhang, & et al, 2017), etc.

The authors developed an application of pre-trained deep neural networks to large vocabulary speech recognition in the study (Navdeep Jaitly, & et al, 2012), etc.

The authors used SOM-based stratified sampling for data splitting for the artificial neural networks in the work (R.J.May, H.R.Maier, & G.C.Dandy, 2010), etc.

The authors presented a novel model of a pattern-recognition technique according to the ARTNEUR-NET for reduction of false positives in computerized detection of lung nodules in low-dose computed tomography in the survey (Kenji Suzuki, & et al, 2003), etc.

We have hoped that there are going to be many surveys of the ARTNEURNET for the MASSDSs in the SEQSYS more and more in the near future, etc.

Furthermore, we have presented the studies of the ARTNEURNET for the LARSCDSs in the PAR-NETSYS as follows:

The authors developed a neural network parallel algorithm in the work (N. Funabiki, & Y. Takefuji, 1992) for channel assignment problems in cellular radio networks, etc.

In the study (Leah L. Rogers, & Farid U. Dowla, 1994), the optimization of groundwater remediation was proposed by using the ARTNEURNET with parallel solute transport modeling, etc.

The authors used and designed massively distributed computers for the ARTNEURNET in the work (Tomas Nordstrom, & Bertil Svensson, 1992), etc.

The authors displayed distribution environment state estimation by using an ARTNEURNET approach for pseudo measurement modeling in the survey (Efthymios Manitsas, & et al, 2012), etc.

The survey developed a parallel neural network architecture for controlling hexapord robot locomotion in (Randall D. Beer, & et al, 2008), etc.

The authors proposed an application of the ARTNEURNET approach in the survey (Qi-quan Li, & et al, 2013). This survey developed a radial basis function neural networks model, combined with principal component analysis, to predict the spatial distribution of SOM content across China, etc.

The parallel environments were developed for implementing neural networks in the work (Manavendra Misra, 1997), etc.

The authors used MapReduce and Cascading Model for the parallelizing back-propagation Neural Network in the survey (Yang Liu, & et al, 2016), etc.

The work used the ARTNEURNET on massively distributed computer hardware in (Udo Seiffert, 2004), etc.

The multicore and GPU parallelization of neural networks were developed for face recognition in the work (Altaf Ahmad Huqqani, & et al, 2013), etc.

The authors designed and performed a distributed software for a hybrid neural network computation in the distributed virtual machine system in the study (Huiwei Guan, & et al, 2002), etc.

The authors used and designed massively distributed computers for the ARTNEURNET in the research (Tomas Nordström, & Bertil Svensson, 1992), etc.

In the "Solutions and Recommendations", we have shown a novel model for the BIGDSs of the ARTNEURNET of the SEMANAL in the SEQSYS and the PARNETSYS, etc.

SOLUTIONS AND RECOMMENDATIONS

We have proposed the significant basic principles as follows:

1. Each sentence has been m words/phrases in English.
2. The maximum number of one sentence in English has been m_max. It has meant that m has been less than m_max, or m has been as equal as m_max.
3. Each document has been n sentences in English.
4. The maximum number of one document in English has been n_max. It has meant that n has been less than n_max, or n has been as equal as n_max.
5. Each sentence has been transformed into one one-dimensional vector (ONEDIMVECT) in English. Therefore, the length of the vector has been m. When m has been less than m_max, each element of the vector from m to m_max-1 has been 0 (zero).
6. Each document in English has been transferred into one MULTDIMVECT. So, the MULTDIMVECT has been n rows and m columns. When n has been less than n_max, each element of the MULTDIMVECT from n to n_max-1 has been 0 (zero vector).

In this proposed survey, we have proposed a new model by using the ARTNEURNET with the MULTDIMVECTs of the sentiment lexicons (SENTLEXs) to classify the opinions (positive, negative, or neutral) of the documents in English in the SEQSYS and the PARNETSYS

We have been the most significant contributions of this novel model briefly as follows:

1. We have believed that the results of this novel approach can be used for many surveys, commercial applications, and etc.

2.   The opinion scores of the words/phrases in English has been identified by using the RUSRAOC through the GOOGSE with the ANDOROPs on the Internet

3.   We have developed the formulas for this proposed survey.

4.   We have built the algorithms for this novel approach.

5.   We have believed that we can certainly apply this study to other languages easily.

6.   The ARTNEURNET has been applicable to the SEMANAL of the natural language processing, etc.

7.   This proposed model has proved that the different areas of the scientific research can be related in many different ways.

8.   This work has successfully handled millions of the documents in English for the SEMANAL.

9.   The SEMANAL has been performed in the SEQSYS and the PARNETSYS

10. We have proposed the significant principles in this survey.

11. We have used the Cloudera distributed network environment (CLOUDISNETEN), the Hadoop Map-M and Hadoop Reduce-R for this novel work successfully.

12. We have believed that this proposed study can be applied to other parallel network systems successfully.

13. We have believed that we can apply this work to many different distributed network environment such as the CLOUDISNETEN, etc.

14. We have believed that we can apply this approach to many parallel functions such as the M and the R, etc.

15. We have developed the algorithms related to the ARTNEURNET in this novel approach.

a. Transferring the Documents Into the MULTDIMVECTs According to the SENTLEXs

We have been the 3 sections for this part as follows:

a.1. Calculating the Valence of the SENTLEXs

We have been at least the 55,000 terms comprising nouns, verbs, adjectives, and etc. in English.

We have identify the semantic score and the polarity of the words or the phrases in English for our basis English opinion dictionary (BEOD) by using the RUSRAOC.

We have been the PMIMEA of the two words wi and wj based on the survey [(Aleksander Bai, & Hugo Hammer, 2014), (P.D.Turney, & M.L.Littman, 2002), (Robert Malouf, & Tony Mullen, 2017), (Christian Scheible, 2010), (Dame Jovanoski, & et al, 2015), (Amal Htait, & et al, 2016), (Xiaojun Wan, 2009), (Julian Brooke, & et al, 2009), (Tao Jiang, & et al, 2015), (Tan, S.; & Zhang, J.; 2007), (Weifu Du, & et al, 2010), (Ziqing Zhang, & et al, 2010), (Guangwei Wang, & Kenji Araki, 2007), (Shi Feng, & et al, 2013), and (Nguyen Thi Thu An, & Masafumi Hagiwara, 2014)] as follows:

$$PMI\left(wi, wj\right) = \log_2\left(\frac{P\left(wi, wj\right)}{P\left(wi\right) \times P\left(wj\right)}\right) \tag{1}$$

and we have been the equation of the SO (sentiment orientation) of word wi

$$SO(wi) = PMI(wi, positive) - PMI(wi, negative) \tag{2}$$

We have been the positive and the negative of Eq. (2) in the works [(Aleksander Bai, & Hugo Hammer, 2014), (P.D.Turney, & M.L.Littman, 2002), (Robert Malouf, & Tony Mullen, 2017), (Christian Scheible, 2010), (Dame Jovanoski, & et al, 2015), (Amal Htait, & et al, 2016), (Xiaojun Wan, 2009), and (Julian Brooke, & et al, 2009)] as follows: negative = { nasty, negative, bad, unfortunate, poor, wrong, inferior}, and positive = {nice, good, excellent, positive, correct, fortunate, superior}.

The AltaVista search engine (ALTVISSE) was used in the PMIMEA in the studies [(P.D.Turney, & M.L.Littman, 2002), (Robert Malouf, & Tony Mullen, 2017), and (Dame Jovanoski, & et al, 2015)]. The authors were used the GOOGSE in the PMIMEA of the works [(Christian Scheible, 2010), (Amal Htait, & et al, 2016), and (Julian Brooke, & et al, 2009)]. The authors also used German in the study (Christian Scheible, 2010). Macedonian was also used in the survey (Dame Jovanoski, & et al, 2015). Arabic was used in the study (Amal Htait, & et al, 2016). Chinese was used in the work (Xiaojun Wan, 2009). Spanish was used in the survey (Julian Brooke, & et al, 2009).

The formula of the JACCCO of the two words wi and wj has been as follows:

$$Jaccard\left(wi, wj\right) = J\left(wi, wj\right) = \frac{\left|wi \cap wj\right|}{\left|wi \cup wj\right|} \tag{3}$$

and other type of the equation of the JACCCO of the two words wi and wj has been as follows:

$$Jaccard\left(wi, wj\right) = J\left(wi, wj\right) = sim\left(wi, wj\right) = \frac{F\left(wi, wj\right)}{F\left(wi\right) + F\left(wj\right) - F\left(wi, wj\right)} \tag{4}$$

and the SO of the word wi has been as follows:

$$SO(wi) = \Sigma\ Sim(wi, positive) - \Sigma\ Sim(wi, positive) \tag{5}$$

We have been the positive and the negative of Eq. (5) in English as follows: negative = {nasty, bad, poor, negative, wrong, unfortunate, inferior}, and positive = {good, nice, excellent, positive, fortunate, correct, superior}.

The authors used the JACCCO with the GOOGSE in English in the surveys [(Shi Feng, & et al, 2013), (Nguyen Thi Thu An, & Masafumi Hagiwara, 2014), and (Xiang Ji, & et al, 2015)]. The authors used the JACCCO in English in the studies (Nihalahmad R. Shikalgar, & Arati M. Dixit, 2014) and (Oded Netzer, & et al, 2012). The authors used the JACCCO in Chinese in the works (Yong REN, & et al, 2014) and (Yong Ren, & et al, 2011). The authors used the JACCCO in Arabic in the survey (Nazlia Omar, & et al, 2013). The authors used the JACCCO and the Chinese search engine in Chinese in the work (Huina Mao, & et al, 2014).

The authors used the Ochiai measure (OCHMEAS) through the GOOGSE with the ANDOROPs to identify the valences of the words in Vietnamese in the study (Vo Ngoc Phu, & et al, 2017a).

The opinion scores of the words in English were calculated by using the Cosine coefficient (COS-COE) through the GOOGSE with the ANDOROPs in the work (Vo Ngoc Phu, & et al, 2017b), etc. The semantic values of the words in English were identified by using the Sorensen coefficient (SORCOE) through the GOOGSE with the ANDOROPs in the research (Vo Ngoc Phu, & et al, 2017c), etc.

According to the above proofs, we have been the information as follows: The authors used the PMIMEA with the ALTVISSE in the languages such as English, Chinese and Japanese, and the authors used the PMIMEA with the GOOGSE in English. The authors used the JACCCO with the GOOGSE in English, Chinese, and Vietnamese. The authors used the OCHMEAS with the GOOGSE in Vietnamese. The authors used the COSCOE and SORCOE with the GOOGSE in English.

Based on the surveys [(Julia V. Ponomarenko, & et al, 2002), (Andréia da Silva Meyer, & et al, 2004), (Snežana Mladenović Drinić, & et al, 2008), (Tamás, Júlia; & et al, 2001), (Vo Ngoc Phu, & et al, 2017a), (Vo Ngoc Phu, & et al, 2017b), (Vo Ngoc Phu, & et al, 2017c), (Vo Ngoc Phu, & et al, 2017d), and (Vo Ngoc Phu, & et al, 2017e)], the PMIMEA, the JACCCO, the COSCOE, the OCHMEAS, the Tominato measure (TOMMEAS), and the RUSRAOC have been the similarity measures of the two words, and they can implement the same functions and the same characteristics. So, the RUSRAOC has been used in identifying the opinion scores of the words. Furthermore, we have proved that the RUSRAOC can be used in determining the semantic value of the word in English through the GOOGSE with the ANDOROPs.

We have been the equation of the RUSRAOC based on the surveys in [(Seung-Seok Choi, & et al, 2010), (Donald A. Jackson, & et al, 1989), (Andréia da Silva Meyer, & et al, 2004), (S. M. Shafer, & D. F. Rogers, 2007), (S. C. Beer, & et al, 1992), (Daniel P. Faith, 1983), (Khan Md. Saiful Islam, & Bhaba R. Sarker, 2000), and (Eviatar Nevo, & et al, 2013)] as follows:

$$RRC\left(a,b\right) = \frac{\left(a \cap b\right)}{\left(a \cap b\right) + \left(\neg a \cap b\right) + \left(a \cap \neg b\right) + \left(\neg a \cap \neg b\right)} \tag{6}$$

with a and b have been the vectors.

According Eq. (1), Eq. (2), Eq. (3), Eq. (4), Eq. (5), and Eq. (6), calculating the valence of the words/phrases in English and their polarity has been identified by using the novel formulas of the RUSRAOC through the GOOGSE.

In Eq. (6), when we have been one element of a only, a has been a word. When we have been one element of b only, b has been a word. In addition, in Eq. (6), we have replaced a by w1, and we have also replaced b by w2.

$$RRC\left(w1,w2\right) = \frac{P\left(w1,w2\right)}{P\left(w1,w2\right) + P(\neg w1,\neg w2) + P\left(\neg w1,w2\right) + P\left(w1,\neg w2\right)} \tag{7}$$

Eq. (1) has been similar to Eq. (7). Furthermore, in Eq. (2), we have replaced Eq. (1) by Eq. (7). We have been Eq. (8) as follows:

$$Valence(w) = SO\_RRC(w) = RRC(w, positive\_query) - RRC(w, negative\_query) \qquad (8)$$

In Eq. (7), w1 has been replaced by w, and w2 has been replaced by position_query. We have been Eq. (9) as follows:

$$RRC\Big(w, positive\_query\Big) = \frac{P\Big(w, positive\_query\Big)}{A9} \qquad (9)$$

with

$A9 = P(w, positive\_query) + P(\neg w, \neg positive\_query) + P(\neg w, positive\_query) + P(w, \neg positive\_query)$

In Eq. (7), w1 has been replaced by w, and w2 has been replaced by negative_query. We have been Eq. (10) as follows:

$$RRC\Big(w, negative\_query\Big) = \frac{P\Big(w, negative\_query\Big)}{A10} \qquad (10)$$

with

$A10 = P(w, negative\_query) + P(\neg w, \neg negative\_query) + P(\neg w, negative\_query) + P(w, \neg negative\_query)$

We have been the information of w, w1, w2, P(w1, w2), and etc. as follows:

1. w, w1, and w2 have been the words/the phrases in English.
2. P(w1, w2) has been the number of the returned results in the GOOGSE by the keyword (w1 and w2). In addition, we have used the API of the GOOGSE to get the number of the returned results in the GOOGSE online by the keyword (w1 and w2).
3. P(w1) has been the number of the returned results in the GOOGSE by the keyword w1. Furthermore, we have used the API of the GOOGSE to get the number of the returned results in the GOOGSE online by the keyword w1.
4. P(w2) has been the number of the returned results in the GOOGSE by the keyword w2. Moreover, we have used the API of the GOOGSE to get the number of the returned results in the GOOGSE online by the keyword w2.
5. Valence(W) = SO_RRC(w) has been the opinion value of the word/the phrase w in English, and it has also been the SO of the word (or the phrase) by the RUSRAOC.
6. positive_query has been { active or good or positive or beautiful or strong or nice or excellent or fortunate or correct or superior } with the positive_query has been the group of the positive words in English.

7. negative_query has been { passive or bad or negative or ugly or week or nasty or poor or unfortunate or wrong or inferior } with the negative_query has been the group of the negative words in English.

8. P(w, positive_query) has been the number of the returned results in the GOOGSE by the keyword (positive_query and w). In addition, we have used the API of the GOOGSE to get the number of the returned results in the GOOGSE online by the keyword (positive_query and w)

9. P(w, negative_query) has been the number of the returned results in the GOOGSE by the keyword (negative _query and w). Furthermore, we have used the API of the GOOGSE to get the number of the returned results in the GOOGSE online by the keyword (negative_query and w)

10. P(w) has been the number of the returned results in the GOOGSE by the keyword w. Moreover, we have used the API of the GOOGSE to get the number of the returned results in the GOOGSE online by the keyword w.

11. P(¬w,positive_query) has been the number of the returned results in the GOOGSE by the keyword ((not w) and positive_query). In addition, we have used the API of the GOOGSE to get the number of the returned results in the GOOGSE online by the keyword ((not w) and positive_query).

12. P(w, ¬positive_query) has been the number of the returned results in the GOOGSE by the keyword: (w and (not (positive_query))). Moreover, we have used the API of the GOOGSE to receive the number of the returned results in the GOOGSE online using the keyword: (w and [not (positive_query)]).

13. P(¬w,¬positive_query) has been the returned results in the GOOGSE by the keyword: ([not w] and [not (positive_query)]). Furthermore, we have used the API of the GOOGSE to receive the returned results in the GOOGSE online using the keyword: ((not w) and (not (positive_query))).

14. P(¬w,negative_query) has been the returned results in the GOOGSE using the keyword: ((not w) and negative_query). Moreover, we have used the API of the GOOGSE to receive the returned results in the GOOGSE online using the keyword: ((not w) and negative_query).

15. P(w,¬negative_query) has been the returned results in the GOOGSE using the keyword: (w and (not (negative_query))). In addition, we have used the API of the GOOGSE to receive the returned results in the GOOGSE online using the keyword: (w and (not (negative_query))).

16. P(¬w,¬negative_query) has been the returned results in the GOOGSE using the keyword: ((not w) and (not (negative_query))). Furthermore, we have used the API of the GOOGSE to receive the returned results in the GOOGSE online using the keyword: ((not w) and (not (negative_query))).

We have identified the semantic score of the word w in English according to the proximity of positive_query with w, the remote of positive_query with w, the proximity of negative_query with w, and the remote of negative_query with w.

When the value RRC(w, positive_query) has been as equal as 1, the word w in English has been the nearest of positive_query.

When the value RRC (w, positive_query) has been as equal as 0, the word w in English has been the farthest of positive_query.

When the value RRC (w, positive_query) has been greater than 0, and the value RRC (w, positive_query) has been less than 1 or as equal as 1, the word w in English has belonged to positive_query being the positive group of the words in English.

When the value RRC (w, negative_query) has been as equal as 1, the word w in English has been the nearest of negative_query.

When the value RRC (w, negative_query) has been as equal as 0, the word w in English has been the farthest of negative_query.

When the value RRC (w, negative_query) has been greater 0, and the value RRC (w, negative_query) has been less than 1 or as equal as 1, the word w in English has belonged to negative_query being the negative group of the words in English.

Therefore, the semantic value of the word w in English has been the value (RRC (w, positive_query)-RRC (w, negative_query)), and in addition, the Eq. (8) has been the equation for identifying the sentiment score of the word w in English

The information of the value RRC has been as follows:

1. RRC (w, positive_query) has been greater than 0 or as equal as 0, and RRC (w, positive_query) has been less than 1 or as equal as 1.
2. RRC (w, negative_query) has been greater than 0 or as equal as 0, and RRC (w, negative_query) has been less than 1 or as equal as 1.
3. When the value RRC (w, positive_query) has been as equal as 0, and the value RRC(w, negative_query) has been as equal as 0, the value SO_RRC(w) has been as equal as 0.
4. When the value RRC (w, positive_query) has been as equal as 1, and the value RRC (w, negative_query) has been as equal as 0, the value SO_RRC(w) has been as equal as 0.
5. When the value RRC (w, positive_query) has been as equal as 0, and the value RRC (w, negative_query) has been as equal as 1, the value SO_RRC(w) has been as equal as -1.
6. When the value RRC (w, positive_query) has been as equal as 1, and the value RRC (w, negative_query) has been as equal as 1, the value SO_RRC(w) has been as equal as 0

Thus, the value SO_ RRC (w) $\geq$ -1 and SO_ RRC (w) $\leq$ 1.

When the value SO_RRC (w) has been greater than 0, the word w in English has been the positive polarity.

When the value SO_RRC (w) has been less than 0, the word w in English has been the negative polarity.

When the value SO_RRC (w) has been as equal as 0, the word w in English has been the neutral polarity.

Furthermore, the opinion score of the word w in English has been SO_ RRC (w).

We have identified the valence and the polarity of the word/the phrase w in English by using a training corpus of approximately one hundred billion words of the web sites, social networks, and etc. in English that have been indexed by the GOOGSE on the internet. The ALTVISSE has been chosen because it has been a NEAR operator. However, the ALTVISSE has been no longer.

In this survey, we have used the GOOGSE which has not been a NEAR operator. The GOOGSE has used the ANDOROPs. The results of identifying the semantic value of the word w in English by using the GOOGSE have been similar to the results of the opinion score of the word w in English by using the ALTVISSE

The BEOD has been more the 55,000 words/phrases in English, and the BEOD has been stored in Microsoft SQL Server 2008 R2.

a.2. Transferring the Documents Into the MULTDIMVECTs in the SEQSYS

In this section, we have transformed the documents of the TESTDSET and the TRAINDSET into the MULTDIMVECTs in the SEQSYS.

We have presented how to transfer one document in English into one MULTDIMVECT according to the SENTLEXs in the SEQSYS firstly. Then, we have applied this to transfer all the documents of the TESTDSET and the TRAINDSET into MULTDIMVECTs in the SEQSYS.

We have proposed the algorithm 1 to transfer one document in English into MULTDIMVECT based on the SENTLEXs in the SEQSYS

Input: one English document

Output one MULTDIMVECT based on the SENTLEXs

1. This document has been separated into the n sentences
2. We have repeated each sentence in the sentences as follows:
3. This sentence has been separated into the n_n meaningful words (or meaningful phrases);
4. We have repeated each term in the n_n terms as follows:
5. We have gotten the semantic value of this term according to the BEOD;
6. Add this term (term, valence) into the one one-dimensional vector;
7. End Repeat- End (4);
8. Add one one-dimensional vector (corresponding to this sentence) into the MULTDIMVECT;
9. End Repeat – End (2);
10. Return the MULTDIMVECT;

a.3. Transferring the Documents Into the MULTDIMVECTs in the PARNETSYS

We have transformed the documents of the TESTDSET and the TRAINDSET into the MULTDIMVECTs in the PARNETSYS

We have displayed how to transfer one document in English into one MULTDIMVECT according to the SENTLEXs in the CLOUDISNETEN. The input of the M in the CLOUDISNETEN has been one document, the SENTLEXs of the BEOD. The output of the M has been one ONEDIMVECT (corresponding to one sentence of this document). The input of the R has been the output of the M. So, the output of the R has been one MULTDIMVECT (corresponding to this document). Then, we have applied this part to transform all the documents of the TESTDSET and the TRAINDSET into the MULTDIM-VECTs in the CLOUDISNETEN.

In the M phase:

Input: One document in English ; The SENTLEXs of the BEOD.

Output: one ONEDIMVECT;

1. Input One English document; and the SENTLEXs of the BEOD into the M in the CLOUDISNETEN.
2. This document has been separated into the sentences;
3. We have repeated each sentence in the sentences as follows:
4. This sentence has been separated into the n_n meaningful words (or meaningful phrases)
5. Each term in the n_n terms, do repeat:
6. Get valence of this term based on the BEOD;

7.   Add this term into the ONEDIMVECT;
8.   End Repeat – End (5);
9.   Return this ONEDIMVECT;
10. The output of the M has been this ONEDIMVECT;

In the R phase:
Input: one ONEDIMVECT of the M (the input of the R has been the output of the M)
Output: one MULTDIMVECT (corresponding to one English document)

1.   Receive one ONEDIMVECT of the M
2.   Add this ONEDIMVECT into the MULTDIMVECT;
3.   Return the MULTDIMVECT;

b. Implementing the ARTNEURNET in the SEQSYS and the PARNETSYS

We have been the two parts of this section as follows: The SEMANAL for the documents of the SEQSYS has been displayed in the first part. The SEMANAL for the documents of the SEQSYS has been presented in the second part.

There have been the two groups of the TRAINDSET as follows: The first group has included the positive documents, and the second group has been the negative documents. The first group has been called the positive cluster, and the second group has been called the negative cluster.

All the documents in both the first group and the second group have gone through the segmentation of words and stop-words removal. Then, they have been transferred into the MULTDIMVECTs (vector representation).

The positive documents of the positive cluster have been transformed into the positive MULTDIM-VECTs which have been called the positive multi-dimensional vector group (POSMULTDIMVECTGR).

The negative documents of the negative cluster have been transformed into the negative MULTDIM-VECTs which have been called the negative multi-dimensional vector group (NEGMULTDIMVECTGR).

Therefore, the TRAINDSET has been the POSMULTDIMVECTGR and the NEGMULTDIMVECTGR.

We have transformed all documents in English into the MULTDIMVECTs in the SEQSYS similar to (a.2), and we have also transferred all the documents in English into the MULTDIMVECTs in the PARNETSYS similar to (a.3).

b.1. The ARTNEURNET in the SEQSYS

The documents of the TESTDSET have been transformed into the MULTDIMVECTs: Each document of the TESTDSET has been transferred into each MULTDIMVECT (each sentence of one document of the TESTDSET has been transformed into the ONEDIMVECT in the SEQSYS similar to (a.2)).

The positive documents of the TRAINDSET have been transferred into the positive MULTDIM-VECTs in the SEQSYS, called POSMULTDIMVECTGR: Each document of the positive documents of the TRAINDSET has been transformed into the ONEDIMVECT in the SEQSYS similar to (a.2)).

The negative documents of the TRAINDSET have been transferred into the negative MULTDIM-VECTs in the SEQSYS, called NEGMULTDIMVECTGR: Each document of the negative documents of the TRAINDSET has been transformed into the ONEDIMVECT in the SEQSYS similar to (a.2)).

We have performed this part as follows: The ARTNEURNET has been implemented to classify one MULTDIMVECT (called A) of the TESTDSET into either the NEGMULTDIMVECTGR or the POS-MULTDIMVECTGR. When A has been classified into the POSMULTDIMVECTGR, this document (corresponding to A) has been the positive polarity. When A has been classified into the NEGMULT-DIMVECTGR, this document (corresponding to A) has been the negative polarity. When A has been classified into neither the NEGMULTDIMVECTGR nor the POSMULTDIMVECTGR, this document (corresponding to A) has been the neutral polarity.

We have developed the algorithms to perform the ARTNEURNET in the SEQSYS.

We have proposed the algorithm 2 to transfer one document in English into one MULTDIMVECT in the SEQSYS: Each document has been separated into the sentences. Each sentence of one document has been transformed into one ONEDIMVECT in the SEQSYS based on (a.2). We have inserted all the ONEDIMVECTs of the sentences into one MULTDIMVECT.

Input: one English document

Output: one MULTDIMVECT

1. Split the English document into many separate sentences based on "." Or "!" or "?";
2. Each sentence in the n sentences of this document, do repeat:
3. Transfer this sentence into one ONEDIMVECT based on (a.2);
4. Add the transferred vector into one MULTDIMVECT
5. End Repeat – End (2)
6. Return one MULTDIMVECT;

We have built the algorithm 3 to create the POSMULTDIMVECTGR in the SEQSYS: Each document of the positive documents of the TRAINDSET has been separated into the sentences. Each sentence of the document has been transferred into one ONEDIMVECT in the SEQSYS according to (a.2). We have inserted all the ONEDIMVECTs of the sentences of the document into one ONEDIMVECT of the document. Then, the positive documents of the TRAINDSET have been transferred into the positive MULTDIMVECTs.

Input: the positive English documents of the TRAINDSET.

Output: the positive vector group POSMULTDIMVECTGR

1. Each document of the positive document of the TRAINDSET, do repeat:
2. OneMultiDimensionalVector:= Call Algorithm 1 with the positive English document of the TRAINDSET;
3. Add OneMultiDimensionalVector into POSMULTDIMVECTGR;
4. End Repeat – End (1)
5. Return POSMULTDIMVECTGR;

We have proposed the algorithm 4 to create the NEGMULTDIMVECTGR in the SEQSYS: Each documents of the negative documents of the TRAINDSET has been separated into the sentences. Each sentence of the document has been transferred into one ONEDIMVECT in the SEQSYS according to (a.2). We have inserted all the ONEDIMVECTs of the sentences of the document into one ONEDIM-VECT of the document. Then, the negative documents of the TRAINDSET have been transformed into the negative MULTDIMVECTs.

Input: the negative English documents of the TRAINDSET.
Output: the negative vector group NEGMULTDIMVECTGR

1. Each document in the negative documents of the TRAINDSET, do repeat:
2. OneMultiDimensionalVector:= Call Algorithm 1 with the negative English document of the TRAINDSET;
3. Add OneMultiDimensionalVector into NEGMULTDIMVECTGR ;
4. End Repeat – End (1);
5. Return NEGMULTDIMVECTGR;

We have developed the algorithm 5 to classify one MULTDIMVECT (corresponding to one document of the TESTDSET) into either the NEGMULTDIMVECTGR or the POSMULTDIMVECTGR in the SEQSYS

Input: one MULTDIMVECT A (corresponding to one English document of the TESTDSET), the POSMULTDIMVECTGR and the NEGMULTDIMVECTGR;

Output: positive, negative, neutral;

1. Implement the ARTNEURNET based on the ARTNEURNET of the surveys [53-67] with the input has been one MULTDIMVECT (corresponding to one English document of the TESTDSET), the POSMULTDIMVECTGR, and the NEGMULTDIMVECTGR;
2. With the results of (1), If the vector is clustered into the positive vector group Then Return positive;
3. Else If the vector is clustered into the negative vector group Then Return negative; End If – End (2)
4. Return neutral;

The ARTNEURNET has used the Euclidean distance to calculate the distance between two vectors

b.2. The ARTNEURNET in the PARNETSYS

All the documents of the TESTDSET and the TRAINDSET have been transformed into all the MULTDIMVECTs in the CLOUDISNETEN.

We have transformed the documents of the TESTDSET into all the MULTDIMVECTs by using the M and the R in the CLOUDISNETEN for the purpose of shortening the execution time of this task.

We have transferred the documents of the TRAINDSET into all the MULTDIMVECTs by using the M and the R in the CLOUDISNETEN for the purpose of shortening the execution time of this task.

The positive documents of the TRAINDSET have been transformed into the positive MULTDIM-VECTs in the CLOUDISNETEN, called POSMULTDIMVECTGR

The negative documents of the TRAINDSET have been transformed into the negative MULTDIM-VECTs in the CLOUDISNETEN, called NEGMULTDIMVECTGR

We have done this part in Figure 1 as follows: One MULTDIMVECT (called A) of the document of the TESTDSET has been classified into either the NEGMULTDIMVECTGR or the POSMULTDIM-VECTGR using the ARTNEURNET in the CLOUDISNETEN. When A has been classified into the POSMULTDIMVECTGR, the document (corresponding to A) has been the positive polarity. When A has been classified into the NEGMULTDIMVECTGR, the document (corresponding to A) has been the negative polarity. When A has been classified into neither the NEGMULTDIMVECTGR nor the POSMULTDIMVECTGR, the document (corresponding to A) has been the neutral polarity.

Figure 1. The ARTNEURNET in the Parallel Network Environment.

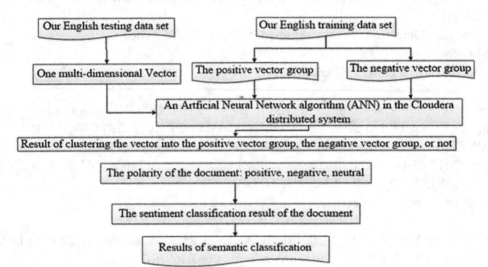

Transferring each document in English into one MULTDIMVECT in the CLOUDISNETEN has been presented in Figure 2. This has been the two phases: the M, and the R. Moreover, the input of the M has been on document, and the output of the M has been many components of a MULTDIMVECT corresponding to the document. This document, the input of the M, has been separated into the sentences. Each sentence in the document has been transformed into one ONEDIMVECT based on (a.3). This has been repeated for all the sentences of the document until all the sentences have been transformed into all the ONEDIMVECTs of the document. Then, the M of the CLOUDISNETEN has automatically transferred the ONEDIMVECT into the R. The input of the R has been the output of the M, and this input has comprised the components (corresponding the ONEDIMVECTs) of the MULTDIMVECT. The output of the R has been a MULTDIMVECT corresponding to the document. In the R of the CLOUDISNETEN, these ONEDIMVECTs have been added into one MULTDIMVECT.

The documents of the TESTDSET have been transferred into the MULTDIMVECTs based on Figure 2.

The ARTNEURNET in the CLOUDISNETEN has been the two main phases: the first main phase has been the M phase in the CLOUDISNETEN, and the second main phase has been the R phase in the CLOUDISNETEN.

In the M of the CLOUDISNETEN, the input of this phase has been the MULTDIMVECT of one English document (which has been classified), the POSMULTDIMVECTGR and the NEGMULTDIMVECTGR. The output of the phase has been the classifying results of the MULTDIMVECT of the document into either the NEGMULTDIMVECTGR or the POSMULTDIMVECTGR.

In the R of the CLOUDISNETEN, the input of the phase has been the output of the M of the CLOUDISNETEN, and this input has been the classifying results of the MULTDIMVECT of the document into either the NEGMULTDIMVECTGR or the POSMULTDIMVECTGR. The output of the phase has been the result of the SEMANAL of the document into either the positive polarity, the negative polarity, or the neutral polarity.

Figure 2. Transforming each English document into one MULTDIMVECT in the CLOUDISNETEN

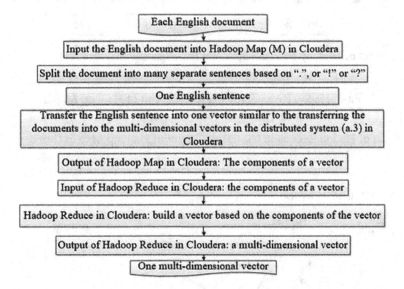

In the R phase, when the MULTDIMVECT has been classified into the POSMULTDIMVECTGR, this document has been classified as the positive semantic. When the MULTDIMVECT has been classified into the NEGMULTDIMVECTGR, this document has been classified as the negative opinion. When the MULTDIMVECT has been classified into neither the NEGMULTDIMVECTGR nor the POSMULTDIMVECTGR, this document has been classified as the neutral sentiment.

In the M phase: We have implemented this phase in Figure 3. The ARTNEURNET in the CLOUD-ISNETEN has been based on the ARTNEURNET of the surveys [(R.J. Kuo, & et al, 2001), (K. P. Sudheer, & et al, 2002), (Carsten Peterson, & et al, 1994), (D.C. Park, & et al, 1991), (Kuo-lin Hsu, & et al, 1995), (Xin Yao, 1999), (B. Samanta, & K.R. Al-Balushi, 2003), (V Brusic, G Rudy, & et al, 1998), (Muriel Gevrey, & et al, 2003), (C. Charalambous, 1992), (K. P. Sudheer, & et al, 2002), (Zhi-Hua Zhou, & et al, 2002), (Laurent Magnier, & Fariborz Haghighat, 2010), (Sovan Lek, & J.F. Guégan, 1999), and (Kyoung-jae Kim, & Ingoo Han, 2000)]. This input has been one MULTDIMVECT of the TESTDSET, the NEGMULTDIMVECTGR and the POSMULTDIMVECTGR of the TRAINDSET. The output of the ARTNEURNET has been the classifying result of the MULTDIMVECT into either the NEGMULTDIMVECTGR or the POSMULTDIMVECTGR.

The main ideas of the ARTNEURNET have been presented one more details.

The ARTNEURNET in our model has included the learning stage and the testing stage. An overview of our ARTNEURNET has been in Figure 4.

In Figure 4, the input of neural network has been a multi-dimensional vector X and the output of network has been +1 or -1. When the output has been +1, this vector of the input has been classified into the POSMULTDIMVECTGR. When the output has been -1, this vector of the input has been classified into the NEGMULTDIMVECTGR

Figure 3. The ARTNEURNET in the M of the CLOUDISNETEN

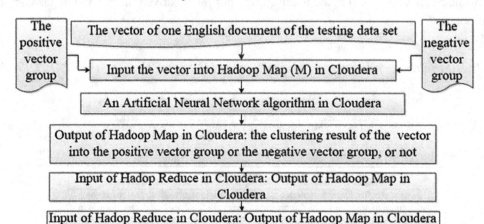

Figure 4. Overview of neural network

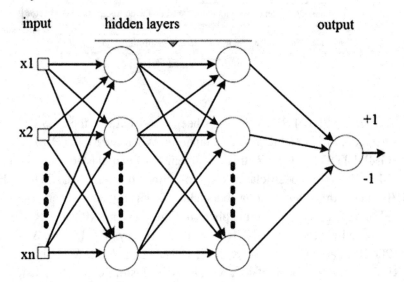

Our learning stage: in this stage, we have used the positive vectors of the POSMULTDIMVECTGR and the negative vectors of the NEGMULTDIMVECTGR to identify the parameters of our neural network, such as weights, outputs, etc.

Our testing stage: with the parameters of our neural network, each vector of the TESTDSET has been the input of our neural network. The following Algorithm 6 is the basic algorithm of the supervised learning of our neural network.

Supervised learning can be considered as mapping approximately: $X \rightarrow Y$, where X is the set of problems and Y is the corresponding set of solutions to that problem. The samples (x, y) with x = (x1, x2,..., Xn) $\in$ X, y = (yl, y2,..., Ym) $\in$ Y be given.

Input: x = (x1, x2,..., Xn) ∈ X,
Output: y = (yl, y2,..., Ym) ∈ Y

begin

1. Build the appropriate structure for neural network, for example with (n+1) neurons input (n neurons for input variables and 1 neuron for threshold x0), m output neurons, and initialize the weights of the network links.
2. Input one vector x in the X training data set input into network
3. Calculate the output vector o of network.
4. Compare the expected output vector y (is the given result of training data set) with the output vector o which network generated; if can be then identify error
5. Adjust the weights in some way so that in the next time, when inputs vector x to the network, the output vector o will resemble y more.
6. Can repeat step 2 to step 5 if want, until converging. The evaluation of error can perform in many different ways, using the most used instant error: Err = (o - y), or Err = | o - y |; mean squared error (MSE: mean-square error): Err = (o- y) 2/2;

end;

There have been two types of errors in the evaluation of a neural network. Firstly, called as clear error, assess approximately the training samples of a network have been trained. Second, called as test error, assess the ability of a total process of a network has been trained, the ability to react with the new input vector.

In this study, we have used back-propagation algorithm of neural network for our new model.

The main ideal of the back-propagation algorithm: we have wanted to train a multi-layer feed-forward network by gradient descent to approximate an unknown function, based on some training data consisting of pairs (x,t). The vector x has represented a pattern of input to the network, and the vector t the corresponding target (desired output). As we have seen before, the overall gradient with respect to the entire training set has been just the sum of the gradients for each pattern; in what follows we would therefore describe how to compute the gradient for just a single training pattern. As before, we would number the units, and denote the weight from unit j to unit i by w_{ij}.

Definitions

The error signal for unit j: $\delta_j = -\partial E/\partial netj$
The (negative) gradient for weight wij: $\nabla \mathcal{M}^{s3} = -9E / 9\mathcal{M}^{s3}$
The set of nodes anterior to unit i: $A_i = \{j: \exists w_{ij}\}$
The set of nodes posterior to unit j: $P_j = \{i: \exists w_{ij}\}$

The Gradient

As we did for linear networks before, we expand the gradient into two factors by use of the chain rule:

$$\Delta w_{ij} = -\frac{\partial E}{\partial net_i}\frac{\partial net_i}{\partial w_{ij}}$$

The first factor is the error of unit i. The second is

$$\frac{\partial net_i}{\partial w_{ij}} = \frac{\partial}{\partial w_{ij}}\sum_{k\in A_i} w_{ik}y_k = y_j$$

Putting the two together, we get

$$\Delta w_{ij} = \delta_i y_j$$

To compute this gradient, we thus need to know the activity and the error for all relevant nodes in the network.

Forward Activation

The activity of the input units is determined by the network's external input x. For all other units, the activity is propagated forward:

$$y_i = f_i\left(\sum_{j\in A_i} w_{ij}y_j\right)$$

Before the activity of unit i can be calculated, the activity of all its anterior nodes (forming the set Ai) must be known. Since feedforward networks do not contain cycles, there is an ordering of nodes from input to output that respects this condition.

Calculating Output Error

Assuming that we are using the sum-squared loss

$$E = \frac{1}{2}\sum_o \left(t_o - y_o\right)^2$$

the error for output unit o is simply

$$\delta o = to - yo$$

Error Backpropagation

For hidden units, we must propagate the error back from the output nodes (hence the name of the algorithm). Again using the chain rule, we can expand the error of a hidden unit in terms of its posterior nodes:

$$\delta_j = -\sum_{i \in P_j} \frac{\partial E}{\partial net_i} \frac{\partial net_i}{\partial y_j} \frac{\partial y_j}{\partial net_j}$$

Of the three factors inside the sum, the first is just the error of node i. The second is

$$\frac{\partial net_i}{\partial y_j} = \frac{\partial}{\partial y_j} \sum_{k \in A_i} w_{ik} y_k = w_{ij}$$

while the third is the derivative of node j's activation function:

$$\frac{\partial y_j}{\partial net_j} = \frac{\partial f_j(net_j)}{\partial net_j} = f'_j(net_j)$$

For hidden units h that use the tanh activation function, we can make use of the special identity

$$f'_h(net_h) = 1 - y_h^2$$

Putting all the pieces together we get

$$\delta_j = f'_j(net_j) \sum_{i \in P_j} \delta_i w_{ij}$$

In order to calculate the error for unit j, we must first know the error of all its posterior nodes (forming the set Pj). Again, as long as there are no cycles in the network, there is an ordering of nodes from the output back to the input that respects this condition. For example, we can simply use the reverse of the order in which activity was propagated forward.

After finishing to cluster the multi-dimensional vector into either the POSMULTDIMVECTGR or the NEGMULTDIMVECTGR, the M has transferred this results into the R in the Cloudera system.

In the R phase:

This phase has been performed in Figure 5: After receiving the classifying result of the M, the R has labeled the opinion polarity for the MULTDIMVECT which has been classified. Then, the output of the R has returned the semantic polarity of one document (corresponding to the MULTDIMVECT) of the TESTDSET. When the MULTDIMVECT has been classified into the POSMULTDIMVECTGR, the document has been the positive polarity. When the MULTDIMVECT has been classified into the NEGMULTDIMVECTGR, the document has been the negative polarity. When the MULTDIMVECT has not been classified into the NEGMULTDIMVECTGR and the POSMULTDIMVECTGR, the document has been the neutral polarity.

We have used an Accuracy (A) measure to identify the accuracy of the results of the SEMANAL of this model.

Figure 5. The ARTNEURNET in the R of the CLOUDISNETEN

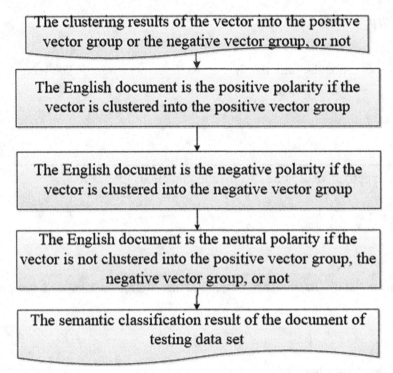

The Java programming language (JAVAPRL) has been used to program for saving the TESTDSET and the TRAINDSET, and for performing our proposed model to classify the documents of the TESTDSET into either the positive, the negative, or the neutral.

The configuration of each server (each node) has been: Intel® Server Board S1200V3RPS, Intel® Pentium® Processor G3220 (3M Cache, 3.00 GHz), 2GB PC3-10600 ECC 1333 MHz LP Unbuffered DIMMs.

The operating system of each node (each server) has been the Cloudera.

The SEQSYS in this novel survey has been 1 node (1 server). The JAVAPRL has been used in programming the ARTNEURNET.

We have implemented the ARTNEURNET in the CLOUDISNETEN: This CLOUDISNETEN has included the 9 nodes (9 servers). The JAVAPRL has been used in programming the application of the ARTNEURNET in the CLOUDISNETEN. All the 9 nodes have been the same configuration information.

The results of the documents of the TESTDSET have been displayed in Table 1.

The accuracy of the SEMANAL of the documents of the TESTDSET has been presented in Table 2.

Table 1. The results of the documents of the TESTDSET

	Testing Dataset	Correct Classification	Incorrect Classification
Negative	500,000	434,759	65,241
Positive	500,000	435,541	64,459
Summary	1,000,000	870,300	129,700

Table 2. The accuracy of the SEMANAL of the documents of the TESTDSET

Proposed Model	Class	Accuracy
Our new model	Negative	87.03%
	Positive	

The average execution times of the SEMANAL of our novel model for the documents of the TES-TDSET have been shown in Table 3.

Table 3. The average execution times of the SEMANAL of our novel model for the documents of the TESTDSET

	The Average Times of the Classification /1,000,000 English Documents
The ARTNEURNET in the sequential environment	5,261,792 seconds
The ARTNEURNET in the CLOUDISNETEN – 3 nodes	1,538,736 seconds
The ARTNEURNET in the CLOUDISNETEN – 6 nodes	854,373 seconds
The ARTNEURNET in the CLOUDISNETEN – 9 nodes	611,784 seconds

Although our new model has been tested on our English data set, it can be applied to other languages certainly.

In this book chapter, our novel model has been tested on the 1,000,000 documents in English of the TESTDSET which has been very small. However, this novel approach can be applied to many large-scale data sets with millions of the documents in English in the shortest time.

In this work, we have developed a novel model to classify the opinions (positive, negative, or neutral) of the documents using the ARTNEURNET in the SEQSYS and the CLOUDISNETEN with the M and the R.

In Table 2, we have already achieved 87.03% accuracy of the TESTDSET of the novel model.

In Table 3, we have been the information of the average execution times of the SEMANAL of our proposed model as follows:

1. The average execution time of the SEMANAL of the ARTNEURNET in the SEQSYS has been 5,261,792 seconds /1,000,000 English documents, and it has been greater than the average execution time of the SEMANAL of the ARTNEURNET in the CLOUDISNETEN – 3 nodes which has been 1,538,736 seconds /1,000,000 documents in English.
2. The time of the SEMANAL of the ARTNEURNET in the CLOUDISNETEN – 9 nodes which has been 611,784 seconds /1,000,000 documents in English has been the shortest time.
3. The average execution time of the SEMANAL of the ARTNEURNET in the CLOUDISNETEN – 6 nodes has been 854,373 seconds /1,000,000 documents in English.

The time of the ARTNEURNET in the CLOUDISNETEN has been dependent on the performance of the CLOUDISNETEN, and it has also been dependent on the performance of each server of the CLOUDISNETEN. It has also been dependent on the number of the nodes (servers) of the CLOUDISNETEN.

FUTURE RESEARCH DIRECTIONS

From those results of this novel model and according to the above proofs, we are going to study this model for applying to billions of English documents in both the SE and the PNE. In addition, we are also going to research this approach for being performed in the PNE with over 50 nodes. Furthermore, the accuracy of this new computational model can be studied to improve certainly.

From the results of this chapter, many algorithms, methods, models, and etc. are going to be developed more and more for handling the massive data sets fully in the near future.

CONCLUSION

In this book chapter, we have already presented the simple concepts of the ARTNEURNET, the BIGDSs, and etc. We have also shown the importance of the ARTNEURNET, the MASSDSs, and etc. in the world. The problems and challenges of the ARTNEURNET, the MASSDSs, and etc. have also displayed on more details, etc.

We have already given an example of the ARTNEURNET of the SEMANAL for the LARSCDSs in this book chapter using the ARTNEURNET, and the MULTDIMVECTs of the SENTLEXs of the RUSRAOC through the GOOGSE with the ANDOROPs in the SEQSYS and the PANETSYS.

From the results of the proposed model, based on our opinion, the ARTNEURNET, the artificial intelligence, the machine learning, and etc. are very crucial for the MASSDS certainly. We believe that there are going to have many important contributions of the ARTNEURNET, the artificial intelligence, the machine learning, and etc. for the BIGDSs fully and successfully.

In addition, this novel model can process billions of the documents in English of the SEMANAL for a MASSDS.

Many algorithms, methods, models, and etc. are going to be developed for the BIGDSs to be applied to the different fields from the results of the proposed approach. This is very significant for many organizations, economies, governments, countries, commercial applications, researches, and etc. in the world.

ACKNOWLEDGMENT

This book chapter has been funded by Institute of Research and Development of Duy Tan University-DTU in Da Nang city in Vietnam

REFERENCES

Andréia da Silva, M., Antonio, A. F. G., Pereira de Souza, A., & Lopes de Souza, C. Jr. (2004). Comparison of similarity coefficients used for cluster analysis with dominant markers in maize (Zea maysL). *Genetics and Molecular Biology, 27*(1), 83–91. doi:10.1590/S1415-47572004000100014

Andréia da Silva, M., Antonio, A. F. G., Pereira de Souza, A., & Lopes de Souza, C. Jr. (2004). Comparison of similarity coefficients used for cluster analysis with dominant markers in maize (Zea mays L). *Genetics and Molecular Biology, 27*(1). doi:10.1590/S1415-47572004000100014

Apache. (2017). Retrieved from http://apache.org

Bai, A., & Hammer, H. (2014). Constructing sentiment lexicons in Norwegian from a large text corpus. *2014 IEEE 17th International Conference on Computational Science and Engineering.* DOI: 10.1109/CSE.2014.73

Beer, R. D., Chiel, H. J., Quinn, R. D., Espenschied, K. S., & Larsson, P. (2008). A Distributed Neural Network Architecture for Hexapod Robot Locomotion. *Neural Computation, 4*(3), 356–365. doi:10.1162/neco.1992.4.3.356

Beer, S. C., Goffreda, J., Phillips, T. D., Murphy, J. P., & Sorrells, M. E. (1992). Assessment of Genetic Variation in Avena sterilis using Morphologicall Traits, Isozymes, and RFLPs. *Crop Science, 33*(6), 1386–1393. doi:10.2135/cropsci1993.0011183X003300060051x

Brooke, J., Tofiloski, M., & Taboada, M. (2009). Cross-Linguistic Sentiment Analysis: From English to Spanish. *International Conference RANLP 2009*, 50–54.

Brusic, V., Rudy, G., Honeyman, G., Hammer, J., & Harrison, L. (1998). Prediction of MHC class II-binding peptides using an evolutionary algorithm and artificial neural network. *Bioinformatics (Oxford, England), 14*(2), 121–130. doi:10.1093/bioinformatics/14.2.121 PMID:9545443

Carrera-Trejo, V., Sidorov, G., Miranda-Jiménez, S., Ibarra, M. M., & Martínez, R. C. (2015). Latent Dirichlet Allocation complement in the vector space model for Multi-Label Text Classification. *International Journal of Combinatorial Optimization Problems and Informatics, 6*(1), 7–19.

Charalambous, C. (1992). Conjugate gradient algorithm for efficient training of artificial neural networks. *IEE Proceedings. Part G. Circuits, Devices and Systems, 139*(3), 301–310. doi:10.1049/ip-g-2.1992.0050

Choi, S.-S., Cha, S.-H., & Tappert, C. C. (2010). A Survey of Binary Similarity and Distance Measures. *Systemics, Cybernetics and Informatics, 8*(1).

Cloudera. (2017). Retrieved from http://www.cloudera.com

Dahl, G. E., Yu, D., Deng, L., & Acero, A. (2012). Context-Dependent Pre-Trained Deep Neural Networks for Large-Vocabulary Speech Recognition. *IEEE Transactions on Audio, Speech, and Language Processing, 20*(1), 30–42. doi:10.1109/TASL.2011.2134090

Dat, Phu, & Chau, Tran, & Nguyen. (2017). STING Algorithm used English Sentiment Classification in A Parallel Environment. *International Journal of Pattern Recognition and Artificial Intelligence, 31*(7). doi:10.11420218001417500215

DictionaryC. E. (2017). Retrieved from http://dictionary.cambridge.org/

DictionaryC. E. (2017). Retrieved from http://www.collinsdictionary.com/dictionary/english

DictionaryL. E. (2017). Retrieved from http://www.ldoceonline.com/

DictionaryO. E. (2017). Retrieved from http://www.oxforddictionaries.com/

Drinić, S. M., Nikolić, A., & Perić, V. (2008). Cluster Analysis of Soybean Genotypes Based on RAPD Markers. *Proceedings. 43rd Croatian and 3rd International Symposium on Agriculture*, 367-370.

Du, W., Tan, S., Cheng, X., & Yun, X. (2010). Adapting Information Bottleneck Method for Automatic Construction of Domain-oriented Sentiment Lexicon. WSDM'10, New York, NY. doi:10.1145/1718487.1718502

English Dictionary of Lingoes. (2017). Retrieved from http://www.lingoes.net/

Faith, D. P. (1983). Asymmetric binary similarity measures. *Oecologia*, *57*(3), 287–290. doi:10.1007/BF00377169 PMID:28309352

Feng, S., Le Zhang, B. L. D. W., Yu, G., & Wong, K.-F. (2013). Is Twitter A Better Corpus for Measuring Sentiment Similarity? *Proceedings of the 2013 Conference on Empirical Methods in Natural Language Processing*, 897–902.

Funabiki & Takefuji. (1992). A neural network parallel algorithm for channel assignment problems in cellular radio networks. *IEEE Transactions on Vehicular Technology, 41*(4), 430-437. Doi:10.1109/25.182594

Gevrey, M., Dimopoulos, I., & Lek, S. (2003). Review and comparison of methods to study the contribution of variables in artificial neural network models. *Ecological Modelling*, *160*(3), 249–264. doi:10.1016/S0304-3800(02)00257-0

Guan, H., Li, C.-K., Cheung, T.-Y., Yu, S., & Tong, W. (2002). Design and implementation of a parallel software for hybrid neural network computation in PVM environment. *Proceedings of Third International Conference on Signal Processing (ICSP'96)*. DOI: 10.1109/ICSIGP.1996.566591

Hadoop. (2017). Retrieved from http://hadoop.apache.org

Hernández-Ugalde, J. A., Mora-Urpí, J., & Rocha, O. J. (2011). Genetic relationships among wild and cultivated populations of peach palm (Bactris gasipaes Kunth, Palmae): Evidence for multiple independent domestication events. *Genetic Resources and Crop Evolution*, *58*(4), 571–583. doi:10.100710722-010-9600-6

Hsu, K., Gupta, H. V., & Sorooshian, S. (1995). Artificial Neural Network Modeling of the Rainfall-Runoff Process. *Water Resources Research*, *31*(10), 2517–2530. doi:10.1029/95WR01955

Htait, A., Fournier, S., & Bellot, P. (2016). LSIS at SemEval-2016 Task 7: Using Web Search Engines for English and Arabic Unsupervised Sentiment Intensity Prediction. *Proceedings of SemEval-2016*, 481–485. 10.18653/v1/S16-1076

Huqqani, A. A., Schikuta, E., Ye, S., & Chen, P. (2013). Multicore and GPU Parallelization of Neural Networks for Face Recognition. *Procedia Computer Science*, *18*, 349–358. doi:10.1016/j.procs.2013.05.198

Islam & Sarker. (2000). A similarity coefficient Measure And Machine-Parts Grouping In Cellular Manufacturing Systems. *International Journal Of Production Research*. Http://Dx.Doi. Org/10.1080/002075400189374

Jackson, Somers, & Harvey. (1989). Similarity Coefficients: Measures of Co-Occurrence and Association or Simply Measures of Occurrence? *American Naturalist, 133*(3).

Jaitly, N., Nguyen, P., Senior, A., & Vanhoucke, V. (2012). Application of Pretrained Deep Neural Networks to Large Vocabulary Speech Recognition. *13th Annual Conference of the International Speech Communication Association*, 2578-2581.

Ji, X., Chun, S. A., Wei, Z., & Geller, J. (2015). Twitter sentiment classification for measuring public health concerns. *Social Network Analysis and Mining, 5*(1), 13. doi:10.100713278-015-0253-5

Jiang, T., Jiang, J., Dai, Y., & Li, A. (2015). Micro–blog Emotion Orientation Analysis Algorithm Based on Tibetan and Chinese Mixed Text. *International Symposium on Social Science (ISSS 2015)*. 10.2991/isss-15.2015.39

Jovanoski, D., Pachovski, V., & Nakov, P. (2015). Sentiment Analysis in Twitter for Macedonian. Proceedings of Recent Advances in Natural Language Processing, 249–257.

Kuo, R. J., Chen, C. H., & Hwang, Y. C. (2001). An intelligent stock trading decision support system through integration of genetic algorithm based fuzzy neural network and artificial neural network. *Fuzzy Sets and Systems, 118*(1), 21–45. doi:10.1016/S0165-0114(98)00399-6

Kyoung-jae, K., & Han, I. (2000). Genetic algorithms approach to feature discretization in artificial neural networks for the prediction of stock price index. *Expert Systems with Applications, 19*(2), 125–132. doi:10.1016/S0957-4174(00)00027-0

Lek, S., & Guégan, J. F. (1999). Artificial neural networks as a tool in ecological modelling, an introduction. *Ecological Modelling, 120*(2–3), 65–73. doi:10.1016/S0304-3800(99)00092-7

Li, Q., Yue, T., Wang, C., Zhang, W., Yu, Y., Li, B., ... Bai, G. (2013). Spatially distributed modeling of soil organic matter across China: An application of artificial neural network approach. *Catena, 104*, 210–218. doi:10.1016/j.catena.2012.11.012

Liu, Y., Jing, W., & Xu, L. (2016). Parallelizing Backpropagation Neural Network Using MapReduce and Cascading Model. *Computational Intelligence and Neuroscience, 2016*, 1–11. doi:10.1155/2016/2842780 PMID:27217823

MacMillanE. D. (2017). Retrieved from http://www.macmillandictionary.com/

Magnier, L., & Haghighat, F. (2010). Multiobjective optimization of building design using TRNSYS simulations, genetic algorithm, and Artificial Neural Network. *Building and Environment, 45*(3), 739–746. doi:10.1016/j.buildenv.2009.08.016

Malouf, R., & Mullen, T. (2017). Graph-based user classification for informal online political discourse. *Proceedings of the 1st Workshop on Information Credibility on the Web*, 1-8.

Manitsas, Singh, Pal, & Strbac. (2012). Distribution System State Estimation Using an Artificial Neural Network Approach for Pseudo Measurement Modeling. *IEEE Transactions on Power Systems, 27*(4), 1888-1896. Doi:10.1109/TPWRS.2012.2187804

Mao, G. Wang, & Bollen. (2014). Automatic Construction of Financial Semantic Orientation Lexicon from Large-Scale Chinese News Corpus. In *7th Financial Risks International Forum*. Institut Louis Bachelier.

May, R. J., Maier, H. R., & Dandy, G. C. (2010). Data splitting for artificial neural networks using SOM-based stratified sampling. *Neural Networks, 23*(2), 283–294. doi:10.1016/j.neunet.2009.11.009 PMID:19959327

Mikolov, T., Deoras, A., Povey, D., Burget, L., & Cernocky, J. (2011). Strategies for Training Large Scale Neural Network Language Models. *2011 IEEE Workshop on Automatic Speech Recognition and Understanding (ASRU)*, 196-201. 10.1109/ASRU.2011.6163930

Misra, M. (1997). Parallel Environments for Implementing Neural Networks. *Neural Computing Surveys, 1*, 48–60.

Netzer, O., Feldman, R., Goldenberg, J., & Fresko, M. (2012). Mine Your Own Business: Market-Structure Surveillance Through Text Mining. *Marketing Science, 31*(3), 521–543. doi:10.1287/mksc.1120.0713

Nevo, E., Fragman, O., Dafni, A., & Beiles, A. (2013). Biodiversity And Interslope Divergence Of Vascular Plants Caused By Microclimatic Differences At "Evolution Canyon", Lower Nahal Oren, Mount Carmel, Israel. *Israel Journal of Plant Sciences, 47*(1), 49–59. doi:10.1080/07929978.1999.10676751

Nguyen, T. T. A., & Hagiwara, M. (2014). Adjective-Based Estimation of Short Sentence's Impression. *Proceedings of the 5th Kanesi Engineering and Emotion Research; International Conference.*

Nordström, T., & Svensson, B. (1992). Using and Designing Massively Parallel Computers for Artificial Neural Networks. *Journal of Parallel and Distributed Computing, 14*(3), 260–285. doi:10.1016/0743-7315(92)90068-X

Nordström, T., & Svensson, B. (1992). Using and designing massively parallel computers for artificial neural networks. *Journal of Parallel and Distributed Computing, 14*(3), 260–285. doi:10.1016/0743-7315(92)90068-X

Omar, N., Albared, M., Al-Shabi, A. Q., & Al-Moslmi, T. (2013). Ensemble of Classification algorithms for Subjectivity and Sentiment Analysis of Arabic Customers' Reviews. *International Journal of Advancements in Computing Technology*, 5.

Park, D. C., El-Sharkawi, M. A., Marks, R. J., Atlas, L. E., & Damborg, M. J. (1991). Electric load forecasting using an artificial neural network. *IEEE Transactions on Power Systems, 6*(2). doi:10.1109/59.76685

Peterson, C., Rögnvaldsson, T., & Lönnblad, L. (1994). JETNET 3.0—A versatile artificial neural network package. *Computer Physics Communications, 81*(1–2), 185–220. doi:10.1016/0010-4655(94)90120-1

Phu, Chau, Ngoc, & Duy. (2017g). A C4.5 algorithm for english emotional classification. *Evolving Systems*. doi:10.100712530-017-9180-1

Phu, V. N., Dat, N. D., Vo, T. N. T., Vo, T. N. C., & Nguyen, T. A. (2017f). Fuzzy C-means for english sentiment classification in a distributed system. *International Journal of Applied Intelligence, 46*(3), 717–738. doi:10.100710489-016-0858-z

Phu, V. N., & Tuoi, P. T. (2014). Sentiment classification using Enhanced Contextual Valence Shifters. *International Conference on Asian Language Processing (IALP),* 224-229. 10.1109/IALP.2014.6973485

Phu, V. N., Vo, T. N. C., Dat, N. D., Vo, T. N. T., & Nguyen, T. A. (2017b). *A Valences-Totaling Model for English Sentiment Classification. International Journal of Knowledge and Information Systems.* doi:10.100710115-017-1054-0

Phu, V. N., Vo, T. N. C., & Vo, T. N. T. (2017c). *Shifting Semantic Values of English Phrases for Classification. International Journal of Speech Technology.* doi:10.100710772-017-9420-6

Phu, V. N., Vo, T. N. C., & Vo, T. N. T. (2017i). *SVM for English Semantic Classification in Parallel Environment. International Journal of Speech Technology.* doi:10.100710772-017-9421-5

Phu, V. N., Vo, T. N. C., Vo, T. N. T., & Dat, N. D. (2017a). *A Vietnamese adjective emotion dictionary based on exploitation of Vietnamese language characteristics. International Journal of Artificial Intelligence Review.* doi:10.100710462-017-9538-6

Phu, V. N., Vo, T. N. C., Vo, T. N. T., Dat, N. D., & Khanh, L. D. D. (2017d). *A Valence-Totaling Model for Vietnamese Sentiment Classification. International Journal of Evolving Systems.* doi:10.100712530-017-9187-7

Phu, V. N., Vo, T. N. C., Vo, T. N. T., Dat, N. D., & Khanh, L. D. D. (2017e). *Semantic Lexicons of English Nouns for Classification. International Journal of Evolving Systems.* doi:10.100712530-017-9188-6

Phu, V. N., & Vo, T. N. T. (2017a). *English Sentiment Classification using Only the Sentiment Lexicons with a JOHNSON Coefficient in a Parallel Network Environment.* American Journal of Engineering and Applied Sciences. doi:10.3844/ajeassp.2017

Phu, V. N., & Vo, T. N. T. (2017b). *A STING Algorithm and Multi-dimensional Vectors Used for English Sentiment Classification in a Distributed System.* American Journal of Engineering and Applied Sciences. doi:10.3844/ajeassp.2017

Phu, V. N., & Vo, T. N. T. (2018a). English Sentiment Classification using A Gower-2 Coefficient and A Genetic Algorithm with A Fitness-proportionate Selection in a Parallel Network Environment. *Journal of Theoretical and Applied Information Technology, 96*(4), 1-50.

Phu, V. N., & Vo, T. N. T. (2018b). English sentiment classification using a Fager & MacGowan coefficient and a genetic algorithm with a rank selection in a parallel network environment. *International Journal of Computer Modelling and New Technologies, 22*(1), 57-112.

Phu, V. N., & Vo, T. N. T. (2018c). Latent Semantic Analysis using A Dennis Coefficient for English Sentiment Classification in A Parallel System. *International Journal of Computers, Communications and Control, 13*(3), 390-410.

Phu, V. N., & Vo, T. N. T. (2018d). English Sentiment Classification using A BIRCH Algorithm and The Sentiment Lexicons-Based One-dimentional Vectors in a Parallel Network Environment. *International Journal of Computer Modelling and New Technologies, 22*(1).

Phu, V. N., & Vo, T. N. T. (2018e). A Fuzzy C-Means Algorithm and Sentiment-Lexicons-based Multi-dimensional Vectors Of A SOKAL & SNEATH-IV Coefficient Used For English Sentiment Classification. *International Journal of Theoretical and Applied Information Technology, 96*(10).

Phu, V. N., & Vo, T. N. T. (2018f). A Self-Training - Based Model using A K-NN Algorithm and The Sentiment Lexicons - Based Multi-dimensional Vectors of A S6 coefficient for Sentiment Classification. *International Journal of Theoretical and Applied Information Technology, 96*(10).

Phu, V. N., & Vo, T. N. T. (2018g). The Multi-dimensional Vectors and An Yule-II Measure Used for A Self-Organizing Map Algorithm of English Sentiment Classification in A Distributed Environment. *Journal of Theoretical and Applied Information Technology, 96*(10).

Phu, V. N., & Vo, T. N. T. (2018h). Sentiment Classification using The Sentiment Scores Of Lexicons Based on A Kuhns-II Coefficient in English. International Journal of Tomography & Simulation, 31(3).

Phu, V. N., & Vo, T. N. T. (2018i). K-Medoids algorithm used for english sentiment classification in a distributed system. *Computer Modelling and New Technologies, 22*(1), 20-39.

Phu, V. N., & Vo, T. N. T. (2018j). A Reformed K-Nearest Neighbors Algorithm for Big Data Sets. *Journal of Computer Science*. Retrieved from http://thescipub.com/abstract/10.3844/ofsp.11819

Phu, V. N., Vo, T. N. T., & Max, J. (2018). A CURE Algorithm for Vietnamese Sentiment Classification in a Parallel Environment. *International Journal of Computer Science*. Retrieved from http://thescipub.com/abstract/10.3844/ofsp.11906

Phu, V. N., Vo, T. N. T., Vo, T. N. C., Dat, N. D., & Khanh, L. D. D. (2017h). A Decision Tree using ID3 Algorithm for English Semantic Analysis. *International Journal of Speech Technology*. doi:10.100710772-017-9429-x

Ponomarenko, J. V., Bourne, P. E., & Shindyalov, I. N. (2002). Building an automated classification of DNA-binding protein domains. *Bioinformatics (Oxford, England), 18*(Suppl 2), S192–S201. doi:10.1093/bioinformatics/18.suppl_2.S192 PMID:12386003

Ren, Y., Kaji, N., Yoshinaga, N., Toyoda, M., & Kitsuregawa, M. (2011). Sentiment Classification in Resource-Scarce Languages by using Label Propagation. In *Proceedings of the 25th Pacific Asia Conference on Language, Information and Computation*. Institute of Digital Enhancement of Cognitive Processing, Waseda University.

Rogers, L. L., & Dowla, F. U. (1994). Optimization of groundwater remediation using artificial neural networks with parallel solute transport modeling. *Water Resources Research, 30*(2), 457–481. doi:10.1029/93WR01494

Samanta, B., & Al-Balushi, K. R. (2003). Artificial Neural Network Based Fault Diagnostics Of Rolling Element Bearings Using Time-Domain Features. *Mechanical Systems and Signal Processing, 17*(2), 317–328. doi:10.1006/mssp.2001.1462

Scheible, C. (2010). Sentiment Translation through Lexicon Induction. *Proceedings of the ACL 2010 Student Research Workshop*, 25–30.

Seiffert, U. (2004). Artificial Neural Networks on Massively Parallel Computer Hardware. *Neurocomputing, 57*, 135–150. doi:10.1016/j.neucom.2004.01.011

S. M. Shafer, & D. F. Rogers. (2007). Similarity and distance measures for cellular manufacturing. Part II. An extension and comparison. *International Journal of Production Research, 31*(6). doi:10.1080/00207549308956793

Shikalgar & Dixit. (2014). JIBCA: Jaccard Index based Clustering Algorithm for Mining Online Review. *International Journal of Computer Applications, 105*(15).

Singh & Singh. (2015). Vector Space Model: An Information Retrieval System. *Int. J. Adv. Engg. Res. Studies, 4*(2), 141-143.

Soucy, P., & Mineau, G. W. (2015). Beyond TFIDF Weighting for Text Categorization in the Vector Space Model. *Proceedings of the 19th International Joint Conference on Artificial Intelligence*, 1130-1135.

Sudheer, K. P., Gosain, A. K., Mohana Rangan, D., & Saheb, S. M. (2002). Modelling evaporation using an artificial neural network algorithm. *Hydrological Processes, 16*(16), 3189–3202. doi:10.1002/hyp.1096

Sudheer, K. P., Gosain, A. K., & Ramasastri, K. S. (2002). A data-driven algorithm for constructing artificial neural network rainfall-runoff models. *Hydrological Processes*. doi:10.1002/hyp.554

Suzuki, Armato III, Li, Sone, & Doi. (2003). Massive training artificial neural network (MTANN) for reduction of false positives in computerized detection of lung nodules in low-dose computed tomography. *The International Journal of Medical Physics Research and Practice, 30*(7), 1602-1617.

Tamás, J., Podani, J., & Csontos, P. (2001). An extension of presence/absence coefficients to abundance data: a new look at absence. *Journal of Vegetation Science, 12*(3), 401–410. doi:10.2307/3236854

Tan, S., & Zhang, J. (2007). An empirical study of sentiment analysis for Chinese documents. *Expert Systems with Applications*. doi:10.1016/j.eswa.2007.05.028

Turney, P. D., & Littman, M. L. (2002). *Unsupervised Learning of Semantic Orientation from a Hundred-Billion-Word Corpus*. arXiv:cs/0212012

Wan, X. (2009). Co-Training for Cross-Lingual Sentiment Classification. *Proceedings of the 47th Annual Meeting of the ACL and the 4th IJCNLP of the AFNLP*, 235–243.

Wang, G., & Araki, K. (2007). Modifying SO-PMI for Japanese Weblog Opinion Mining by Using a Balancing Factor and Detecting Neutral Expressions. *Proceedings of NAACL HLT 2007*, 189–192. 10.3115/1614108.1614156

Yao, X. (1999). Evolving artificial neural networks. *Proceedings of the IEEE, 87*(9). doi:10.1109/5.784219

Yong, R., Nobuhiro, K., Naoki, Y., & Masaru, K. (2014). Sentiment Classification in Under-Resourced Languages Using Graph-based Semi-supervised Learning Methods. *IEICE Transactions on Information and Systems, E97–D*(4). doi:10.1587/transinf.E97.D.1

Zhang, R., Deng, W., & Zhu, M. Y. (2017). Using Deep Neural Networks to Automate Large Scale Statistical Analysis for Big Data Applications. *Proceedings of Machine Learning Research, 77,* 311–326.

Zhang, Z., Ye, Q., Zheng, W., & Li, Y. (2010). Sentiment Classification for Consumer Word-of-Mouth in Chinese: Comparison between Supervised and Unsupervised Approaches. *The 2010 International Conference on E-Business Intelligence.*

Zhou, Z.-H., Wu, J., & Tang, W. (2002). Ensembling neural networks: Many could be better than all. *Artificial Intelligence, 137*(1–2), 239–263. doi:10.1016/S0004-3702(02)00190-X

This research was previously published in the Handbook of Research on Big Data and the IoT; pages 406-439, copyright year 2019 by Engineering Science Reference (an imprint of IGI Global).

APPENDIX: ABBREVIATIONS

Artificial Intelligence: ARTINT
large-scale data sets: LARSCDSs
big data sets: BIGDSs
massive data sets: MASSDSs
sequential system: SEQSYS
parallel network system: PARNETSYS
multi-dimensional vectors: MULTDIMVECTs
RUSSELL & RAO coefficient: RUSRAOC
international search engine – Google: GOOGSE
And and Or operator: ANDOROPs
semantic analysis: SEMANAL
testing data set: TESTDSET
training data set: TRAINDSET
Artificial Neural Network: ARTNEURNET
artificial neurons: ARTNEURs
Point-wise Mutual Information measure: PMIMEA
unsupervised learning: UNSUPLERN
sentiment orientation: SO
Jaccard coefficient: JACCCO
one-dimensional vector: ONEDIMVECT
sentiment lexicons: SENTLEXs
positive multi-dimensional vector group: POSMULTDIMVECTGR
negative multi-dimensional vector group: NEGMULTDIMVECTGR
Cosine coefficient: COSCOE
Ochiai measure: OCHMEAS
Sorensen coefficient: SORCOE
Tominato measure: TOMMEAS
Cloudera distributed network environment: CLOUDISNETEN
Hadoop Map: M
Hadoop Reduce: R
basis English opinion dictionary: BEOD
Sentiment orientation: SO
AltaVista search engine: ALTVISSE
Bing search engine: BINGSE
Java programming language: JAVAPRL

Chapter 7
Development and Performance Analysis of Fireworks Algorithm–Trained Artificial Neural Network (FWANN):
A Case Study on Financial Time Series Forecasting

Sarat Chandra Nayak
CMR College of Engineering and Technology, Hyderabad, India

Subhranginee Das
KIIT University, Bhubaneswar, India

Bijan Bihari Misra
Silicon Institute of Technology, India

ABSTRACT

Financial time series are highly nonlinear and their movement is quite unpredictable. Artificial neural networks (ANN) have ample applications in financial forecasting. Performance of ANN models mainly depends upon its training. Though gradient descent-based methods are common for ANN training, they have several limitations. Fireworks algorithm (FWA) is a recently developed metaheuristic inspired from the phenomenon of fireworks explosion at night, which poses characteristics such as faster convergence, parallelism, and finding the global optima. This chapter intends to develop a hybrid model comprising FWA and ANN (FWANN) used to forecast closing prices series, exchange series, and crude oil prices time series. The appropriateness of FWANN is compared with models such as PSO-based ANN, GA-based ANN, DE-based ANN, and MLP model trained similarly. Four performance metrics, MAPE, NMSE, ARV, and R2, are considered as the barometer for evaluation. Performance analysis is carried out to show the suitability and superiority of FWANN.

DOI: 10.4018/978-1-6684-2408-7.ch007

INTRODUCTION

The process of predicting the future data based on current and past data of a financial time series is known as financial time series forecasting. Financial time series are highly nonlinear and their movement is quite unpredictable due to economical, political, natural, and global phenomena. Accurate forecasting model design is the keen objective of researchers, financial experts, and speculators. Several conventional as well as advanced computing-based forecasting models have been developed and applied to financial domain. In early days a quite good number of mathematical as well as statistical models are suggested to model the financial time series (Contreras, Espinola, Nogales, & Conejo, 2003; Leigh, Hightower, & Modani, 2005; Swider & Weber, 2007; Kung & Yu, 2008). These models are based on the assumption of the linearity of current and previous variables and are not efficient in handling highly non-linear time series data.

With the exponential growth in computing technologies, the process of financial forecasting becomes faster and more powerful. The advancement in the electronic communication and popularity of internet technologies made the access of financial data easy. Conventional computing, i.e. hard computing requires a lot of computation time and precisely stated analytic model. However, soft computing is tolerant of imprecision, partial truth, uncertainty and approximation. It mimics the human brain as it represents ideas that seem to emulate intelligence to solve commercial problems. In soft computing the tolerance for uncertainty and imprecision is exploited to achieve tractability, lower computation cost, robustness, high machine Intelligence quotient and economy of computation. Soft computing techniques are better suited to deal with the uncertainty and irregularity involved in financial time series. Hence, they are widely used for analyzing and forecasting the financial data. They can be broadly categories as: Artificial Neural Network, Evolutionary Algorithms, and Fuzzy Logic System.

Artificial Neural Network (ANN) has the analogy with the thinking capacity of human brain and thus mimicking it. Introduction about ANN can be found in (Haykin, 2010; Kecman, 2006; Rajasekaran & Pai, 2007; Aliev, Fazlollahi & Aliev, 2004). The ANN can imitate the process of human behavior and solve nonlinear problems, which have made it popular and are widely used in calculating and predicting complicated systems. ANNs are found to be good universal approximator which can approximate any continuous function to desired accuracy. These are considered to be an effective modeling procedure for mapping input-output containing both regularities and exceptions as the case of financial time series. These advantages of ANN attract researchers to forecast financial time series with ANN based models. Dealing with uncertainty and nonlinearity associated with financial time series with ANN based forecasting method primarily involves recognition of patterns in the data and using such patterns to predict future event.

The adjustment of neuron weight and bias of ANN is the key factor of ANN training and is a crucial task. The performance of ANN based models are solely depends upon the adjustment of weight and bias vectors. To circumvent the limitations of gradient descent-based ANN training, large number of nature and bio-inspired optimization techniques are proposed and applied (N. Shadbolt). Evolutionary computing techniques are based on the behavior of nature. Normally these algorithms are motivated by biological evolution and termed as evolutionary algorithms of metaheuristic. The ideas of imitating concepts from nature have great potential in developing algorithms to solve engineering problems. In recent past, applications of these techniques have achieved popularity in wide area of engineering, computer science, medicine, economics, finance, social networks and so on. Their performance depends upon several algorithm specific control parameters and there is no single technique performing well on all problems. Evolutionary training algorithms such as GA (Goldberg, 1989), PSO (Kennedy & Eberhart, 2001), DE (Price, Storn, & Lampinen, 2005), Ant colony optimization (Dorigo & Stutzle, 2004), FWA (Tan & Zhu, 2010) etc. are capable of searching optimal solutions better than gradient descent based search techniques.

Fireworks algorithm (FWA) is a recently developed metaheuristic which simulates the phenomenon of fireworks explosion at night (Tan & Zhu, 2010). Like other nature inspired optimization it is also a population based evolutionary algorithm. It tries to find the best fit solution in the search space through the explosion of fireworks. Several applications of FWA are found in the literature for solving real data mining problems. Meantime, there are some improved and enhanced version of FWA proposed and their superiority have been established. However its application toward financial time series is limited.

The main objective of this chapter is to develop and performance analysis of FWA based ANN (FWANN) hybrid model on financial time series. We used three real financial time series such as stock closing prices series, exchange rate series and crude oil price series for evaluating FWANN. The hybrid model employed FWA to optimize the weight and bias vector of an ANN. Each location (individual) of FWA can be viewed as a possible weight and bias vector for an ANN. The FWA applies local as well as global search techniques in the form of fireworks explosion to explore the optimal weight and bias vector in the potential search space. The proposed hybrid FWANN model is evaluated in forecasting one step ahead data point of three financial time series in terms of four error statistics MAPE, NMSE, R2 and ARV. The performance of the model is compared with that of four other models such as PSO-ANN, GA-ANN, DE-ANN, and MLP trained similarly. The major contributions of this chapter are:

- A brief introduction to FWA metaheuristic
- Discussion about financial time series and their importance
- Developing hybrid model FWANN
- Developing other hybrid models using PSO, DE, GA etc.
- Designing adaptive models
- Experimenting on three financial time series such as stock closing prices, exchange rate series and crude oil price series.
- Rigorous performance analysis of the proposed hybrid models.

Fireworks Algorithm Metaheuristic

Fireworks algorithm (FWA) is a recently proposed optimization technique which simulates the explosion process of fireworks (Tan & Zhu, 2010). It tries to select certain number of locations in a search space for explosion of fireworks to produce set of sparks. Locations with qualitative fireworks are considered for the next generation. The process continues iteratively up to a desired optimum or reaching the stopping criterion. The process mainly comprises three steps: setting off N fireworks at N selected locations, obtaining the locations of sparks after explosion and evaluating them, stop on reaching optimal location or select N other locations for the next generation of explosion. An explosion of fireworks can be viewed as a search process in the local space. According to the basic FWA, for each firework x_i, the amplitude of explosion (A_i) and number of sparks (s_i) are defined as follows:

$$A_i = \hat{A} \cdot \frac{f(x_i) - f_{min} + \varepsilon}{\sum_{j=1}^{p} \left(f(x_j) - f_{min} \right) + \varepsilon} \tag{1}$$

$$S_i = \frac{m \cdot f_{max} - f(x_i) + \varepsilon}{\sum_{j=1}^{p} \left(f_{max} - f(x_j) \right) + \varepsilon} \tag{2}$$

where $\hat{A}$ is the maximum explosion amplitude. f_{max} and f_{min} are the maximum and minimum objective function values among the p fireworks. m is a controlling parameter for total number of sparks generated by a firework and ε is a constant used to avoid zero division error. Bounds are imposed on s_i to overcome the devastating effects of marvelous fireworks as follows:

$$S_i = \begin{cases} s_{max}, & \text{if } s_i > s_{max} \\ s_{min}, & \text{if } s_i < s_{min} \\ s_i, & \text{otherwise} \end{cases} \tag{3}$$

The location of each spark x_j generated by x_i is calculated by setting z directions randomly and for each dimension k setting the component x_j^k based on x_i^k, where $1 £ j £ s_i$, $1 £ k £ z$.

The setting of x_j^k can be done in two ways as follows:

- For most sparks, a displacement is added to x_j^k as:

$$x_j^k = x_i^k + A_i \cdot rand(-1,1) \tag{4}$$

- To maintain diversity, for few specific sparks, an explosion coefficient based on Gaussian distribution is applied to x_j^k as:

$$x_j^k = x_i^k \cdot Gaussian(1,1) \tag{5}$$

When a new location falls out of the search space, it is mapped to the potential space as follows:

$$x_j^k = x_{min}^k + \left| x_j^k \right| \% \left(x_{max}^k - x_{min}^k \right) \tag{6}$$

where % is the modulo operator.

The next step is selection of another N location for the fireworks explosion. This step always keeps the current best location x^* for the next generation. Remaining N-1 locations are considered on the basis of their distance to other locations. The distance between a location x_i and other locations (K) can be calculated as the sum of Euclidean distance between them and as follows:

$$Distance(x_i) = \sum_{j \in K} x_i - x_j \tag{7}$$

A location xi is selected for the next generation based on a probability value as follows:

$$prob(x_i) = \frac{Distance(x_i)}{\sum_{j \in K} Distance(x_j)} \tag{8}$$

Based on the above concepts, the basic FWA is formulated and represented in Algorithm 1.

Algorithm 1. *FA framework*

Select N locations randomly for fireworks;
while (stopping criteria == false)
Set off N fireworks at N locations
for each firework x_i
Calculate number of sparks s_i using Equation3
Obtain locations of s_i sparks of firework x_i using Equation4.
end for
for k = 1: m
Select a firework x_j randomly
Generate a specific spark using Equation5.
end for
Select the best location x* and keep it for next generation
Select remaining *N-1* locations randomly based on a probability using Equation8.
end while

Since the sparks suffer from the power of explosion, they move along z directions simultaneously. This makes FWA to achieve faster convergence. Also, it avoids the premature convergence with the two types of spark generation methods and specific location selection method (Tan & Zhu, 2010). The advantages of FWA over standard PSO and its improved variants are demonstrated in the research work (Tan & Zhu, 2010).

Financial Time Series Forecasting

A time series can be viewed as a sequence of values/data points/events separated/occurred by equal interval of time. It can be represented as a set of discrete values $\{x_1, x_2, x_3, \ldots, x_n\}$, where n is the total number of observations. A time series possess both deterministic as well as stochastic components characterized by noise interference. The forecasting process can be mathematically represented as:

$$y_{t+1} = f(y_t, y_{t-1}, y_{t-2}, \cdots, y_{t-n}) \tag{9}$$

where y_t is the observation at time t, n is the number of past observations and y is the value to be forecasted.

However, financial time series show random fluctuations compared to ordinary time series. It is characterized with high nonlinearity, non-stationary and chaotic in nature. It is often desirable to monitor the price behavior frequently to understand the probable development of the prices in the future. Daily closing prices, exchange rates of a stock market and oil prices are few examples of financial time series. Financial time series forecasting is the process of making prediction about future performance of a stock market based on existing market behavior. Financial time series behaves like a random walk process. Due to the influence of uncertainties, financial time series forecasting is regarded as a difficult task.

Forecasting Models

The most popular statistical methods are moving averages (MA), auto-regressive integrated moving average (ARIMA), auto-regressive heteroscedastic (ARCH), generalized ARCH (GARCH) etc. (Contreras, Espinola, Nogalesn & and Conejo, 2003; Leigh, Hightower & Modani, 2005; Swider & Weber, 2007; Kung & Yu, 2008). These models are based on the assumption of the linearity of current and previous variables. However, these models are inefficient in handling highly non-linear time series data. They can't be automated easily and require expert interpretation and development at every stage. The poor capabilities of these models in capturing the nonlinearity of the financial time series forces the researchers to develop efficient models adopting soft and evolutionary computing methodologies which include artificial neural network (ANN), fuzzy neural networks, rough set theory, genetic algorithm etc.

The ANNs are applied to many areas such as data mining, stock market analysis, medical and many other fields. Some earlier use of ANN for the financial forecasting purpose can be found in the research works (Kumar & Bhattacharya, 2006; Cao, Leggio, & Schniederjans, 2005; Leigh, Hightower & Modani, 2005; Chen, Leung & Daouk, 2003; Yu, Wang, & Lai, 2009). During last few decades, the rapid growth in economical situations of developed countries has amplified the requirement of more competent and sophisticated forecasting models. In order to outperform the conventional statistical methods, several artificial intelligent systems have been developed and found to be experimentally efficient (Nayak, Misra, & Behera, 2018; Gu, Kelly, & Xiu, 2018; Board, 2017; Nayak, Misra & Behera, 2017; Guan, Dai, Zhao, & He, 2018; Nayak, Misra, & Behera, 2013; Nayak, Misra, & Behera, 2017). Authors used ANN models and linear regression models for New York stock exchange composite index (Leigh, Hightower & Modani, 2005). Results were robust and informative as to the role of trading volumes in the stock market. Group decision making models for economic interpretations are presented by the researchers in (Li, Kou & Peng, 2016; Zhang, Kou, & Peng, 2019). A survey on existing researches and methodologies on assessment and measurement of financial systemic risk combined with machine learning technologies is found in (Kou, Chao, Peng, Alsaadi, & Herrera-Viedma, 2019). Higher order and polynomial neural networks are proposed for financial time series forecasting in (Nayak, Misra, & Behera, 2016; Nayak & Misra, 2018). For improvement in forecasting accuracy of ANN based models several research works suggested for exploration and incorporation of virtual data positions in the original financial time series (Nayak, Misra, & Behera, 2017; Nayak, Misra & Behera, 2017; Nayak, Misra, & Behera, 2016). Analysis and improvement of fireworks algorithm is suggested in research work (Li, Han, & Gong, 2017). A cooperative framework for fireworks algorithm is suggested in (Zheng, Li, Janecek & Tan, 2017). An enhanced version of fireworks algorithm is proposed in for standard benchmark functions (Zheng, Janecek & Tan, 2013). Adaptive fireworks algorithm and dynamic search in fireworks algorithm are introduced by authors in (Li, Zheng, & Tan, 2014; Zheng, Janecek, Li & Tan, 2014).

Proposed FWANN Based Forecasting

The intention of this chapter is to study the suitability of FWA on searching the optimal weight and bias vector of an ANN based forecasting model. The mathematical description of ANN is beyond the scope of this chapter. We present only the description of ANN model used in this study and the forecasting process. ANN architecture with one hidden layer of neurons is used as the base neural architecture as shown in Figure 1. Since there is no rule to choose the optimal number of layer and neurons, we choose them on experimental basis.

Figure 1. FWANN based forecasting model

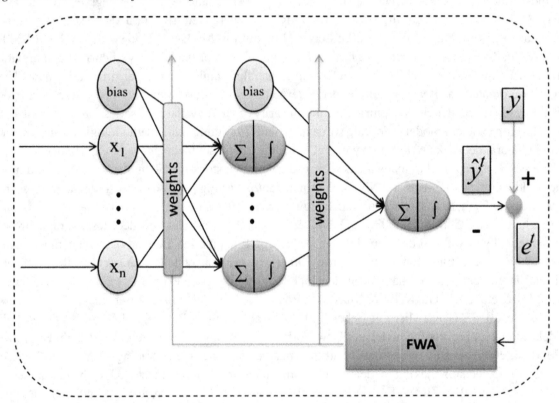

The error correction learning in this case is supervised learning, i.e. the target response for the system is presented at the output neuron. This model consists of a single output unit to estimate one-day-ahead data point in the financial time series. The neurons in the input layer use a linear transfer function, the neurons in the hidden layer and output layer use sigmoidal function as follows:

$$y_{out} = \frac{1}{1 + e^{-\lambda y_{in}}} \tag{10}$$

where yout is the output of the neuron, λ is the sigmoidal gain and yin is the input to the neuron. The first layer corresponds to the problem input variables with one node for each input variable. The second layer is useful in capturing non-linear relationships among variables. At each neuron, j in the hidden layer, the weighted output Z is calculated using Equation 11.

$$Z = f\left(B_j + \sum_{i=1}^{n} V_{ij} * O_i \right) \tag{11}$$

where O_i is the ith component of the $N{\times}M$ input vector, V_{ij} is the synaptic weight value between i^{th} input neuron and j^{th} hidden neuron and B_j is the bias value and f is a nonlinear activation function. The output y at the single output neuron is calculated using Equation 12.

$$y = f\left(B_0 + \sum_{j=1}^{m} W_j * Z \right) \tag{12}$$

where W_j is the synaptic weight value from j^{th} hidden neuron to output neuron, Z is the weighted sum calculated as in Equation 7, and B_0 is the output bias. This output y is compared to the target output and the error is calculated by using Equation 13.

$$Err_i = |\, Target_i - Estimated_i\, | \tag{13}$$

where ERR_i is the error signal, $Target_i$ is the target signal for ith training pattern and $Estimated_i$ is the calculated output for ith pattern. The error signal $Err(i)$ and the input vector are employed to the weight update algorithm to compute the optimal weight vector. During the training, the network is repeatedly presented with the training vector and the weights as well as biases are adjusted by FWA till the desired input-output mapping occurs. The error is calculated by Equation 13 and the objective is to minimize the total error as in Equation 14 with an optimal set of weight and bias vector of the ANN.

$$Error(i) = \frac{1}{2} \sum_{i=1}^{N} Err(i)^2 \tag{14}$$

Here, the FWA is used to train the ANN model. A location (individual) of FWA can be viewed as a potential weight and bias vector for the ANN in the search space. At beginning, a set of such location is initialized and for each such location, two types of explosion are carried. The exploration as well as exploitation of the search space is achieved by these explosion methods. The locations are then evaluated in terms of error signal generation. The location with lowest error signal is considered as the best location. The selection process is then carried out with inclusion of this best location and remaining locations. The above process continues till an optimal location found and the search process then terminates. The best location is the optimal weight and bias vector for the ANN model.

CASE STUDY ON FINANCIAL TIME SERIES FORECASTING

This section performs a case study on financial time series. As we mentioned earlier, this chapter aims to develop an ANN based forecasting model trained by FWA. The proposed FWANN model is evaluated on forecasting three financial time series: (1) daily closing prices series of Bombay stock exchange, (2) exchange rate series of Indian rupees to US dollar, and (3) crude oil price series.

Description of Experimental Data

The BSE indices are collected from the source https://in.finance.yahoo.com/ for each financial day starting from 1st January 2003 to 12th September 2016. The closing prices series is shown by Figure 2. Real data from Bombay stock exchange are collected from the source www.forecasts.org. The series contains the monthly exchange rate of (Indian) Rupees against USA Dollar. The data are recorded on the first day of each month during the period 1999 to 2016 comprising 214 data points in the series. The series is presented by Figure 3. The crude oil prices (Dollars per Barrel) are retrieved from US Department of energy: Energy Information Administration web site: http://www.eia.doe.gov/ during the period Jan 02 1986 to Feb 11 2019. The crude oil price series is shown by Figure 4. The descriptive statistics from three financial time series considered are presented in Table 1.

Table 1. Descriptive statistics from three financial time series

Financial time series	Descriptive statistics						
	Minimum	Maximum	Mean	Standard deviation	Skewness	Kurtosis	Jarque-Bera test statistics
Closing price series	792.1800	1.1024e+004	4.6235e+003	2.6947e+003	0.1154	1.7908	236.0430(h=1)
Exchange rate series	39.2680	68.2400	49.5192	7.5903	1.0952	2.9765	42.7875 (h=1)
Crude oil prices series	10.4200	145.2900	42.8112	28.6656	1.0111	2.8953	1.5390e+03 (h=1)

Experimental Setup

All the experiments are carried out in MATLAB-2015 environment, with Intel ® core TM i3 CPU, 2.27 GHz processing and 2.42 GB memory size. A sliding window of fixed size is used for selecting input for the forecasting model. In this method rather than selecting all of the data seen so far, or on some sample, decision is made based only on some recent data points. On each sliding of the window, a new data point is incorporated and the oldest one is discarded. The window moves through whole financial time series and the selection of size of window is a matter of experimentation.

Figure 2. Closing prices series of BSE

Figure 3. Exchange rate series (Indian Rupees to US Dollar)

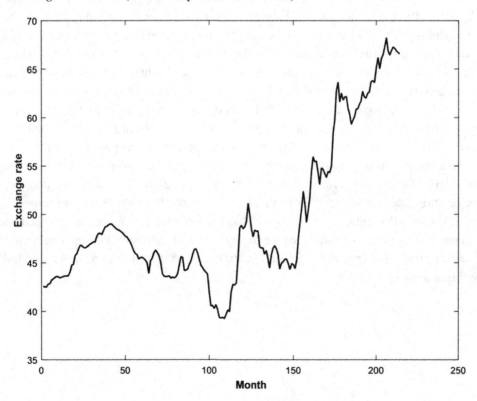

Figure 4. Crude oil prices series

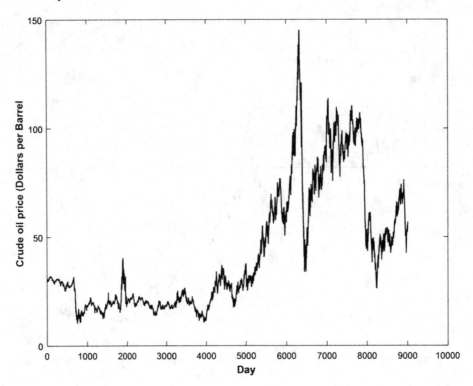

All the three financial time series are normalized before feeding them to the ANN model (Nayak, Misra, & Behera, 2014). The normalized data are then used to form a training bed for the network model. The model is simulated for 20 times for each training set and the average error is considered for comparative analysis of results. Since each time the sliding window moves one step ahead, only one new closing price data has been included into the training set. So there may not be significant change in nonlinearity behavior of the training data set. For that reason, instead of considering another random weight set (i.e. set of locations), we used the previously optimized weight set for the successive training. In this way, after the first training set, the number of iteration has been fixed to a small value, hence significant reduction in training time. During experimentation, different possible values for the model parameters were tested and best values are recorded. The parameters of FWA are set as suggested in (Tan & Zhu, 2010). The average performance of the models over 20 runs are considered for comparison.

The four performance metrics used for evaluating the forecasting models are as follows:

The Mean Absolute Percentage Error (MAPE) has been considered as the first performance metric in order to have a comparable measure across experiments with different dataset. The closer the value of MAPE towards zero, the better is the prediction ability of the model. The formula for MAPE is represented by Equation 15.

$$MAPE = \frac{1}{N}\sum_{i=1}^{N}\frac{\left|x_i - \hat{x}_i\right|}{xi} \times 100\% \qquad (15)$$

The second performance metric is the mean of squared error calculated on the normalized data sets and known as Normalized Mean Squared Error (NMSE). The closer the value of it to zero, better is the prediction ability of the model. The NMSE can be calculated as in Equation 16.

$$NMSE = \frac{1}{N} \sum_{i=1}^{N} \left(x_i - \hat{x}_i \right)^2 \tag{16}$$

The third performance metric considered here is known as the coefficient of determination, or the coefficient of multiple determinations for multiple regressions represented as R2. R-squared is a statistical measure of how close the data are to the fitted regression line. The definition of R-squared is presented by Equation 17. The ideal value of R2 is 1(one). 0 values indicate that the model explain none of the variability of the response data around its mean whereas 1 indicates that the model explains all the variability of the response data around its mean.

$$R^2 = 1 - \frac{SS_{res}}{SS_{tot}} \tag{17}$$

where SSres is the sum of squares of residuals or residual sum of squares and represented as in Equation 18.

$$SS_{res} = \sum_{i=1}^{N} \left(x_i - \hat{x}_i \right)^2 \tag{18}$$

Similarly, SStot is the total sum of squares which is proportional to the variance of the data and calculated as in Equation 19.

$$SS_{tot} = \sum_{i=1}^{N} \left(x_i - \bar{X} \right)^2 \tag{19}$$

The fourth evaluation measure is the Average Relative Variance (ARV). The ARV can be calculated as in Equation 20.

$$\frac{\sum_{i=1}^{N} \left(\hat{x}_i - x_i \right)^2}{\sum_{i=1}^{N} \left(\hat{x}_i - \bar{X} \right)^2} \tag{20}$$

If the ARV value of the forecasting model is equal to 1, then it is same as considering the mean of the financial time series. The model is considered as performing worst as compared to mean if the ARV value is greater than 1. However, the model can be considered as performing better than simply calculating the mean if its ARV value is less than 1. Hence, the closer the value to 0, the forecasting model tends to be more accurate.

For all the above calculations, x_i is the observed data, $\hat{x}_i$ is the estimated data, $\bar{X}$ is the mean of observed data and N is the total number of observations.

Experimental Results and Discussion

For comparative purpose we developed another four models such as PSO-ANN, GA-ANN, DE-ANN, and MLP trained similarly. The input data for all five models are same. We conducted experiments for short term (1-step-ahead) and long term (7-step-ahead) forecasting. The results from these experiments are summarized in Table 2 – 3 respectively. The error convergence graph of five forecasting models from closing price dataset is shown in Figure 5. From this curve it can be observed that the proposed FWANN model converges very fast compared to others.

Figure 5. Error convergence graph of forecasting models (from closing price dataset)

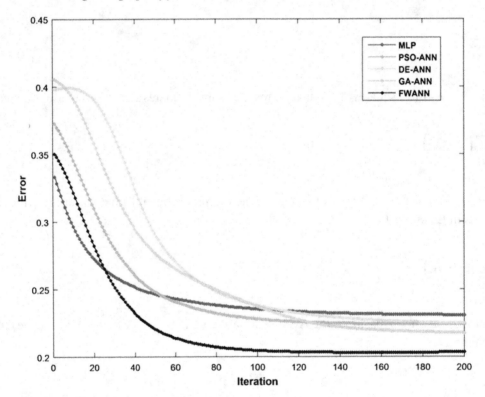

Table 2. Results from 1-step-ahead forecasting

Financial time series	Model	MAPE	NMSE	R^2	ARV
Closing price series	FWANN	0.036825	0.054783	0.937643	0.018639
	PSO-ANN	0.057547	0.085746	0.913125	0.027685
	GA-ANN	0.073648	0.082853	0.852965	0.070833
	DE-ANN	0.079900	0.058593	0.926455	0.055747
	MLP	0.108353	0.087985	0.894785	0.082845
Exchange rate series	FWANN	0.064675	0.013521	0.925400	0.047785
	PSO-ANN	0.068830	0.016468	0.903503	0.061354
	GA-ANN	0.075902	0.026863	0.873525	0.065503
	DE-ANN	0.079475	0.050522	0.901275	0.071685
	MLP	0.095355	0.065455	0.887435	0.088635
Crude oil prices series	FWANN	0.085700	0.063315	0.935427	0.085635
	PSO-ANN	0.089265	0.120127	0.900075	0.088557
	GA-ANN	0.097285	0.157500	0.846522	0.089655
	DE-ANN	0.136885	0.079822	0.890711	0.090755
	MLP	0.262384	0.095665	0.865184	0.254845

Table 3. Results from 7-step-ahead forecasting

Financial time series	Model	MAPE	NMSE	R^2	ARV
Closing price series	FWANN	0.039875	0.074478	0.920784	0.026865
	PSO-ANN	0.060754	0.089749	0.905028	0.027990
	GA-ANN	0.078004	0.088855	0.822977	0.073802
	DE-ANN	0.079985	0.070858	0.900655	0.067745
	MLP	0.178344	0.100780	0.874722	0.200285
Exchange rate series	FWANN	0.069679	0.030655	0.905372	0.054985
	PSO-ANN	0.082835	0.036465	0.883525	0.068355
	GA-ANN	0.078955	0.027986	0.833563	0.085750
	DE-ANN	0.079864	0.057505	0.900200	0.078060
	MLP	0.099384	0.216545	0.807839	0.090636
Crude oil prices series	FWANN	0.089688	0.084810	0.917542	0.088699
	PSO-ANN	0.089697	0.127225	0.917583	0.089506
	GA-ANN	0.099728	0.159204	0.840065	0.091965
	DE-ANN	0.256566	0.079974	0.832871	0.090827
	MLP	0.472385	0.295632	0.807518	0.290488

As shown in Table 2, the FWANN model generated lower error signals in terms of all four metrics. Its performance is better than other models. However, in case of crude oil price prediction it shown inferior result compared to closing price and exchange rate time series. The performance of PSO-ANN, GA-ANN, and DE-ANN are acceptable but inferior to FWANN. All four hybrid models have shown better results than the MLP. To ascertain the validity of FWANN model, we also conducted experiments for long-term (7-step-ahead) forecasting and the results are summarized in Table 3. In this case also the FWANN performed better to other models. As the time step increases the error signals from the forecasting model also increases. However, in both cases the FWANN model shown lower error signals which indicates that the forecasted values are very closer to the actual values. For more clarity the estimated v/s actual values are plotted and shown by Figures 6 - 8. From Figure 6 and 7, it is observed that the estimated values by FWANN model are very close to the actual. But, in case of oil price dataset, the estimated values are slightly deviated from the actual. However, the model is capable in following the trend of the time series.

Figure 6. Actual closing price v/s estimated closing price by FWANN

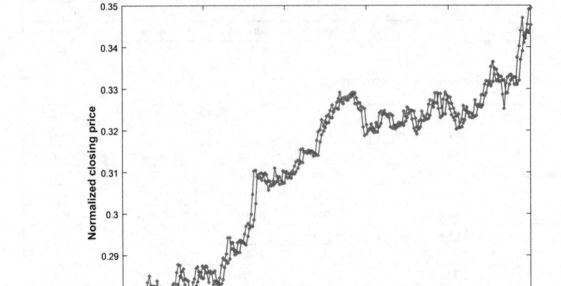

Figure 7. Actual exchange rate v/s estimated exchange rate by FWANN

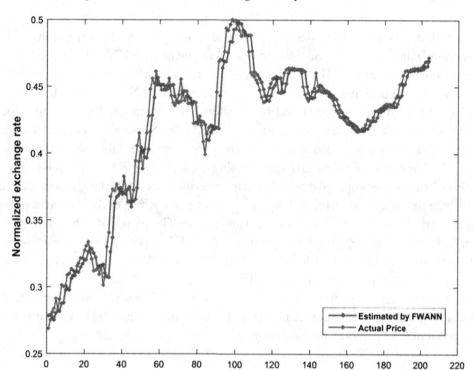

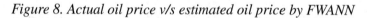

Figure 8. Actual oil price v/s estimated oil price by FWANN

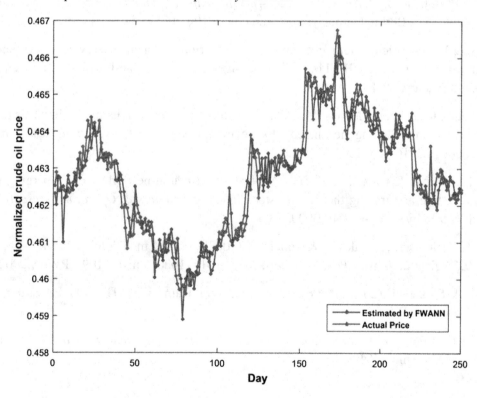

CONCLUSION

Fireworks algorithm is a recently proposed metaheuristic which simulates the explosion process of fireworks as an optimization technique. Several successful applications of FWA have been demonstrated in the literature since its inception. The adjustment of neuron weight and bias of ANN is the key factor of ANN training and is a decisive assignment. The performance of ANN based models are exclusively depends upon the adjustment of weight and bias vectors. To circumvent the limitations of gradient descent-based ANN training this chapter developed a hybrid FWANN model where the synaptic weight and bias vector of an ANN is searched with FWA. The hybrid model exhibits the better generalization capability of ANN as well as fast and efficient learning capacity of FWA, hence robust in nature. To validate the efficiency of the proposed model the chapter performed a case study on financial time series forecasting. Three financial time series such as daily closing price series, exchange rate series, and daily crude oil price time series are considered for experimentation. The proposed hybrid FWANN model is evaluated in forecasting one step ahead and seven-step-ahead data point of three financial time series in terms of four error statistics such as MAPE, NMSE, R2 and ARV. The performance of the model is compared with that of four other models such as PSO-ANN, GA-ANN, DE-ANN, and MLP trained in similar manner. From experimental studies it is observed that the FWANN model performed better to other models and competent to capture the nonlinear behavior of the financial time series. The applications of the model may be explored in other domain.

REFERENCES

Aliev, R. A., Fazlollahi, B., & Aliev, R. R. (2004). *Soft computing and its applications in business and economics* (Vol. 157). Berlin, Germany: Springer. doi:10.1007/978-3-540-44429-9

Board, F. S. (2017). Artificial intelligence and machine learning in financial services. November, available at http://www. fsb. org/2017/11/artificialintelligence-and-machine-learning-in-financialservice/ (accessed 30th January, 2018).

Cao, Q., Leggio, K., & Schniederjans, M. (2005). A comparison between Fama and French's model and artificial networks in predicting the Chinese stock market. *Computers & Operations Research*, *32*(10), 2499–2512. doi:10.1016/j.cor.2004.03.015

Chen, A., Leung, M., & Daouk, H. (2003). Application of neural networks to an emerging financial market: Forecasting and trading the Taiwan stock index. *Computers & Operations Research*, *30*(6), 901–923. doi:10.1016/S0305-0548(02)00037-0

Contreras, J., Espinola, R., Nogales, F., & Conejo, A. (2003). ARIMA models to predict next-day electricity prices. *IEEE Transactions on Power Systems*, *18*(3), 1014–1020. doi:10.1109/TPWRS.2002.804943

Dorigo, M., & Stutzle, T. (2004). *Ant colony optimization*. Cambridge: The MIT Press. doi:10.7551/mitpress/1290.001.0001

Goldberg, D. E. (1989). *Genetic algorithms in search, optimization, and machine learning*. Boston, MA: Addison-Wesley Longman Publishing.

Gu, S., Kelly, B., & Xiu, D. (2018). *Empirical asset pricing via machine learning (No. w25398).* National Bureau of Economic Research.

Guan, H., Dai, Z., Zhao, A., & He, J. (2018). A novel stock forecasting model based on High-order-fuzzy-fluctuation Trends and Back Propagation Neural Network. *PLoS One*, *13*(2). doi:10.1371/journal. pone.0192366 PMID:29420584

Haykin, S. (2010). *Neural Networks and Learning Machine.* Upper Saddle River, NJ: Pearson Education.

Kecman, V. (2006). *Learning and Soft Computing.* Upper Saddle River, NJ: Pearson Education.

Kennedy, J., & Eberhart, R. C. (2001). *Swarm intelligence.* San Francisco, CA: Morgan Kaufmann Publishers.

Kou, G., Chao, X., Peng, Y., Alsaadi, F. E., & Herrera-Viedma, E. (2019). Machine learning methods for systemic risk analysis in financial sectors. *Technological and Economic Development of Economy*, *§§§*, 1–27.

Kumar, K., & Bhattacharya, S. (2006). Artificial neural network vs. linear discriminant analysis in credit ratings forecast. *Review of Accounting and Finance*, *5*(3), 216–227. doi:10.1108/14757700610686426

Kung, L., & Yu, S. (2008). Prediction of index futures returns and the analysis of financial spillovers-A comparison between GARCH and the grey theorem. *European Journal of Operational Research*, *186*(3), 1184–1200. doi:10.1016/j.ejor.2007.02.046

Leigh, W., Hightower, R., & Modani, N. (2005). Forecasting the New York stock exchange composite index with past price and interest rate on condition of volume spike. *Expert Systems with Applications*, *28*(1), 1–8. doi:10.1016/j.eswa.2004.08.001

Leigh, W., Hightower, R., & Modani, N. (2005). Forecasting the New York stock exchange composite index with past price and interest rate on condition of volume spike. *Expert Systems with Applications*, *28*(1), 1–8. doi:10.1016/j.eswa.2004.08.001

Li, G., Kou, G., & Peng, Y. (2016). A group decision making model for integrating heterogeneous information. *IEEE Transactions on Systems, Man, and Cybernetics. Systems*, *48*(6), 982–992. doi:10.1109/TSMC.2016.2627050

Li, J., Zheng, S., & Tan, Y. (2014, July). Adaptive fireworks algorithm. *2014 IEEE Congress on evolutionary computation (CEC)* (pp. 3214-3221). IEEE. doi:10.1109/CEC.2013.6557813

Li, X. G., Han, S. F., & Gong, C. Q. (2017). Analysis and improvement of fireworks algorithm. *Algorithms*, *10*(1), 26. doi:10.3390/a10010026

Nayak, S. C., & Misra, B. B. (2018). Estimating stock closing indices using a GA-weighted condensed polynomial neural network. *Financial Innovation*, *4*(1), 21. doi:10.118640854-018-0104-2

Nayak, S. C., Misra, B. B., & Behera, H. S. (2013, September). Hybridzing chemical reaction optimization and artificial neural network for stock future index forecasting. *Proceedings 2013 1st International Conference on Emerging Trends and Applications in Computer Science* (pp. 130-134). IEEE. 10.1109/ICETACS.2013.6691409

Nayak, S. C., Misra, B. B., & Behera, H. S. (2014). Impact of data normalization on stock index forecasting. *Int. J. Comp. Inf. Syst. Ind. Manag. Appl, 6*, 357–369.

Nayak, S. C., Misra, B. B., & Behera, H. S. (2016). An adaptive second order neural network with genetic-algorithm-based training (ASONN-GA) to forecast the closing prices of the stock market. [IJAMC]. *International Journal of Applied Metaheuristic Computing, 7*(2), 39–57. doi:10.4018/IJAMC.2016040103

Nayak, S. C., Misra, B. B., & Behera, H. S. (2016). Efficient forecasting of financial time-series data with virtual adaptive neuro-fuzzy inference system. *International Journal of Business Forecasting and Marketing Intelligence, 2*(4), 379–402. doi:10.1504/IJBFMI.2016.080132

Nayak, S. C., Misra, B. B., & Behera, H. S. (2017). Artificial chemical reaction optimization of neural networks for efficient prediction of stock market indices. *Ain Shams Engineering Journal, 8*(3), 371–390. doi:10.1016/j.asej.2015.07.015

Nayak, S. C., Misra, B. B., & Behera, H. S. (2017). Artificial chemical reaction optimization based neural net for virtual data position exploration for efficient financial time series forecasting. *Ain Shams Engineering Journal*.

Nayak, S. C., Misra, B. B., & Behera, H. S. (2017). Exploration and incorporation of virtual data positions for efficient forecasting of financial time series. *International Journal of Industrial and Systems Engineering, 26*(1), 42–62. doi:10.1504/IJISE.2017.083179

Nayak, S. C., Misra, B. B., & Behera, H. S. (2017). Efficient financial time series prediction with evolutionary virtual data position exploration. *Neural Computing & Applications*, 1–22.

Nayak, S. C., Misra, B. B., & Behera, H. S. (2018). ACFLN: artificial chemical functional link network for prediction of stock market index. Evolving Systems, 1-26.

Price, K., Storn, R., & Lampinen, J. (2005). *Differential evolution: a practical approach to global optimization*. Berlin, Germany: Springer.

Rajasekaran, S., & Pai, G. A. V. (2007). *Neural Networks, Fuzzy Logic and Genetic Algorithms Synthesis and Application*. Delhi, India: PHI Learning Private Limited.

Shadbolt, N. (2004). Nature-Inspired Computing. *IEEE Intelligent Systems, 19*(1), 2–3. doi:10.1109/MIS.2004.1265875

Swider, D. J., & Weber, C. (2007). Extended ARMA Models for Estimating Price Developments on Day- ahead Electricity Markets. *Electric Power Systems Research, 77*(5-6), 583–593. doi:10.1016/j.epsr.2006.05.013

Tan, Y., & Zhu, Y. (2010, June). Fireworks algorithm for optimization. *Proceedings International conference in swarm intelligence* (pp. 355-364). Berlin, Germany: Springer.

Yu, L., Wang, S., & Lai, K. K. (2009). A neural-network-based nonlinear metamodeling approach to financial time series forecasting. *Applied Soft Computing, 9*(2), 563–574. doi:10.1016/j.asoc.2008.08.001

Zhang, H., Kou, G., & Peng, Y. (2019). Soft consensus cost models for group decision making and economic interpretations. *European Journal of Operational Research*.

Zheng, S., Janecek, A., Li, J., & Tan, Y. (2014, July). Dynamic search in fireworks algorithm. *Proceedings 2014 IEEE Congress on evolutionary computation (CEC)* (pp. 3222-3229). IEEE. 10.1109/CEC.2014.6900485

Zheng, S., Janecek, A., & Tan, Y. (2013, June). Enhanced fireworks algorithm. *Proceedings 2013 IEEE Congress on evolutionary computation* (pp. 2069-2077). IEEE.

Zheng, S., Li, J., Janecek, A., & Tan, Y. (2017). A cooperative framework for fireworks algorithm. [TCBB]. *IEEE/ACM Transactions on Computational Biology and Bioinformatics*, *14*(1), 27–41. doi:10.1109/TCBB.2015.2497227 PMID:26552094

This research was previously published in the Handbook of Research on Fireworks Algorithms and Swarm Intelligence; pages 176-194, copyright year 2020 by Engineering Science Reference (an imprint of IGI Global).

Chapter 8
Meta–Heuristic Parameter Optimization for ANN and Real–Time Applications of ANN

Asha Gowda Karegowda
Siddaganga Institute of Technology, India

Devika G.
(iD) https://orcid.org/0000-0002-2509-2867
Government Engineering College, Mandya, India

ABSTRACT

Artificial neural networks (ANN) are often more suitable for classification problems. Even then, training of ANN is a surviving challenge task for large and high dimensional natured search space problems. These hitches are more for applications that involves process of fine tuning of ANN control parameters: weights and bias. There is no single search and optimization method that suits the weights and bias of ANN for all the problems. The traditional heuristic approach fails because of their poorer convergence speed and chances of ending up with local optima. In this connection, the meta-heuristic algorithms prove to provide consistent solution for optimizing ANN training parameters. This chapter will provide critics on both heuristics and meta-heuristic existing literature for training neural networks algorithms, applicability, and reliability on parameter optimization. In addition, the real-time applications of ANN will be presented. Finally, future directions to be explored in the field of ANN are presented which will of potential interest for upcoming researchers.

INTRODUCTION

There are umpteen number of standard machine learning algorithms that are developed during previous decades to cater the day to day activities in various domains which demand pattern recognition, prediction, decision making and many others. But still there is a gap between the domain specific applications and solving algorithms. Furthermore, there is need for parameter optimization of various machine learning

DOI: 10.4018/978-1-6684-2408-7.ch008

algorithms, so as to achieve faster convergence with minimum iterations, which in turn increases the efficiency of an algorithm, both in terms of execution time and accuracy. In recent years, many nature-inspired meta-heuristic optimization algorithms (MHOA) were developed, which have been successfully applied for optimization of various machine learning algorithms like artificial neural network (ANN), extreme learning machine, deep learning machine, support vector machine, Radial basis neural network, etc. Few of the MHOAs use memory to keep track of the search process and find the optimal solution based on the previous solutions stored in the memory. Based on the search process, these MHOAs are broadly classified as single solution based and population based algorithms. The search process in the single solution based algorithm starts with one candidate solution (search agent/ object) and progresses over a specific number of iterations. Contrary to single solution, in the population based solution, the search process starts with a set of candidate solutions which gets upgraded in next iterations and finally the best fit candidate is chosen as the optimal solution. This chapter mainly focuses on how MHOAs can be applied to optimize various parameters of ANN in particular connection weights. Furthermore, various applications of ANN in the field of textile, tourism and educations are elaborated. In addition, applications of MHOA optimized ANN are also elucidated.

ANNs has significant advantages over statistical models when both are relatively compared. There is no prerequisite demand of hypothesis for testing as needed for statistical methods. In addition, ANNs are robust enough to handle noisy data, provide desired results, are scalable and suitable for handling nonlinear data. ANN processing is reassuring in numerous areas including medical analysis, (Catalogna, 2012, Raval, 2018), education, agriculture, industry, weather forecasting, tourism, textile, manufacturing industry, defense and many more. Surveys provided on ANN till date is limited to tools survey or ANN with specific application. Comparatively this chapter will provide a deeper insights of design techniques of ANN with respects to parameter optimization of ANN using meta heuristic method and also will discuss applications of ANN and MHOAs optimized ANN for umpteen number of real time applications.

Highlights of the chapter are briefed below:

- An overview of ANN weights optimization using two meta-heuristic algorithms: Genetic algorithm and Particle swarm optimization is provided.
- Brief discussion on ANN for few applications namely education, textile, tourism is provided which is not commonly found in literature. Most of the work published covers common applications of ANN restricted to medical field and agriculture domain.
- GA optimized ANN and PSO optimized ANN is covered in detail for umpteen numbers of applications.
- Summarized information of various meta heuristic methods for optimizing ANN and its applications is also deliberated.
- Recent advances and future applications of NNs are briefed.

OVERVIEW OF ANN

The ANN is a feed forward neural network (FFNN) structure which mostly has three layers namely input layer, hidden layer and output layer (figure 1). The training of ANN is the continuous optimization which is the mapping of input layer to output layer by setting the optimal set of weights and biases so as solve the problem in minimum number of iterations and minimum classification error. The outcome of the training a ANN is the connection weight matrix/ synaptic weights which decides the perfomance of ANN during test phase(Fan, 2012; Saravan, 2014). The back-propagation network (BPN) is the most popular traditional learning algorithm that is gradient-based used to train the ANN by back propagating the error estimated as the difference between the actual output and expected output at the output layer . The major loopholes of BPN are getting trapped in local minimum and slow convergence rates (Porchas, 2016;Abid, 2014). Other popularly used training methods include Newton method, Conjugate gradient, Quasi-Newton method and Levenberg-Marquardt algorithm.

Figure 1. Feed forward neural network of 3-4-1 topology

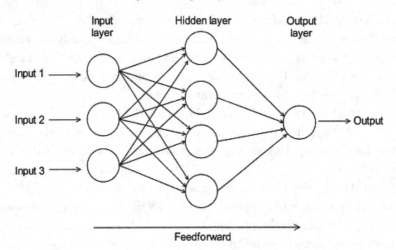

For ANN modeling, the first and foremost operation is to define ANN topology/ architecture. It comprises of deciding the number of nodes in input layer (which is usually the number of input features for the given data set), number of hidden layers, number of nodes in each hidden layer, number of nodes in the output layer(representing the number of class labels for given data or the values to be predicted). Apart from topology, we need to set bias and connection weights based (usually set randomly) on defined ANN topology, momentum and the learning rate. The commonly used approach to train the ANN is back propagation, which involves updating the initially assigned random weights by back propagating the error at the output layer in the reverse order. The training process is repeated till the ANN produces desired minimum classification/prediction error or the user specified number of iterations(epochs) are reached. The variants of ANN include multilayer feed forward neural networks (MLFNN), time-delay neural networks (TDNN), recurrent neural networks (RNN), convolution neural networks (CNN), deep belief networks (DBN), radial basis function neural networks (RBFNN), wavelet neural networks (WNN), fuzzy neural networks (FNN) and many more.

META-HEURISTIC APPROACH TO OPTIMIZE ANN

The various ANN parameters can be optimized using MHOA which include: number of nodes in input layer (identify significant features which will decide the size of input layer), number of hidden layers, number of nodes in each hidden layer, bias, connection weights, momentum and learning rate. Learning most often is modeled as an optimization process, wherein the error is minimized as the learning takes place. Various nature inspired or soft computing-based algorithms have resolved intricate optimization problems where traditional or classical problem-solving methods fail. In recent years, enormous work has been done to optimize connection weights of ANNs using evolutionary algorithms, especially Evolution Strategy, Differential Evolution, and swarm-intelligent based approaches (Sharma, 2015). Green II et al. proposed a Central Force Optimization (CFO) method for training ANNs and found it performed better than PSO in terms of algorithm design, computational complexity, and natural basis. (Bolaji, 2016) proposed the fireworks algorithm and compared it against other established algorithms using different benchmark datasets. Faris et al. proposed the Lightening Search Algorithm (LSA) for finding optimal results and tested it with different measurements. (Karaboga, 2007) contributed Artificial Bee Colony (ABC) for optimizing weights in ANNs. (Aljarah,2016), developed the whale optimization algorithm to find optimal connection weights in MLP ANNs, which showed superior performance to those of other benchmark algorithms.

In this section, we will attempt to understand how MHOA are used to optimize connection weights for simple feed forward NN using (i) Genetic algorithm and (ii) particle swam optimization. In general, population based algorithm of MHOA is used to optimize the connection weights. The type of population depends on the optimization algorithm selected. Each member or search agent (P) of the population is considered as a K-dimensional vector (indicating K connection weights) and K is calculated as, $K=(I*H)+(H*O)$, where I, H, and O are the number of nodes in input layer, hidden layer and output layer; (I*H) indicates the number of connection weights between input layer and output layer; (H*O) indicates the number of connection weights between the hidden and output layer. If we want to optimize the bias, leaning rate and momentum in addition to weights then the dimension of population member or agent will be

$$K = (I*H) + (H*O) + (H+O) + 2;$$

where $(I*H)+(H*O)$ is number of connection weights as explained above, $(H+O)$ for number of bias in hidden nodes and output layer, and 2 is one each for momentum and learning rate. The good optimization algorithm should maintain a proper trade-off between exploration and exploitation while maintaining its efficient search behavior to find "global" most optimal solution. The major objective of MHOA is to make sure that, the ANN does not get entangled in local optimum and avoid premature convergence. Since lot of literature exist on fundamentals of GA and PSO, henceforth details of working of GA and PSO is not covered in this chapter, instead a direct explanation of GA and PSO for optimizing FFN weights is explicated.

GA Optimized FFN Connection Weights (GAFFN)

GA has been used for optimizing the NN parameters which include: architecture (deciding the number of hidden layers and number of nodes in each hidden layer), and connections weights, bias, significant feature selection, activation function, learning rate, momentum and numbers of iterations. (Asha, 2013) have applied GA for optimizing the connection weights of FFN: GAFFN for diagnosis of PIMA diabetic dataset. The functioning of GAFFN for optimizing connection weights of FFN is briefed as follows.

1. The original population is a set of randomly generated N chromosomes. For a FFN with single hidden layer with H hidden nodes, I inputs nodes and O output nodes, the number of connection weights is equal to $(I*H) + (H*O)$. Each chromosome is made up of number of genes equal to total number of connection weights of FFN. Genes are represented by real number encoding method. For example, Figure 2 shows sample chromosome with 10 genes representing $(3*2+2*2)$ connection weights for 3-2-2 topology network.

2. Repeat steps (c) - (f) until termination condition (80% of the chromosomes converge to the same fitness value or user set maximum iterations is reached.

3. Fitness of each chromosome is computed by maximum fitness method. For optimal connection weights, Fitness function is computed $(Ci) = 1/E$, for each chromosome Ci of the population, where E is the error computed as mean square error (MSE) at the output layer. Less the MSE, more fit is the chromosome.

4. The best-fit chromosomes (lowest MSE) replace the worst fit chromosomes (Reproduction step).

5. Crossover step is implemented using single point crossover, two-point crossover and multi point crossover and mixed crossover is used. In mixed crossover, given M number of generation, multi-point crossover is applied for the first 60% of generation, followed by two point crossover for the next 20% generation and finally one point crossover for the remaining generations.

6. Mutation is applied by changing the weights of randomly selected chromosomes by multiplying it with a random number to generate the new population.

Figure 2. Chromosome in GA / Particle in PSO representing weights for 3-2-2 topology

W14	W15	W16	W24	W25	W26	W46	W47	W56	W57

The weights represented by the fittest chromosome (with least MSE) in the final population are the optimized connection weights of the FFN. Functioning of GAFFN is shown in Figure. 3(a).

Particle Swarm Optimization Algorithm (PSO)

For a FFN with single hidden layer with m nodes in hidden layer, I inputs nodes and O output nodes, the number of connection weights is given by $(I*H) +(H*O)$. The total number of connection weights of the FFN decides the number of dimensions of the PSO particle. The proposed PSOFFN algorithm is explained below (Asha 2013).

1. Initialize the original population as set of N particles (each particle representing connection Weights of NN), which is initially generated randomly.

2. Train the NN using particle (set connection weights using each particle figure 2).

3. Compute the learning error at output layer of NN. Fitness of each particle is computed by maximum optimization method. Compute Fitness $(Pi) = 1/E$ for each particle of the population, where

E is the error computed as *MSE* at the output layer of NN as the difference between expected and estimated output.

4. Compare the particles current fitness value with particles *Pbest*. If the current fitness value of particle is better than the previous *Pbest* then set *Pbest* as current fitness value. If the current best fitness value is better than the previous *Gbest* then set *Gbest* as best current fitness value.

5. Compute the velocity and update position of each particle based on *Gbest* value (lowest learning error found in entire learning process so far) and *Pbest* value (each particles lowest learning error so far)

6. Repeat steps (b) - (e) until terminating condition is reached (user defined maximum iterations or minimum error criterion).

The *Gbest* positioned particle, represents the optimized connection weights for FFN. The performance of PSOFFN is measured using percentage of correctly classified test data. Functioning of PSOFFN is shown in Figure. 3(b)

Figure 3. (a) GA optimized of FFN weights (b) PSO optimized FFN weights (Asha 2013)

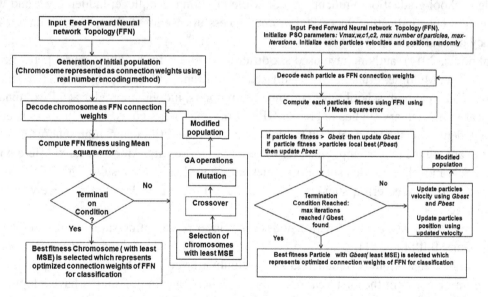

FEW APPLICATIONS OF ANN IN EDUCATION SECTOR, TEXTILE AND TOURISM INDUSTRY

Having understood the basic functioning of ANN, in previous sections, this section covers ANN application to real-world problem in education sector, textiles and tourism Industry all of which play a vital role in national economy.

Application of ANN in Education

It is found that a substantial percentage of students are dropping out from colleges for various causes, which include lack of finance, family background, lack of interest, poor academic background etc. This results in loss of revenue to the institutes as well as reducing the percentage of graduates for the nation as whole. Hence in this regard lot of research is employed to study the student data so as to predict enrollment rates, perseverance rates, and/or graduation rates. The educational performance of students is one of the major benchmark to associate the eminence of university students. ANN can play a major role in education to improve the proficiency of students in attaining high academic which in turn improves the ranking of the institution and standard of nation at global level.

In (Barker, 2004), ANNs and Support Vector Machines are applied to classify graduation rate of students at a 4-year course at an institution using total of 59 input features to describe each student in terms of demographic, academic, and attitudinal information. Both SVM and ANN resulted in accuracy rate of 63.4% for test data.

In (Stamos, 2008), authors have applied ANN with the following 11 input parameters: Ethnic Code, Gender, Current Age, Graduated High schools Code, Intention for enrolling college as intent code, Disability, Boolean variables Need disability services and Need support services, Zip code, Country, Age during high school graduation, Student's major while enrolling to college; hidden layer and with two nodes at output layer indicating Successful or not Successful case for student. The test data resulted in an accuracy of 70.27%.

In (Suknovic, 2014), authors have used six different methods for building neural network models: Quick, Dynamic, Multiple, Prune, RBFN and Exhaustive Prune with 15 input features (student gender, high school GPA and high school type, entrance exam points, individual grades at 11 examinations of the first year of elementary studies to predict GPA at the end their studies. They further experimented the work by identifying the top 6 relevant (which included grades at 11 exam, high school GPA and high school type) among the total 15 input features to get improved results. Among the six different methods of building NN model, the Exhaustive Prune method showed superior results with 0.253, 0.317, and 0.890 as absolute average error, standard deviation, and Linear correlation respectively with top six relevant features.

In (Oancea, 2017) ANN is used with 7 nodes input layer representing students age, gender (0/1 for M/F), part time/ full time (0/1), points scored at high school, break in number of years between high school and higher education; two hidden layers and output layer with three nodes, to predict GPA (as poor, medium or good) in the first year of study of higher education. Authors have adopted various training algorithms: backpropagation, quick propagation, classical resilient propagation, scaled conjugate gradient and got superior results using version of Resilient backpropagation called RPROP with an overall accuracy of 86%.

In (Mason,2017), authors aim to adopt probabilistic neural network (PNN) to study engineering student attrition. This data consist of student attributes related to demographics and academic background of engineering student attrition. Among the various attributes collected, the following 14 selected were selected: First term end exam Cumulative GPA, Maths GPA, total credit, highest math course, cumulative earned hours at the end of first term, Summation score, ACT math imputed, Age, total expenses for first term, Financial aid semester award amount, Financial aid offer accepted (yes/no), Income levels Scale and College division of major Categorical. Results are compared with logistic regression, a multi-layer perceptron artificial neural network, and PNN. Performance is measured using accuracy, sensitivity, specificity and overall results. The sensitivity (detecting non-retained students) was found to be 65.4%, 72.2% and 76.9% for the logistic regression model, MLP and PNN respectively. Prediction accuracy of PNN was found be less compared to other two models, but PNNs better sensitivity was more important to detect a student who will, without intervention, eventually leave engineering.

In (Lau, 2019), the ANN with 11-30-30-1 topology with hyperbolic tangent function is used with following 11 input nodes in input layer pertaining to students background information like gender, location, repeating or not repeating students, earlier school location, occupation of parents, and entrance exam results for five subjects: Chinese, English, Maths, Comprehensive Science and Proficiency test and one single node in output layer for prediction of students CGPA. The principle component analysis is used to reduce the dimensionality and for this data resulted in five best components so to avoid over-fitting. The performance was measured using Mean Square Error (MSE), regression analysis, error histogram, the area under the ROC curve (AUC) and confusion matrix. Levenberg–Marquardt algorithm is used to determine the optimal weights of ANN during training phase and resulted in prediction accuracy of 84.8% and AUC value of 0.86.

In (AYbek, 2018), authors have used MLP and RBF for predicting the final exam scores and pass/fail rates of the students taking the Basic Information Technologies Basic Information Technologies course as part of Open Education System (OES) of Anadolu University. The following input features were identified for the work which included: Demographic(Year of birth, TR identity no, Nationality, Gender, Province), Educational Background (Year of Graduation from the High School, University entrance score (UES), High school type, High school code, High School GPA, Foreign Language, UES Score type, Quota type, University placement ranking), Open education system(Mid-term exam, final exam, letter grade), and Other (Mid-term exam, final exam, letter grade). 12 MLPs were executed with different combination of six parameters which include number of hidden layers, number of nodes in hidden layer, batch training (weights updates at end of all training data) or online training (weights updates at end of each training record), activation function: hyperbolic tangent and sigmoidal, data standardized (data range [0,1] or normalized (data range in [-1,1]). The RBF was also executed with four various combinations of three parameters: Hidden Layer, Activation Function and scaling of Continuous Variables. Importance levels, correlation and determination coefficients of the independent variables are used to evaluate the performance of both MLP and RBF. MLP was found to make better prediction of pass/fail rates of students compared to RBF. It was also observed that few of input features namely mid-term exam scores, university entrance scores and secondary school graduation year proved to play a vital role in elucidation of prediction of final exam scores and pass/fail rates of the students.

Teaching professional career need to acquire large number of competencies and skills, pressure to handle various students and their parents, completion with peers leads to lot of physical and mental stress and hence resulting in teacher's burnout Syndrome. (Ilda, 2017) have applied ANN to predict professional burnout issues related to teachers. They collected the various parameters related to science teachers which include: Sureness on the field information of science teachers, Sureness on the performance of science teacher, Sureness on the lab knowledge of science teacher, Competence of science teacher, Depersonalization in science teachers and Personal achievement in science teachers. The work resulted in performance of ANN network with 40%, 50%, 20% and 80% for prediction of Emotional exhaustion, Personal success, Depersonalization and Competence respectively.

There is tremendous hike in the percentage of students involved in online learning. MLP has been used by (Zacharis, 2016) to predict students performance and resulted in an accuracy of 98.3% using four learning activities as inputs from the Moodle server: communication via emails, collaborative content creation with wiki, content interaction measured by files viewed and self-evaluation through online quizzes. The authors claim that the model can be further extended to help the instructors to plan accordingly to enhance the success rates of students based on predicted results.

RBF, MLP, PNN, and SVM has been applied to predict the learning performances of medical students (Dharmasaroja, 2016). The data related to medical neuroscience course, in two academic years was garnered which includes demographics -gender, high-school backgrounds, first-year grade-point averages, and composite scores of examinations (normalized T-scores of raw scores of MCQ examinations, laboratory examinations, laboratory post-tests, and post-tests of small-group /PBL/TBL sessions) during the course have been applied to predict the learning performance of medical students. Performance is measured in terms of accuracy, sensitivity, specificity, positive predictive value (PPV), negative predictive value (NPV), F-measure, and areas under the receiver operating characteristic (ROC) curves (AUC). Accuracies of RBF, MLP, PNN, and SVM were almost same (in between 98.1 to 99.5%).

ANN Applications in Textiles Industry

ANN and logistic regression have been extensively used by research fraternity for predicting different kinds of yarn and fabric properties. Drape is the ability of a fabric to fall under its own weight into wavy folds. From the designer point of view, the drape property has a vital role in aesthetic appeal of fabric and hence of great importance in textile market. Drapability of fabric is accessed manually and hence differs based on individual skill and experience. In (Amine, 2018), ANN has been used to predict fabric drapability using fabric mechanical properties measured by the Fabric Assurance by Simple Testing (FAST). The following seven input features: Warp count (tex), Weft count (tex), Picks per centimeter, Ends per centimeter, Weight (g/m2), Formability on weft direction in mm2 and Formability on warp direction in mm2 were provided to ANN to predict the five grades of the Drapability from 1 as low drapability to 5 as excellent drapability. A high positive correlation coefficient of 0.86 was obtained between actual and ANN predicted drapability.

Tensile strength is the key characteristic that discriminates it from non-woven and knitted fabric. The more is the crimp in the yarn, the more extensible is the fabric. The air permeability, is mainly dependent on fabrics weight, thickness and porosity, and is equally vital factor to access the quality of few textile materials and is in particular given more importance for clothing which include parachutes, sails, vacuum cleaner, fabrics for air bags and industrial filter fabrics. Tensile properties, breaking extension and air permeability of woven fabrics were anticipated using ANN and regression models (Ghada, 2015). The input layer has three variables: weft yarn count (Ne), twist multiplier and weft density (ppi). Dependent variables used to predict the tensile strength, breaking extension and air permeability. The outcomes of the work clearly states that ANN outperformed regression modes in terms of RMSE, absolute error and correlation coefficient R2 value. The RMSE was found to be 4.477 and 1.08; and R2 as 0.951 and 1.0 for regression model and ANN respectively for prediction of air permeability of the woven fabrics. In addition the RMSE was found to be 1.24 and 0.0006; and R2 as 0.67 and 0.99 for regression model and ANN respectively for prediction of breaking extension of the woven fabrics. Furthermore, the RMSE was found to be 3.072 and 0.0; and R2 as 0.87 and 1.0 for regression model and ANN respectively for prediction of tensile strength.

Core-spun yarns are structures entailing 2 constituent fibers: corn yarn (marks the mechanical properties of yarn, enhances yarn strength) and sheath or covering (causes surface physical and esthetic properties). The tensile properties of core-spun yarn is widely used to measure the performance various post-spinning operations like warping, weaving, knitting, final textile products etc., henceforth there is need for precise prediction of tensile properties. ANN and logistic regression has been used (Almetwally, 2014) to predict the tensile properties of cotton core-spun. ANN model with 3-12-1 topology with one-neuron output layer at a time, aiming on tensile properties of cotton/spandex corespun yarn, i.e. breaking strength (cN), breaking elongation (%), and work of rupture (N cm). The input layer has three nodes representing: linear density of core part (spandex linear density, dtex), drawing ratio of the spandex fila-ment (%), and twist multiplier. The RMSE was 4.87 and 27.45 ; Mean bias error (MBE) was 1.35 and 1.81; and correlation coefficient was 0.99 and 0.71 for ANN and multiple regression model respectively.

In addition to food industry, textile industry also plays a vital role in the increase of foreign exchange. Manual assessment of fabric quality is done with human eye which is not only time consuming but also erroneous. The manual inspection volume may not balance with production volume and hence has impact on the consumer demand. Image processing and ANN is used to classify defects in the fabric as substitute for human inspection and henceforth reduces the inspection time and upsurge the accuracy level of defect identification. ANN has been applied to classify the fabric as normal, wrap defect, empty feed defect and oil defect by using GLCM features (Mulyana, 2017). Accuracy result obtained for test data was 88.75% with an average inspection time for classification of 80 data in real time as 0.56 seconds when compared to average manual scanning time of 19.87 seconds.

Woven fabric properties mainly include yarn parameters: yarn count, twist factor, twist direction, spinning type, and the fabric constructional parameters: weave structure, warp density, cover factor, weft yarn density and tightness factor. Among these parameters, the Tightness factor also known fabric firmness is the key parameter which prominently affects the woven fabric properties. (Nassif, 2018) attempted to predict the tightness degree of cotton-spandex stretchable woven fabric at various levels of spandex ratio and linear density using ANN (3-20-1 topology), linear and logarithmic regression models. A total of 36 woven cotton stretchable fabrics with different weave structures (plain 1/1, twill 2/2 and satin 5), spandex draw ratio (four different draw ratios, i.e. 2, 3, 4 and 5 y) and spandex linear density were woven (20,40 and 80 dtex) was identified as input to ANN to predict the tightness factor The learning method of the ANN is accomplished using Levenberg–Marquardt algorithm, sigmoid as activation function. RMSE values 0.00013, 0.02825 and 0.0268; correlation coefficient R^2 values 0.999, 0.867 and 0.891; and MBE of 0.00009, 0.02431 and 0.0239 was obtained with ANN, multiple regression and logarithmic regression respectively.

Even though fabrics are distributed to garment manufacturers from finishing facilities with the desired values, it is found that during the cloth take-up process and cloth spreading process throughout garment manufacturing increase total internal tensions in the fabric and henceforth the garment manufacturers complain about the dimensional change issues. In this context, ANN has been used to correctly esti-mate the dimensional changes in fabrics and accordingly estimate dimensional changes in a garment. Kalkanci(2017) used dimensional measure properties of T-shirts using ANN. The ANN has 5 nodes in the input layer representing fabric type, fabric code, measurement table for sizes, ironed, measurement point. The fabric type were of four types (S[Single, jersey], LS[single,sersey, lykra], INT[interlock], LINT[interlock/lykra]) coded as 1,2,3,4). The fabric code was represented as numbers in the range of 1 to 18 and measurement size as XS, M and XL represented as 37, 41 and 47. The ironed parameter was taken as 1 and 2 for before ironing and after ironing so as determining the ironing effect. The measure-ment point such as chest, waist, hips, Length from shoulder, Shoulder to shoulder, Arm hole, Arm length, Sleeve hem, Collar pit, Front collar drop, Back collar drop, were replaced with numerical values of 1,

2, 3, 4, 5, 6, 7, 8, 9, 10 and 11, respectively. ANN resulted in correlation coefficient R2 of 0.99872 and MSE of 0.60535.

Yarn strength depends on roving's characteristics and spinning process. During yarn spinning process one of the vital parameters to be controlled is yarn strength. Technicians predict the Yarn strength using knowledge about various fiber parameters like fiber strength, the fiber length, the twist yarn, the yarn count, and the fineness. The laborious task is solved by (Furferi, 2010) using ANN for predicting the yarn strength and achieved a mean error less than 4%. The data considered for work has 6 different families of roving's for different type of fabrics with values of fiber strength, fiber length, twist yarn, and yarn. Results proved to better that multiple regression model.

Bleach washing and use of enzymatic treatment are two conventional technologies used in fabric industry to create design by fading of color. Cotton Denim fabric used for jeans uses cellulase as part of enzymatic treatment to create good color. This method has various drawback, to list a few are difficult to apply, time consuming, not easy to create new design, difficult to get the color effect to all textile surface and in application, and resulting in poor quality fabric if the process is out of control. An ANN with Bayesian regulation back propagation (Kan, 2013) was applied to predict the color properties and color yield of cotton denim fabric after undergoing the cellulase treatment. The fabric yarn twist level and the following cellulase treatment processing factors: treatment temperature (temperature), treatment time (time), pH (pH), and mechanical agitation (MA) formed the input layer of the ANN model. The output layer had six nodes representing color-ks, color-l, color-a, color-b, color-candcolor-h to be predicted. Work was done with changing the number of hidden nodes and adopting both one and two hidden layers. The ANN results proved to excellent compared to that of linear regression model. Figure 4 illustrate how ANN model predicted are matching with and actual values for color-l compared to that of linear regression model prediction. Similar results were obtained for the other colors also.

Figure 4. (a) ANN model fitting for color-l (b) Linear regression model fitting for color-l (Kan, 2013)

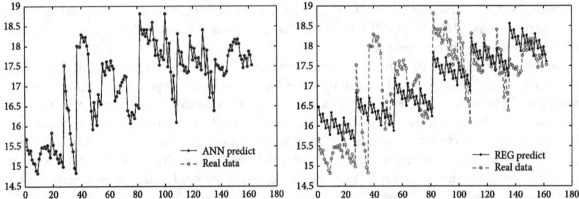

Applications of ANN for Tourism

In addition to food industry, fabric industry, and many more applications, Tourism also plays a vital role in national economy. In fact, tourism industry is one of the world largest employer option. Hence there is tremendous need for development strategy for Tourism to accurately predict the tourism demand. There are many factors affecting the tourism demand which include: population, gross national product, financial status, Qualification, age, weather, travel distance and time, prices, etc. Xiaofeng(2019) have used the following factors as input to ANN model Number of inbound tourists, Currency exchange rate, Per capita GDP of both source and destination countries, Total import and export of goods, Population, Virtual variables(special events), Per capita GDP of the destination country to predict the tourism demand. Performance is measured using MSE and determination coefficient R2. ANN (trained using back propogation) model results outperformed results of support vector machine (SVM) and autoregressive integrated moving average (ARIMA) model at a regional level.

Cankurt (2016) have compared the performance of 3 methods: multiple linear regression (MLR), MLP regression, and support vector regression (SVR) for multivariate tourism forecasting for Turkey. The dataset was collected during Jan 1996 to Dec 2013 (67 time series) with respect to Turkey for 26 major tourism clients. SVR resulted in better results with relative absolute error (RAE) of 12.34% and root relative squared error (RRSE) of 14.02% (figure 5).

Figure 5. ANN model fitting for number of tourists using MLR, MLP, SVR and Actual (Cankurt, 2016)

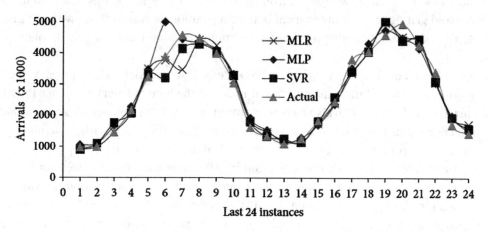

Panarat(2017) have applied feed forward network of 8-1-1 topology to forecast the airline passengers. Data during 1993-2016 was collected with input parameters of world GDP, world population growth, world jet fuel prices, world air fares (proxy for air travel cost), Australia's tourism attractiveness, outbound flights, Australia' s unemployment levels, the Australian and United States foreign exchange rate and three dummy variables (Sydney Olympics, 9/11 and the 2006 Commonwealth Games) to predict the Australia's Outbound Passenger Air Travel Demand. The following five measures were used in the present study: mean square error (MSE), the root mean square error (RMSE), mean absolute error (MAE), mean absolute percentage error (MAPE), and correlation coefficient (R) goodness-of-fit measures: mean absolute error (MAE), mean square error (MSE), root mean square errors (RMSE), AND mean absolute percentage errors (MAPE). ANN obtained R-value of 0.99733 proving its efficient predictive capability.

APPLICATIONS OF PSO OPTIMIZED ANN

This section covers few of applications of PSO optimized ANN.

Since several water bodies are drying, Iran faces water scarcity problem, henceforth there was a need to develop precise model to simulate the rainfall -runoff processing in Karaj basin so as to support the related administrations to handle water scarcity problem. The proper water resource planning depends on the precise forecasting of river flow on daily basis. In (Hamed, 2017), ANN has been applied for reliable rainfall runoff model which can provide information for water planning and supervision for Kajra river in Iran. The 5 years data pertaining to daily precipitation and runoff recorded by gauges were used. The data were collected from hydrometric station and the rain gauge. Performance of PSO optimized ANN weights and biases resulted in R2 of 0.88 and 0.78 for 1 and 2 days ahead runoff forecasting compared to that of Levenberg-Mrquadt(LM) trained ANN model.

Among the tool condition monitoring, drill failure is one of the major areas of research in manufacturing industry. There are various factors associated with drill failure, henceforth there is a need to estimate the drill were accurately. Saurabh(2014) have used PSO trained ANN to predict flank wear in drilling. Results are compared with ANN trained used traditional BP. High speed steel (HSS) drills is employed for drilling on mild steel workpieces, by varying cutting conditions. For each case, the RMS value of spindle motor current as well as the average flank wear is noted. It was observed that the PSO trained ANN avoid getting trapped in the local optimum solution as was the case with BP trained NN. Drill diameter(mm), Spindle speed(rpm), Feed rate (mm/rev), Motor current sensor value (rpm) are input nodes.

Zhang(2000), have adopted two interleaved PSO: outer PSO (particle with integer values) for architecture optimization (to optimize the number of nodes in the hidden layer) and inner PSO for MLP weight optimization. (Marcio, 2000) also have used two interleaved PSO as used by Zhang(2000) with a small alteration done in use of weight decay heuristic in the inner PSO for the MLP weight adjustment. Work is carried out on commonly used benchmark medical data for classification problems of Cancer, Diabetes and Heart from machine learning repository. 50% training data was used for inner PSO to optimize weights, 25% validation data was used by outer PSO for architecture optimization (with one hidden layer) and remaining 25% for testing the MLP network. Results obtained by (Marcio, 2000) are better compared to those obtained by Zhang(2000). Results were also compared with other methods which include Evolutionary Programming (EP), Genetic Algorithm trained MLP, Tabu Search(TS), Simulated Annealing(SA) and Yamazaki Methodology(TS +SA). The proposed method results were in between those obtained by EP and GA. Performance was evaluated using Mean Classification Error Percentage (CEP) and standard deviation (σ) for each algorithm.

The slope stability can used as measure to ensure a safe and low cost design of the various structures. Hence prediction of slope stability is one the major concern in geotechnical engineering during earthquake. (Behrouz, 2016) have used PSO trained ANN to predict factor of safety (FOS) of homogenous slope. The input for the PSO-ANN model was slope height, gradient, cohesion, friction angle and peak ground acceleration. The performance of proposed PSO-ANN was compared with ANN using RMSE, VAF and R2 measures. R2 values obtained was 0.915 and 0.986 for ANN and PSO–ANN model.

One of the major subjects of interest for investors and decision makers in predicting failures in financial sector. Fathima(2019) proposed solution for banking sector bankruptcy prediction using ANN trained via 3 different combination of PSO and Simulated Annealing (SA) as depicted in figure 6. In all the three methods, the outer PSO is used to find the optimal number of hidden nodes for ANN. In PSO-

PSO method, inner PSO for ANN weight optimization. In PSO-PSO-SA method, the inner PSO with SA is used to find optimal ANN weights. In PSO-improved PSO-SA, the inner improved PSO with SA is used to find the ANN optimal weights. The improved PSO is based on the assumption that learning process is based on bad experiences in addition to good experiences. Multivariate Discriminant Analysis (MDA), Logistic Regression (LR) and Decision Tree (DT) are used to find significant features as input for input layer of ANN. Number of features selected by DA, LR and DT was 8, 13 and 16 respectively. Among the different combination, the best results for Bankrupt and Non-bankrupt prediction was found to be 73.5% and 92.2% respectively using PSO-improved PSO-SA with DT identified features.

Figure 6. PSO & SA based ANN optimization with features extracted by MDA, LR & DT
(Fathima, 2019)

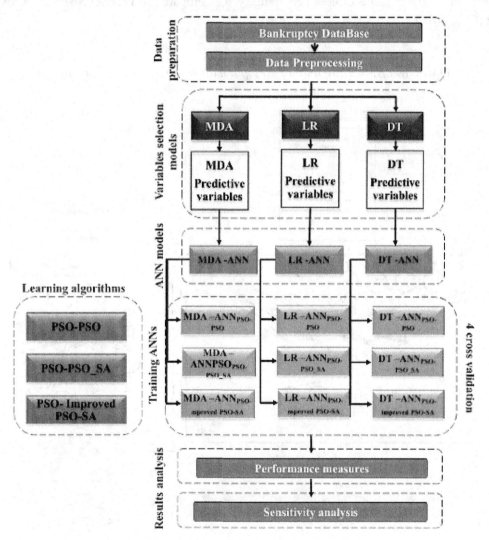

Metal Bending is one of the activities which consumes lot of time. Springback happens owing to residual stress in the metal sheet while bending process. After removal of punch on the metal, the springback takes place and the change in the wall angle 'a', is defined to be a measure of distortion. Therefore, a suitable prediction method is required to predict the springback angle. Springback is subjective to various parameters like thickness of the sheet, grease conditions, tooling geometry and material properties. Sathish(2018) have used PSO optimized ANN weights for predicting the springback effect of metal sheet while bending of the sheet (Sathish, 2018)

The plastic injection cost comprises of design/R&D cost, mold cost, and molding products cost. Che(2010) have used amalgamation of factor analysis (FA), PSO and ANN with 2 BPNs (shown in figure 7) called FAPSO-TBP (shown in figure 8) and one BPN called FAPSO-SBP to predict the mold cost and molding product cost for plastic injection molding. FAPSO-TBP showed better and stable results (shown in figure 9,10) in terms of cost Percentage error compared to FAPSO-SBP and ANN trained using BP (Che, 2010).

Figure 7. FAPSO with two BPN using total of 16 input features to predict product and mold cost (Che,2010)

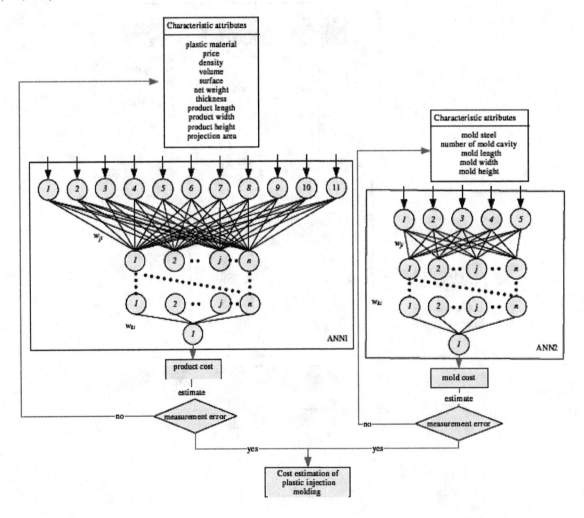

Figure 8. FAPSO with single BPN using 13 input features to predict product & mold cost (Che,2010)

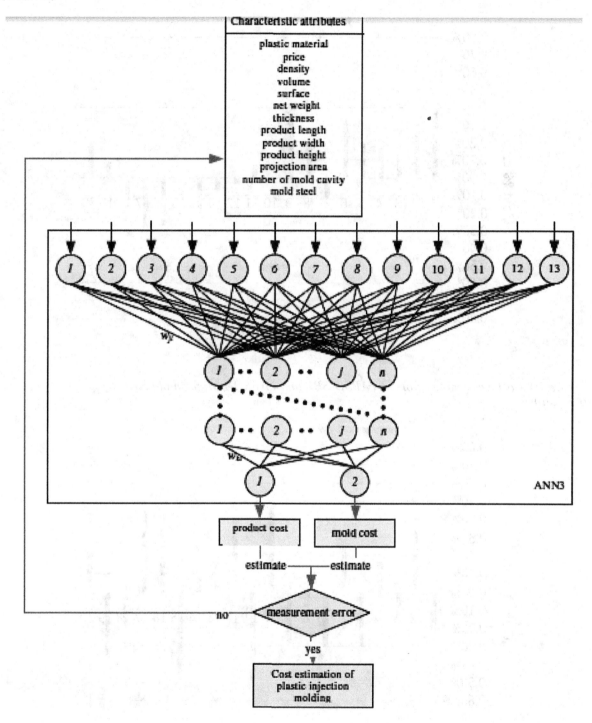

Figure 9. Cost Percentage Errors of FAPSO-SBP and FAPSO-TBP for product cost
(Z.H. Che(2010)

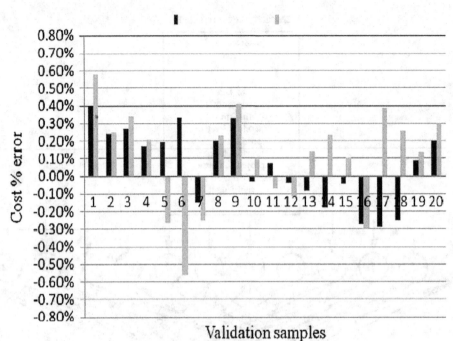

Figure 10. Cost percentage errors of FAPSO-SBP and FAPSO-TBP for mold cost
(Che, 2010)

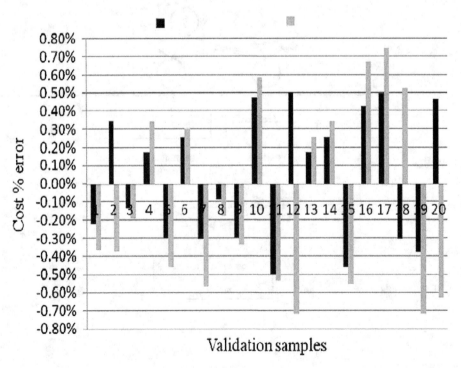

Huge amount of chlorophenol compounds which are exceedingly toxic and resistant to biological degradation are found in wastewater produced from various industry. Electro-oxidation is very costly but rapid, efficient, environment friendly method, and doesn't use extra reagents to remove chlorophenol compounds from wastewater. Compared to traditional mathematical models, ANN model are found to be more reliable for predicting the behavior of electrochemical oxidation processes at low energy cost. Yu Mei(2019) have used PSO trained ANN to predict (i) COD removal efficiency & (ii) total energy consumption (TEC) of electro-oxidation (Mei, 2019). The proposed PSO-ANN model (figure 11) provide appreciable results with R2 of 0.99 and 0.9944 for COD removal efficiency and TEC, and MSE values of 0.0015526 and 0.0023456 respectively for the testing dataset. The weight matrix of PSO-ANN provided the relative importance of input variables (with current density: 18.85%, original pH:21.11%, electrolyte concentration: 19.69%, electro-oxidation time: 21.30%, ORP 19.05%) on the value of COD removal efficiency and TEC.

Figure 11. PSO-ANN model for predicting COD removal efficiency and total energy consumption (Yu Mei, 2019)

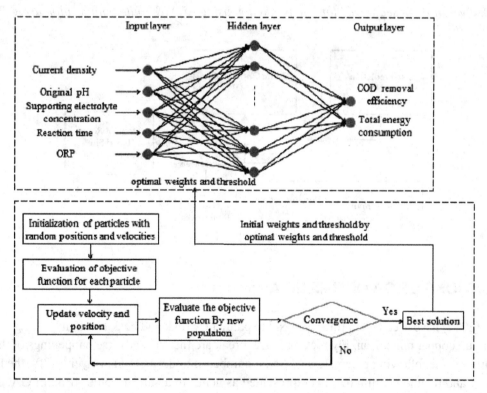

Tourist wish to cover maximum tourist spots on each day of trip in tourist city. It is important to have proper selection of tourist spots, in order to visit those spots and optimal route to those spots to make trip worth for the tourist. In this context, Sehrish Malik(2019) have proposed optimal route recommendation to (i) predict the next tourist attraction using ANN using input parameters: past routes, season, day, time & vehicles on route and (ii) predict the optimal route (with input parameters as distance, road congestion, weather conditions, route popularity, and user preference) to the foretold location by ANN using PSO. These can be used in navigation applications by drivers to get better routes for their trips. Distance, road congestion, weather conditions, route popularity, and user preference are used as route parameters as input to objective function for the route Optimization. In this work PSO, is not used to optimize ANN parameters but an amalgamation of ANN (to predict optimal tourist spot) and PSO (to find optimal route to ANN predicted tourist spot) is done to assist tourist to cover maximum spots in minimum time. Work is carried on tourism data form 2016-17 of Jeju Island of South Korea. The data used is the tourism data of Jeju Island from December. Overall model is presented in figure 12. Detailed design of ANN for prediction of next tourist spot is shown in figure 13. Detailed design of optimal route to ANN predicted next tourist spot is shown in figure 14. Both the algorithms gave same optimized route as output using the proposed objective function. Prediction accuracy of next tourist spot of PSO optimized ANN was superior than ANN, SVM, random forest, (RF), and naive Bayes (NB). In the similar lines they have used GA optimized ANN to find optimal path to the next tourist spot. Performance of both GA and PSO were good. Compared to PSO, GA took more number of iterations and hence more time to find optimal route.

Figure 12. Overall proposed model for Site prediction using ANN & route optimization using PSO (Sehrish Malik, 2019)

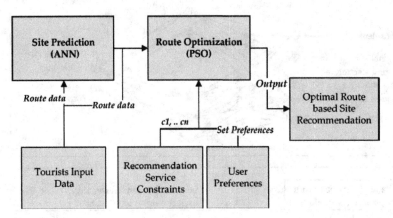

APPLICATIONS OF GA OPTIMIZED ANN

Monjenzi (2012) have used GA optimized ANN to predict fly rock and back break in blasting operation of the Sungun copper mine, Iran. Fly rock and back break are the most adverse happenings of the blasting operations. The following parameters of ANN: number of nodes in hidden layer (1-30), the learning rate (0 to1), and the momentum (0-1) is represented as genes in a chromosome string of GA. The GA identified optimal number of hidden layer was nodes found to be 16 with 0.58 and 0.46 learning rate and momentum. The following 9 parameters are the inputs: Hole diameter (mm) as D, Hole length (m) as L, Spacing (m) as S, Burden (m) as B, Stemming (m) as T, Powder factor (kg/ton) as Pf, Specific drilling(m/m3) as SD, Charge per Delay (kg) as Ch and RMR) Output Fly rock (m) Fly rock 20–100 to GA-ANN model to predict fly rock and back break (figure 15). Performance was measured using MSE, NMSE, and determination coefficient R2. Multivariable regression analysis resulted in R2 value of 0.58 showing poor correlation between the parameters and flyrock ; and 0.42 for backbreak. Contrary to this, GA-ANN showed a very high correlation (0.978) between predicted and measured flyrock ; 0.958 for backbreak.

Figure 13. Detailed model for predicting next tourist spot using ANN
(Sehrish Malik, 2019)

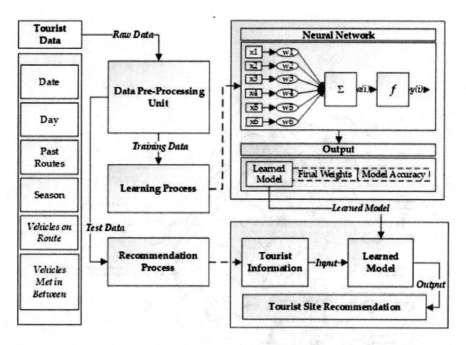

Figure 14. Detailed route optimization using PSO to tourist spot predicted by ANN
(Sehrish Malik, 2019)

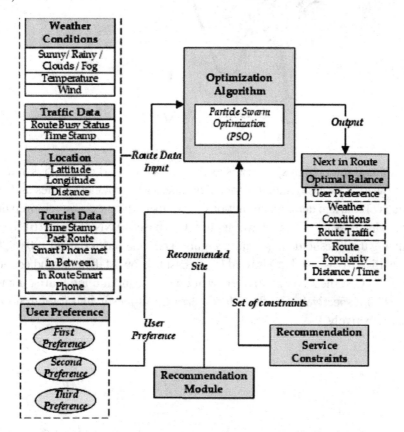

Figure 15. GA-ANN (optimized number of hidden nodes, learning rate and momentum) to predict flyrock and backbreak
(Monjenzi 2012)

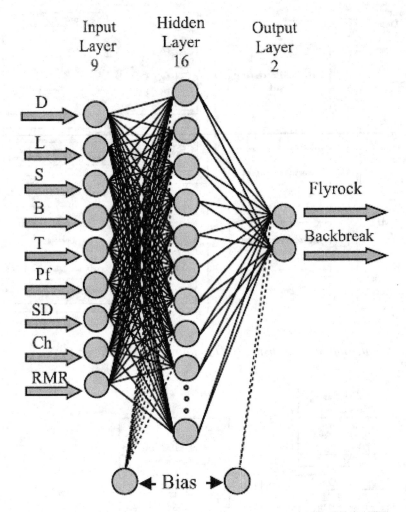

International standard refers high speed rails as the one with speed above 250km/hr. China aims to achieve 38000 km by 2025 to strengthen the connection between provinces, cities and countries. Since the traditional means of tourism demand prediction cannot meet the precision requirements of the high-speed railway era, Meiyu Wang (2019) have applied GA based ANN (figure 16) to predict tourism demand by optimizing the threshold values and weights. The time series data (1990 to 2014 samples as training data and 2015-2016 as test data) is used to forecast the tourist demand and economic growth of Sanjiang County. With GA, the ANN relative error of domestic and foreign tourist population is found to be 12.23 and 4.95% respectively and the relative error of domestic and foreign tourism income as 1.84% and 1.82% respectively.

Figure 16. Meiyu Wang(2019) proposed GA-ANN to optimize weights and thresholds to predict tourist demand and economic growth

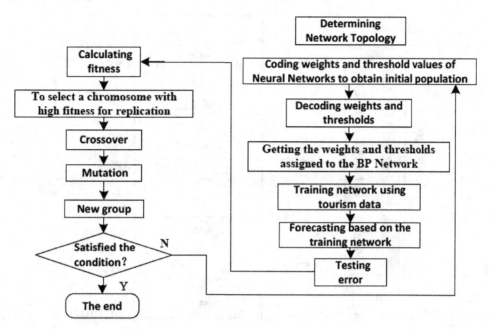

There is noteworthy rise of ultraviolet radiation (UVR) due to depletion of Ozone layer in the atmosphere; henceforth there is increase in the prevalence of skin cancers in countries like Australia and South Africa which have high solar exposure. One of the solutions to this problem is to cover skin by clothing. There are various parameters which influence the UV protection capacity which include fiber type, yarn structure, fabric cover factor, fabric areal density, fabric thickness, finishing process, coloration process and presence of UVR absorbers. Ultraviolet protection factor (UPF) indicates the UV protective capacity of fabric. A comfortable fabric must allow transmission of air permeability (AP) and moisture vapor transmission rate (MVTR) in addition to UV protective property. The major problem is by increasing UPF, reduces the fabric comfort factor of AP and MVTR. Thus Fabric designing is a multi-objective problem to have sought after levels of conflicting to each other parameter: UPF, AP and MVTR simultaneously. Abhijit(2015) have endeavored the above mentioned fabric multi objective problem by finding optimal combination of UPF, AP and MVTR using GA based ANN (figure 17) with following input parameters: fiber blend proportion in yarn, yarn count (warp and weft) and thread density (ends per inch and picks per inch). Separate ANN models with one hidden layer (4 hidden nodes) was trained by Levenberg–Marquardt algorithm. The result of ANN was compared with GA trained ANN. The encoding of GA chromosome representing the search space with five input variables (each of 14 bits) indicating the overall proportion of polyester in fabric. Example of the 30 bit binary encoded chromosome indicating the binary values of five inputs is shown in figure 18. Results prove, the hybrid ANN–GA system was precise in attaining targeted fabric functional properties.

Noersasongko(2016) have used GA to optimize the 3 parameters of BPNN: learning rate, training cycle and momentum to predict tourist arrival. The findings reveal that GA-ANN resulted in very small RMSE compared to BPNN, K-Nearest Neighbor (KNN) and Multiple Linier Regression (MLR).

Figure 17. Hybrid ANN–GA Model to predict the optimal combination of UPF, AP and MVTR (Abhijit 2015)

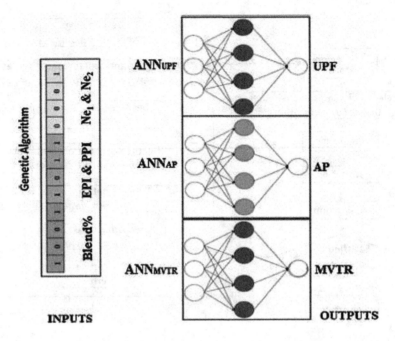

Figure 18. Sample binary encoded chromosome of size 30 representing the five genes of 6 bits each for five input features (Abhijit 2015).

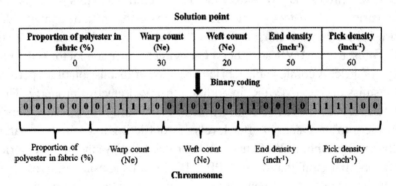

One of the major sources of electric power industry which is both low cost as well as environment friendly is wind power. Precise prediction of wind power production is used for various tasks which include optimal generation scheduling, maintenance scheduling, load shedding and various diction making process. Yordanos (2018) have proposed hybrid GA and PSO algorithms to optimize the weights and bias of ANN model for predicting wind power. The dataset has wind speed and the corresponding turbine output power data of the aforesaid period. Initially the ANN model starts with randomly generated weights and bias which decide the size of candidate solution for both PSO and GA. The fitness function of both GA and PSO are compared. If PSO best particle is better than the GA best chromosome, then the genes of best chromosome is replaced by PSO solution. If GA solution is best then, best particle's variables are replaced by the genes of best GA chromosome. In either case for the next new iteration, both GA and PSO begin with the best global solution among the both. Mean squared error (MSE), root mean square error (RMSE), mean absolute error (MAE), normalized mean absolute error (NMAE), and mean absolute percentage error (MAPE) are used as performance evaluation measures. Results prove that prediction of wind power using hybrid PSO-GA-ANN are better (with highest and lower errors of 12.55% and 1.2% respectively) than PSO-ANN and GA-ANN model. The proposed hybrid model yielded highest and lowest errors of 12.55% and 1.2% respectively

Arya (2018) have used GA to optimize the ANN weights to predict rainfall for Goa region. As part of data pre-processing, the missing values in the time series data was handled using List wise deletion method followed by use PCA to extract five significant input features: SST, SLP, Humidity, U-wind, V-wind of IO region. SOM and k-mediods are used to cluster rainfall values. SOM resulted in better clusters than k-mediods. Finally the GA-ANN is used to predict the rainfall. The accuracy of BPNN and GA-NN was found to be 92.78 and 98.78

Lalita(2009) applied GA to optimize the various parameters of ANN to predict yarn properties in spinning process of Textile industry. Each chromosome is encoded as to include the following NN parameters to be optimized: number of nodes in hidden layers, transfer function, learning rate, momentum and number of epochs with MSE as the fitness function. GA resulted in NN which can predict the fiber properties from given yarn properties Uniformity Ratio, Tenacity, Elongation, Count, Thin, Thick, Neps and CSP respectively. The quality of any yarn spun from cotton depends on fiber quality chiefly, Span Length(SL), Uniformity Ratio(UR), Short Fibre Index(SFI), Micronaire(MIC), Strength(STR) and Trash(TR), henceforth selection of cotton is very important for a better end product design.

In textile industry, yarn tenacity is most vital property of yarn production. Dasti(2014) have used GA to find the optimal input values to obtain desired yarn tenacity keeping minimum production cost. Seven fibers characteristics are used as input: Fiber Tenacity (CN/Tex), Fiber Elongation, %50 Average Length, length uniformity, Micronaire Reflection Degree, Yellownes. Firstly, the ANN is trained independent of GA using backpropagation to find the optimal NN topology. As part of second step, GA is used on NN topology of first step to determine optimal input values to attain the desired yarn tenacity at minimum production cost. Performance is measured error value and coefficient determination. The fitness function of GA is multigoal problem, keeping the production cost as minimum and attaining the tenacity of produced yarn to be equal and more than the desired tenacity. One can use the proposed model by first determining the desired tenacity of yarn, followed by assigning the weights of input material propositional to the cost of material. The GA will be used to predict the amount of input material needed for yarn production keeping two goals: minimum production cost and produced yarn has desired yarn tenacity. GA is not used to optimize the ANN weights in the proposed method.

Eutrophication is excess contents of nutrients in water body which leads to growth of aquatic plants, henceforth create problems for water supply, fishery etc. Nitrogen and phosphorus are the two major controllable nutrients loads used to control eutrophication. Jan-Tai (2006) have applied ANN to simulate watershed nutrient model based on data from nutrient loads, average and maximum rainfall in the watershed, and outflow to forecast phosphorus concentration in the reservoir. The GA is applied with ANN model to optimize nutrient control from the watershed to forecast the total phosphorus concentration in the reservoir and compared with total phosphorus (TP) model figure 19. The fitness of each chromosome is assessed using an objective function which comprises of one measure to represent the minimum treatment level (i.e. sum of the square of the phosphorus reduction rates is the minimum).

Figure 19. GA based ANN for water quality model

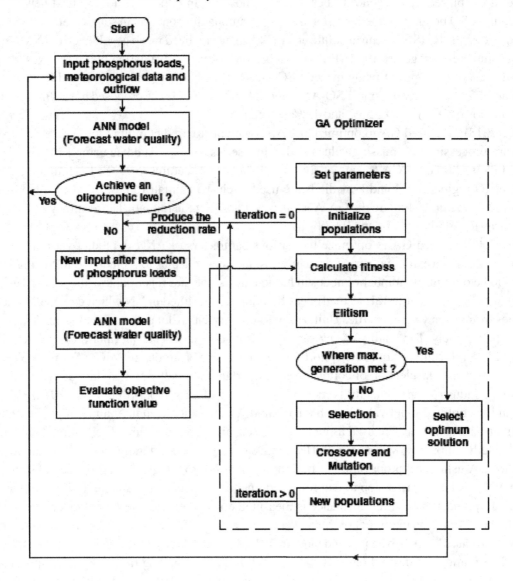

The GA-ANN method provides precise information which can be used by decision makers to manage reservoir eutrophication control.

Dezdemona(2014) have applied GA optimized neural network to forecast the tourist number and to regulate the trends of the future tourist inflow; henceforth serving Albania tourism agencies in financial decision. A total of 99 months data (number of tourist) from Jan 2005 to June 2013, was collected for the work. Results of both ANN and GA-ANN were compared with Exponential Smoothing model to validate their accuracy. Han-chen(2017) applied GA to find the optimal number of hidden nodes of ANN to predict Air ticket sales revenue (T month). GA identified ANN optimal network architecture was 12-142-1. The 12 input nodes represented NTD/USD exchange rate, the number of people traveling abroad from Taiwan each month, the international oil price, the Taiwan stock market weighted index, Taiwan's monthly monitor indicator, Taiwan's monthly composite leading index, Taiwan's monthly composite coincident index, and W travel agency's monthly air ticket sales(T-1~T-18). The GA identified optimal number of hidden nodes for ANN resulted in mean absolute relative error (MARE) of 10.51% and correlation coefficient of 0.913.

Brief applications of few more MHOA for optimizing ANN parameters in summarized in table 1.

Table 1. Summary of MHOA optimized ANN for various applications

Author &Year	Meta Heuristic Approach	Purpose	Application	Function/DATASET
Conforth, 2014	Ant Colony Optimization +PSO	Ant Colony Optimization(ACO) is applied to optimize ANN topology, Particle Swarm Optimization (PSO) is applied to adjust ANN connection weights.	reinforcement learning	SWIRL, the XOR and double pole balance Problem
Ojha, 2017	Ant Colony Optimization	To explore the impact of The optimization of the individual transfer function parameters On the performance of NN.	Classification	Iris, Breast Cancer (Wdbc) and Wine
Weingaertner, 2002	Artificial Bee colony (ABC)	Means of choosing various transfer function at the hidden Layers and the output layers of a NN	Pattern classification	Heart
Sheg, 2010	ABC	Means of choosing various transfer function at the hidden Layers and the output layers of a NN	Activation function optimization	Xor, Decoder-Encoder and 3-Bit Parity Problems
Ozturk, 2011	ABC+LM(Levenberq-Marquardt)	To find global Optimistic result	Training	Xor, Decoder-Encoder and 3-Bit Parity problems.
Karaboga, 2007	ABC	To train feed-forward artificial neural Networks for classification purpose	Classification	XOR, 3-Bit Parity and 4-Bit Encoder-Decoder problems
Johm, 2007	ABC	To optimize two key neural network BP learning parameters, Namely the random initial weight range and the single learning rate	Weight optimization and Comparison	Thyroid, heart, horse, soybean, gene, digits
Noor, 2017	ABC+PSO	To train neural networks using optimal weight set to obtain better results	pattern-classification	Iris, Cancer, Diabetes and Glass
Ozkan, 2011	ABC+LM(Levenberq-Marquardt)	To Train feed-forward neural networks on classi¯cation	oil spill detection	132 Oil pollution Radarsat-1 images of Lebanese coast, 2007
Cheg,2007	ACO	To construct the relationship function among response, inputs And parameters of a dynamic system, which is then used to predict the responses of the System.	Parameter design with dynamic charcteristics	crystal nanobalance (QCN) gas sensor, motor controller test circuit
Suamn, 2010	Binary ACO	To achieve the Optimal FNN model in terms of neural complexity minimization of hidden layers and cross-entropy error	classification	Iris, Liver disorders Diabetes, Yeast, Breast Cancer, Wine Hepatitis, Thyroid, Mushroom Horse colic, Ionosphere, Arcene
Meil, 2009	ACO	To achieve continuous optimization, which includes Global searching, local searching and definite searching	Find relation function	Two exponential functions
Michalis, 2013	ACO	To use global optimization algorithms to provide BP with good initial connection weights	Prediction	Cancer, Diabetes, Heart

continues on following page

Table 1. Continued

Author &Year	Meta Heuristic Approach	Purpose	Application	Function/DATASET
Salman, 2014	ACO	To achieve Topological improvement	Construct topology of FNN	20 benchmark pattern classification datasets, from UCI
Michalis, 2014	ACO	To train feed-forward neural networks for pattern classification	Pattern classification	Cancer, Diabetes, Heart
Rahul, 2007	ACO	To eliminate the variables that produce noise Or, are strictly correlated with other already selected variables	feature subset selection	Thyroid, Dermatology, breast cancer
Socha, 2007	ACO	To achieve continuous optimization	Pattern classification	Cancer, diabetes, heart
Valiant, 2011	Cuckoo search	To adopted best fitness function	Optimization of parameters	20 benchmark pattern classification datasets, from UCI
Nawi, 2013	Cuckoo search	For faster convergence and local minima avoidance	classification	Heart
Nawi, 2014	Cuckoo search + Levenberg Marquardt	To adopted improved fitness function	classification	Wisconsin Breast Cancer D
Yi, 2014	Cuckoo search	to simultaneously optimize the initial weights and bias of BP network	classification	Wine data
Nandy, 2012	Firefly Optimization Algorithm (FOA)	to optimize its performance index	classification	Iris, wine, liver
Mirjalili,, 2015	Grey wolf optimizer	To adopted improved fitness function	Function approximation and classification	3 XOR, balloon, iris, breast cancer, heart
Brajevic, 2013	Firefly Optimization Algorithm (FOA)	To improve function	Activation function optimization	Sin, sigmoid
Alweshah, 2014	Firefly Optimization Algorithm (FOA)	To improve fitness function for better classification	Parameter optimization	UCR time series characteristics
Tang, 2014	Wolf search algorithm	to produce the weight values for BPN to train	Activation function optimization	Griewangk, sphere, rastrign, moved axis parallel hyper, Bohachevsky, Michalewiz, Rosenbrook function
Saha, 2014	Gravitational search algorithm (GSA)	for the faster convergence towards global optima	classification	Iris, glass, wine, cancer, crab
Mirjalili, 2014	Gravitational search algorithm (GSA)	To generate adaptive weight	Function approximation and classification	3 XOR, balloon, iris, breast cancer, heart
Rashedi, 2009	Gravitational search algorithm (GSA)	To minimization of MSE is the objective function	Optimization of activation function	3 Linear Functions
Hadi, 2016	Bacterial foraging optimization algorithm	To improve activation function	Parameter estimation	Cancer, balloon
Kaur, 2014	Bacterial foraging optimization algorithm	To improve weights	Classification of software defect	Ant 1.7
Nawi, 2014	Bat inspired	To improve activation function	Parameter optimization	2-bit XOR, 3-bit XOR, 4-OR
Jaddi, 2014	Bat inspired	Optimize ANN structure	Function optimization	
Mirjalili, 2014	Biogeography-based optimization	To optimize fitness function To optimize the number of weights and biases	Classification	Iris, Breast Cancer (Wdbc) and Wine
Askarzadeh, 2013	Bird mating optimizer	to identify the weights for training ANN	Parameter optimization	UCR time series characteristics

continues on following page

Table 1. Continued

Author &Year	Meta Heuristic Approach	Purpose	Application	Function/DATASET
Yu, 2011	Chemical reaction optimization	To improve fitness function and to achieve local minima in minimum duration	?????	Functions of ANN
Yumany, 2015	Moth-flame optimization algorithm	the objective function used to find the optimal solution	Classification	XOR, balloons, iris, heart, breast cancer
Cuves, 2013	Social Spider optimization	the objective function used to find the optimal solution to reduce mean square error	Search agents	
Balamurugan, 2018	social spider optimization	to separate the categorical and non-categorical data pre-processing	Classification of micro array data as normal or abnormal data	breast cancer, leukemia, lung cancer, lymphoma and ovarian
Kose, 2018	Ant-lion optimization	the objective function used to find the optimal solution to reduce mean square error and mean absolute error	Electroencephalogram (EEG) Prediction	10 different EEG datasets recorded at State Hospital, Isparta, Turkey
Saghatforoush, 2007	Ant colony optimization (ACO)	for prediction and optimization of flyrock and back-break induced by blasting,	Mining prediction	data from the mine, burden, spacing, hole length, stemming, and powder factor were selected as input parameters. The R2 values of 0.994 and 0.832 for testing datasets of flyrock and back-break
Li, 2019	Firefly Optimization algorithm (FOA)	the objective function used to find the optimal solution	Daily Tourism Demand Forecasting with Web Search Data	validated with the data of bus line Jiading 3 in Shanghai, China
Haitao, 2019	Glowworm	the objective function used to find the optimal solution, adn parameters set methods	Traffic prediction	Yangjiang inbound tourism
Mais, 2018	Dragon fly and ABC	To optimize NN weights	Medical data classification	Cleveland Clinic heart disease, the hepatitis, diabetes, Wisconsin Diagnostic breast cancer and blood donations dataset from the Blood Transfusion Service Center in Taiwan

FUTURE DIRECTIONS

There are still many more MHOA algorithms which are yet to explored to optimize the various parameters of ANN, and other machine learning algorithms for solving diverse applications. The upcoming research scholars can focus on the few of the imminent research areas in machine learning listed below.

- Integration of fuzzy logic and ANN: Fuzzy logic is a type of logic that recognizes more than simple true and false values, hence better simulating the real world. For example, the statement today is sunny might be 100% true if there are no clouds, 80% true if there are a few clouds, 50% true if it's hazy, and 0% true if rains all day. Hence, it takes into account concepts like -usually, somewhat, and sometimes. Fuzzy logic and neural networks have been integrated for uses as diverse as automotive engineering, applicant screening for jobs, the control of a crane, and the monitoring of glaucoma.

- In recent years, data from neurobiological experiments have made it increasingly clear that biological neural networks, which communicate through pulses, use the timing of the pulses to transmit information and perform computation. This realization has stimulated significant research on pulsed neural networks, including theoretical analyses and model development, neurobiological modeling, and hardware implementation.

- Amalgamation of two or more MHOA to optimize the NN parameters
- Apply MHOA to optimize various machine learning algorithms apart from ANN: SVM, RBF etc.
- Apply MHOA to find the best input feature set for machine learning algorithms
- Apply MHOA to optimize parameters of Convolutional Neural Network (CNN), Long short-term memory (type is an artificial recurrent neural network (RNN) architecture) and other deep learning algorithms.
- Apply MHOA to optimize unsupervised algorithms.

CONCLUSION

ANN has been widely used for classification and prediction in umpteen number of fields since it is robust to handle voluminous, noisy and nonlinear data. The performance of the ANN depends on various parameters among which the connection weights play a vital role. This chapter elucidates how ANN weights optimization can be obtained using two most common MHOA: GA and PSO. Various real time applications of ANN for textile, education and tourism is also briefed. Real time applications of GA optimized ANN, PSO optimized ANNs, and many more MHOA are covered. These applications will definitely help the research fraternity to carry out further work using MHOA optimized ANN for further more domains. There is lot of scope for optimizing many more ANN parameters using emerging MHOA; as well for optimizing the upcoming deep learning algorithms.

REFERENCES

Abid, F., & Hamami, L. (2018). A survey of neural network based automated systems for human chromosome classification. *Artificial Intelligence Review*, *49*(1), 41–56. doi:10.100710462-016-9515-5

Abou-Nassif. (2015). Predicting the Tensile and Air Permeability Properties of Woven Fabrics Using Artificial Neural Network and Linear Regression Models. *J Textile Sci Eng, 5*(5). DOI: .doi:10.4172/2165-8064.1000209

Abou-Nassif, A. (2018). Comparison among artificial neural network, linear and logarithmic regression models as predictors of stretchable woven fabric tightness. *International Journal of Chemtech Research*, *11*(01), 41–49.

Admuthe, L., Apte, S., & Admuthe, S. (2009). Topology and Parameter Optimization of ANN Using Genetic Algorithm for Application of Textiles. *IEEE International Workshop on Intelligent Data Acquisition and Advanced Computing Systems: Technology and Applications*, 21-23. 10.1109/IDAACS.2009.5342981

Al-Hadi & Hashim. (2016). Bacterial foraging optimization algorithm for neural network learning enhancement. *Int. J. of Innovative Computing*, *1*(1), 8–14.

Al Nuaimi & Abdullah. (2017). Neural network training using hybrid particle-move artificial bee colony algorithm for pattern classification. *Journal of ICT, 16*(2), 314–334.

Aljarah, I., Faris, H., & Mirjalili, S. (2016). Optimizing connection weights in neural networks using the whale optimization algorithm. *Soft Computing, 22*(1), 1–15. doi:10.100700500-016-2442-1

Almetwally, A. A., Idrees, H. M. F., & Hebeish, A. A. (2014). Predicting the tensile properties of cotton/spandex core-spun yarns using artificial neural networkand linear regression models. *Journal of the Textile Institute, 105*(11), 1221–1229. doi:10.1080/00405000.2014.882043

Alweshah, M. (2014). Firefly Algorithm with Artificial Neural Network for Time Series Problems. *Research Journal of Applied Sciences, Engineering and Technology, 7*(19), 3978–3982. doi:10.19026/rjaset.7.757

Arya & Pai. (2018). Rainfall Prediction Using an Optimised Genetic-Artificial Neural Network Model. *National Journal of Pure and Applied Mathematics, 119*(10), 669-678.

Asha Gowda Karegowda, M.A. (2013). Significant Feature Set Driven and Optimized FFN for Enhanced Classification. *International Journal of Computational Intelligence and Informatics, 2*(4), 248–255.

Askarzadeh, A., & Rezazadeh, A. (2013). Artificial neural network training using a new efficient optimization algorithm. *Applied Soft Computing, 13*(2), 1206–1213. doi:10.1016/j.asoc.2012.10.023

Azayite, F., & Achchab, S. (2019). A hybrid neural network model based on improved PSO and SA for bankruptcy prediction. *International Journal of Computer Science Issues, 16*(1).

Balamurugan & Nanc. (2018). Basis Function Neural Network. *International Journal of Uncertainty, Fuzziness and Knowledge-Based Systems, 26*(5), 695–715. Doi:10.1142/S0218488518500320695

Barker, K., Trafalis, T., & Rhoads, T. R. (2004). Learning from Student Data. *Proceedings of the 2004 IEEE Symposium on Systems and information Engineering Design*, 79-86. 10.1109/SIEDS.2004.239819

Bolaji, A. L., Ahmad, A. A., & Shola, P. B. (2016). Training of neural network for pattern classification using fireworks algorithm. *Int. J. Syst. Assur. Eng. Manag.*, 9(1), 208–215. doi:10.100713198-016-0526-z

Brajevic, I., & Tuba, M. (2013). Training feed-forward neural networks using firefly algorithm. *Recent Advances in Knowledge Engineering and Systems Science: Proc. of the 12th Int. Conf. Artificial Intelligence, Knowledge Engineering and Data Bases (AIKED'13)*, 156-161.

Bullinaria & Alyahya. (2014). Artificial Bee Colony Training of Neural Networks: Comparison with Back-Propagation. *Journal Memetic Computing*. Doi:10.100712293-014-0137-7

Cankurt, S., & Subas, A. (2016). Tourism demand modeling and forecasting using data mining techniques in multivariate time series: A case study in Turkey. *Turkish Journal of Electrical Engineering and Computer Sciences, 24*, 3388–3404. doi:10.3906/elk-1311-134

Carvalho, M. (2000). Particle Swarm Optimization of Neural Network Architectures and Weights. Academic Press.

Catalogna,, M., Cohen,, F., & Fishman,, S., Halpern, Nevo, U., & Ben-Jacob, E. (.(2012). ANN based controller for gloucose monitoring during, clamp test. *PLoS One, 7*, e44587. doi:10.1371/journal. pone.0044587 PMID:22952998

Chang, Chen, & Chen. (2007). Dynamic parameter design by ant colony Optimization and neural networks. *Asia-Pacific Journal of Operational Research, 24*(3), 333–351.

Che, Z. H. (2010). PSO-based back-propagation artificial neural network for product and mold cost estimation of plastic injection molding. *Computers & Industrial Engineering, 58*(4), 625–637. doi:10.1016/j. cie.2010.01.004

Conforth & Meng. (2014). *Toward Evolving Neural Networks using Bio-Inspired Algorithms*. Academic Press.

Cuevas, E., Cienfuegos, M., Zald'ıvar, D., & P'erez-Cisnero, M. (2013). A swarm optimization algorithm inspired in the behavior of the social-spider. *Expert Systems with Applications, 40*(16), 6374–6384. doi:10.1016/j.eswa.2013.05.041

Dashti, M., Derhami, V., & Ekhtiyari, E. (2014). Yarn tenacity modeling using artificial neural networks and development of a decision support system based on genetic algorithms. *Journal of Artificial Intelligence and Data Mining, 2*(1), 73–78.

Dharmasaroja, P., & Kingkaew, N. (2016). Application of Artificial Neural Networks for Prediction of Learning Performances. *12th International Conference on Natural Computation, Fuzzy Systems and Knowledge Discovery (ICNC-FSKD)*. 10.1109/FSKD.2016.7603268

Fan, W., Bouguila, N., & Ziou, D. (2012). Variational learning for finite Dirichlet mixture models and applications. *IEEE Transactions on Neural Networks and Learning Systems, 23*(5), 762–774. doi:10.1109/ TNNLS.2012.2190298 PMID:24806125

Furferi, Gelli, & Yarn. (2010). Strength Prediction: A Practical Model Based on Artificial Neural Networks. *Advances in Mechanical Engineering*. doi:10.1155/2010/640103

Garg, S., Patra, K., & Pal, S. K. (2014). Particle swarm optimization of a neural network model in a machining process. *Sadhana, 39*(3), 533–548. doi:10.100712046-014-0244-7

Gjylapi & Durmishie. (2014). Albania Artificial neural networks in forecasting tourists' flow, an intelligent technique to help the economic development of tourism in Albania. *Academicus - International Scientific Journal, 10*(14). Doi:10.7336/academicus.2014.10.14

Gordan, B., Armaghani, D. J., Hajihassani, M., & Monjezi, M. (2016). Prediction of seismic slope stability through combination of particle swarm optimization and neural network. *Engineering with Computers, 32*(1), 85–97. doi:10.100700366-015-0400-7

Haykin, S. S. (2001). Kalman Filtering and Neural Networks. Wiley.

Hilal, S. Y. A., & Okur, M. R. (2018). Predicting Achievement with Artificial Neural Networks: The Case of Anadolu University Open Education System. *International Journal of Assessment Tools in Education, 5*(3), 474–490. doi:10.21449/ijate.435507

Huang, H.-C., & I Hou, C. (2017). Tourism Demand Forecasting Model Using Neural Network. *International Journal of Computer Science & Information Technology*, 9(2), 19–29. doi:10.5121/ijcsit.2017.9202

Jaddi, N. S., Abdullah, S., & Hamdan, A. R. (2015). Multi-population cooperative bat algorithm-based optimization of artificial neural network model. *Journal of Information Science*, *294*, 628–644. doi:10.1016/j.ins.2014.08.050

Kalkanci, M., Kurumer, G., Öztürk, H., Sinecen, M., & Kayacan, Ö. (2017). Artificial Neural Network System for Prediction of Dimensional Properties of Cloth in Garment Manufacturing: Case Study on a T-Shirt. *Fibres & Textiles in Eastern Europe*, *4*(14), 135–140. doi:10.5604/01.3001.0010.2859

Kan, C. W., Wong, W. Y., Song, L. J., & Law, M. C. (2013). Prediction of Color Properties of Cellulase-Treated 100% Cotton Denim Fabric. *Journal of Textiles*. Advance online publication. doi:10.1155/2013/962751

Karaboga, D., Akay, B., & Ozturk, C. (2007). Artificial bee colony (ABC) optimization algorithm for training feed-forward neural networks. In *Modeling Decisions for Artificial Intelligence* (pp. 318–329). Springer. doi:10.1007/978-3-540-73729-2_30

Karaboga, D., Akay, B., & Ozturk, C. (2007). Artificial Bee Colony (ABC) Optimization Algorithm for Training Feed-Forward Neural Networks. *LNAI*, *4617*, 318–329.

Kaur, R., & Kaur, B. (2014). Artificial neural network learning enhancement using bacterial foraging optimization algorithm. *International Journal of Computers and Applications*, *102*(10), 27–33. doi:10.5120/17852-8812

Kose, U. (2018). An Ant-Lion Optimizer-Trained Artificial Neural Network System for Chaotic Electroencephalogram (EEG). *Prediction. Appl. Sci.*, *8*(9), 1613. Advance online publication. doi:10.3390/app8091613

Kuoa, J.-T., Wanga, Y.-Y., & Lungb, W.-S. (2006). A hybrid neural–genetic algorithm for reservoir water quality management. *Water Research*, *40*(7), 1367–1376. doi:10.1016/j.watres.2006.01.046 PMID:16545860

Lau, Sun, & Yang. (2019). SN Modelling, prediction and classification of student academic performance using artificial neural networks. *Applied Sciences, 1*, 982-989. doi:10.100742452-019-0884-7

Li, H. (2019). Network traffic prediction of the optimized BP neural network based on Glowworm Swarm Algorithm. *Systems Science & Control Engineering.*, *7*(2), 64–70. doi:10.1080/21642583.2019.1626299

Li, K., Lu, W., Liang, C., & Wang, B. (2019). Intelligence in Tourism Management: A Hybrid FOA-BP Method on Daily Tourism Demand Forecasting with Web Search Data. *Mathematics*, *7*(6), 531–542. doi:10.3390/math7060531

Majumdar, A., Das, A., Hatua, P., & Ghosh, A. (2015). *Optimization of woven fabric parameters for ultraviolet radiation protection and comfort using artificial neural network and genetic algorithm.* Neural Comput & Applic. doi:10.100700521-015-2025-6

Malik, S. (2019). Optimal Travel Route Recommendation Mechanism Based on Neural Networks and Particle Swarm Optimization for Efficient Tourism Using Tourist. *Sustainability*, *11*, 3357. doi:10.3390u11123357

Martínez-Porchas, M., Villalpando-Canchola, E., & Vargas-Albores, F. (2016). Significant loss of sensitivity and specificity in the taxonomic classification occurs when short 16S rRNA gene sequences are used. *Heliyon, 2*(9), e00170. doi:10.1016/j.heliyon.2016.e00170 PMID:27699286

Mason, C., Twomey, J., Wright, D., & Whitman, L. (2017). Predicting Engineering Student Attrition Risk Using a Probabilistic Neural Network and Comparing Results with a Backpropagation Neural Network and Logistic Regression. *Research in Higher Education*. Advance online publication. doi:10.100711162-017-9473-z

Mavrovouniotis & Yang. (2014). *Training neural networks with ant colony optimization algorithms For pattern classification*. Springer-Verlag.

Mei, Y., Yang, J., Lu, Y., Hao, F., Xu, D., Pan, H., & Wang, J. (2019). BP–ANN Model Coupled with Particle Swarm Optimization for the Efficient Prediction of 2-Chlorophenol Removal in an Electro-Oxidation System. *International Journal of Environmental Research and Public Health, 16*(14), 2454. doi:10.3390/ijerph16142454 PMID:31295918

Mei & Wang. (2009). Ant Colony Optimization for Neural Network. *Key Engineering Materials, 392*, 677-681.

Mirjalili, S. (2015). How effective is the Grey Wolf optimizer in training multi-layer perceptrons. *Applied Intelligence, 43*(1), 150–161. doi:10.100710489-014-0645-7

Mirjalili, S., Mirjalili, S. M., & Lewis, A. (2014). Grey wolf optimizer. *Advances in Engineering Software, 69*, 46–61. doi:10.1016/j.advengsoft.2013.12.007

Mirjalili, S., Mirjalili, S. M., & Lewis, A. (2014). Let a biogeography-based optimizer train your Multi-Layer Perceptron. *Information Sciences, 269*, 188–209. doi:10.1016/j.ins.2014.01.038

Monjezi, Amini Khoshalan, Yazdian, Arab, & Geosci. (2012). Prediction of flyrock and backbreak in open pit blasting operation. *A Neuro-Genetic Approach, 5*, 441–448. DOI doi:10.100712517-010-0185-3

Motahari. (2017, January). Development of a PSO-ANN Model for Rainfall-Runoff Response in Basins, Case Study: Karaj Basin, Civil. *Engineering Journal (New York), 3*(1), 35–44.

Nandy, S., Sarkar, P. P., & Das, A. (2012). Analysis of a nature inspired firefly algorithm based back-propagation neural network training. *International Journal of Computers and Applications, 43*, 8–16. doi:10.5120/6401-8339

Nawi, N. M., Khan, A., & Rehman, M. Z. (2013). New back-propagation neural network optimized with cuckoo search algorithm. *Proc. Int. conf. Computational Science and Its Applications, ICCSA-2013*, 413-426. 10.1007/978-3-642-39637-3_33

Nawi, N. M., Khan, A., & Rehman, M. Z. (2014). *Data classification using metaheuristic Cuckoo Search technique for Levenberg Marquardt back propagation (CSLM) algorithm*. AIP Conference Proceedings.

Nawi, N. M., Rehman, M. Z., & Khan, A. (2014). A new bat based back-propagation (BAT-BP) algorithm. In J. Swiatek, A. Grzech, P. Swiatek, & J. Tomczak (Eds.), *Advances in Systems Science, Advances in Intelligent Systems and Computing* (pp. 395–404). Springer. doi:10.1007/978-3-319-01857-7_38

Noersasongko, E., Julfia, F. T., Syukur, A., Purwanto, R. A. P., & Supriyanto, C. (2016, January). A Tourism Arrival Forecasting using Genetic Algorithm based Neural Network. *Indian Journal of Science and Technology, 9*(4). Advance online publication. doi:10.17485/ijst/2016/v9i4/78722

Oancea, B., Dragoescu, R., & Ciucu, S. (2017). *Predicting students' results in higher education using a neural network.* https://mpra.ub.uni-muenchen.de/72041/

Obeid. (2018). Optimizing Neural Networks using Dragonfly Algorithm for Medical Prediction. *2018 8th International Conference on Computer Science and Information Technology (CSIT).*

Ojha, Abraham, & Sn'aˇsel. (2017). *Simultaneous Optimization of Neural Network Weights and Active Nodes using Metaheuristics.* arxiv:1707.01810v1

Özdemir & Polat. (2017). Forecasting With Artificial Neural Network Of Science Teachers. *Professional Burnout Variables. Int. J. Educ. Stud., 04*(03), 49–64.

Ozkan, Ozturky, Sunarz, & Karaboga. (2011). The artificial bee colony algorithm In training artificial neural Network for oil spill detection. *ICS AS CR 2011.*

Ozturk & Karaboga. (2011). *Hybrid Artificial Bee Colony Algorithm For Neural Network Training.* IEEE.

Rashedi, E., Nezamabadi-pour, H., & Saryazdi, S. (2009). GSA: A gravitational search algorithm. *Information Sciences, 179*(13), 2232–2248. doi:10.1016/j.ins.2009.03.004

Raval, D., Bhatt, D., Kumhar, M. K., Parikh, V., & Vyas, D. (2016). Medical diagnosis system using machine learning. *International Journal of Computer Science & Communication, 7*(1), 177–182.

Sadeghyan & Asadi. (2010). *Ms-baco: a new model selection algorithm using binary ant Colony optimization for neural complexity and error reduction.* Academic Press.

Saghatforoush, A., Monjezi, M., Shirani, R., & Faradonbeh, D. J. A. (2007). Combination of neural network and ant colony optimization algorithms for prediction and optimization of flyrock and back-break induced by blasting. *Engineering with Computers.* Advance online publication. doi:10.100700366-015-0415-0

Saha, S., Chakraborty, D., & Dutta, O. (2014). Guided convergence for training feed-forward neural network using novel gravitational search optimization. *Proc. 2014 International Conference on High Performance Computing and Applications (ICHPCA)*, 1-6. 10.1109/ICHPCA.2014.7045348

Salama, K., & Abdelbar, A. M. (2014). A Novel Ant Colony Algorithm for Building Neural Network Topologies. *Springer International Publishing Switzerland LNCS, 8667*, 1–12. doi:10.1007/978-3-319-09952-1_1

Saravanan, K., & Sasithra, S. (2014). Review on classification based on artificial neural networks. *Int. J. Ambient Syst. Appl., 2*(4), 11–18.

Sathish, T. (2018). Prediction of springback effect by the hybridisation of ANN with PSO in wipe bending process of sheet metal. Progress in Industrial Ecology –. *International Journal (Toronto, Ont.), 12*(1), 112–119.

Semero, Y. K., Zhang, J., Zheng, D., & Wei, D. (2018). A GA-PSO Hybrid Algorithm Based Neural Network Modeling Technique for Short-term Wind Power Forecasting. *Distributed Generation & Alternative Energy Journal*, *33*(4), 26–43. doi:10.1080/21563306.2018.12029913

Shadika & Rendra. (2017). Optimizing Woven Curtain Fabric Defect Classification using Image Processing with Artificial Neural Network Method at PT Buana Intan Gemilang. *MATEC Web of Conferences, 135*. Doi:10.1051/matecconf/201713500052

Sharma, K., Gupta, P., & Sharma, H. (2015). Fully informed artificial bee colony algorithm. *Journal of Experimental & Theoretical Artificial Intelligence*, *281*, 403–416.

Sheng, Z., Xiuyu, S., & Wei, W. (2010). An ann model of optimizing activation Functions based on constructive algorithm and gp. In *Computer Application And System Modeling (ICCASM), 2010 International Conference On*, 420–424.

Shi, X. (2019). Tourism culture and demand forecasting based on BPNN mining algorithms. *Personal and Ubiquitous Computing*. Advance online publication. doi:10.100700779-019-01325-x

Sivagaminathan, R. K., & Ramakrishnan, S. (2007). A hybrid approach for feature subset selection using neural Networks and ant colony optimization. *Expert Systems with Applications*, *33*(1), 49–60. doi:10.1016/j.eswa.2006.04.010

Socha & Blum. (2007). An ant colony optimization algorithm for continuous Optimization: application to feed-forward neural network. *Neural Comput & Applic.*, (16), 235–247. DOI doi:10.100700521-007-0084-z

Srisaeng, P., & Baxter, G. (2017). Modelling Australia's Outbound Passenger Air Travel Demand Using An Artificial Neural Network Approach. *International Journal for Traffic and Transport Engineering*, *7*(4), 406–423. doi:10.7708/ijtte.2017.7(4).01]

Stamos, T. Karamouzis and Andreas Vrettos. (2008). An Artificial Neural Network for Predicting Student Graduation Outcomes. *Proceedings of the World Congress on Engineering and Computer Science*.

Suknovic, M., & Isljamovic, S. (2014). Predicting Students' Academic Performance Using Artificial Neural Network: A Case Study From Faculty Of Organizational Sciences. *The Eurasia Proceedings of Educational & Social Sciences (EPESS)*, 68-72.

Taieb, A. H., Mshali, S., & Sakli, F. (2018). Predicting Fabric Drapability Property by Using an Artificial Neural Network. *Journal of Engineered Fibers and Fabrics*, *13*(3). Advance online publication. doi:10.1177/155892501801300310

Tang, R., Fong, S., Yang, X. S., & Deb, S. (2014). Wolf search algorithm with ephemeral memory. *Proc. Seventh International Conference on Digital Information Management (ICDIM 2012)*, 165-172.

Valian, E., Mohanna, S., & Tavakoli, S. (2011). Improved cuckoo search algorithm for feedforward neural network training. *Int. J. of Artificial Intelligence & Applications*, *2*. Advance online publication. doi:10.5121/ijaia.2011.2304

Wang, M., Zhang, H., & Wu, Z. (2019). Forecast and Application of GA Optimization BP Neural Network Tourism Demand in High-speed Railway Era. *IOP Conf. Series: Materials Science and Engineering, 569.* doi:10.1088/1757-899X/569/4/042053

Weingaertner, D., Tatai, V. K., Gudwin, R. R., & Von Zuben, F. J. (2002). Hierarchical evolution of heterogeneous neural networks. in Evolutionary Computation, CEC'02. *Proceedings of the 2002 Congress On, 2,* 1775–1780.

Yamany, W., Fawzy, M., Tharwat, A., & Hassanien, A. E. (2015). Moth-flame optimization for training Multi-Layer Perceptrons. *Proc. 2015 11th International Computer Engineering Conference (ICENCO),* 267-272. 10.1109/ICENCO.2015.7416360

Yang. (2013). *Evolving Neural Networks using Ant Colony Optimization with Pheromone Trail Limits.* IEEE.

Yi, Xu, & Chen. (2014). *Novel Back Propagation Optimization by Cuckoo Search Algorithm.* Hindawi Publishing Corporation. doi:10.1155/2014/878262

Yu, J. J. Q., Lam, A. Y. S., & Li, V. O. K. (2015). Evolutionary artificial neural network based on chemical reaction optimization. *Proc. IEEE Congress of Evolutionary Computation (CEC),* 2083-2090.

Yu, W., He, H., & Zhang, N. (2009). Advances in Neural Networks. *ISNN 2009 6th International Symposium.*

Zacharis, N. Z. (2016). Predicting Student Academic Performance In Blended Learning Using Artificial Neural Networks. *International Journal of Artificial Intelligence and Applications, 7*(5). Advance online publication. doi:10.5121/ijaia.2016.7502

Zhang, C., & Shao, H. (2000). An ANN's Evolved by a New Evolutionary System and Its Application. *Proceedings of the 39th IEEE Conference on Decision and Control, 4*(1), 3562-3563. 10.1109/CDC.2000.912257

This research was previously published in Applications of Artificial Neural Networks for Nonlinear Data; pages 227-269, copyright year 2021 by Engineering Science Reference (an imprint of IGI Global).

Chapter 9
Evaluation of Parameter Settings for Training Neural Networks Using Backpropagation Algorithms:
A Study With Clinical Datasets

Leema N.
Anna University, Chennai, India

Khanna H. Nehemiah
Anna University, Chennai, India

Elgin Christo V. R.
Anna University, Chennai, India

Kannan A.
Anna University, Chennai, India

ABSTRACT

Artificial neural networks (ANN) are widely used for classification, and the training algorithm commonly used is the backpropagation (BP) algorithm. The major bottleneck faced in the backpropagation neural network training is in fixing the appropriate values for network parameters. The network parameters are initial weights, biases, activation function, number of hidden layers and the number of neurons per hidden layer, number of training epochs, learning rate, minimum error, and momentum term for the classification task. The objective of this work is to investigate the performance of 12 different BP algorithms with the impact of variations in network parameter values for the neural network training. The algorithms were evaluated with different training and testing samples taken from the three benchmark clinical datasets, namely, Pima Indian Diabetes (PID), Hepatitis, and Wisconsin Breast Cancer (WBC) dataset obtained from the University of California Irvine (UCI) machine learning repository.

DOI: 10.4018/978-1-6684-2408-7.ch009

INTRODUCTION

Researchers aim to build a computing system that will operate intelligently like a human brain. The Artificial Neural Network (ANN) facilitates the information processing in an intelligent manner (Akinyokun, 2002; Bezdek, 1993), and is inspired by the biological neural system. A biological nervous system is a large interconnection of neurons located within the brain. The functional equivalent of an artificial neuron is known as computational neuron or a node (Eluyode, Akomolafe & MNCS, 2013). These neurons are structured hierarchically by layers and interconnected between them like the biological nervous systems. Artificial neural network determines the rate of adjustment required for internal network parameters. This adjustment is known as learning or training the network. The neuron functions are described by the activation function. Activation functions are used in the hidden and the output layer. Hidden layer implements the non-linear activation function, whereas the output layer implements the linear activation function. Linear activation function used in neural network training is purelin and the non-linear activation functions are hardlim, sigmoid and logistic (Sharma, 2014).

Parameters of both biological and Artificial Neural Networks are structures, layers, number of neurons, the functional capabilities of neurons, their learning capabilities, processing elements, connections, strength, processing speed, style of computation, information storage, signal transduction, information transmission communication media selection and fault tolerance. Major difficulty faced in correlating artificial neural networks with biological neural networks are adjusting weights and synaptic strengths. Weights are altered mathematically in an ANN, based on differences in error values. Synaptic strengths are modified in response to synaptic activity. A simple feed-forward system behaves similar to biological neurons and they are used for pattern recognition. Once input values are given to the input layer, neuron computes the output, layer by layer. The dependence of output values and input values require adjusting every weight, and threshold, which can be complex and time consuming. After training is complete, the network is able to give reasonable outputs for any type of input, even if the test data does not match with the training data. This is referred to as the generalization capability of the network. In that case, the ANN attempts to determine the best output depending on its training method.

Based on the structure, ANN is divided into two types, namely, single layer neural network and multilayer neural network. Single layer neural network is used for linearly separable problems, whereas the multilayer neural network is used for linearly non separable problems. One major drawback of a single layer network is that it can predict the output, which is similar to the input pattern. For many practical problems, very similar input patterns may have very different output requirements (FFNN, 2010). To overcome the above limitation multilayer neural network has been developed with one or more hidden layers, called multi-layer perceptron (MLP) networks. Hidden layer in the MLP is used to deal with nonlinear relationships between input features and the output layer is used to obtain the predicted output. This MLP can be used to solve many real world problems like predicting the future trends based on the historical data (Kosko, 1994.). ANN have been implemented in many science and engineering fields such as, decision making and control, biological modeling, health care and medicine, marketing, engineering and manufacturing for classification task (Krasnopolsky & Dé ricChevallier, 2003; Coppin, 2004; Basheer & Hajmeer, 20007; He, Wu & Gong, 1992).

In machine learning, Backpropagation (BP) is a supervised learning algorithm for training the Artificial Neural Network (ANN). Most of the researchers used different BP algorithms to train ANN without knowing the performance of different BP algorithms and network parameter adjustments. Backpropagation training algorithms receive the inputs, adjust the weights and produce the required output.

The commonly used supervised training algorithm is gradient descent backpropagation in which the weights are altered based on the quadratic error function (Rumelhart, Hinton & Wiliams, 1986b). The BP algorithm is a universal approximator, which can approximate any smooth function to an arbitrary degree of accuracy, when the network parameters are optimized. Hence the training process needs the appropriate combination of network parameters to obtain higher accuracy in classification. ANN is usually designed for specific applications such as data classification, pattern recognition, optimization, time series prediction, curve fitting, sensitivity analysis, dynamic modeling and the control of systems over time (Rajasekaran & Pai, 2003).

This work provides the comparative study and discusses the impact of various network parameter combinations using twelve different backpropagation training algorithms. The different combination of network parameters was tested. For each combination, training was carried out ten times, and minimum mean squared error was found out. The performance of each BP trained network is evaluated based on the accuracy, convergence rate and MSE. From the evaluation results, the most appropriate combination of network parameters and the best type of BP algorithm are identified.

The rest of the paper is organized as follows: Section 2 presents an overview of related research. Section 3 provides necessary background materials and methods used in the comparative study carried out. The implementation and comparative analysis of the results are discussed in section 4. Section 5 deals with conclusions and scope for future work.

RELATED WORK

Related works carried out by researchers using backpropagation algorithm for training the neural network is discussed below.

Rosenblatt (1958) developed a hypothetical nervous system called perceptron, that answered the questions of "how the information about physical world is sensed", "in what form, the information is remembered" and "how does the information retained in memory influence recognition". This work provides the relationship between psychology and biophysics and predicts the learning curves from neurological variables and vice versa. Rumelhart, Hinton & Wiliams (1986a) introduced a multilayer feed forward network with an error backpropagation method to train the network. The algorithm back-propagates the error repeatedly by adjusting the weights in the network. The weight adjustments to the hidden nodes are independent of input and output features.

Verma & Mulawka (1994) developed a modified Backpropagation (BP) algorithm, which was based on solving the weight matrix in the output layer using the theory of equations and least square techniques. This overcomes the drawback of long training process in the BP algorithm. Drago, Morando & Ridella(1995) developed an adaptive momentum BP algorithm for achieving fast minimum search. In this work, the network weight updation rule is chosen to accelerate the faster convergence in the training process using adaptive momentum term to reduce the error function. This achieves high convergence speed and generalization of the network.

Bossan, Seixas, Caloba,Penha & Nadal(1995) developed a modified BP algorithm for neural classifiers. This method reduced the time to achieve the low Mean Squared Error, by ignoring patterns in the sparse regions in very populated regions of the pattern space until a large number of training epochs occurred. Yu & Chen (1997) considered efficient BP learning using dynamically optimal learning rate and momentum factor. This approach uses the products with respect to the momentum factor and learning rate. The learning rate and momentum term were adjusted using conjugate gradient method at each iteration to reduce the training time. This provides faster convergence to achieve the low mean squared error.

Fukuoka, Matsuki,Minamitani & Ishida (1998) modified the BP algorithm to avoid local minima. The modification is done by multiplying a factor within the range of (0,1) at a constant interval of each connected weight in a network during the training process. This method uses sigmoid activation function when the error rate is high. This overcomes the problem of local minima. Ng, Leung & Luk(1999) developed the generalized BP algorithm with constant learning rate. The network weights in the generalized BP algorithm are approximated by using OrdinaryDifferential Equation (ODE).When the learning rate increases from zero, the generalized backpropagation algorithm provides faster convergence and overcomes the local minima problem.

Zweiri, Whidborne & Seneviratne (2003) introduced a third term in BP algorithm for ANN training. The existing BP algorithm uses two terms for training namely, learning rate and momentum factor. The author introduced the third term named as proportional factor, which speedup the weight updating process. This overcomes the slow convergence and local minima problem of the existing BP algorithm. Zhang & Suganthan (2016) did a survey on training neural networks using randomized algorithms. The drawback of the existing neural network training algorithms is that it tunes the parameters iteratively. This suffers from local minima and slow convergence. This training approach uses randomization either to change the data distribution or to change network configuration.

Christopher, Nehemiah & Kannan (2015) developed a rule based clinical decision support system to diagnose the presence or absence of allergic rhinitis. The developed clinical decision support system is based on the results of an intradermal skin test. This framework compares the efficiency of five traditional classification approaches namely, k-nearest neighbourclassifier (KNN), Decision tree classifier (C4.5), Multi-layer perceptron classifier Support Vector Machine and Naïve Bayes classifier (NB). The rule based approach presents the knowledge model in an IF-THEN rule format. As rule based Clinical Decision Support System (CDSS) provides better comprehensibility than other classification approaches, physicians prefer them.The clinical decision support system achieved an accuracy of 88.31% for diagnosis of allergic rhinitis. Furthermore, the clinical decision support system can be used as an aid for decision support for junior clinicians in the absence of allergy specialist.

Nahato, Nehemiah & Kannan (2016) developed a classifier which combines fuzzy logic and Extreme Learning Machine (ELM). The classifier was tested with UCI machine learning repository datasets namely, Cleveland Heart disease (CHD), Pima Indian Diabetes (PID) and Statlog Heart Disease (SHD). The datasets were preprocessed by using the nearest neighbor method based on Euclidian distance. Fuzzification of selected features was done using Trapezoidal Membership Function. The ELM uses single hidden layer feed forward neural network for classification. The classifier achieved 73.77%, 93.55%, 94.44% and 92.54% accuracies for CHD with five class labels, CHD with two class labels SHD and PID datasets respectively.

Nahato, Nehemiah & Kannan (2015) used rough set with backpropagation neural network for classification of clinical datasets. The clinical datasets were obtained from the University of California Irvine (UCI) machine learning repository. Missing values from the clinical dataset was handled by either imputing or rejecting based on the percentage of the missing values. Handling missing values and selection of attributes are performed using indiscernibility relation. The selected attributes are used to train back propagation neural network. The network is a single hidden layer feed forward neural network having Tangent sigmoid activation function applied to the hidden neuron and linear activation function applied to the output neuron. The accuracy obtained from their proposed method is 97.3%, 98.6%, and 90.4% for hepatitis, Wisconsin Breast Cancer, and Cleveland Heart Disease datasets respectively.

Leema, Nehemiah & Kannan (2016) developed a optimization technique for training neural network using differential evolution with global information (DEGI) with BP algorithm for clinical datasets. The DEGI was developed by drawing the relative advantages of particle swarm optimization's (PSO) global search ability and differential evolution's modified mutation operation is used to improve the search exploration of PSO. The DEGI algorithm is used for global search and the BP algorithm is used for local search. This optimization technique overcomes drawback of the local minima problem of BP and premature convergence due to stagnation problem of PSO. The classifier performance was tested using three datasets namely, Pima Indian Diabetes, Cleveland Heart Disease and Wisconsin Breast Cancer obtained from the UCI machine learning repository. The developed classifier provides 98.52%, 85.71% and 86.66% of accuracies for the above datasets.

Elgin, Nehemiah, Minu & Kannan (2019)developed a framework for clinical decision support system (CDSS) which uses Correlation based ensemble feature selection and gradient descent back propagation neural network for classification. The Hot deck imputation has been used for handling missing values and min max-normalization was used to transformation. Correlation based ensemble feature selector is performed to get the optimal feature set by the rejection of high similarity features from majority voting on the output of Differential evolution, LION optimization and glow-worm swarm optimization. The CDSS was experimented on Hepatitis dataset and Wisconsin Diagnostic Breast Cancer (WDBC) dataset from University of California Irvine (UCI) Machine Learning repository and was observed that it was obtained an accuracy of 95.51% for Hepatitis and 98.47% WDBC.

Wu, Zhao, Zhang, Sang, Dong, & Jiang (2020, January) proposed a framework for diagnosing early diabetic retinopathy detection using back-propagation artificial neural network (BP-ANN) improved by a priori knowledge. The retinal blood vessels are segmented using a fuzzy clustering algorithm based on texture features. Based on the a priori knowledge obtained from the experienced ophthalmologists, geometric features of blood vessels namely, width and tortuosity are extracted. A total of 72 retinal vessel features were extracted and are classified using an Improved BP Neural Network Classifier. A total of 240 fundus images were used for experimentation which were obtained from 120 early-stage DR and 120 normal participants. The average accuracy of 10 randomization tests with different hidden neurons based on BP-ANN were obtained. The maximum accuracy obtained for BP-ANN using a priori knowledge was 98.46%.

Geetha, Aprameya & Hinduja (2020) proposed a diagnostic system for diagnosing dental caries from digital radiographs. The framework comprised of preprocessing steps such as Laplacian filtering, window based adaptive threshold, morphological operations, statistical feature extraction. Back propagation neural network used to classify a tooth surface as normal or having dental caries. The dataset consists of 49 caries and 56 sound dental X-ray images obtained from SJM Dental College Chitradurga, India using intra oral Gendex X-ray machine with RVG sensor was experimented. The system achieved an accuracy of 97.1%.

Sudha (2017) developed a CDSS that uses Genetic algorithm based rough set method for selecting relevant features and Back Propagation Neural Network for classification. The CDSS named as Application Specific Intelligent Computing (ASIC) decision support system. The CDSS has been tested with breast cancer, fertility diagnosis and heart disease data set from UCI machine learning repository. Sigmoid function is used as the activation function and MSE is used the fitness function for BPNN. The CDSS provides 93%, 97.61% and 92.3% for the above datasets respectively.

Helwan, Idoko & Abiyev (2017) proposed an automated Breast tissue classifier using two different neural networks namely feed forward neural network using the Backpropagation learning algorithm (BPNN) and Radial Basis Function Network (RBFN) . Breast Tissue dataset from the UCI machine learning repository is used for experimentation. Feature selection is performed through a filter approach by computing the information gain. Seventy percentage of the samples were used for training and thirty percentage for testing. The performance of BPNN and RBFN are compared in terms of accuracy. The classification accuracies obtained from the BPNN and RBFN are 93.39% and 94.33% respectively. It can be inferred that the Radial basis function network outperformed the back propagation network for classifying six different breast tissues. The performance of the classifier is measured in terms of accuracy, minimum error, maximum epochs and training time.

Desai, Giraddi, Narayankar, Pudakalakatti & Sulegaon (2019) performed a comparison of two classifiers namely BPNN and Logistic Regression (LR). The performance of the classifier is tested with Cleveland Hear Disease (CHD) dataset obtained from UCI machine learning repository. The accuracies of the classifier is 85.074% and 92.58% for BPNN (nonparametric) and LR (parametric) models, respectively. The BPNN used MSE as the optimization function with 10-fold cross validation.

Ravindra, Sriraam & Geetha (2018, February) in their work have developed a BPNN classifier for the diagnosis of Chronic Kidney Disease. Details of 230 patients collected from a local hospital in Karnataka, India is used for experimentation. The objective of the work is to discriminate between chronic kidney disease and non-chronic kidney disease. The BPNN is used MSE as the optimization function and Tan-sigmoid as the activation function. Levenberg-marquardt back propagation algorithm is used for the training of neural network. The developed method provides an accuracy of 95.3% for the diagnosis of Chronic Kidney Disease.

Tarle & Jena (2017, August) have proposed a BPNN for the diagnosis of heart disease. Experiments were conducted on CHD dataset from UCI machine learning repository. The BPNN used sigmoid function as the activation function and MSE as the optimization criterion. Min-max Normalization was used to normalize the dataset. The performance of the classifier is evaluated using Five-fold cross validation. The accuracy obtained from their proposed method is 83% for CHD dataset.

Paing, Hamamoto, Tungjitkusolmun & Pintavirooj (2019) in their work, have proposed a Computer Aided Diagnosis (CAD) system for detecting and staging lung cancer from computedtomography (CT) images. The proposed CAD system has two stages of classification; the first stage discriminate the true tumour nodules from other false lesions. The second stage intents to classify the associated stages of the truly predicted tumours. The proposed CAD was developed and tested using 1560 CT exams from four popular public datasets: LIDC-IDRI, NSCLC-Radiomics-Genomics, NSCLC-Radiomics and NSCLC Radio genomics. The BPNN is used in both the stages of classification. The developed CAD achieved a detection accuracy of 92.8%, a sensitivity of 93.6%, a specificity of 91.8%, a precision of 91.8%, a F-score of 92.8%, and an AUC of 96.8%. For the staging, the proposed CAD achieved an accuracy of 90.6%, a sensitivity of 77.4%, a specificity of 97.4%, a precision of 93.8%, an F1-score of 79.6% and an AUC of 84.6% respectively.

Agharezaei, Agharezaei, Nemati, Bahaadinbeigy, Keynia, Baneshi & Agharezaei (2016) proposed a CDSS to assist diagnosis and prediction of the risk level of pulmonary embolism in patients, by means of artificial neural network. Two types of artificial neural networks, namely Feed-Forward Back Propagation and Elman Back Propagation were used for the research. 294 Patients admitted in educational hospitals affiliated with Kerman University of Medical Sciences, located in the south eastern Iran were used for experimentation. 80 percent of the dataset is randomly assigned as training data and 20 percent is assigned as testing data. Both Feed-Forward Back Propagation and Elman Back Propagation ended up with the same performance (93.23% accuracy). The advantage of Feed-Forward Back Propagation Network has a higher convergence speed and requires fewer neurons in its hidden layer.

This work provides a comparative study on variations in various network parameters using different BP algorithms. The training algorithms are tested using three clinical datasets obtained from the UCI machine learning repository. The experimental results show, which combination of network parameter values and the training algorithms provides faster convergence and minimum error in the classification process.

MATERIALS AND METHODS

In this section, the materials and methods that have been used to investigate the performance of twelve different BP algorithms with the impact of variations in network parameter values for neural network training are discussed.

Mean Square Error

The MSE computes the difference between the neural network output and the target value. The main objective of ANN training is to minimize the MSE and improve the ability of classification. The MSE (E_k) is computed using Equation (1):

$$E_k = \sum_{i=1}^{O} \left(z_i^k - C_i^k \right)^2 \tag{1}$$

where z_i^k is the neural network output from the network, C_i^k is the target output and E_k is the mean squared error of the network. The error is backpropagated until minimum mean square error is achieved. Although several algorithms are used to train the ANN, most commonly used supervised algorithm is backpropagation algorithm.

Backpropagation (BP) Algorithms

BP algorithm was introduced by Rumelhart, Hinton and Wiliams (1986a). BP algorithm is a supervised learning algorithm for training the ANN. The BP training includes the following steps: initialization of weights, MSE computation, optimization of weights and backpropagation of errors. The BP algorithm is classified into two types namely, faster and slower training algorithms (Bezdek, 1993.). The faster training algorithms falls into two main categories, namely, heuristic and standard numerical optimization. Heuristic techniques are developed from the performance analysis of the standard steepest descent algorithm.

The heuristic techniques are further divided into two types, namely, Gradient Descent with variable learning rate BP and Resilient BP. The standard numerical optimization algorithms are divided into three types such as, Conjugate Gradient algorithms, Quasi Newton and Levenberg-Marquardt. The Conjugate

Gradient algorithms are further divided into four types namely, Conjugate Gradient backpropagation with Fletcher-Reeves updates, Conjugate Gradient backpropagation with Polak-Ribiere updates and Conjugate Gradient backpropagation with Powell-Beale Restarts and Scaled Conjugate Gradient. The Quasi Newton algorithm is further divided into two types such as BFGS algorithm and One Step Secant algorithm.

The slower training algorithms are gradient descent algorithms and are not used for solving practical problems, because the training process is very slow. The gradient descent algorithms has two modes, they are, incremental mode and batch mode. The input is applied to the network and then, the weights are updated and gradient is computed in the incremental mode of training. In the batch mode of training, all inputs are applied before the network weights are updated. The BP training strongly depends on the network parameters and training algorithms (Eluyode, Akomolafe & MNCS, 2013).

ANN Parameters

The ANN parameters used to train BPNN are namely, initial weights and biases, number of hidden layers and the number of neurons per hidden layer, activation function, number of training epochs, learning rate, minimum error and momentum term. Selection of optimal set of initial weights and biases for training the neural network reduces the training time and initial error. Hidden layer is used to solve complex non-linearly separable problem.

Multiple hidden layers and the number of neurons in the hidden layer are used, when accuracy is the main criteria and there is no limitation for the complexity of the network and training time. During training, the learning rate controls the rate of change in weights and biases of the network. Momentum parameter prevents the system from converging to local minima. The activation function determines the complexity and performance of the network. It plays a major role in the convergence of the learning algorithms. If the network parameters are not chosen properly, then the network slows down the training process.

Initial Weight Selection

The training algorithms are very sensitive to the random selection of initial weight values. Selection of an optimal set of initial weight values for neural network training reduces the training time and initial error. Training iterations are reduced, if the initial weights chosen are closer to the true minimum. An inappropriate choice of initial weights leads to getting stuck in local minima.

Researchers introduced several weight initialization techniques. Yam & Chow (2000) implemented a weight initialization technique for feed forward networks based on a linear algebraic method and Cauchy's inequality. This method ensures the hidden neuron's output is in the active region, which means the activation function's derivative has a larger value. When the optimal initial weights are chosen, this method reduces the initial error and increases the convergence rate. Hence the number of iterations to reach the error criterion is significantly reduced.

Masters (1993) used least square method for weight initialization. The researcher had used neural networks with one hidden layer and the weights between input and hidden layer are initialized by using simulated annealing and genetic algorithm. The output layer weights are calculated using singular value decomposition. Nguyen &Widrow (1990) developed an algorithm for weight initialization where all the hidden nodes are scattered uniformly in the input space, which results in substantial improvement of the learning speed of the network. The initial weights and biases in the region of interest are distributed by dividing into smaller intervals. As the initial weights are divided into smaller intervals, the input pattern is learned quickly by the network.

Number of Hidden Layers and Number of Neurons Per Hidden Layer

The hidden layer is an intermediate layer between the input and the output layer. Hidden layer is a collection of neurons and an activation function is applied to it. If the problem is linearly separable, then there is no need for the hidden layer. Hence an activation function is used in the input layer to solve linearly separable problems. In case of non-linearly separable problems, there is a need for one or more hidden layers with activation function applied to it. If the number of neurons in the hidden layer is too low, then underfitting occurs. If the number of neurons in the hidden layer is too high, then overfitting or memorization of the training dataset will occur (Alsmadi, Omar & Noah, 2009; Karsoliya, 2012). Different approaches have been followed by other researchers in the computation of number of hidden layers and number of neurons in each hidden layer.

Boger & Guterman (1997) suggested that the hidden layer size is $2/3^{rd}$ of the input layer. Berry & Linoff (1997) suggested that the hidden layer size should be less than twice the size of the input layer. Blum (1992) stated that the hidden layer size is in between the input layer and the output layer. Morshed & Kaluarachi (1998) demonstrated that the size of the hidden layer is $(2n+1)$, where n is the number of neurons in the input layer. The size of the hidden layer can be determined by the activation function used in the neurons, the training algorithm, the neural network architecture and training samples in the dataset. Multiple hidden layers are used in applications, where there are no limitations on training time and accuracy is the main criteria. The limitation of using multiple hidden layers in the neural network leads to the problem of local minima (Liu, Starzyk & Zhu 2007).

Activation Function

The activation function strongly influences the complexity and performance of neural networks and plays a major role in the convergence of the learning algorithms (Chandra & Singh, 2004; Duch & Jankowski1999; 2001; Saduf, 2013; Singh & Chandra, 2003.). Several activation functions are used in the ANN training such as Linear, Sigmoid, Sigmoid Stepwise, Sigmoid Symmetric, Sigmoid Symmetric Stepwise, Gaussian, Gaussian Symmetric, Elliot, Elliot Symmetric, Linear Piecewise and Linear Piece Symmetric (Sibi, Jones & Siddarth, 2013). To increase the speed of the training process, several modifications have been done by researchers in the activation functions. Masters (1993) determined that the local minima problem arises when the error saturation in the hidden layer occurs. To overcome the local minima problem, the author introduced a new algorithm by adjusting the sigmoid activation functions in the hidden layer of each neuron, which provides slight modification of weights between the hidden and the output layer. The sigmoid function is adjusted by varying the gain parameter of the hidden neurons. The gain parameter modification is done according to the degree of approximation of the desired output in the output layer.

Nguyen & Widrow (1990) introduced an improvement to the basic BP by adjusting the slope of the activation function of the output layer nodes and using different learning rates for the hidden and output layer nodes. Wang, Tang, Tamura, Ishii & Sun, (2004) implemented an algorithm for modifying the gradient based search direction by adaptively varying the slope parameter (gain) of the sigmoid function.

Learning Rate (η)

The learning rate is a tunable factor that controls the speed of the training process. The sigmoid activation function used in the BP algorithm will slow down the training process, when the output is near to 0 or 1, as the learning rate is very small and results only in a slight change in the weight adjustments. Lee, Chen & Huang (2001) found the error saturation condition is the main cause for the premature convergence. To overcome the error saturation problem, the author introduced an error saturation prevention function (ESP) which is a parabolic function to the learning rate in the nodes of the output layer. The ESP function scales up the learning rate within the range of [0, 1]. However the learning rate for the hidden layer is very small when the actual output of a unit reaches the saturation area of 0 or 1. The learning rate with constant value of 0.01 is used to overcome the above drawback (Wani, 2014). This constant value was chosen after analyzing many experimental results whereas to improve the learning speed and faster convergence.

Momentum

In BP learning, the impact of learning rate reveals that a smaller learning rate gives smaller changes of weights in the network from one iteration to the next. If the learning rate is too large, it results in larger change in weights and makes the network unstable. To overcome this problem, a momentum term (m) is added to the weight updation rule. The momentum affects the weight to be tuned in up slope instead of down slope. To overcome the above limitations in learning, researchers have introduced dynamically varying momentum term. Swanston, Bishop & Mitchell, (1994) introduced an adaptive momentum approach by considering the current negative gradient and the last weight changes. If the current weight change vector is similar in direction to the previous weight change, then the momentum term is increased. If the current weight change is in opposite direction to previous weight change, then the momentum is reduced to zero.

Limitations of BP Algorithms

'Over-fitting' or memorization of data and slow learning problems will occur, when the number of hidden layers and neurons in the hidden layer are too high. When the number of hidden layers and neurons in the hidden layer are too low, 'under-fitting' or unable to learn the data will occur. If the learning rate is too small, the learning process is done slowly and can easily get stuck in the local minima. If the learning rate is too big, instability or poor performance will occur in the network. The parameters are fixed in the network using trial and error method. Hence successful application of BPNN requires time and experience.

Data Set Description

The BP training methods has been experimented with three clinical datasets namely, Pima Indian Diabetes (PID), Hepatitis and Wisconsin Breast Cancer (WBC) dataset obtained from the UCI machine learning repository (Lichman, 2013). The description of clinical dataset is presented in Table 1 to Table 3.

Pima Indian Diabetes

The PID dataset is the result of a research survey carried out in the National Institute of Diabetes and Digestive and Kidney Diseases (NIDDK), United States. PID dataset samples are taken from Pima Indian Heritage, which contains the details of female patients having gestational diabetes of age group greater than 21 years. The dataset samples were collected during the first trimester of pregnancy.The PID data set has 768 samples with eight features and one class label is associated with each sample to indicate whether the individual is affected with Gestational diabetes or not. Among 768 samples collected, 268 samples (34.9%) had been diagnosed with Gestational diabetes and 500 samples (65.1%) without Gestational diabetes. The description of the attributes in PID dataset is shown in Table 1.

Table 1. Description of attributes in Pima Indian Diabetes Dataset

S.No.	Attribute	Description
1	Preg	Number of pregnancies
2	Plas	Plasma glucose concentration in an oral glucose tolerance test
3	Pres	Diastolic blood pressure
4	Skin	Triceps skin fold thickness
5	Insu	2-Hour serum insulin
6	Mass	Body mass index
7	Pedi	Diabetes pedigree function
8	Age	Age of an individual
	Class	Tested positive / negative

Hepatitis

Hepatitis dataset was donated by the Jozef Stefan Institute. Hepatitis dataset consist of 155 instances with 19 features including class label.The class label Histology describes whether the patient with hepatitis will live or not. The dataset has 123 instances with 'Live' class and 32 instances with 'Die' class. Six features have numerical data type and the remaining thirteen attributes have binary data type. The description of attributes in the Hepatitis dataset is shown in Table 2.

Wisconsin Breast Cancer

Wisconsin Breast Cancer (WBC) dataset has been created by Dr. William H. Wolberg from the University of Wisconsin hospitals. The WBC dataset has 699 instances with nine features from breast fine needle aspiration. The class label for an instance can be Malignant (Cancerous) and Benign (non cancerous). The dataset has 241 instances with malignant class and 458 instances with benign class. All features have numerical data type ranging from 1 to 10. The description of attributes in the WBC dataset is shown in Table 3.

Table 2. Description of attributes in Hepatitis Dataset

S.No.	Attribute	Description
1	Age	Age of an individual
2	Sex	Gender
3	Steroid	Use of anabolic steroids
4	Antivirals	Use of Anti-virals
5	Fatigue	Extreme tiredness
6	Malaise	A vague feeling of bodily discomfort
7	Anorexia	Lack or loss of appetite for food
8	Liver big	Enlargement of Liver
9	Liver firm	Firmness of the liver
10	Spleen palpable	Enlargement of spleen
11	Spiders	Blood vessels near the skin's surface due to the increased estrogen levels
12	Ascites	Accumulation of fluid in the peritoneal cavity
13	Varices	Bleeding from varices
14	Bilirubin	Amount of bilirubin in a blood sample
15	Alk phosphate	Level of alkaline phosphatase
16	SGOT	Amount of serum glutamic oxaloacetic transaminase in blood
17	Albumin	Amount of serum albumin protein in the clear liquid portion of the blood.
18	Protime	Time taken for blood plasma to clot
	Histology	Die or Live

Table 3. Description of attributes in Wisconsin Breast Cancer Dataset

S.No.	Attribute	Description
1	Clump Thickness	Assesses if cells are mono or multi-layered.
2	Uniformity of Cell Size	Evaluates the consistency in size of the cells in the sample.
3	Uniformity of Cell Shape	Estimates the equality of cell shapes and identifies marginal variances.
4	Marginal Adhesion	Quantifies how much cells on the outside of the epithelium tend to stick together.
5	Single Epithelial Cell Size	Relates to cell uniformity, determines if epithelial cells are significantly enlarged.
6	Bare Nuclei	Presence and size of nuclei
7	Bland Chromatin	Rates the uniform "texture" of the nucleus in a range from fine to coarse.
8	Normal Nucleoli	Determines whether the nucleoli are small and barely visible or larger, more visible, and more plentiful.
9	Mitoses	Describes the level of mitotic (cell reproduction) activity.
	Class	benign, malignant

DESIGN AND IMPLEMENTATION

This research work investigates the parameter settings for twelve different BPNN training is carried out. The system framework consists of preprocessing subsystem, training subsystem and classification subsystem.

Preprocessing Subsystem

The preprocessing subsystem handles noisy, missing and irregular values. Table 4 presents the number of features, classes and instances of the three clinical datasets obtained from the UCI machine learning repository.

Table 4. Number of features, classes and instances

S.No.	Dataset	Number of Features	Number of Classes	Number of Instances
1	WBC	9	2	683
2	PID	8	2	768
3	Hepatitis	19	2	155

Handling Missing Values

Hepatitis and Wisconsin Breast Cancer datasets have missing values, whereas Pima Indian Diabetes dataset has no missing values. In this research work, missing values are handled by rejecting or imputing using the steps given below.

Input: Clinical Dataset
Process:
Step 1: Count missing values for each feature.
Step 2: Eliminate features where missing values are greater than 25%, else retain the feature.
Step 3: Count missing values in each instance.
Step 4: Eliminate instances with greater than 25% missing values, otherwise retain them.
Step 5: Impute the missing values of the remaining instances with most frequent feature values corresponding to that class.
Output: Clinical dataset without missing values.

The Hepatitis dataset has 167 missing values. The features alkphosphate and protime have the missing values greater than 25%, hence they are removed from the dataset. The WBC dataset has 16 missing values. The feature Bare Nuclei have 16 missing values. These missing values are handled by imputing the most frequent values of the corresponding class. The PID dataset has no missing values, but there are noisy values in the dataset. In hepatitis dataset six samples have missing values greater than 25%, hence these samples are rejected from the dataset. The dataset is reduced to 149 samples from 155 samples. Table 5 shows the number of missing values in each dataset.

Table 5. Details about the number of missing values in each dataset

S.No.	Data Set	Presence of Missingness	Number of Missing Values	Number of Noisy Values
1	WBC	YES	16	-
2	PID	NO	-	432
3	Hepatitis	YES	167	-

Smooth Noisy Data

In Pima Indian Diabetes dataset, the value zero corresponds to each feature is considered as noisy value. In this research work, noisy values are handled by eliminating or imputing attribute values using the steps below.

Input: Clinical dataset without missing values.
Process:
Step 1: Count noisy values for each feature.
Step 2: Eliminate features where noisy values are greater than 25%, else retain the feature.
Step 3: Count noisy values in each instance.
Step 4: Eliminate instances with greater than 25% noisy values, otherwise retain them.
Step 5: Impute the noisy values of the remaining instances with most frequent feature values corresponding to that class.

In Pima Indian Diabetes dataset, among the 768 samples in the dataset 432 samples have one or more zero values associated with it. The number of instances greater than 25% features having value 0, is 256. The number of instances is reduced from 768 to 512. Among 512, 176 instances have feature value zero. The value zero is replaced by frequently occurring values of an attribute belonging to that class. From the 512 instances, 343 instances indicate the absence of diabetes (class 0) and 169 instances indicate the presence of diabetes (class 1). There is no noisy value in the WBC and hepatitis datasets.

Output: Clinical dataset without noisy values.

Data Normalization

Input: Clinical dataset without noisy values.
Process:

Normalize irregular feature values in the clinical dataset into a specified range using Min-Max normalization (Kamber, Han & Pei, 2012) which is presented in Equation (2):

$$Normalized\left(X\right) = \frac{E - E_{min}}{E_{max} - E_{min}}\left(E_{new\_max} - E_{new\_min}\right) + E_{new\_min} \tag{2}$$

where E is the feature value to be normalized, X is the normalized feature value, E_{min} is the minimum value of the feature, E_{max} is the maximum value of the feature, E_{new_max} and E_{new_min} represents the normalized value within the range [0,1].

Output: Normalized Clinical Dataset

Training Subsystem

The training subsystem uses multi layer feed forward neural network with one hidden layer for training the neural network classifier. The input layer corresponds to each feature in the dataset. The hidden layer neurons is structured using Equation (6) and the output layer with output nodes corresponding to the class label. The activation function used is sigmoid. The following Equations (2) and (3) are used to compute the sigmoidal activation functions (Mhaskar & Micchelli, 1994):

$$\log sig(n) = 1/(1 + exp(-n))$$ (3)

$$\tan sig(n) = 2/(1 + exp(-2*n)) - 1$$ (4)

where n is the number of input features in the network.

Backpropagation Training Algorithm

Notations Used

Input: Training Dataset
Process:
Step 1: Initialize the input layer with n input nodes, the hidden layer with H hidden nodes and the output layer with O output nodes.
Phase 1: Feed Forward Phase
Step 2: Compute the output of the jth hidden node using Equation (5):

$$f\left(y_j\right) = \left. 1 \middle/ \left(1 + \exp\left(-\left(\sum_{i=1}^{n} w_{ji} x_i - \theta_j\right)\right)\right), \quad j = 1, 2..., H \right.$$ (5)

Step 3: Compute the output of the output layer using Equation (6):

$$z_k = \sum_{j=1}^{H} w_{kj} f\left(y_j\right) k = 1,2,...,O$$ (6)

Step 4: The number of hidden nodes in the hidden layer is represented in Equation (7):

$$H = (2n +)$$ (7)

Step 5: Compute Mean Squared Error (MSE) E_k using Equation (8):

$$E_k = \sum_{i=1}^{O} \left(z_i^k - C_i^k \right)^2 \tag{8}$$

Phase 1: Backpropagation of Error

Step 6: Compute the error in the network with respect to the weights and biases increment, which is represented in Equation (9):

$$\Delta w_k = \eta(zi - ci)xi \tag{9}$$

Phase 1: Weight and Bias Update

Step 6.1: The error in the network with respect to weights and biases are computed and is updated using **Gradient Descent BP** algorithm. The updation is a negative gradient of the performance function and is represented in Equation (10):

$$\Delta w_k = -\eta.gk \tag{10}$$

Step 6.2: Compute the error in the network weights and biases. They are updated using **Gradient Descent with Momentum** algorithm. The momentum term is added by a fractional change of the new weight, which is represented in Equation (11):

$$\Delta w_k = -\eta_k.g_k + p\Delta w_{k-1} \tag{11}$$

Step 6.3: Compute the error in the network with respect to the weights and biases increment using **Gradient Descent Variable Learning Rate BP** which is represented in Equation (12):

$$\Delta w_k = \eta.\frac{\Delta E_k}{\Delta w_k} \tag{12}$$

Step 6.4: Compute the error in the network with respect to the weights and biases. The increments are calculated using **Gradient Descent with Momentum and Variable Learning Rate BP** algorithm, in which the variable learning rate and the momentum term are added using Equation (13):

$$\Delta w_k = p\Delta w_{k-1} + \eta.p.\frac{\Delta E_k}{\Delta w_k} \tag{13}$$

Step 6.5: Compute the error in the network with respect to the weights and biases. This computation is performed during **Resilient BP** algorithm. the temporal behavior of sign function in this algorithmis used to determine the direction of the weight update.Weightupdation is calculated using Equation (14):

$$\Delta w_k = -sign\left(\frac{\Delta E_k}{\Delta w_k}\right).\Delta w_{k-1} \tag{14}$$

Step 6.6: Compute the error in the network with respect to the weights and biases. The increments are computed using **Conjugate Gradient Backpropagation with Fletcher-Reeves Updates** algorithm. In this algorithm, the line search starts in the steepest descent direction. The line search method determines the optimal current search direction α. The next search direction β is determined by conjugate to previous search directions. This produces faster convergence than steepest descent directions and is represented in Equation (15) to (18):

$$p0 = -g0 \tag{15}$$

$$\Delta w_k = \alpha k\, pk \tag{16}$$

$$p_k = -g_k + \beta_k p_{k-1} \tag{17}$$

$$\beta_k = \frac{g_k^{'}\, g_k}{g_{k-1}^{'}\, g_{k-1}} \tag{18}$$

Step 6.7: Compute the error in the network with respect to the weights and biases increment using **Conjugate Gradient Backpropagation with Polak-Ribiere Updates** algorithm. In this algorithm, new search direction is computed as the product of the previous change in the gradient with the current gradient divided by the square of the previous gradient and is represented in Equation (18).

Step 6.8: Compute the error in the network with respect to the weights and biases increment using **Conjugate Gradient Backpropagation with Powell-Beale Restarts** algorithm. In this algorithm, the direction of search periodically resets to the negative of the gradient and is represented in Equation (19):

$$\left|g_{k-1}^{'} g_k\right| \geq 0.2 g_k^{2} \tag{19}$$

Step 6.9: Compute the error in the network with respect to the weights and biases increment using **Scaled Conjugate Gradient (SCG)** algorithm. The algorithm is based on conjugate directions calculated using Equations (18) and (19).

Step 6.10: Compute the error in the network with respect to the weights and biases increment using **Quasi-Newton BFGS** algorithm. In this algorithm the second derivative of the Hessian matrix is computed using Equation (20):

$$\Delta w_k = -H_k' g_k \tag{20}$$

Step 6.11: Compute the error in the network with respect to the weights and biases increment using **One Step Secant** algorithm. The search starts in the negative direction of the performance gradient. The next search direction is computed from the new gradient and the previous gradient according to the Equation (21):

$$\Delta w_k = -g_k + z_{k-1} * \Delta w_{k-1} + \beta_k * \Delta g_{k-1} \tag{21}$$

Step 6.12: Compute the error in the network with respect to the weights and biases increment using **Levenberg-Marquardt** algorithm which is represented in Equation (20), (22) and (23):

$$H' = J'J \tag{22}$$

$$g = J'E_k \tag{23}$$

Output: Backpropagation Trained Neural Network Classifier.

Classification Subsystem

The classification subsystem uses the BP trained ANN classifier for disease diagnosis. The efficiency of the developed BP trained ANN classifier has been tested with three clinical datasets namely, Wisconsin Breast Cancer, Pima Indian Diabetes and Hepatitis obtained from the UCI machine learning repository.

Input: Testing Samples
Process:
Step 1: Preprocessthe input features using the steps given in section 4.1.
Step 2: Preprocessed samples are given as the inputs to the backpropagation trained ANN classifier to obtain diagnostic results.
Output: Diagnostic Results.

EXPERIMENTAL RESULTS AND DISCUSSION

This section presents the results of the experiments along with analysis of BPNN classifier. The expriments were conducted on personal compute with Intel (R) core (TM) 2 Duo CPU E7500 processor with speed of 2.93 GHz and 2.00 GB ram the BPNN classifier is implemented using the neural network toolbox MATLAB R2013a computing platform. The steps of this comparative BPNN classifier are demonstrated by showing the outputs considering the input clinical datasets. The developed BPNN classifier has been experimented on three different clinical datasets obtained from the UCI machine learning repository namely, Pima Indian Diabetes, Hepatitis, and Wisconsin Breast Cancer.

From Table 6, it can be inferred that, the neural network experimented with (2n+1) hidden neurons and the activation function used in the hidden and the output layer are logsig-logsig and tansig-logsig respectively. For PID dataset, the LM algorithm converges to 48 epochs in 0.01 seconds to get the MSE less than 0.01. The gradient descent with adaptive learning rate BP algorithm does not converge at maximum epochs (500) with the MSE 0.265, but it achieves maximum accuracy 83.4% for PID dataset. For WBC dataset, the Polak-Ribiere and One Step Secant BP algorithm exceeds maximum of 500 epochs with MSE of 0.006, this yields highest accuracy of 98.6% for WBC dataset. For Hepatitis dataset, the classification accuracy is low for all twelve BP algorithms, as the number of samples in the dataset is low. BFGS algorithm provides an accuracy of 45.8% for hepatitis dataset. The parameters that work well for Wisconsin Breast Cancer and Pima Indian Diabetes dataset has given an average result for Hepatitis dataset. However, changing these parameters may yield a better result for Hepatitis dataset.

Table 6. Performance evaluation of twelve BP algorithms for three clinical datasets

Performance Analysis

The classifier results are compared against the statistical measures namely, accuracy, sensitivity and specificity. The statistical measures are evaluated using metrics derived from confusion matrices such as True Positives (TP), True Negatives (TN), False Positives (FP) and False Negatives (FN). The elements are determined as follows:

TP – Diseased sample correctly identified as Diseased.
TN – Normal sample correctly identified as Normal.
FP – Diseased sample incorrectly identified as Normal.
FN – Normal sample incorrectly identified as Diseased.

The performance measures are computed using Equations (24) through (26) and the results are presented in Table 7:

$$Accuracy = \frac{TP + TN}{\left(TP + FP + FN + TN\right)} \tag{24}$$

$$Sensitivity = \frac{TP}{\left(TP + FN\right)} \tag{25}$$

$$Specificity = \frac{TN}{\left(FP + TN\right)} \tag{26}$$

CONCLUSION

In this work, an analytic study has been performed to evaluate the network parameter values for backpropagation neural network training. The investigation is performed on the network parameters namely, number of neurons in the hidden layer, activation function used in the hidden and the output layer, learning rate, number of training epochs and mean square error while training the twelve different Backpropagation Neural Network (BPNN). The performance of the twelve BPNN classifier has been evaluated using three clinical datasets namely Pima Indian diabetes, Wisconsin Breast cancer and Hepatitis obtained from the UCI machine learning repository. From the comparative study it can be inferred that the accuracy of the classifier depends upon the type of backpropagation algorithm chosen, the combination of network parameter values chosen and the dataset chosen. This work can serve as a guideline to design network parameters for any neural network based CDSS.

Table 7. Classification performance comparison of twelve BP algorithms for three clinical datasets

MSE	Accuracy (%)	Sensitivity (%)	Specificity (%)	MSE	Accuracy (%)	Sensitivity (%)	Specificity (%)	MSE	Accuracy (%)	Sensitivity (%)	Specificity (%)
	WBC				Hepatitis				PID		
1. Levenberg – Marquardt (trainlm)											
0.00015	97.9	98.1	97.0	0.0005	33.9	100	32.8	0.01	74.1	93.7	29
2. Gradient descent Backpropagation (traingd)											
0.0501	83.9	93.0	54.5	0.0940	15.3	100	13.8	0.201	68.3	97.2	1.6
3. Gradient Descent with Momentum Backpropagation (traingdm)											
0.0529	95.7	98.6	86.4	0.0737	20.3	100	19	0.180	71.7	90.0	27.4
4. Gradient Descent with adaptive Learning Rate Backpropagation (traingda)											
0.00798	97.1	98.1	93.9	0.00098	33.9	100	32.8	0.132	79.5	85.3	66.1
5. Gradient Descent with Momentum and adaptive Learning Rate Backpropagation											
0.0005	97.5	98.1	95.5	0.00089	40.7	100	39.7	0.115	83.4	88.1	72.6
6. Resilient Backpropagation (trainrp)											
0.0008	96.8	97.2	95.5	0.00079	25.4	100	24.1	0.0421	76.1	84.6	56.5
7. Conjugate gradient Backpropagation with Fletcher – Reeves Updates (traincgf)											
0.002	98.2	98.6	97	0.00077	40.7	100	39.7	0.0302	76.6	83.2	61.3
8. Polak – Ribiere (traincgp)											
0.0009	98.6	98.6	98.5	0.00019	35.6	100	34.5	0.0277	76.1	81.1	64.5
9. Conjugate gradient Backpropagation with Powell – Beale Restarts (traincgb)											
0.002	98.2	98.1	98.5	0.00057	33.9	100	32.8	0.0196	76.1	81.1	64.5
10. Scaled Conjugate Gradient (trainscg)											
0.0007	97.5	98.6	93.9	0.00061	40.7	0	41.4	0.0130	76.1	81.8	62.9
11. Quasi – Newton Algorithms – BFGS Algorithm (trainbf)											
0.0081	97.9	98.1	97	0.00069	45.8	100	44.8	0.0420	78	81.8	69.4
12. One Step Secant Algorithm (trainoss)											
0.002	98.6	98.6	98.5	0.00037	32.2	100	31	0.0362	76.6	81.8	64.5

REFERENCES

Agharezaei, L., Agharezaei, Z., Nemati, A., Bahaadinbeigy, K., Keynia, F., Baneshi, M. R., & Agharezaei, M. (2016). The prediction of the risk level of pulmonary embolism and deep vein thrombosis through artificial neural network. *Acta Informatica Medica*, *24*(5), 354. doi:10.5455/aim.2016.24.354.359 PMID:28077893

Akinyokun, O. C.(2002). Neuro-Fuzzy Expert System for Human Resource Performance Evaluation. *First Bank of Nigeria Plc Endowment Fund Public Lecture, Series 1*.

Alsmadi, M. K. S., Omar, K. B., & Noah, S. A. (2009). Back propagation algorithm: The best algorithm among the multi-layer perceptron algorithm. *International Journal of Computer Science and Network Security*, *9*(4), 378–383.

Basheer, I. A., & Hajmeer, M. (2000). Artificial neural networks: Fundamentals, computing, design, and application. *Journal of Microbiological Methods*, *43*(1), 3–31. doi:10.1016/S0167-7012(00)00201-3 PMID:11084225

Berry, M. J., & Linoff, G. (1997). *Data mining techniques: for marketing, sales, and customer support*. John Wiley & Sons, Inc.

Bezdek, J. C. (1993). A review of probabilistic, fuzzy, and neural models for pattern recognition. *Journal of Intelligent & Fuzzy Systems*, *1*(1), 1–25. doi:10.3233/IFS-1993-1103

Blum, A. (1992). *Neural networks in C*. Wiley.

Boger, Z., & Guterman, H. (1997). Knowledge extraction from artificial neural network models. In Systems, Man, and Cybernetics. *IEEE International Conference on Computational Cybernetics and Simulation*, *4*, 3030-3035. 10.1109/ICSMC.1997.633051

Bossan, M. C., Seixas, J. M., Caloba, L. P., Penha, R. S., & Nadal, J. (1995). A modified backpropagation algorithm for neural classifiers. *Proceedings of the 38th Midwest SymposiumIn Circuits and Systems*, *1*, 562-565.

Chandra, P., & Singh, Y. (2004). An activation function adapting training algorithm for sigmoidal feed-forward networks. *Neurocomputing*, *61*, 429–437. doi:10.1016/j.neucom.2004.04.001

Christopher, J. J., Nehemiah, H. K., & Kannan, A. (2015). A clinical decision support system for diagnosis of Allergic Rhinitis based on intradermal skin tests. *Computers in Biology and Medicine*, *65*, 76–84. doi:10.1016/j.compbiomed.2015.07.019 PMID:26298488

Coppin, B. (2004). *Artificial intelligence illuminated*. Jones & Bartlett Learning.

Desai, S. D., Giraddi, S., Narayankar, P., Pudakalakatti, N. R., & Sulegaon, S. (2019). Back-propagation neural network versus logistic regression in heart disease classification. *Advanced Computing and Communication Technologies*, 133-144. doi:10.1007/978-981-13-0680-8_13

Drago, G. P., Morando, M., & Ridella, S. (1995). An adaptive momentum back propagation (AMBP). *Neural Computing & Applications*, *3*(4), 213–221. doi:10.1007/BF01414646

Duch, W., & Jankowski, N. (1999). Survey of neural transfer functions. *Neural Computing Surveys*, *2*(1), 163–212.

Duch, W., & Jankowski, N. (2001). Transfer functions: hidden possibilities for better neural networks. ESANN, 81-94.

Elgin Christo, V. R., Khanna Nehemiah, H., Minu, B., & Kannan, A. (2019). Correlation-Based Ensemble Feature Selection Using Bioinspired Algorithms and Classification Using Backpropagation Neural Network. *Computational and Mathematical Methods in Medicine*, *2019*, 1–17. doi:10.1155/2019/7398307 PMID:31662787

Eluyode, O. S., & Akomolafe, D. T., & MNCS, M. (2013). Comparative study of biological and artificial neural networks. *European Journal of Applied Engineering and Scientific Research*, *2*(1).

FFNN. Feed-forward Neural Networks. (2010). *Short Notes*. http://www.cs.nott.ac.uk/~pszqiu/Teaching/G53MLE/ffnets-note.pdf

Fukuoka, Y., Matsuki, H., Minamitani, H., & Ishida, A. (1998). A modified back-propagation method to avoid false local minima. *Neural Networks*, *11*(6), 1059–1072. doi:10.1016/S0893-6080(98)00087-2 PMID:12662775

Geetha, V., Aprameya, K. S., & Hinduja, D. M. (2020). Dental caries diagnosis in digital radiographs using back-propagation neural network. *Health Information Science and Systems*, *8*(1), 1–14. doi:10.100713755-019-0096-y PMID:31949895

Hamamoto, Tungjitkusolmun, & Pintavirooj. (2019). Automatic Detection and Staging of Lung Tumors using Locational Features and Double-Staged Classifications. *Applied Sciences*, *9*(11), 2329.

He, Z., Wu, M., & Gong, B. (1992). Neural network and its application on machinery fault diagnosis. *IEEE International Conference on Systems Engineering*, 576-579.

Helwan, A., Idoko, J. B., & Abiyev, R. H. (2017). Machine learning techniques for classification of breast tissue. *Procedia Computer Science*, *120*, 402–410. doi:10.1016/j.procs.2017.11.256

Kamber, M., Han, J., & Pei, J. (2012). *Data mining: Concepts and techniques*. Elsevier.

Karsoliya, S. (2012). Approximating number of hidden layer neurons in multiple hidden layer BPNN architecture. *International Journal of Engineering Trends and Technology*, *3*(6), 714–717.

Kosko, B. (1994). *Neural Network and Fuzzy Systems* (1st ed.). Prentice Hall of India.

Krasnopolsky, V. M., & Chevallier, F. (2003). Some neural network applications in environmental sciences. Part II: Advancing computational efficiency of environmental numerical models. *Neural Networks*, *16*(3), 335–348. doi:10.1016/S0893-6080(03)00026-1 PMID:12672429

Lee, H. M., Chen, C. M., & Huang, T. C. (2001). Learning efficiency improvement of back-propagation algorithm by error saturation prevention method. *Neurocomputing*, *41*(1), 125–143. doi:10.1016/S0925-2312(00)00352-0

Leema, N., Nehemiah, H. K., & Kannan, A. (2016). Neural network classifier optimization using Differential Evolution with Global Information and Back Propagation algorithm for clinical datasets. *Applied Soft Computing*, *49*, 834–844. doi:10.1016/j.asoc.2016.08.001

Lichman, M. (2013). *UCI Machine Learning Repository*. University of California, School of Information and Computer Science.

Liu, Y., Starzyk, J. A., & Zhu, Z. (2007). Optimizing number of hidden neurons in neural networks. *Artificial Intelligence and Applications (Commerce, Calif.)*, *2*, 138–143.

Masters, T. (1993). *Practical neural network recipes in C*. Morgan Kaufmann.

Mhaskar, H. N., & Micchelli, C. A. (1994). How to choose an activation function. *Advances in Neural Information Processing Systems*, 319–319.

Morshed, J., & Kaluarachchi, J. J. (1998). Parameter estimation using artificial neural network and genetic algorithm for free-product migration and recovery. *Water Resources Research*, *34*(5), 1101–1113. doi:10.1029/98WR00006

Nahato, K. B., Harichandran, K. N., & Arputharaj, K. (2015). Knowledge mining from clinical datasets using rough sets and backpropagation neural network. *Computational and Mathematical Methods in Medicine*, *2015*, 1–13. doi:10.1155/2015/460189 PMID:25821508

Nahato, K. B., Nehemiah, K. H., & Kannan, A. (2016). Hybrid approach using fuzzy sets and extreme learning machine for classifying clinical datasets. *Informatics in Medicine Unlocked*, *2*, 1–11. doi:10.1016/j.imu.2016.01.001

Ng, S. C., Leung, S. H., & Luk, A. (1999). Fast convergent generalized back-propagation algorithm with constant learning rate. *Neural Processing Letters*, *9*(1), 13–23. doi:10.1023/A:1018611626332

Nguyen, D., & Widrow, B. (1990). Improving the learning speed of 2-layer neural networks by choosing initial values of the adaptive weights. *International Joint Conference In Neural Networks*, 21-26.

Rajasekaran, S., & Pai, G. V. (2003). *Neural networks, fuzzy logic and genetic algorithm: synthesis and applications (with cd)*. PHI Learning Pvt. Ltd.

Ravindra, B. V., Sriraam, N., & Geetha, M. (2018, February). Chronic kidney disease detection using back propagation neural network classifier. *2018 International Conference on Communication, Computing and Internet of Things (IC3IoT)*, 65-68. 10.1109/IC3IoT.2018.8668110

Rosenblatt, F. (1958). The perceptron: A probabilistic model for information storage and organization in the brain. *Psychological Review*, *65*(6), 386–408. doi:10.1037/h0042519 PMID:13602029

Rumelhart, D. E., Hinton, G. E., & Wiliams, R. J. (1986b). Learning representations by back-propagating errors. *Nature*, *323*(6088), 533–536. doi:10.1038/323533a0

Rumelhart, D. E., Hinton, G. E., & Williams, R. J. (1986a). Learning internal representations by error propagation. *Parallel Distributed Processing*, *1*, 318–362.

Saduf, M. A. W. (2013). Comparative study of back propagation learning algorithms for neural networks. *International Journal of Advanced Research in Computer Science and Software Engineering*, *3*(2), 1151–1156.

Sharma, B. (2014). Comparison of neural network training functions for hematoma classification in brain CT images. *IOSR Journals*, *1*(16), 31–35. doi:10.9790/0661-16123135

Sibi, P., Jones, S. A., & Siddarth, P. (2013). Analysis of different activation functions using back propagation neural networks. *Journal of Theoretical and Applied Information Technology*, *47*(3), 1264–1268.

Singh, Y., & Chandra, P. (2003). A class+ 1 sigmoidal activation functions for FFANNs. *Journal of Economic Dynamics & Control*, *28*(1), 183–187. doi:10.1016/S0165-1889(02)00157-4

Sudha, M. (2017). Evolutionary and neural computing based decision support system for disease diagnosis from clinical data sets in medical practice. *Journal of Medical Systems*, *41*(11), 178. doi:10.100710916-017-0823-3 PMID:28956226

Swanston, D. J., Bishop, J. M., & Mitchell, R. J. (1994). Simple adaptive momentum: New algorithm for training multilayer perceptrons. *Electronics Letters*, *30*(18), 1498–1500. doi:10.1049/el:19941014

Tarle, B., & Jena, S. (2017, August). An artificial neural network based pattern classification algorithm for diagnosis of heart disease. *2017 International Conference on Computing, Communication, Control and Automation (ICCUBEA)*, 1-4. 10.1109/ICCUBEA.2017.8463729

Verma, B. K., & Mulawka, J. J. (1994). A modified backpropagation algorithm. *IEEE World Congress on Computational Intelligence*, *2*, 840-844.

Wang, X., Tang, Z., Tamura, H., Ishii, M., & Sun, W. D. (2004). An improved backpropagation algorithm to avoid the local minima problem. *Neurocomputing*, *56*, 455–460. doi:10.1016/j.neucom.2003.08.006

Wani, M. A. (2014). Comparative Study of High Speed Back-Propagation Learning Algorithms. *International Journal of Modern Education and Computer Science*, *6*(12), 34–40. doi:10.5815/ijmecs.2014.12.05

Wu, H., Zhao, S., Zhang, X., Sang, A., Dong, J., & Jiang, K. (2020, January). Back-propagation Artificial Neural Network for Early Diabetic Retinopathy Detection Based On A Priori Knowledge. *Journal of Physics: Conference Series*, *1437*(1), 012019. doi:10.1088/1742-6596/1437/1/012019

Yam, J. Y., & Chow, T. W. (2000). A weight initialization method for improving training speed in feedforward neural network. *Neurocomputing*, *30*(1), 219–232. doi:10.1016/S0925-2312(99)00127-7

Yu, X. H., & Chen, G. A. (1997). Efficient backpropagation learning using optimal learning rate and momentum. *Neural Networks*, *10*(3), 517–527. doi:10.1016/S0893-6080(96)00102-5

Zhang, L., & Suganthan, P. N. (2016). A survey of randomized algorithms for training neural networks. *Information Sciences*, *364*, 146–155. doi:10.1016/j.ins.2016.01.039

Zweiri, Y. H., Whidborne, J. F., & Seneviratne, L. D. (2003). A three-term backpropagation algorithm. *Neurocomputing*, *50*, 305–318. doi:10.1016/S0925-2312(02)00569-6

This research was previously published in the International Journal of Operations Research and Information Systems (IJORIS), 11(4); pages 62-85, copyright year 2020 by IGI Publishing (an imprint of IGI Global).

Chapter 10
Hybrid Particle Swarm Optimization With Genetic Algorithm to Train Artificial Neural Networks for Short-Term Load Forecasting

Kuruge Darshana Abeyrathna

Centre for Artificial Intelligence Research, University of Agder, Grimstad, Norway

Chawalit Jeenanunta

Sirindhorn International Institute of Technology, Thammasat University, Pathumthani, Thailand

ABSTRACT

This research proposes a new training algorithm for artificial neural networks (ANNs) to improve the short-term load forecasting (STLF) performance. The proposed algorithm overcomes the so-called training issue in ANNs, where it traps in local minima, by applying genetic algorithm operations in particle swarm optimization when it converges to local minima. The training ability of the hybridized training algorithm is evaluated using load data gathered by Electricity Generating Authority of Thailand. The ANN is trained using the new training algorithm with one-year data to forecast equal 48 periods of each day in 2013. During the testing phase, a mean absolute percentage error (MAPE) is used to evaluate performance of the hybridized training algorithm and compare them with MAPEs from Backpropagation, GA, and PSO. Yearly average MAPE and the average MAPEs for weekdays, Mondays, weekends, Holidays, and Bridging holidays show that PSO+GA algorithm outperforms other training algorithms for STLF.

DOI: 10.4018/978-1-6684-2408-7.ch010

INTRODUCTION

STLF is vital for many utility activities: security analysis, fuel purchasing, generator scheduling, and maintenance scheduling (Rana & Koprinska, 2016). Forecasting errors can negatively affect the monetary savings regardless of whether its positive or negative. Over forecasting causes producing or purchasing extra electricity. Under forecasting causes revenue reduction by not having of enough electricity to cover the customer demand (Ismail, Yahya, & Mahpol, 2009). However, STLF is difficult due to the nonlinear behavior of the load consumption. Load consumption depends on many factors such as weather conditions, human behavior, and commercial and social activities (Singh & Singh, 2001). Therefore, contemplating the significance and the difficulty of STLF, a number of Artificial Intelligence (AI) and statistical based techniques have been suggested by researchers (Hassan, Khosravi, & Jaafar, 2015). Even though, statistical based forecasting techniques such as Regression Analysis (Dudek, 2016) and Stochastic Time Series (Clements, Hurn, & Li, 2016) abound in STLF, these are good at forecasting linear time series. Since electricity load consumption is highly nonlinear, AI based forecasting techniques such as Deep Learning (Coelho et al., 2016; Dedinec, Filiposka, Dedinec, & Kocarev, 2016; Qiu, Ren, Suganthan, & Amaratunga, 2017), Fuzzy Logic (Hassan, Khosravi, Jaafar, & Khanesar, 2016), machine learning based models (Jurado, Nebot, Mugica, & Avellana, 2015), and Artificial Neural Networks (ANNs) (Chae, Horesh, Hwang, & Lee, 2016; Ding, Benoit, Foggia, Bésanger, & Wurtz, 2016) are better for STLF.

ANN is introduced to STLF as a pattern matching technique. Recognizing and learning nonlinear patterns in data and adjusting its weights based on them to work with unseen data is the principal operation of ANN. Due to its continues accuracy for STLF, use of ANN is ample in the field. However, forecasting capabilities of ANN have been proved by comparing it with other forecasting techniques: Gajowniczek and Ząbkowski (Gajowniczek & Ząbkowski, 2014) use Multi-Layer Perceptron (MLP) and Support Vector Machines (SVM) in their research for electricity forecasting and show that MLP performs better compared to SVM. ANN and Box-Jenkins methods for electricity forecasting are compared by (Ramakrishna, Boiroju, & Reddy, 2011). Results of their research show that ANN performs better in electricity demand forecasting than Box-Jenkins method. Ringwood et et., (Ringwood, Bofelli, & Murray, 2001) also use ANN for forecasting Irish electricity demand. They find that ANN is better for forecasting all three time horizons: Short-Term Load Forecasting (STLF) for next hour to one week, Medium-Term Load Forecasting (MTLF) for one week to one month, and Long-Term Load Forecasting (LTLF) for one months to several years.

However, ANN has some limitations and continues monitoring is required to minimize their effect on forecasting outcomes (Singh & Singh, 2001): ANN takes large computational times as it requires many training cycles to learn the patterns in large datasets, forecasts depend on the random initial values, difficulty of selecting inputs and targets, and determining the number of hidden units (layers and neurons). One of the most highlighted limitations with ANN is, training likely to stops at local minima. The standard training algorithm to adjust the weights and bias of ANNs is Backpropagation (Shayeghi, Shayanfar, & Azimi, 2009). Nevertheless, Backpropagation is a gradient search algorithm and these kind of training algorithms tend to get trapped at local minima (Sarangi, Singh, Swain, Chauhan, & Singh, 2009; Shayeghi et al., 2009) and are sensitive to the random initial parameters (Bashir & El-Hawary, 2007).

To overcome the above limitations, meta-heuristic optimization techniques are used to train ANNs: Genetic Algorithm (GA) and Particle Swarm Optimization (PSO). GA and PSO are population-based global optimization techniques which are used to solve complex nonlinear objective functions (Subbaraj & Rajasekaran, 2008). The ability of training ANNs with GA and PSO for electricity forecasting has been highlighted in many research (Jeenanunta & Abeyrathn, 2017; Jeenanunta & Abeyrathna, 2017; Mishra & Patra, 2008).

Although the attempt of applying meta-heuristic techniques solve the problem up to a considerable level, the training error, which decides the forecasting performances, can be further reduced by combining their individual properties. Therefore, this research brings a new training algorithm which has both GA and PSO properties to train the ANN for STLF. GA operations are applied to perturb the particles of PSO when it traps in local minima. This helps PSO to create a completely different particle set while they keep the previous personal best and global best values. In case newly created particle can beat the current personal best or the global best, these values are updated and carried to the next generation.

The rest of the paper is arranged as follows: First, the basics of the ANNs and training algorithms (Backpropagation, GA, PSO, and PSO+GA) are explained. The data cleaning process, data arrangement, and training the suggested ANN with different training algorithms are explained under the Design of Experiment. Finally, the conclusion is made after discussing the results of the experiment.

ARTIFICIAL NEURAL NETWORKS AND TRAINING ALGORITHMS

Many researchers (Demiroren & Ceylan, 2006; Krunic, 2000; Senjyu, Tamaki, Takara, & Uezato, 2002) use ANN for electricity load demand forecasting since its ability of recognizing and learning inherent patterns in historical data. As a causal forecasting technique, many external series can be included in ANN such as temperature and time variables. The basic structures of ANNs consist of input nodes, output nodes, and hidden layers. Input nodes are given to represent the external inputs to the network. Output nodes represent the output from the ANNs or the ANNs' results. Hidden layers consist with neurons and all the layers are connected by their specific weights from one neuron to another. When the number of hidden layers and neurons in the hidden layers are increased, the number of weights in the structure are also increased. The weights that connect each node are adjusted during the training phase. The job of the training algorithm is adjusting the weights of the network so that it gives the minimum error between the network output for the training inputs and the target data. The weights adjusting procedure is different from one training algorithm to another.

Backpropagation is the most common training method among researchers (Demiroren & Ceylan, 2006; Rumelhart, 1986; Senjyu, Tamaki, Uezato, Tomonobu, 2001; Shayeghi et al., 2009). 'Backward Propagation of Errors' has been abbreviated to Backpropagation. Backpropagation adjusts weights based on the given target series. Therefore, this method is called as supervised training algorithm.

Algorithm starts giving random values for weights. Inputs pass through these weights and hidden neurons to get the network outputs. These network outputs are compared with the given target values to calculate the errors. These errors are propagated back to the previous layers and during the process weights are adjusted to minimize the errors. This process runs until the output error becomes less than a predetermined value or stop after running predetermined number of cycles (epochs). After stopping the weights adjusting process, the network is ready to work with unseen data.

Genetic algorithm is used to solve complex optimization problems. This method is based on the natural selection or it has been derived from biological evolution (Survival of the Fittest) which was first introduced by Charles Darwin (Sarangi et al., 2009). GA starts with a random population. This population includes a set of individual solutions (Chromosomes). Random values for variables of the objective function bring different objective values or solutions. These random values in chromosomes are called as Genes. Then, GA calculates fitness values of each chromosome. The best chromosomes based on their fitness values are selected as parents. GA uses these parents in the current population to produce children for the next generation. This is how GA expects to get better and better fitness values over the generations. Over successive generations, chromosomes in the populations evolve toward an optimal solution.

PSO has some similarities with GA. Both methods start with random solutions for the given objective function (fitness function). In PSO, individual solutions in the population are called particles. Both methods check the conditions of each individual by calculating the fitness value of them. Based on the calculated fitness values, they produce the next population until they meet the stopping conditions. But PSO does not have evolution operators like in GA: producing crossover and mutation children. Its individuals follow the best particles from their solution space and run until they reach to the target. Since it has few parameters to adjust, it is easier to use and control than GA (Shayeghi et al., 2009).

Generally, PSO shows poor performances as it still has a chance to trap in local minima in the solution space. Since all the particles follow its own personal best and the global best particle within certain generations, all particles would trap at particular solutions. However, several researchers have attempted to combine PSO with some other techniques to increase its performance: Leboucher et al. combine PSO with Evolutionary Game Theory to solve a resources allocation problem (Leboucher, Chelouah, Siarry, & Le Ménec, 2012), Kumar and Singh combine PSO with Bacterial Foraging Optimization for Biometric Feature Optimization (Kumar & Singh, 2017), and Hein and the team apply reinforcement learning with PSO in their research to solve complex optimization problems (Hein, Hentschel, Runkler, & Udluft, 2016). Concurrently, we combine PSO with GA to train ANNs and the detailed producer is given in the next section.

Research discussed in the previous sections are summarized in Table 1. For instance, we found different STLF techniques in the literature and out of them one research uses regression and three use Deep Learning and so on.

Table 1. Summary of the previous attempts

Concern	Details (The Number of Attempts)					
STLF techniques	Regression (1)	Deep Learning (3)	Stochastic Time Series (1)	Fuzzy Logic (1)	Machine Learning (1)	ANNs (5)
Compare ANN with	Box-Jenkins	Support Vector Machines				
Limitations of ANN	difficulty of determining parameters	requires large computational times	Performances rely on the random initial values	Training likely to stops at local minima		
ANNs' training algorithms	Backpropagation (4)	Genetic Algorithm (1)	Particle Swarm Optimization (2)			
Hybridize PSO with	Evolutionary Game Theory	Bacterial Foraging Optimization	Reinforcement Learning Approaches			

In addition to the STLF techniques, Table 1 presents the techniques that used to compare the results of ANNs, limitations of ANNs, training algorithms of ANNs, and other techniques used with PSO to create hybridize algorithms.

DESIGN OF EXPERIMENT

Data Cleaning

The research is arranged to forecast the days in 2013 using one-year training data in the training phase. Therefore, a sample data set (1st January 2012 to 31st December 2013) is selected from the data gathered by Electricity Generating Authority of Thailand. However, abnormal behavior of data due to holidays, bridging holidays, and outliers reduce the forecasting accuracy. Therefore, the sample data set is cleaned before use them to train the ANN. At the beginning, calendar holidays and bridging holidays which is a day between two holidays or between a holiday and a weekend are replaced by the same-day-of-the-week from previous two weeks as given in Equation (1). Only the latest two weeks are used to avoid the unnecessary variation in the patterns from old data:

$$L^p_t(d) = w_1 L_t(d-7) + w_2 L_t(d-14) \tag{1}$$

where, $L^p_t(d)$ is the estimated demand and $L_t(d)$ is the actual load demand at time t on day d. Giving the priority for the most recent week, w_1 and w_2 are optimally set to 0.7 and 0.3, respectively.

Data is separated into different time windows considering the similar load behavior of the same time period of the same-day-of-the-week. Four period moving average ($k=4$) and the standard deviation of each time window is used to create the Time-Window based filtering band for each time window as given in Equation (2). All the data outside the filtering band are identified as outliers:

$$B_t(d) = \frac{\left[\sum_{i=1}^{k} L_t(d-7 \times i)\right]}{k} \pm N \times SD(V_t(d)); \quad t = 1,\dots 48 \tag{2}$$

where:

$$V_t(d) = \left[L_t(d'), L_t(d'-7), L_t(d'-14),\dots L_t(d'-7 \times m)\right] \tag{}$$

where:

$$d \in \{d', d'-7,\dots, d'-7m\}, d' \text{ is the last 7 days in the data set} \tag{3}$$

and $B_t(d)$ indicates the Time-Window based filtering band of day d, at time period t. The N defines the size of the band width and $V_t(d)$ is the Time-Window containing all loads of the same period t that also include $L_t(d)$. $SD(V_t(d))$ is the standard deviation of all periods in Time-Window $V_t(d)$. m of Time-Window $V_t(d)$ is the number of weeks and equal to 105 when the day of week is Sunday, Monday, and Tuesday. m is equal to 104 for all the other vectors.

Outliers identified by the Time-Window based technique are replaced using the Equation (1) according to the following conditions:

$$L^p_t(d) = \begin{cases} w_1 L_t(d-7) + w_2 L_t(d-14), & if \ L_t(d) \notin B_t(d) \\ L_t(d), & otherwise \end{cases} \tag{4}$$

Data Arrangement

A sample data set is arranged in segment to forecast each time period t of each day d separately for the year, 2013. The similar load behavior of the same time periods of the previous day and the same-day-of-the-week is considered. Also, the concept of similar temperature behavior of the same time period of the previous day and the forecasted temperature values for the forecasting day are used. One-year data is used to train the network each time for forecasting each time period of each day in 2013. The notion of walking-forward testing routine is applied to forecast each time period where the same amount of training sets is used while forecasting each time period of each day. Considering Monday as an example, for forecasting the time periods of Mondays in 2013, the ANN is trained with one-year data so that only Mondays are in the target series, which gives only 52 training sets to forecast each Monday in 2013. Likewise, 52 training sets are used to forecast each Sunday in 2013 and 51 training sets for forecasting all the other days.

Training the ANN

According to the data arrangement, electricity demand values from two days $\left(L^p_t(d-7)\right)$ and $L^p_t(d-1)$ of the same time period t and temperature values from two days ($T^p_t(d-1)$ and $T^p_t(d)$) of the same time period t are given as inputs to the network as given in Figure 1.

One hidden layer with four neurons is added to the network. The network has 16 weights to connect input nodes and hidden neurons and 4 weights to connect hidden neurons and the output node. All hidden neurons and output nodes have bias. Therefore, 5 bias can be found in the network (4+1). All these weights and bias are variables and adjusted during the training phase. Therefore, total of 25 (16 + 4 + 5) variables can be found from the suggested network. This suggested ANN structure is illustrated by Figure 1 $L^p_t(d)$ represents the cleaned load of day d, at time t. Likewise, $T^p_t(d)$, and $F^p_t(d)$ represent cleaned temperature and forecasted load of day d, at time t, respectively.

Train With Backpropagation

When the network and the data set is ready, backpropagation algorithm start adjusting the weights and bias of the network. Only the stopping conditions have to be set. These stopping conditions are namely the minimum error (MSE) between the network outputs and the target series and the maximum number of epochs that the algorithm should run. Until one of these conditions are met, backpropagation algorithm adjusts the weights and bias based on the current error. Therefore, expecting the maximum performance, the minimum or the target error is set to zero and the maximum number of epochs is set to 1000.

Figure 1. The suggested ANN structure

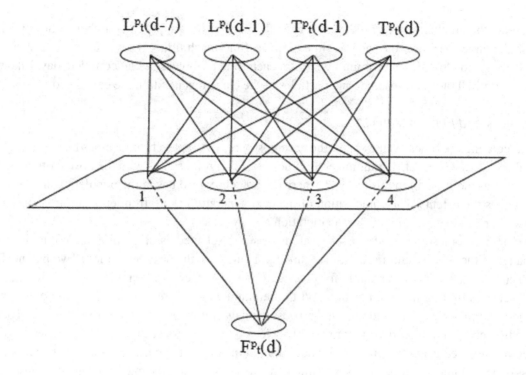

Train With GA, PSO, and PSO+GA

Encoding

Before training the weights and bias of the ANN using GA and PSO, all the weights and bias have to be taken into chromosomes and particles. These weights and bias represent specific genes in the chromosomes and particles. According to the suggested structure in the previous section, 25 genes should have in each chromosome and particle. First 16 genes of the chromosomes and particles belong to the weights that connect input nodes and neurons of the hidden layer. The bias of the hidden neurons ($b_{(1,1)}$ - $b_{(1,4)}$) are placed just after the first 16 weights. Since there is 1 output node, there are 4 weights to connect hidden neurons and the output node. These weights are placed after the bias of the hidden neurons and then the bias of output node ($b_{(2,1)}$) is placed.

Fitness Values Calculation

Mean Squared Error (*MSE*) between the target series $\left(L^p_t(d)\right)$ and the training outputs $\left(F^p_t(d)\right)$ is used as the fitness function. Therefore, weights and bias are adjusted and updated at every generation while minimizing the error between the target and training output series. *MSE* between target series and the training outputs is given by:

$$MSE^d{}_t = \frac{1}{n} \sum_{s=1}^{n} \left(L^p{}_t (d - 7s) - F^p{}_t (d - 7s) \right)^2, \quad for \ n \ training \ sets \tag{5}$$

n represents the number of data sets used to train the network or simply the number of days we have given in the target series for the specific time period t. Since each time period is forecasted separately, t varies from 1 to 48 with a new training data set each time to forecast a one complete day. Likewise, fitness vales of all the chromosomes and particles in the current generation are calculated.

Parameters and Functions in GA

After calculating the fitness values of all the chromosomes, GA ranks chromosomes based on their fitness values. Since GA wants to minimize the fitness value, chromosomes with the lowest fitness values are selected as the parents. In this research, there are 100 chromosomes in the population and best 30% is selected as the parents. The composition of the next generation is 5% from elite children, 50% from the crossover children, and 45% from the mutation children.

The top 5 chromosomes of the ranked parents' list are selected as elite children. Without making any change in them, these chromosomes are directly included to the next generation. Two parents from the selected list are selected randomly for producing the crossover children. Genes from the first parent are selected up to a random position and the remaining genes are selected from the other parent for generating the crossover children. This process runs until it creates 50 crossover children. Total of 45 mutation children are produced by randomly selected parents. As each chromosome has 25 genes, 5 randomly selected genes are changed by adding random values from the Gaussian distribution. The process of generating new populations is terminated when GA reaches the maximum generations of 200, the minimum fitness of 0, or the stall generations of 20 where there is no or minor improvement of the fitness value over successive generations.

Parameters and Functions in PSO

The number of elements in each particle is already defined when the ANN structure is made. The number of particles in a population are varied on how difficult the problem is. This research sets 100 particles for a generation. For updating the velocity of each particle for the next generation ($V^i(t+1)$) as given in Equation (6), the inertia weight w, random values *rand1* and *rand2*, and the learning factors *c1* and *c2* have to be set. The inertia weight is set to 0.6 so that the current velocity has a higher impact on the velocity of the next generation. Two random values between 0 and 1 created and assigned to *rand1* and *rand2*. Learning factors are set to 2 and 0.5, respectively so that each particle gets higher impact from the personal best than the global best. The updated velocity is used to update the position of each particle ($X^i(t+1)$):

$$V^i(t+1) = w \times V^i(t) + c1 \times rand\,1 \times \left(p - X^i(t) \right) + c2 \times rand\,2 \times \left(g - X^i(t) \right) \tag{6}$$

$$X^i\left(t+1\right) = X^i\left(t\right) + V^i\left(t+1\right) \tag{7}$$

Same as in GA, PSO algorithm is terminated when it reaches the maximum generations of 200, the minimum fitness of 0, or the stall generations of 20.

Apply GA on PSO

When the fitness value shows minor improvements over successive generations, we assume that it has reached to a local minimum or the global minimum and stars counting the stall generations. When stall generations reach to 20, GA operations are applied to perturb the particles of PSO. Since the size of the population is 100, fifty mutation and fifty crossover children are produced. Fifty particles from the last generation are selected randomly for producing the mutation children. Random values between -1 and 1 are added to the randomly selected 5 elements of each selected particle. For producing crossover children, the same method applied in GA is used where a new particle is created using a random number of genes of a randomly selected particle from the previous generation and remaining genes from another randomly selected particle. The phases of the proposed algorithm are highlighted in the following flowchart (Figure 2).

Figure 2. Flowchart which connect the phases of the PSO+GA training algorithm

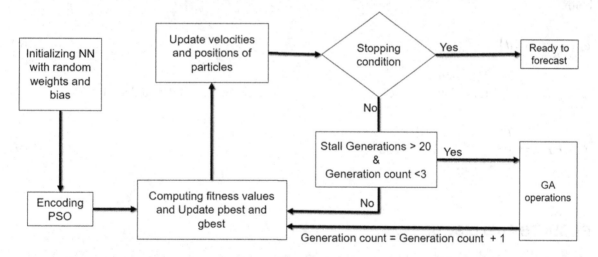

GA operations help PSO to create completely a different particle set while they keep the previous personal best and global best values. In case newly created particle can beat the current personal best or the global best, these values are updated and carried to the next generation. After applying these GA operations, PSO starts performing its regular activities for finding the global best. Likewise, GA operations are applied two times in PSO over one training period in order to minimize the training error without stopping it at a local minimum.

Parameters used at each training algorithm are summarized in Table 2. Since the same ANN was used at each phase to train with different training algorithms, variables, which should be optimized, are equal to for all training algorithms and their target training error is 0.

Table 2. Training parameters of each training algorithm

Parameter	Backpropagation	GA	PSO	PSO+GA
No. of ANN variables	25	25	25	25
Target Training Error	0	0	0	0
Training Epochs/ No. of Generations	1000	200	200	200
Population	-	100	100	100
No. of Stall Generations	-	20	20	20
Elite children	-	5%	-	-
Crossover Children	-	50%	-	50%
Mutation Children	-	45%	-	50%

Evaluating the Accuracy

Forecasting accuracy of the testing data set is presented in terms of the Mean Absolute Percentage Error (MAPE) for each day, separately (48 values at a time) as in Equation (9). Forecasted outputs are denoted as $F_t^p(d)$, where t is the time intervals of day d. These forecasted series are compared with actual demand series after cleaning the data, $L_t^p(d)$. Therefore, the error series can be calculated as given below:

$$e_t^p(d) = L_t^p(d) - F_t^p(d) \tag{8}$$

Then the MAPE for day d is calculated by the following equation and denoted as $MAPE_d^p$:

$$MAPE_d^p = [\left(\frac{1}{48}\right) \sum_{t=1}^{48} \left| \frac{e_t^p(d)}{L_t^p(d)} \right| \times 100] \tag{9}$$

RESULTS AND DISCUSSION

Table 3 gives the monthly average $MAPE^p$ of 15 runs for different training algorithms. Average for each column has been calculated to get the average $MAPE^p$ for the year 2013 by each training algorithm. Average yearly $MAPE^p$ helps to select the best training algorithm to train the ANNs for forecasting short term load demand. Therefore, considering the yearly average $MAPE^p$, the training algorithm which combines GA and PSO methods performs better compared to the other training algorithms. The yearly average $MAPE^p$ with the PSO+GA algorithm is 2.867 and this is the smallest $MAPE^p$ compared to other yearly $MAPE^p$: 3.108 with GA, 3.430 with PSO, and 3.759 with Backpropagation.

The minimum and the maximum monthly average $MAPE^p$ with the hybridized algorithm are 2.164 (April) and 6.761 (December), respectively. These values when GA is used with the ANN are 2.442 (September) and 7.069 (December). The minimum (2.556) and maximum (8.636) monthly average MA-

PE^p with PSO training algorithm belong to November and December, respectively. The Backpropagation training algorithm which gives the highest yearly average $MAPE^p$ has its minimum monthly average $MAPE^p$ in August (2.541) and the maximum monthly average $MAPE^p$ in December (8.466).

Table 3. Monthly (2013) average MAPE^p for different training algorithms

	Monthly Average $MAPE^p$			
	PSO+GA	**GA-ANN**	**PSO-ANN**	**BP-ANN**
January	2.638	2.926	3.137	3.836
February	2.836	3.040	3.215	3.479
March	2.886	3.104	3.494	4.254
April	2.164	2.491	2.603	3.394
May	2.411	2.643	2.938	3.416
June	2.843	3.112	3.202	3.594
July	2.392	2.612	2.931	3.172
August	2.173	2.453	2.573	2.541
September	2.265	2.442	2.611	2.655
October	2.746	2.929	3.259	3.388
November	2.293	2.470	2.556	2.917
December	6.761	7.069	8.636	8.466
Average	2.867	3.108	3.430	3.759

Only December has higher than 3.00 average monthly $MAPE^p$ when the ANN trains with the hybridized training algorithm. Average monthly $MAPE^p$s are higher than 3.00 in February, March, June, and December when ANN uses GA. January, February, March, June, October, and December have over 3.00 average monthly $MAPE^p$s with PSO while only August, September, and November give less than 3.000 $MAPE^p$ values with backpropagation. The difference of the forecasts over the actual demand of a sample day (24th of April, 2013) is given in Figure 3.

Regardless of the training algorithm, average monthly $MAPE^p$s in December are higher compared to the other months. The reason is, although holidays, bridging holidays, and outliers from the sample data set are replaced with the estimated data, still the load consumption in December is much lower compared to the other months. When the ANN is trained with higher consumption values from other months, it forecasts assuming that December has similar consumption values.

Figure 4 summarizes the yearly average $MAPE^p$s of different categories of days: Weekdays, Mondays, Weekends, Holidays, and Bridging holidays with different training algorithms. The best yearly average $MAPE^p$ for all the categories comes with the hybridized training algorithm, while the maximum yearly average $MAPE^p$ for all the categories belongs to backpropagation training algorithm. Considering the expansion of boxes and maximum $MAPE^p$s of each category, promising results can be expected for Weekdays, regardless of the training method. However, the average $MAPE^p$s and error expansions are higher when the network forecasts Holidays and Bridging Holidays. The highest maximum errors come with the Monday forecasting, regardless of the training method.

Figure 3. Actual vs. Forecasted load with different training algorithms for April 24, 2013 (Wednesday)

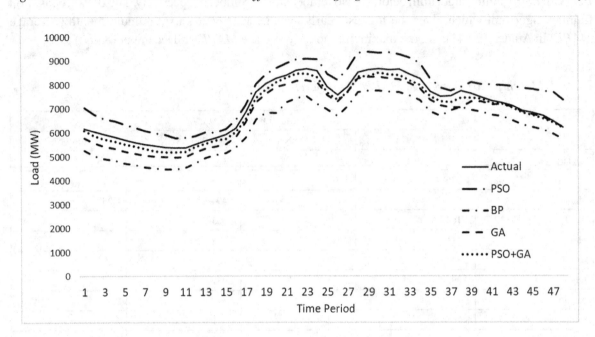

Figure 4. Box plot of yearly average MAPE's of different categories of days by different training algorithms

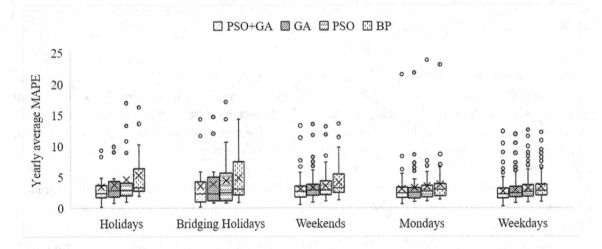

CONCLUSION

The objective of the research is to identify the best way of training ANNs for improving forecasting outcomes by minimizing the training error. Due to the limitations of using the backpropagation training algorithm, where it can trap in local minima, two meta-heuristic techniques (GA and PSO) are suggested for further reducing the training error. Another training algorithm is created using the qualities of both GA and PSO techniques. PSO cannot get out of the local minima in case it traps in one. When it traps in a local minimum, crossover and mutation functions of GA are introduced to perturb the positions of each particle in the solution space and to help getting out from the local minimum. These theoretical concepts have been proved with the arranged experiments for Short Term Load Forecasting for the case of Thailand. According to the daily forecasting results for 2013 with the suggested ANN, the best training algorithm to get a good forecasting outcome is the hybridized training algorithm (PSO+GA). GA also gives competitively good results compared to the hybridized training algorithm. However, PSO and Backpropagation training algorithms are fairly good compared to the other two training algorithms.

Regardless of the training algorithm, the hardest month to forecast is December. Due to the low electricity consumption in December, all the forecasting outcomes are higher than the actual electricity consumption. Other than December, February, March, and June are also difficult to forecast according to the monthly average $MAPE^p$ of those months.

Days of the sample set are categorized into five sections based on the patterns of the consumption curves. Out of them, forecasting results of weekdays except Mondays are promising. Therefore, the research can be further extended to improve the forecasting outcomes of the other categories: Mondays, Weekends, Holidays, and Bridging holidays. Also, some strategies have to be used for forecasting the demands in December. These could be achieved by creating new training algorithms, new ANN feature arrangements, and/or with new data arrangements which help to capture the seasonal variations of data.

REFERENCES

(2000). An improved neural network application for short-term load forecasting in power systems. *Electric Machines & Power Systems*, *28*(8), 703–721. doi:10.1080/07313560050082703

Bashir, Z., & El-Hawary, M. (2007). Short-term load forecasting using artificial neural network based on particle swarm optimization algorithm. *Paper presented at the Canadian Conference on Electrical and Computer Engineering CCECE 2007*. 10.1109/CCECE.2007.74

Chae, Y. T., Horesh, R., Hwang, Y., & Lee, Y. M. (2016). Artificial neural network model for forecasting sub-hourly electricity usage in commercial buildings. *Energy and Building*, *111*, 184–194. doi:10.1016/j. enbuild.2015.11.045

Clements, A. E., Hurn, A., & Li, Z. (2016). Forecasting day-ahead electricity load using a multiple equation time series approach. *European Journal of Operational Research*, *251*(2), 522–530. doi:10.1016/j. ejor.2015.12.030

Coelho, V. N., Coelho, I. M., Rios, E., Alexandre Filho, S., Reis, A. J., Coelho, B. N., ... Guimarães, F. G. (2016). A Hybrid Deep Learning Forecasting Model Using GPU Disaggregated Function Evaluations Applied for Household Electricity Demand Forecasting. *Energy Procedia*, *103*, 280–285. doi:10.1016/j. egypro.2016.11.286

Dedinec, A., Filiposka, S., Dedinec, A., & Kocarev, L. (2016). Deep belief network based electricity load forecasting: An analysis of Macedonian case. *Energy*, *115*, 1688–1700. doi:10.1016/j.energy.2016.07.090

Demiroren, A., & Ceylan, G. (2006). Middle anatolian region short-term load forecasting using artificial neural networks. *Electric Power Components and Systems*, *34*(6), 707–724. doi:10.1080/15325000500419284

Ding, N., Benoit, C., Foggia, G., Bésanger, Y., & Wurtz, F. (2016). Neural network-based model design for short-term load forecast in distribution systems. *IEEE Transactions on Power Systems*, *31*(1), 72–81. doi:10.1109/TPWRS.2015.2390132

Dudek, G. (2016). Pattern-based local linear regression models for short-term load forecasting. *Electric Power Systems Research*, *130*, 139–147. doi:10.1016/j.epsr.2015.09.001

Gajowniczek, K., & Ząbkowski, T. (2014). Short term electricity forecasting using individual smart meter data. *Procedia Computer Science*, *35*, 589–597. doi:10.1016/j.procs.2014.08.140

Hassan, S., Khosravi, A., & Jaafar, J. (2015). Examining performance of aggregation algorithms for neural network-based electricity demand forecasting. *International Journal of Electrical Power & Energy Systems*, *64*, 1098–1105. doi:10.1016/j.ijepes.2014.08.025

Hassan, S., Khosravi, A., Jaafar, J., & Khanesar, M. A. (2016). A systematic design of interval type-2 fuzzy logic system using extreme learning machine for electricity load demand forecasting. *International Journal of Electrical Power & Energy Systems*, *82*, 1–10. doi:10.1016/j.ijepes.2016.03.001

Hein, D., Hentschel, A., Runkler, T. A., & Udluft, S. (2016). Reinforcement learning with particle swarm optimization policy (PSO-P) in continuous state and action spaces. *International Journal of Swarm Intelligence Research*, *7*(3), 23–42. doi:10.4018/IJSIR.2016070102

Ismail, Z., Yahya, A., & Mahpol, K. (2009). Forecasting peak load electricity demand using statistics and rule based approach. *American Journal of Applied Sciences*, *6*(8), 1618–1625. doi:10.3844/ajassp.2009.1618.1625

Jeenanunta, C., & Abeyrathn, K. D. (2017). Combine Particle Swarm Optimization with Artificial Neural Networks for Short-Term Load Forecasting. *ISJET*, *8*, 25.

Jeenanunta, C., & Abeyrathna, K. D. (2017). Neural Network with Genetic Algorithm for Forecasting Short-Term Electricity Load Demand. *International Journal of Energy Technology and Policy*.

Jurado, S., Nebot, À., Mugica, F., & Avellana, N. (2015). Hybrid methodologies for electricity load forecasting: Entropy-based feature selection with machine learning and soft computing techniques. *Energy*, *86*, 276–291. doi:10.1016/j.energy.2015.04.039

Kumar, S., & Singh, S. K. (2017). Hybrid BFO and PSO swarm intelligence approach for biometric feature optimization. In Nature-Inspired Computing: Concepts, Methodologies, Tools, and Applications (pp. 1490-1518). Hershey, PA: IGI Global. doi:10.4018/978-1-5225-0788-8.ch057

Leboucher, C., Chelouah, R., Siarry, P., & Le Ménec, S. (2012). A swarm intelligence method combined to evolutionary game theory applied to the resources allocation problem. *International Journal of Swarm Intelligence Research*, *3*(2), 20–38. doi:10.4018/jsir.2012040102

Mishra, S., & Patra, S. K. (2008). Short term load forecasting using neural network trained with genetic algorithm & particle swarm optimization. *Paper presented at the First International Conference on Emerging Trends in Engineering and Technology ICETET'08*. 10.1109/ICETET.2008.94

Qiu, X., Ren, Y., Suganthan, P. N., & Amaratunga, G. A. (2017). Empirical mode decomposition based ensemble deep learning for load demand time series forecasting. *Applied Soft Computing*, *54*, 246–255. doi:10.1016/j.asoc.2017.01.015

Ramakrishna, R., Boiroju, N. K., & Reddy, M. K. (2011). Forecasting daily electricity load using neural networks. *International Journal of Mathematical Archive, 2*(8).

Rana, M., & Koprinska, I. (2016). Forecasting electricity load with advanced wavelet neural networks. *Neurocomputing*, *182*, 118–132. doi:10.1016/j.neucom.2015.12.004

Ringwood, J. V., Bofelli, D., & Murray, F. T. (2001). Forecasting electricity demand on short, medium and long time scales using neural networks. *Journal of Intelligent & Robotic Systems*, *31*(1-3), 129–147. doi:10.1023/A:1012046824237

Rumelhart, D. E., Hinton, G. E., & Williams, R. J. (1986). Learning representations by back-propagating errors. nature, 323(6088), 533. doi:10.1038/323533a0

Sarangi, P. K., Singh, N., Swain, D., Chauhan, R., & Singh, R. (2009). Short term load forecasting using neuro genetic hybrid approach: Results analysis with different network architectures. *Journal of Theoretical and Applied Information Technology*, 109-116.

Senjyu, H. S., Tamaki, Y., & Katsumi Uezato, T. (. (2001). Next-day load curve forecasting using neural network based on similarity. *Electric Power Components and Systems*, *29*(10), 939–948. doi:10.1080/15325000152646541

Senjyu, T., Tamaki, Y., Takara, H., & Uezato, K. (2002). Next day load curve forecasting using wavelet analysis with neural network. *Electric Power Components and Systems*, *30*(11), 1167–1178. doi:10.1080/15325000290085398

Shayeghi, H., Shayanfar, H., & Azimi, G. (2009). STLF based on optimized neural network using PSO. *Iranian Journal of Electrical and Computer Engineering*, *4*(10), 1190–1199.

Singh, D., & Singh, S.D. Singh, S. P. Singh. (2001). A self-selecting neural network for short-term load forecasting. *Electric Power Components and Systems*, *29*(2), 117–130. doi:10.1080/153250001300003386

Subbaraj, P., & Rajasekaran, V. (2008). Evolutionary techniques based combined artificial neural networks for peak load forecasting. *World Academy of Science, Engineering and Technology*, *45*, 680–686.

This research was previously published in the International Journal of Swarm Intelligence Research (IJSIR), 10(1); pages 1-14, copyright year 2019 by IGI Publishing (an imprint of IGI Global).

Chapter 11
Reconstruction of Missing Hourly Precipitation Data to Increase Training Data Set for ANN

Hema Nagaraja
Department of Computer Science, Jaypee Institute of Information Technology, Noida, India

Krishna Kant
Manav Rachna International University, Faridabad, India

K. Rajalakshmi
Jaypee Institute of Information Technology, Noida, India

ABSTRACT

This paper investigates the hourly precipitation estimation capacities of ANN using raw data and reconstructed data using proposed Precipitation Sliding Window Period (PSWP) method. The precipitation data from 11 Automatic Weather Station (AWS) of Delhi has been obtained from Jan 2015 to Feb 2016. The proposed PSWP method uses both time and space dimension to fill the missing precipitation values. Hourly precipitation follows patterns in particular period along with its neighbor stations. Based on these patterns of precipitation, Local Cluster Sliding Window Period (LCSWP) and Global Cluster Sliding Window Period (GCSWP) are defined for single AWS and all AWSs respectively. Further, GCSWP period is classified into four different categories to fill the missing precipitation data based on patterns followed in it. The experimental results indicate that ANN trained with reconstructed data has better estimation results than the ANN trained with raw data. The average RMSE for ANN trained with raw data is 0.44 and while that for neural network trained with reconstructed data is 0.34.

DOI: 10.4018/978-1-6684-2408-7.ch011

1. INTRODUCTION

Meteorological data are a set of climatic information, which describes the characteristics of the atmosphere. Meteorological station records climatic parameters like air temperature, dew point temperature, atmospheric pressure, rainfall, wind speed, wind direction, maximum temperature, minimum temperature and sunshine hours in minutes. These data are available on the hourly or daily basis. Meteorological data are very important in hydrological analysis and for agricultural purpose. Measuring instrument or infrastructural failures creates missing data in the measurements. These missing data may be significant portions and can be random in space and time. This paper proposes to reconstruct the missing hourly rainfall and how this increased data set will help in improving estimation of precipitation.

Water reservoir system, flood warning systems, domestic usage planning, irrigation calculation, industry usage planning and planning of hydropower generation (Mays, 2010) required accurate hourly rainfall data. Real-time smart irrigation system requires accurate and complete hourly rainfall data from past and present hour to schedule the timely and right amount of irrigation as described in "Specification for Weather-Based Irrigation Controllers" by WaterSense (July, 2012). Incomplete rainfall data provided to real-time irrigation system will lead to over or under irrigation for that particular irrigation cycle.

Filling of missing values can be based on the same site or use nearby sites to estimate values. Estimation is based on time dimension, space dimension or a combination of both depending on the pattern of missing data and its correlation with each other (Gao et al., 2015). Higher the correlation better estimation of missing values (Graham, 2012). The selection of interpolation method mainly depends on the type of data that are used to fill the gaps. Rainfall data are spatiotemporal variable and uses deterministic and geostatistical methods for estimation of missing rainfall data (Piazza et al., 2015). Understanding of precipitation patterns is important for appropriate selection of interpolation method.

A study by Deshpande et al. (2012) provides the characteristics of the hourly rainfall over India based on a large network of Self Recording Rain Gauge Stations with 25 years of data. Study shows that area of our interest Delhi, India has rainfall of minimum 200 hr/yr and a maximum of 600 hr/yr. During non-monsoon season that is for January to May and October to December the average rainfall is less than 10 cm and during monsoon season average rainfall is between 50 cm to 100 cm. Characteristics of acquired data from Delhi validates the characteristics defined by Deshpande et al. (2012).

For experimentation purpose, real data has acquired from 14th January 2015 to 28th February 2016 from eleven Automatic Weather Stations (AWS) located in Delhi. Approximate annual rainfall for all eleven AWS has summarized in Table 1. Column 1 of Table 1 is a total number of rainfall hours for each of eleven AWS's for the year 2015 to 2016. The average rainfall is 577 hr, and is falling within the range defined by Deshpande et al. (2012). Column 2 of Table 1 has a total number of hours of rainfall occurred in a non-monsoon season of the year 2015-16. On average 172 hours of rainfall has occurred in a non-monsoon season, with average rainfall range of 1-9 mm/hr. Monsoon has frequent rainfall with an average of 406 hr with a range of 1-55 mm/hr.

Rain gauges used in AWS is of tipping bucket type. The range of the sensor is the 0 to the 1023mm/hr with an accuracy of ±5%. Rain gauge's recorded data is hourly cumulative and refreshed at 3:00 UTC. Indian Meteorological Department (IMD) Delhi (semi-arid region) data from eleven AWS's has following hourly rainfall characteristics:

- Most of the time there is no precipitation and data read from the meteorological station are 0 mm.
- Single AWS showing rainfall has a low intensity of precipitation in the range of 1-6 mm/hr.

243

- When rainfall starts, precipitation data are in increasing values.
- When rainfall about to stop, precipitation data are in decreasing values.
- In between start and stop of rainfall, data has a steady and consistent pattern.
- During heavy rainfall majority of nearby weather station also shows precipitation for the same time stamp with different patterns.

Table 1. Summary of approximate annual rainfall in hours for Delhi, India

Stations	Annual Rainfall in hr	non-monsoon season rainfall in Hr	Non-Monsoon Rainfall Range in mm	Monsoon season rainfall in hr	Monsoon Rainfall Range in mm
AWS-1	630	282	1-8	348	1-73
AWS-2	554	160	1-8	394	1-103
AWS-3	543	180	1-9	363	1-47
AWS-4	610	160	1-5	450	1-35
AWS-5	531	119	1-4	412	1-55
AWS-6	856	311	1-13	545	1-45
AWS-7	531	112	1-17	419	1-52
AWS-8	538	167	1-6	371	1-40
AWS-9	565	178	1-8	387	1-64
AWS-10	560	107	1-12	453	1-41
AWS-11	421	106	1	315	1-43
Average	**577**	**172**	**1-9**	**406**	**1-55**

Above rainfall, characteristics are used to define Precipitation Sliding Window Period (PSWP) algorithm. PSWP classifies rainfall into different classes based on all AWS with zero precipitation, or single AWS precipitation, or a majority of AWS is having different precipitation patterns at same time stamp or hourly changing precipitation data for same time stamp. Each AWS has local cluster sliding window period (LCSWP) whose size is defined based on the time stamp in which precipitation patterns are same.

Global cluster sliding window (GCSWP) period size is defined before filling missing precipitation data. GCSWP period is obtained based on the mode or means of all LCSWP period size. Most of the missing rainfall data have been reconstructed using PSWP except for the following cases

- Hourly changing precipitation patterns
- Precipitation that is missing in transition windows
- Continuous missing precipitation data.

Due to above, said reason PSWP is unable to reconstruct complete data, in addition to PSWP other interpolation techniques are required. Artificial Neural Network (ANN) interpolation technique is more suitable for filling missing precipitation data. In particular time stamp, the nearby weather station rainfall patterns are correlation with each other and hence ANN is suitable interpolation technique. Accurate correlation can be obtained by nearby weather station only when all their corresponding hourly data are available. Out of 11 AWS, even if one of the AWS's data is missing then complete record will be discarded from the analysis. The dropping of records is happening due to these filtrations and hence reduces the dataset from the analysis in the study.

As initial data processing techniques, PSWP is used to reconstruct most of the missing rainfall data. Further, this increased data set from PSWP is used by ANN to estimate missing data. It is very important to increase data set to obtain the accurate estimations especially for ANN. Experiments conducted on study area Delhi shows that accuracy of ANN estimation improves with increased data set which are reconstructed from PSWP method.

Next section presents already existing methods used in the reconstruction of missing precipitation data. Section 3 presents a description of the study area and observed precipitation data characteristics. Section 4 presents our proposal of PSWP method for reconstruction of missing data. This section provides various algorithms to create local and GCSWP for different patterns and filling of missing data.

After reconstruction of missing precipitation data, next step is to validate how these increased data set used by neural networks is improving the accuracy of estimation. Section 5 describes back-propagation neural network used for experiments. Section 6 demonstrates results of a neural network trained with raw data set and reconstructed data set for all eleven AWSs. Root Mean Square Error (RMSE) is used to represent estimation error and Section 7 concludes the paper and address the future work..

2. RELATED WORK ON RECONSTRUCTION OF MISSING DATA

Estimation of missing meteorological data depends on data from the same location or its neighboring stations. Estimation of data series interval depends on application need which varies typically from annual, monthly, weekly, daily to hourly data. Hourly precipitation estimation is more challenging than daily, weekly, monthly and annual precipitation.

Hourly precipitation estimation has higher error association and we need careful selection of interpolation techniques. Therefore, the choice of an interpolation method for missing data mainly depends on the quality of observed data, whether study area is arid or semi-arid regions and size of sampled data set.

The review by Ly et al. (2013), discusses the existing methods of interpolation of rainfall data used in hydrological modeling. The review discussed that spatial interpolation has two main methods of deterministic and geostatistical techniques. Under deterministic techniques the Thiessen polygon (THI), IDW, polynomial interpolation, spline interpolation, moving window regression methods have been used. Under geostatistical techniques the various methods of Kriging and semi-variogram have been used. For annual and monthly precipitation estimation both deterministic and geostatistical techniques are used in which geostatistical methods outperform deterministic methods.

Geostatistical and non-geostatistical approaches are applied for daily precipitation estimation. In this approach the kriging and IDW methods are better estimators. Hourly estimation by Verworn and Haberlandt (2011), has used a multivariate geostatistical method like Kriging with External Drift (KED) along with radar data as the second variable.

Kim and Pachepsky (2010), concludes that instead of using stand-alone regression trees and artificial neural networks, if they are used in combination for reconstruction of missing daily precipitation data then there is a significant improvement in the accuracy of the estimation. Lee and Kang (2015), proposes five different kernel functions to estimate missing daily precipitation data. A result demonstrates that kernel interpolation is a better estimator than KNN regression.

Another interesting study by Ramos-Calzado et al. (2008), proposes a new method of filling monthly precipitation gaps in the climatological series for a target station using precipitation data from neighboring stations with a similar precipitation pattern. The proposed approach uses the uncertainty of rainfall measurement for filling missing data which is highly variable and depends on precipitation rate. The presented paper uses a similar approach of precipitation pattern but we are using the intersection of both local station as well as its neighbor stations precipitation patterns. Using this intersection, a window is created and classified according to the patterns and then filling of missing data takes place.

Ferrari and Ozaki (2014), discuss filling of daily precipitation gaps using regular interpolation technique of Inverse Distance Weighted (IDW) method and Linear Regular Regression method. Results conclude that IDW provides better estimation than Linear Regression techniques. Also, there is quality control of the estimated data whether it is consistent or not. Further, this estimated and quality controlled data are used for drought estimation which helps farmer for planning the crop and cash.

Velasco-Forero et al. (2009), focus on hourly precipitation by using a non-parametric technique based on fast Fourier transform (FFT) along with radar observations to directly obtain the correlograms. Due to this, correlation maps can be automatically obtained on hourly basis and can be used for real-time applications. Cross-validation and spatial pattern analysis showed that KED gives accurate results.

Teegavarapu et al. (2012), proposes new mathematical programming models to estimate daily missing precipitation data. These models use both nonlinear and mixed-integer nonlinear mathematical programming formulations (using Genetic Algorithm) with binary variables, which overcome the limitation of spatial interpolation methods. The results from this method are superior to naive approaches, multiple linear regression, nonlinear least-square optimization, kriging, and global and local trend surface and thin-plate spline models.

Back-propagation neural network is the effective and popular model used for the complex multi-layered neural network. It uses supervised learning algorithm and trains complex input with output patterns. They are not only used for filling of missing precipitation but also for forecasting of precipitation. Ilunga (2010), has used feed-forward ANN techniques to infill annual rainfall data. The standard and the generalized back-propagation technique is used and back-propagation technique showed better estimation.

Only a few literatures are available for estimation of hourly precipitation. Simple and accurate estimate of hourly precipitation is a need for hydrological models. Climate-based smart irrigation products need complete hourly precipitation data for more accurate and timely irrigation.

3. DESCRIPTION OF STUDY AREA AND DATA

Eleven AWSs located in Delhi is considered as a study area to fill missing precipitation data. The locations of AWS installed in Delhi region are as follows:

- South West Delhi: Najafgarh, Jafarpur
- South Delhi: Ayanagar
- North West: Narela, Pitampura
- North Delhi: Delhi University
- East Delhi: Akshardham, National Centre for Medium Range Weather Forecasting (NCMRWF)
- Central Delhi: New Delhi, Pusa and Sports Complex Delhi

Figure 1 shows the placement of AWSs in the Delhi locality. Table 2 shows the latitude and longitude of these places and they are within 50 km of radius.

Figure 1. Delhi, AWS Location MAP

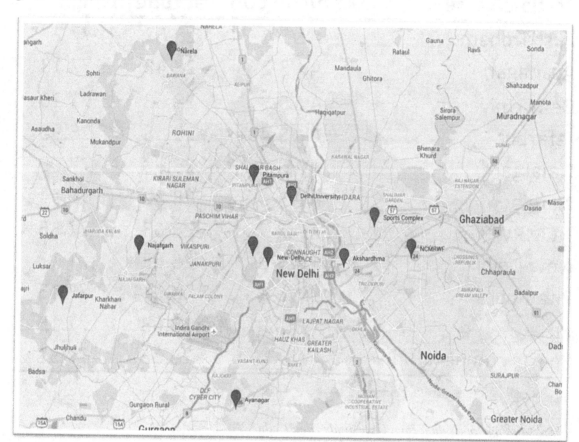

Rainfall data are available in a one-hour time interval and are available at Indian Meteorological Department (IMD) website "http://www.imdaws.com/ViewAwsData. aspx". The desired state, district and location can be accessed through IMD website and data are available for week duration. Total of 675 AWS was installed across India during 2008-2010 as articulated by Giri et al. (2014).

To demonstrate filling of data, we have considered precipitation data from January 2015 to Feb 2016. Data acquired in this period is around 63,514 hours. Out of this acquired hourly data, around 9,530 hours of data are missing. That is a total of 15.00% of precipitation data are missing from observed data. All weathers station having zero-precipitation with the different time stamp is around 44,913 hours. Single AWS having precipitation with the different time stamp is around 8,602 hours. 473 hours has random hourly precipitation at different time stamp. 9,526 hours has a mixture of different precipitation (zero or non-zero) pattern at the same period. Table 3 shows filling of missing precipitation data using PSWP in hours for each AWS.

Table 2. Latitude and Longitude of the Case Study Area Delhi

Station Name	Station Abbreviation	Latitude	Longitude
Akshardham	AWS-1	28.62	77.27
Ayanagar	AWS-2	28.48	77.13
Delhi University	AWS-3	28.68	77.20
Jafarpur	AWS-4	28.58	76.90
Najafgarh	AWS-5	28.63	77.00
Narela	AWS-6	28.82	77.04
NCMRWF	AWS-7	28.63	77.36
New Delhi	AWS-8	28.62	77.17
Pitampura	AWS-9	28.7	77.15
Pusa	AWS-10	28.63	77.15
Sports complex Delhi	AWS-11	28.66	77.31

Table 3. Missing hour's data from Case Study Area Delhi

Stations	Missing hours
AWS-1	1139
AWS-2	415
AWS-3	574
AWS-4	512
AWS-5	605
AWS-6	2110
AWS-7	559
AWS-8	2248
AWS-9	606
AWS-10	509
AWS-11	253
Total	**9530**

4. PROPOSED RECONSTRUCTION METHOD: PRECIPITATION SLIDING WINDOW PERIOD

IMD hourly precipitation data is available for all seasons and length of this time series data is considered to be L. The maximum number of AWSs is denoted by max. Each AWS is denoted by A_j, where j is the AWS number 0 to max–1. Let c be the common timestamp period for precipitation patterns observed over all AWSs.

Precipitation data has organized in such a way that each column represents individual AWS data and each row represents hourly precipitation data for all AWS. For individual AWS a Local Cluster Sliding Window Period (LCSWP) is defined which are having same precipitation patterns. Global Cluster Sliding Window (GCSWP) is common sliding window period defined for all AWS's for particular time stamp period based on precipitation patterns. The mode of all AWS's LCSWP size forms GCSWP. In this common GCSWP, individual AWS may have more than one LCSWP period.

Precipitation sliding window period (PSWP) method classifies rainfall pattern into four major GCSWP cases as follows:

A. Window having all AWS with zero precipitation
B. Window having single AWS with non-zero precipitation
C. Window having all AWS with random hourly precipitation
D. Window having mixed precipitation

Algorithms to obtain GCSWP for each case are discussed in next section. Some common notations used are as follows:

- Length of LCSWP is denoted by l_{A_j}, where $2 < l_{A_j} \leq L$
- Length of GCSWP is denoted by g_c.
- P_{A_j} represents precipitation data of jth AWS.
- $P_{A_j}[t]$ refers to t^{th} hour precipitation data for j^{th} AWS, where $t£L$.
- g_t represents total number hours for which global cluster sliding window has been created and traversed. g_t is sum the of g_c until t reaches L. Initially $g_t = 0$
- Initially missing values in the array $P_{A_j}[t]$ is blank.

Before defining GCSWP we have to obtain LCSWP for each AWS. Algorithm 1 gives steps to obtain LCSWP. Filling of missing precipitation takes place after defining GCSWP period. If the GCSWP size is equal to LCSWP period then filling of missing precipitation value uses the same pattern as that of LCSWP. If the LCSWP size is not equal to GCSWP then traverse the only LCSWP to fill the missing precipitation.

Next section discusses algorithms to obtain GCSWP for all four cases and filling of missing precipitation in each case. Missing values has following occurrences in obtained g_c:

1. Column missing values i.e. missing of complete AWS data.
2. Missing values in rows i.e. missing data for all AWS's.

3.   Random missing in column and row.

The accuracy of filled data depends on the missing occurrence type. For random row and column missing data, the accuracy will be high as filling values considers previous and next hour precipitation i.e. uses the pattern defined in LCSWP. For continuous missing values of columns and rows, the accuracy of filling data is low.

4.1. Case A: Obtaining Global Cluster Window with Zero Precipitation

The study area is mainly semi-arid region and in annual precipitation data, maximum hours have zero precipitation. Algorithm 2 follows simple steps to obtain GCSWP g_c for case-A. GCSWP size depends on the maximum occurrence of LCSWP size of all AWSs. Once GCSWP is obtained, all missing values are majorly filled by zero values.

Algorithm 1: Steps to obtain LCSWP size l_{A_j}

   For all j from 0 to max–1

1.   Initially l_{A_j} for j^{th} AWS is zero.
2.   Loop t from g_t to L–1.
3.   Add $P_{A_j}[t]$ to LCSWP, increment l_{A_j} to 1.
4.   Increment t to read next hour precipitation data. If $\left| P_{A_j}[t+1] - P_{A_j}[t] \right| = 0$ or $P_{A_j}[t+1] = missing\ data$ then add $P_{s_j}[t+1]$ into the current sliding window and increment l_{A_j} by 1.
5.   Keep repeating step-D until $\left| P_{A_j}[t+1] - P_{A_j}[t] \right| \neq 0$. This non-zero indicates change in rainfall value in LCSWP.
6.   If there is change in precipitation data that is $P_{A_j}[t+1] \neq P_{A_j}[t]\ and \neq blank$ then stop iterations. Return the value of l_{A_j}, if $l_{A_j} > 2$.
7.   Else, if $l_{A_j} < 2$, then return null. (LCSWP can't be defined).
8.   Increment value of j and repeat the steps A to H.

4.1.1. Filling of Missing Values for Case-A

Once GCSWP is defined, next step is to fill the missing precipitation data. In GCSWP, all precipitation values are either zero precipitation values or missing values. Filling of few continuous rows, few continuous columns and random row column values are with zero precipitation. Probabilities of these missing values to be zero's are high.

Algorithm 2: Steps to obtain GCSWP for Zero Precipitation
   For all j from 0 to max–1

1.   Using algorithm-1 obtain l_{A_j} for all AWS

2.   Repeat A and B till all AWS has obtained LCSWP
3.   Obtain minimum of all AWS's l_{A_j} to obtain g_c. Minimum size LCSWP decides size of g_c.
4. $g_t = g_t + g_c$, return g_t.

By applying algorithm-2 on data set we have obtained 44,933 hours of precipitation data falling under this category. Experimental dataset has a total of 71 different sized GCSWP. Around 15.10% (6788 hr) of data was missing in this category, they are filled with zero precipitation. Whereas, if the length of missing data in column is equal to g_c, then error may be associated in filling zero precipitation is as shown in Table 4. This error is due to reason of single AWS showing precipitation whereas its neighbour AWS showing no sign of precipitation. Around 8,602 hr of data falls in the category-B of single precipitation data.

Table 4 shows error influence while filling with zero precipitation. For example, in Table 4 the AWS-1 shows 129 hours of precipitation while no other stations have precipitation at that time. Error influence is 1.5% (129 hr precipitation in single precipitation data set).

Table 4. Error that may influence on Case A and B while filling missing data

Stations	Single AWS Precipitation	% Error influence
AWS-1	129	1.50
AWS-2	31	0.36
AWS-3	90	1.05
AWS-4	74	0.86
AWS-5	10	0.12
AWS-6	261	3.03
AWS-7	32	0.37
AWS-8	38	0.44
AWS-9	57	0.66
AWS-10	38	0.44
AWS-11	29	0.34

4.2. Case B: Obtaining Global Cluster Window with Single AWS Precipitation

For single AWS precipitation, Algorithm 3 follows simple steps to obtain GCSWP g_c. Once GCSWP is obtained all missing values are majorly filled by zero values other than non-zero precipitation station. Any missing value in non-zero precipitation station will be filled with pattern that has occurred in g_c.

Algorithm 3: Steps to obtain GCSWP for single precipitation station
    For all *j* from 0 to max−1

A.   Using algorithm-1 obtain l_{A_j} for all AWS
B.   Repeat A and B till all AWS's LCSWP have obtained.

C.   Obtain the length l_{A_j} of non-zero precipitation station and assign that to g_c.

D. $g_t = g_t + g_c$, return g_t.

4.2.1. Filling of Missing Values for Case-B

In case-B there can be two types of missing data, one is single precipitation AWS and another one is zero precipitation AWSs. Since the length of single precipitation AWS's LCSWP is equal to GCSWP, any missing data in it must have the same pattern as that of LCSWP. Therefore, all missing data in single precipitation is filled with the same pattern as that of LCSWP's pattern. For rest of the AWSs, missing data is filled with zero precipitation. Missing data may be a continuous row, column or random row and column. Filling of few continuous row, random row and column with zero are more accurate, but for complete column filling with zero precipitation may not be accurate. The reason is due to the error associated with zero filling similar to that of case-A. By applying algorithm-3 on data set we have obtained 8,602 hours of precipitation data falling under this category B. Total of 62 different sized GCSWP was obtained on experimental data set for case B. Around 18.78% (1616 hr) of data was missing in this category which is filled with zero and non-zero precipitation.

Example 1: Precipitation data from 3ʳᵈ July 2015 4:00 to 4ᵗʰ July 3:00 is considered for a demonstration of PSWP method. The table has three GCSWP two with all AWSs with zero precipitation and another with single AWS precipitation.

In Table 5, LCSWP period is calculated for each AWS as

$$l_{A_0} = 24, \ l_{A_1} = 11, \ l_{A_2} = 24, \ l_{A_3} = 24, \ l_{A_4} = 24,$$
$$l_{A_5} = 24, \ l_{A_6} = 24, \ l_{A_7} = 24, \ l_{A_8} = 24, \ l_{A_9} = 24 \text{ and } l_{A_{10}} = 24.$$

Minimum is applied on all LCSWPs size to obtain GCSWP period size (g_c) which is 11 ($c = 11$). Eight hours of data is missing in this GCSWP and they are filled with zero precipitation.
In the second iteration for Table 5, g_t will start at 11. LCSWP period is calculated as

$$l_{A_0} = 22, \ l_{A_1} = 13, \ l_{A_2} = 22, \ l_{A_3} = 22, \ l_{A_4} = 22, \ l_{s_5} = 22,$$
$$l_{s_6} = 22, \ l_{s_6} = 22, \ l_{s_7} = 22, \ l_{s_8} = 22, \ l_{s_9} = 22 \text{ and } l_{s_{10}} = 22. \ (\text{max}{-}1)$$

Stations has zero precipitation therefore GCSWP g_n is defined using LCSWP size of non-zero precipitation station which is 13 ($c = 13$). Five hours missing value has to be filled with zero precipitation in this iteration. Traversed Sliding window $g_t = 24$.
In the third iteration for Table 5, calculation of LCSWP period for each AWS is

$$l_{A_0} = 10, \ l_{A_1} = 10, \ l_{A_2} = 10, \ l_{A_3} = 10, \ l_{A_4} = 10,$$
$$l_{A_5} = 10, \ l_{A_6} = 10, \ l_{A_7} = 10, \ l_{A_8} = 10, \ l_{A_9} = 10 \text{ and } l_{A_{10}} = 10.$$

Minimum is applied on all LCSWPs size to obtain GCSWP period size (g_c) which is 10 $(c= 10)$. Three hours of data is missing in this GCSWP and they are filled with zero precipitation.

Table 5. Precipitation data from 3rd July 2015 4:00 to 4th July 3:00, B denotes blank/Missing data

Sr. No.	Date	Time	AWS-1	AWS-2	AWS-3	AWS-4	AWS-5	AWS-6	AWS-7	AWS-8	AWS-9	AWS-10	AWS-11
1	03-Jul-15	4:00	0	0	0	0	0	0	0	0	0	0	0
2	03-Jul-15	5:00	0	0	B	0	0	0	0	0	0	0	0
3	03-Jul-15	6:00	0	0	B	0	0	0	0	0	0	0	0
4	03-Jul-15	7:00:	0	0	0	0	0	0	B	0	0	0	0
5	03-Jul-15	8:00:	0	0	0	0	0	0	0	0	0	0	0
6	03-Jul-15	9:00:	0	0	0	0	0	0	0	0	B	0	0
7	03-Jul-15	10:00	0	0	0	0	0	0	0	0	0	0	0
8	03-Jul-15	11:00	0	0	0	0	B	B	0	0	0	0	0
9	03-Jul-15	12:00	0	0	0	0	0	0	0	0	0	B	0
10	03-Jul-15	13:00	0	0	B	0	0	0	0	0	0	0	0
11	03-Jul-15	14:00	0	0	0	0	0	0	0	0	0	0	0
12	03-Jul-15	15:00	0	4	0	0	0	0	0	0	0	0	0
13	03-Jul-15	16:00	0	4	0	0	0	0	0	0	0	B	0
14	03-Jul-15	17:00	0	4	B	0	0	B	0	0	0	0	0
15	03-Jul-15	18:00	0	4	0	0	0	0	0	0	0	0	0
16	03-Jul-15	19:00	0	4	0	0	0	0	0	0	0	0	0
17	03-Jul-15	20:00	0	4	0	B	0	0	0	0	0	0	0
18	03-Jul-15	21:00	0	4	0	0	0	0	0	0	0	0	0
19	03-Jul-15	22:00	0	4	0	0	0	0	0	0	0	0	0
20	03-Jul-15	23:00	0	4	0	0	0	0	0	0	0	0	0
21	04-Jul-15	0:00	0	4	0	0	0	0	B	0	0	0	0
22	04-Jul-15	1:00	0	4	0	0	0	0	0	0	0	0	0
23	04-Jul-15	2:00	0	4	0	0	0	0	0	0	0	0	0
24	04-Jul-15	3:00	0	4	0	0	0	0	0	0	0	0	0
25	04-Jul-15	4:00	0	0	0	0	0	0	0	0	0	0	0
26	04-Jul-15	5:00	0	0	0	0	0	0	0	0	0	0	0
27	04-Jul-15	6:00	0	0	0	0	0	0	0	0	0	0	0
28	04-Jul-15	7:00	0	0	0	B	0	0	0	0	0	0	0
29	04-Jul-15	8:00	0	0	0	B	0	0	0	0	0	0	0
30	04-Jul-15	9:00	0	0	0	0	0	0	0	0	0	0	0
31	04-Jul-15	10:00	0	0	0	0	0	0	0	0	0	0	0
32	04-Jul-15	11:00	0	0	0	0	0	0	0	0	0	0	B
33	04-Jul-15	12:00	0	0	0	0	0	0	0	0	0	0	0
34	04-Jul-15	13:00	0	0	0	0	0	0	0	0	0	0	0

4.3. Case C: Obtaining Global Cluster Window for Mixed Precipitation

For different pattern precipitation, Algorithm 4 is used to obtain GCSWP g_c. The size of GCSWP depends on the maximum occurrence of pattern length in each AWS. Once GCSWP is obtained, most of missing values are filled with pattern followed in their LCSWP. In this window, at least two AWS will have non-zero precipitation.

4.3.1. Filling of Missing Values for Case-C

In this case filling of missing values in few continuous rows, random row and column are more accurate than any other interpolation techniques because filling uses pattern followed in their LCSWP. The major problem with this case C is that complete column missing values can't be filled using PSWP method. Also, missing values in the boundary of LCSWP and its length < 2 can't be filled using this PSWP method.

While filling of missing values in few continuous rows, correlation with its non-zero precipitation neighbor is obtained to see the similarity in the pattern of precipitation then accordingly missing data will be filled. By applying Algorithm-4 on data set, we have obtained 9,504 hours of precipitation data in category C. Total of 95 different sized GCSWP was obtained on experimental data set for case C. Around 10.86% (1033 hr) of data was missing in this category out of which still 6.48% of data is still missing. That is a total of 417 hours of missing data was filled in the case C.

Algorithm 4: Steps to obtain GCSWP for mixed Precipitation
  For all j from 0 to max−1

A. Using algorithm-1 obtain l_{A_j} for all AWS

B. Repeat A and B till all AWS's LCSWP have obtained.

C. Apply *mode* to array of l_{A_j} (whose sum of precipitation is not equal to zero) to obtain g_c. Maximum repeated occurrence of l_{A_j} decides size of g_c.

D. $g_t = g_t + g_c$, return g_t.

4.4. Case D: Obtaining Global Cluster Window for Random Hourly Precipitation

The last category of GCSWP is case D in which window is defined for hourly changing precipitation. Algorithm 5 is called when algorithm 1-4 are not called. Sixteen different sized GCSWP was obtained on experimental data set for case D. Also, any undefined LCSWP is put into this category D due to which the length of most of the GCSWP will be one. This hourly change in precipitation is observed during start and end of heavy precipitation.

LCSWP can't be defined for most of the AWS due to hourly change in precipitation values and no consistent patterns are followed in it. Case D is the worst case of the PSWP method to fill the missing data. Experiment data set has 473 hours of data falling into this category and has 93 hours of missing data in it. Total missing data is 19.66% and filled data is 2.53%. Still missing values is 81 hours i.e. 17.12%.

Algorithm 6 is the main algorithm which calls others algorithm (1-4) to obtain GCSWP and to fill the missing values. In this Algorithm 6 for each AWS's LCSWP and its corresponding sum of precipitation is considered to call Algorithm 1-5.

Example 2: Precipitation data from 5th Aug 2015 9:00 to 5th Aug 20:00 is considered for a demonstration of PSWP method. The table has three GCSWP, where two with random hourly precipitation and another one with mixed precipitation patterns.

Algorithm 5: Steps to obtain GCSWP for hourly random precipitation
For all j from 0 to max-1

1. Using algorithm-1 obtain l_{A_j} for all AWS
2. Repeat A and B till all AWS's LCSWP have obtained.
3. Apply mode to array of l_{A_j} to obtain g_c. Maximum repeated occurrence of l_{A_j} decides size of g_c.
4. $g_t = g_t + g_c$, return g_t.

In Table 6, LCSWP period is calculated for each AWS as

$$l_{A_0} = 2, \ l_{A_1} = 12, \ l_{A_2} = 1, \ l_{A_3} = 2, \ l_{A_4} = 1, \ l_{A_5} = 0,$$
$$l_{A_6} = 5, \ l_{A_7} = 1, \ l_{A_8} = 1, \ l_{A_9} = 8 \text{ and } l_{A_{10}} = 2$$

By taking mode of all LCSWP, we get GCSWP $g_c = 1(c=1)$. One hour of data is missing in this GCSWP and it is unable to estimate.

In next iteration for Table 6, LCSWP period is calculated for each AWS as

$$l_{A_0} = 1, \ l_{A_1} = 11, \ l_{A_2} = 1, \ l_{A_3} = 1, \ l_{A_4} = 1, \ l_{A_5} = 0,$$
$$l_{A_6} = 4, \ l_{A_7} = 11, \ l_{A_8} = 1, \ l_{A_9} = 7 \text{ and } l_{A_{10}} = 1$$

By taking mode of all LCSWP, we get GCSWP $g_c = 1(c=1)$. Two hours of data is missing in this GCSWP and they are unable to estimate.

Algorithm 6: Main algorithm to fill missing values

1. Initially all missing values in the array $P_{s_j}[t]$ is blank.
2. Algorithm-1 is called to get LCSWP l_{A_j} for all AWSs.
3. For all j stations if $\sum_{t=w_t}^{t=l_{A_j}} P_{s_j}[t] = 0$, then call Algorithm-1 to obtain g_c and then fill values for Case-A.
4. For all $j-1$ stations if $\sum_{t=g_t}^{t=l_{A_j}} P_{s_j}[t] = 0$, then call Algorithm-2 to obtain g_c then fill values for Case-B.

5. For at least two AWS if $\sum\limits_{t=g_t}^{t=l_{A_j}} P_{s_j}[t] \neq 0$, then call Algorithm-3 to obtain g_c then fill values for Case-C.

6. For all j AWS if mode of l_{A_j} can't be defined or all undefined windows, call Algorithm-4 to obtain g_c then fill values for Case-D.

7. $g_t = g_t + g_c$, if traversed index $g_t < L-1$, then repeat steps 2 to 7.

In the last iteration for Table 6, LCSWP period is calculated for each AWS as

$$l_{A_0} = 10,\ l_{A_1} = 10,\ l_{A_2} = 1,\ l_{A_3} = 10,\ l_{A_4} = 1,$$
$$l_{A_5} = 0,\ l_{A_6} = 3,\ l_{A_7} = 10,\ l_{A_8} = 10,\ l_{A_9} = 6 \text{ and } l_{A_{10}} = 10.$$

By taking mode of all LCSWP expect one with zero precipitation, we get GCSWP $g_c=10(c=10)$. Thirteen hours of data is missing in this GCSWP in which 11 hours are unable to estimate. Reason for this is because either they are falling in boarder of changing window or complete column values are missing. Whereas, in AWS-3 at 20th hour missing value is filled with 27mm precipitation which is average precipitation of LCSWP in that GCSWP. AWS-9 is filled with 30mm precipitation at 11th hour which is the average precipitation of LCSWP in that GCSWP.

Table 7 gives a summary of each case with their corresponding total number of GCSWP's obtained, the total number of hours falling in each case, the total number of missing hours for each AWS's and total number filled hours for each AWS's. From the Table 7 it can be seen that most of the missing data under Case-A and Case-B are reconstructed while in Case-C and Case-D still some of the data are not filled.

Table 8 gives an overall summary of data filled using PSWP method. A total of 15% (9,530 hours) of data was missing from acquired data in which 8,833 hours of data are reconstructed using PSWP. Remaining 1.10% of data (697 hours) has to be reconstructed using other interpolation techniques.

From reconstruction results, it is understood that not all data can be reconstructed using PSWP method. To fill rest of the data it is proposed to use Artificial Neural Network (ANN) using back propagation algorithm as the majority of hourly precipitation show pattern in their precipitation. Next section discusses the application of ANN technique to estimate missing precipitation.

5. ANN WITH BACK-PROPAGATION ALGORITHM TO ESTIMATING MISSING PRECIPITATION DATA

Existing literature shows the exhaustive practice of using the artificial neural network (ANN) for a different aspect of hydrology (Feng and Hong, 2008), (Dawson and Wilby, 2001). Mainly, due to the capability of self-learning, self-organizing, and self-adapting structure of ANN. The ANN main application in hydrology includes forecasting of precipitation, flood flow forecasting, time series rainfall estimation, and real-time rainfall estimation.

Table 6. Precipitation data from 5th Aug 2015 9:00 to 5th Aug 20:00 2015, B denotes blank/Missing data

Sr. No.	Date	Time	AWS-1	AWS-2	AWS-3	AWS-4	AWS-5	AWS-6	AWS-7	AWS-8	AWS-9	AWS-10	AWS-11
1	05-Aug-15	9:00	0	0	0	0	1	B	0	0	4	1	0
2	05-Aug-15	10:00	B	0	3	0	2	B	0	1	8	1	0
3	05-Aug-15	11:00	7	0	26	2	12	B	0	1	B	1	11
4	05-Aug-15	12:00	7	0	27	2	15	B	0	1	30	1	11
5	05-Aug-15	13:00	7	0	27	2	15	B	B	1	30	1	11
6	05-Aug-15	14:00	7	0	27	2	15	B	1	1	30	1	11
7	05-Aug-15	15:00	7	0	27	2	15	B	1	1	30	1	11
8	05-Aug-15	16:00	7	0	27	2	15	B	1	1	30	1	11
9	05-Aug-15	17:00	7	0	27	2	15	B	1	1	30	0	11
10	05-Aug-15	18:00	7	0	27	2	15	B	1	1	30	0	11
11	05-Aug-15	19:00	7	0	27	2	15	B	1	1	30	0	11
12	05-Aug-15	20:00	7	0	B	2	15	B	1	1	30	0	11

Table 7. Summary of all cases with their GCSWP's size, missing hours, filled hours

	Case-A 71 GCSW		Case-B 62 GCSW		Case-C 95 GCSW		Case-D 18 GCSW	
	Total Hrs 44933	Missing Hrs 6788	Total Hrs 8602	Missing Hrs 1818	Total Hrs 9504	Missing Hrs 1033	Total Hrs 473	Missing Hrs 93
Stations	Missing Hrs	Filled Hrs	Missing Hrs	Filled Hrs	Missing Hrs	Filled Hrs	Missing Hrs	Filled Hrs
AWS-1	860	860	158	158	114	52	7	0
AWS-2	304	304	78	78	29	28	4	1
AWS-3	350	350	118	118	94	68	12	1
AWS-4	342	342	126	126	35	30	9	1
AWS-5	377	377	154	154	66	30	8	1
AWS-6	1400	1400	265	265	421	41	24	1
AWS-7	433	433	101	101	22	21	3	2
AWS-8	1697	1697	380	380	176	79	15	1
AWS-9	482	482	96	96	25	20	3	2
AWS-10	380	380	101	101	24	23	4	1
AWS-11	163	163	59	59	27	25	4	1

Table 8. Overall summary of data filled using PSWP method

Stations	Missing hours	Reconstructed Data using PSWP	Still missing	% Missing Data before PSWP	Percentage Missing %
AWS-1	1139	1070	69	19.7	1.2
AWS-2	415	411	4	7.2	0.1
AWS-3	574	537	37	9.9	0.6
AWS-4	512	499	13	8.9	0.2
AWS-5	605	562	43	10.5	0.7
AWS-6	2110	1707	403	36.5	7
AWS-7	559	557	2	9.7	0.0
AWS-8	2248	2137	111	38.9	1.9
AWS-9	606	600	6	10.5	0.1
AWS-10	509	505	4	8.8	0.1
AWS-11	253	248	5	4.4	0.1
Total	9530	8833	697	15.00	1.10

A study by Hsu et al. (1997) uses an adaptive-ANN model that estimates rainfall tariff using infrared satellite imagery and automated meteorological data. Another study by Rajurkar et al. (2004) and Dawson and Wilby (1998) has designed rainfall-runoff modeling for flood events using ANN. ANN is also used for real-time rainfall estimation using satellite data as discussed by Grimes (2003). ANN is also popularly in forecasting precipitation (Hung, 2008). The presented study uses the approach of the back-propagation neural network for estimation and details working of this network are discussed as follows.

ANN is a nonlinear statistical tool used to model the complex relationships between inputs and outputs or to find patterns in data. ANN initially takes set of the input pattern and their corresponding output pattern data to train the network and later uses the same network to predict unknown values using a known set of input pattern (Jain, 1996). ANN has set of the input layer, hidden layers and output layers as shown in Figure 2. Back-propagation is a supervised learning technique used for training ANN.

In Back-propagation algorithm the predicted output of ANN is compared with observed output, error difference is propagated backward from output layer to inner layer, so that output error can be reduced to a threshold value (Zhu, 2003).

In this study, we have used Back-propagation neural network with k^{th} input layer having K nodes, m^{th} hidden layer having M nodes and i^{th} output layer having I nodes. In Back-propagation neural network, each connection between layers has weights assigned to it. Initially, random weights will be assigned which later will be modified to reduce the error in the output. Figure 3, shows the transformation of a weighted sum of its inputs via a function (which is nonlinear), into an activation level called as "output."

Equation (1) is weighted sum x_m of input y_k and passes into activation function given in equation (2) to produce output y_m.

$$x_j = \sum_{k \in K_m} w_{km} y_k \tag{1}$$

Figure 2. Artificial Neural Network with k-input layer and m-hidden layer and i-output layer

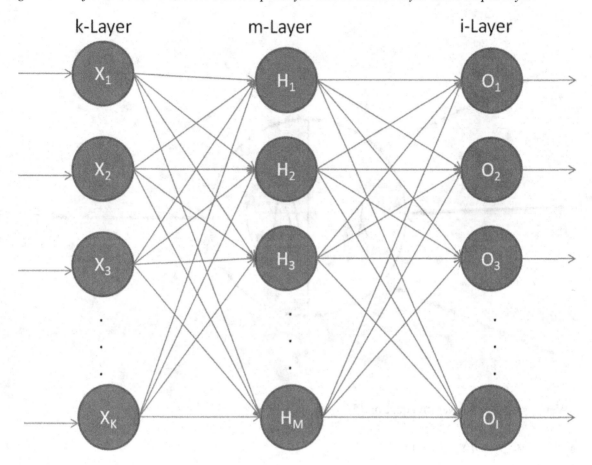

$$y_m = f(x_m) \tag{2}$$

Different activation function such as linear, sigmoid, Gaussian, Hyperbolic tangent, are popular activation function and are discussed in (Sibi et al., 2013). The sigmoid activation function will only generate positive value in range 0 and 1. The sigmoid activation function is useful for training data which also ranges between 0 and 1. It is one of the most used activation functions as shown in equation (3).

$$f\left(x_j\right) = \frac{1}{1 + e^{-\gamma x m}} \tag{3}$$

Where γ control the shape of the activation function. Back-propagation is a gradient-descent method to minimize the squared-error cost function as given in equation (4)

$$E := \frac{1}{2}\sum_{m=1}^{M}\left(t_m - y_m\right)^2 \tag{4}$$

Figure 3. Activation of weighted sum of inputs and passes into activation function to produce output y_m

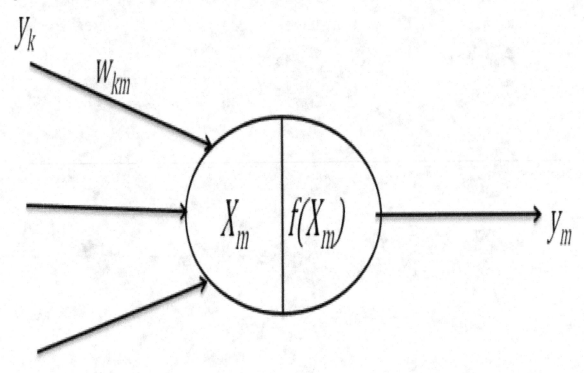

Weights update is given in equation (5) by (Rojas, 1996).

$$\Delta w_{km}(n) = \alpha \delta_m y_k + \eta \Delta w_{km}(n-1) \tag{5}$$

where:

α is the learning rate and ranges between 0 and 1;
y_k is the activation of the node in layer k,
n and $n-1$ refers to the iteration through the loop;
η is the momentum, with range between 0 and 1;
δ_m is the "error term" associated with the node after the weight

If m is output layer, the error is computed as given in equation (6), where y_m is the actual activation of an output node and t_m is the desired output for that node.

$$\delta_m := (t_m - y_m)y_m(1 - y_m) \tag{6}$$

If m is hidden layer, then error is computed as given in equation (7)

$$\delta_m 6 = \left(\sum_{i \in I_m} \delta_m w_{mi} \right) y_m \left(1 - y_m \right) \tag{7}$$

6. EXPERIMENTS AND RESULTS

In our experiment, we have taken precipitation of 10 AWSs as input nodes, 25 hidden nodes and single output as the target node for which precipitation estimation has to be done using back-propagation algorithm. For training purposes, we have considered precipitation data from Jan 2015 to Feb 2016 and acquired data is around about 63,514 hours of data. In this data set around 9,530 hours of data is missing in random positions of rows and columns. To train the network it is required to have records without any missing fields (any AWS). After filtering missing field records, we have obtained around 15,081 hours of data for training purpose. This data set is raw data obtained without applying any filling method.

Using proposed PSWP algorithm most of the missing data are reconstructed which is adding up to 8,833 hours of data. Again, this filled data are at random rows and columns. Further, filtering of missing field records we have obtained around 57,112 hours of data for training purpose. This data set which is obtained will be used for training the neural network.

Table 9 shows the correlation of all AWS for raw data set and reconstructed data set. The majority of the correlation coefficient of the reconstructed data set has increased showing that increased data set has increased dependency with its neighbor. In few cases like AWS-1, AWS-5 and AWS-10 overall correlation coefficient with other AWS has decreased with reconstructed data due to single AWS precipitation. The increased correlation coefficient is due to filling of zero precipitation and filling of random missing precipitation data.

Back-propagation neural networks are trained with two sets of data. One is using raw data which is obtained after filtering missing records and another one is reconstructed data using PSWP method. Nearby (max–1) AWS precipitation data are used to train output of individual AWS precipitation. Total of 22 different training and testing are performed to see the estimation errors for both raw and reconstructed data.

For testing purposes, we have used a new set of data from March 2016. A total of random 45 hours of data is tested against the trained networks. Learning rate of the neural network of all experiments is 0.25, error threshold is 0.2, momentum is 0.9 and activation function used is sigmoidal.

The Root Mean Square Error (RMSE) has been used as one of the standard statistical metrics to measure model performance in meteorology, air quality, and other climate research studies as discussed in (Chai and Draxler, 2014). Estimation error are defined using RMSE and has formula as defined in equation (8).

$$\text{RMSE} = \sqrt{\frac{1}{L} \sum_{j=1}^{L} \left(P_j - \hat{P}_j \right)^2} \tag{8}$$

Where, L is total number of hours of precipitation, P_j is the estimated precipitation for j^{th} AWS and $\hat{P}_j$ is the observed precipitation of the jth AWS.

Table 9. Correlation of Raw Data and Reconstructed Data

Correlation for RAW data of all AWS										
AWS-1	0.09	0.61	0.06	0.35	-0.06	0.76	0.37	0.78	0.37	0.86
0.10	AWS-2	0.62	0.13	0.67	-0.03	0.23	0.93	0.16	0.83	0.25
0.56	0.66	AWS-3	0.20	0.53	-0.07	0.57	0.79	0.72	0.74	0.73
0.07	0.27	0.38	AWS-4	0.42	0.60	-0.04	0.19	0.31	0.01	0.07
0.33	0.56	0.49	0.69	AWS-5	0.05	0.14	0.75	0.19	0.52	0.22
-0.03	0.01	0.00	0.39	0.05	AWS-6	-0.08	-0.04	0.16	-0.01	-0.06
0.72	0.24	0.56	0.02	0.13	-0.03	AWS-7	0.41	0.69	0.56	0.86
0.36	0.91	0.79	0.34	0.64	0.00	0.41	AWS-8	0.38	0.90	0.46
0.71	0.28	0.77	0.40	0.26	0.18	0.66	0.48	AWS-9	0.40	0.90
0.38	0.78	0.67	0.06	0.38	0.03	0.60	0.82	0.41	AWS-10	0.50
0.82	0.30	0.74	0.20	0.25	-0.02	0.84	0.49	0.90	0.51	AWS-11
Correlation for reconstructed data using PSWP										

Table 10 shows the summary of experiments conducted with their error represented in RMSE. Except for AWS-5, AWS-8 and AWS-10 all other AWS are showing reduced error from reconstructed data. RMSE of AWS-5 has increased with increased data set because in test sample had a condition where its entire neighbor had precipitation, but AWS-5 itself didn't have precipitation. Though we need a large set of data to train a neural network for accurate estimation, a small increase in set data using PSWP has decreased significant error (9.96%) in training. The overall experiment shows that estimation errors are reduced significantly with reconstructed data.

Table 10. RMSE for Raw Data (without PSWP) and Reconstructed Data

Stations	RMSE without PSWP	RMSE with PSWP	Difference in RMSE
AWS-1	0.67	**0.23**	0.44
AWS-2	0.37	**0.19**	0.18
AWS-3	0.49	**0.19**	0.30
AWS-4	0.76	**0.13**	0.63
AWS-5	**0.36**	0.72	-0.36
AWS-6	0.18	**0.18**	0.00
AWS-7	0.50	**0.48**	0.02
AWS-8	**0.42**	0.43	-0.01
AWS-9	0.37	**0.37**	0.00
AWS-10	**0.62**	0.72	-0.10
AWS-11	0.11	**0.09**	0.02
Total	0.44	**0.34**	0.10

7. CONCLUSION AND FUTURE WORK

This paper discusses how proposed reconstruction algorithm increases precipitation data set for estimation using neural networks. The advantage of the increased data set, is demonstrated by estimating missing data using two data sets namely raw and reconstructed precipitation data. First, the raw data set is acquired from the automatic weather station. Secondly, the reconstructed data set is obtained from proposed PSWP algorithm.

The missing data estimation is done using a back-propagation neural network. We have considered data from Jan 2015 to Feb 2016 for training the neural network. Further, for testing March 2016 data is considered. One of the data set is raw data, which is obtained after filtering records that are having missing fields within records. Such data set has lesser records for training the neural network. On the other hand, the reconstructed data set has significantly increased the data size. Moreover, this provides sufficiently larger data set for training the neural network.

Acquired precipitation data is around 63,514 hours of data in which 9,530 hrs of data is missing in a random position of rows and column. After removing records that are having missing fields, we obtained 15,081 hrs of raw data (23.74%) which is used for training a neural network for the first set of experiment. By using proposed PSWP method, we have reconstructed 8,833 hours of precipitation data, which has increased data set to 57,112 hrs (89.92%). It is observed, that reconstruction has added 66% of additional data to the raw data set, exhibits enhanced performance by PSWP algorithm. This reconstructed data is used to train the neural network for the second set of experiments. The average RMSE for ANN trained with raw data is 0.44 and while that for neural network trained with reconstructed data is 0.34. Results prove that estimation error measured in RMSE has reduced by 9.96% by using reconstructed data from PSWP method.

Neural networks need large training data set to obtain the accurate estimation of precipitation. Using PSWP method, dataset size can be increased which further improves the estimation results. PSWP is novel reconstruction method to fill the missing data. This method uses the space and time to classify the rainfall pattern to create different windows to fill the missing precipitation data.

As a future scope, PSWP method needs further improvements while dealing with boundary data of different classified windows. Also, when data are continuously missing for hours, then in addition to PWSP, some traditional interpolation algorithms may be used to reconstruct such continuous missing data. The accuracy obtained in PSWP in such cases is low.

REFERENCES

Chai, T., & Draxler, R. R. (2014). Root mean square error (RMSE) or mean absolute error (MAE)?–Arguments against avoiding RMSE in the literature. *Geoscientific Model Development*, 7(3), 1247–1250. doi:10.5194/gmd-7-1247-2014

Dawson, C. W., & Wilby, R. (1998). An artificial neural network approach to rainfall-runoff modelling. *Hydrological Sciences Journal*, 43(1), 47–66. doi:10.1080/02626669809492102

Dawson, C. W., & Wilby, R. L. (2001). Hydrological modelling using artificial neural networks. *Progress in Physical Geography*, 25(1), 80–108. doi:10.1177/030913330102500104

Deshpande, N. R., Kulkarni, A., & Krishna Kumar, K. (2012). Characteristic features of hourly rainfall in India. *International Journal of Climatology*, *32*(11), 1730–1744. doi:10.1002/joc.2375

Feng, L., & Hong, W. (2008). On hydrologic calculation using artificial neural networks. *Applied Mathematics Letters*, *21*(5), 453–458. doi:10.1016/j.aml.2007.06.004

Ferrari, G. T., & Ozaki, V. (2014). Missing data imputation of climate datasets: Implications to modeling extreme drought events. *Revista Brasileira de Meteorologia*, *29*(1), 21–28. doi:10.1590/S0102-77862014000100003

Gao, Z., Cheng, W., Qiu, X., & Meng, L. (2015). A missing sensor data estimation algorithm based on temporal and spatial correlation. *International Journal of Distributed Sensor Networks*, *11*(10), 435391. doi:10.1155/2015/435391

Giri, R. K., Pradhan, D., & Sen, A. K. (2015). Rainfall Comparison Of Automatic Weather Stations And Manual Observations Over Bihar Region. *International Journal of Physics and Mathematical Sciences*, *5*(2), 1–22.

Graham, J. W. (2012). *Missing data: analysis and design. Statistics for social and behavioral sciences*. Springer-Verlag New. doi:10.1007/978-1-4614-4018-5

Grimes, D. I. F., Coppola, E., Verdecchia, M., & Visconti, G. (2003). A neural network approach to real-time rainfall estimation for Africa using satellite data. *Journal of Hydrometeorology*, *4*(6), 1119–1133. doi:10.1175/1525-7541(2003)004<1119:ANNATR>2.0.CO;2

Hsu, K. L., Gao, X., Sorooshian, S., & Gupta, H. V. (1997). Precipitation estimation from remotely sensed information using artificial neural networks. *Journal of Applied Meteorology*, *36*(9), 1176–1190. doi:10.1175/1520-0450(1997)036<1176:PEFRSI>2.0.CO;2

Hung, N. Q., Babel, M. S., Weesakul, S., & Tripathi, N. K. (2008). An artificial neural network model for rainfall forecasting in Bangkok, Thailand. *Hydrology and Earth System Sciences Discussions*, *5*(1), 183–218. doi:10.5194/hessd-5-183-2008

Ilunga, M., 2010: Infilling annual rainfall data using feedforward back-propagation Artificial Neural Networks (ANN): application of the standard and generalised back-propagation techniques: technical paper. *Joernaal van die Suid-Afrikaanse Instituut van Siviele Ingenieurswese [Journal of the South African Institution of Civil Engineering]*, *52*(1), 2-10.

Jain, A. K., Mao, J., & Mohiuddin, K. M. (1996). Artificial neural networks: A tutorial. *IEEE Computer*, *29*(3), 31–44. doi:10.1109/2.485891

Kim, J. W., & Pachepsky, Y. A. (2010). Reconstructing missing daily precipitation data using regression trees and artificial neural networks for SWAT streamflow simulation. *Journal of Hydrology (Amsterdam)*, *394*(3), 305–314. doi:10.1016/j.jhydrol.2010.09.005

Lee, H., & Kang, K. (2015). Interpolation of missing precipitation data using kernel estimations for hydrologic modeling. Advances in Meteorology.

Ly, S., Charles, C., & Degré, A. (2013). Different methods for spatial interpolation of rainfall data for operational hydrology and hydrological modeling at watershed scale. A review. *Biotechnologie, Agronomie, Société et Environnement, 17*(2), 392.

Mays, L. W. (2010). *Water resources engineering.* John Wiley & Sons.

Piazza, A. D., Conti, F. L., Viola, F., Eccel, E., & Noto, L. V. (2015). Comparative analysis of spatial interpolation methods in the Mediterranean area: Application to temperature in Sicily. *Water (Basel), 7*(5), 1866–1888. doi:10.3390/w7051866

Rajurkar, M. P., Kothyari, U. C., & Chaube, U. C. (2004). Modeling of the daily rainfall-runoff relationship with artificial neural network. *Journal of Hydrology (Amsterdam), 285*(1), 96–113. doi:10.1016/j.jhydrol.2003.08.011

Ramos-Calzado, P., Gómez-Camacho, J., Pérez-Bernal, F., & Pita-López, M. F. (2008). A novel approach to precipitation series completion in climatological datasets: Application to Andalusia. *International Journal of Climatology, 28*(11), 1525–1534. doi:10.1002/joc.1657

Rojas, R. 1996: The backpropagation algorithm. Neural Networks: A Systematic Introduction (pp. 149-182). Springer Berlin Heidelberg. doi:10.1007/978-3-642-61068-4_7

Sibi, P., Jones, S. A., & Siddarth, P. (2013). Analysis of different activation functions using back propagation neural networks. *Journal of Theoretical and Applied Information Technology, 47*(3), 1264–1268.

Teegavarapu, R. S., & Chandramouli, V. (2005). Improved weighting methods, deterministic and stochastic data-driven models for estimation of missing precipitation records. *Journal of Hydrology (Amsterdam), 312*(1), 191–206. doi:10.1016/j.jhydrol.2005.02.015

Velasco-Forero, C. A., Sempere-Torres, D., Cassiraga, E. F., & Gómez-Hernández, J. J. (2009). A nonparametric automatic blending methodology to estimate rainfall fields from rain gauge and radar data. *Advances in Water Resources, 32*(7), 986–1002. doi:10.1016/j.advwatres.2008.10.004

Verworn, A., & Haberlandt, U. (2011). Spatial interpolation of hourly rainfall - effect of additional information, variogram inference and storm properties. *Hydrology and Earth System Sciences, 15*(2), 569–584. doi:10.5194/hess-15-569-2011

Zhu, Q. M. (2003). A back propagation algorithm to estimate the parameters of non-linear dynamic rational models. *Applied Mathematical Modelling, 27*(3), 169–187. doi:10.1016/S0307-904X(02)00097-5

This research was previously published in the International Journal of Agricultural and Environmental Information Systems (IJAEIS), 9(1); pages 62-84, copyright year 2018 by IGI Publishing (an imprint of IGI Global).

Chapter 12

Evaluating the Effects of Size and Precision of Training Data on ANN Training Performance for the Prediction of Chaotic Time Series Patterns

Lei Zhang

https://orcid.org/0000-0003-0535-998X

University of Regina, Regina, Canada

ABSTRACT

In this research, artificial neural networks (ANN) with various architectures are trained to generate the chaotic time series patterns of the Lorenz attractor. The ANN training performance is evaluated based on the size and precision of the training data. The nonlinear Auto-Regressive (NAR) model is trained in open loop mode first. The trained model is then used with closed loop feedback to predict the chaotic time series outputs. The research goal is to use the designed NAR ANN model for the simulation and analysis of Electroencephalogram (EEG) signals in order to study brain activities. A simple ANN topology with a single hidden layer of 3 to 16 neurons and 1 to 4 input delays is used. The training performance is measured by averaged mean square error. It is found that the training performance cannot be improved by solely increasing the training data size. However, the training performance can be improved by increasing the precision of the training data. This provides useful knowledge towards reducing the number of EEG data samples and corresponding acquisition time for prediction.

INTRODUCTION

In the age of big data, it seems that both data scientists and machine learning experts have been unanimously advocating for infinitely increasing the amount of training data and contributing excessive time and effort on data collection from all sources (Deng, 2009; Wu, 2014; Labrinidis, 2012). The training

DOI: 10.4018/978-1-6684-2408-7.ch012

outcomes with a mere few percentage point improvement in the learning accuracy can be considered hugely satisfying, and sufficient for raising a toast to the developing of convolutional neural network (CNN) (Simonyan, 2014) and the advancing of deep learning (LeCun, 2015). In the light of artificial neural network (ANN) technology inspired by brain research (Schalkoff, 1997), with scientific prudence and inquisition, this paper offers some alternative perspectives on improving the training efficacy by using smaller training data size with better data precision and employing optimized ANN architecture with less computational cost. It has been reported that deep learning (Krizhevsky, 2017) has triumphed human brain in terms of achieving better accuracy in image classification. It is however necessary to point out that human brain is by far the most energy efficient design of evolution, of which the ultimate goal is to save energy for survival instead of sparing it to achieve some impressive but impractical accuracy. Although there are approximately a billion neurons and a trillion neural connections in a human brain, they are only activated partially when necessary, in that specific brain functions only activate the related brain region. That is perhaps why people often feel exhausted after trying to multi-task, while creativity and innovation can be better cultivated by allowing the brain to focus intensively on a dedicated single task. For a normal daily task such as face recognition, a human brain can easily succeed in feature detection and classification accurately and efficiently, with a very short period of time and a negligible amount of energy. In a real-life scenario, the ambitious may be willing to spend extra effort to achieve extraordinary performance in remembering thousands of faces in detail, while some may be able to get by with much less energy strategically by distinguishing a small number of key features. In this research, the goal is to investigate the "get by" solution for the generation and prediction of chaotic time series patterns using ANN by improving the quality instead of the quantity of the training data. This can consequently reduce the number of Electroencephalogram (EEG) samples and correspondingly the data acquisition time required for ANN training (Zou et al., 2011), meanwhile lower the energy consumption for the hardware implementation of a real-time prediction system for brain research (Wang et al., 2010).

From a practical point of view, it is difficult to acquire EEG signals with big data size as it is time consuming to setup EEG equipment with multi-channel wet electrodes and the collected EEG signals are generally noisy and individually dependent. Therefore, it is necessary to first simulate the EEG signals with ANN-based chaotic system generator model for theoretical research purpose; then to evaluate the training performances using data with various sizes and precisions to define the optimal training data for ANN training; and additionally to optimize ANN architecture to improve the training efficacy with reduced number of EEG signals. Lorenz system can be used for modeling many real-world chaotic phenomena such as in weather prediction. This study uses Lorenz system as the research subject, with the potential to apply the research method and outcomes to other similar chaotic systems in general.

The rest of the paper provides the research background and explains the research approach of using ANN-based chaotic system generator to simulate and predict EEG signals for brain research; describes the generation of the training data; demonstrates and discusses the generation of different training data sets and the corresponding training results; and finally summarizes the research work.

BACKGROUND

ANN-Based Chaotic System Generator

ANN can be trained by training data with a sufficient number of training samples in order to generate targeted outputs. The network interconnections of ANN architecture are inspired by and resemble the brain neural networks. Chaotic systems are nonlinear dynamic systems, the outputs of which demonstrate chaotic features and are highly sensitive to initial values. The outputs of chaotic systems can be generated using a number of system equations. It is reported in previous research that brain activities demonstrate chaotic behaviors (Pereda, 2005; Falahian, 2015). Recently several related research works have successfully generated the chaotic time series outputs of Lorenz systems based on ANN model (Zhang, 2017a, 2017b). The training samples are generated by three differential equations of the Lorenz system. The training performances for various ANN architectures have also been investigated. The combined knowledge obtained from previous research outcomes offers a promising opportunity to simulate brain dynamics in order to fully understand brain functionalities and advance brain research. As the acquisition of big EEG data from large population is empirically impractical, and the available EEG signals are limited and highly individually dependent, the developed ANN-based chaotic system model can be used to generate pseudo EEG chaotic patterns to compensate for the lack of empirically EEG signals and fill the gaps of theoretical study for brain research and cognitive informatics (Wang et al., 2015).

NAR Model and ANN Architecture

The ANN training is carried out using MATLAB neural network time series tool (*ntstool*) and the Non-linear Autoregressive (NAR) model. The NAR model can be used for solving non-linear time series problems. The NAR model is trained in open loop with delayed target outputs as feedback inputs during the training process instead of using the outputs of the network under training. Figure 1 shows two NAR open loop ANN models. The first ANN (n = 3, d = 4) shown in Figure 1(a) has 3 hidden neurons and 4 feedback delays. The second ANN (n = 6, d = 1) shown in Figure 1(b) has 6 hidden neurons and 1 feedback delay.

Figure 1. NAR open loop models (a) 3 hidden neurons and 4 delays (b) 6 hidden neurons and 1delay

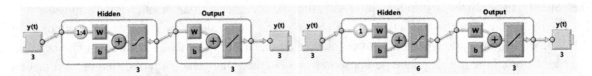

A completed post-training closed loop NAR model includes delayed feedback outputs connected to the input to predict future values from past values of one or more time series. It is used for generating and prediction Lorenz chaotic system with predefined invariant initial values and system parameters. A closed loop NAR model for ANN (n = 4, d = 3) is shown in Figure 2. Adding an input delay is equivalent to adding a neuron to the input layer of the ANN. The training performances of various ANN architectures are evaluated for different training data sets generated by Lorenz system equations, in order to investigate the feasibility of using reduced training data size required for representing Lorenz chaotic system in the training process to improve the training efficacy. The ANN architecture consists of one input, one hidden and one output layer. Different ANN architectures with 3 to 16 hidden neurons and 1 to 4 feedback input delays are evaluated using each data set.

Figure 2. Simulink closed loop model with 4 hidden neurons and 3 delays

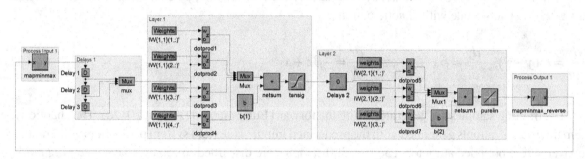

Training Performance and Training Algorithm

The average mean square errors (MSEs) between the ANN outputs and the target outputs are used to measure the training performance. Better training performance is indicated by smaller MSE values. Random initial values are assigned to all weights and bias in the ANN by the MATLAB *ntstool* and the MSE value varies for each training iteration, even with the same ANN architecture and training data set. The ANN training for a combination of selected ANN architecture and training data set is carried out for 2 iterations. The smaller MSE is used for evaluating training performance among various training data. This can eliminate the abnormal big MSE value when the calculated gradient in back propagation training stops to decrease and causes the training process to stop at a local minimum (Atakulreka, 2007). The training algorithm *trainlm* of the MATLAB *ntstool* is used for ANN training. With *trainlm*, the ANN weight and bias values are updated based on Levenberg-Marquardt (LM) optimization (Hegan, 1994). It is reported in previous related research that this training algorithm has much better performance than the *trainscg* algorithm. It has similar performance as the *trainbr* algorithm but with a much faster training time. The training parameters of the *trainlm* algorithm are configured in the same way as listed in (Zhang, 2017c).

Training Data

The effect of training data on the training performance for a selected ANN architecture is investigated from two aspects: the number of training samples (data size) and the precision of the training samples (step size).

Training Data Generation

The Lorenz system differential equations used for generating the training data are listed in equation (1). The system has three outputs x, y and z, which are the target outputs of the ANN training, hence there are three neurons in both the input and output layers of the NAR ANN model. σ, ρ and β are three system parameters. Chaotic systems can be in chaotic, periodic or stable states depending on the setup of initial values and system parameters. In this study, all training data sets are generated with the same initial values $x0 = y0 = z0 = 10$, and system parameters $\sigma=10$, $\rho=28$, $\beta=8/3$, which will set the Lorenz attractor in chaotic state with chaotic outputs.

$$\frac{dx}{dt} = \sigma(y-x), \quad \frac{dy}{dt} = \rho x - y - xz, \quad \frac{dz}{dt} = -\beta z + xy \tag{1}$$

The training samples are generated using the forward Euler method (Zhang, 2017d). The chaotic system time series outputs generated with the predefined initial values and system parameters will gradually converge to a bounded attractor. The first 300 samples are discarded to remove the con*verging path of the time series outputs*, which is not part of the bounded attractor of the chaotic system. The MATLAB codes are given below:

```
% The Forward Euler Method
x0 = 10; y0 = 10; z0 = 10;          % Initial Values
sig = 10; r = 28; b = 8/3;        % System Parameters
dt = 0.02;                         % Step Size
Ns = 300;                                % Start Sample
N = 2300;                        % Total Samples
  for i = 1:N
    dxdt = sig * (y0 - x0);
    dydt = r * x0 - y0 - x0 * z0;
    dzdt = x0 * y0 - b * z0;
    dx = dxdt*dt;
    dy = dydt*dt;
    dz = dzdt*dt;
    x = x0 + dx;
    y = y0 + dy;
    z = z0 + dz;
    time_series(:, i) = [x;y;z];
    x0 = x;
    y0 = y;
    z0 = z;
  end;
```

The generated training samples are randomly divided into 3 subsets for training (70%), validation (15%) and testing (15%) using the 'dividerand' function. During the ANN training process, the training subset is used for computing the gradient and updating the weights and biases to gradually reduce the MSE. The validation set is used to measure network generalization and stop the training if the training performance fails to generalize. The training MSE should gradually decreases during a training process, so does the validation MSE. Otherwise, if the validation MSE starts to increase successively for 6 training epochs, it indicates that the network is overfitting on the training data, and the training will stop. The network weights and biases are saved at the minimum validation MSE. The testing subset is used to independently measure the network performance during and after the training, usually for comparing the results of different network models. It can also detect poor division of training samples among the three data subsets when the minimum MSEs of the testing data and validation data occur at a significantly different training epoch.

Training Data Size

Two training data sets with 1,000 (1k) and 2,000 (2k) training samples are used respectively for training different ANN architectures with 3 to 16 hidden neurons and 1 to 4 input delays. It is noted that the generated training data sets with limited number of samples can only represent small segments of the Lorenz attractor. The intention is to examine the training performance and determine if these partial representations of the chaotic system are sufficient for the ANN training to extract the features associated with the system parameters and generate the target outputs. Given there are 3 to 16 hidden neurons (14) and 1 to 4 input delays (4), the total number of ANN architectures is 56. As each architecture is trained for 2 iterations, the total number of training iterations for each training algorithm is 112. The total training time is measured in seconds for different training data sizes.

Training Data Step Size

Three step sizes (dt) 0.02, 0.01 and 0.005 are used for generating up to 2k training samples of Lorenz system using the forward Euler method. The length of the time series segment depends on the product of the step size and the number of training samples. For example, the 1k samples data set with dt = 0.01 only represents the first half time series segment of the 1k data set with dt = 0.02, but the former has better precision. The 2k samples data set with dt = 0.005 can represent the same time series segment as the 1k sample data set with dt = 0.01, again the former has better precision. In another word, there is a tradeoff between data size and step size for representing the same time series segment.

The Lorenz time series segments are generated using the Euler method with step size (dt) at 0.02, 0.01 and 0.005 respectively. The time series segments with 1k samples are plotted in Figure 3 (a), (b) and (c). The first 300 samples of the generated time series are removed and the following 1k samples are used. Each data set contains 1k samples of three system outputs (x, y and z). It can be observed that when a smaller step size is used to generate the training samples, the precision of the representation is better and the plotted time series is smoother, but the time series segment generated is shorter using the same number of samples. Figure 3(a) shows a good range coverage of the Lorenz 'butterfly' with 1k samples but the time series are inaccurate due to the big step size (dt = 0.02). In fact, the outputs will diverge quickly to infinity if a bigger step size (i.e., 0.027) is used. Figure 3(b) shows that the length of the generated time series segment is halved for dt = 0.01 with 1k samples, but the data precision is twice better. The same tradeoff is demonstrated by Figure 3(c) for dt = 0.005. The training samples with 2k samples are plotted in Figure 3 (d), (e) and (f) for step size 0.02, 0.01 and 0.005, respectively.

Figure 3. Training data of two data sizes (1k/2k samples) and three precisions (dt = 0.02/0.01/0.005)

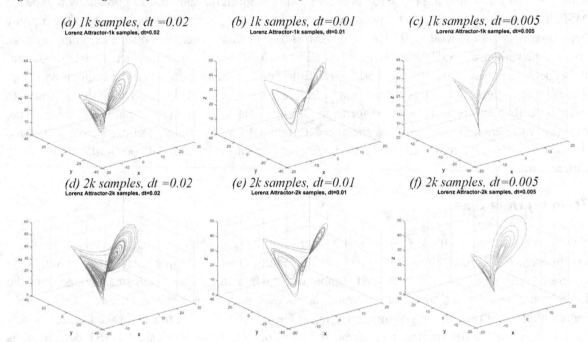

(a) 1k samples, dt =0.02
Lorenz Attractor-1k samples, dt=0.02

(b) 1k samples, dt=0.01
Lorenz Attractor-1k samples, dt=0.01

(c) 1k samples, dt=0.005
Lorenz Attractor-1k samples, dt=0.005

(d) 2k samples, dt =0.02
Lorenz Attractor-2k samples, dt=0.02

(e) 2k samples, dt=0.01
Lorenz Attractor-2k samples, dt=0.01

(f) 2k samples, dt=0.005
Lorenz Attractor-2k samples, dt=0.005

Table 1. Best MSE with 1k/2k samples, 1~ 4 input delays, 3~16 hidden neurons at precision dt = 0.02

Neurons	1k Samples				2k Samples			
	delay 1	delay 2	delay 3	delay 4	delay 1	delay 2	delay 3	delay 4
3	4.05E-02	1.14E-02	1.23E-03	1.17E-03	5.39E-02	1.69E-02	3.57E-03	1.13E-03
4	1.19E-03	1.48E-03	3.17E-04	1.14E-04	1.36E-02	6.65E-04	3.10E-04	1.24E-04
5	1.17E-05	8.29E-05	1.97E-05	6.03E-05	1.49E-05	1.94E-04	4.32E-05	5.42E-05
6	6.57E-06	6.74E-05	1.03E-05	1.34E-05	1.17E-05	2.03E-05	3.79E-05	9.81E-06
7	3.21E-06	3.31E-06	1.87E-06	6.78E-06	4.41E-06	1.66E-05	1.45E-05	3.93E-06
8	2.44E-06	4.62E-06	3.40E-06	1.80E-06	7.74E-07	3.62E-06	3.70E-07	3.36E-07
9	2.56E-06	6.72E-07	9.22E-07	5.35E-08	3.28E-06	8.80E-07	3.89E-06	2.41E-07
10	2.69E-06	8.82E-07	9.86E-07	5.69E-08	8.05E-07	1.95E-06	7.60E-07	2.28E-07
11	3.57E-07	2.27E-07	8.57E-08	9.15E-08	1.42E-06	7.46E-07	1.01E-07	1.44E-07
12	1.51E-07	8.33E-07	1.64E-07	2.28E-08	1.78E-07	8.22E-07	1.25E-07	4.98E-08
13	1.66E-07	4.14E-07	5.34E-08	4.30E-08	5.06E-07	1.44E-07	1.12E-07	3.90E-08
14	2.54E-06	3.47E-07	1.08E-08	2.91E-08	1.79E-07	6.67E-08	1.24E-07	3.58E-08
15	2.58E-07	7.38E-09	1.01E-07	7.95E-08	1.87E-07	4.88E-08	1.71E-09	1.54E-08
16	2.05E-07	6.19E-09	4.02E-09	4.17E-09	1.12E-07	1.23E-07	6.35E-09	3.18E-09

ANN Training Results

The overall training performances are measured by the average MSE of all training samples (70% for training, 15% for validation and 15% for testing). The better performance (smaller MSE) of iteration I and II is selected to eliminate the abnormal bad performance iteration, which is caused by local minimum of the gradient as the initial weights and bias values for the ANN are randomly generated. The best training performance of the two training iterations for different ANN architectures using either 1k or 2k training samples are compared in Table 1, 2 and 3 at dt = 0,02, 0.01 and 0.005, respectively.

Table 2. Best MSE with 1k/2k samples, 1~ 4 input delays, 3~16 hidden neurons at precision dt = 0.01

Neurons	1k Samples				2k Samples			
	delay 1	delay 2	delay 3	delay 4	delay 1	delay 2	delay 3	delay 4
3	8.56E-03	4.88E-04	1.83E-05	3.17E-06	7.56E-03	4.75E-04	1.92E-05	3.86E-06
4	1.05E-03	7.40E-05	4.99E-06	5.95E-07	2.82E-04	4.61E-05	8.73E-06	2.48E-06
5	1.06E-05	8.12E-06	5.64E-07	1.47E-06	2.11E-05	1.26E-05	8.79E-07	6.16E-07
6	5.65E-06	5.13E-06	1.23E-06	1.51E-07	2.75E-06	7.44E-07	2.46E-07	1.49E-07
7	4.93E-07	3.81E-07	4.24E-07	7.58E-08	4.74E-06	8.62E-07	1.53E-07	1.97E-07
8	6.84E-07	8.61E-07	1.76E-08	1.10E-09	8.08E-07	9.86E-07	1.56E-07	4.47E-07
9	1.14E-06	6.87E-08	2.55E-08	1.29E-07	1.60E-07	3.72E-07	6.23E-08	1.80E-09
10	2.36E-07	2.27E-07	2.00E-08	6.25E-09	3.83E-07	6.80E-09	2.39E-09	2.69E-08
11	1.57E-07	5.81E-08	5.96E-09	4.06E-08	1.00E-07	1.73E-07	2.63E-08	1.59E-08
12	3.50E-08	2.39E-08	1.76E-09	9.26E-10	1.43E-07	1.46E-09	7.24E-11	2.08E-08
13	1.52E-07	2.52E-08	1.58E-09	1.72E-09	1.38E-07	1.47E-09	2.41E-09	1.54E-10
14	1.94E-07	1.54E-09	9.97E-10	6.69E-10	2.14E-07	1.67E-09	1.86E-11	1.42E-10
15	1.33E-08	2.21E-08	5.13E-09	8.69E-11	7.91E-08	3.00E-10	1.63E-10	9.95E-10
16	2.77E-07	5.64E-09	7.98E-10	1.27E-09	3.01E-07	1.87E-09	1.34E-11	2.76E-09

Training Results of 1,000 Samples

The best overall training performances using two data sizes of 1k & 2k samples and three precisions at dt = 0.02, 0.01 & 0.005 are measured for different ANN architectures with 3 to 16 hidden neurons and 1 to 4 input delays. The training results are plotted in Figure 4 (a)~(f), respectively.

It is shown that the training performance for a given ANN architecture can be improved by using the same number of training samples (1k) generated with a smaller step size, which provides better precision. It is also shown that in general, the training performance can be improved by optimizing the ANN architecture with increased number of hidden neurons or/and input delays. Moreover, when a smaller step size is used to generate more accurate training data, the number of inputs delays can have a relatively bigger impact on the performance of ANN with a given number of hidden neurons. For instance, by adding 4 input delays to the ANN with 3 hidden neurons, the performance using the training data generated with step size 0.005 is 3.45E-07, compared to 1.17E-03 using the training data generated with step size 0.02.

Therefore, the step size, aka, the data precision, is an important factor to be considered for the fixed-point representation in hardware implementation, which requires simplifying the ANN architecture by using a minimum number of hidden neurons. It can also be observed that the training performance of ANN architectures with 3 to 5 hidden neurons can be improved by adding up to 4 feedback input delays, at all three step sizes. However, the effect of added input delays becomes less apparent for the ANN with 6 hidden neurons as the best training performance stops improving at the level of 1E-07.

Table 3. Best MSE with 1k/2k samples, 1~ 4 input delays, 3~16 hidden neurons at precision dt = 0.005

Neurons	1k Samples				2k Samples			
	delay 1	delay 2	delay 3	delay 4	delay 1	delay 2	delay 3	delay 4
3	4.35E-03	1.03E-05	1.10E-06	3.45E-07	2.56E-03	2.04E-05	1.17E-06	4.12E-07
4	1.26E-04	4.24E-06	2.37E-07	2.85E-07	1.83E-04	7.14E-06	7.77E-07	2.17E-07
5	3.15E-06	4.33E-07	2.11E-07	1.69E-07	1.04E-05	3.53E-06	1.92E-07	1.97E-07
6	3.66E-07	7.85E-07	1.63E-07	1.47E-07	3.25E-06	6.22E-07	1.20E-07	1.66E-07
7	7.85E-07	4.05E-08	3.52E-08	5.20E-09	8.23E-07	4.98E-07	1.93E-07	3.85E-08
8	7.05E-07	2.39E-07	7.61E-09	2.33E-09	8.24E-07	6.98E-08	4.31E-09	2.75E-08
9	1.29E-07	2.28E-08	2.17E-09	2.12E-10	1.48E-06	4.98E-08	1.56E-09	2.47E-08
10	2.06E-07	5.71E-08	9.60E-09	1.57E-10	1.15E-07	6.10E-09	1.60E-08	8.32E-10
11	2.70E-07	2.52E-10	8.24E-10	1.00E-10	9.42E-08	2.49E-08	2.80E-11	1.45E-11
12	8.07E-08	1.84E-08	5.04E-09	1.25E-09	4.50E-08	4.41E-10	9.35E-10	8.17E-10
13	2.33E-07	2.17E-08	1.22E-09	1.20E-10	5.81E-08	2.55E-10	9.37E-10	5.39E-09
14	1.15E-07	1.09E-10	7.43E-11	8.72E-12	1.83E-07	1.99E-10	1.51E-09	8.43E-10
15	1.45E-08	1.47E-09	6.69E-11	6.54E-11	5.70E-08	7.28E-10	7.70E-09	7.72E-10
16	2.40E-09	1.75E-11	3.26E-08	5.05E-11	3.88E-08	1.99E-08	7.40E-11	6.84E-11

Training Results of 2,000 Samples

It is generally advised that the training performance can be potentially improved by adding more training data. Hence, 2k training samples are generated and used following the same training process as done with 1k training samples in the previous subsection. The training time is more than doubled compared to that of using 1k training samples. It was expected that the training performance would improve with the doubled training samples, but the training results show neither significant nor consistent improvement, and are subject to ANN architecture.

Figure 4. Best training performances of ANN with 1k/2k samples, 1~ 4 input delays, 3~16 hidden neurons and 3 precisions (dt = 0.02, 0.01 & 0.005)

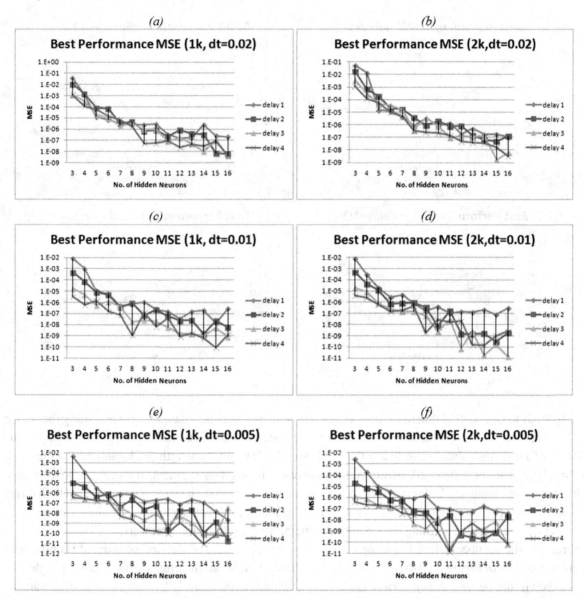

Training Results of Equivalent Time Series Segments

In order to further evaluate the effect of training data size and precision on the training performances, two pairs of training data sets with equivalent time series segments are compared:

- 1k Samples, dt = 0.02 Verses 2k Samples, dt = 0.01
- 1k Samples, dt = 0.01 Verses 2k Samples, dt = 0.005

Figure 5. Best MSE for equivalent time series segments: 1k samples, dt = 0.02 Vs. 2k samples, dt = 0.01

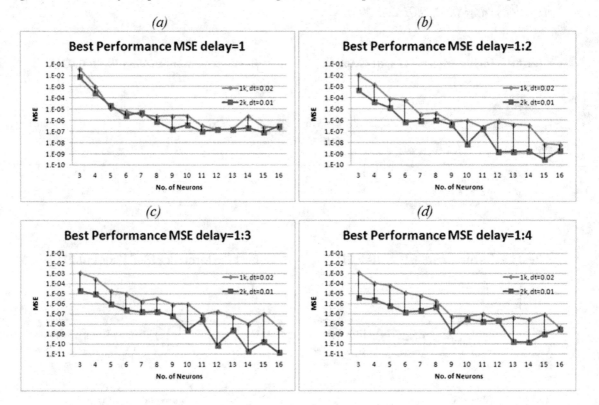

It needs to be clarified that these time series segments are considered equivalent regarding the length of the time series, which balances the trade-off between the data size and step size. For example, the length of 1k samples data set with dt = 0.02 is 1k*0.02 = 20; and the length of 2k samples data set with dt = 0.01 is also 2k*0.01 = 20. However, the equivalent time series segments are not identical because they are generated using Euler method with different step sizes, which cause the time series to diverge. Nevertheless, the comparison results show that the training performance can be improved by increasing the precision of the training data without reducing the length of the time series. This will result in increasing the number of training samples. The best performances of the first equivalent training data sets are shown in Figure 5(a)~(d), separately for different ANN architectures with 1 to 4 input delays. It is shown that better training performance can be achieved consistently by using the training data set (2k, dt = 0.01) compared to the training data set (1k, dt = 0.02). The same conclusion can be drawn from the other pair of training data sets as shown in Figure 6.

Training Results using Increased Data Sizes

In order to further investigate the effect of training data size on the training performance, two selected ANN architectures (n = 3, d = 4) and (n = 6, d = 1) are trained with training data size from 1k to 10k samples at 1k sample increment. The training samples are generated with dt = 0.01. As before, two training iterations are carried out for each ANN architecture and each data size. The best training performances are plotted in Figure 7. The extended training results have reinforced the conclusion made from the comparison between using training data of 1,000 and 2,000 samples. That is, the training performance cannot be improved by simply increasing the number of training samples. The results also indicate that the ANN (n = 3, d = 4) architecture has a more consistent training performance compared with the ANN (n = 6, d = 1) architecture, which may be potentially benefited from adding input delays.

Figure 6. Best MSE for equivalent time series segments: 1k samples, dt = 0.01 Vs. 2k samples, dt = 0.005

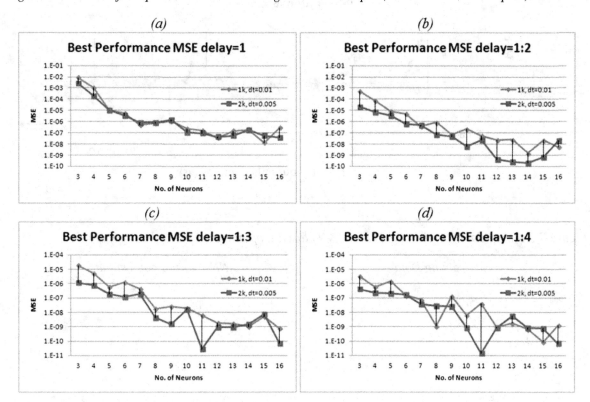

Time Series Prediction using Closed Loop ANN

The ANN (n = 6, d = 1) architecture is trained with different training data sets in open loop mode. The closed loop ANN is used to generate 2k samples outputs for the simulation and prediction of Lorenz chaotic time series patterns. Figure 8 displays the 1k training data at dt = 0.02 and the 2k closed loop ANN outputs. Figure 9 displays the 1k data at dt = 0.01 and the 2k closed loop ANN outputs. With the same number of training samples (1k), the second training data set has twice better precision (dt = 0.01) but covers only half of the trajectory range compared to the first training data set (dt = 0.02). And the 2k samples closed loop outputs are apparently distorted when the ANN is trained with the first training data set at dt = 0.02. In fact, due to the intrinsic chaotic characteristic of the system, a very small increment of the step size can cause the output to diverge to infinity. In comparison, the 2k samples closed loop outputs plotted in Figure 9 depicts a much smoother and more accurate representation of the Lorenz chaotic time series pattern, regardless of the halved trajectory range covered by the training data.

Figure 7. Best MSE of two ANN architecture using 1k to 10k samples

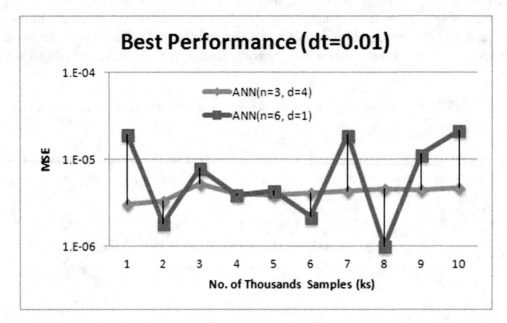

Figure 8 Training data (1k, dt = 0.02) and ANN closed loop outputs for ANN (n = 6, d = 1)

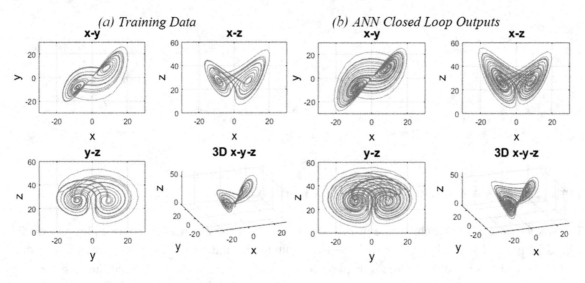

Figure 10 and Figure 11 display the other two training data sets with 2k samples at dt = 0.02 and 0.01, respectively, as well as the 2k samples closed loop ANN outputs. Similarly, with the same number of training samples (2k), the second training data set has twice better precision (dt = 0.01) but covers only half of the trajectory range compared to the first training data set (dt = 0.02), and the accuracy of closed loop outputs is dominantly determined by the precision of the training data, rather than the number of the training samples. Additionally, since both training data and the closed loop outputs contain 2k samples, a closer comparison can be drawn between the training data and the closed loop outputs. It can be seen in both Figure 10 and Figure 11 that the outputs are more divergent than the training data, and the divergence is more significant with lower data precision.

Figure 9 Training data (1k, dt = 0.01) and ANN closed loop outputs for ANN (n = 6, d = 1)

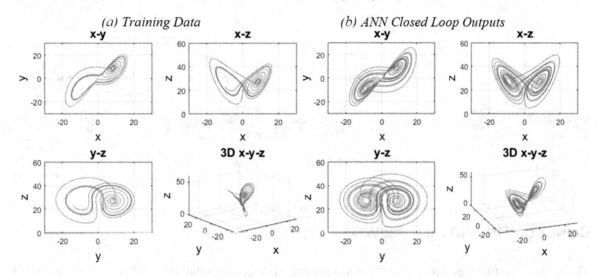

Figure 10 Training data (2k, dt = 0.02) and ANN closed loop outputs for ANN (n = 6, d = 1)

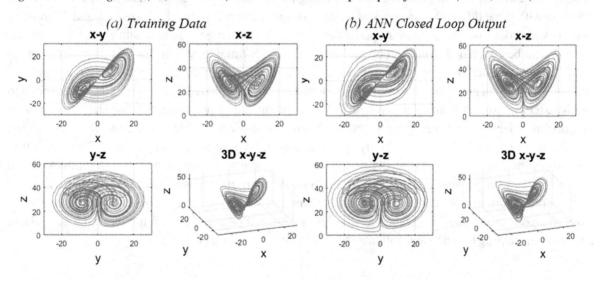

Figure 11 Training data (2k, dt = 0.01) and ANN closed loop outputs for ANN (n = 6, d = 1)

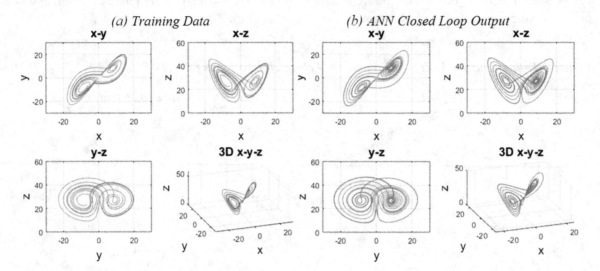

CONCLUSION AND FUTURE WORK

The research results reported in this paper has proven the hypothesis that ANN can be trained with relatively small training data size to preserve the information represented by the system equations of Lorenz chaotic system. The training data is generated using the Lorenz system equations and the forward Euler method with three different data step sizes: 0.02, 0.01 and 0.005 and two data sizes: 1k and 2k training samples in order to evaluate training performance based on the precision and data size of the training data. It can be concluded from the comparison of the ANN training results that in this application for chaotic system generation and prediction using ANN: 1) The ANN training performance is dominantly affected by the data precision. The training performance can be improved by using training data generated with better precision, i.e., smaller step size. 2) Given the same data precision, the data size does not have significant effect on the training performance. Therefore, it is reasonable to conclude that the training performance cannot be improved simply by increasing the size of the training data. 3) The simulation outputs of the closed loop NAR model show that a small time series segment (1k or 2k samples) of the Lorenz system can provide sufficient information for ANN training to generate and predict the time series. In the follow-up research, other performance metrics such as standard deviation of averaged MSE, as well as other chaotic systems such as Rössler system will be used in the future research to evaluate the general training efficacy and validate the results reported in this paper.

REFERENCES

Atakulreka, A., & Sutivong, D. (2007, December). Avoiding local minima in feedforward neural networks by simultaneous learning. In *Australasian Joint Conference on Artificial Intelligence* (pp. 100-109). Springer. doi:10.1007/978-3-540-76928-6_12

Deng, J., Dong, W., Socher, R., Li, L., Li, K., & Fei-Fei, L. (2009). ImageNet: A large-scale hierarchical image database. In *2009 IEEE Conference on Computer Vision and Pattern Recognition*. 10.1109/CVPR.2009.5206848

Falahian, R., Dastjerdi, M. M., Molaie, M., Jafari, S., & Gharibzadeh, S. (2015). Artificial neural network-based modeling of brain response to flicker light. *Nonlinear Dynamics*, *81*(4), 1951–1967. doi:10.100711071-015-2118-x

Hagan, M., & Menhaj, M. (1994). Training feedforward networks with the Marquardt algorithm. *IEEE Transactions on Neural Networks*, *5*(6), 989–993. doi:10.1109/72.329697 PMID:18267874

Krizhevsky, A., Sutskever, I., & Hinton, G. E. (2017). ImageNet classification with deep convolutional neural networks. *Communications of the ACM*, *60*(6), 84–90. doi:10.1145/3065386

Labrinidis, A., & Jagadish, H. V. (2012). Challenges and opportunities with big data. *Proceedings of the VLDB Endowment International Conference on Very Large Data Bases*, *5*(12), 2032–2033. doi:10.14778/2367502.2367572

Lecun, Y., Bengio, Y., & Hinton, G. (2015). Deep learning. *Nature*, *521*(7553), 436–444. doi:10.1038/nature14539 PMID:26017442

Pereda, E., Quiroga, R. Q., & Bhattacharya, J. (2005). Nonlinear multivariate analysis of neurophy6siological signals. *Progress in Neurobiology*, *77*(1-2), 1–37. doi:10.1016/j.pneurobio.2005.10.003 PMID:16289760

Schalkoff, R. J. (1997). *Artificial neural networks* (International ed). New York: McGraw-Hill.

Simonyan, K. & Zisserman, A. (2014). Very Deep Convolutional Networks for Large-Scale Image Recognition.

Wang, Y., Ngolah, C. F., Zeng, G., Sheu, P. C., Choy, C. P., & Tian, Y. (2010). The Formal Design Model of a Real-Time Operating System (RTOS+): Conceptual and Architectural Frameworks. *International Journal of Software Science and Computational Intelligence*, *2*(2), 105–122. doi:10.4018/jssci.2010040106

Wang, Y., Rolls, E. T., Howard, N., Raskin, V., Kinsner, W., Murtagh, F., ... Shell, D. F. (2015). Cognitive Informatics and Computational Intelligence: From Information Revolution to Intelligence Revolution. *International Journal of Software Science and Computational Intelligence*, *7*(2), 50–69. doi:10.4018/IJSSCI.2015040103

Wu, X., Zhu, X., Wu, G., & Ding, W. (2014). Data mining with big data. *IEEE Transactions on Knowledge and Data Engineering*, *26*(1), 97–107. doi:10.1109/TKDE.2013.109

Zhang, L. (2017a). Artificial Neural Network model design and topology analysis for FPGA implementation of Lorenz chaotic generator. In *2017 IEEE 30th Canadian Conference on Electrical and Computer Engineering (CCECE)* (pp. 216-219). doi:10.1109/ccece.2017.7946635

Zhang, L. (2017b). Artificial neural networks model design of Lorenz chaotic system for EEG pattern recognition and prediction. In *2017 IEEE Life Sciences Conference (LSC)* (pp. 39-42). 10.1109/LSC.2017.8268138

Zhang, L. (2017c). Design and implementation of neural network based chaotic system model for the dynamical control of brain stimulation. In *The Second International Conference on Neuroscience and Cognitive Brain Information (BRAININFO 2017)* (pp. 14–21).

Zhang, L. (2017d). System generator model-based FPGA design optimization and hardware co-simulation for Lorenz chaotic generator. In *2017 2nd Asia-Pacific Conference on Intelligent Robot Systems (ACIRS)* (pp. 170-174). doi:10.1109/acirs.2017.7986087

Zou, L., Wang, X., Shi, G., & Ma, Z. (2011). EEG Feature Extraction and Pattern Classification Based on Motor Imagery in Brain-Computer Interface. *International Journal of Software Science and Computational Intelligence*, *3*(3), 43–56. doi:10.4018/ijssci.2011070104

This research was previously published in the International Journal of Software Science and Computational Intelligence (IJSSCI), 11(1); pages 16-30, copyright year 2019 by IGI Publishing (an imprint of IGI Global).

Chapter 13
Development of the Enhanced Piece–Wise Linear Neural Network Algorithm

Veronica K. Chan
Faculty of Engineering and Applied Science, University of Regina, Canada

Christine W. Chan
Faculty of Engineering and Applied Science, University of Regina, Canada

ABSTRACT

This chapter discusses development, application, and enhancement of a decomposition neural network rule extraction algorithm for nonlinear regression problems. The dual objectives of developing the algorithms are (1) to generate good predictive models comparable in performance to the original artificial neural network (ANN) models and (2) to "open up" the black box of a neural network model and provide explicit information in the form of rules that are expressed as linear equations. The enhanced PWL-ANN algorithm improves upon the PWL-ANN algorithm because it can locate more than two breakpoints and better approximate the hidden sigmoid activation functions of the ANN. Comparison of the results produced by the two versions of the PWL-ANN algorithm showed that the enhanced PWL-ANN models provide higher predictive accuracies and improved fidelities compared to the originally trained ANN models than the PWL-ANN models.

INTRODUCTION

Artificial neural network (ANN) is a popular data mining approach because of its high classification or predictive accuracy, and resistance to noise. However, in addition to high prediction accuracy, researchers often need to gain better understanding of the problems at hand, and ANNs are black boxes that cannot be interpreted. To overcome this deficiency, the rule extraction approach can be adopted so as to generate explicit information from the analysis results of the trained ANNs. The objective of this study is to develop a decompositional neural network rule extraction algorithm for non-linear regression

DOI: 10.4018/978-1-6684-2408-7.ch013

problems. The approach adopted is to model a given dataset using the ANN approach and the originally trained model is assumed to be a three-layer feed-forward backpropagation neural network with a sigmoid activation function. Since these are the most common types of neural network models, this will be the target models on which rule extraction will be performed. Also, based on experience, one hidden layer in an ANN is typically sufficient to solve most non-linear problems without overfitting. Although the pedagogical type of rule extraction algorithms are better in terms of computational complexity and generality than decompositional algorithms, the decompositional approach is the focus because the objective is to explore the trained neural network and "open the black box". The algorithm approximates the activation functions of a given ANN model with piece-wise linear (PWL) equations and generates explicit information in the form of numerical formulae. The targeted problems are regression problems related to engineering domains. In terms of expressive power, we aim to generate "rules" expressed as linear numeric functions in the form of

$$Y = a_1 x_1 + a_2 x_2 + \dots + b.$$

Since one of the research objectives is to understand the working mechanisms of the trained neural network model, fidelity to the trained ANN will be the primary evaluation criterion of the developed algorithm.

This paper is organized as follows: Section 2 discusses some background literature related to the area of ANN rule extraction algorithms and applications of artificial neural network modeling to engineering domains. Section 3 discussed the methodology of the PWL-ANN algorithm. Section 4 discusses some results from application of the PWL-ANN algorithm and their analysis. Section 5 presents the methodology of the Enhanced PWL-ANN algorithm as well as some application results and their analysis. Section 6 describes a comparison of the performances of the two versions of the PWL-ANN algorithms in terms of predictive accuracy and fidelity. Section 7 gives the conclusion and some directions for future work.

BACKGROUND LITERATURE

On ANN Rule Extraction

There are three approaches to ANN rule extraction: (1) decompositional, which extracts rules by examining the activation and weights of the hidden layer neurons; (2) pedagogical, which extracts rules by mapping the relationships between the inputs and outputs as closely as possible to those given by the trained ANN model without opening up the "black-box" of the ANN models; and (3) eclectic, which is a hybrid of the two previous approaches. Most studies on ANN rule extraction focus on classification problems (Augasta & Kathirvalavakumar, 2012), when in reality many problems encountered in the real world contexts are regression problems. In classification problems, the output variables are class labels, whereas in regression problems, the output variables are continuous values.

Rule extraction algorithms for ANN can be classified into three approaches based on the criterion of translucency of the algorithm: decompositional, pedagogical and eclectic (Andrews, Diederich & Tickle, 1995). The approach of decompositional algorithms aims to extract rules by examining activation functions and weights of the hidden layer neurons, and this type of algorithms are considered to be completely translucent. On the other end of the translucency spectrum is the pedagogical approach, which extracts rules by mapping the relationship between the inputs and outputs as closely as possible to that given by the trained ANN model without exploring the ANN models. The underlying ANN models are still viewed as a "black-box" and "translucency" is not a priority. The eclectic approach is a hybrid of the other two approaches and lies in the middle on the translucency spectrum.

Since decompositional algorithms involve examining the underlying ANN model, they generally involve more complex computation than pedagogical algorithms. Some of the proposed decompositional algorithms generate rules by clustering the weighted links between the input and hidden neurons with similar values (Towell & Shavlik, 1993; Setiono & Liu, 1995; Setiono & Liu, 1997; Odajimi *et al.*, 2008). Others involve finding the combination of input value weights to the neuron (Krishnan *et al*, 1999). In Kim & Lee (2000), rules were generated by replacing the neurons in the first hidden layer with logic gates. The pedagogical approach maps the relationships between the inputs and outputs as closely as possible to those given by the ANN model without analysing the underlying ANN model. In Thrun (1993), Thrun mapped the input/output relationships using Validity Interval Analysis, which is similar to sensitivity analysis. In Craven & Shavlik (1996) and deFortuny & Martens (2012), the trained ANN was used as an oracle to construct a decision tree, and/or other "white-box" algorithms. Saad and Wunsch (2007) extracted rules by finding the hyperplanes that represent the NN decision boundary using NN inversion techniques. A reversed engineering approach was also used (Augasta & Kathirvalayakumar, 2012). An eclectic approach is generally any approach that lies in the middle on the translucency spectrum between the decomposition and pedagogical approaches. Some sample work of the eclectic approach include Hruschka & Ebecken (2006), which proposed clustering the activation values using a genetic algorithm (GA), Mohamed (2011) which employed GA for solving the optimization problem of the output function, and Al Iqban (2011), which extracted rules by replacing each of the hidden neurons with a decision tree.

Most of the proposed ANN rule extraction algorithms target classification problems, which are problems that involve categorical variables as outputs. However, in many engineering problems, the output variables involve numeric or continuous values. Some studies that aim to extract rules by approximating the hidden sigmoid activation functions into some piece-wise linear functions include Setiono et al. (2002), Setiono & Thong (2004) and Wang et al. (2011), and the approximation is illustrated in Figure. 1. The differences among the algorithms proposed in Setiono et al. (2002), Setiono & Thong (2004) and Wang et al. (2011) lie in the method each used to solve the PWL approximation. In order to generate sets of rules with high fidelity to the underlying neural network, the accuracy of the PWL approximation is crucial. While Setiono et al. (2002) solved the PWL approximation by "minimizing the area bounded by the hyperbolic tangent function and the linear approximating function", Setiono & Thong (2004) generated the PWL equations by minimizing the sum of squared errors between the activation function and the PWL functions. By contrast, Wang et al. (2011) suggested that neither of the previous methods gave desirable approximation accuracies, and proposed solving the approximation problem with the least squares approach. The approach was applied on one UCI (University of California Irvine (Lichman, 2013)) dataset and the results gave lower values of the mean absolute error (MAE) and root mean absolute error (RMAE) compared to the two algorithms suggested in Setiono et al. (2002) and Setiono & Thong (2004).

Most decompositional algorithms suggest grouping the hidden activation values into classes. By contrast, the PWL approximation approach groups the activation values into linear functions. This makes the algorithm useful for regression problems and is an interesting approach. However, a weakness with the approach in Wang et al. (2011) is that the authors only demonstrated their algorithm on a simple

UCI dataset. In this study, an improved version of the algorithm based on the one proposed in Wang et al. (2011) has been developed for modeling more complicated regression problems. The improved version of the algorithm, which is called the piece-wise linear neural network (PWL-ANN) algorithm is presented in Section 3.

Figure 1. Approximating the activation function (sigmoid function) with a three-piece linear approximation function.

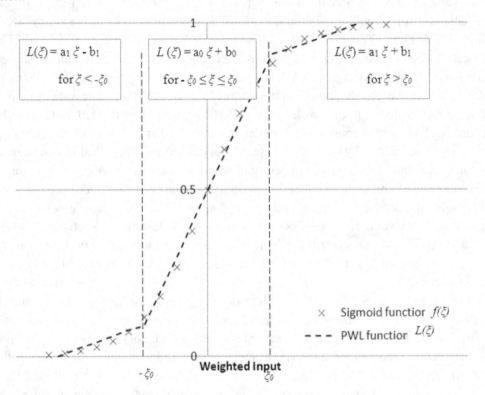

On Applications of ANN Modeling in Engineering Domains

Many research studies were done on applications of ANN technologies for modeling parameters in engineering domains, with the research objective of providing accurate predictions of specific parameters when some other predictor parameters are known. The machine learned or predicted results are then compared with results generated from empirical modeling. For example, Pouryousefi, Idem, Supap & Tontiwachwuthikul. (2016) aimed to predict the physical properties of density, viscosity, refractive index, heat capacity, thermal conductivity and thermal diffusivity of two quaternary amine systems for carbon dioxide (CO_2) capture based on the predictor parameters of the mole fractions of the components and temperature. The back-propagation neural network (BPNN) and radial basis function neural network (RBFNN) approaches were used and the predicted results were compared with results generated from empirical modeling based on the Weiland, Nissan-Grunberg, Gladston-Dale, and Redlich-Kister models. The comparison reveals that the neural network predicted results were accurate within 1% deviation for all the properties of the amine systems, and the empirically derived results were less accurate. Liu

& Chan (2016) investigated the carbon dioxide equilibrium solubility of seven tertiary amine solvents using both the empirical modeling and artificial neural network approaches. The study was conducted at the amine concentration of 2.0 mol/L, over the temperature range of 298-333K, and over the CO_2 partial pressure range of 3-101kPa. The thermodynamic models adopted for correlation and prediction of the experimental results of CO_2 equilibrium solubility in the seven tertiary amine solutions included the new K2 correlation Helei-Liu model and Liu et al. model. A comparison of the performances of the empirical and ANN models in predicting CO_2 solubility showed that the Liu et al. and the ANN models gave the best performances in predicting the CO_2 equilibrium solubility in the newly formulated amine solutions. Fu et al. (2014) similarly employed BPNN and RBFNN to predict the mass transfer performance of carbon dioxide absorption in random and structured packed columns using amine as an absorbent. The predictor parameters include gas flow rate, liquid flow rate, solvent concentration, carbon dioxide loading in liquid, mole fraction of carbon dioxide, temperature, and packing area, and the predicted parameter is the mass transfer of carbon dioxide. The results from the neural network modeling was compared with those from numerical correlations and the former approach was found to be more accurate. Among the two methods, the RBFNN approach was found to generate more accurate results than the BPNN approach. Similarly, Fotoohi, Amjad-Iranagh, Golzar & Modarress (2016) also studied pure and binary gas adsorption on activated carbon using ANN compared with equations of state, and the results produced by the ANN approach was found to be more accurate than the equations of state.

Therefore, the surveyed works revealed that using the ANN approach for prediction of parameter values in engineering domains was often found to be a feasible and accurate method. However, these research studies often aimed only for accurate prediction of some parameters and ignored the need for explication or interpretation of the modelled relationships among the parameters. In fact, studies that adopt interpretability as an objective are scarce. Some studies that adopted the rule extraction approach for achieving interpretability in engineering problem domains include Krishnan et al. (1999), Setiono et al. (2002, 2004), and Wang et al. (2011), which adopted the decompositional rule extraction approach, and Thrun (1993) and de Fortuny & Martens (2012), which employed the pedagogical rule extraction approach for extracting information about the domains. In this chapter, we aim to fill this gap in research and present our work on development and application of two versions of the PWL-ANN algorithm for modeling nineteen sets of data. Some preliminary results were presented in Chan & Chan (2017a, 2017b).

METHODOLOGY

The PWL-ANN algorithm is built on two concepts. First, the piece-wise linear (PWL) algorithm is responsible for approximating the hidden activation functions of a trained neural network. Secondly, the neural network with the hidden layer replaced by the generated PWL equations is called the piece-wise linear neural network (PWL-ANN). Rapidminer (trademark of Rapidminer) has been used to train the neural network, and the rule extraction algorithm is written in R. The main steps of the PWL-ANN algorithm are as follows:

Step 1. Training the neural network for a given dataset.

The data is first normalized to the range of [-1, 1] before training and Rapidminer's neural network model (trademark of Rapidminer) was used to model the dataset. The model uses a sigmoid function and a linear function as the activation functions for the hidden layer and the output layer, respectively.

The training cycles were set to 500 with a learning rate of 0.3 and a momentum of 0.2, both are default settings. Only a single hidden layer is considered, and the number of nodes in the hidden layer by default in Rapidminer is given by: (number of input attributes + number of output attributes)/2 +1. The model is trained with a 20-fold cross-validation, and Rapidminer provides information on the trained ANN model and its performance in terms of the root mean squared error. The weights of the nodes of the trained model given by Rapidminer are used in the PWL approximation algorithm.

Step 2. Approximating the activation functions of the hidden neurons of the trained ANN model using the three-piece linear (3PL) functions. The activation function used in the hidden layer is assumed to be a sigmoid function, $f(\xi)$:

$$f(\xi) = \frac{1}{1+e^{-\xi}}$$

where ξ is the sum of the weighted input:

$$\xi = \sum_{i=1} w_i x_i + \theta$$

where w_i are the weights and θ is the bias.

The sigmoid function can be approximated using a three-piece linear function, $L(\xi)$; such that:

$$L(\xi) = \begin{cases} -a_1 + b_1\xi, & if\ \xi > \xi_0 \\ b_0\xi, & if\ -\xi_0 \geq \xi \geq \xi_0 \\ a_1 + b_1\xi, & if\ -\xi_0 > \xi \end{cases}$$

As shown in Figure 1, ξ_0 and $-\xi_0$ are called the breakpoints (BPs) of the piece-wise linear equations. The challenge of finding an accurate 3PL equation lies in locating the breakpoints, which can be found by performing a brute-force search on the dataset. The steps involved in approximating the activation functions are as follows:

Let M be the total number of data points in a given dataset,

1. Sort the data points in ascending order.
2. Divide the dataset into M/d number of subsets, where d is the number of data points per subset and this value determines how frequently the data points within the dataset are tested. Each tested point becomes a potential breakpoint, in other words, the break points are the points at which the function changes. For example, d=1 means each point will be tested and d=10 means every 10 points of the dataset will be tested.
3. For each subset, consider the last data entry of the subset, ξ_i, as the breakpoint. Solve the linear equations for the data entries in the subintervals of $[0, \xi_i]$ and $[\xi_i, \xi_{max}]$ using the least squares approach. Record the mean squared error (MSE) given by the two lines.
4. Repeat step (iii) with all the subsets.

The set of equations with the lowest value of MSE is considered the best solution.

Due to the symmetry of the sigmoid function, it is only necessary to locate one breakpoint, ξ_0, and the other breakpoint will be $-\xi_0$. Based on this constraint, two possible approaches can be adopted to solve the 3PL equations:

1. Either the dataset that lies on the left, i.e. negative ξ values, or right, i.e. positive ξ values, hand side of the y-axis is used, the choice favors the side that has the larger set of data.
2. The absolute values of ξ are used to solve the linear equations and it is necessary to locate only one breakpoint, ξ_0. The $L(\xi)$ values of negative ξ can be obtained by $1 - L(\xi)$.

Step 3. Extracting rules from the approximated linear functions.

After the activation functions of the hidden neurons are approximated using 3PL equations, the sigmoid functions are replaced with the 3PL functions and the PWL-ANN model is derived. Then rules in the form of linear functions can be extracted from the PWL-ANN model.

To illustrate the result of the algorithm, consider a neural network with three inputs and three hidden neurons as shown in Figure 2.

Figure 2. A trained neural network with three inputs, three hidden neurons and one output.

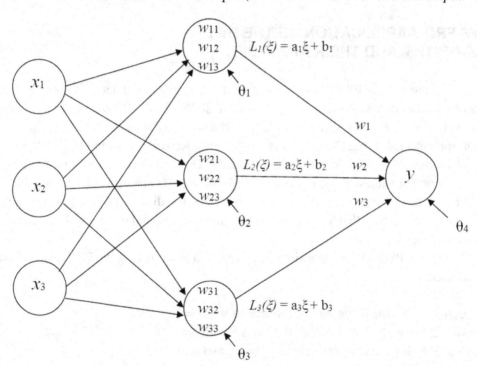

By approximating the activation functions with linear equations, the output can be expressed in terms of the inputs as a linear equation:

$$y = w_1(a_1(w_{11}x_1 + w_{12}x_2 + w_{13}x_3 + \theta_1) + b_1) + w_2(a_2(w_{21}x_1 + w_{22}x_2 + w_{23}x_3 + \theta_2) + b_2) + w_3(a_3(w_{31}x_1 + w_{32}x_2 + w_{33}x_3 + \theta_3) + b_3) + \theta_4$$

which can be simplified as

$$y = Ax_1 + Bx_2 + Cx_3 + D$$

$$A = w_1 a_1 w_{11} + w_2 a_2 w_{21} + w_3 a_3 w_{31}$$

$$B = w_1 a_1 w_{12} + w_2 a_2 w_{22} + w_3 a_3 w_{32}$$

$$C = w_1 a_1 w_{13} + w_2 a_2 w_{23} + w_3 a_3 w_{33}$$

$$D = w_1(a_1\theta_1 + b_1) + w_2(a_2\theta_2 + b_2) + w_3(a_3\theta_3 + b_3) + \theta_4$$

For each of the given input, we can now find the corresponding multiple linear equation that calculates the output. These linear equations become the output "class" of the dataset and if-then rules can be generated based on these classes.

RESULTS FROM APPLICATION OF THE PWL-ANN ALGORITHM AND THEIR ANALYSIS

To assess performance of the PWL-ANN algorithm, it was tested on 19 datasets, among which 15 datasets were obtained from the UCI repository (Lichman, 2006) and the Weka project (Hall et al., 2009), and 4 datasets (number 16 – 19) were obtained from the post-combustion carbon dioxide capture process system implemented at the Clean Energy Technology Research Institute (CETRI) located at the University of Regina, in Regina, Saskatchewan, Canada. These datasets were chosen because they all have continuous output values. The characteristics of the datasets are summarized in Table 1. For the discrete attributes, dummy variables were used to represent the different classes of that attribute. For example, for an input attribute that has the classes of sunny, cloudy, and windy, with the dummy coding, the classes are labeled as 1, 2 and 3.

Based on the same PWL-ANN algorithm, three approaches in solving the PWL approximation process were adopted:

1. Approach 1: Using the larger half of the dataset with d=10;
2. Approach 2: Using the larger half of the dataset with d=3;
3. Approach 3: Using the absolute values of the dataset with d=3.

As mentioned in Section 1, the primary evaluation criterion is fidelity of the generated rule sets to the originally trained ANN. While accuracy of the PWL-ANN algorithm is also considered, the predictive accuracy of the PWL-ANN model is constrained by the predictive accuracy of the trained ANN model. In other words, if the trained ANN model has low accuracy, then the PWL-ANN model of this trained ANN model would also have low accuracy. To evaluate fidelity, the values of R^2 and mean square error

(MSE) given by the ANN and the PWL-ANN models are compared. MSE measures the deviation of the predicted value to the actual value; and R^2 shows how close the actual values are to the fitted line. The values of R^2 and MSE can be calculated as follows:

$$R^2 = 1 - \frac{\sum_i \left(y_i - \hat{y}_i\right)^2}{\sum_i \left(y_i - \bar{y}\right)^2}$$

where y_i = the expected output of the ith dataset, $\bar{y} = \frac{1}{n}\sum_{i=1}^{n} y_i$ and $\hat{y}$ = predicted output.

$$MSE = \frac{\sum_i \left(y_i - \hat{y}_i\right)^2}{n}$$

Table 1. Characteristics of the datasets

	Dataset	Data size	No. of input nodes	No. of hidden nodes
#1	Energy Efficiency Heat loading (UCI)	767	8	6
#2	Energy Efficiency Cool loading (UCI)	767	8	6
#3	Airfoil Self-noise (UCI)	1503	5	4
#4	CCPP (UCI)	9568	4	4
#5	Housing (UCI)	506	13	8
#6	Yacht Hydrodynamics (UCI)	308	6	5
#7	Bodyfat (Weka)	252	9	9
#8	pwLinear (Weka)	200	14	7
#9	AutoPrice (Weka)	159	15	9
#10	Parkinson (UCI)	5873	19	12
#11	Concrete (UCI)	1030	8	6
#12	ERA (Weka)	1000	4	4
#13	Pollution (UCI)	60	15	9
#14	ESL (Weka)	488	4	4
#15	CPU (UCI)	209	7	7
#16	CO_2 production rate	10421	8	6
#17	Heavy Duty	10421	8	6
#18	Lean Loading	10421	8	6
#19	Absorption Efficiency	10421	8	6

Since an important research objective is to generate explicit information from the ANN models, the evaluation criterion adopted is that the PWL-ANN algorithm would produce similar values of R^2 and MSE as those produced by the ANN model on all the datasets. In order to more easily compare the results from the applications of the algorithm to the datasets, the percentage difference between the MSE given by the proposed PWL-ANN algorithm is compared to the MSE given by the trained ANN. Table 2 and 3 summarize the MSE and R^2 given by the ANN and the PWL-ANN approaches, respectively, which show the accuracies of the ANN and PWL-ANN models.

Table 2. MSE given by the ANN model and the PWL-ANN approaches

	ANN	PWL-ANN Approach 1	PWL-ANN Approach 2	PWL-ANN Approach 3
#1	9.52E-01	4.51E+00	1.29E+00	1.10E+00
#2	3.54E+00	3.92E+00	3.54E+00	3.57E+00
#3	1.61E+01	1.66E+01	1.66E+01	1.65E+01
#4	2.47E+01	2.53E+01	2.53E+01	2.54E+01
#5	6.81E+00	7.72E+00	7.70E+00	7.67E+00
#6	1.49E+00	4.02E+00	3.96E+00	3.95E+00
#7	6.26E-01	7.49E-01	7.60E-01	7.61E-01
#8	1.40E+00	1.47E+00	1.46E+00	1.46E+00
#9	1.88E+06	2.21E+06	2.15E+06	2.19E+06
#10	1.93E+01	1.98E+01	1.98E+01	1.97E+01
#11	5.51E+01	5.84E+01	5.88E+01	5.85E+01
#12	3.56E+00	3.54E+00	3.60E+00	3.58E+00
#13	4.98E+02	5.98E+02	5.99E+02	5.94E+02
#14	4.59E-01	3.69E-01	3.67E-01	3.64E-01
#15	1.78E+01	7.09E+01	4.57E+01	4.78E+01
#16	1.24E-03	1.40E-03	1.40E-03	1.40E-03
#17	4.89E+07	5.13E+07	5.12E+07	5.02E+07
#18	3.04E-03	3.03E-03	3.03E-03	3.04E-03
#19	6.44E-03	6.73E-03	6.74E-03	6.72E-03

Table 4 summarizes the percentage differences between the MSE given by the trained ANN models and the PWL-ANN models and the results are plotted in Figure 3. It can be seen that the percentage differences are low: aside from dataset #1 (approach 1 and 2), #6, #7, #13 and #15, most of the datasets demonstrate reasonable fidelity to the original ANN with a percentage difference in MSE of below 20%. The low percentage differences between the two MSE's demonstrate good fidelity of the PWL-ANN model to the original trained ANN.

When the percentage difference between the MSE's is high, it means the PWL-ANN model demonstrates poor fidelity to the original ANN model. The analysis of the percentage difference between the MSE's and R^2's has two objectives. First, the analysis aims to determine which of the three approaches listed earlier gives the best general performance. Secondly, it aims to investigate the causes for the poor performance of the algorithm on a particular dataset; the approach adopted is to analyze the performance of the three approaches on each individual dataset. The datasets identified with high percentage differences between the MSE's and R^2 will be the focus of the analysis, and the analysis is presented as follows.

Table 3. R^2 given by the ANN model and the PWL-ANN approaches

	ANN	PWL-ANN Approach 1	PWL-ANN Approach 2	PWL-ANN Approach 3
#1	0.9907	0.9557	0.9874	0.9892
#2	0.9609	0.9566	0.9609	0.9605
#3	0.6618	0.6509	0.6208	0.6522
#4	0.9150	0.9130	0.9130	0.9129
#5	0.9193	0.9086	0.9088	0.9092
#6	0.9935	0.9825	0.9827	0.9828
#7	0.9910	0.9893	0.9891	0.9891
#8	0.9298	0.9261	0.9298	0.9266
#9	0.9454	0.9355	0.9373	0.9362
#10	0.8311	0.8271	0.8271	0.8277
#11	0.8023	0.7904	0.7893	0.7900
#12	0.0949	0.0981	0.0838	0.0875
#13	0.8691	0.8429	0.8426	0.8439
#14	0.7724	0.8172	0.8182	0.8195
#15	0.9993	0.9970	0.9981	0.9980
#16	0.9359	0.9276	0.9276	0.9276
#17	0.7541	0.7422	0.7426	0.7478
#18	0.7709	0.7716	0.7715	0.7709
#19	0.7804	0.7704	0.7703	0.7707

Overall Performance of the Three Approaches

In both approaches 2 and 3, a small value of d is used, which means more data points are tested as the potential break points. Using these approaches ensure a more fine-grained approximation of the curve is implemented. Hence, the performances of Approach 2 and 3 can be expected to be better than Approach 1. This hypothesis is valid and it can be seen in Table 5 that approach 1 gives the best fidelity for only 3 datasets, while approaches 2 and 3 give the best performance for 6 and 9 datasets, respectively. The difference between approach 2 and 3 is that approach 2 uses half of the values on the sigmoid curve, whereas approach 3 uses the absolute values and all the data points on the sigmoid curve. Since approach 3 outperforms approach 2, we can conclude that among the three approaches, the best performance is given when the full range of values is included and when a finer grained approximation is used. Thus, in future work, the absolute values and a small value of d will be used for the PWL approximation.

Performance of the Three Approaches on Each Individual Dataset

An analysis of the R^2 values in Table 3 reveals that the PWL-ANN models give close performances to the ANN models on all datasets, even for the dataset on which the ANN model did not give good predictive performance. Based on the premise that a R^2 value that is close to 1 indicates higher predictive accuracy of the model, it can be seen from Table 3 that the R^2 given by dataset #12 is only 0.0949, which reflects low accuracy, and the values given by the PWL-ANN models are 0.0981, 0.0838 and 0.0875, which show similar performance to the ANN model.

Table 4 and Figure. 3 show that aside from dataset #1 (approach 1 and 2), #6, #7, #13 and #15, most of the datasets demonstrate reasonable fidelity to the original ANN with a percentage difference in MSE of below 20%. The analysis aims to identify the causes for the poor performances of the PWL-ANN algorithms. The datasets with a MSE percentage difference greater than 150% include (aside from dataset #1) datasets #6 and #15, as shown in italics in Table 4 and indicated by the tall columns in Figure 3. These datasets deserve careful examination because of their high MSE percentage differences. Dataset #1 will not be examined because its performance was improved from 373.75% in approach 1 to 15.52% in approach 3. Similarly, datasets #6 and #7 will not be examined because their MSE percentage differences are just over 20%, which can be considered acceptable. Thus, the datasets to be examined include only datasets #6 and #15.

Table 4. MSE percentage difference between ANN and the three PWL-ANN approaches

	PWL-ANN Approach 1	PWL-ANN Approach 2	PWL-ANN Approach 3
#1	373.75%	35.25%	15.52%
#2	10.94%	0.00%	0.81%
#3	3.20%	3.16%	2.83%
#4	2.43%	2.40%	2.56%
#5	13.31%	13.06%	12.61%
#6	*169.59%*	*165.72%*	*164.96%*
#7	19.75%	21.53%	21.66%
#8	5.25%	4.05%	4.52%
#9	17.99%	14.75%	16.76%
#10	2.37%	2.37%	2.00%
#11	6.04%	6.59%	6.21%
#12	-0.35%	1.23%	0.82%
#13	*20.02%*	20.28%	*19.25%*
#14	-19.65%	-20.11%	-20.67%
#15	*298.94%*	*156.78%*	*168.77%*
#16	13.01%	12.99%	12.99%
#17	4.84%	4.67%	2.57%
#18	-0.27%	-0.24%	0.02%
#19	4.56%	4.58%	4.42%

Table 5. Performances of the PWL-ANN models

Approach	1	2	3
No. of dataset with the best performance	3	6	9

Note: Data #16 is a draw for both Approach 2 and 3.

In some of the cases, the PWL-ANN models even outperformed the ANN models in terms of accuracies: in dataset #14, the PWL-ANN models give higher R^2's than the ANN model. As pointed out by Zhou (2004), the criteria of accuracy and fidelity can be contradictory. If the assumption is that the underlying ANN model gives good accuracies, then if the proposed rule extraction algorithm has a high fidelity to the ANN model, the rule extraction algorithm will also demonstrate good accuracy. This will fulfill both of the objectives on fidelity and accuracy. However, if there is a dataset for which the underlying ANN model does not predict well, then the rule extraction algorithm can only accomplish one of the two objectives: either it models the ANN model very well, such that the algorithm also gives poor prediction, or it generates a set of rules that gives good accuracy; and the result of data #14 demonstrates this contradiction. Since our primary evaluation criterion is fidelity, it is not expected that the PWL-ANN model should outperform the ANN model. Therefore, the PWL-ANN modeling result of dataset #14 is considered not satisfactory.

Figure 3. MSE percentage difference between the ANN models and the PWL-ANN models

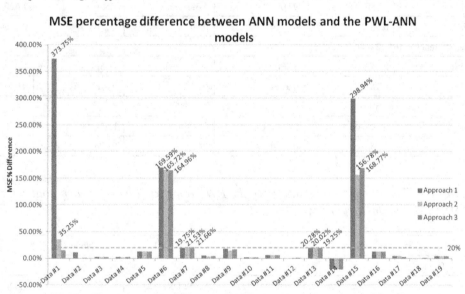

Two Hypotheses to Explain Poor Performance of the PWL-ANN Algorithm

Hypothesis 1: If the PWL approximation of all nodes are highly accurate (with $R^2 > 0.99$), then the fidelity of the PWL-ANN model should be high.

This hypothesis suggests a causal relationship between the accuracy of the PWL approximation as indicated by the R^2 and MSE values and the fidelity of the PWL-ANN mode to the original ANN model. Tables 6 and 7 illustrate this relationship for datasets #6 and #15. The two tables show the values of MSE and R^2 of each node given by the PWL equations in the three approaches for datasets #6 and #15, respectively. It is assumed that if the PWL approximation is highly accurate as indicated by a R^2 value of greater than 0.99, then the PWL-ANN model generated by the algorithm will demonstrate high fidelity to the original ANN, and this will be indicated by a low percentage difference value. This hypothesis was supported by dataset #6 but not by dataset #15. By analyzing the R^2 values in Table 6, it can be seen that some of the nodes in dataset #6 have an R^2 of less than 0.99 (the values are indicated in italics). In this case, the PWL-ANN models demonstrate poor fidelity to the original ANN models. By contrast, in Table 7, approaches 2 and 3 both gave R^2 values that are greater than 0.99 for all the nodes in dataset #15, and yet the MSE percentage differences are still above 150%. This shows that high fidelity of the PWL-ANN model to the original ANN model cannot be guaranteed even when each individual node has been accurately approximated.

Table 6. Dataset #6: Comparison of accuracies of the PWL approximation for each node with fidelity of the PWL-ANN model to the original ANN model

	Node 1	Node 2	Node 3	Node 4	Node 5
Approach 1% difference = 169.59%					
MSE	2.58E-04	9.20E-06	5.30E-06	1.56E-04	1.62E-05
R^2	*0.9878*	0.9974	0.997	*0.9768*	0.9964
Approach 2% difference = 165.72%					
MSE	2.54E-04	9.20E-06	5.30E-06	1.55E-04	1.62E-05
R^2	*0.988*	0.9974	0.997	*0.9769*	0.9964
Approach 3% difference = 164.96%					
MSE	2.54E-04	9.20E-06	5.30E-06	1.55E-04	1.62E-05
R^2	*0.988*	0.9974	0.997	*0.9769*	0.9964

Table 7. Data #15: Comparison of accuracies of the PWL approximation for each node with fidelity of the PWL-ANN model to the original ANN model

	Node 1	Node 2	Node 3	Node 4	Node 5
Approach 1% difference = 298.94%					
MSE	2.25E-05	3.00E-07	8.90E-06	6.34E-05	2.00E-05
R^2	0.9986	0.9997	0.9993	*0.988*	0.9987
Approach 2% difference = 156.78%					
MSE	2.16E-05	3.00E-07	8.60E-05	4.45E-05	1.93E-05
R^2	0.9986	0.9997	0.9994	0.9916	0.9987
Approach 3% difference = 168.77%					
MSE	2.16E-05	3.00E-07	8.60E-06	4.73E-05	1.93E-05
R^2	0.9986	0.9997	0.9994	0.991	0.9987

Hypothesis 2: Insufficiency of the three-piece linear equation approximation

Since it has been established from the analysis for hypothesis 1 that accurate approximation of each individual node of the original ANN model cannot guarantee good fidelity of the PWL-ANN model to the original ANN model, the analysis now turns to investigate more specific values within the nodes. The second hypothesis assumes that the poor performance of the PWL-ANN algorithm is due to insufficiency of the three-piece linear equation in approximating the curve in the sigmoid functions. In other words, while some of the data values that fall on the curve of the sigmoid functions in some of the hidden nodes have significant influences on the overall performance of the PWL-ANN, these points on the curve are not adequately modelled. As a consequence, the PWL-ANN model shows poor fidelity to the original ANN model. It is important to note that this hypothesis does not assume that omission of all the points that lie in the curves of all the hidden nodes cause the poor fidelity to the original ANN model. Rather, the omission of some combination of points in some nodes is the culprit. If this hypothesis is true, a more fine-grained PWL approximation, such as a five-piece linear approximation, on the appropriate hidden nodes would improve performance of the algorithm.

To test the hypothesis on the insufficiency of the three-piece linear equations, the data points that lie in the curve of the hidden nodes are removed one at a time and these subsets of data are used to generate new sets of 3-piece linear equations for the PWL-ANN models. The data points are eliminated one hidden node at a time so as to reveal which sets of data points have positive effects on the MSE of the PWL-ANN model. Since application of the PWL-ANN algorithm to dataset #6 demonstrated poor performance, this elimination process was applied to dataset #6. The results are shown in Table 8, whose left column indicates the modelled dataset, and the right column indicates the MSE values given by the subsets. The first row of Table 8 shows the MSE values derived from applying the PWL-ANN algorithm to the original dataset using Approach 3. Subset 1 refers to the dataset that has the data points lying on the curve of the first hidden node removed and Subset 2 refers to the data points lying on the curve of the second node removed and so on.

Table 8. MSE's given by PWL-ANN modeling for original dataset #6 and its subset

	MSE	% difference with MSE from Approach 3
Approach 3	3.95	--
Subset 1	2.62	-33.59%
Subset 2	3.96	0.29%
Subset 3	3.95	0.00%
Subset 4	4.18	5.79%
Subset 5	3.21	-18.80%

It can be seen from Table 8 that by removing the data points that lie on the curves of nodes 1 and 5, the MSE's of the PWL-ANN models have decreased and improved from that given by the original model, while removing data points from node 2 and 4 increased the MSE values from 3.95 to 3.96 and 4.18, respectively. Based on these results, we generate a new subset, called subset B, which is produced by removing data points that lie on the curves of node 1 and 5, because these nodes caused improvement on the MSE value. The MSE given by applying the PWL-ANN algorithm to subset B is significantly lower than that given by approach 3, as shown in Table 9. The percentage difference between the MSE given by the PWL-ANN model and the original ANN model also decreased from 164.96% to 42.42%.

Table 9. Performance of PWL-ANN modeling on subset B of dataset #6 using approach 3

	PWL-ANN MSE	MSE % diff. with ANN
Approach 3	3.95	164.96%
Subset B	2.08	42.42%

The result from this analysis suggests hypothesis 2 is valid. It shows that the accuracy and fidelity of the PWL-ANN model can be improved by better approximating the sigmoid function. This observation echoed findings in some relevant literature. Setiono et al. (2002) suggested a 5-piece approximation algorithm in their work and their results showed that the 5-piece approximation outperformed the 3-piece approximation. However, their work suffered from several weaknesses, which include: (i) their application dataset has less than 700 data points, and (ii) the complexity of the 5-piece linear application algorithm was not considered. In fact, a 5-piece linear approximation requires significantly more computation time, and this is especially true for industrial datasets, e.g. the CO_2 capture plant datasets in our study have over 10,000 data points. A promising direction for enhancement is to extend the brute-force search algorithm for locating more break points. Instead of locating only one breakpoint for a 3-piece approximation because of symmetry of the sigmoid function, a 5-piece linear approximation will require locating more than one breakpoint. It will also be necessary to examine and consider the computing time required to process a 3-piece (1 breakpoint) and a 5-piece (2 breakpoints) approximation on different sizes of datasets. Therefore, the enhanced version of the PWL-ANN algorithm would aim to increase the "pieces" in the piece-wise linear equation from 3 to more pieces so that approximation of the sigmoid function curves in the hidden nodes can be improved.

Methodology of the Enhanced-PWL-ANN Algorithm

The objective of developing the enhanced version of the PWL-ANN algorithm was to extend the original PWL-ANN algorithm and enable it to increase the number of pieces in the piece-wise linear equations. The enhanced PWL-ANN algorithm consists of the same three steps as the original PWL-ANN algorithm, which are:

1. Training the neural network model for a given dataset, and the ANN model obtained is called the originally trained ANN model.
2. Approximating the activation functions of the hidden neurons of the originally trained ANN model and generate the PWL-ANN models.
3. Extracting rules from the generated PWL-ANN models

However, while Steps 1 and 3 remain unchanged from the PWL-ANN algorithm, step 2 of the enhanced version was modified for the purpose of improving predictive accuracy and fidelity of the enhanced PWL-ANN models compared to the originally trained ANN model. Specifically, step 2 of the PWL-ANN algorithm was modified to incorporate the following features:

1.   Instead of locating only two breakpoints (BPs), the brute force search is extended to locate N number of breakpoints and therefore, the hidden activation functions can be approximated by not three but (N+1)-piece linear equations;
2.   A sampling algorithm is included as an option to manage computation time of the algorithm;
3.   A sensitivity analysis (SA) algorithm is implemented to determine the number of breakpoints used in each of the hidden nodes of the originally trained ANN model.

   The pseudo code of the steps involved in approximating the activation functions and finding the optimal set of piecewise linear equations is shown in Figure 4. For implementation, the software platform of Rapidminer (trademark of Rapidminer) was used to train the original neural network model from a given dataset, and the enhanced-PWL-ANN algorithm was written in R (trademark of R).

Figure 4. Process diagram for approximating the hidden activation function

Input:
Input data, Actual Output, ANN Output, Hidden weight values, Output weight values, Activation function (Sigmoid or Hyperbolic), minimum distance between breakpoints (I), maximum number of breakpoints (maxBP), Sampling = TRUE or FALSE, Sampling size ($D_{sampling}$), Error (E).
Output:
PWL equations for each nodes with number of BPs less than or equal to maxBP, and the MSE outputs of the PWL-ANN model within E% with the ANN output.

Begin:
1. Calculate weighted input:
    weighted input = Input x hidden weight
2. Calculate activation function value:
    activation value = activation function(weighted input)

/* Sampling algorithm
3. If(sampling = TRUE)
    X = data size / sampling size data
    Take every x sample from weighted input and activation values
else
    data = weighted input and corresponding activation values

4. /* Brute-force search algorithm for locating breakpoints
4.1. Generate SSR matrix
4.2. Search through SSR matrix to locate breakpoints

5. Calculate PWL-ANN output using 2BP for all nodes, and find MSE
If(MSE < E)
    Return PWL-ANN with 2BP for all nodes

6. /* Sensitivity Analysis
Else
    6.1/* increase the number of breakpoints one node at a time
    /* i keeps count of the nodes
    For(i = ; i = i+1; i < no. of nodes){
        /* j keeps count of the number of breakpoints,
        /* and j is always an even number
        For(j = 4, j = j+2, j < maxBP){
            Calculate PWL-ANN output using j number of BP for node i, and 2 BP for all the other nodes, and MSE.

            Record number of BP per node and the corresponding MSE to the SA matrix.
        }
    }

    6.2 If(any of the MSE in SA matrix < E)
        Return that combination of PWL equations.
    6.3 Else
        /* Find a combination that will give MSE < E
        /* m keeps count of the number of breakpoints
        For(m=4; m = m+2; m<maxBP){
            /* k keeps count of the number of nodes
            For(k=1; k+1; k<no of node){
                Increase number BP of node k to m

                Calculate PWL-ANN output and MSE

                If(MSE < E)
                    Return that combination of PWL equations
            }
        }
        Return combination with minimum MSE

With the modifications made in step 2, the enhanced PWL-ANN algorithm effectively adopted different techniques compared with the original PWL-ANN algorithm; the newly incorporated techniques are discussed as follows.

1. The brute force search in the PWL-ANN algorithm [22] can only locate two breakpoints in the hidden sigmoid functions; it then approximates each hidden sigmoid function with a set of 3-piece linear equations. On the other hand, the brute-force search algorithm in the Enhanced-PWL-ANN algorithm can locate N possible breakpoints and the activation function in each hidden node is approximated with a set of (N+1)-piece of linear equations. By increasing the number of breakpoints, the accuracy and fidelity of the models are improved. A sampling algorithm is included as an option in the Enhanced PWL-ANN algorithm; this enables the user to manage the computation time required to locate N possible breakpoints.
2. A sensitivity analysis is included as part of the Enhanced PWL-ANN algorithm, and the sensitivity analysis can determine the number of breakpoints applicable for each of the hidden nodes in the originally trained ANN model. This feature enables the user to decide on the trade-off between model fidelity and comprehensibility of the extracted rule set.

To demonstrate the improvement in performance between the preliminary and enhanced versions of the PWL-ANN algorithm, the Enhanced PWL-ANN algorithm was applied to the three datasets for which the preliminary PWL-ANN algorithm failed to provide satisfactory results in [22].

The characteristics of the three datasets are summarized in Table 10.

Table 10. Characteristics of the datasets

	Dataset	Data size	No. of input nodes	No. of hidden nodes
#6	Yacht Hydrodynamics (UCI)	308	6	5
#7	Bodyfat (Weka)	252	9	9
#15	CPU (UCI)	209	7	7

Since Approach #3 was found to give the best results, this approach was adopted for comparison between the original and enhanced versions of the PWL-ANN algorithm. A comparison of the parameter settings for generating the PWL-ANN and the enhanced-PWL-ANN models are summarized in Table 11.

The two sets of models were compared in terms of their predictive accuracies and fidelities of the models to the original ANN models. The size of the sample dataset or "sample data size" is indicated as "N/A" for the PWL-ANN models in Table 11 because the original PWL-ANN algorithm does not include a sampling algorithm and the application involved the entire data set.

Table 11. Parameter settings of the PWL-ANN and enhanced-PWL-ANN models

	PWL-ANN models	Enhanced-PWL-ANN models
Number of breakpoints	2	Maximum of 6
Minimum distance between breakpoints	1	1
Sample data size	N/A	300
Desired error rate in terms of MSE percentage difference	< 20%	< 20%

Comparison of Predictive Accuracy and Fidelity of the two Versions of the PWL-ANN Models

The values of R^2 and mean square error (MSE) were used to compare the accuracies of the PWL-ANN and enhanced PWL-ANN models. Since a lower MSE value indicates less deviation of the predicted from the actual values, and a R^2 value close to 1 indicates that the fitted line is close to the actual values, therefore a low MSE value and a R^2 value that is close to 1 are desired. The same primary evaluation criterion of fidelity to the originally trained ANN model adopted for the PWL-ANN models in [22] was also adopted for evaluation of the enhanced-PWL-ANN models. A high fidelity model means that the generated model produces similar values of R^2 and MSE as those produced by the originally trained ANN models. The measure adopted to evaluate fidelity of the generated models produced by the PWL-ANN and the enhanced PWL-ANN algorithms to the originally trained ANN model is the percentage difference between the mean square errors (MSE) given by the respective generated models and the ANN models.

Table 12 summarizes the MSE and R^2 values associated with the three models: (i) the originally trained ANN models (called model #1), (ii) the PWL-ANN models (called model #2) and (iii) the enhanced-PWL-ANN models (called model #3). It can be observed from Table 5 that the MSE values given by Model #3 are lower than those given by Model #2 and the values of R^2 given by Model #3 is closer to 1 than those given by Model #2. This demonstrates an improvement in terms of predictive accuracy given by the enhanced-PWL-ANN algorithm. A comparison of models #1 and #3 shows that Model #1 has the highest accuracy because it consistently has the lowest MSE values and a R^2 value closest to 1 for the three applications. It can be seen from Table 12 that the predictive accuracies given by Model #3 are close to those given by Model #1 and all the R^2 values are within 0.001 differences, which are negligible. Hence, not only do Models #3 demonstrate similar predictive abilities compared to Models #1, Models #3 have the advantage of interpretability while Models #1 are opaque.

Table 12. MSE and R^2 given by Model #1, Model #2 and Model #3

	MSE			R^2		
	Model #1	Model #2	Model #3	Model #1	Model #2	Model #3
#6	1.49E+00	3.95E+00	1.65E+00	0.9935	0.9828	0.9928
#7	6.26E-01	7.61E-01	6.70E-01	0.9910	0.9891	0.9904
#15	1.78E+01	4.78E+01	1.96E+01	0.9993	0.9980	0.9993

Table 13 summarizes the MSE percentage differences between Model #1 and Model #2, and between Model #1 and Model #3 and the number of breakpoints (BPs) per hidden node in these models. Using Dataset #6 as an example, the numbers of BPs for each hidden node in Model #3 are (6, 2, 2, 4, 2), which means the model has 5 nodes in the hidden layer, and the first node has 6 BPs, the second, third and fifth nodes each has 2, and the fourth node has 4 BPs.

A low MSE percentage difference indicates high fidelity between the models, and the desired difference is set at less than 20%. For all three datasets, it can be seen from Table 6 that the MSE percentage differences of the datasets between Model #1 and Model #2 are respectively 164.96%, 21.66%, and 168.77%, which are all over 20%. Hence, they do not satisfy the desired MSE percentage difference of below 20%. However, by increasing the number of breakpoints to a maximum of 6 using the enhanced-PWL-ANN algorithm, the MSE percentage differences for the three applications drop to 10.45%, 7.11%, and 10.44% respectively, which are all below 20%. In other words, applying the enhanced PWL-ANN algorithm was able to reduce the MSE percentage difference for dataset #6 from 164.96% to 10.45%, for dataset #7 from 21.66% to 7.11%, and for dataset #15 from 168.77% to 10.44%. Hence, it can be concluded that the enhanced-PWL-ANN algorithm achieves its objective of improving fidelities of the generated models such that compared with the originally trained ANN model, the MSE percentage differences are all below 20%.

Table 13. Comparison of 3 datasets: MSE percentage differences given by PWL-ANN models and Enhanced-PWL-ANN models

	MSE % difference between Model #1 and		No. of BP per hidden node	
	Model #2	Model #3	Model #2	Model #3
#6	164.96%	10.45%	2, 2, 2, 2, 2	6, 2, 2, 4, 2
#7	21.66%	7.11%	2, 2, 2, 2, 2, 2, 2, 2, 2	2, 2, 4, 2, 2, 2, 2, 2, 2
#15	168.77%	10.44%	2, 2, 2, 2, 2	4, 2, 2, 6, 2

It can also be observed from Table 13 that compared with Model #1, the predictive accuracies and fidelities of Model #3 are both higher than those of Model #2 due to the fact that the number of breakpoints for some of the hidden node functions was increased. As shown in Table 13, the MSE percentage difference of dataset #7 given by Model #2, where the number of BP was 2, was at the borderline value of 21.66%. By increasing the number of breakpoints to 4 in the third hidden node, the MSE percentage difference between Model #1 and Model #3 dropped from 21.66% to 7.11%. For datasets #6 and #15, the MSE percentage difference between Model #1 and Model #2 are more than 15 times greater than those between Model #1 and Model #3. Hence, it was necessary to increase the breakpoints of more than one hidden node in order to decrease the MSE percentage difference. For dataset #6, the number of breakpoints in the first and fourth hidden of the originally trained ANN models were increased to 6 and 4, respectively. As a result, the MSE percentage difference was decreased from 164.96% to 10.45%. Similarly for dataset #15, the number of breakpoints in the first and fourth hidden nodes of the originally trained ANN model were increased to 4 and 6, respectively, and as a result, the MSE percentage difference was decreased from 168.77% to 10.44%. All these applications demonstrate that by improving the accuracies of the PWL approximation on select hidden nodes, the accuracies of the enhanced-PWL-ANN models were improved. For datasets #6 and #15, it can be seen that when fidelity to the originally trained ANN model is extremely low, i.e. when the MSE percentage difference is over 150%, the breakpoints of a combination of nodes need to be increased in order to achieve the desired fidelity of the enhanced-PWL-ANN models (or Models #3) to the original ANN models (or Models #1).

CONCLUSION AND FUTURE WORK

This study aims to present the original and enhanced versions of the PWL-ANN algorithm, and compare the techniques and performances of two versions. The original PWL-ANN algorithm was not able to give satisfactory results when it was used for modelling three datasets in Chan & Chan (2017a). The Enhanced PWL-ANN algorithm was developed so as to improve upon the original PWL-ANN algorithm in terms of predictive accuracy and fidelity, and better model the three datasets. By comparing the application performances of the two algorithms on the three datasets, it can be seen that the Enhanced PWL-ANN algorithm is able to generate models with higher predictive accuracy and better fidelity to the originally trained ANN models than the PWL-ANN algorithm. The enhanced version of the algorithm supports increasing the number of breakpoints in some select hidden nodes of the original ANN model. While the PWL-ANN models have MSE percentage differences that exceed 20% compared to the originally trained ANN models, the enhanced-PWL-ANN models have MSE percentage differences that are less than 20% compared to the originally trained ANN models. In other words, the enhanced PWL-ANN models demonstrated higher fidelity to the originally trained ANN models. However, there is likely to be a trade-off between fidelity of the enhanced-PWL-ANN models and comprehensibility of the generated rule sets. Depending on the characteristics of the dataset, the user needs to determine if increasing the number of breakpoints of select hidden nodes is justifiable because doing so may compromise or reduce comprehensibility of the generated rule set

For future work, the extracted rules can be used for specific problem solving cases in diverse engineering domains. For example, the user may need to achieve a target value of a predicted parameter Y and all the predictor parameter values are known except for two parameters, called X1 and X2. The problem then becomes one of determining the values of the unknown predictor attributes, i.e. X1 and X2, that would achieve the target predicted value of Y. To determine the two unknown predictor parameter values, the equations that cover the values of the known attributes can be identified and used for solving for the unknown parameters. The algorithm to support this scenario of back calculation will be tackled in the next step of this study. Another direction for future work is to try to generate rules that can be directly applied to the original data values of the studied problem so that the normalization and de-normalization steps are no longer necessary.

ACKNOWLEDGMENT

The first author is grateful for the scholarships and generous support from the Faculty of Graduate Studies and Research, University of Regina and from the Canada Research Chair Program. The authors also wish to acknowledge the contributions of Dr. Raphael Idem and Dr. Paitoon Tontiwachwuthikul for their insights and for allowing us to use the datasets on the carbon dioxide capture process system of the Clean Energy Technology Research Institute in Saskatchewan, Canada.

REFERENCES

Al Iqbal, R. (2011). Eclectic extraction of propositional rules from neural networks. *14th International Conference on Computer and Information Technology*, 234–239. 10.1109/ICCITechn.2011.6164790

Andrews, R., Diederich, J., & Tickle, A. B. (1995). Survey and critique of techniques for extracting rules from trained artificial neural networks. *Knowledge-Based Systems*, 8(6), 373–389. doi:10.1016/0950-7051(96)81920-4

Augasta, M. G., & Kathirvalavakumar, T. (2012). Rule Extraction from Neural networks - a Comparative Study. *Proceedings of the International Conference on Pattern Recognition, Informatics and Medical Engineering*.

Chan, V., & Chan, C. (2017b). Learning from a carbon dioxide capture process system: Application of the piecewise linear neural network algorithm. *Petroleum Journal: Special Issue on Carbon Dioxide Capture and Utilization*, 3(1), 56–67. doi:10.1016/j.petlm.2016.11.004

Chan, V., & Chan, C. W. (2017a). Towards development of a piece-wise linear neural network algorithm for rule extraction. *International Journal of Cognitive Informatics and Natural Intelligence*, 11(2), 57–73. doi:10.4018/IJCINI.2017040104

Craven, M. W., & Shavlik, J. W. (1996). Extracting tree-structured representations of trained neural networks. *Advances in Neural Information Processing Systems*, 8, 24–30.

de Fortuny, E. J., & Martens, D. (2012). Active Learning Based Rule Extraction for Regression. *2012 IEEE 12th International Conference on Data Mining Workshops*, 926–933.

Fotoohi, F., Amjad-Iranagh, S., Golzar, K., & Modarress, H. (2016). Predicting pure and binary gas adsorption on activated carbon with two-dimensional cubic equations of state (2-D EOSs) and artificial neural network (ANN) method. *Physics and Chemistry of Liquids*, 54(3), 281–302. doi:10.1080/00319104.2015.1084877

Fu, K., Chen, G., Liang, Z., Sema, T., Idem, P., & Tontiwachwuthikul, P. (2014). Analysis of Mass Transfer Performance of Monoethanolamine-Based CO2 Absorption in a Packed Column Using Artificial Neural Networks. *Industrial & Engineering Chemistry Research*, 53(11), 4413–4423. doi:10.1021/ie403259g

Hall, M., National, H., Frank, E., Holmes, G., Pfahringer, B., Reutemann, P., & Witten, I. H. (2009). The WEKA Data Mining Software : An Update. *SIGKDD Explorations*, 11(1), 10–18. doi:10.1145/1656274.1656278

Hruschka, E. R., & Ebecken, N. F. F. (2006). Extracting rules from multilayer perceptrons in classification problems: A clustering-based approach. *Neurocomputing*, 70(1-3), 384–397. doi:10.1016/j.neucom.2005.12.127

Kim, D., & Lee, J. (2000). Handling Continuous-Valued Attributes in Decision Tree with Neural Network Modelling. *Machine Learning: ECML 2000, 11th European Conference on Machine Learning*, 211–219.

Krishnan, R., Sivakumar, G., & Bhattacharya, P. (1999). A search technique for rule extraction from trained neural networks. *Pattern Recognition Letters*, 20(3), 273–280. doi:10.1016/S0167-8655(98)00145-7

Lichman, M. (2013). *UCI Machine Learning Repository*. Irvine, CA: University of California, School of Information and Computer Science.

Liu, H., Chan, C., Tontiwachwuthikul, P., & Idem, R. (2019). Analysis of carbon dioxide equilibrium solubility of seven tertiary amine solvents using thermodynamics and ANN models. *Fuel*, *249*, 61–72. doi:10.1016/j.fuel.2019.02.088

Mohamed, M. H. (2011). Rules extraction from constructively trained neural networks based on genetic algorithms. *Neurocomputing*, *74*(17), 3180–3192. doi:10.1016/j.neucom.2011.04.009

Odajima, K., Hayashi, Y., Tianxia, G., & Setiono, R. (2008). Greedy rule generation from discrete data and its use in neural network rule extraction. *Neural Networks*, *21*(7), 1020–1028. doi:10.1016/j.neunet.2008.01.003 PMID:18442894

Pouryousefi, F., Idem, R., Supap, T., & Tontiwachwuthikul, P. (2016). Artificial Neural Networks for Accurate Prediction of Physical Properties of Aqueous Quaternary Systems of Carbon Dioxide (CO2)-Loaded 4-(Diethylamino)-2-butanol and Methyldiethanolamine Blended with Monoethanolamine. *Industrial & Engineering Chemistry Research*, *55*(44), 11614–11621. doi:10.1021/acs.iecr.6b03018

Saad, E. W., & Wunsch, D. C. II. (2007). Neural network explanation using inversion. *Neural Networks*, *20*(1), 78–93. doi:10.1016/j.neunet.2006.07.005 PMID:17029713

Setiono, R., Leow, W. K., & Zurada, J. M. (2002). Extraction of rules from artificial neural networks for nonlinear regression. *IEEE Transactions on Neural Networks, 13*(3), 564–577.

Setiono, R., & Liu, H. (1995). Understanding Neural Netowrks via Rule Extraction. In *Proceeding of 14th International Joint Conference on Artificial Intelligence* (pp. 480 – 485). Academic Press.

Setiono, R., & Liu, H. (1997). Neurolinear: From neural networks to oblique decision rules. *Neurocomputing*, *17*(1), 1–24. doi:10.1016/S0925-2312(97)00038-6

Setiono, R., & Thong, J. Y. L. (2004). An approach to generate rules from neural networks for regression problems. *European Journal of Operational Research*, *155*(1), 239–250. doi:10.1016/S0377-2217(02)00792-0

Thrun, S. B. (1993). *Extracting provably correct rules from artificial neural networks*. University of Bonn. Retrieved from http://citeseerx.ist.psu.edu/viewdoc/download?doi=10.1.1.2.2110&rep=rep1&type=pdf

Towell, G. G., & Shavlik, J. W. (1993). Extracting refined rules from knowledge-based neural networks. *Machine Learning*, *13*(1), 71–101. doi:10.1007/BF00993103

Wang, J., Qin, B., Zhang, W., & Shi, W. (2011). Regression rules extraction from artificial neural network based on least squares. In *Proceedings - 2011 7th International Conference on Natural Computation, ICNC 2011,* (pp. 203–207). 10.1109/ICNC.2011.6021906

Zhou, Z. (2004). Rule extraction: Using neural networks or for neural networks? *Journal of Computer Science and Technology*, *19*(2), 249–253. doi:10.1007/BF02944803

This research was previously published in Innovations, Algorithms, and Applications in Cognitive Informatics and Natural Intelligence; pages 104-126, copyright year 2020 by Engineering Science Reference (an imprint of IGI Global).

Chapter 14
The Role of Neural Networks and Metaheuristics in Agile Software Development Effort Estimation

Anupama Kaushik

Maharaja Surajmal Institute of Technology, Delhi, India; Indira Gandhi Delhi Technical University for Women, Delhi, India

Devendra Kumar Tayal

Indira Gandhi Delhi Technical University for Women, Delhi, India

Kalpana Yadav

Indira Gandhi Delhi Technical University for Women, Delhi, India

ABSTRACT

In any software development, accurate estimation of resources is one of the crucial tasks that leads to a successful project development. A lot of work has been done in estimation of effort in traditional software development. But, work on estimation of effort for agile software development is very scant. This paper provides an effort estimation technique for agile software development using artificial neural networks (ANN) and a metaheuristic technique. The artificial neural networks used are radial basis function neural network (RBFN) and functional link artificial neural network (FLANN). The metaheuristic technique used is whale optimization algorithm (WOA), which is a nature-inspired metaheuristic technique. The proposed techniques FLANN-WOA and RBFN-WOA are evaluated on three agile datasets, and it is found that these neural network models performed extremely well with the metaheuristic technique used. This is further empirically validated using non-parametric statistical tests.

DOI: 10.4018/978-1-6684-2408-7.ch014

INTRODUCTION

In software development firms, two development approaches are present, the traditional software development approach and agile software development approach. In traditional software development approach requirements are well understood and there are predefined stages of development. This type of development is driven by process and tool. The requirements once decided is difficult to change and the customer's involvement is limited in this development. Here, the iterations are longer and the working software is not quickly available.

In agile software development approach customers can do modifications until late in project's life. They are people and collaboration driven. So, there is a continuous involvement of customers'. This development approach is more user friendly and follows incremental and iterative development. The iterations are shorter here and working software is available quickly. Now-a-days, software development firms are moving towards adopting agile methodologies (Dingsøyr, Nerur, Balijepally, & BredeMoe, 2012; Papadopoulos, 2015).

The success of a software project mainly depends upon the accuracy of estimation of its resources like effort, schedule etc. There are many effort estimation studies for traditional software development present in literature (Nguyen, Boehm &LiGuo, 2019; Venkataiah, Mohanty, Pahariya & Nagaratna, 2017; Kaushik, Verma, Singh & Chabbra, 2017; Kaushik, Tayal, Yadav & Kaur, 2016). These studies are based on algorithmic and non-algorithmic approach. The COCOMO model (Boehm, 1994) commonly used for effort estimation in traditional software development uses algorithmic approach. The non-algorithmic approach uses various soft computing techniques like fuzzy logic, neural network, genetic algorithms etc.

In agile software development approach, not much of work has been done in estimation of resources for the projects but a lot of work is going on for developing agile methodologies (Curiel, Jacobo, Alfaro, Zepeda & Delgado, 2018; Tolfo, Wazlawick, Ferreira & Forcellini, 2018; Perkusich, Gorgônio, Almeida, & Perkusich, 2017).This work is dedicated towards estimation of effort for agile projects using story point approach which finds the effort of a project in terms of story points. In the past, few researchers have applied various machine learning techniques for effort estimation using story point approach (Satapathy, Panda & Rath, 2014; Panda, Satapathy & Rath, 2015; Satapathy & Rath, 2017).

The current work integrates artificial neural networks (ANN) with a metaheuristic technique for effort estimation of projects following agile methodologies. The ANN used are RBFN and FLANN and, the metaheuristic technique used is whale optimization algorithm (WOA).

The ANN models incorporated have no relationship with each other and they are evaluated independently. These models are used as they have their own advantages. The major advantages of FLANN are: it has less computational complexity, faster convergence and handles the non-linear data (Mishra & Dehuri, 2007) ; and the major advantages of RBFN are: its easy design, good generalization, strong tolerance to input noise and has faster online learning ability (Yu, Xie, Paszczyñski & Wilamowski, 2011). These models are also chosen as no earlier study exists based on these models for agile environment.

Now-a-days metaheuristic techniques have come up. These are the optimization techniques which mimics the biological or physical phenomenon to solve various engineering problems. They can even find the solutions for the problems with very less and incomplete information. Many new metaheuristic algorithms are developed and many researchers (Kaushik, Tayal, Yadav, & Kaur, 2016; Kaushik, Verma, Singh, & Chhabra, 2017; Benala & Mall, 2018) have used these techniques in estimations for traditional software development environment, but according to the best of our knowledge these techniques have not been explored for resource estimations in agile software development. So the current work is an attempt to introduce metaheuristic techniques in effort estimation for agile software development environment. Here, whale optimization algorithm (WOA) is the metaheuristic approach used with ANN due to its striking features which are at par than other optimization methods (Mirjalili & Lewis, 2016). The study also examines the effort estimation accuracy of the selected ANN models by incorporating WOA.

The paper consists of literature review section which discusses the work done by the researchers concerning software effort estimation in agile environment, followed by the section on background concepts used in the current work. After that, innovation in the paper is discussed in research contribution section followed by simulation and results section. Finally, conclusion of the study is presented.

LITERATURE SURVEY

Few of the effort estimation studies related to agile software development are discussed below.

Lang, Conboy and Keaveney (2011) discussed four case studies to explain the cost estimation process, causes of inaccurate estimates and steps to improve the process in agile software development. They also discussed, how agile handles the classical problems which affects the cost estimation in comparison to traditional information system development. Their study recommended three points for agile projects and they are: estimation models are not necessarily required, documentation of past project data and experience, and fixed price budgets.

Coelho and Basu (2012) discussed effort estimation in agile software development in detail using story points and directed further scope of improvement. They also provided various size estimation techniques used traditionally, discussed user stories prioritization and delivery date estimations. They concluded that some hidden factors were also responsible for the delay in software project deployment.

Ziauddin, Tipu and Zia (2012) provided a software effort estimation model based upon user stories. This model included all the characteristics of agile software development. The model used various equations and demonstrated its effectiveness using data collected from 21 software projects. They provided guidelines to measure user story size and complexity in the scale of 1-5. They also discussed various factors affecting the projects velocity and provided a way to handle uncertainty in calculation of completion time.

Choudhari and Suman (2012) proposed an effort estimation model for software maintenance which was validated using various types of maintenance projects. This was based on story points to calculate the volume of maintenance and value adjustment factors. The model was developed in order to help the project managers to estimate the software maintenance for agile and extreme programming environment.

Hussain, Kosseim and Ormandjieva (2013) used COSMIC standard to approximate the functional size in early effort estimation in agile processes. Their methodology used supervised text mining approach where COSMIC function size is calculated from the textual requirements and it was also able to recognize the striking features of the functional processes in order to determine their size.

Popli and Chauhan (2014) provided an estimation method for projects using agile methodologies. The algorithm efficiently proposed effort, cost and duration for small and medium sized agile projects. They also discussed already existing methods of agile estimation along with their limitations. Their estimation model was based on story point approach and a case study was discussed with the proposed model.

Satapathy, Panda and Rath (2014) used Support Vector Regression (SVR) for effort estimation method using story point approach. They optimized the result of story point approach using SVR kernel methods for better prediction accuracy. The kernel methods used by them were linear, polynomial, Radial Basis

Function (RBF) and Sigmoid kernels. They concluded that RBF kernel based SVR was at par than the rest of the three kernel methods for effort estimation.

Panda, Satapathy and Rath (2015) used different types of Neural Networks to increase the accuracy estimation of agile projects using story point approach. The parameters used by them in estimation were story points, velocity and actual effort. They used dataset of 21 projects to validate their approach and used Mean Square Error (MSE), squared correlation coefficient (R^2), Mean Magnitude of Relative Error (MMRE) and Prediction Accuracy (PRED) as the evaluation criteria.

Garg and Gupta (2015) proposed a cost estimation method where they identified the key attributes that have maximum impact on development cost using principal component analysis. In order to satisfy the criteria imposed by agile manifesto they further used constraint solving approach. Their model also worked in absence of historical data and expert opinion. The model provided lower MMRE value in comparison to planning poker and mapped the agile manifesto.

Tanveer (2016) provided a hybrid methodology with tool support for effort estimation which handled change impact analysis, expert judgement and software visualization. They proposed that agile projects were usually estimated using expert judgement which was not accurate and reliable. So a new technique was proposed by them to improve the estimation process in agile environment.

Raslan, Darwish and Hefny (2015) proposed an effort estimation methodology using fuzzy logic. They used story point approach and trapezoidal membership functions to represent the input parameters which consisted of Story Points (SP), Implementation Level Factor (ILF), FRiction factors (FR), and Dynamic Forces (DF). They designed the proposed fuzzy inference system in MATLAB and calculated the effort.

Dragicevic, Celar and Turic (2017) proposed an effort prediction model for agile projects using bayesian network. They validated their technique on the agile project data of a single company. The model was further assessed using various statistical parameters. The model could be used with any agile methodology in the initial planning phase. It basically provided task effort estimation based on various parameters like working hours, requirements complexity, developer's skills etc.

Salmanoglu, Hacaloglu, and Demirors (2017) evaluated three case studies on agile projects to compare effort estimation using COSMIC and story points. They found that effort estimation models developed using COSMIC size performed better on all the three case studies. They also concluded that COSMIC provided better productivity for the data which was less dispersed than story points. They also shared their datasets for future research.

Satapathy and Rath (2017) improved the prediction accuracy of story point approach using various machine learning techniques and compared the proposed techniques with the existing techniques in the literature. The machine learning techniques used were decision tree (DT), stochastic gradient boosting (SGB) and Random forest (RF). They developed this estimation model considering scrum projects. The technique SGB gave the best results than the rest of the two techniques on the examined dataset.

Tanveer, Vollmer and Braun (2018) proposed an estimation technique for agile development teams. They designed a hybrid method where the impact of change is analysed and incorporated for effort estimation. They also proposed an estimation technique using boosted trees and discussed their methodology using a case study on a German software company. Their method was more effective and accurate than the expert based methods.

Usman, Britto, Damm and Borstler (2018) identified and analysed the effort estimation process in large scale distributed agile projects. They also identified various factors effecting the effort of such projects. They devised a two stage effort estimation and restimation process to improve the accuracy of estimation in such projects. They concluded that effort overruns in large scale distributed agile projects could be limited by considering various factors like requirements size, its priorities, maturity and team distribution of agile projects.

Martínez, Noriega, Ramírez, Licea and Jiménez (2018) proposed a Bayesian network model to handle the complexity and importance associated with the user stories used for estimation of scrum projects. Their model could replace the traditional planning poker used in estimations and could be used by an inexperienced or a new developer. They used estimations provided by students and professionals in order to validate the model. They found professionals' estimation more correlated to the proposed model than the students' estimation as the proposed model included various factors considered in real world application.

Mensah, Keung, Bosu, and Bennin (2018) designed a duplex output model for software effort estimation. The first output here was software effort and the second output was the classification of effort in order to identify the level of effort. The study was motivated by conclusion instability problem faced by effort estimation models. They did comparison of six different regression-based techniques which included the state-of-the-art baseline model (ATLM) and ElasticNet regression to solve conclusion instability. They found ElasticNet regression providing superior accuracy than the rest of the techniques.

Bilgayian, Das and Mishra (2019) solved effort estimation problem for agile projects by using back propagation neural networks and Elman neural networks. They validated the model on Zia dataset using standard evaluation criteria used in software effort estimation. They simulated their model using MATLAB and found feed forward back propagation neural networks performed better than Elman neural networks and cascade correlation network present in the literature.

Tanveer, Vollmer, Braun and Ali (2019) proposed a hybrid model based on gradient boosted trees (GBT) which estimates the effort including the impact of changes on the existing system. They evaluated their model in a German software company. The results showed that their model provided more accurate estimates than expert based and model based techniques.

The given literature review reveals that there are many effort estimation studies present but the studies using metaheuristic techniques are still unavailable. All the above studies have their strengths and weaknesses. As the plethora of new techniques are introduced every year, there is always a scope of improvement which exists.

BACKGROUND CONCEPTS USED

In this section the background concepts used are reviewed.

Story Point Approach

In agile environment story point is the most commonly used unit of measure followed for effort estimation. In story point approach the user story is the term for requirements (Cohn, 2005). The effort of a particular user story is determined by its size and complexity and based upon that a story point value is assigned (Ziauddin, Tipu, & Zia, 2012). The commonly used assignment criteria for story points are t-shirt sizing, Fibonacci sequence or simply small vs. needs-to-be-split. Story point is the amount of effort completed in a unit time. For agile projects the unit of Effort is Story Point (SP) (Ziauddin, Tipu, & Zia, 2012). Agile velocity is the amount of work done by a project team in a single sprint. It is calculated based upon the effort and sprint time. Sprint time is the time period during which a particular work is completed by the project team and the work is available for review.

In all the effort estimation studies based upon story point approach and using machine learning techniques and neural networks, the input parameters are story points and velocity, and the output is the effort of a project (Popli & Chauhan, 2014; Satapathy, Panda & Rath, 2014; Panda, Satapathy & Rath, 2015; Satapathy &Rath, 2017; Bilgayian, Das & Mishra, 2019).

Functional Link Artificial Neural Networks (FLANN)

FLANN consists of three layers i.e. first, middle and the last layer. As the name goes by, FLANN uses various functions like Power Series polynomials, Boubaker polynomials, Fibnocci polynomials, Chebyshev polynomials and Legendre polynomials etc. to expand the input pattern supplied to it. The input data is supplied to the first layer, which navigates it to middle layer where the polynomial function is applied which converts the n-dimensional input data to K dimensions where $n < K$. These data values are represented in the matrix form and are combined linearly after multiplying with the weight matrix. This provides a scalar quantity which forms the required output. The current work uses Chebyshev polynomial function which is defined as:

Chebyshev polynomials: $F_0(z)=1$

$$F_1(z)=z \quad F_2(z) = 2z^2 - 1 \quad F_3(z) = 4z^3 - 3z \quad F_4(z) = 8z^3 - 8z^2 + 1 \tag{1}$$

These polynomials are further generated as:

$$F_n\left(z\right) = 2zF_{n-1}\left(z\right) - F_{n-2}\left(z\right), n^32 \tag{2}$$

Chebyshev polynomials were also used by early researchers in software cost estimations and are considered as a basis function in this field (Benala, Korada, Mall, & Dehuri, 2013).

Radial Basis Function Network (RBFN)

RBFN is a three layer neural network consisting of the first, middle and the last layer (Idri, Zahi, Mendes, & Zakrani, 2007; Kaushik, Soni, & Soni, 2013). The input supplied to the network is first clustered and its output is provided to the middle layer neurons where the Gaussian radial basis function as given by (3) is applied.

$$f\left(y\right) = e^{\left(-\frac{\|y-v_i\|^2}{\sigma_i^2}\right)} \tag{3}$$

Here, y is the input, v_i and σ_i are the center and the wideness of the ith neuron of the middle layer respectively. $\|.\|$ denotes the Euclidean distance. Intutionistic Fuzzy C-Means (IFCM) clustering algorithm (Bezdek, 1981; Kaur, Soni, & Gossain, 2012; Chaira, 2011; Atanassov, 1983) is used to determine v_i and σ_i is calculated using p-nearest neighbour heuristic (Moody, & Darken, 1989).

In this study, the weights of ANNs are obtained using whale optimization algorithm and updated using delta rule. The delta rule is a learning rule for updating the weights of the neurons using gradient descent learning which minimizes the error between the target value and the estimated value.

Whale Optimization Algorithm (WOA)

Mirjalili and Lewis (2016) framed this algorithm on hump back whales for optimization which modelled the spiral bubble-net feeding behaviour of these whales. The basic phases are:

Encircling Prey

Hump back whales encircles their prey after recognizing them. Here, the prey which is targeted, is assumed as the current best candidate solution and a best explore agent is defined. This is shown by:

$$\vec{E} = \left| \overrightarrow{D}. \overrightarrow{K_p}(l) - \vec{K}(l) \right| \tag{4}$$

$$\overrightarrow{K}(l+1) = \overrightarrow{K_p}(l) - \vec{B}.\vec{E} \tag{5}$$

Where, $\vec{B}$ and $\vec{D}$ are the coefficient vectors, l is the current iteration, K_p is the position vector of the predator, $\vec{K}$ is the position vector of the whale. $\vec{B}$ and $\vec{D}$ are calculated as follows:

$$\vec{B} = 2\overrightarrow{b_1}.\overrightarrow{s_1}.\overrightarrow{b_1} \tag{6}$$

$$\vec{D} = 2.\overrightarrow{s_2} \tag{7}$$

Where, $\overrightarrow{b_1}$ is linearly reduced from 2 to 0 over the course of iterations and $\overrightarrow{s_1}$, $\overrightarrow{s_2}$ are the random vectors in [0, 1].

Bubble Net Attacking Method

In this method bubbles are formed by the whales to attack their prey either along a circle or 9 shaped path. It is mathematically modelled using two approaches:

Shrinking Encircling Mechanism

It is obtained by decreasing $\overrightarrow{b_1}$ in (6). It also affects the range of $\vec{B}$ which is in [-1, 1]. It finds the new location of an explore agent.

Spiral Updating Position

It finds the distance between the whale and prey and mimics the spiral motion of whales as shown in (8):

$$\vec{K}(l+1) = \overrightarrow{E'}.e^{ol}.\cos(2\pi l) + \overrightarrow{K_p}(l) \tag{8}$$

Where, $\overrightarrow{E'} = \left| \overrightarrow{K_p}(l) - \vec{K}(l) \right|$ and gives the distance of the ith whale to the predator, o is constant that represents the shape of the logarithmic spiral, l is a random number in [-1, 1].

Search for Prey

The $\vec{B}$ vector is varied between [-1, 1], to allow these hump back whales to randomly search for their predator according to position of each other. WOA performs global search as the location of the explore agent is upgraded according to randomly chosen explore agent which is given as:

$$\vec{E} = \left| \vec{D}.\overrightarrow{K_{rand}} - \vec{K} \right| \tag{9}$$

$$\vec{K}(t+1) = \overrightarrow{K_{rand}} - \vec{B}.\vec{E} \tag{10}$$

Where, $\overrightarrow{K_{rand}}$ is a random position vector (a random whale) which is chosen from the current population.

This algorithm was tested on 29 mathematical optimization functions by the authors Mirjalili and Lewis (2016) in order to test its efficiency and it gave the best results for all the problems. The function used in algorithm for the current work is given in (11) (Mirjalili & Lewis, 2016):

$$F5(y) = \sum_{i=1}^{n-1} \left[100\left(y_{i+1} - y_i^2\right)^2 + \left(y_i - 1\right)^2 \right] \tag{11}$$

This function is used as a cost function in WOA to create the optimized weights of range [0, 1]. There are various reasons for choosing WOA over other metaheuristic algorithms. WOA exhibits high exploration, exploitation, local optima avoidance and convergence speed. The whales randomly move around each other initially and their positions get updated. This represents the high exploration behaviour of WOA as given in (10).In later iterations they exhibit high exploitation and convergence. As these two phenomenon are separately performed by whales, this leads to high local optima avoidance (Mirjalili & Lewis, 2016).

RESEARCH CONTRIBUTION

Effort estimation is an important issue faced by the project managers. A good estimation model will always help the managers to estimate accurately which will lead the project to success. The work presented in this paper contributes to effort estimation of agile projects following the story point approach. The novelty here is the integration of a metaheuristic technique and neural networks. There are limited studies present in the literature for effort estimation of agile projects based on machine learning and neural networks (Popli & Chauhan, 2014; Satapathy, Panda & Rath, 2014; Panda, Satapathy & Rath, 2015; Satapathy &Rath, 2017; Bilgayian, Das & Mishra, 2019) and none of them have used FLANN and RBFN for agile effort estimation, also no study has incorporated any metaheuristic technique in their estimation model. The models proposed in the current work are FLANN-WOA and RBFN-WOA described subsequently.

FLANN-WOA

In this framework, first the input data to be trained is supplied as an input to the first layer of the neural network. The data is expanded by FLANN using Chebyshev polynomials as shown in (1) and (2). After applying Chebyshev expansion, the non-linear outputs become the nodes for the middle layer. The estimated effort is then calculated by multiplying these nodes with the weight vector calculated using WOA. The block diagram is represented in Figure 1.

Figure 1. FLANN-WOA block diagram

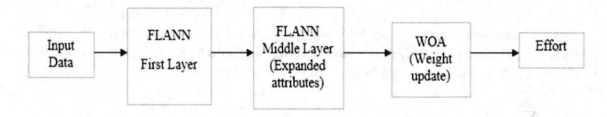

The procedure of FLANN-WOA is given in Figure 2:

RBFN-WOA

The input neurons of the first layer of RBFN receives the input data and, the gaussian radial basis function as given by (3) is applied to form the middle layer. The nodes of the middle layer is multiplied by the weight values obtained using WOA and the weighted sum is obtained to get the required output. This is demonstrated in Figure 3.

The procedure for RBFN –WOA is given below in Figure 4.

Both the above models are described by taking examples from the datasets in the next section.

Figure 2. FLANN-WOA

```
FLANN-WOA
Step 1: Preprocess the input data.
Step 2: Split the input data into training and testing data.
Step 3: For all the training and testing data do
        {
                Expand the input data using Chebyshev polynomial expansion.
                While (the stopping condition not met)
                {
                        For each expanded input pattern
                        {
                                •   Call WOA () and assign the best position between the second layer and the last layer as
                                    the weight.
                                •   Calculate the weighted sum and generate the estimated output at the last layer.
                                •   Generate the difference between the actual output and the calculated output.
                                •   Upgrade the weights between the second and the last layer.
                        }
                }
        }
```

Figure 3. RBFN-WOA block diagram

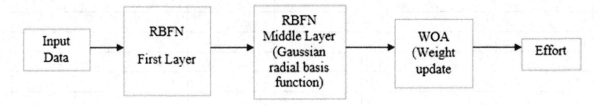

Figure 4. RBFN-WOA

```
RBFN-WOA
Step 1: Preprocess the input data.
Step 2: Split the input data into training and testing data.
Step 3: For all the training and testing data do
        {
            Feed the input data to the first layer.
             While(the stopping criteria not met)
            {
                    •   Generate the middle layer by injecting the Gaussian function on input neurons.
                    •   Call WOA () and assign the best position between the second layer and the last layer as the
                        weight.
                    •   Produce the estimated output at the last layer by calculating the weighted sum.
                    •   Generate the difference between the actual output and the calculated output.
                    •   Upgrade the weights between the second and the last layer.
            }
        }
}
```

SIMULATION AND RESULTS

The proposed approaches FLANN-WOA and RBFN-WOA are evaluated on three datasets. The input datasets are Zia dataset, Company Dataset -1 (CD1) and Company Dataset-2 (CD2).The first dataset is taken from Zia (Ziauddin, Tipu, & Zia, 2012). This dataset was a collection of 21 agile software projects taken from 6 software houses. The features of the dataset used in the study is given in Table 1.

Table 1. Zia dataset

P.No	Effort	V	Actual Time (*months*)
1	156	2.7	63
2	202	2.5	92
3	173	3.3	56
4	331	3.8	86
5	124	4.2	32
6	339	3.6	91
7	97	3.4	35
8	257	3	93
9	84	2.4	36
10	211	3.2	62
11	131	3.2	45
12	112	2.9	37
13	101	2.9	32
14	74	2.9	30
15	62	2.9	21
16	289	2.8	112
17	113	2.8	39
18	141	2.8	52
19	213	2.8	80
20	137	2.7	56
21	91	2.7	35

Here, the first dimension is P.No showing the project number, the second is Effort in developing the project, the third one shows the velocity values for different projects and the fourth gives the actual time in completing a project.

As the agile studies lack in availability of public datasets, the second and third dataset as given in Table 2 and Table 3, is shared by a company in Delhi NCR on special request. The information provided by the datasets is on two different projects only. The Company Dataset -1 (CD1) consists of a project with 23 issues and the Company Dataset-2 (CD2) points to a project with 25 issues. Both the datasets are mapped according to the requirement of the existing study by calculating the estimated effort of various issues using the proposed methodologies.

In Table 2 and 3, the first dimension is the Issue Number of various issues, the second gives the Effort values for these issues, the third and fourth dimension provides the time and story point values for these issues.

Table 2. Company dataset-1

Issue No.	Effort	Time *(minutes)*	Story Point
1	5600	93600	9
2	4879	15000	8
3	7200	15000	7
4	7654	14000	9
5	5674	22200	6
6	8900	23400	8
7	57600	25800	8
8	8432	18000	7
9	28800	136800	8
10	7896	10800	8
11	9879	25200	5
12	3789	28800	8
13	9756	9000	9
14	8763	14400	8
15	3567	12600	12
16	9875	25200	8
17	8945	21600	8
18	5678	10800	8
19	5699	12780	9
20	4321	11900	8
21	8754	8600	8
22	7542	9300	7
23	9050	7800	8

Table 3. Company Dataset-2

Issue No.	Effort	Time *(minutes)*	Story Point
1	8700	99800	9
2	6487	76000	8
3	7872	25000	9
4	9876	19000	9
5	6675	56200	13
6	3489	23500	9
7	7876	15800	9
8	7832	28000	12
9	52880	128800	10
10	3487	20600	9
11	8987	15200	7
12	7785	12800	8
13	7785	5000	6
14	5769	24200	12
15	4356	22600	11
16	6879	15200	8
17	8843	25600	8
18	8671	20800	8
19	8856	12880	8
20	2352	12600	9
21	7651	6800	9
22	3542	6300	7
23	4550	8800	7
24	6879	4800	6
25	8543	6500	6

In order to test the validity of the proposed estimation models leave-one-out (LOO) sampling method, which is a type of K-fold Cross-Validation is used. Here K equals to N, the number of data points in the dataset. This sampling method is employed due to its advantages over N-Way sampling (Kocaguneli & Menzies, 2013).

Overfitting is another issue faced by the estimation models. It is important to recognize and manage this issue otherwise our models will not be able to generalize well and make predictions on the unseen data. An important technique to handle it is the resampling technique which is, LOO in our case.

Before running the procedures of FLANN-WOA and RBFN-WOA, the three datasets are pre-processed. The following three steps are used for data pre-processing:

Step 1: Check whether the data is normally distributed or not. It is found that for the given datasets, the data values were not normally distributed, so logarithmic transformation is done on the data values in order to make it normally distributed.

Step 2: Normalize the input data between [0 1] to discard the scaling effects on various dimensions.

Step 3: Partition the dataset into training and testing datasets.

Now, both the procedures, FLANN-WOA and RBFN-WOA are called individually on the pre-processed data as discussed in the previous section. The results are recorded and evaluated using the commonly used evaluation criteria used in software cost estimations (Foss, Stensrud, Kitchenham, & Myrtveit, 2003; Stensrud, Foss, Kitchenham, & Myrtveit, 2002) . They are Magnitude of Relative Error (MRE), Mean Magnitude of Relative Error (MMRE), Prediction (t) and Median Magnitude of Relative Error (MdMRE) which are given below:

$$MRE = \frac{|Actual\,Data - Estimated\,Data|}{Actual\,Data} \tag{12}$$

MMRE is the average of all the MRE values.

$$MMRE = \frac{1}{N}\sum_{X=1}^{N}MRE \tag{13}$$

$$MdMRE = Median(MRE) \tag{14}$$

$$Pred(t) = \frac{k}{n} \tag{15}$$

Where, n shows the total number of projects and k is the number of projects with MRE less than or equal to 0.25 (Rao et al., 2009).

All the above evaluation criteria are the accuracy measurers. They show how close a measurement is to an existing value that has already been known.

Table 4 lists the initialization of parameters done for WOA for both FLANN and RBFN.

Let us consider the dataset CD1 to explain FLANN-WOA. In this dataset for Issue No. 2, the normalized input values for story points and velocity are 0.4285 and 0.3252 respectively. This data is mapped to the input layer of FLANN which expands it using Chebyshev polynomial expansion given in (1). The WOA algorithm is then called with the parameters given in Table 4 which provided the best value as 0.3387 in this case. This value is now assigned as a weight between the hidden layer and the output layer. The weighted sum is now calculated using the weight and hidden layer values to produce the estimated output. It is then tuned by reducing the error as given in Step 3 of Figure 2 to calculate the final estimated output which is 0.02399, whereas the normalized actual effort is 0.02428. So, the estimated effort is very near to the actual effort.

In order to explain RBFN-WOA, let us consider the Zia dataset given in Table 1. In this dataset for P. No. 4, the normalized inputs provided to RBFN-WOA are 0.984 and 0.778. These values are provided as input to the first layer of RBFN. The Gaussian Radial Basis Function given in (3) is then applied to form the middle layer. Now the WOA algorithm is called which provided the best value as 0.2768. This value is used as a weight between the middle layer and the final layer. The estimated output is obtained by finding the weighted sum of middle layer inputs and the weight. This value is fine-tuned as given in Step 3 of Figure 4 to calculate the final estimated effort which is 0.950 and the normalized actual effort is 0.971. Here also, there is not much difference between the estimated and the actual output.

In this manner all the datasets are processed using FLANN-WOA and RBFN-WOA techniques to obtain the estimated effort. They are further assessed using evaluation criteria and the results are recorded in Table 5, 6 and 7.

Table 4. Initialization of parameters for WOA

Parameters Initialization
SearchAgents_no 30
Max_iteration 500
o 1
l [-1 1]
q [0 1]
$\overrightarrow{S_1}$ [0 1]
S_2 [0 1]

Table 5. Results on Zia Dataset

Approaches Used	MMRE		MdMRE		PRED(0.25)	
	Train Data	Test Data	Train Data	Test Data	Train Data	Test Data
FLANN	.619	.672	.49	.510	.33	.34
FLANN-WOA	.180	.193	.167	.179	.869	.859
RBFN	.548	.512	.243	.232	.571	.587
RBFN-WOA	.196	.201	.172	.174	.876	.882

Table 6. Results on Company Dataset 1

Approaches used	MMRE		MdMRE		PRED(0.25)	
	Train Data	Test Data	Train Data	Test Data	Train Data	Test Data
FLANN	.612	.623	.449	.412	.394	.412
FLANN-WOA	.183	.192	.109	.172	.890	.874
RBFN	.721	.730	.77	.78	.26	.29
RBFN-WOA	.153	.185	.128	.143	.869	.871

Table 7. Results on Company Dataset 2

Approaches used	MMRE		MdMRE		PRED(0.25)	
	Train Data	Test Data	Train Data	Test Data	Train Data	Test Data
FLANN	.425	.487	.2	.294	.642	.631
FLANN-WOA	.123	.138	.17	.185	.912	.893
RBFN	.283	.311	.224	.247	.566	.581
RBFN-WOA	.151	.160	.191	.182	.882	.870

The output after applying the proposed approaches are demonstrated in Table 5, 6 and 7 respectively. There is a comparison of FLANN to FLANN-WOA and RBFN to RBFN-WOA in order to judge whether the performance of FLANN and RBFN improves upon integration with WOA, as the current work discusses the role of neural networks and metaheuristics in agile software development effort estimation. From the results it is found that the performance of FLANN-WOA and RBFN-WOA are at par than FLANN and RBFN.

In order to have more clarity and representation of facts the performance of FLANN, FLANN-WOA, RBFN and RBFN-WOA is depicted graphically in Figure 5, 6 and 7 for the three datasets respectively. Satapathy and Rath (2017) provided results on Zia dataset for effort estimation using story points on agile software development. The results are from the techniques Decision Tree (DT), Stochastic Gradient Boosting (SGB) and Random Forest (RF) which are compared with the results of the proposed techniques and depicted in Table 8.

From, the given data in Table 8 it can be seen that FLANN-WOA and RBFN-WOA gave better results than the techniques used by researchers, except for Stochastic Gradient Boosting (SGB) technique. The SGB technique provided better results than FLANN-WOA and RBFN-WOA for MMRE and MdMRE criterias.

So, it can be concluded that by integrating WOA with FLANN and RBFN has definitely enhanced the performance of FLANN and RBFN. This is also statistically validated.

Statistical validation is required to confirm the validity of any proposed approach. The statistical tools allow researchers to know whether the results evaluated with the proposed approaches can be accepted with confidence or rejected. These tools allow one to trust the new developed method. Therefore, it is necessary and valuable to compare FLANN to FLANN-WOA and RBFN to RBFN-WOA using these tests.

Figure 5. Performance of FLANN, FLANN-WOA, RBFN and RBFN-WOA on ZIA dataset

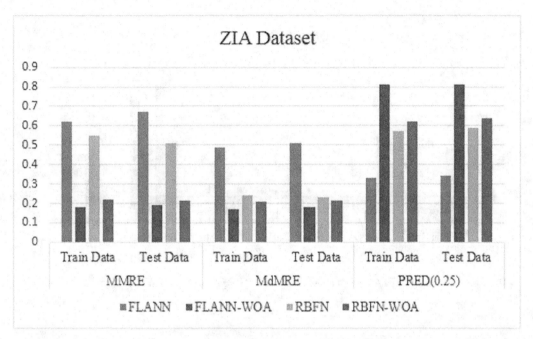

Figure 6. Performance of FLANN, FLANN-WOA, RBFN and RBFN-WOA on Company Dataset-1

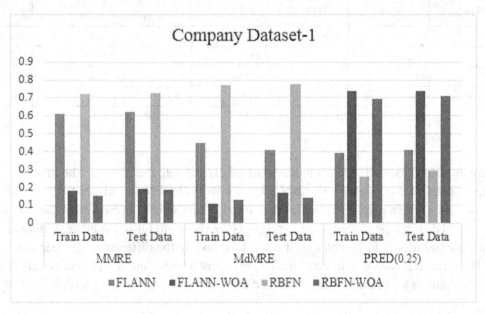

Statistical inferential tests are categorized into three kinds: parametric, semi-parametric and non-parametric. The parametric statistical tests relies on prior information. They make an assumption about the population parameters and its probability distribution whereas the non-parametric tests doesn't assume anything about the population parameters and its distribution. The merits of both the parametric and non-parametric tests are present in semi-parametric tests.

Figure 7. Performance of FLANN, FLANN-WOA, RBFN and RBFN-WOA on Company Dataset-2

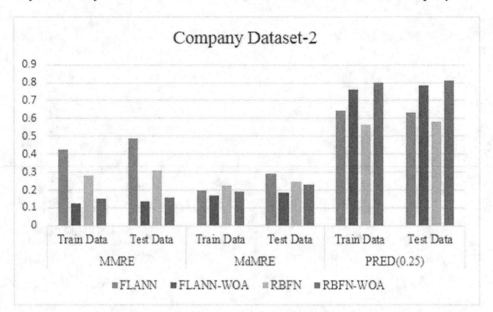

Table 8. Comparison with earlier approaches on ZIA dataset

Techniques	MMRE	MdMRE	PRED (25)	PRED (50)	PRED (75)	PRED (100)
DT	.382	.289	38.095	71.428	80.952	90.476
SGB	.163	.115	85.714	95.238	95.238	95.238
RF	.251	.203	66.666	80.952	90.476	95.238
FLANN-WOA	.186	.173	86.4	95.238	100	100
RBFN-WOA	.198	.173	87.9	95.238	100	100

The existing study uses IBM SPSS tool to statistically validate the models. The input to the tool is MRE values obtained after applying FLANN, FLANN-WOA, RBFN and RBFN-WOA on the datasets. Tests of normality is then performed on this data through SPSS and it is found that the data is not following a normal distribution. So, non-parametric tests are chosen to further validate the model. The first non-parametric test used is Friedman test. It is used for finding the differences between several related samples. Here, this test is used in order to initially compare whether the two techniques are different or not. The test statistics for Friedman test is defined as:

$$\chi_F^2 = \frac{12Q}{n(n+1)} \left[\sum_{j=1}^{n} R_j^2 - \frac{n(n+1)^2}{4} \right] \tag{16}$$

With, R_j, the average rank of algorithms $j=1,2,....n$ over Q datasets.

Here, the null hypotheses and alternate hypotheses for both FLANN and RBFN are:

(a) *Null Hypotheses:* Performance of FLANN = FLANN-WOA
    Alternate Hypotheses: Performance of FLANN ¹FLANN-WOA
(b) *Null Hypotheses:* Performance of RBFN = RBFN-WOA
    Alternate Hypotheses: Performance of RBFN ¹ RBFN-WOA

Table 9 provides the output of Friedman test on all the three datasets.

Table 9. Test statistics of Friedman test on all the datasets

Test Statistics	ZIAFLANN & ZIAFLANN-WOA	ZIARBFN & ZIARBFN-WOA	CD1FLANN & CD1FLANN-WOA	CD1RBFN & CD1RBFN-WOA	CD2FLANN & CD2FLANN-WOA	CD2RBFN & CD2RBFN-WOA
N	21	21	23	23	25	25
Chi-Square	5.000	7.200	8.909	4.545	6.000	10.667
DF	1.0	1.0	1.0	1.0	1.0	1.0
Asy. Sig.	.025	.007	.003	.033	.014	.001

Here, N is the total data in each dataset, Chi-Square is the value of test statistics calculated by the test, DF is the degree of freedom which is 1 as DF= n-1 . As there are two approaches to be tested on all the datasets, here n is 2 and DF is 2-1 = 1.The last row gives the Asymptotic Significant values calculated by the test. The $\chi 2$ (Chi-Square) value for DF= 1 and $\alpha = 0.05$ is 3.841. If $\chi 2$ (Chi-Square) in our test statistics is greater than 3.841 for asymptotic significant (p-value) less than 0.05 then the null hypothesis is rejected. From the Chi-Square and asymptotic significant values present in Table 9, the null hypotheses is rejected and alternate hypotheses is accepted.

To further confirm the performance of FLANN-WOA and RBFN-WOA, a second non-parametric test is applied which is Wilcoxon matched pair's test. It ranks the two models by calculating the positive and negative differences of ranks and is calculated as:

$$\min\left(\sum_{d_i>0} R(d_i) + \frac{1}{2}\sum_{d_i=0} R(d_i), \sum_{d_i<0} R(d_i) + \frac{1}{2}\sum_{d_i=0} R(d_i)\right) \tag{17}$$

Where, $R(d_i)$ is the difference of ranks of performance between two models, ignoring signs. The null hypotheses and alternate hypotheses are:

Null Hypotheses: Median difference between pairs of observations is zero i.e. there is no difference in performance of FLANN and RBFN with and without WOA.

Alternate Hypotheses: Median difference between pairs of observations is not zero i.e. there is difference in performance of FLANN and RBFN with and without WOA.

Table 10 gives the result of the test. Here, for all the instances the null hypothesis is not accepted as the asymptotic significant values are less than 0.05. It is also found that for all the cases the approach with WOA has lower mean rank than its counterpart.

Table 10. Test statistics of Wilcoxon Matched Pairs test on all the datasets

	Mean Rank	Asymptotic Significance
ZIAFLANN ZIAFLANN-WOA	12.13 5.60	0.004
ZIARBFN & ZIARBFN-WOA	11.25 7.50	0.005
CD1FLANN CD1FLANN-WOA	11.83 10	0.005
CD1RBFN CD1RBFN-WOA	14.13 4.50	0.001
CD2FLANN CD2FLANN-WOA	13.72 8.83	0.006
CD2RBFN CD2RBFN-WOA	7.25 13.55	0.001

So after applying statistical tests it is observed that FLANN and RBFN performed differently with and without WOA and the performance of FLANN-WOA and RBFN-WOA is higher than FLANN and RBFN.

CONCLUSION

Effort estimation forms an integral part of any software development. A good estimation model is always the need of the hour. The paper has proposed effort estimation models for the projects using agile methodology. There are few studies existing in the literature based on neural networks for effort estimation of agile projects but none of the study has explored the fusion of ANN and a metaheuristic algorithm. The proposed study integrates ANN models, FLANN and RBFN with a metaheuristic algorithm, Whale Optimization Algorithm (WOA). Both FLANN-WOA and RBFN-WOA are evaluated on three agile datasets, one is Zia dataset and the rest two datasets are gathered through a firm in Delhi NCR incorporating agile software development. The details of these datasets are shared so that it can be used for future work. The study uses MMRE, MDMRE and PRED (0.25) as the evaluation parameters. The experimental results demonstrated that the ANN models provided excellent results by integrating with the metaheuristic technique used. This is further validated by using two statistical tests i.e. Friedman test and Wicoxon test. Though the techniques performed well but due to lack of availability of public datasets on agile software development methodology the proposed approaches are evaluated on limited datasets. So, the future work can include evaluating these techniques on more number of agile datasets.

REFERENCES

Atanassov, K. T. (1983). Intuitionistic fuzzy set. VII ITKR's Session, Sofia, 983. (Deposed in Central Science –Technology Library of Bulgaria Academy of Science, 1697/84)

Benala, T. R., Korada, C., Mall, R., & Dehuri, S. (2013). A particle swarm optimized functional link artificial neural networks (PSO-FLANN) in software cost estimation. In Proceedings of the International Conference on Frontiers of Intelligent Computing: Theory and Applications (FICTA) Advances in Intelligent Systems and Computing (vol. 199, pp. 59-66). Academic Press.

Benala, T. R., & Mall, R. (2018). DABE: Differential evolution in analogy-based software development effort estimation. *Swarm and Evolutionary Computation, 38*, 158–172. doi:10.1016/j.swevo.2017.07.009

Bezdek, J. C. (1981). *Pattern Recognition with Fuzzy Objective Function Algorithm.* New York: Plenum. doi:10.1007/978-1-4757-0450-1

Bilgayian, S., Mishra, S., & Das, M. (2019). Effort estimation in agile software development using experimental validation of neural network models. *International Journal of Information Technology, 11*(3), 569–573. doi:10.100741870-018-0131-2

Boehm, B. W. (1994). *Software Engineering Economics.* Englewood Cliffs, NJ: Prentice-Hall.

Chaira, T. (2011). A novel intuitionistic fuzzy C means clustering algorithm and its application to medical images. *Applied Soft Computing, 11*(2), 1711–1717. doi:10.1016/j.asoc.2010.05.005

Choudhari, J., & Suman, U. (2012). Story Points Based Effort Estimation Model for Software Maintenance. *Procedia Technology, 4*, 761–765. doi:10.1016/j.protcy.2012.05.124

Coelho, E., & Basu, A. (2012). Effort estimation in agile software development using story points. *International Journal of Applied Information System, 3*(7), 7–10. doi:10.5120/ijais12-450574

Cohn, M. (2005). *Agile Estimating and Planning.* Addison-Wesley.

Curiel, I.E.E., Jacobo, J.R., Alfaro, E.V., Zepeda J.A.F., & Delgado D.F. (2018). Analysis of the changes in communication and social interactions during the transformation of a traditional team into an agile team. *The Journal of Software Evolution and Process.* doi:10.1002mr.1946

Dingsøyr, T., Nerur, S., Balijepally, V., & Moe, N. B. (2012). A decade of agile methodologies: Towards explaining agile software development. *Journal of Systems and Software, 85*(6), 1213–1221. doi:10.1016/j.jss.2012.02.033

Dragicevic, S., Celar, S., & Turic, M. (2017). Bayesian network model for task effort estimation in agile software development. *Journal of Systems and Software, 127*, 109–119. doi:10.1016/j.jss.2017.01.027

Foss, T., Stensrud, E., Kitchenham, B., & Myrtveit, I. (2003). A simulation study of the model evaluation criterion MMRE. *IEEE Transactions on Software Engineering, 29*(11), 985–995. doi:10.1109/TSE.2003.1245300

Garg, S., & Gupta, D. (2015). PCA based cost estimation model for agile software development projects. In *Proceedings of International Conference on Industrial Engineering and Operations Management* (pp. 1–7). 10.1109/IEOM.2015.7228109

Hussain, I., Kosseim, L., & Ormandjieva, O. (2013). Approximation of COSMIC functional size to support early effort estimation in Agile. *Data & Knowledge Engineering*, *85*, 2–14. doi:10.1016/j.datak.2012.06.005

Idri, A., Zahi, A., Mendes, E., & Zakrani, A. (2007). Software cost estimation models using radial basis function neural networks. In *Proceedings of International Conference on Software process and product measurements*, (vol. 4895, pp. 21–31). 10.1007/978-3-540-85553-8_2

Kaur, P., Soni, A. K., & Gossain, A. (2012). Novel intuitionistic fuzzy C means clustering for linearly and nonlinearly separable data. *WSEAS Transactions on Computers*, *11*(3), 65–76.

Kaushik, A., Soni, A. K., & Soni, R. (2013). Radial basis function network using intuitionistic fuzzy C means for software cost estimation. *International Journal of Computer Applications in Technology*, *47*(1), 86–95. doi:10.1504/IJCAT.2013.054305

Kaushik, A., Tayal, D. K., Yadav, K., & Kaur, A. (2016). Integrating firefly algorithm in artificial neural network models for accurate software cost predictions. *Journal of Software Evolution and Process*, *28*(8), 665–688. doi:10.1002mr.1792

Kaushik, A., Verma, S., Singh, H. J., & Chhabra, G. (2017). Software Cost Optimization Integrating Fuzzy System and COA-Cuckoo Optimization Algorithm. *International Journal of System Assurance Engineering and Management*, *8*(S2), 1461–1471. doi:10.100713198-017-0615-7

Kocaguneli, E., & Menzies, T. (2013). Software effort models should be assessed via leave-one-out validation. *Journal of Systems and Software*, *86*(7), 1879–1890. doi:10.1016/j.jss.2013.02.053

Lang, M., Conboy, K., & Keaveney, S. (2011). Cost Estimation in Agile Software Development Projects. In *Proceedings of International Conference on Information Systems Development* (pp. 1-12). Prato, Italy: Academic Press.

Martínez, J. L., Noriega, A. R., Ramírez, R. J., Licea, G., & Jiménez, S. (2018). User stories complexity estimation using bayesian networks for inexperienced developers. *Journal of Cluster Computing*, *21*(1), 715–728. doi:10.100710586-017-0996-z

Mensah, S., Keung, J., Bosu, M. F., & Bennin, K. E. (2018). Duplex output software effort estimation model with self-guided interpretation. *Information and Software Technology*, *94*, 1–13. doi:10.1016/j.infsof.2017.09.010

Menzies, T., Chen, Z., Hihn, J., & Lum, K. (2006). Selecting best practices for effort estimation. *IEEE Transactions on Software Engineering*, *32*(11), 883–895. doi:10.1109/TSE.2006.114

Mirjalili, S., & Lewis, A. (2016). The Whale Optimization Algorithm. *Advances in Engineering Software*, *95*, 51–67. doi:10.1016/j.advengsoft.2016.01.008

Mishra, B. B., & Dehuri, S. (2007). Functional Link Artificial Neural Network for classification task in Data Mining. *Journal of Computational Science*, *3*(12), 948–955. doi:10.3844/jcssp.2007.948.955

Moody, J., & Darken, C. J. (1989). Fast learning in networks of locally tuned processing units. *Neural Computation*, *1*(2), 281–294. doi:10.1162/neco.1989.1.2.281

Nguyen, V., Boehm, B., & Huang, L. G. (2019). Determining relevant training data for effort estimation using window based COCOMO calibration. *Journal of Systems and Software*, *147*, 124–146. doi:10.1016/j.jss.2018.10.019

Panda, A., Satapathy, S. M., & Rath, S. K. (2015). Empirical Validation of Neural Network Models for Agile Software Effort Estimation based on Story Points. In *Proceedings of 3rd International Conference on Recent Trends in Computing* (*vol. 57*, pp.772 – 781). Procedia Computer Science. 10.1016/j.procs.2015.07.474

Papadopoulos, G. (2015). Moving from Traditional to Agile Software Development Methodologies Also on Large, Distributed Projects. *Procedia: Social and Behavioral Sciences*, *175*, 455–463. doi:10.1016/j.sbspro.2015.01.1223

Perkusich, M., Gorgônio, K. C., Almeida, H., & Perkusich, A. (2017). Assisting the continuous improvement of Scrum projects using metrics and Bayesian networks. *Journal of Software Evolution and Process*, *29*(6), e1835. doi:10.1002mr.1835

Popli, R., & Chauhan, N. (2014). Cost and Effort estimation in agile software development. In *Proceedings of International conference on Reliability, Optimization and Information Technology* (pp. 57-61). Faridabad, India: Academic Press. 10.1109/ICROIT.2014.6798284

Rao, B. T., Dehuri, S., & Mall, R. (2012). Functional link artificial neural networks for software cost estimation. *International Journal of Applied Evolutionary Computation*, *3*(2), 62–82. doi:10.4018/jaec.2012040104

Rao, B. T., Sameet, B., Swathi, G. K., Gupta, K. V., Ravi Teja, Ch., & Sumana, S. (2009). A novel neural network approach for software cost estimation using functional link artificial neural network (FLANN). *International Journal of Computer Science and Network Society*, *9*(6), 126–131.

Raslan, A. T., Darwish, N. R., & Hefny, H. A. (2015). Towards a fuzzy based framework for effort estimation in agile software development. *International Journal of Computer Science and Information Security*, *13*(1), 37–45.

Salmanoglu, M., Hacaloglu, T., & Demirors, O. (2017). Efort Estimation for Agile Sofware Development: Comparative Case Studies Using COSMIC Functional Size Measurement and Story Points. In Proceedings of IWSM /Mensura'17 (pp.42-50). Gothenberg, Sweden: Academic Press.

Satapathy, S. M., Panda, A., & Rath, S. K. (2014). Story point approach based agile software effort estimation using various SVR kernel. In *Proceedings of 26th International Conference on Software Engineering and Knowledge Engineering* (pp. 304–307). Vancouver: Academic Press.

Satapathy, S. M., & Rath, S. K. (2017). Empirical assessment of machine learning models for agile software development effort estimation using story points. *Innovations in Systems and Software Engineering*, *13*(2-3), 191–200. doi:10.100711334-017-0288-z

Stensrud, E., Foss, T., Kitchenham, B. A., & Myrtveit, I. (2002). An empirical validation of the relationship between the magnitude of relative error and project size. In *Proceedings of the IEEE 8th metrics symposium* (pp. 3–12). Ontario: Academic Press. 10.1109/METRIC.2002.1011320

Tanveer, B. (2016). Hybrid Effort Estimation of Changes in Agile Software Development. *Lecture Notes in Business Information Processing, 251, 316-320*. doi:10.1007/978-3-319-33515-5_33

Tanveer, B., Vollmer, A. M., & Braun, S. (2018). A hybrid methodology for effort estimation in Agile development: An industrial evaluation. In *Proceedings of International Conference on Software and System Process* (pp. 21-30). 10.1145/3202710.3203152

Tanveer, B., Vollmer, A. M., Braun, S., & Ali, N. B. (2019). An evaluation of effort estimation supported by change impact analysis in agile software development. *Journal of Software Evolution and Process.* . doi:10.1002mr.2165

Tolfo, C., Wazlawick, R.S., Ferreira, M.G.G., & Forcellini, F.A. (2018). Agile practices and the promotion of entrepreneurial skills in software development. *Journal of Software Evolution and Process.* . doi:10.1002mr.1945

Usman, M., Britto, R., Damm, L. O., & Borstler, J. (2018). Effort estimation in large scale software development: An industrial case study. *Journal of Information and Software Technology.*, *99*, 21–40. doi:10.1016/j.infsof.2018.02.009

Venkataiah, V., Mohanty, R., Pahariya, J. S., & Nagaratna, M. (2017). Application of ant colony optimization techniques to predict software cost estimation. In Computer Communication, Networking and Internet Security. Springer. doi:10.1007/978-981-10-3226-4_32

Yu, H., Xie, T., Paszczyñski, S., & Wilamowski, B. (2011). Advantages of Radial Basis Function Networks for Dynamic System Design. *IEEE Transactions on Industrial Electronics*, *58*(12), 5438–5450. doi:10.1109/TIE.2011.2164773

Ziauddin, T. S. K., & Zia, S. (2012). An effort estimation model for agile software development. *Advances in Computer Science and Its Applications*, *2*(1), 314-324.

This research was previously published in the International Journal of Information Technology Project Management (IJITPM), 11(2); pages 50-71, copyright year 2020 by IGI Publishing (an imprint of IGI Global).

Chapter 15
Artificial Neural Network Training Algorithms in Modeling of Radial Overcut in EDM:
A Comparative Study

Raja Das
VIT University, India

Mohan Kumar Pradhan
Maulana Azad National Institute of Technology, India

ABSTRACT

This chapter describes with the comparison of the most used back propagations training algorithms neural networks, mainly Levenberg-Marquardt, conjugate gradient and Resilient back propagation are discussed. In the present study, using radial overcut prediction as illustrations, comparisons are made based on the effectiveness and efficiency of three training algorithms on the networks. Electrical Discharge Machining (EDM), the most traditional non-traditional manufacturing procedures, is growing attraction, due to its not requiring cutting tools and permits machining of hard, brittle, thin and complex geometry. Hence it is very popular in the field of modern manufacturing industries such as aerospace, surgical components, nuclear industries. But, these industries surface finish has the almost importance. Based on the study and test results, although the Levenberg-Marquardt has been found to be faster and having improved performance than other algorithms in training, the Resilient back propagation algorithm has the best accuracy in testing period.

DOI: 10.4018/978-1-6684-2408-7.ch015

INTRODUCTION

Due to the increasing trend of using lightweight, lean, and compact components in recent years, there has been growing interest in the advanced and tailor-made materials, with better properties such as high strength, high stiffness, good damping capability, low thermal expansion, higher fatigue characteristics. Besides, components made with these materials demands stringent design and close tolerances during manufacturing. The traditional manufacturing processes are unable to cope up the challenges exhibit by these advanced materials owing to the improved mechanical properties (Abbas, Solomon, & Bahari, 2007; Ho & Newman, 2003). They are hard and 'difficult to machine', strict high precision, higher surface quality standards lead to increase the scrap and rework that leads to increase the machining price. For the last seven decades, electrical discharge machining (EDM) has been extending inimitable capabilities to ma- chine "difficult to machine" materials with desired shape, size and required dimensional accuracy. It has been impressively applied for machining in the advance industries like automotive, medical, aerospace, consumer electronics and optoelectronic industries development. In the past, with the continuing advances of technology, there has been a significant enhancement in EDM technology also, to improve productivity, accuracy and the versatility of the process. The key interest in the active research was to choose the optimal setting of the process parameters in such a way that accuracy should increase and, concurrently, overcut or gap, tool wear and surface roughness should reduce (Pradhan, 2012; Anitha, Das, & Pradhan, 2012; Pradhan & Kumar, 2012). Moreover, a process can be identified better when a model replicates its behavior by its vital parameters. The factors that are significant for the system are to be recognized and different aspects of the process are to be correlated while constructing the model. It is expensive, unpractical or impossible to experiment directly with the process so a good model can be cost-effective to predict the actual process very closely (Das & Pradhan, 2014; Jena, Pradhan, Das, Acharjya, & Mishra, 2014; Pradhan & Das, 2015).

Experimental Setup and Procedure

To collect the data experiments were performed using a CNC Electrical discharge die sinking machine set up "Electronica Electraplus PS 50ZNC" presented in Figure 1. A pure copper electrode (99.9% Cu) of a diameter of 30 mm was used to machine the AISI D2 Tool steel, the photographic view of the specimen is depicted in Figure 2, and a commercial grade EDM oil (specific gravity = 0.763, freezing point= 94°C) was used as dielectric fluid, the power supply was linked with the tool electrode (Tool: positive polarity, work piece: negative polarity). Dielectric was pumped through the tube electrode laterally as shown in Figure 3, for effective flushing of machining debris from the working gap region with a pressure of 0.4 kgf/cm^2. Work piece material was initially circular bar of diameter 100 mm and was cut into specimens of thickness 10 mm. the top and bottom faces of the work piece were ground to make it flat and good quality surface finish before experimentation. the bottom of the cylindrical electrode was polished by a very fine grade emery sheet before each experimental run. every treatment of the experiment was run for 15 minutes and the time was measured with a stopwatch of accuracy 0.1s. The work piece as well because the tool was detached from the machine, clean and dried up, to form it free from the dirt, trash and dielectric. They were weighed, before and after machining, on a precision electronics balance (maximum capacity = 300 g, precision = 0.001 g). The diameter of the cavity machined on work piece was measured by a tool maker microscope (make: Carl Zeiss, Germany) with an accuracy of 1 μ m.

Artificial Neural Network

An ANN is a biologically inspired computational model that processes information. ANN has been shown to be highly flexible modeling tool with capability of learning the mathematical mapping between input and output. ANN is formed from several layers of neurons. The input layer of neurons is connected to the output layers of neurons through one or more hidden layers of neurons. Initially, ANN is trained and tested with experimental data to reach at an optimum topology and weights. A multilayer perceptron (MLP) is feed forward neural network with one or more hidden layers. During the training process ANN adjusts its weights to minimize the errors between the predicted result and actual output by using different back-propagation algorithms.

The Back-Propagation Neural Network (BPNN) with n input nodes, r output nodes and a single hidden layer of m nodes are shown in Figure 1. Each interconnection between the nodes has a weight associated with it. The Transfer function of the hidden and output nodes are tan-sigmoid S($\bullet$) and linear, respectively.

According to Figure 1 the net input to the jth hidden neuron is given by

$$y_j\left(x\right) = \sum_{i=1}^{n} w1_{ji} x_i + b1_j \tag{1}$$

where $w1_{ji}$ is the weight between the ith node of input layer and jth node of hidden layer and $b1_j$ is the bias at jth node of hidden layer. The output of the jth hidden node is defined by

$$z_j\left(x\right) = 2\big/\left(1 + \exp\left(-2x\right)\right) - 1 \tag{2}$$

Given an input vector x, the output, value $o_k(x)$ of the kth node of output layer is equal to the sum of the weighted outputs of the hidden nodes and the bias of the kth node output layer, and is given by

$$o_k = \sum_{j=1}^{m} w2_{kj} z_j + b2_k \tag{3}$$

where $w2_{kj}$ is the weight between the jth node of hidden layer and kth node of output layer (3), $b2_k$ is biasing term at the kth output node.

The output of ANN is determined by giving the inputs and computing the output from various nodes activation and interconnection weights. The output is compared to the experimental output and Mean Squared Error is calculated. The error value is then propagated backwards through the network and changes are made to the weights at each node in each layer by three different training algorithms.

ANN Training Algorithms

The present work describes three different artificial neural network (ANN) training algorithms Levenberg- Marquardt, conjugate gradient and resilient back propagation used in the study. This was done with a view to see which algorithm produces better results and has faster training for the application under consideration.

Figure 1. Architecture of BPNN with single hidden layer

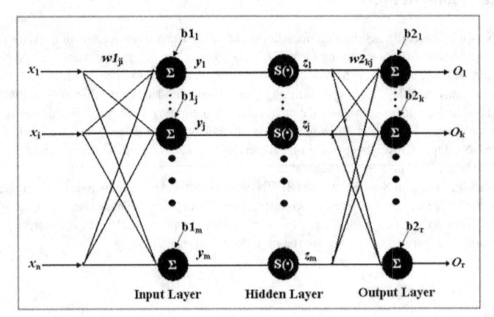

The objective of training is to reduce the global error E defined as

$$E = \frac{1}{P}\sum_{p=1}^{P} E_p$$

where P is the total number of training dataset; and E_α is the error for p*t*h training data, E_p is calculated by the following formula

$$E_\alpha = \frac{1}{2}\sum_{q=1}^{r}\left(o_q - t_q\right)^2 \tag{4}$$

where r is the total number of output nodes, o_q is the network output at the qth output node, and t_q is the target output at the qth output node.

In every training algorithm, an attempt is made to reduce this global error (4) by adjusting the weights and biases.

Levenberg- Marquardt (LM) Algorithm

The approximated Hessian matrix $J^T J + \mu I$ is invertible; Liebenberg-Marquardt algorithm introduces another approximation to Hessian matrix.

$H = J^T J + \mu I$ (5) where J is the Jacobian matrix which contains first derivative of the network errors with respect to the weights and bias, μ is always positive, called combination coefficient and I *is* the identity matrix.

The Levenberg-Marquardt algorithm uses this approximation to the Hessian matrix in the following Newton-like update:

$$w_{k+1} = w_k - \left(J_k^T J_k + \mu I\right)^{-1} J_k e_k \tag{6}$$

where w is the weight vector and e is the error vector.

As the combination of the steepest descent algorithm and the Gauss–Newton algorithm, the Levenberg–Marquardt algorithm switches between the two algorithms during the training process. When the combination coefficient μ is very small (nearly zero), Gauss–Newton algorithm is used. When combination coefficient μ is very large, the steepest descent method is used. The Levenberg- Marquardt optimization technique is more powerful than the conventional gradient descent techniques.

Conjugate Gradient (CG) Algorithm

The standard conjugate gradient method is to minimize the differentiable function E by generating a sequence of approximation w_{k+1} iteratively according to

$$w_{k+1} = w_k + \alpha_k d_k$$

The scalar α_k is the step length, known in neural network notation as learning rate. The step length α_k can be determined by line search techniques in the way that $E(w_k + \alpha_k d_k)$ is minimize along the direction d_k, given w_k and d_k fixed.

The standard conjugate gradient algorithm begins the minimization process with initial estimate w0 and an initial search direction

$$d_0 = -\nabla E(w_0) = -g_0$$

Each direction d_{k+1} is chosen to be linear combination of the steepest direction $-g_{k+1}$ and the previous direction d_k. We write

$$d_{k+1} = -g_{k+1} + \beta_k d_k$$

where the scalar β_k is to be determined by the requirement that dk and d_{k+1} must fulfill the conjugate property. There are many formulae for the parameters β_k. One of them is Fletcher-Reeves formula and is given by

$$\beta_k = \frac{g_k^T g_k}{g_{k-1}^T g_{k-1}}$$

Conjugate gradient method has a second order convergence property without complex calculation of the Hessian matrix. A faster convergence established than first order steepest descent approach.

Resilient Back- Propagation (RP) Algorithm

The individual update value $\Delta_{ij}(k)$ for each weight $w_{ij}(k)$ can be expressed according to the learning rule for each case based on the observed behavior of the partial derivative during two successive weight-steps by the following formula:

$$\Delta_{ij}(k) = \begin{cases} \eta^+ \Delta_{ij}(k-1), & if\ \dfrac{\partial E}{\partial w_{ij}}(k).\dfrac{\partial E}{\partial w_{ij}}(k-1) > 0 \\[2ex] \eta^- \Delta_{ij}(k-1), & if\ \dfrac{\partial E}{\partial w_{ij}}(k).\dfrac{\partial E}{\partial w_{ij}}(k-1) < 0 \\[2ex] \Delta_{ij}(k-1) & else \end{cases}$$

where $0 < \eta^- < 1 < \eta^+$.

It is evident that whenever that partial derivative of the equivalent weight w_{ij} varies its sign, which indicates that the last update was large in magnitude and the algorithm has skipped over a local minima, the update-value $\Delta_{ij}(k)$ is decreased by the factor η^-. If the derivative holds its sign, the update-value will to some extent increase in order to speed up the convergence.

When the update-value for each weight is settled in, the weight updates by a very simple rule.

$$w_{ij}(k + 1) = w_{ij}(k) + \Delta w_{ij}(k)$$

where

$$\Delta w_{ij}(k) = \begin{cases} -\Delta_{ij}(k), & if\ \dfrac{\partial E}{\partial w_{ij}}(k) > 0 \\[2ex] \Delta_{ij}(k), & if\ \dfrac{\partial E}{\partial w_{ij}}(k) < 0 \\[2ex] 0, & else \end{cases}$$

If the partial derivative changes sign that is the previous step was too large and the minimum was missed, the previous weight-update is reverted:

$$\Delta w_{ij}(k) = -\Delta w_{ij}(k-1),\ if\ \frac{\partial E}{\partial w_{ij}}(k).\frac{\partial E}{\partial w_{ij}}(k-1) < 0$$

In order to avoid a double penalty of the update-value, there should be no adaptation of the update value in the succeeding step. In practice, this can be done by setting $\dfrac{\partial E}{\partial w_{ij}}\left(k-1\right)=0$ in the Δ_{ij} update rule above.

Hence, the partial derivative of the errors must be accumulated for all training data. This indicates that the weights are updated only after the presentation of all of the training data. It is noticed that resilient back-propagation is much faster than the standard steepest descent algorithm.

Result and Discussion

In the present BPNN model, the inputs of the model are Ton, τ, Ip, V. The output of the model is Radial Overcut. In general, the architecture of multi-layer BPNN can have many layers where a layer represents a set of parallel processing units (or nodes). The three layers BPNN used in this study contain only one intermediate (hidden) layer. Multi-layer BPNN can have more than one hidden layer; however theoretical works have shown that a single hidden layer is sufficient for BPNN to approximate any complex non-linear functions. Indeed, many experimental results seem to confirm that one hidden layer may be enough for most forecasting problems. Therefore, in this study, one hidden layered ANNs with 6, 14 and 15 neurons for LM, CG and RP training algorithms respectively were used as shown in Figure 2. 44 set of data under EDM process was used for training, validation and testing for three ANNs. Out of 44 experimental data, 26 training, 9 validation, and 9 testing data sets are considered for the three ANNs to compare the performance. Three MATLAB language codes were written for the ANN algorithms.

Figure 2. Mean square error for ANNs with different training algorithms

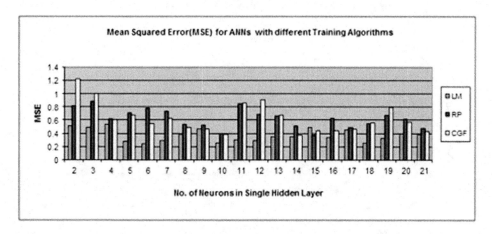

The ANN algorithms were compared according to mean squared errors (MSE) and mean percentile error (MPE) criteria. These criteria are defined as

$$Mean\ Squared\ Error = \frac{1}{N}\sum_{i=1}^{N}\left(Ra_{observed} - Ra_{predicted}\right)^{2}$$

$$Mean\ Percentile\ Error = \frac{1}{N}\sum_{i=1}^{N}\frac{\left|Ra_{observed} - Ra_{predicted}\right|}{Ra_{observed}} \times 100$$

For each combination ANN was trained using three different algorithms, that is, LM, CG, and RP. After training was over, the weights were saved and used to test network performance. The ANN results were transformed back to the original domain and MSE was computed. The iterations were stopped when the difference between two epochs was too small. The experimental results and predicted results of 'Ra' by the LM, CG and RP were plotted on the same scale, as shown in Figure 4. The performance of three neural network models is studied with the special attention to their regression plot and it is presented in Figure 3 (a)-3(b). The ANN with training algorithm LM has the best R value.

ANNs are compared separately with results obtained by experiments and the average absolute error obtained for all the three networks. ANNs with CG and RP models are poorer in predicting Radial Overcut. The test result accuracy measured in terms of MAE and MPE for nine test data are given in Table 1.

Figure 3. Regression analysis for ANN with CG

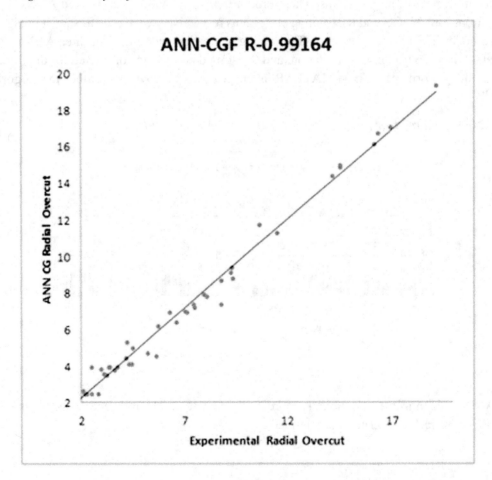

Figure 4. Regression analysis for ANN with LM

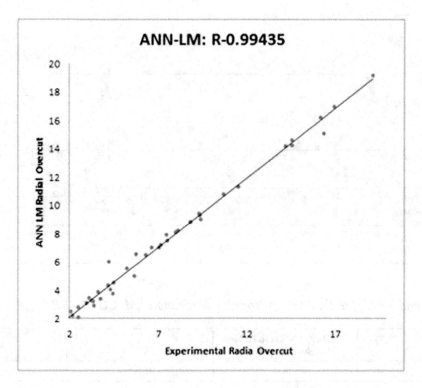

Figure 5. Regression analysis for ANN with RP

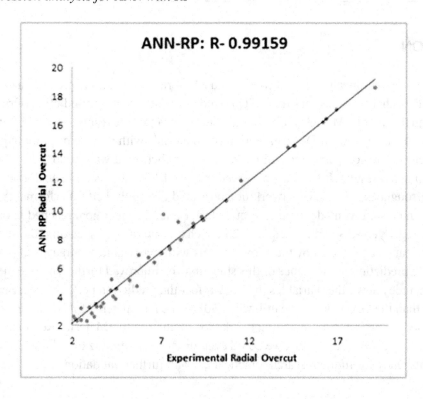

Figure 6. Comparison of ANNs with experimental values

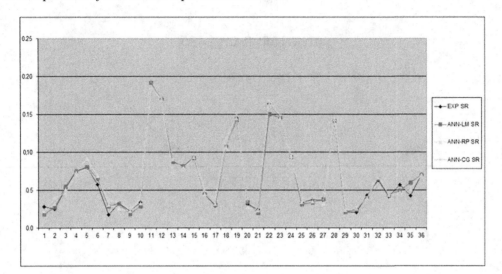

Table 1. MAE and MPE of testing data for training algorithms LM, CG and RP

	Number of Nodes in Hidden Single Layer	MAE	MPE
LM	6	0.243	9.674
CG	14	0.366	27.635
RP	15	0.370	11.634

CONCLUSION

In this chapter, three training algorithms LM, CG and RP were applied for the prediction of radial overcut of the Electrical discharge machined surface. This study indicated that the prediction of radial overcut is possible through the use of LM, CG and RP based neural network. The results obtained from widespread experiments conducted on ANSI D2 steel work piece materials with diverse machining parameters using copper electrode are compared and validate with the prediction. It was found to be close correlation with the experimental results. It was also observed that the LM model is quite analogous with CG and RP for surface roughness. The LM network demonstrated a slightly better performance compared to other models. And also, LM model predicted quite faster than the error goal reached in only 10 epochs while CG required 18 epochs and RP required 23 epochs. Conclusively speaking, the surface finish of EDMed surface cane be predicted by the above models with reasonable accuracy.

However, the prediction performance of this study may be improved further in three means. The first method is to include a few other variables that may affect the prediction performance. Second, optimal methods other than the GA may also be utilized to adjust the parameters of ANN model. We may even use models based on probabilistic neural networks for predicting the Material Removal Rate, Surface Roughness and Radial Overcut. Lastly, we could even propose an optimization based on the prediction outcomes of this study for future research, practical use and further validation.

REFERENCES

Anitha, J., Das, R., & Pradhan, M. K. (2012). Comparison of Neural Network Learning Algorithms for Prediction of Surface Roughness in EDM. *Journal of Mechatronics and Intelligent Manufacturing*, *3*(1/2), 3.

Das, R., & Pradhan, M. K. (2014). General Regression Neural Network and Back Propagation Neural Network Modeling for Predicting Radial Overcut in EDM: A Comparative Study. *Mechatronic and Manufacturing Engineering*, *8*(4), 799–805.

Ho, K. H., & Newman, S. T. (2003). State of the art electrical discharge machinings (EDM). *International Journal of Machine Tools & Manufacture*, *43*(13), 1287–1300. doi:10.1016/S0890-6955(03)00162-7

Jena, A. R., Pradhan, M. K., Das, R., Acharjya, D. P., & Mishra, M. (2014). Prediction of Radial Overcut in Electro-Discharge Machining through Artificial Neural Network. In *Advancements and Current Trends in Industrial Mechanical and Production Engineering*.

Mohd Abbas, N., Solomon, D. G., & Fuad Bahari, M. (2007, June). A review on current research trends in electrical discharge machining (EDM). *International Journal of Machine Tools & Manufacture*, *47*(7-8), 1214–1228. doi:10.1016/j.ijmachtools.2006.08.026

Pradhan, D., & Kumar, M. (2012). Multi-objective optimization of MRR, TWR and Radial Overcut of EDMed AISI D2 tool steel using response surface methodology, grey relational analysis and entropy measurement. *Journal for Manufacturing Science & Production*, *12*(1), 51–63. doi:10.1515/jmsp-2012-0004

Pradhan, M. K. (2012). Multi-objective optimization of MRR, TWR and radial overcut of EDMed AISI D2 tool steel using response surface methodology, grey relational analysis and entropy measurement. *J. Manuf. Science and Production*, *12*(1), 51–63.

Pradhan, M. K. (2010). *Experimental investigation and modelling of surface integrity, accuracy and productivity aspect in EDM of AISI D2 steel* [Ph.D. thesis]. National Institute of Technology, Rourkela, India.

Pradhan, M. K., & Das, R. (2015). Application of a general regression neural network for predicting radial overcut in electrical discharge machining of AISI D2 tool steel. *International Journal of Machining and Machinability of Materials*, *17*(3-4), 355–369. doi:10.1504/IJMMM.2015.071998

Pradhan, M. K., & Das, R. (2015). Application of ann modeling of radial overcut in electrical discharge machining. *Journal of Manufacturing Technology Research*, *7*(1/2), 39.

Chapter 16
To Design a Mammogram Edge Detection Algorithm Using an Artificial Neural Network (ANN)

Alankrita Aggarwal

https://orcid.org/0000-0002-0931-1118

Panipat Institute of Engineering and Technology, Samalkha, India

Deepak Chatha

Panipat Institute of Engineering and Technology, Samalkha, India

ABSTRACT

An artificial neural network (ANN) is used to resolve problems related to complex scenarios and logical thinking. Nowadays, a cause for concern is the mortality rate among women due to cancer. Generally, women to around 45 years old are the most vulnerable to this disease. Early detection is the only hope for the patient to survive, otherwise it may reach an unrecoverable stage. Currently, there are numerous techniques available for the diagnosis of such diseases out of which mammography is the most trust-worthy method for detecting early stage cancer. The analysis of these mammogram images is always difficult to analyze due to low contrast and non-uniform background. The mammogram images are scanned, digitized for processing, nut that further reduces the contrast between region of interest (ROI) and the background. Furthermore, presence of noise, glands, and muscles leads to background contrast variations. The boundaries of the suspected tumor area are always fuzzy and improper. The aim of this article is to develop a robust edge detection technique which works optimally on mammogram images to segment a tumor area.

INTRODUCTION

The flow diagram consists of three major steps i.e. bilateral filtering, entropy multithresholding and artificial neural network (ANN) based edge detection (Sharifi, Fathy, & Mahmoudi, 2002). The acquired image is preprocessed by using bilateral filter to smoothen any spurious pixels present in acquired image.

DOI: 10.4018/978-1-6684-2408-7.ch016

As mammographic images have low contrast and single thresholding Binarization is not inadequate for mammogram images. Therefore, three threshold levels are calculated by using entropy technique for binarization (Heindel, Wige, & Kaup, 2016). This multi threshold entropy binarization method helps to manifest maximum detail out of low contrast breast images. The true edges are filtered out by using Artificial Neural Network which is trained by using 3 × 3 Binary images. Finally, the output of ANN is edge map of lessen masses present in mammogram images. The complete details of these steps are described in following subsections. (Joshi, Yadav, & Allwadhi, 2016).

The detail flow diagram of proposed method is shown in Figure 1.

BACK PROPAGATION NEURAL NETWORK (BPNN)

Back propagation neural network (BPNN) is a multi-layer network introduced. It is basically a supervised network use to train the network for edge detection by using the different Training Samples. Training means adjustment of Weights and Biases of Neural Network according to different input and output relation (Chickanosky & Mirchandani, 1998).

Suppose x is input training sample where $x = (x_1, x_2, \ldots, x_n)$, t is the output target given by $t = (t_1, t_2, \ldots, t_m)$. δ_k is the error at output unit y_k, δ_j is the error at hidden unit z_j, α is the learning rate, v_{oj} is the bias of hidden layer neuron j, w_{ok} is the bias of hidden layer neuron k, z_j and y_k is the output of hidden layer and output neuron.

Output of hidden layer neuron is given by

$$z_{inj} = v_{oj} + \sum_{i=1}^{n} x_i v_{ij} \tag{1}$$

f is the activation function and output of jth hidden neuron which is given by

$$z_j = f(z_{inj}) \tag{2}$$

$$y_{ink} = v_{oj} + \sum_{j=1}^{p} z_j w_{jk} \tag{3}$$

And output of kth output node is given by

$$y_k = f(y_{ink}) \tag{4}$$

Error at k^{th} output node is given by

$$\delta_k = (t_k - y_k) f^1(y_{ink}) \tag{5}$$

Figure 1. Flow diagram of proposed algorithm

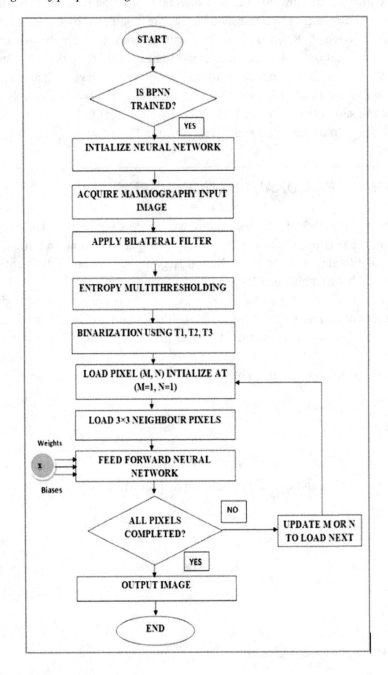

Each hidden neuron sums its error delta inputs as

$$\delta_{inj} = \sum_{k=1}^{m} \delta_j w_{jk} \tag{6}$$

$$\delta_j = \delta_{inj} f'(z_{inj}) \tag{7}$$

The weight and bias correction term of hidden layer with updated weight and bias is given by

$$\Delta w_{jk} = \alpha \delta_k z_j \text{ and } \Delta w_{ok} = \alpha \delta_k \tag{8}$$

$$w_{jk}(\text{New}) = w_{jk}(\text{Old}) + \Delta w_{jk} \text{ and } w_{ok}(\text{New}) = w_{ok}(\text{Old}) + \Delta w_{ok} \tag{10}$$

Similarly, weight and bias correction term of output layer with updated weight and bias is given by

$$\Delta v_{ij} = \alpha \delta_j x_i \text{ and } \Delta v_{oj} = \alpha \delta_j \tag{11}$$

$$v_{ij}(\text{New}) = v_{ij}(\text{Old}) + \Delta v_{ij} \text{ and } v_{oj}(\text{New}) = v_{oj}(\text{Old}) + \Delta v_{oj} \tag{12}$$

The BPNN is provided with total 237 different samples to train it. Each sample is of size 3×3 in binary format and output is either 0 or 1 depending on central pixel of sample is an edge or not as shown in Figure 2.

The flow diagram of Back propagation Neural Network is shown in Figure 3. The architecture of Back propagation Neural Network (BPNN) is consisting of 9 input nodes, 12 hidden nodes and 1 output node. The input layer nodes and output layers are interconnected through hidden nodes forming mesh type networks. These nodes and interconnections are characterized by weights and biases. The input samples are given to input nodes one by one and output is generated, this output is compared with actual output value and error term is generated. This error is back propagated from output layer to input layer and adjustment of weights and biases is done by using back propagation learning technique. The maximum epochs used for BPNN learning is 128. Once learning is completed i.e. when error becomes less than 0.001 as shown in Figure 4, then weight and biases are saved in some variable say X. This learning of BPNN is passed on to Feed Forward Neural Network to generate the edge map of acquired image (Neil, 1963).

IMAGE ACQUISITION

Image acquisition is the foremost step of any image processing task, so does in the proposed algorithm. It is the process of acquiring images for problem domain that are captured using image sensors like CCD/CMOS. For this algorithm, the test images from online MIAS dataset are used (Umbaugh, 2005; Lakshminarayana & Sarvagya, 2015; Lu, Kot, & Shi, 2004).

Image Pre-Processing

The proposed edge detection algorithm is designed to work on 8-bit gray scale image. (Liu, 2009). In Image processing step, image is filtered using bilateral filter and then pixels values are normalized. A bilateral filter is a non-linearsmoothing filter which preserves the edge information of the image. The pixel intensity in an image is recalculated by a weighted average (Gaussian distribution) of intensity values from surrounding pixels. The weights depend on both Euclidean distances and radiometric differences (Shrivakshan & Chandrasekhar, 2012).

Figure 2. Flow diagram of BPNN learning

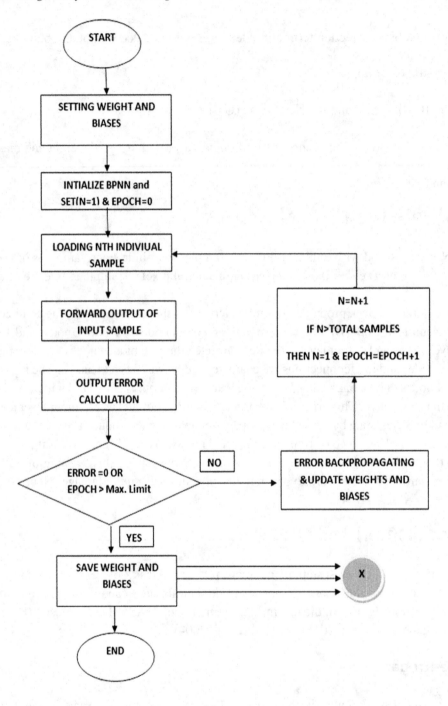

After Bilateral filtering the Gray scale image is normalized to the range of [0, 1] by using equation 16.

$$NormalizedPixel = \frac{PixelValue - Min.Pixelvalue}{Max.Pixelvalue - Min.Pixelvalue} \qquad (13)$$

Figure 3. Training samples

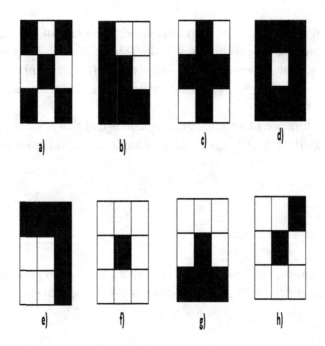

Figure 4. Error Reduction during BPNN learning

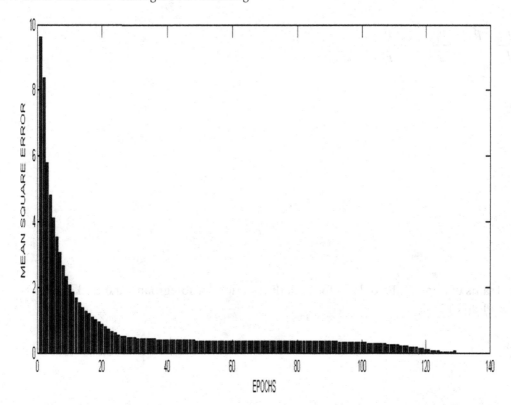

MULTI-THRESHOLDING

As Single level threshold results in loss of prominent structural details of input gray scale image during binary conversion. So, proposed algorithm uses Multi-Thresholding technique to find more than one threshold levels. This algorithm determines by Tsallis entropy (i.e. Principle of maximum entropy), to compute three threshold levels (T1, T2, T3). Tsallis entropy is actually a generalization of Boltzmann-Gibbs statistics.

Let the pixel intensity function of acquired gray scale image of size $M \times N$ is $f(x,y)$ where $x \in \{1,2,3,\dots ,M\}$, $y \in \{1,2,3,\dots ,N\}$. Let $P = p_1, p_2, p_3, \dots, p_k$ is the probability distribution of k different gray intensity levels which must satisfy.

$$\sum_{i=1}^{k} p_i = 1 \tag{14}$$

To compute Tsallis entropy, two probability distributions for the foreground object (p_A) and for the background (p_B) are calculated [20] as given by equation 3 & 4 respectively.

$$p_A : \frac{p_1}{P_A}, \frac{p_2}{P_A}, \frac{p_3}{P_A}, \dots, \frac{p_t}{P_A} \tag{15}$$

$$p_B : \frac{p_{t+1}}{P_B}, \frac{p_{t+2}}{P_B}, \frac{p_{t+3}}{P_B}, \dots, \frac{p_k}{P_B} \tag{16}$$

Where,

$$P_A = \sum_{i=1}^{t} p_i \tag{17}$$

$$P_B = \sum_{i=t+1}^{k} p_i \tag{18}$$

The Tsallis entropy of the order q for each distribution for foreground and background is given by equation 11 and 12.

$$S_q^A (t) = \frac{1}{q-1}\left(1 - \sum_{i=1}^{t} p_A^q \right) \tag{19}$$

$$S_q^B\left(t\right) = \frac{1}{q-1}\left[1 - \sum_{i=t+1}^{k} p_B^q\right] \tag{20}$$

The gray scale intensity level that correspond to maximum Sq(t) is considered to be the optimum threshold value t(q) which is given by equation 1.

$$t\left(q\right) = Arg\ \max\left[S_q^A\left(t\right) + S_q^B\left(t\right) + \left(1-q\right).S_q^A\left(t\right).S_q^B\left(t\right)\right] \tag{21}$$

Computation of Tsallis Entropy for Multi-Thresholding:
The steps to compute three Threshold levels (T_1, T_2, T_3) using Tsallis Entropy are:

Step 1: Calculate the probability distribution p_i, for input gray scale image $g(x,y)$ of size $M\times N$.
Step 2: For all t ∈ {0, 1...255}, apply Equation 7, 8, 9, and 10 to calculate P_A, P_B, p_A, p_B.
Step 3: Use Equation 13 to get first optimal Threshold level (T_1).
Step 4: Split the whole histogram into two parts i.e. from 0 to T_1 (part1) and from T_1 to 255 (part2).
Step 5: Apply step 2 and 3 on part 1 of histogram to get second optimal threshold level T_2.
Step 6: Again apply step 2 & 3 on part2 to get third optimal threshold level T_3.

BINARIZATION

Binarization is the process to convert the input gray scale image, where each pixel attains 256 different values, into binary image where each pixel must contain either 0 or 1. This is governed by some well define rules depending upon single or multiple threshold levels. Image binarization is the method to classify the image into two classes of foreground and background. It plays important role in image feature and dimension reduction The three threshold levels i.e. T_1, T_2, T_3 computed by tsallis entropy, are used for binarization by using equation 14 where $f(x,y)$ is input grayscale intensity function and $g(x,y)$ is output binary intensity function. (Gotas, Ntirogiannis, & Pratikakis, 2011).

$$g\left(x,y\right) = \begin{cases} 0, & if\ f\left(x,y\right) < T_2 \\ 1, & if\ T_2 < f\left(x,y\right) < T_1 \\ 0, & if\ T_1 < f\left(x,y\right) < T_3 \\ 1, & if\ f\left(x,y\right) > T_3 \end{cases} \tag{22}$$

CONCLUSION

Artificial neural network (ANN) is a robust network which is designed and trained for any nonlinear problem. Edge detection is itself a very complex problem as the performance of edge detectors may get affected due to several factors. (Sun & Wang, 2005), Binarization plays an important role in data reduction step in any edge detection algorithm. This data reduction step also leads to information loss which may be minimized by using Multi-level thresholding instead of single-level thresholding.

REFERENCES

Joshi, K., Yadav, R., & Allwadhi, S. (2016). PSNR and MSE Based Investigation of LSB. In *Proceedings of the 2016 International Conference on Computational Techniques in Information and Communication Technologies (ICCTICT)* (pp. 280-285). Academic Press. 10.1109/ICCTICT.2016.7514593

Lu, H., Kot, A. C., & Shi, Y. Q. (2004). Distance-Reciprocal Distortion Measure For Binary Document Images. *IEEE Signal Processing Letters*, *11*(2), 228–231. doi:10.1109/LSP.2003.821748

Gotas, B., Ntirogiannis, K., & Pratikakis, I. (2011). DIBCO 2009: Document Binarization Contest. *IJDAR*, *14*(1), 35–44. doi:10.100710032-010-0115-7

Sun, W., & Wang, Y. (2005). Segmentation Method of MRI Using Fuzzy Gaussian Basis Neural Network Neural Information Processing. *Letters and Reviews*, *8*(2), 19–24.

Heindel, A., Wige, E., & Kaup, A. (2016). Low- Complexity Enhancement Layer Compression For Scalable Lossless Video Coding Based HEVC. *IEEE Transactions on Circuits and Systems for Video Technology*, *99*, 1–1.

Lakshminarayana, M., & Sarvagya, M. (2015). Random Sample Measurement And Reconstruction Of Medical Image Signal Using Compressive Sensing. In *Proceedings of the IEEE International Conference on Computing and Network Communications* (pp. 255-262). IEEE Press. 10.1109/CoCoNet.2015.7411195

Liu, A. (2009). Evaluation of Gray Image Definition Based on Edge Kurtosis in Spatial Domain. In *Proceedings of the First International Workshop on Education and Computer Science* (Vol. 3, pp. 472-475). Academic Press. 10.1109/ETCS.2009.634

Shrivakshan, G.T. & Chandrasekhar, C. (2012). A Comparison Of Various Edge Detection Techniques Used In Image Processing. *International Journal of Computer Science Issues*, *9*(5), 269–276.

Neil, R. O. (1963). Convolution Operators And L(P, Q) Spaces. *Duke Mathematical Journal*, *30*(1), 129–142. doi:10.1215/S0012-7094-63-03015-1

Umbaugh, S. E. (2005). *Computer Imaging: Digital Image Analysis and Processing*. CRC Press.

Chickanosky, V., & Mirchandani, G. (1998, May). Wreath products for edge detection. In *Proceedings of the 1998 IEEE International Conference on Acoustics, Speech and Signal Processing ICASSP'98* (Vol. 5, pp. 2953-2956). IEEE.

Sharifi, M., Fathy, M., & Mahmoudi, M. T. (2002). A Classified and Comparative Study of Edge Detection Algorithms. In *Proceedings of IEEE International Conference on Information Technology: Coding and Computing (ITCC)* (pp. 117-120). IEEE Press. 10.1109/ITCC.2002.1000371

This research was previously published in the International Journal of Distributed Artificial Intelligence (IJDAI), 11(1); pages 34-43, copyright year 2019 by IGI Publishing (an imprint of IGI Global).

Chapter 17
A Framework for an Artificial–Neural–Network–Based Electronic Nose

Mudassir Ismail
University of Bahrain, Bahrain

Ahmed Abdul Majeed
University of Bahrain, Bahrain

Yousif Abdullatif Albastaki
 https://orcid.org/0000-0002-6866-2268
Ahlia University, Bahrain

ABSTRACT

Machine odor detection has developed into an important aspect of our lives with various applications of it. From detecting food spoilage to diagnosis of diseases, it has been developed and tested in various fields and industries for specific purposes. This project, artificial-neural-network-based electronic nose (ANNeNose), is a machine-learning-based e-nose system that has been developed for detection of various types of odors for a general purpose. The system can be trained on any odor using various e-nose sensor types. It uses artificial neural network as its machine learning algorithm along with an OMX-GR semiconductor gas sensor for collecting odor data. The system was trained and tested with five different types of odors collected through a standard data collection method and then purified, which in turn had a result varying from 93% to 100% accuracy.

DOI: 10.4018/978-1-6684-2408-7.ch017

BACKGROUND

Technology has boomed over the past few decades bringing us all kinds of comfort and accessibility. The screens that we had once that used to be black and white are now colorful and the methods of interacting with a computer using a mouse and keyboard has now been complimented by touch, and even through motion and air gestures.

These advances have had the researchers work on different ways and methods to add more ways to interact with the computer and somehow give it more 'senses'. This vision has led to development of various types of sensors through which computers can interact with users and the environment around them. Developments have been made in the fields of various types of interactions such as touch/pressure, measuring temperature and even giving computers a 'vision' through cameras and image recognition. These advances have led to various applications in many industries.

One of these 'senses' has been enabling the computer to 'smell' or detect odor. Imagine being on a video call with a friend over another continent and being able to smell what perfume they are wearing. Or having the ability to not only take pictures and keep them as memories but also the smell of different places and occasions. Or walking through a Virtual world with an ability to know what it smells like.

The efforts of researchers in this field led to creating of an odor-sensing electronic nose first introduced in 1982 (Lee, et al., 2012) which utilized a multi-sensor array of gas sensors combined to classify odors by the detection of different gases present. Since then until now over a period of over three decades, many advancements have been made in the hardware technology of electronic noses with more sensors being introduced and many being created for very specific purposes such as detection of leakage in natural gas factories, analyzing amount of carbon dioxide in an environment. Though less as compared to special purpose sensors, there has been developments in general purpose sensors consisting of a wider array of different types of sensors as well.

Given the wide range of needs of detecting 'odors' and electronic noses still being developed. Humans were utilized in food factories and many other industries to differentiate spoiled from unspoiled food and in other applications. This approach can be unreliable at times due to the limitations of the range of odors a human nose can detect. An alternate that is used are dogs, but the cost of their training is high and they have a short life span.

OBJECTIVES OF THE RESEARCH WORK

As humans, our sense of smell is very important, and we rely on it for various tasks and functions some of which are daily activities and others which can be more important. Despite the importance of this sense, our sense of smell is usually limited both in its capabilities and can be influenced by external factors such as flu, our surroundings and other factors. Our human sense of smell can also only detect a limited number of gases due to which must be facilitated by adding compounds to different gases for humans to be able to detect it (Lee, et al., 2012).

These limitations of human olfactory system make it difficult to rely on humans for the job of odor detection in Industries. Moreover, the odor detection of dangerous gases, even though possible by humans, may be fatal. An alternate approach is to train and utilize dog for odor sensing. This too has limitations as it is expensive to train dogs, and their life span is short and limited. These limitations have led to the development of electronic noses which try to mimic the human olfactory system. Electronic noses have proved their significance in various fields of health and industries and have been used as sensors for detection of food spoilage and in diagnosis of various diseases and much more (Gurney, 1997). Despite advances in the hardware of electronic noses, there hasn't been much attention paid to the software side of electronic noses.

This research aims to develop a general purpose Artificial Neural Network that can be used in various kinds of application from differentiating between markers, detecting food spoilage and diagnosing diseases.

As discussed in the previous section, the research and development on the software side of Odor sensing systems has been relatively less compared to its hardware. Moreover, these developments have been for very specific purposes and uses.

This chapter aims on developing an Odor sensing system using Electronic nose as a hardware and Artificial Neural Network as software for general odor sensing and identifying different odors as shown in Figure 1.

Figure 1. The odor sensing system

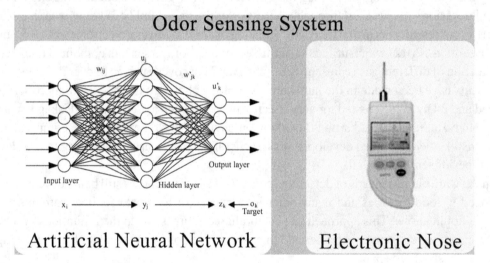

ARTIFICIAL INTELLIGENCE TECHNIQUES

Various Artificial Intelligence techniques have been developed and are used in different fields. For this research, the researchers analyzed three most relevant techniques which are as follows:

- **Artificial Neural Networks:** An ANN is made up of nodes in different layers. The layers are input layer, intermediate hidden layer(s) and the output layer as shown in figure 2. The links between nodes of adjacent layers have weights. The goal of training is to assign correct weights for these edges. These weights determine the output vector for a given input vector (Wilson & Baietto, 2009).

At the start, all the edge weights are randomly assigned. For every input in the training dataset, the ANN is executed. The output obtained is compared with the intended output that is already known, and if there is an error then the error is propagated back to the previous layer. The weights are adjusted according to the error. This process is repeated until the output error is equal to or below a predetermined threshold.

Figure 2. Architecture of an Artificial Neural Network

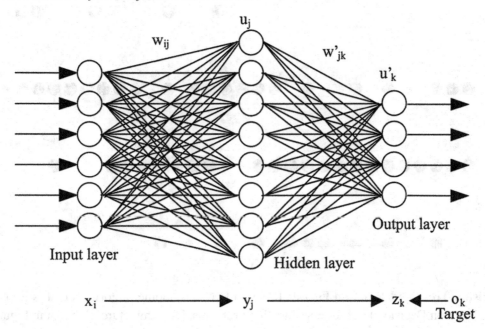

Once the algorithm terminates, we have a trained ANN. We consider that the ANN is ready to work with new inputs. This ANN can then be trained further by providing more input data and therefore making the results more accurate.

- **Decision Trees and XGBoost:** Classification or regression models in the form of a tree structure are built using a decision tree. It breaks down a dataset into smaller and smaller subsets while incrementally developing an associated decision tree at the same time. The result is a tree with decision nodes and leaf nodes. A decision node has two or more branches. Leaf node represents a classification or decision. The uppermost decision node in a tree which corresponds to the best predictor is called root node. Both categorical and numerical data can be handled by decision trees.

XGBoost stands for eXtreme Gradient Boosting. It is an implementation of gradient boosted decision trees designed for performance and speed. Its architecture is shown in Figure 3. It uses the technique of gradient boosting where new models are created that predict the residuals or errors of prior models and then added together to make the final prediction (Friedman, 2001).

Figure 3. Architecture of decision trees algorithm

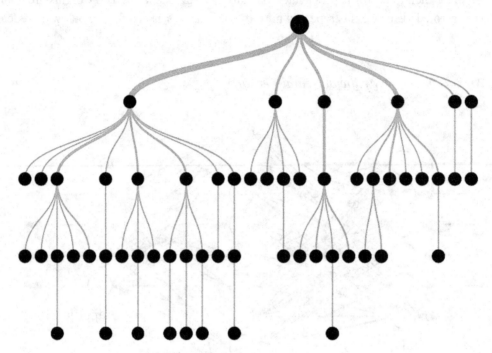

- **Decision Trees and Random Forest:** Random Forest is another algorithm that is implemented together with Decision trees for classification problems, its architecture is shown in Figure 4.

Figure 4. Architecture of decision trees and random forest algorithm

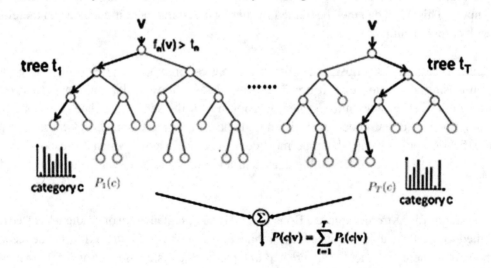

The random forest is an aggregate approach that is used by combining many decorrelated random trees. It is an aggregate approach that can thought of as a form of nearest neighbor predictor. For this algorithm, a large set of sample data is taken, and then random subset of these data are generated. From these subsets, decision trees and classifier classes are created to classify the data. Random forest algorithms are used when the data set is very large and there is a possibility of missing data existing.

- **Choice of Algorithm:** For this research, the algorithm the authors choose is Artificial Neural Networks over Decision Trees with XGBoost and Decision Trees with Random Forest. The reason behind this are as follows. Firstly, Artificial Neural Networks (ANN) are more flexible in terms of their outputs, and can be used for Single or multiple outputs. Moreover, ANN provide the feature of 'Back propagation' due to which it requires minimal supervision and only needed to be provided with input data for it to train itself making it much simpler to train for large number of data and more flexible for various types of applications due to which giving the ability to use the same network in different fields. Finally, with more training, the 'weights' of the nodes of an ANN are adjusted automatically whenever trained to give more precise results, this feature can lead to simplifying our application, so it could be used by less tech-savvy people hence increasing its utility.

SCOPE OF THE WORK

The scope of the research, as shown in Figure 5, is to create a general odor sensing system able to differentiate between sampled odors using OMX-GR sensor as the hardware and Artificial Neural Network (ANN) as software.

Figure 5. The scope of the research

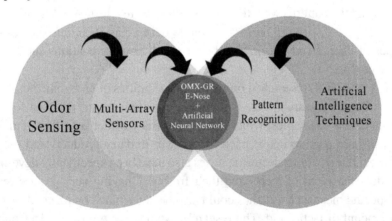

The working of the hardware and the implementation details of the software are described in coming sections of this chapter.

RELATED WORKS

Many researches have been done on the electronic noses and their applications in various fields such as diagnosis, food industries, and as sensors. Some of these reviewed works are as follows.

- **Di Natale, and et al.** (2003) researched on the diagnosis of lung cancer using an electronic nose. The diagnosis system used a LibraNose electronic nose. The data collection was done in the premises of the hospital and samples of patients having diagnosed with lung cancer and those that had its symptoms were taken. The analysis of this data was done through partial least squares discriminant analysis. A result of 94% accuracy was obtained by the research in diagnosis of lung cancer.
- **Thaler, and et. al.** (2006) used a smell sensor for the diagnosis of sinnusitis. The smell sensor used by the research was a Cyranose 320. Patients with known sinnusitis were taken and samples were collected from them. Five samples each were collected from the patients with a rest-time of five minutes between each sample for the sensor to recover. For the analysis of this data, Support Vector Machine (SVM) algorithm was used. This resulted in an accuracy of 72% due to the limitations of the smell sensor.
- **Mohamed, and et. al.** (2002) used a smell sensor for the diagnosis of diabetes. The researchers took urine samples from patients with known diabetes and healthy patients. These urine samples were then processed through a smell sensor and fed into an Artificial Neural Network, and also analyzed using Logistic regression and Principal Component analysis. This led to an accuracy of 92% when an Artificial Neural Network and Logistic regression was used and 88% when using Principal Component analysis.
- **Ampeuro, and et. al.** (2003) tested smell sensors in the applications of classifying dairy products, specifically, different kinds of cheese and milk. The research focused on different between different kinds of cheese, detecting molds of bacteria on cheese, classifying bacteria cultures in milk, aging of dairy products and detection of cheese that is gone bad. Various sensors were used to gather the data and the patterns were then analyzed to see results using Artificial Neural Networks. The results were mixed with the sensors unable to detect classifications such as defective cheese, different types of cheese and performing better on other classifications such as determining the age of a diary product.
- **Wilson, and et. al.** (2009) researched on various applications of electronic noses in different fields and industries. Per the research, there is intensive use of electronic nose sensors to determine the ripeness of fruits and vegetables, which has an accuracy of between 86% and 100%. Electronic noses have also been used to detect bacterial growth in dairy products and their shelf-lives and have done so accurately. Some electronic noses also have been specifically developed for detecting spoilages in different types of meats and their freshness having very precise results. The sweet/sourness of specific meat such as fishes could also be determined by using electronic noses for the detection of amount of lactic acid. The research also focuses on use of electronic noses in medicine and health where they have been used to detect traces of blood in urine samples and had an accuracy of 86.6% in doing so.
- **Pearce, and et. al.** (2006) in their research designed an electronic nose system that can be used to determine the quality of indoor-air. The system is composed of a hardware Metal Oxide Gas sensor and a fuzzy logic pattern recognition algorithm to determine the data from the sensor. These

devices were low power and low cost and yielded high accuracy when tested for the detection of Nitrogen Oxide and Carbon dioxide gases in the indoor-air.

- **Luo, and et. al.** (2004) used a Cyranose 320 smell sensor with artificial neural network to detect the difference between different brands of cigarette. Four types of cigarettes from different brands were taken and data was gathered through the electronic nose. Three different artificial networks were trained on this data. These networks had similar characteristics except the input size, which varied between 32 or 35 inputs. After analysis, the network with the most inputs had better results with an accuracy varying between 80-100% for the given brands.

- **Gardener, and et. al.** (2000) in their research used a modified FOX 2000 smell sensor and CellFacts liquid analysis instrument to gather data to detect the presence of various bacteria such as Legionalla pneumphilia, Staphylococcus and Escherichia coli (E. coli). They gathered this data in strict lab conditions using various lab equipment to purify the sample before feeding it into the sensor. They analyzed the patterns of the collected data after gathering it and achieved 80.6% accuracy in detecting the presence of these bacteria. They also suggested that this result could've been improved on by using an artificial neural network.

- **D'Amico, and et. al.** (2010) used a custom made electronic nose to use for the detection of lung cancer. They took various breath samples from both healthy and cancer inflicted patients. Their samples mainly consisted of the last part of breath before a person ran out of breath to ensure that the air being collected was from the deeper part of the lungs. Moreover, the participants were required to fast for 9 hours before the samples were taken. The analysis of the data collected led a precision of 85.7% in detecting of lung cancer.

- **Hanson, and et. al.** (2005) developed a smell sensor with an array of 32 sensors for the detection of severity of pneumonia in Ventilator-associated pneumonia patients. They gathered samples from various patients in hospitals directly from their ventilators to ensure external factors did not affect the samples. The samples then were analyzed using Statistical analysis and each was given a 'Pneumonia score' based on the stage and the type of the bacteria present. The results were only partially convincing due to the limitations of the smell sensor used.

Summary of Review

Reviewing the literature in the field of electronic nose and its use in odor sensing shows that various smell sensors have been used for the different purposes alongside different methods of analysis which were mainly statistical in nature and not artificially intelligent. Moreover, the trend of using custom smell sensors is also seen, with many being developed for very specific purposes to detect specific odors only. An overview of this is given in the Table 1.

Reviewing the aforementioned researches, this research uses a general-purpose sensor in form of OMX-GR and Artificial Neural Network for analysis due to its ability of being trained and being general purpose. The details of the working of the sensor and those of the Artificial Neural Network are given in coming sections.

Table 1. An overview of different technology used in reviewed literature

Research Paper	Smell Sensor Used	Method/Algorithm for Odor Sensing	Accuracy
Lung cancer identification by the analysis of breath by means of an array of non-selective gas sensors. (Di Natale, et al., 2003)	LibraNose	Partial Least Squares Discriminant Analysis	94%
Use of an electronic nose to diagnose bacterial sinusitis. (Thaler & Hanson, 2006)	Cyranose 320	Support Vector Machine	76%
Predicting Type 2 diabetes using an electronic nose-based artificial neural network analysis. (Mohamed, et al., 2002)	Custom Smell Sensor	Artificial Neural Network	92%
Detecting quality of indoor-air using electronic nose. (Pearce, Schiffman, Nagle, & Gardner, 2006)	Custom Smell Sensor	Fuzzy Logic Pattern Recognition	90%-100%
Application of ANN with extracted parameters from an electronic nose in cigarette brand identification. (Luo, Hosseini, & Stewart, 2004)	Cyranose 320	Artificial Neural Network	80-100%
An electronic nose system to diagnose illness. (Gardner, Shin, & Hines, 2000)	Fox 2000	Statistical Analysis	80.6%
An investigation on electronic nose diagnosis of lung cancer. Lung Cancer. (D'Amico, et al., 2010)	Custom Smell Sensor	Partial Least Squares Discriminant Analysis	85.7%
Electronic nose prediction of a clinical pneumonia score: biosensors and microbes. (Hanson & Thaler, 2005)	Custom Smell Sensor	Statistical Analysis	<50%

BACKGROUND THEORY

In the previous section, related works was discussed. In this chapter, the functioning of electronic noses (e-noses), and an algorithm developed to mimic the biological neural network structure of the human brain known as artificial neural network will be discussed (Zhang, Patuwo, & Y. Hu, 1998).

Electronic-Nose

Electronic-nose or e-nose is a device intended to detect and classify odor. It's engineered to emulate the human olfactory system (Zhang, Patuwo, & Y. Hu, 1998). Interest among the scientists in the field of electronic-nose was recorded in the early 20th century when scientist Alexander Graham Bell famously said that "if you are ambitious to found a new science, measure a smell." (Bell, 1914). Nonetheless, developments in the field took place approximately 50 years later after Bell had put forth the idea of a new science. During the recent years, a lot of discoveries have been made in the field, yet there is a lot more to be learnt and explored.

- **Brief History of Electronic-Nose:** Electronic-Nose is a relatively new field, whose earliest developments can be dated back to 1961 when Moncrieff (1961) developed a mechanical nose to detect odors. Wilkens and Hatman (1964) built on the work of Moncrieff to create the first reported electronic nose in 1964. However, it was the work of Persaud and Dodd that introduced electronic nose as a system of chemical array sensor system in 1982 (Persaud & Dodd, 1982) and (Gardner & Barlett, 1994). It was also during the 1980's that the term 'electronic nose' started to appear, its specific usage can be dated to 1987 when it was used in the 8th International Congress of European Chemoreception Research Organization at the University of Warwick (Gardner J., 1987), (Lang, et al., 2007) and (Li, 2009).

- **The Term Electronic-Nose:** With the evolution of electronic-nose field, the term used for the electronic-nose device has also evolved. Initially, mechanical nose was used as the instrument was mechanical and currently, electronic-nose, artificial-nose and odor-sensing system are being interchangeably used for the same device (Al-Bastaki, 2009), (Moncrieff, 1961), (Gardner & Barlett, 1994), (Lang, et al., 2007) and (Li, 2009). Gardner and Barlett (Gardner & Barlett, 1994) defined electronic nose as an instrument, that is made up of an array of electronic chemical sensors having partial specificity and an appropriate pattern-recognition system which can recognize simple or complex odors. An array of electronic chemical sensors having partial specificity is a vital part of the definition as it implies that devices with only one sensor or the ability to identify only one compound or odor are not electronic-noses (Wilson & Baietto, 2009) and (Gardner & Barlett, 1994). Furthermore, Gardner and Barlett (1994) list the following components that are depicted in figure 6, as the basics of an electronic-nose:

  - An odor delivery system that transfers the molecules of the source material to the sensor array system.
  - A chamber where the sensors are located, usually having a fixed temperature and humidity, so that the absorption of the molecules is not affected.
  - A transducer that converts chemical input to an electrical signal.
  - A converter that converts electrical to digital signal.
  - A pattern recognition system that takes the digital signal and predicts the odor.

Figure 6. Components of an electronic-nose

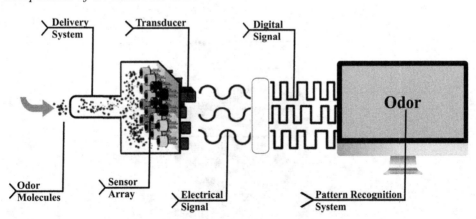

The first four components generally form the smell sensor (Li, 2009) and (Kalita, Saikia, & Singh, 2015). Many smell sensors have already been developed and are going under constant improvements (Li, 2009). The last component can be either a microprocessor with an embedded algorithm or an application for pattern recognition. (Tang, et al., 2010) and (Wilson & Baietto, 2009). The smell sensor used in this research and the pattern recognition system are discussed in the following sections.

OMX-GR Handheld Odor Meter

An OMX-GR smell sensor as shown in the Figure 7 was used for odor sensing. It uses two semiconductor gas sensors to detect odors (Shinyei, n.a.). Strength and classification (ID) of the odor that are calculated using an original method of Shinyei technology are displayed on the screen through its LCD display (Shinyei, n.a.). There is no correlation between the indicated value of OMX-GR and the value of human sense of odor intensity. The ID is an integer with a range of 0 to 90 and the strength is also an integer with a range of 0 to 999 (Shinyei, n.a.). It has a different response rate to different compounds and liquids (Shinyei, n.a.) as follows:

- Ethanol 100ppm in 20 seconds.
- Methyl Mercaptan 0.16ppm in 50 seconds.
- Xylene 46ppm in 50 seconds.

Figure 7. OMX-GR handheld odor meter

A RS-232 cable was used to connect and read the strength and ID of odors from the sensor through the custom-made application.

Pattern Recognition System

The final component of the electronic-nose from its definition is its Pattern Recognition System. The pattern recognition system uses computer algorithms to find regularities and key features in the output of the smell sensor to identify odor and to classify it into different categories (Bishop, 2006). For odor classification various algorithms have been used which include principal component analysis, cluster analysis, k-nearest neighbor, genetic algorithms, discriminant function analysis, canonical discriminant analysis, statistical pattern recognition, radial basis function and artificial neural networks (Nagle, Gutierrez-Osuna, & Schiffman, 1998), (Schaller, Bosset, & Escher, 1998), (Gardner & Bartlett, 1992), (Penza, Cassano, Tortorella, & Zaccaria, 2001), (Bicego, Tessari, Tecchiolli, & Bettinelli, 2002) and (Kim, et al., 2012). Among these the researchers will be using Artificial Neural Network (ANN) for the advantages mentioned in section Artificial Intelligence Techniques. A summary of ANN was given in Artificial Intelligence Techniques section, in the subsequent section ANN is discussed in detail.

Artificial Neural Network

Artificial neural network also known as neural network, has been an area of great interest ever since the discovery that the human brain works in a completely different way as compared to the conventional digital computer (Haykin, 2009). Moreover, the human brain does recognition computation much faster than the fastest computers in existence today (Haykin, 2009). On average, it can detect a familiar face among unfamiliar faces 10 times faster than a computer (Nagarajan & Stevens, 2008). Advantages like these have led to the efforts of simulating the brain electronically, thus it's important to understand the basic functioning of the human brain as described in the following section.

The Human Neural Network

The average human brain is composed of approximately 100 billion (1×10^{11}) tiny nerve cells called neurons (Herculano-Houzel, 2009), (Bartheld, Bahney, & Herculano-Houzel, 2016) and (Spitzer, 2006). These neurons have about 10 connections with each of the 1000 neurons that it is connected to, thus having 10, 000 connections individually and one quadrillion (1×10^{15}) connections collectively (Spitzer, 2006). The communication through the connections takes place through electrochemical signals (Ma, Forbes, Llano, Berger-Wolf, & Kenyon, 2016). Initially, the cell body of the neuron called a soma shown in Figure 8 collects and combines incoming information from other neurons, this information is passed as electrical signals to the axon hillock, which decides whether to fire an action potential or not based on a certain threshold. If an action potential is fired, then electrical signals are passed through the axon to the terminal endings which contain synapses. Synapses convert the incoming electrical signals to chemical signals. They then send signals to a dendrite of another neuron, these synaptic signals maybe inhibitory or excitatory i.e., they will make the next neuron less or more likely to fire their action potential (Madan & Dandina, 1994) and (Wan, 1993). It's due to the various sequences of the firing these neurons that humans can see, move, hear, smell, taste, touch, reason, think, dream, remember, plan and do all the things that we do through our brain (Solomon D, 2015). To make use of the neurons incredible abilities these neurons are electronically imitated as explained in artificial neural network model section.

Figure 8. Schematic diagram of a neuron and an ANN node

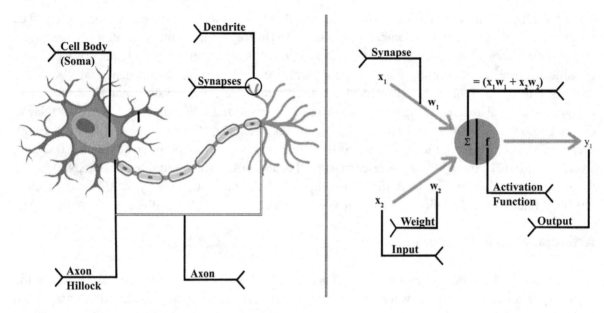

ARTIFICIAL NEURAL NETWORK MODEL

After covering the human neural network in the previous section, in this section the various components of an artificial neural network will be covered. Starting off with the artificial equivalent of the human neurons that are represented as nodes or units as shown in figure 8 (Gurney, 1997).

ANN Nodes

Like the neurons, the nodes also have synapses. However, the synapse of nodes functions a bit differently, each synapse is assigned a weight to it and the synapse takes the input from the nodes in the previous layer, and multiplies it with its weight. The product of all inputs with their respective weight is then summed together and passed to an activation function that works like the axon hillock of a human neuron and it is applied to obtain the output of the node.

Types of Networks

The inter-linking of the nodes through input, hidden and output layer results in an artificial neural network as displayed on the left side of Figure 9. Input and output layers can have any number of nodes however, both have only one layer. Hidden layer on the other hand, in addition to any number of nodes can also have any number of layers. When the number of layers in the hidden part of the network is greater than 1, then the network is known as a deep neural network as shown on the right side of Figure 9. Deep neural networks are used when transformations are required between layers i.e., in image processing the first hidden layer may be used to detect the edges of an image and the second layer may be used to extract the object from the obtained edges of the first layer.

Figure 9. An Artificial Neural Network and a Deep Neural Network

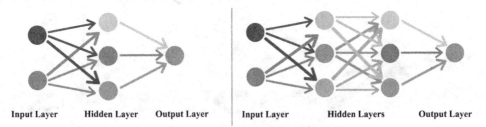

Back to neural networks with a single layer, in the next subsection the activation function mentioned in section ANN nodes is explained in detail.

Activation Functions

Activation functions are sometimes called a transfer function or a squashing function. Its role is to limit the range of output (Haykin, 2011) and (Demuth, Beale, De Jess, & Hagan, 2014). Depending upon the chosen activation function the output range of a node is usually in the interval of [0,1] or [-1,1]. In neural networks, various activation functions are used. The choice of activation function comes down to the requirements of the network. Therefore, instead of covering majority of the activation functions, only the sigmoid activation function will be covered. But before covering the sigmoid function, let's first define the notations that will be used as illustrated in figure 10:

- x_{ij}: The input of the jth neuron in the ith layer.
- w_{ijk}: The weight coming from the kth neuron in the $(i-1)^{th}$ layer to the jth neuron in the ith layer.
- y_{ij}: The output produced by the activation function for the jth neuron in the ith layer.
- z_{ij}: The activation value before the activation function is applied, which is equal to the sum of the product of all inputs with their respective weights coming into the jth neuron in the ith layer i.e.,

$$\sum_k \left(x_{(i-1)k} * w_{ijk} \right).$$

Sigmoid Activation Function

The sigmoid activation function takes the input and applies the following formula to it:

$$y_{ij} = \frac{1}{1 + e^{-\left(z_{ij}\right)}}$$

These results are shown in Figure 11.

Figure 10. Illustration of notations used for sigmoid activation function

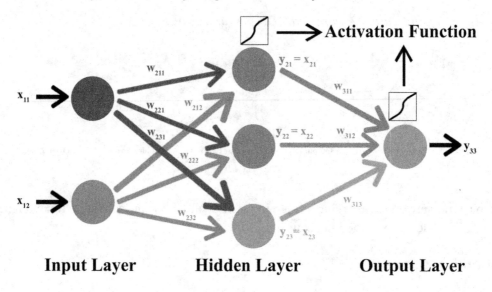

Figure 11. Graph of the Sigmoid Function
Plotted using desmos.com.

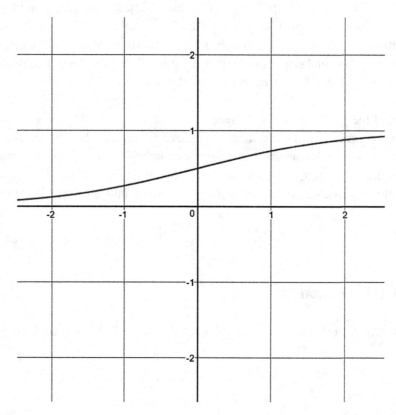

As visible in the graph 11, the sigmoid function takes input between minus and plus infinity and squashes it to a number between 0 and 1.

After covering the sigmoid activation function, in the next section the basics of feed forward algorithm will be covered.

Feed Forward Algorithm

The feed forward algorithm is used to carry the inputs obtained in the input layer to the hidden and then to the output layer to obtain an output from the network. The algorithm starts by assigning random numbers to the weights. It then takes in the inputs and does matrix multiplication of inputs with the weights coming into the 2nd layer. Next sigmoid activation function is applied to each element obtained from the matrix multiplication, the new values represent the input to the next layer. This whole process of matrix multiplying the inputs with the weights and applying activation function is repeated till the algorithm reaches the output layer.

With the network now capable of producing an output, the training of the network that is done using the backpropagation algorithm is covered in the next subsection.

Backpropagation Algorithm

The backpropagation algorithm is a method used for training a multilayer neural network. Using the backpropagation algorithm, the weights in the network are modified to produce the expected outputs. First, feed forward algorithm described in previous section is used to produce an output. A cost function like the mean squared error i.e., $E = \sum \left(y - \hat{y} \right)^2$ is then used to calculate how far or close was the produced output ($\hat{y}$) to the expected one (y). The weights are then updated to minimize this cost function and the whole process is repeated till a satisfactory error rate is obtained.

DATA COLLECTION, ANALYSIS, AND RESULTS

After covering the background theory, data collection and its analysis will be discussed in this section. The discussion will start with data collection, in which the issues faced in data collection will be examined and solved. After which the collected data will be analyzed, processed and finally, the results will be discussed.

Data Collection

Odor data was collected using the OMX-GR sensor discussed in OMX-GR handheld odor meter section. However, many issues were faced in the collection of data as the sensor was more than a decade and half old, and couldn't be replaced with a new one due to limited budget of the research.

First, the authors realized that the sensor wasn't having a standard response time to the odors even when the odors were presented to the sensor from a uniform distance. This meant that the response time of odors couldn't be used as an input parameter to the neural network, which could've led to more accurate results. Response time of three odors is mentioned in the manual of the sensor (Shinyei, n.a.), from which it can be concluded that the sensor originally had a standard response time. Nonetheless, as the sensor had gotten old, its response time might have been affected.

Next, when different odors were read in quick succession, the sensor was giving completely different readings to the previously obtained readings of the odors. After researching, the authors came to know that different sensors have different recovery times in addition to response time (Wilson & Baietto, 2009) and (Bochenkov & Sergeev, 2010). However, unlike response time the recovery time wasn't mentioned on the sensor's manual. Therefore, to identify the recovery time, the researchers started by allowing the sensor a recovery time of 5 seconds and checked the consistency of the readings. The consistency of the readings didn't improve, so the recovery time was further increased, this continued till the recovery time was increased to 10 minutes and the readings' consistency hadn't improved, as sometimes the sensor wouldn't respond to an odor even after 10 minutes of recovery time. Therefore, the researchers concluded that the sensor no longer had a standard response or recovery time.

Then, it also came to our knowledge that environmental factors i.e., temperature and humidity affect readings of the sensors. This has also been confirmed in various researches (Wilson & Baietto, 2009), (Bochenkov & Sergeev, 2010) and (Powers, 2004). To reduce the effect of environmental factors pipes of varying sizes were used to expose odors directly to the sensor and restrict the environment's effect on them.

Even after taking all the previous mentioned steps to improve the readings, consistent readings weren't obtained. Therefore, the following purification method was used to obtain consistent readings.

1. Each substance's reading should be taken from a specific distance every time.
2. The readings should be taken through the pipe chambers.
3. The sensor should be given a recovery time of at least 10 minutes after every reading.
4. A reading is considered acceptable only if the reading's ID has a range difference of 3 for 60 seconds and this reading is consistent with previous readings of the same substance.

5 readings of various substances were taken, each for 60 seconds, however due to the sensor's limitation only 5 substances, namely, HiGeen Papaya hand sanitizer, Glue Stick, Obama perfume, Faber-Castell permanent marker and Pentel permanent marker gave acceptable readings for the purification method. The acceptable readings are discussed and analyzed in the following section.

Data Analysis

In data analysis, the readings of the 5 odors will be analyzed. A total of 300 readings were taken for each odor over 5 sessions of 60 readings each. Each reading has an ID as shown in Figure 12 and a strength value as shown in Figure 13.

Figure 12 shows the ID values of the odor readings. At the bottom of the figure the ID values of Obama perfume are represented by round dotted dashes. The ID values of Obama perfume range between 53 and 55. Above it we have the ID values of Glue Stick are shown that range between 57 and 59. In the middle the Pentel marker's ID values are shown that range between 77 and 79. At the top, the overlapping range values of HiGeen hand sanitizer and Faber-Castell marker are displayed. HiGeen's values range between 86 and 88, while Faber-Castell's values range between 87 and 89.

Figure 12. Odors IDs

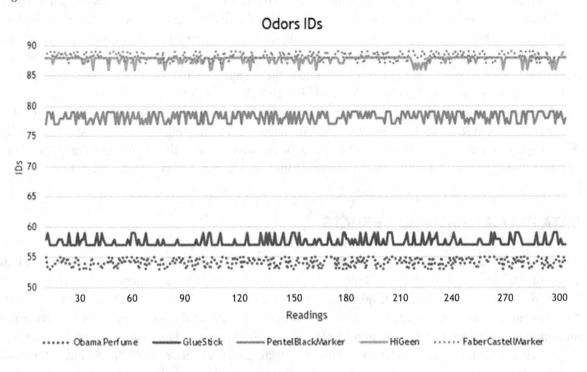

Figure 13. Odors strengths

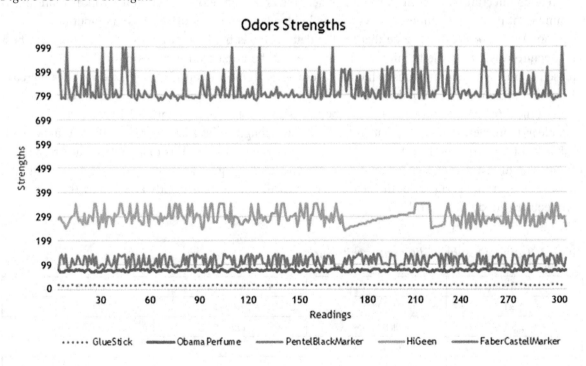

In Figure 12 strengths (the intensity) of the odors are plotted. Glue Stick's strength readings are shown at the bottom of the figure through round dotted dashes. Its readings gave a uniform strength reading that ranged between 16 and 19. Above the Glue Stick, we have the strength readings for Obama perfume that ranged between 70 and 82. The perfume's readings overlap a bit with the strength readings of Pentel marker that ranged between 80 and 143. In the middle, the strength readings of HiGeen that range between 241 and 352 are illustrated. Finally, at the top Faber-Castell marker's strength readings are shown that range between 779 and 999. The first two odors discussed i.e., Glue Stick and Obama perfume display uniform changes in strength. However, the strength range of the remaining odors vary widely especially the strength of Faber-Castell. This could be due to the reason that when these substances are exposed to air, their strength reduces as their odor disperses (Mukhtar, Ullman, Carey, & Lacey, 2004).

DATA PROCESSING AND RESULTS

For processing the data and identifying the odors using the neural network the readings were divided into a ratio of 20, 70 and 30 for validation, training and testing according to the findings of Data Division for Neural Networks (Shahin, Maier, & Jaksa, 2004). This means that 20% out of the total readings (1500) was selected randomly for validation set. Out of the remaining 1200 readings 70% were selected randomly for training the network and the remaining 360 readings (30%) were used for testing the trained network.

To train the neural network different architectures were used to evaluate which one would be the most appropriate. Training was done till an error rate of 0.1000 was obtained. The details of trainings using different architectures are given in Table 2, where the architecture of the neural network is represented as number of input layer: number of neurons in hidden layer: number of neurons in output layer.

From Table 2 we can conclude that for the data that was presented to the neural network the best architecture was 2:6:1. The training time decreased as the number of neurons in hidden layer was increased till the number of neurons in hidden layer was 7. Number of epochs decreased with the increase of number of neurons in the hidden layer. However, no significant change was seen in the validation rate, yet the 2:6:1 architecture acquired the best validation rate too. A simple 2:2:1 architecture was not suitable as there were overlapping data in both ID and Strength values, and therefore, the neural network took a lot of time to train itself to achieve a max error rate of 0.1000. It is to be noted that irrespective of which architecture is chosen for training, if it achieves the required max error rate while training, the testing and querying accuracy of the neural network will not be significantly affected by the network's architecture (Foody & Arora, 1997).

Table 2. Training results of different architectures

Architecture	Training Time	Epochs Completed	Validation Rate
2:2:1	1h 29m 14s	3,640,445	0.04680
2:3:1	0h 04m 45s	179,849	0.03773
2:4:1	0h 02m 19s	68,189	0.03816
2:5:1	0h 02m 07s	66,257	0.03841
2:6:1	0h 01m 39s	39,876	0.03752
2:7:1	0h 01m 52s	36,593	0.03791

After training the network with the purified data, testing was performed to test the performance of the network. All 360 testing samples were correctly classified by the neural network, which meant that a 100% accuracy rate was obtained as shown in Figure 14 generated by the program.

Figure 14. Testing performance report

Network Testing Performance Report

Network Details

Name:	ANNeNose
Type:	ActivationNetwork
Layout:	6-1
Function:	SigmoidFunction
Description:	

Network Schema

Inputs:	ID, Strength
Outputs:	*Output*

* Underlined fields indicates a categorical (non numeric) field

Training Details

Training Entries:	840
Validation Entries:	300
Training Deviation:	0.0999998878999852

Testing Summary

Testing Entries:		360
Testing Items:		360
Hits:	360	100.00%
Correct:	360	100.00%
Incorrect:	0	0.00%
Errors:	0	0.00%

CONCLUSION AND FINDINGS

With advancements in technology and the never-ending goal of making life easier for humans, it is evident that odor sensing could lead to a better tomorrow. This paper discussed the various applications odor sensing could be used in and has been used for. Various researches have been done in this field using various other techniques to help develop this field of research. Most of research has been specifically focused on a single industry or field of application. Our paper focused on and developed a system using Artificial Neural Network with an E-Nose and laid the foundation for a general-purpose system which can be used for various applications and in various industries.

The smell sensor used in this research was an OMX-GR sensor which is a semiconductor based gas sensor. Along with the smell sensor as hardware, Artificial Neural Network was used as software which was built on top of Sinapse framework and the framework itself was heavily modified as well to fit the needs of the project. Due to the sensor being old, and its other various limitations. Many methods had to be tried for data collection. Adjustments had to be made to the distance between sample and the sensor while collecting readings, to its recovery times, and to other external factors to ensure the readings were precise. The data was also cleaned and went through a purification process as mentioned in detail in the previous sections.

After collecting data and its purification, it was fed to the ANN to train on and then the Artificial Neural Network was tested for accuracy. This process was repeated for all the samples that were taken. Backpropagation algorithm was used for the training and adjustment of weights to ensure the results were precise and accurate.

- **Findings:** The system developed in this research could differentiate between various types of odors with an accuracy of between 93-100%. It suggests that Artificial Neural Networks can be very efficiently utilized with smell sensors for the detection of various odors due to the large amount of data involved in the nature of the problem and the capability of ANN to learn and train further as more data is provided and hence increasing its precision.
- **Limitations:** There were various limitations that affected the research, mainly, those related to the smell sensor. The smell sensor used in this research is an OMX-GR sensor which was produced a decade and half ago. Due to this, data collection method had to be adapted per the sensor's limitation. Some of these limitations were related to connectivity issues as the Serial Port of the sensor uses legacy drivers which are rare to find. Therefore, necessary drivers had to be implemented within the system to make the sensor compatible. Furthermore, due to the lack of extensive documentation of the sensor, various experimentation and tweaks had to be made to the data collection methods to ensure the most accurate data was collected. Some of the data collection issues were related to the recovery and response time of the sensor.

Some software related limitations were the limitation of the framework used as well. This led to creation of various new functions to make the system perform better and faster and to make it much easier to use.

- **Future Implementations:** In the future, work could be done to test the system with various other sensors that are modern and precise to get readings of more odors with more parameters i.e., response time, to have a high accuracy with higher number of odors. Moreover, the ability to create a cloud-based datahub on which various researches could contribute with their data and samples to train the ANN could as well lead to further developments in the field of odor sensing. In terms of the developed software, it can be improved by combining the ANN with a Genetic algorithm to overcome getting stuck in local minima while training.

REFERENCES

Al-Bastaki, Y. (2009). An Artificial Neural Networks-Based on-Line Monitoring Odor Sensing System. *Journal of Computational Science*, *11*, 878–882.

Ampuero, S., & Bosset, J. O. (2003). The electronic nose applied to dairy products: A review. *Sensors and Actuators. B, Chemical*, *94*(1), 1–12. doi:10.1016/S0925-4005(03)00321-6

Bartheld, C., Bahney, J., & Herculano-Houzel, S. (2016). The search for true numbers of neurons and glial cells in the human brain: A review of 150 years of cell counting. *The Journal of Comparative Neurology*, *524*(18), 3865–3895. doi:10.1002/cne.24040 PMID:27187682

Bell, A. (1914). *Discovery and Invention*. Washington, DC: National Geographic Society.

Bicego, M., Tessari, G., Tecchiolli, G., & Bettinelli, M. (2002). A comparative analysis of basic pattern recognition techniques for the development of small size electronic nose. *Sensors and Actuators. B, Chemical*, *85*(1), 137–144. doi:10.1016/S0925-4005(02)00065-5

Bishop, C. (2006). *Pattern recognition and Machine Learning*. Springer.

Bochenkov, V., & Sergeev, G. (2010). Sensitivity, selectivity, and stability of gas-sensitive metal-oxide nanostructures. *Metal Oxide Nanostructures and Their Applications*, *3*, 31-52.

D'Amico, A., Pennazza, G., Santonico, M., Martinelli, E., Roscioni, C., Galluccio, G., & Di Natale, C. (2010). An investigation on electronic nose diagnosis of lung cancer. *Lung Cancer (Amsterdam, Netherlands)*, *68*(2), 170–176. doi:10.1016/j.lungcan.2009.11.003 PMID:19959252

Demuth, H. B., Beale, M. H., De Jess, O., & Hagan, M. T. (2014). *Neural network design*. Martin Hagan.

Di Natale, C., Macagnano, A., Martinelli, E., Paolesse, R., D'Arcangelo, G., Roscioni, C., & D'Amico, A. (2003). Lung cancer identification by the analysis of breath by means of an array of non-selective gas sensors. *Biosensors & Bioelectronics*, *18*(10), 1209–1218. doi:10.1016/S0956-5663(03)00086-1 PMID:12835038

Foody, G., & Arora, M. (1997). An evaluation of some factors affecting the accuracy of classification by an artificial neural network. *International Journal of Remote Sensing*, *18*(4), 799–810. doi:10.1080/014311697218764

Friedman, J. (2001). Greedy function approximation: A gradient boosting machine. *Annals of Statistics*, *29*(5), 1189–1232. doi:10.1214/aos/1013203451

Gardner, J. (1987). Pattern recognition in the Warwick Electronic Nose. *8th International Congress of European Chemoreception Research Organization*.

Gardner, J., & Barlett, P. (1994). A Brief History of Electronic Noses. *Sensors and Actuators. B, Chemical*, *18*(1-3), 211–220. doi:10.1016/0925-4005(94)87085-3

Gardner, J., & Bartlett, P. (1992). Pattern recognition in odour sensing. *Sensors and sensory systems for an electronic nose*, 161-179.

Gardner, J. W., Shin, H. W., & Hines, E. L. (2000). An electronic nose system to diagnose illness. *Sensors and Actuators. B, Chemical, 70*(1), 19–24. doi:10.1016/S0925-4005(00)00548-7

Gurney, K. (1997). *An introduction to neural networks*. CRC Press. doi:10.4324/9780203451519

Hanson, C. W., & Thaler, E. R. (2005). Electronic nose prediction of a clinical pneumonia score: Biosensors and microbes. *The Journal of the American Society of Anesthesiologists, 102*(1), 63–68. PMID:15618788

Haykin, S. (2009). *Neural networks and learning machines*. Upper Saddle River, NJ: Pearson.

Haykin, S. (2011). *Neural Networks and Learning Machines* (3rd ed.). Pearson.

Herculano-Houzel, S. (2009). The human brain in numbers: A linearly scaled-up primate brain. *Frontiers in Human Neuroscience, 3*(31). PMID:19915731

Kalita, P., Saikia, M., & Singh, N. (2015). Electronic-Nose Technology and its Application -A Systematic Survey. *International Journal of Innovative Research in Electrical Electronics Instrumentation and Control Engineering, 3*(1), 123–128. doi:10.17148/IJIREEICE.2015.3126

Kim, E., Lee, S., Kim, J. H., Kim, C., Byun, Y. T., Kim, H. S., & Lee, T. (2012). Pattern recognition for selective odor detection with gas sensor arrays. *Sensors (Basel), 12*(12), 16262–16273. doi:10.3390121216262 PMID:23443378

Lang, H. P., Braun, T., Schmid, D., Hunziker, P., Jung, C., Hegner, M., & Gerber, C. (2007). An Artificial Nose Based on Microcantilever Array Sensors. *Journal of Physics: Conference Series, 61*, 663–667. doi:10.1088/1742-6596/61/1/133

Lee, S. H., Kwon, O. S., Song, H. S., Park, S. J., Sung, J. H., Jang, J., & Park, T. H. (2012). Mimicking the human smell sensing mechanism with an artificial nose platform. *Biomaterials, 33*(6), 1722–1729. doi:10.1016/j.biomaterials.2011.11.044 PMID:22153868

Li, S. (2009). Overview of Odor Detection Instrumentation and the Potential for Human Odor Detection in Air Matrices. *MITRE Innovation Program and US Government Nano-enabled Technology Initiative*, 5-43.

Luo, D., Hosseini, H. G., & Stewart, J. R. (2004). Application of ANN with extracted parameters from an electronic nose in cigarette brand identification. *Sensors and Actuators. B, Chemical, 99*(2), 253–257. doi:10.1016/j.snb.2003.11.022

Ma, C., Forbes, A., Llano, D., Berger-Wolf, T., & Kenyon, R. (2016). Swordplots: Exploring neuron behavior within dynamic communities of brain networks. *Electronic Imaging, 60*(1), 1–13.

Madan, M., & Dandina, H. (1994). *Neuro-Control Systems: Theory and Applications*. IEEE Press.

Mohamed, E. I., Linder, R., Perriello, G., Di Daniele, N., Pöppl, S. J., & De Lorenzo, A. (2002). Predicting Type 2 diabetes using an electronic nose-based artificial neural network analysis. *Diabetes, Nutrition & Metabolism, 15*(4), 215–221. PMID:12416658

Moncrieff, R. (1961). An instrument for measuring and classifying odours. *Journal of Applied Physiology, 16*, 742–749. PMID:13771984

Mukhtar, S., Ullman, J., Carey, J., & Lacey, R. (2004). A review of literature concerning odors, ammonia, and dust from broiler production facilities: 3. Land application, processing, and storage of broiler litter. *Journal of Applied Poultry Research, 13*(3), 514–520. doi:10.1093/japr/13.3.514

Nagarajan, N., & Stevens, C. (2008). How does the speed of thought compare for brains and digital computers? *Current Biology, 18*(17), 756–758. doi:10.1016/j.cub.2008.06.043 PMID:18786380

Nagle, H. T., Gutierrez-Osuna, R., & Schiffman, S. S. (1998). The How and Why of Electronic Noses. *IEEE Spectrum, 35*(9), 22–24. doi:10.1109/6.715180

Pearce, T. C., Schiffman, S. S., Nagle, H. T., & Gardner, J. W. (2006). *Handbook of machine olfaction: electronic nose technology*. John Wiley & Sons.

Penza, M., Cassano, G., Tortorella, F., & Zaccaria, G. (2001). Classification of food, beverages and perfumes by WO 3 thin-film sensors array and pattern recognition techniques. *Sensors and Actuators. B, Chemical, 73*(1), 76–87. doi:10.1016/S0925-4005(00)00687-0

Persaud, K., & Dodd, G. (1982). Analysis of discrimination mechanisms in the mammalian olfactory system using a model nose. *Nature, 299*(5881), 352–355. doi:10.1038/299352a0 PMID:7110356

Powers, W. (2004). *The science of smell, part 3: odor detection and measurement*. Iowa State University Extension PM.

Schaller, E., Bosset, J. O., & Escher, F. (1998). 'Electronic Noses' and Their Application to Food. *Lebensmittel-Wissenschaft + Technologie, 31*(4), 305–316. doi:10.1006/fstl.1998.0376

Shahin, M., Maier, H., & Jaksa, M. (2004). Data division for developing neural networks applied to geotechnical engineering. *Journal of Computing in Civil Engineering, 18*(2), 105–114. doi:10.1061/(ASCE)0887-3801(2004)18:2(105)

Shinyei. (n.d.). *Handheld Odor Meter OMX-GR Operation Manual*. Kyomachi: Shinyei.

Solomon, D. A. (2015). Neuron the Memory Unit of the Brain. *IOSR Journal of Computer Engineering, 17*(14), 48–61.

Spitzer, M. (2006). Brain research and learning over the life cycle. In Schooling for tomorrow: Personalising education (pp. 47-62). Academic Press. doi:10.1787/9789264036604-4-en

Tang, K. T., Chiu, S. W., Pan, C. H., Hsieh, H. Y., Liang, Y. S., & Liu, S. C. (2010). Development of a Portable Electronic Nose System for the Detection and Classification of Fruity Odors. *Sensors (Basel), 10*(10), 9179–9193. doi:10.3390101009179 PMID:22163403

Thaler, E. R., & Hanson, C. W. (2006). Use of an electronic nose to diagnose bacterial sinusitis. *American Journal of Rhinology, 20*(2), 170–172. PMID:16686381

Wan, E. (1993). *Finite impulse response neural networks with applications in time series prediction* (Doctoral dissertation). Stanford University, Stanford, CA.

Wilkens, W., & Hatman, A. (1964). An electronic analog for olfactory processes. *Journal of Food Science, 29*(3), 372–378. doi:10.1111/j.1365-2621.1964.tb01746.x PMID:14220555

Wilson, A., & Baietto, M. (2009). Applications and Advances in Electronic-Nose technologies. *Sensors (Basel)*, *9*(7), 5099–5148. doi:10.339090705099 PMID:22346690

Zhang, G., Patuwo, E., & Hu, Y., M. (1998). Forecasting with artificial neural networks: The state of the art. *International Journal of Forecasting*, *14*, 35–60. doi:10.1016/S0169-2070(97)00044-7

Chapter 18
Artificial Neural Network (ANN) Modeling of Odor Threshold Property of Diverse Chemical Constituents of Black Tea and Coffee

Jillella Gopala Krishna
NIPER Kolkata, Kolkata, India

Probir Kumar Ojha
(iD) https://orcid.org/0000-0003-4796-3915
Jadavpur University, Kolkata, India

ABSTRACT

The authors have developed an artificial neural network model using odor threshold (OT) property data for diverse odorant components present in black tea (76 components) and coffee (46 components). The models were validated in terms of both internal and external validation criteria signifying acceptable results. The authors found the significant features controlling the OT property using Mean Absolute Error (MAE)-based criteria in a backward elimination of descriptors, one in each turn. The present results well-corroborated the previously published PLS-regression based chemometric model results.

1. INTRODUCTION

Tea is the most commonly consumed nonalcoholic beverage after water. The consumption of tea is a very ancient habit. In 1978, an Archeological research reported by Jelinek suggested that the infusion of leaves from the tea tree was probably practiced more than 500 000 years ago (Gutman, & Ryu, 1996). Black tea is originated from the two varieties such as *Camellia assamica* and *Camellia sinensis*. Black tea and green tea are produced from the same plant *Camellia sinensis* but the name varies due to how the

DOI: 10.4018/978-1-6684-2408-7.ch018

plant's leaves are processed (Hara, Luo, Wickremashinghe, & Yamanishi, 1995). Black tea is grown and processed all over the world in varying geographies and climates. Though, China is the largest producer of tea, but India, Sri Lanka and Africa are the top three producers of black tea today (Mary, & Robert, 2011). Among the different varieties of tea, black tea is most widely used worldwide due to its flavour. In case of black tea preparation, before the heat processing and drying, the leaves are allowed to oxidize fully which turn the leaves from the rich dark brown to black colour for which black tea leaves are famous for. The change of colour occurs due to the interactions between the tea plant cell walls and oxygen. This oxidation process alters the flavor profile of black tea. The enzyme, catechol oxidase, acts as a catalyst in the oxidation process leading to the formation of theaflavins and thearubigins from flavanols which are responsible for the characteristic colour and flavor of fermented tea (Robertson, 1992; Borse, Rao, Nagalakshmi, & Krishnamurthy, 2002; Bhattacharyya et al., 2008). Thus, the characteristics flavour is the key element for identification or evaluation of tea. Flavour of black tea is due to the presence of taste and aroma active components. Volatile components (around 600 volatile compounds have been reported in tea leaves) like aldehydes, alcohols, ketones, furans, and aromatic compounds control the aroma of black tea while the non-volatile components like organic acids, polyphenols, sugars, caffeine, catechin, theaflavins, thearubigins and free amino acids, among others are responsible for taste of black tea (Wang et al., 2011; Rawat et al., 2007; Bondarovich et al., 1967). Though, the volatile components are present in minute amount, but these have high impact to regulate the flavour of the black tea due to their low threshold values (Rawat et al., 2007).

Like tea, coffee, though young, is also an important beverage used worldwide due to its flavour as well as its potential health benefit (Balentine, Wiseman, & Bouwens, 1997; Halder et al., 2005). Coffee is prepared from roasted coffee beans, the seeds of berries from certain *Coffea* species. This is one of the major sources of income for many countries like Brazil, Vietnam, Colombia, Indonesia, Ethiopia, India, Honduras, Uganda, Mexico, Guatemala, Peru, etc. As of 2018, Brazil is producing one-third of the world total coffee (Coffee Annual Brazil - USDA GAIN reports, 2018). The worldwide popularity of this beverage is due to some factors, among which, flavour is the main reason. Thus, distinctive characteristics of smell can help in the identification of different food and beverages. This is also very helpful in case of perfume and beverage industries for masking the obnoxious odor of chemicals used in different food, pharmaceuticals and cosmetic products. An odor is the impression in the brain obtained by the recognition of a volatile compound at a very low concentration by odorant receptors (ORs) which is perceived by the sense of olfaction of human or other animals.

1.1. Odor Threshold and Evaluation

The odor threshold (OT) is the minimum concentration at which all panelists have been able to recognize the odor sensitivity (Leonardos, Kendall, & Barnard, 1969). A trained Panel of four staff members of the Food and Flavor Section of Arthur D. Little, Inc. was used for determining the odor threshold of each chemical. The Panel members were selected from a pool of approximately fifteen observers with more than one year of analytical odor work. Only one chemical was observed per day by the panel. Before the observations of a chemical, the Panel examined the odor at diverse dilutions to familiarize with the odor type. Each chemical was examined with the five different concentrations. The first odor observation of the day was the background level of test room. A concentration range was selected for inclusion of the odor threshold. The Panel members were not informed of the concentration of the chemical in the test room. The results obtained from each panelist were examined separately. Each Panel member was required to be present for all the odor examinations scheduled for the day, as a different concentration was evaluated at each session. The Panel members were not allowed to make continuous observations, every observation was separated within 25 minutes. Afterwards, range and concentration were decided by the Panel members. A positive response is indicated for each concentration at which the Panelist described the odor of the chemical. The concentration ranges were changed on a random basis, the threshold concentration for each subject was determined by recording positive responses as a function of the concentration. The threshold is the least concentration, i.e., when the Panelist could define the odor and it would be constantly observed in higher concentrations. Chemical odor is compiled in this manner for each Panel member. The odor threshold reported is the concentration at which all four panel members could positively recognize the odor of the chemical (Leonardos, Kendall, & Barnard, 1974). This property is typical attribute for individual component and has been reliable in their response at all higher test concentrations. Since there is no such modern technology which can mimic the efficiency of human nose and can characterize different types of odor with the similar sensitivity.

1.2. Why Machine Learning Approach?

In this regard, *in silico* tool can be applied for the prediction of OT property of odorants. Quantitative structure-activity relationships (QSARs) have been used for prediction of biological activity/property/ toxicity to understand of the mechanism(s) of action (Hansch, Kurup, Garg, & Gao, 2001). Sometimes, it is very difficult to explain all the sources of variability due to the complexity between the molecular structure and activity/property/toxicity. In this complex situation, machine learning approach like artificial neural networks (ANNs) may be used for the predictions (Haykin, 1994; Agatonovic-Kustrin, & Beresford, 2000). However, most of the common drawback of machine learning approaches is failure to interpret the relationships between the independent variables and the response variables (Polishchuk, 2017).

In the present work, we have developed ANN models separately using OT property data for diverse chemical classes of odor active components present in black tea and coffee and tried to found out the significant features controlling OT property using Mean Absolute Error (MAE) based criteria. The ANN models were developed in this study keeping in mind the principles of Organization for Economic Co-operation and Development (OECD) (http://www.oecd.org/dataoecd/33/37/37849783.pdf).

2. METHODS AND MATERIALS

2.1. Dataset

The present work deals with modeling of the OT property data for diverse chemical classes (aldehydes, acids, esters, furans, sulfur containing compounds, thiols, thiophenes, thiazoles, furanones, ketones, norisoprenoids, phenolic compounds, pyrazines, pyridines, terpenes, etc.) of compounds present in black tea and coffee collected from the published literature (Yeretzian, 2017; Magagna et al., 2017). The whole datasets of black tea (76 compounds) and coffee (46 compounds) are presented in Tables 6 and 7 respectively in Supplementary Section. Here, we have developed two multi-layer perceptron (MLP) based ANN models separately using the odor active components present in black tea and coffee. The odor threshold (OT) of compounds present in black tea and coffee are expressed in mmol/kg and in µmol/kg respectively. The OT values are taken in the negative logarithmic scale [log(1/OT)] leading to Y values ranging from -0.935 to 7.677 (in case of black tea) and -1.736 to 5.532 (in case of the coffee). The initial modelling analysis identified one compound as potential outlier (based on a high residual value) in case of the tea dataset. Thus, the final ANN model was developed using 76 components present in black tea.

2.2. Descriptor Calculation

We have drawn individually all compounds in the data sets using Marvin Sketch software (http://www.chemaxon.com). Descriptors are "numerical values associated with chemical constitution for correlation of chemical structure with various physical properties, chemical reactivity or biological activity". Using the drawn structures, we have calculated the descriptors using three software tools namely Dragon software version 6 (http://www.talete.mi.it/products/dragondescription.htm), PaDEL-Descriptor (http://www.yapcwsoft.com/dd/padeldescriptor) software and Cerius 2 version 4.10 software (http://www.accelrys.com). Dragon software was used to calculate constitutional indices, ring descriptors, connectivity indices, functional group counts, atom centered fragments, atom type E-state indices and 2D atom pairs descriptors while PaDEL-descriptor software was used to calculate extended topochemical atom (ETA) indices (Das, & Roy, 2016). Before computation of 3D descriptors, all structures were optimized using the "optimal search method" available in Cerius2 software version4.10 (http://www.accelrys.com). All the 3D descriptors were calculated using geometry optimized molecules. Thus, the models were developed in this work using a pool of both 2D and 3D descriptors. From the initial pool of descriptors, we have removed those descriptors having constant and near constant values (standard deviation less than 0.0001), variables with at least one missing value, descriptors with all missing values and descriptors with (absolute) pair correlation larger than or equal to 0.95.

2.3. Division of the Dataset: Selection of Training and Test Sets

We have employed a clustering technique, "Modified *k*-medoids" (Park,& Jun, 2009), using a tool developed in our laboratory (http://teqip.jdvu.ac.in/QSAR_Tools/DTCLab) for division of the datasets. Seven clusters were generated in case of components present in black tea, and four clusters were generated in case of components present in coffee based on the properties available for the respective dataset components. Based on the clusters, we have taken approximately 75% compounds randomly from each cluster for the training set (57 compounds and 36 compounds in case of the tea and coffee datasets respectively) and remaining 25% compounds for the test set (19 compounds in case of the tea dataset and 10 compounds for the coffee dataset). The ANN model was developed using the training set compounds, and the test set compounds were used to validate the ANN models. Note that we have used same division pattern of the data sets for development of final ANN models as reported in the paper published previously by our group (Ojha, & Roy, 2018).

2.4. Descriptor Selection

Using the whole pool of descriptors, first we have performed stepwise regression for selection of the descriptors. We have removed the selected descriptors after the first run of stepwise regression, and rerun stepwise regression using remaining pool of descriptors. In this way, we have selected 48 descriptors in case of the tea and 40 descriptors in case of the coffee dataset as also discussed in our previous paper (Ojha, & Roy, 2018). This reduced pool of descriptors was used for the development of the final ANN models.

2.5. Optimization of Parameters and Development of ANN Models

Artificial Neural Network (ANN) is a multilayered architecture made up of one or more hidden layers placed between the input and output layers (Agatonovic-Kustrin, & Beresford, 2000). In the present work, a multilayer perceptron (MLP) neural network with the Broyden-Fletcher-Goldfarb-Shanno (BFGS) algorithm (Head, & Zerner, 1985) was used to construct ANN models. BFGS is also known as variant of Gradient descent method which overcomes the limitations of plain gradient descent by seeking the second derivative (a stationary point) of the cost function (Liu, & Nocedal, 1989). Hence, this domain is created to predict odorant property of black tea and coffee. The network requires iterative training phases, which may be slow, but the networks are quite compact, execute quickly once trained and in most cases yield better results than the other types of networks (Zuvela, David, & Wong, 2018). In this study, the same methodology of ANN was used to generate separately the predictive models correlating a set of reduced pool molecular descriptors and odorant properties of the components present in black tea and coffee using STATISTICA software (version 13.4) (Statistica, 2016). The process starts with splitting of the (training) datasets with subset variable sampling method. The training process is a feed forward network. The input layer contains all the relevant descriptors obtained after reducing the initial pool of descriptors in order to investigate the prediction capability of the proposed ANN methods. The next one is a hidden layer. The performance of neural network depends on the number of hidden layers and number of neurons in the hidden layers. In this study, the neural network architecture is trained with different combinations of hidden layers and single output layer with 5 types of activation functions/ Transfer functions namely Identity, Logistic, Tanh, Exponential and Sine which are available for hidden and output layers. The final ANN model was developed using 3 nodes with Logistic activation function in case of the black tea dataset and 2 nodes with identity activation function in case of the coffee dataset. Basically, Identity function is the operation of artificial neural network which sum up the product of the associated weight and the input signal and produce an output (Godfrey, & Gashler, 2015). The second one is sigmoid or logistic activation function which normalizes the data between0to1. Therefore, it is especially used for models to predict the probability as an output. Sigmoid is the right choice because it is differentiable, that means, we can find the slope of the sigmoid curve at any two points (Godfrey, & Gashler, 2015). The third one in the process is Tanh activation function, also known as hyperbolic tangent activation function. It is like logistic or sigmoid function, but better predictions are possible. The range of Tanh functions is from -1 to 1. The next activation function is the exponential activation function, which speeds up learning in neural networks and leads to higher classification accuracies. Here, α is an exponential hyper parameter, which controls the value to which an Exponential activation saturates for negative net inputs. This function diminishes the vanishing gradient effect like rectified linear units (ReLUs) and leaky ReLUs (LReLUs). The vanishing gradient problem is alleviated because the positive part of these functions is the identity. Therefore, their derivative is one and it is not contractive. In contrast, the exponential function has negative values which push the mean of the activations closer to zero. Mean activations that are closer to zero enable faster learning as they bring the gradient closer to the natural gradient. The exponential activation function saturates to a negative value when the argument gets smaller. Saturation means a small derivative which decreases the variation and the information that is propagated to the next layer (Clevert, Unterthiner, & Hochreiter, 2015). The final activation function of the process is *Sine*. It is a periodic function, and unlike other activation functions it is non-quasiconvex and non-monotonic. This means that for a periodic activation function, as the correlation with the input increases, the activation will oscillate between stronger and weaker activations. This apparently undesirable behavior might suggest that periodic functions might be just as undesirable as activation functions in a typical learning task (Parascandolo, Huttunen, & Virtanen, 2016). After selection of activation function, another pivotal parameter is the Weights of neural network. For the optimized predictive model, always less weight is preferable. An increase in weights may cause over fitting problem. Weights in the hidden layers and the output layer maintained uniformly throughout the process. Here, for the development of the final ANN models, we have selected the network weight decay in hidden and output layer is 0.0001-0.001. The training process is continued to develop the model until error reaches performance goal (minimum error and maximum accuracy) that will be decided by Initialization. It is an iterative process where the user defined the seed number to decide how many times the process need to be cycled. In this work, we have used 1000 iterations for the development of ANN model in case of the tea dataset and 120 iterations in case of the coffee dataset. During the process of training, the software provides summary details about the networks being built including the type of network, the activation functions utilized, the training cycle configuration and the appropriate error terms. Once the training process of neural network is completed, the results are displayed. The active neural networks grid will show the top five networks generated during the training in which only one predictive model will be selected based on the training set and test set performances.

2.6. Strategy Used to Find Out the Significant Descriptors

After selection of the optimized model, we wanted to see the relative importance of different descriptors used in model development employing MAE based criteria (Roy et al., 2016). To achieve that, every time one descriptor is removed and the model is rebuilt with the rest of the descriptors without interrupting the network architecture used to develop the parent model. In this way,48 individual descriptor omission models are constructed in case of the black tea dataset and 40 models are constructed in case of the coffee dataset. After that, we have calculated Mean Absolute Error (MAE) for models obtained from individual descriptor omissions in case of both the black tea and coffee datasets and checked the MAE variations in each case after comparing with the MAE of the parent models. Furthermore, based on the MAE variation, all the input descriptors were divided into three types, category-I (significant descriptors: MAE changes>+0.01), category-II (redundant descriptors: MAE varies between +0.01 to -0.01) and category-III (noisy descriptors: MAE changes<-0.01).

2.7. Statistical Validation Parameters and Applicability Domain (AD)

The developed ANN model was validated in terms of both internal (R^2_{train}) and external (Q^2_{F1}) validation parameters (Ojha, & Roy, 2011; Roy, Ambure, Kar, & Ojha, 2018; Ojha, & Roy, 2018; Roy, Ghosh, Ojha, & Roy, 2018; Ojha, Kar, Roy, & Leszczynski, 2018). The parameters obtained for the final ANN models are depicted in Table 1. The AD of a QSAR model is represented by the chemical space which is provided by the molecular properties of the training set compounds. The AD criteria help to check whether a query compound lies inside the domain of chemical space of the training set compounds or not. In this work, we have checked the applicability domain of test set compounds of the developed ANN models employing the standardization approach using the software developed in our laboratory

(Roy, Kar, & Ambure, 2015). The reliability of prediction of a QSPR model is considered good if the molecules are present within the region of the chemical space of the training set molecules.

The methods employed for the development of ANN models are represented graphically in Figure 1.

Figure 1. Schematic representation of the steps involved in the development of final ANN models

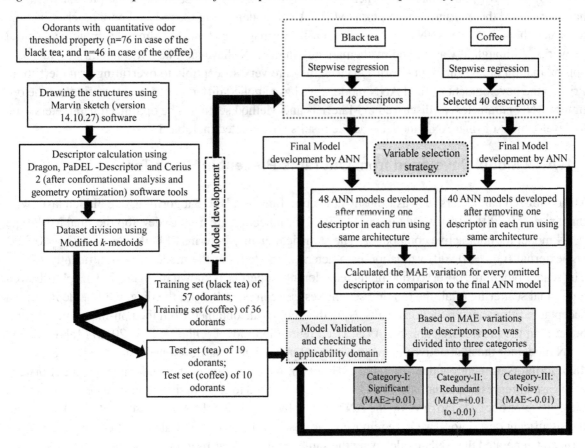

2.8. Software Used

Marvin sketch (version 14.10.27) software (http://www.chemaxon.com/) was used to draw the chemical structures. Dragon version 6 (http://www.talete.mi.it/products/dragondescription.htm), Cerius 2 (version 4.0) (http://www.accelrys.com) and PaDEL-Descriptor (http://www.yapcwsoft.com/dd/padeldescriptor) software tools were used to calculate the molecular descriptors. Modified *k*-medoid (http://teqip.jdvu.ac.in/QSAR_Tools/DTCLab) cluster analysis was performed by employing the software developed in our laboratory. The stepwise regression analysis was performed by using MINITAB software (version 14.13) (http://www.minitab.com/en-US/default.aspx). STATISTICA software (version 13.4) was used to develop the ANN models.

3. RESULTS AND DISCUSSION

To model the relationships between the molecular structure and the odor threshold (OT) property of black tea and coffee separately, we have employed *a-priori* selected reduced pool of molecular descriptors. The reduced pool descriptors were selected using various strategies as discussed in our previously published work (Ojha, & Roy, 2018) as well as here in Materials and methods section. In the present work, we have developed the multilayer perceptron (MLP) ANN models using the reduced pool descriptors only to reduce the noise. The ANN as a powerful non-linear mapping technique simulates biological neural networks. Although, it was proved mathematically that ANNs have an inherent capability of universal approximation of any function (Hornik, 1991), they are very susceptible to overfitting or underfitting. Prior to the development of final ANN models, we have applied different conditions to find out the optimum ANN parameters as discussed in Materials and Method section. The optimized parameters used to development of final ANN models and the results are depicted in Table 1.

3.1. ANN Model Developed from Odorants Present in Black Tea

The optimized parameters such as Logistic activation function, BFGS algorithm, one hidden layer with three nodes, 0.0001-0.001 weight decay and 1000 initialization are used to develop the final MLP type ANN model for odor active compounds. The statistical quality in terms of both internal (R^2_{train} =0.823) and external (Q^2_{F1} = 0.900) validation parameters suggested that the model was significantly robust. The scatter plot of the observed and predicted odorant properties is shown in Figure 2. This plot showed a minimal scattering of all the training set and test set compounds from the diagonal line depicting an acceptable fitting and prediction results. Note that the results obtained from the non-linear model is far better than the previously published PLS based regression model (Ojha, & Roy, 2018) (Table 1). The ANN model for the odor active compounds present in black tea was developed using the priori selected 48 descriptors as mentioned in the Table 2. However, interpretation of the model is not straightforward as in case of regression equations. In this work, we have tried to explore the significant descriptors from the descriptor pool used to develop the ANN model by employing the MAE based criteria. To find out the significant descriptors, we have removed one descriptor from the initial pool of descriptors in each turn, and generated the ANN model using the same architecture as used in the development of the final ANN model and calculated the variation of MAE for removing that particular descriptor. In this way, we have generated ANN models one by one for every omitted descriptor and calculated the MAE variation in each case. After removing the particular descriptor, if the MAE value is found to be higher as compared to that of the parent model then we can say that the impact of that particular descriptor is high. Based on the variation of MAE, we have divided the descriptors pool in three categories namely category-I, category-II and category-III (Table 2). The category-I (MAE varies +0.01 and above) descriptors are the most significant descriptors, category-II (MAE varies between +0.01 to -0.01) depicts redundant descriptors and the third category descriptors i.e., category-III (MAE varies -0.01 and lesser) are defined as noisy descriptors. In the black tea dataset, out of 48 descriptors, we have found out 26 descriptors as significant, 8 descriptors as redundant and 14 descriptors as noisy descriptors. Our results also well corroborated the previously published work by our group as out of six descriptors (obtained from the PLS regression-based model published previously by our group), five descriptors were identified as significant descriptors in the present work.

Table 1. The statistical results obtained from ANN-model of TEA and Coffee

MLP	Activation function	Weight. decay		Network	Initialization	Q2F1	$r^2_{m(test)}$	$\overline{r}^2_{m(test)}$	RMSEP	Training set		Test set	
(2-3 Hidden layers)		Hidden layer	Output layer		(seedcontrol)								
										MAE (100%)	MAE (95%)	MAE (100%)	MAE (95%)
Tea	Logistic	0.0001-0.001	0.0001-0.001	48-3-1	1000	0.781	0.716	0.14	0.596	0.801	0.707	0.401	0.351
Coffee	Identity	0.0001-0.001	0.0001-0.001	40-2-1	120	0.947	0.911	0.021	0.4	0.708	0.646	0.299	0.23

Table 2. Categorical list of descriptors obtained from the ANN model based on MAE (95%) in case of black tea dataset

Category	Sl. No	Descriptor removed	Definition	Type	Architecture	MAE (95%)	Changes in MAE
Category-1: Significant descriptors	1	H-051	H attached to alpha-C	Atom centred fragments	47-3-1	0.591	0.113
	2	F10[C-O]	Frequency of C-O at topological distance 10	2DAtomPairs	47-3-1	0.584	0.106
	3	Jurs-RPSA	Relative polar surface area: total polar surface area divided by the total molecular solvent-accessible surface area	Spatial descriptor	47-3-1	0.582	0.104
	4	ETA_dAlpha_B	DaB	ETA descriptor	47-3-1	0.57	0.092
	5	nRCHO	number of aldehydes (aliphatic)	Functional group counts	47-3-1	0.568	0.09
	6	H-047	H attached to C1(sp3)/C0(sp2)	Atom centred fragments	47-3-1	0.566	0.088
	7	SssssC	Sum of ssssC E-states	Atom-type E-state indices	47-3-1	0.562	0.084
	8	Hbond donor	Represents number of hydrogen bond donor	Structural descriptor	47-3-1	0.56	0.082
	9	Jurs-RASA	Relative hydrophobic surface area: total hydrophobic surface area divided by the total molecular solvent-accessible surface area	Spatial descriptor	47-3-1	0.557	0.079
	10	F04[C-C]	Frequency of C-C at topological distance 4	2DAtomPairs	47-3-1	0.557	0.079
	11	nCq	number of total quaternary C(sp3)	Functional group counts	47-3-1	0.555	0.077
	12	AlogP	Ghose-Crippenoctanol-water partition coeff. (logP)	Molecular properties	47-3-1	0.552	0.074

continues on following page

Table 2. Continued

Category	Sl. No	Descriptor removed	Definition	Type	Architecture	MAE (95%)	Changes in MAE
	13	Jurs-RPCG	Relative positive charge: charge of most positive atom divided by the total positive charge		47-3-1	0.55	0.072
	14	ETA_dEpsilon_C	DeC	Extended Topological Atom	47-3-1	0.545	0.067
	15	Jurs-RNCG	Relative negative charge: charge of most negative atom divided by the total negative charge	Spatial descriptor	47-3-1	0.54	0.062
	16	B03[C-O]	Presence/absence of C-O at topological distance 3	2DAtomPairs	47-3-1	0.538	0.06
	17	ETA_dPsi_A	DyA	Extended Topological Atom	47-3-1	0.533	0.055
	18	ETA_Eta_F	hF	Extended Topological Atom	47-3-1	0.528	0.05
	19	ETA_Shape_X	(Sa)X /Sa	Extended Topological Atom	47-3-1	0.528	0.05
	20	ETA_BetaP_ns	Sbns	Extended Topological Atom	47-3-1	0.524	0.046
	21	Jurs-WNSA-3	Surface-weighted charged partial surface areas	Spatial descriptor	47-3-1	0.516	0.038
	22	LUMO	Lowest unoccupied molecular orbitals	Electronic descriptors	47-3-1	0.512	0.034
	23	SssO	Sum of ssO E-states	Atom-type E-state indices	47-3-1	0.505	0.027
	24	nCconj	Number of non-aromatic conjugated C(sp2)	Functional group counts	47-3-1	0.504	0.026
	25	MR	Molar refractivity	Fragment constants descriptor	47-3-1	0.496	0.018
	26	nROH	number of hydroxyl groups	Functional group counts	47-3-1	0.491	0.013
Category-II: Redundant descriptors	27	X5Av	average valence connectivity index of order 5	Connectivity indices	47-3-1	0.486	0.008
	28	nRCOOH	number of carboxylic acids (aliphatic)	Functional group counts	47-3-1	0.479	0.001
	29	C-001	CH3R / CH4	Atom-centred fragments	47-3-1	0.475	-0.003
	30	H-049	"H" attached to C3(sp3)/C2(sp2)/C3(sp2)/C3(sp)	Atom-centredfragments	47-3-1	0.474	-0.004
	31	X3A	average connectivity index of order 3	Connectivity indices	47-3-1	0.473	-0.005
	32	B07[C-C]	Presence/absence of C-C at topological distance 7	2DAtomPairs	47-3-1	0.473	-0.005
	33	ETA_Psi_1	Y1	Extended Topological Atom	47-3-1	0.472	-0.006

continues on following page

Table 2. Continued

Category	Sl. No	Descriptor removed	Definition	Type	Architecture	MAE (95%)	Changes in MAE
	34	Jurs-RPCS	Relative positive charge surface area: solvent-accessible surface area of the most positive atom divided by descriptor	Spatial descriptor	47-3-1	0.469	-0.009
Category-III: Noisy descriptors	35	NdssC	Number of atoms of type dssC	Atom-type E-state indices	47-3-1	0.465	-0.013
	36	H-052	H attached to C0(sp3) with 1X attached to next C	Atom-centred fragments	47-3-1	0.461	-0.017
	37	O-060	Al-O-Ar / Ar-O-Ar / R..O..R / R-O-C=X	Atom-centred fragments	47-3-1	0.459	-0.019
	38	F04[C-O]	Frequency of C-O at topological distance 4	2DAtomPairs	47-3-1	0.454	-0.024
	39	X5A	average connectivity index of order 5	Connectivity indices	47-3-1	0.452	-0.026
	40	ETA_Epsilon_2	ε2	Extended Topological Atom	47-3-1	0.446	-0.032
	41	ETA_AlphaP	Sa/NV	Extended Topological Atom	47-3-1	0.445	-0.033
	42	NssssC	Number of atoms of type ssssC	Atom-type E-state indices	47-3-1	0.427	-0.051
	43	nDB	number of double bonds	Constitutional indices	47-3-1	0.422	-0.056
	44	F03[C-O]	Frequency of C-O at topological distance 3	2DAtomPairs	47-3-1	0.42	-0.058
	45	Jurs-PNSA-1	Partial negative surface area: sum of the solvent-accessible surface areas of all negatively charged atoms	Spatial descriptor	47-3-1	0.416	-0.062
	46	nR=Cs	number of aliphatic secondary C(sp2)	Functional group counts	47-3-1	0.412	-0.066
	47	B06[C-C]	Presence/absence of C-C at topological distance 6	2D Atom Pairs	47-3-1	0.412	-0.066
	48	B04[C-C]	Presence/absence of C-C at topological distance 4	2D Atom Pairs	47-3-1	0.391	-0.087

*MAE (95%): determined after removing 5% test or training sets chemicals with high residual values in order to obviate the possibility of any outlier predictions; MAE (100%): Determined using all training and test sets chemicals.

Table 3. Comparison of numerical values of the descriptors with odorant property of five most potent and five less potent odorants present in black tea

No.	NAME	log (1/OT)	H-051	Jurs-RPSA	ETA_dAlpha_B	nRCHO	H-047	SssssC	Hbond donor	Jurs-RASA	F04 [C-C]	AlogP
Five most potent odorants present in black tea												
68	β-Damascenone	7.677	0	0.072	0.012	0	4	-0.018	0	0.928	14	3.934
51	(E,Z)-2,6-Nonadienal	7.663	0	0.134	0.017	1	4	0	0	0.866	5	2.370
26	(Z)-4-heptenal	6.272	2	0.152	0.021	1	2	0	0	0.848	3	1.374
56	E,E)-2,4-Nonadienal	5.936	0	0.121	0.017	1	4	0	0	0.879	5	2.370
47	Linalool	5.410	0	0.076	0.015	0	4	-0.702	1	0.924	6	2.517
Five leastpotent odorants present in black tea												
12	2-Methyl propanoic acid	1.037	1	0.377	0.056	0	0	0	1	0.623	0	1.023
41	Benzyl alcohol	1.034	0	0.168	0.021	0	7	0	1	0.832	1	1.634
11	Propanoic acid	0.569	2	0.450	0.067	0	0	0	1	0.550	0	0.460
8	Acetic acid	0.080	3	0.561	0.083	0	0	0	1	0.439	0	-0.168
2	Acetone	-0.935	6	0.211	0.042	0	0	0	0	0.789	0	0.379

According to the MAE variation as depicted in Table 2, it is clear that the descriptors like H-051, F10[C-O], Jurs-RPSA, ETA_dAlpha_B, nRCHO, H-047,SssssC, Hbond donor, Jurs-RASA, F04[C-C], AlogP,Jurs-RPCG,ETA_dEpsilon_C,Jurs-RNCG,B03[C-O],ETA_dPsi_A,ETA_Eta_F,ETA_Shape_X, ETA_BetaP_ns, Jurs-WNSA-3, LUMO, SssO, nCconj, MR and nROH play dominant role to regulate the odorant property of black tea. To find out the relationship between the odorant property and the molecular properties, we have selected five higher odorant property containing compounds and five lower odorant property containing compounds and checked the trend of changes of the numerical values of significant descriptors (here we have mentioned only 10 descriptors in Table 3) and odorant property of the constituents present in black tea. It has been found that the trend is very similar, i.e., for the higher active compounds, the numerical values of the descriptors are either in higher range or in lower range based on the descriptors and vice versa (Table 3). As for example, in case of H-051 descriptor (Table 3), only one compound out of the five most potent odorant molecules have a nonzero descriptor value (compound number 26) while four compounds (compounds 12, 11, 8 and 2) have nonzero descriptor values out of the five least potent odorant molecules. Thus, the trend is like that potent odorants have lower descriptor values for H-051 and less potent odorants bear higher descriptor values.A similar trend is also observed in case of JURS-RPSA, ETA_dAlpha_B and Hbond donor descriptors. As shown in Table 3, in case of nRCHO, H-047, SssssC, Jurs-RASA, F04[C-C] and AlogP descriptors, the trend or pattern of changes of the numerical values of these descriptors is similar i.e., the potent odorants contain higher range of descriptor values and less potent odorants bear a lower range of numerical values. We have checked the applicability domain of the ANN model using the standardization approach. We found that all the test set compounds are within the applicability domain of the developed model.

Figure 2. The scatter plot of the observed and the predicted odorant properties [log(1/OT)] for the final ANN model developed from the components present in black tea. The dashed line indicates the best fit line based on test set compounds and the solid line indicates the best fit line based on the training set compounds.

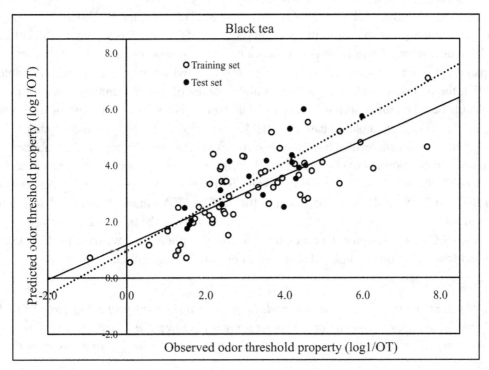

3.2. ANN Model Developed from Odorants Present in Coffee

The optimized parameters used to model the odorant properties of the components present in coffee are Identity as activation function, BFGS algorithm, 2 hidden layers, 0.0001-0.001 weight decay and 120 initialization. The model quality in terms of both internal (R^2_{train} = 0.908) and external (Q^2_{F1} = 0.980) validation parameters confirmed that the model was statistically robust (Table 1).The scatter plot of the observed and predicted odorant properties of the components present in coffee are shown in Figure 3, which showed limited deviations of the fitted values or predictions from the experimental values for the model confirming the acceptability of the model. The results obtained from the ANN models are better than those obtained from the previously published PLS based regression models (Ojha, & Roy, 2018). The ANN model for the odor active compounds present in coffee was developed by using the priori selected 40 descriptors as mentioned in the Table 4. We have found out the significant descriptors among the 40 descriptors used initially as input employing the same protocol as used in case of development of ANN model of odorant components present in black tea. Here also, we have divided the descriptors in three categories based on MAE variation in the same way as discussed earlier in case of the tea dataset. The MAE variation after removing each descriptor from the parent model is summarized in Table 4. Based on MAE variation, out of 40 descriptors as input, we have found out 24 descriptors as significant (category-I), 8 descriptors as redundant (category-II) and 8 descriptors as noisy descriptors (category-III). This results also well corroborated with the previously published work by our group as out of six descriptors (obtained from the PLS regression-based model published previously by our group), five descriptors were identified as significant descriptors here. According to the MAE variation as depicted in Table 4, it can be suggested that the descriptors like F01[C-S], C-024, B07[C-C], nS, B04[C-C], F05[C-C], B07[C-O], S-106, nRCO, Jurs-WPSA-2, ETA_Shape_P, C-040, Apol, nHDon, H-049, B02[C-S], nH, nRCOOH, B01[C-O], Jurs-RNCS, ETA_dAlpha_B, F04[C-N], ETA_Eta and B01[C-S] play a crucial role to control the odorant property of the components present in coffee. In this case, we have also selected five most potent odorants and five least potent odorants present in coffee and compared the trend of changes in the descriptors values with the odorant property (Table 5). We observed that the descriptor values are either in higher range or in lower range in case of potent odor active molecule based on the descriptors, and a similar pattern is also shown in case of least potent odor active molecules. As for example, in case of F01[C-S] descriptor (Table 5), two compounds out of the five most potent odorant molecules having non-zero descriptor value (compound numbers 19 and 16) while none of the compounds having non-zero descriptor values in case of five least potent odorant molecules. This pattern (i.e., higher descriptors value in the potent odor active molecules) is also shown in case of B07[C-C], nS, B04[C-C], F05[C-C], S-106, nRCO, ETA_Shape_P and Apol descriptors. The opposite pattern (i.e., lower or less number of descriptors value in the potent odor active molecules) is shown in case of C-024 descriptor. To check the domain of applicability, we have used standardization approach and found only one compound (compound number 14) as outlier.

Figure 3. The scatter plot of the observed and the predicted odorant properties [log(1/OT)] for the final ANN model developed from the components present in coffee. The dashed line indicates the best fit line based on test set compounds and the solid line indicates the best fit line based on the training set compounds.

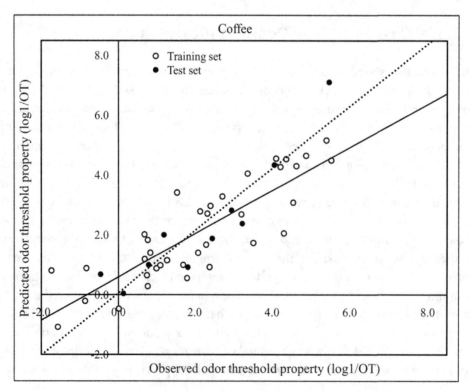

Table 5. Comparison of numerical values of the descriptors with odorant property of five most potent and five less potent odorants present in coffee

Compound no.	NAME	F01 [C-S]	C-024	B07 [C-C]	nS	B04 [C-C]	F05 [C-C]	S-106	nRCO	ETA_Shape_P	Apol
Five most potent odorants present in black tea											
19	3-Methyl-2-butene-1-thiol	1	0	0	1	0	0	1	0	0.550	4706.700
30	(E)-Beta-damascenone	0	0	1	0	1	8	0	1	0.341	8070.440
41	2-Methoxy-3-isopropylpyrazine	0	0	0	0	1	5	0	0	0.292	5317.440
16	3-Mercapto-3-methylbutyl formate	1	0	0	1	1	2	1	0	0.481	5704.260
27	1-Octen-3-one	0	0	1	0	1	3	0	1	0.308	5015.620
Five least potent odorants present in black tea											
43	Pyridine	0	3	0	0	0	0	0	0	0.000	2999.580
8	3-Methylbutyric acid	0	0	0	0	0	0	0	0	0.526	3506.000
35	2,3-Dimethylpyrazine	0	0	0	0	1	0	0	0	0.263	3946.120
42	Ethyl pyrazine	0	0	0	0	1	1	0	0	0.132	3946.120
12	5-Methyl-2-furancarboxyaldehyde	0	2	0	0	1	0	0	0	0.227	3878.500

4. CONCLUSION

The MLP based ANN model for the odor active components present in black tea and coffee were developed using a priori selected descriptors. We have used a variable selection strategy to extract the significant descriptors prior to development of the final models thus reducing the noise. The ANN models were developed keeping in mind the OECD principles. The statistical results obtained from the ANN models justify the reliability and robustness of the developed models. The statistical results in terms of both internal and external validation parameters obtained from the ANN models are far better than the previously published PLS-regression based QSPR model. However, interpretation of the non-linear model is not straightforward as in case of regression equations. In this work, we have tried to explore the significant descriptors from the descriptor pool used to develop the ANN model by employing the MAE based criteria in a backward elimination of descriptors one in each turn. In case of the black tea dataset, we have found out 28 significant descriptors while in case of the coffee dataset we have found out 24 significant descriptors. As compared with the previously published PLS-regression based models, out of six descriptors as in case of both tea and coffee models, five common descriptors are found to be significant descriptors based on the respective ANN models. The present ANN models corroborate the findings of the previously published PLS-regression based chemometric models (Ojha, & Roy, 2018). Thus, the present approach can be used to find out the significant descriptors used for development of ANN models.

Table 4. Categorical list of descriptors obtained from the ANN model based on MAE (95%) in case of coffee dataset

Category	Sl. No.	Descriptor removed	Definition	Type	Architecture	MAE (95%)	Change in MAE
Category-I: Significant descriptors	1	F01[C-S]	Frequency of C-S at topological distance 1	2D Atom Pairs	39-2-1	0.444	0.191
	2	C-024	R--CH--R	Atom-centred fragments	39-2-1	0.404	0.151
	3	B07[C-C]	Presence/absence of C-C at topological distance 7	2DAtom Pairs	39-2-1	0.399	0.146
	4	nS	number of Sulfur atoms	Constitutional indices	39-2-1	0.399	0.146
	5	B04[C-C]	Presence/absence of C-C at topological distance 4	2DAtom Pairs	39-2-1	0.339	0.086
	6	F05[C-C]	Frequency of C-C at topological distance 5	2D Atom Pairs	39-2-1	0.326	0.073
	7	B07[C-O]	Presence/absence of C-O at topological distance 7	2DAtom Pairs	39-2-1	0.326	0.073
	8	S-106	R-SH	Atom-centred fragments	39-2-1	0.318	0.065
	9	nRCO	number of ketones(aliphatic)	Functional group counts	39-2-1	0.317	0.064
	10	Jurs-WPSA-2	Surface-weighted charged partial surface areas	Spatial descriptor	39-2-1	0.315	0.062
	11	ETA_Shape_P	$(\Sigma\alpha)_p / \Sigma\alpha$	Extended Topological Atom	39-2-1	0.312	0.059
	12	C-040	R-C(=X)-X / R-C#X / X=C=X	Atom-centred fragments	39-2-1	0.308	0.055
	13	Apol	Sum of atomic polarizabilities.	Electronic descriptors	39-2-1	0.303	0.050
	14	nHDon	number of donor atoms for H-bonds (N and O)	Functional group counts	39-2-1	0.302	0.049
	15	H-049	H attached to (sp3)/C2(sp2)/ C3(sp2)/C3(sp)	Atom-centred fragments	39-2-1	0.294	0.041
	16	B02[C-S]	Presence/absence of C - S at topological distance 2	2DAtom Pairs	39-2-1	0.294	0.041
	17	nH	number of Hydrogen atoms	Constitutional indices	39-2-1	0.292	0.039
	18	nRCOOH	number of carboxylic acids (aliphatic)	Functional group counts	39-2-1	0.289	0.036
	19	B01[C-O]	Presence/absence of C - O at topological distance 1	2DAtom Pairs	39-2-1	0.289	0.036
	20	Jurs-RNCS	Relative negative charge surface area: solvent-accessible surface area of most negative atom divided by descriptor	Spatial descriptor	39-2-1	0.284	0.031
	21	ETA_ dAlpha_B	$\Delta\alpha_B$	Extended Topological Atom	39-2-1	0.275	0.022
	22	F04[C-N]	Frequency of C - N at topological distance 4	2DAtom Pairs	39-2-1	0.266	0.013
	23	ETA_Eta	η	Extended Topological Atom	39-2-1	0.266	0.013
	24	B01[C-S]	Presence/absence of C - S at topological distance 1	2DAtom Pairs	39-2-1	0.263	0.010

continues on following page

Table 4. Continued

Category	Sl. No.	Descriptor removed	Definition	Type	Architecture	MAE (95%)	Change in MAE
Category-II: Redundant descriptors	25	X1v	valence connectivity index of order 1	Connectivity indices	39-2-1	0.260	0.007
	26	B03[O-S]	Presence/absence of O - S at topological distance 3	2DAtom Pairs	39-2-1	0.257	0.004
	27	C-006	CH2RX	Atom-centred fragments	39-2-1	0.256	0.003
	28	nR=Ct	number of aliphatic tertiary C(sp2)	Functional group counts	39-2-1	0.252	-0.001
	29	F04[C-C]	Frequency of C - C at topological distance 4	2DAtom pairs	39-2-1	0.251	-0.002
	30	S-107	R2S / RS-SR	Atom-centred fragments	39-2-1	0.250	-0.003
	31	ETA_EtaP	η/N_v	Extended Topological Atom	39-2-1	0.248	-0.005
	32	C-029	R--CX--X	Atom centred fragments	39-2-1	0.246	-0.007
Category-III: Noisy descriptors	33	nCsp3	number of sp3 hybridized Carbon atoms	Constitutional indices	39-2-1	0.241	-0.012
	34	Jurs-RNCG	Relative negative charge: charge of most negative atom divided by the total negative charge	Spatial descriptor	39-2-1	0.240	-0.013
	35	C-027	R--CH--X	Atom centred fragments	39-2-1	0.237	-0.016
	36	nROH	number of hydroxyl groups	Functional group counts	39-2-1	0.233	-0.020
	37	SssO	Sum of ssO E-states	Atom-type E-state indices	39-2-1	0.233	-0.020
	38	nArOR	number of ethers (aromatic)	Atom centred fragment	39-2-1	0.232	-0.021
	39	H-050	H attached to heteroatom	Atom centred fragment	39-2-1	0.227	-0.026
	40	nArCHO	number of aldehydes (aromatic)	Functional group counts	39-2-1	0.212	-0.041

ACKNOWLEDGMENT

PKO would like to thanks the UGC, New Delhi for financial assistance in the form of a fellowship (Letter number and date: F./PDFSS-2015-17-WES-11996; dated: 06/04/2016).JGK thanks the Ministry of Chemicals & Fertilizers, Department of Pharmaceuticals, Government of India and the National Institute of Pharmaceutical Education and Research Kolkata (NIPER-Kolkata) for providing financial assistance in the form of a fellowship.

REFERENCES

Agatonovic-Kustrin, S., & Beresford, R. (2000). Basic concepts of artificial neural network (ANN) modeling and its application in pharmaceutical research. *Journal of Pharmaceutical and Biomedical Analysis*, 22(5), 717–727. doi:10.1016/S0731-7085(99)00272-1

Balentine, D. A., Wiseman, S. A., & Bouwens, L. C. (1997). The chemistry of tea flavonoids. *Critical Reviews in Food Science and Nutrition*, *37*(8), 693–704. doi:10.1080/10408399709527797

Bhattacharyya, N., Bandyopadhyay, R., Bhuyan, M., Tudu, B., Ghosh, D., & Jana, A. (2008). Electronic nose for black tea classification and correlation of measurements with "Tea Taster" marks. *IEEE Transactions on Instrumentation and Measurement*, *57*(7), 1313–1321. doi:10.1109/TIM.2008.917189

Bondarovich, H. A., Giammarino, A. S., Renner, J. A., Shephard, F. W., Shingler, A. J., & Gianturco, M. A. (1967). Volatiles in tea some aspects of the chemistry of tea. *Journal of Agricultural and Food Chemistry*, *15*(1), 36–47. doi:10.1021/jf60149a011

Borse, B. B., Rao, L. J. M., Nagalakshmi, S., & Krishnamurthy, N. (2002). Fingerprint of black teas from India: Identification of the regio-specific characteristics. *Food Chemistry*, *79*(4), 419–424. doi:10.1016/S0308-8146(02)00191-7

Cerius2 Version 4.10 [Software]. (2005). Accelrys Inc., San Diego, CA. Retrieved from http://www.accelrys.com

Clevert, D. A., Unterthiner, T., & Hochreiter, S. (2015). Fast and accurate deep network learning by exponential linear units (elus). arXiv:1511.07289

Das, R. N., & Roy, K. (2016). Computation of chromatographic lipophilicity parameter logk0 of ionic liquid cations from "ETA" descriptors: Application in modeling of toxicity of ionic liquids to pathogenic bacteria. *Journal of Molecular Liquids*, *216*, 754–763. doi:10.1016/j.molliq.2016.02.013

Godfrey, L. B., & Gashler, M. S. (2015, November). A continuum among logarithmic, linear, and exponential functions, and its potential to improve generalization in neural networks. In *Proceedings of the 2015 7th International Joint Conference on Knowledge Discovery, Knowledge Engineering and Knowledge Management (IC3K)* (Vol. 1, pp. 481-486). IEEE. doi:10.5220/0005635804810486

Gutman, R. L., & Ryu, B.-H. (1996). Rediscovering tea. An exploration of the scientific literature. *Herbal Gram*, *37*, 33–48.

Halder, A., Raychowdhury, R., Ghosh, A., & De, M. (2005). Black tea (Camellia sinensis) as a chemopreventive agent in oral precancerous lesions. *Journal of Environmental Pathology, Toxicology and Oncology*, *24*(2), 141–144. doi:10.1615/JEnvPathToxOncol.v24.i2.70

Hansch, C., Kurup, A., Garg, R., & Gao, H. (2001). Chem-bioinformatics and QSAR: A review of QSAR lacking positive hydrophobic terms. *Chemical Reviews*, *101*(3), 619–672. doi:10.1021/cr0000067

Hara, Y., Luo, S. J., Wickremashinghe, R. L., & Yamanishi, T. (1995). Botany (of tea). *Food Reviews International*, *11*, 371–374.

Haykin, S. (1994). *Neural networks: a comprehensive foundation. Macmillan*. New York: Prentice Hall PTR.

Head, J. D., & Zerner, M. C. (1985). A Broyden—Fletcher—Goldfarb—Shanno optimization procedure for molecular geometries. *Chemical Physics Letters*, *122*(3), 264–270. doi:10.1016/0009-2614(85)80574-1

Hornik, K. (1991). Approximation capabilities of multilayer feedforward networks. *Neural Networks*, *4*(2), 251–257. doi:10.1016/0893-6080(91)90009-T

Leonardos, G., Kendall, D., & Barnard, N. (1974). Odor threshold determination of 53 odorant chemicals. *Journal of Environmental Conservation Engineering, 3*(8), 579–585. doi:10.5956/jriet.3.579

Liu, D. C., & Nocedal, J. (1989). On the limited memory BFGS method for large scale optimization. *Mathematical Programming, 45*(1-3), 503–528. doi:10.1007/BF01589116

Magagna, F., Cordero, C., Cagliero, C., Liberto, E., Rubiolo, P., Sgorbini, B., & Bicchi, C. (2017). Black tea volatiles fingerprinting by comprehensive two-dimensional gas chromatography–Mass spectrometry combined with high concentration capacity sample preparation techniques: Toward a fully automated sensomic assessment. *Food Chemistry, 225*, 276–287. doi:10.1016/j.foodchem.2017.01.003

Mary, L. H., & Robert, J. H. (2011). The Story of Tea: *A Cultural History and Drinking Guide*. Minitab Inc. Retrieved from http://www.minitab.com/en-US/default.aspx

Ojha, P. K., Kar, S., Roy, K., & Leszczynski, J. (2018). Toward comprehension of multiple human cells uptake of engineered nano metal oxides: Quantitative inter cell line uptake specificity (QICLUS) modeling. Nanotoxicology, 1–21. doi:10.1080/17435390.2018.1529836

Ojha, P. K., & Roy, K. (2011). Comparative QSARs for antimalarial endochins: Importance of descriptor-thinning and noise reduction prior to feature selection. *Chemometrics and Intelligent Laboratory Systems, 109*(2), 146–161. doi:10.1016/j.chemolab.2011.08.007

Ojha, P. K., & Roy, K. (2018). PLS regression-based chemometric modeling of odorant properties of diverse chemical constituents of black tea and coffee. *RSC Advances, 8*(5), 2293–2304. doi:10.1039/C7RA12914A

Ojha, P. K., & Roy, K. (2018). Development of a robust and validated 2D-QSPR model for sweetness potency of diverse functional organic molecules. *Food and Chemical Toxicology, 112*, 551–562. doi:10.1016/j.fct.2017.03.043

Parascandolo, G., Huttunen, H., & Virtanen, T. (2016). Taming the waves: sine as activation function in deep neural networks.

Park, H. S., & Jun, C. H. (2009). A simple and fast algorithm for K-medoids clustering. *Expert Systems with Applications, 36*(2), 3336–3341. doi:10.1016/j.eswa.2008.01.039

Polishchuk, P. (2017). Interpretation of quantitative structure–activity relationship models: Past, present, and future. *Journal of Chemical Information and Modeling, 57*(11), 2618–2639. doi:10.1021/acs.jcim.7b00274

Rawat, R., Gulati, A., Babu, G. K., Acharya, R., Kaul, V. K., & Singh, B. (2007). Characterization of volatile components of Kangra orthodox black tea by gas chromatography-mass spectrometry. *Food Chemistry, 105*(1), 229–235. doi:10.1016/j.foodchem.2007.03.071

Robertson, A. (1992). The chemistry and biochemistry of black tea production—the non-volatiles. In *Tea* (pp. 555–601). Dordrecht: Springer; . doi:10.1007/978-94-011-2326-6_17

Roy, J., Ghosh, S., Ojha, P. K., & Roy, K. (2018). Predictive Quantitative Structure-Property Relationship (QSPR) Modeling for Adsorption of Organic Pollutants by Carbon Nanotubes (CNTs). *Environmental Science. Nano*.

Roy, K., Ambure, P., Kar, S., & Ojha, P. K. (2018). Is it possible to improve the quality of predictions from an "intelligent" use of multiple QSAR/QSPR/QSTR models? *Journal of Chemometrics*, *32*(4), e2992.

Roy, K., Das, R. N., Ambure, P., & Aher, R. B. (2016). Be aware of error measures. Further studies on validation of predictive QSAR models. *Chemometrics and Intelligent Laboratory Systems*, *152*, 18–33. doi:10.1016/j.chemolab.2016.01.008

Roy, K., Kar, S., & Ambure, P. (2015). On a simple approach for determining applicability domain of QSAR models. *Chemometrics and Intelligent Laboratory Systems*, *145*, 22–29. doi:10.1016/j.chemolab.2015.04.013

Statistica version 13.4. (2016). STATSOFT Inc., USA, Available at http://www.statsoft.com

Talete. (2010). Dragon (Version 6). Retrieved from. http://www.talete.mi.it/products/dragondescription.htm

USDA. (2018). Brazil Coffe Annual 2018. Retrieved from https://gain.fas.usda.gov/Recent%20GAIN%20Publications/Coffee%20Annual_Sao%20Paulo%20ATO_Brazil_5-15-2018.pdf

Wang, K., Liu, F., Liu, Z., Huang, J., Xu, Z., Li, Y., ... Yang, X. (2011). Comparison of catechins and volatile compounds among different types of tea using high performance liquid chromatograph and gas chromatograph mass spectrometer. *International Journal of Food Science & Technology*, *46*(7), 1406–1412. doi:10.1111/j.1365-2621.2011.02629.x

Yapcwsoft. (n.d.). PaDEL-Descriptor. Retrieved from http://www.yapcwsoft.com/dd/padeldescriptor

Yeretzian, C. (2017). *Hand book of Odor* (A. Buettner, Ed.). Springer.

Žuvela, P., David, J., & Wong, M. W. (2018). Interpretation of ANN-based QSAR models for prediction of antioxidant activity of flavonoids. *Journal of Computational Chemistry*, *39*(16), 953–963. doi:10.1002/jcc.25168

This research was previously published in the International Journal of Quantitative Structure-Property Relationships (IJQSPR), 4(4); pages 27-49, copyright year 2019 by IGI Publishing (an imprint of IGI Global).

APPENDIX: SUPLEMENTRY TABLES

Table 6. List of aroma components present in black tea with observed and model derived odor threshold property

Compound no.	Structure Name	Observed value (log(1/OT))	Predicted value
1	2-Methyl propanal	4.496	3.770
2	Acetone	-0.935	0.595
3	Butanal	3.603	3.514
4	Ethyl acetate	1.972	1.830
5	1-Butanol	2.694	3.013
6	3-Methyl butanal	3.821	3.825
7	2-Methyl butanal	3.935	4.021
8	Acetic acid	0.080	1.078
9	1-Penten-3-ol	2.333	2.488
10	Pentanal	3.333	2.900
11	Propanoic acid	0.569	1.191
12	2-Methyl propanoic acid	1.037	1.320
13	(E)-2-Pentenal	2.448	3.102
14*	1-Pentanol	1.468	1.538
15	Butanoic acid	2.565	1.233
16*	Hexanal	3.098	3.041
17	Furfural	1.506	1.345
18	3-Methyl butanoic acid	2.164	1.335
19	2-Methyl butanoic acid	2.164	1.437
20*	(E)-2-Hexenal	2.369	3.269
21	(Z)-3-hexen-1-ol	1.825	1.948
22	(E)-2-hexen-1-ol	1.302	1.661
23*	1-Hexanol	2.407	1.841
24*	Pentanoic acid	1.532	0.945
25	2-Heptanone	2.581	2.385
26	(Z)-4-heptenal	6.272	3.617
27	Heptanal	2.359	3.326
28*	(E,E)-2,4-Hexadienal	3.983	3.465
29	(E)-2-Heptenal	4.351	3.656
30	Benzaldehyde	2.482	2.160
31	1-Heptanol	4.588	3.159
32	1-Octen-3-ol	3.409	4.149
33	6-Methyl-5-hepten-2-one	2.101	2.780
34	2-Octanone	2.400	3.061

continues on following page

Table 6. Continued

Compound no.	Structure Name	Observed value (log(1/OT))	Predicted value
35*	Hexanoic acid	1.588	0.922
36*	2-Pentyl furan	4.362	3.893
37	(Z)-3-Hexen-1-ol acetate	4.250	4.492
38*	Octanal	2.603	3.587
39	(E,E) 2,4-Heptadienal	2.486	4.013
40*	Limonene	4.134	3.861
41	Benzyl alcohol	1.034	1.432
42*	Phenyl acetaldehyde	4.280	3.164
43	(E)-2-Octenal	4.499	4.088
44	(E,E)-3,5-Octadien-2-one	5.395	3.955
45	1-Octanol	3.073	3.761
46*	Heptanoic acid	1.638	0.977
47	Linalool	5.410	6.018
48	6-Methyl-3,5-heptadien-2-one	2.514	3.298
49	Nonanal	2.977	3.643
50	2-Phenyl ethanol	2.087	1.843
51	(E,Z)-2,6-Nonadienal	7.663	4.752
52	(E)-2-Nonenal	2.193	4.136
53*	1-Nonanol	3.460	3.858
54	Octanoic acid	1.682	1.364
55	Decanal	2.381	3.533
56	(E,E)-2,4-Nonadienal	5.936	4.721
57*	β-Cyclocitral	4.484	4.885
58	Geraniol	4.683	4.543
59*	(E)-2-Decenal	4.188	3.948
60	Geranial	3.677	4.606
61	Nonanoic acid	1.722	1.573
62	2-Undecanone	4.386	3.089
63*	(E,Z)-2,4-Decadienal	4.183	4.446
64*	Undecanal	4.532	3.566
65	(E,E)-2,4-Decadienal	2.927	4.457
66	Dihydro-5-pentyl-2(3H)-Furanone	3.717	4.257
67	Decanoic acid	1.236	1.091
68	β-Damascenone	7.677	6.142
69	Vanillin	3.881	3.851
70	Dodecanal	4.965	3.610
71	α-Ionone	4.585	5.698
72	Geranyl acetone	3.510	3.507

continues on following page

Table 6. Continued

Compound no.	Structure Name	Observed value (log(1/OT))	Predicted value
73*	β-Ionone	5.983	5.507
74	Dodecanoic acid	1.302	1.321
75*	Tetradecanal	3.549	3.667
76	Tetradecanoic acid	1.359	1.581

*denotes test set compounds

Table 7. List of aroma components present in coffee with observed and model derived odor threshold property

Compound No.	Structure name	Observed value ((log(1/OT))	Predicted value
1*	2-Methylbutanal	1.821	1.853
2	3-Methylbutanal	2.391	1.859
3*	(E)-2-Nonenal	3.244	3.096
4	Acetaldehyde	1.799	0.456
5	4-Methoxybenzaldehyde	0.703	0.541
6	Propanal	0.764	0.920
7	2-Methylbutyric acid	1.009	-0.356
8	3-Methylbutyric acid	-0.836	-0.357
9	Ethyl-2-methylbutyrate	2.412	2.028
10	Ethyl-3-methylbutyrate	2.333	1.959
11*	Furfural	-0.464	-0.834
12	5-Methyl-2-furancarboxyaldehyde	-1.736	-1.086
13	Dimethyl trisulfide	4.101	3.497
14*	Bis(2-methyl-3-furyl)disulfide	5.474	5.461
15	Methional	2.717	3.609
16	3-Mercapto-3-methylbutyl formate	4.627	5.767
17*	2-Furfuryl thiol	4.058	4.528
18	2-Methyl-3-furanthiol	4.212	4.163
19	3-Methyl-2-butene-1-thiol	5.532	4.973
20	Methanethiol	3.381	3.003
21	Dihydro-2-methyl-3(2H)-furanone	4.302	3.477
22	2-Ethyl-4-hydroxy-5-methyl-3(2H)-furanone	0.852	1.309
23*	3-Hydroxy-4,5-dimethyl-2(5H)-furanone	0.807	0.859
24	4-Hydroxy-2,5-dimethyl-3(2H)-furanone	1.108	0.711
25	5-Ethyl-3-hydroxy-4-methyl-2(5H)-furanone	1.278	0.701
26	5-Ethyl-4-hydroxy-2-methyl-3(2H)-furanone	2.092	1.325
27	1-Octen-3-one	4.545	3.333
28*	2,3-Butanedione	2.458	1.603

continues on following page

Table 6. Continued

Compound No.	Structure name	Observed value ((log(1/OT))	Predicted value
29	2,3-Pentanedione	0.700	1.310
30	(E)-Beta-damascenone	5.404	5.387
31	Guaiacol	1.696	1.015
32	4-Ethyl Guaiacol	0.785	2.447
33	4-Vinyl Guaiacol	2.302	1.971
34	Vanillin	0.784	0.245
35	2,3-Dimethylpyrazine	-0.869	-0.411
36*	2,5-Dimethylpyrazine	0.131	-0.337
37	2,3-Diethyl-5-methylpyrazine	3.223	2.519
38	2-Ethyl-3,5-dimethylpyrazine	3.532	1.537
39*	2-Ethyl-3,6-dimethyl-pyrazine	1.200	1.613
40	2-Methoxy-3,5-dimethylpyrazine	4.362	4.062
41	2-Methoxy-3-isopropylpyrazine	4.881	4.795
42	Ethylpyrazine	-1.568	-0.644
43	Pyridine	0.012	-1.038
44*	Linalool	2.958	2.642
45	Limonene	1.532	2.780
46	Geraniol	2.147	2.907

*denotes test set compounds

Section 3
Tools and Technologies

Chapter 19
Tool Condition Monitoring Using Artificial Neural Network Models

Srinivasa P. Pai
iD https://orcid.org/0000-0002-3858-6014
NMAM Institute of Technology, India

Nagabhushana T. N.
S. J. College of Engineering, India

ABSTRACT

Tool wear is a major factor that affects the productivity of any machining operation and needs to be controlled for achieving automation. It affects the surface finish, tolerances, dimensions of the workpiece, increases machine down time, and sometimes performance of machine tool and personnel are affected. This chapter deals with the application of artificial neural network (ANN) models for tool condition monitoring (TCM) in milling operations. The data required for training and testing the models studied and developed are from live experiments conducted in a machine shop on a widely used steel, medium carbon steel (En 8) using uncoated carbide inserts. Acoustic emission data and surface roughness data has been used in model development. The goal is for developing an optimal ANN model, in terms of compact architecture, least training time, and its ability to generalize well on unseen (test) data. Growing cell structures (GCS) network has been found to achieve these requirements.

INTRODUCTION

Manufacturing industries have seen lot of changes in the last few years. The focus is on reducing cost, improving productivity, by reducing downtime, losses and waste. Machining is an important process used by manufacturing industries. It can be classified as traditional and non-traditional. In traditional machining, turning, planning, shaping etc., uses a single point cutting tool and milling, drilling, grinding etc., are multi-point cutting tool operations. They can be used to machine metals or nonmetals, including

DOI: 10.4018/978-1-6684-2408-7.ch019

composites. Cutting tool is an important part of the machining process. It contributes significantly to the total machining costs. Further the goal in manufacturing is towards automation. In this effort, there is a need to continuously monitor the condition of the cutting tool, so that machine tool and cutting tool are not affected. Cutting tool condition monitoring can include detection of the tool condition in terms of tool wear and fracture or breakage (Chelladurai et al., 2008). Tool breakage is a major reason for unscheduled stopping of operations in a machining centre (Rehorn et al., 2005). Traditional methods of monitoring the condition of the cutting tool has been more dependent on the operator. Hence, he or she was not able to detect the condition of the tool, when it was subjected to sudden failure or more wear. As a result, cutting tools were either underutilized or overutilized. To avoid this problem there is a need to use various types of sensing techniques, which can assist the operator in taking proper decisions. Traditionally tool condition monitoring methods are grouped as 'direct' or 'indirect'. Direct methods involve assessing material removal from cutting tool in terms of mass or volume and tend to be offline in nature, as the tool has to be removed from the machining process for measurement. Hence it takes lot of timetool failure development is not clearly visible. Indirect methods can be implemented online, as it involves measurement of 'signals' generated during machining, which have a direct relation with tool condition and includes cutting force, temperature, vibration, acoustic emission etc. (Pai, 2004).

The focus these days is on automated TCM systems, which will recognize the status of the tool, without the interruption of the machining process, under minimum human supervision. Thus, the goal is to achieve 'unattended' machining systems, which can improve the utilization of the capital equipment and substantially reduce the machining costs. For this, there is a need for an "Intelligent sensor system", as described by Dornfeld (1986) as follows, "an integrated system consisting of sensing elements, signal conditioning devices, signal processing algorithms and signal interpretation and decision-making procedures". "Finally, the effort is towards developing an Automated / Intelligent monitoring system, which should have the capabilities of sensing, analyzing, knowledge learning and error correction".

According to Elbestawi et al. (2006), to replicate human intervention, a typical TCM system should have the following components:

(i) Sensing technique – use of different sensing signals like cutting forces, vibrations, acoustic emission. There is a need to combine data from different sensors and locations, to maximize yield of useful information.

(ii) Feature extraction – there is a need to extract information from the signals to differentiate different process and tool conditions and also to remove noise from the signals.

(iii) Decision making – strategies, which use the extracted features and map it to a tool condition.

(iv) Knowledge learning – in order to make correct decisions, learning algorithms have to be used.

"The automated TCM systems, have to learn from past information and also learn from the new information generated from the machining process" (Elbestawi, & Dumitrescu, 2006) (Elbestawi & Ng, 2006).

Monitoring systems which are based in laboratories, are multisensory based are require the need for complex Artificial Intelligence (AI) based systems, which can integrate information, extract features and make reliable decisions about the status of the tool (Balazinski et al., 2002). Multi sensor fusion has some benefits for TCM and include – since the signals get distorted by noise during measurement, using multiple signals can maximize the amount of information available for decision making process and since more signals are considered, the certainty of the estimated parameter value improves (Pai, 2004). "Artificial Neural Networks (ANN) and neuro-fuzzy techniques have been extensively studied from the AI domain" (Balazinski et al., 2002). According to Elbestawi et al. (2006), there are two types of monitoring methods: (i) Model-based methods – "this involves finding a model that fits the process and monitors specific parameters in the model to detect changes". They can be considered as failure detection methods. (ii) Feature-based monitoring methods – relates the tool status to the signal features and includes techniques like ANN, expert systems, fuzzy logic etc. These methods have two phases – learning and classification (Elbestawi, & Dumitrescu, 2006) (Elbestawi & Ng, 2006). Proper selection of features is very important for any application and depending upon the application, the process can become complicated and there is a need for sophisticated feature selection techniques, which can improve the performance of the classifier or modeling technique. For e.g. Kumar et al. (2018) propose the use of exponential spider monkey optimization to select best possible features from a high dimensional feature set for automated plant disease detection system. Standard methods like SPAM have been used to generate the high dimensional features and the features selected by the optimization has been fed to support vector machine (SVM) for classifying the plants into diseased and non-diseased (Kumar et al., 2018a). In another study, the authors develop an automated system for grouping soil data sets using images, which can help in taking decisions regarding crops. A Bag-of-words and chaotic spider monkey optimization methods have been used. The optimization algorithm shows good convergence and improved global search over other methods. It has been further used to cluster the key points in Bag-of-words method for soil prediction. The proposed system gave 79% accuracy and the optimization algorithms perform better than other meta-heuristic methods (Kumar et al., 2018b)

Artificial Neural Networks (ANN) has been preferred for fusion of information from multiple sensors in TCM. Conventional methods are not effective enough to provide the desired level of accuracy. In spite of using sensor fusion, where various signals provide different sensitivity to tool condition, the changes in the signals with changes in tool condition or tool wear are non-linear and non-monotonic. Some features of the signals will be correlated with certain levels of tool wear, but not others. Further, the signals are distorted due to noise, which is common in a shop floor environment. Due to this inherent complexity and variability, the underlying distributions in the signal data are either unknown or not clearly understood. In such scenarios, ANN works well. They are not dependent on the distribution governing the data or any other assumptions to model or predict the responses and their relationship with the inputs. They have the capability to understand and develop relationships between the inputs and outputs in the data. "They estimate the functional relationship between the sensed signals and its features and the levels of tool wear / tool condition adaptively using training data via a learning algorithm. This extracted knowledge is stored in the massively parallel interconnected architecture and is generalized for interpretation of novel sensor signals in terms of tool wear / condition" (Pai, 2004). The recent developments in ANN in terms of using deep learning networks for sophisticated applications make this field very interesting and useful. These networks work well, when the data available for training / modeling is very large. For e.g. Solanki & Pandey (2019) used deep convolutional neural network model for musical instrument recognition. The eight layered network was able to achieve an accuracy of 92.8% (Solanki & Pandey, 2019).

This chapter is focused towards development of a best possible ANN based model for predicting tool wear in face milling using indirect and direct signal features, which is compact, has good generalization capability and takes least time for training.

BACKGROUND

"ANN are computing systems that are made up of a number of simple, highly interconnected processing elements, called neurons, that provide the system the capability of self-learning" (Elbestawi, & Dumitrescu, 2006). "It generally has three layers, an input layer, which receives information from the external world, a hidden layer that processes the information and an output layer, which presents the information back to the external world". Fig. 1 shows a general ANN architecture.

Figure 1.

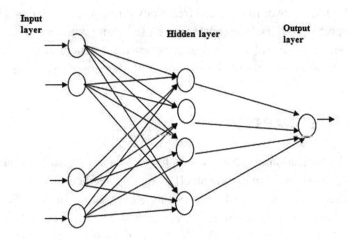

"There are two classifications- (i) Supervised learning networks – In these types of networks, both input and the corresponding output data are given to the network during training. E.g. Multilayer perceptron (MLP) trained using Back Propagation (BP) algorithm" (Haykin, 1998).

(ii)   Unsupervised learning networks – This involves presentation of only the input patterns. The network learns the similarity in the input data through any learning algorithm. E.g. Kohonen's Self-organizing map (Haykin, 1998).

CURRENT STATUS

Multilayer Perceptron (MLP), a frequently used feed forward model generally has three layers – input, hidden and output. It has been widely used in TCM applications. Different aspects of MLP in terms of error prediction level, convergence, difference in architecture etc. has been studied. Dimla et al. (1997) did a focused evaluation of use of ANN for TCM and MLP was widely used. Sick, B. (2002) presented another critical study of 138 publications dealing with online and indirect tool wear monitoring in turning using ANN. Some other researchers who have used MLP for TCM include: Panda, S.S., et al. (2008) monitored drill flank wear using MLP and RBFNN. They used thrust force, torque and vibration signals as inputs. The inclusion of vibration signals improved the prediction accuracy of the wear. MLP was better than RBFNN. But RBFNN is faster in learning and works well for on-line tool wear monitoring. Chelladurai et al. (2008) monitored tool wear using vibration and strain signals in coated carbide inserts, while turning EN-8 steel. The ANN model was built using the data. The model was developed using MATLAB tool box and trainrp algorithm was found to be robust, along with the use of logsig and tansig activation functions for modeling and predicting flank wear. Chen & Chen (2005) developed an ANN-based in-process tool wear prediction (ANN-ITWP) system to predict tool wear. The inputs included feed rate, depth of cut and average peak force in the y direction. The average peak force in y direction was a significant input, the minimum error made was ± 0.037 mm and there were some limitations to be overcome. Cho et al. (2010) studied the development of an effective multisensory based TCM, while machining 4340 steel using coated carbide end mill cutter. The signals used include force, vibration, acoustic emission and spindle power in time and frequency domain. The MLP and RBF neural network models along with support vector machine (SVM) were used along with feature level and decision level fusion. SVM outperformed MLP and RBFNN as it is based on structural risk minimization. Further use of correlation-based feature selection (CFS) improved the accuracy and robustness of classification.

MAIN FOCUS OF THE CHAPTER

This chapter deals with application of ANN models for tool wear estimation (flank wear) for TCM in milling applications on En-8 (medium carbon steel) using uncoated carbide inserts. Acoustic emission is measured online, whereas tool wear and surface roughness are measured offline during the experiments conducted for different cutting speed, feed and depth of cut. Different ANN models starting with MLP, followed by RBFNN, Resource Allocation Network and Growing Cell structures are investigated to propose an optimal model for tool wear estimation, which is robust, compact, takes least training time and generalizes well on unseen (test) data.

Experimental Details

Face milling operations were performed on a Bharat Fritz Werner (BFW) make vertical milling machine under three different cutting speeds (low – 71 m/min, medium – 112 m/min and high – 176 m/min), a wide range of feed / tooth (0.04 mm, which is the lowest and 0.4 mm, which is the highest) and a fixed depth of cut of 0.8 mm (equal to the tool tip radius of the insert). En-8 steel was used for experiments (medium carbon steel, 0.4711% C and 115 RHB hardness). The face milling cutter used was WIDAX M650 High shear milling cutter using uncoated carbide inserts (SEKN 12 03 AFN TTMS grade, ISO grade P15-P30carbide grades). Fig.2 shows the experimental setup used (Pai, 2004).

Signals Measured For TCM

(a) *Acoustic emission (AE)* – "AE are stress waves generated by dynamic processes in materials". "The emissions occur as a release of a series of short impulsive energy packets". "This energy traverses as a spherical wavefront, which can be picked up from the surface of a structure using a highly sensitive transducer (piezoelectric), which converts mechanical signal into electrical signal. This signal can be processed to understand and reveal useful information about the source" (Pai, 2004).

According to Dornfeld (1989), "the typical sources of AE in metal cutting include plastic deformation of the workpiece, plastic deformation in the chip, friction between tool flank and workpiece resulting in flank wear, friction between the tool rake face and chip resulting in crater wear, collisions between the chip and tool, chip breakage and tool fracture". AE signal sources from machining can be classified as continuous and transient, which have distinctly different characteristics. "Continuous signals are associated with shearing in the primary zone, whereas transient signals can be from tool wear, tool fracture or chip breakage" (Xiaoli, 2002).

The AE signals are non-stationary in nature and can be evaluated by extracting features from the signal, which are of interest and can be correlated with tool condition. These can be analyzed either in time or frequency domain. Some of the features of interest are: ring down count, event, rise time, event duration, peak amplitude, RMS voltage, energy etc. (Xiaoli, 2002) (Pai, 2004).

"Since milling is discontinuous in nature, there are some additional sources of AE like tool entry into and exit from the workpiece, chip thickness variation, chip congestion and multi-teeth cutting configuration" (Pai et al., 2002).

In the current work, the AE signals were captured online during machining using the Babcock & Wilcox AET 5500 system. It is a computer based, multi-channel data acquisition and analysis system. It consists of a sensor (piezoelectric transducer with a resonant frequency of 750 kHz), preamplifier (160 B model, with a gain of 60 dB, with a wide band filter (30 kHz- 2 MHz)), cables and AET mainframe, which performs all the signal processing, with the necessary hardware and software (Pai, 2004).

The AE signal parameters considered in this study for modeling using ANN include –ring down count, rise time, RMS voltage, energy, event duration and mean rise time(Pai, 2004).

(b) *Surface roughness*–In a typical machining operation, surface quality is an important parameter and surface roughness is widely used as its indicator. It is a result of process parameters namely tool geometry and cutting conditions (Ozel & Karpat, 2005). The condition of the cutting tool has a significant influence on the surface roughness and thus it can be used as an indicator of the tool condition. Among the numerous parameters that influence surface roughness, some are controllable and include cutting conditions, cutting tool geometry, machine tool setup etc., whereas uncontrollable include cutting tool, workpiece, machine vibrations, tool wear and tool and workpiece material variability (Pai, 2004). The surface topography of the machined workpiece provides relevant information about the machining process. Thus, by monitoring the same and using necessary information, the machining and tool condition can be monitored (Zeng et al., 2009).

In milling operation, the most notable surface defect, in the absence of BUE are the feed marks. The surface roughness has both large and small wavelengths. The large wavelengths are related to macrophenomenon like cutting conditions, tool vibration etc. The small wavelengths are related to microscopic effects like lamellar formation and shear fronts, depending on the material being cut. The final surface profile may be due to the cumulative effects of factors like BUE, side flow, tearing, tool wear and tool vibrations (Pai, 2004). The surface parameters can be classified as amplitude, spacing, hybrid and other parameters (Zeng et al., 2009). Among these amplitude parameters are most common and include R_a, R_q or R_t, R_z and R_{max}. And these parameters have been used in the current work for modeling purposes.

(i) R_a – arithmetic mean deviation from the mean line of the profile.

(ii) R_q or R_t- root mean square value.

(iii) R_z – ten point heights of irregularities.

(iv) R_{max} - maximum height of irregularity (Jain, 2009).

The surface roughness measurement was done using a M4Pi Perthometer. It is a compact, mains-independent roughness measuring instrument. It can be used for mobile purposes in shop floor applications. The measurements are taken using a stylus. After every two cutting cycles, the surface roughness is measured on the workpiece. The sampling length / tracing length has been selected looking at R_a value.

(c) *Flank wear* - It is commonly occurring wear phenomenon in cutting tools, due to the friction between the tool flank and workpiece. "It is gradual or progressive tool wear phenomenon and involves wear on the nose and primary cutting edge with the accompanying notch". It is a regular wear, as it is always present in a machining operation and have regular cutting time related growth characteristics. The wear on the insert is measured as VB_{max} (maximum flank wear) using a tool maker's microscope (LABO make). The measurement is made for two decimal accuracy, as the least count of the micrometers used for measurement is 0.01 mm. The wear is recorded after each machining pass and the wear value for replacement is taken as 0.4 mm based on the tool manufacturer specification (Pai, 2004).

ANN Model Development

In this work, different ANN models have been investigated and include multilayer perceptron, RBFNN, RAN and GCS, with a goal towards developing a network with compact architecture, faster training time and good generalization ability for TCM application in face milling operation (Pai, 2004).

Multilayer Perceptron

A three-layer MLP model has been developed with input layer, one hidden layer and output layer. The input layer consists of 12 neurons, corresponding to 12 features namely 6 AE features (ring down count, rise time, RMS voltage, energy, event duration and mean rise time), 4 surface roughness features (R_a, R_q or R_t, R_z and R_{max}) and 2 cutting conditions (cutting speed and feed per tooth). The output layer has one neuron corresponding to flank wear (VB_{max}). The training set consisted of 69 patterns and test set 15 patterns.

The data has been suitably normalized, since the input and output parameters are of differing magnitude. To avoid problems like giving preference to a few variables and facilitate proper functioning of different activation functions, normalization is necessary. "The normalization method adopted is very simple: normalized variable $x_{i,norm} = x_i / x_{i,max}$, where x_i is the value of the variable and $x_{i,max}$ is the maximum value of the variable and i represents each pattern".

Training and Testing Results

The focus in use of MLP in TCM applications and in this work, is to study the influence of the nature of the machining data generated from live experiments on the network performance. Accordingly, the data has been formulated in three different formats and the network has been trained as per the requirement.

(i)   Type 1 data: both input and output data has been normalized as described before.
(ii) Type 2 data: Input data, that has been normalized has been encoded as binary bits and thus 12 features have been converted into 36 input dimensions, representing each feature using 3 bits.
(iii) Type 3 data: Input data remains in the normalized format and the output, ie., flank wear on the tool has been encoded using 3 bits, representing three classification states of the tool - '0 0 1' - flank wear (< = 0.2 mm), the tool condition is called 'initial', '0 1 0' – flank wear between 0.2 and 0.4 mm, the tool condition is called 'normal' and '0 1 1' – flank wear (> 0.4 mm), the tool condition is called 'abnormal'.

Table 1 shows the sample normalized input data and output data

Table 1. Sample input-output data

Pattern No.	RDC	Rise Time	Rms voltage	Energy	Event duration	Mean Rise Time	R_a	R_t or R_q	R_z	R_{max}	Cutting speed	Feed
1	0.2114	0.2260	0.9778	0.2379	0.2166	0.8731	0.4603	0.5292	0.6504	0.6772	0.3977	0.10
2	0.1430	0.2747	1.0000	0.2199	0.1499	0.9836	0.4226	0.4927	0.5735	0.6724	0.3977	0.10
3	1.0000	1.0000	0.0504	1.0000	1.0000	1.0000	0.7406	0.7299	0.6231	0.5969	0.3977	0.10
4	0.2172	0.0384	0.0805	0.2728	0.2035	0.0142	0.4433	0.4928	0.7760	0.6787	0.6364	0.09
5	0.4468	0.5745	0.1237	0.5590	0.5314	0.1055	0.2874	0.3207	0.4487	0.4249	0.6364	0.09
Test												
1	0.6546	0.7468	0.3547	0.7647	0.7114	0.7336	0.3399	0.2598	0.3764	0.3930	0.6364	0.25
2	0.6359	0.7605	0.3903	0.8122	0.7208	0.9990	0.3077	0.2126	0.4779	0.3805	0.6364	0.25
3	0.5769	0.6913	0.3157	0.7992	0.6855	0.6796	0.2805	0.1859	0.5735	0.4276	0.6364	0.25
4	0.2802	0.0413	0.0201	0.3304	0.2739	0.1967	0.4279	0.4499	0.6269	0.6215	0.3977	0.14
5	0.4020	0.2253	1.0000	0.5151	0.4180	0.7110	0.5673	0.5746	0.6667	0.8224	0.3977	0.14

The MLP network has been trained by changing the number of neurons in the hidden layer and it has been done on a trial and error basis. A single hidden layer has been used in the current work. The performance of the network is dependent on the activation function used in the hidden and output neuron, the rate of learning and momentum term. The backpropagation algorithm provides an approximation to the error trajectory in the weight space computed using the method of gradient descent. There is a need to select the learning rate parameter carefully, to prevent too slow or too fast learning. An efficient method to change the rate of learning, without causing any instability is to use the momentum term (Haykin, 1998). The selection of these two parameters have been done in this work on trial and error basis to minimize the mean squared error

$$E^\mu = 1 / 2 \, \Sigma_\mu \, (\zeta^\mu_i - O^\mu_k)^2.$$

Where $\mu = 1,2,....n$ are the number of patterns, k = 1, number of output neuron, ζ^μ_k, target output, $O^\mu_k = 1/ (1 + e^{-(\Sigma w_{kj} V_j)})$, is the network output (Nagabhushana, 1996).

The training results are as given in Table 2 for different values of hidden neurons, learning rate parameter and momentum term for Type 1 data.

Table 2.Results of Training

No. of Hidden neurons	10	20	24	30
No. of Epochs	160237	129830	122692	119234

i) For η=0.85 α=0.05 Error = 0.01

The mean squared error required for convergence is 0.01. The target for the maximum number of epochs is 175000 (considering old Pentium machine and using Borland C compiler for running the MLP codes). After several trial and error, the learning rate parameter (η) has been fixed as 0.85 and the momentum term (α) as 0.05. In the first part of the table, it is clear that as the number of hidden neurons increase, the number of training epochs decrease. Further in the second part of the table, as the η value increases, the number of training epochs decrease, becomes minimum for 0.85 and then increases. Similarly, in the last part of the table, as the α value increases, the error increases, with no change in the number of training epochs. Thus, the final simulation parameters selected for Type 1 data is: Network architecture 12-24-1, no. of training epochs 122692, η 0.85 and α 0.05. Fig. 2 shows the changes in error with epochs. The error drops quickly in the first 50000 epochs from more than 0.35 to less than 0.05 and then gradually decreases to 0.01 in the 122692 epochs.

Figure 2.

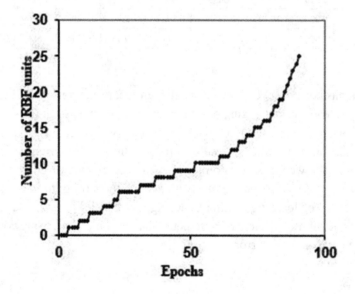

The network output for Type 1 data is considering two classes based on the tool flank wear value. Flank wear is less than or equal to 0.4 mm – if (network output is less than or equal to 0.4) - 'Normal'

Flank wear greater than 0.4 mm – if (network output is greater than 0.4) - 'Abnormal'.

Based on this interpretation of the network output, the classification accuracy on training data is 100% on training data and 87% on test data. Figure 3 shows the changes in actual and network output for test data. There is close correlation between the two, though there is some deviation for a few test data.

Figure 3.

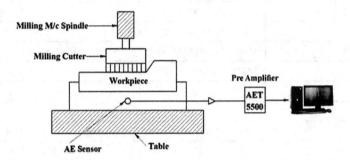

For type 2 data, where the input normalized data has been converted into binary strings. Accordingly, the input dimension of the MLP network is 36. The number of hidden neurons and the learning rate parameter and the momentum term has been varied to decide the optimal value in terms of performance. The optimal values are: No. of hidden neurons -10, $\eta= 0.85$ and $\alpha= 0.05$. The network reached the error of 0.14 in 175000 epochs. Thus, it did not converge to the target error of 0.01. The network gave an accuracy of 91% on training data, whereas on test data it was 60%. This is poor, which can be attributed to the format of the data fed as input to the MLP.

For type 3 data, only the output data was coded into binary bits and the interpretation is as described above. The optimal simulation parameters are $\eta= 0.85$ and $\alpha= 0.05$ and the number of hidden neurons is 12 and the number of epochs taken is 36389. This data format gave the best possible performance in terms of a having a compact network with only 12 hidden neurons, taking least training time and the model gave a result comparable to type 1 data namely 100% on training data and 87% on test data. The binary representation of output leads to better results, as it increased the number of output neurons to three. Also, the representation in the binary format is very useful as it is similar to the real-world interpretation of the tool condition. The tool can be in any one of the three states at any point in time and it's belonging to one state will be more compared to the other states (Pai et al., 2002). Table 3 presents the testing results for sample training and test data.

The MLP network architecture developed for three data formats have resulted in good performance, with type 3 format giving the best possible performance in terms of classification accuracy of 100% on training data and 87% on test data. A compact network was generated with only 12 hidden neurons.

Table 3. Testing results for type 3 data

Pattern No.	Desired output	Network output	Classification error
Training data			
1	0 0 1	0.000274 0.00246 0.990788	4.549072×10^{-5}
2	0 0 1	5.840795×10^{-5} 0.0001520.999986	1.336634×10^{-8}
3	0 1 0	0.000122 0.999951 0.001304	8.589129×10^{-7}
4	0 1 1	9.118312×10^{-5} 0.981859 0.996363	0.000171
5	0 1 1	0.000129 0.999954 0.986036	9.750266×10^{-5}
6	0 1 1	0.000139 0.999963 0.99998	1.055429×10^{-8}
7	0 1 1	0.000134 0.999414 0.999978	1.809107×10^{-7}
8	0 1 1	0.000142 0.999978 0.99897	5.418951×10^{-7}
9	0 0 1	6.581895×10^{-5} 0.018284 0.99881	0.000168
10	0 1 1	0.000109 0.994654 0.999201	1.461647×10^{-5}
Test data			
1	0 1 0	6.0325234×10^{-5} 4.899139×10^{-5} 0.999987	0.999938
2	0 1 0	7.348684×10^{-5} 0.000143 0.966013	0.966448
3	0 1 0	9.057237×10^{-5} 0.967371 0.352656	0.062715
4	0 1 0	0.000103 0.995516 0.017462	0.000163
5	0 1 0	9.264296×10^{-5} 0.931347 0.004932	0.002369

Radial Basis Function Network

"A typical RBFNN consists of three layers, an input layer, a hidden layer and an output layer. The neurons in the hidden layer has a Gaussian activation function with a center and width". There is a need to initialize the centers, width and the number of hidden neurons. The width of the centers can be fixed using a heuristic like P-nearest neighbor or it can be fixed randomly, where the width values are kept constant for all the hidden neurons (Haykin, 1998) (Pai, 2004).

"The learning process taking place in an RBFNN can be understood as – the weights in the output layer vary on a different 'time scale' compared to the nonlinear activation functions in the hidden neurons. These evolve slowly according to some non-linear optimization strategy, whereas the weights in the output layer evolve rapidly through a linear optimization strategy" (Haykin, 1998).

"Three different learning strategies have been chosen for fixing the number of hidden neurons namely fixed centers selected at random, self-organized selection of centers using Batch Fuzzy C means algorithm and initialization of centers using Gradient descent approach" (Haykin, 1998).

Model development: Results and Discussion

(i) Fixed centers selected at random

The simulation parameters used for weights change in the output layer are fixed as $\eta = 0.85$ and $\alpha = 0.05$ and is maintained constant for all studies. The upper limit on the number of training epochs is 175000.

The widths determined using P-nearest neighbor heuristic (with different width value for each RBF unit) has been used. Table 4 shows the corresponding results.

As the number of RBF units increase, the error decreased, reached a minimum for 66 and then started to increase. The drop-in error with number of epochs is very gradual and the target error set is 0.01.

Table 4. Change of error with number of RBF units

No. of RBF units	30	60	66	69
Error	0.387277	0.268209	0.2507	0.253681

Further to understand the effect of keeping the widths constant for all the RBF units, different values are studied and the outcomes are given in Table 5.

Table 5. Change of error with different width values for 66 RBF units

Width value	0.5	0.9	1.5	3.0
Error	0.020268	0.144388	0.429346	0.775172

The error increased with width and the optimum value of width is 0.5 for the lowest error value of 0.020268.

The testing results for different number of RBF units is as shown in Table 6. Further results for different width values is given in Table 9 for 66 hidden neurons.

Table 6. Performance of RBFNN for different number of hidden neurons

No. of RBF units	30	60	66	69
Accuracy on training data	94%	96%	97%	97%
Accuracy on test data	80%	93%	93%	93%

Table 7. Performance of RBFNN with 66 hidden units for different widths

Width value	0.5	0.9	1.5	3.0
Accuracy on training data	100%	99%	97%	90%
Accuracy on test data	87%	93%	93%	80%

As the number of RBF units increases, the accuracy improves for both training and test data and for number of centers equal to number of input training data, there is no change in the classification accuracies. The best performance on training and test data is for 0.9 width. Hence the optimal RBFNN architecture is 12-66-1.

(ii)   Self-organized selection of centers – use of batch fuzzy-c means algorithm

Batch fuzzy-c means algorithm has been used to initialize the centers of the hidden units. "Bezdek developed this algorithm based on fuzzy extensions of the least square criterion" (Pai et al., 2003). The number of units have been initialized randomly. For training this algorithm, the mean squared error has been fixed as 0.001. The number of centers and its location after being established by this algorithm has been used in training and testing the RBFNN. To facilitate learning in the network, the number of training epochs is limited to 175000 and the simulation parameters have been fixed as before. In batch fuzzy-c means algorithm, it is found that as the number of RBF units increases, the error decreases and it is found to be minimum for 50 RBF units, beyond which is starts to increase. The maximum squared error reached is 0.313969 and the drop in the error is gradual (Pai, 2004).

Table 8 gives the details of the results of testing the developed RBFNN for the considered number of RBF units.

Table 8. Performance of RBFNN with centers selected using Batch fuzzy-c means

No. of RBF units	20	30	50	60
Accuracy on training data	96%	94%	97%	97%
Accuracy on test data	87%	93%	93%	93%

The improvement in test performance with changes in number of RBF units is till 50, beyond which there is no much improvement.

(iii)   Center selection using Gradient descent approach

In this strategy, all the free parameters of the network have been modified using gradient descent approach to build the neural network model. Karayiannis (1999) proposed a supervised learning procedure for training reformulated RBF networks. "These networks were generated using linear and exponential generator functions". It was found that use of gradient descent resulted in RBFNN models, which performed better than conventional RBFNN.

In the implementation of this model, the widths of all the hidden units were fixed at 0.9 initially. The RBF units were changed after every 5000 epochs and the widths were calculated using P-nearest neighbor heuristic, which resulted in different width values for different units. The error decreased with increase in the number of RBF units and reached a minimum for 60, and thereafter there was no change. The developed RBFNN was tested for different number of centers and for 60 centers, the accuracy on training data was 91% and on test data was 87%. Further increase in centers showed no variation and afterwards there was a drop in the accuracy.

Thus, this research work focused mainly on use of RBFNN for tool condition monitoring application. Different learning strategies were investigated for selecting the number and location of centers and the widths of the Gaussian RBF units in the hidden layer. This was a focused work related to use of RBFNN for a specific application. Table 9 shows a comparison of different learning strategies.

Table 9. Comparison of RBFNN models for TCM

RBFNN model	Network architecture	Accuracy on Training data	Accuracy on Test data	No. of Epochs
Fixed centers selected at random	12-66-1	97%	93%	175000
Batch fuzzy-c means algorithm	12-50-1	97%	93%	175000
Use of Gradient descent approach	12-60-1	91%	87%	175000

Random selection of centers requires several trials to fix the right number of centers. Batch fuzzy-c means is a robust and effective method to establish the optimal location and number of centers. It uses membership functions to finalize the centers and it will prevent the degradation of the modeling results of the RBFNN, particularly when the data is noisy, as in a shop floor environment. The use of gradient approach has resulted in simultaneous updation of all free parameters of the network, its possibility to be stuck in local minimum is more. Among the three learning strategies, the use of batch fuzzy-c means algorithm has resulted in a compact architecture with 50 centers and has achieved high classification accuracy of 97% and 93% on training and test data for the same training time. Thus, RBFNN are potential neural network models, which can be effectively used in TCM applications (Pai et al., 2002). Table 10 gives sample testing results for RBFNN using batch fuzzy-c means algorithm.

Resource Allocation Network (RAN)

"It is a sequential learning, Gaussian Radial basis function network". While developing a basic RBFNN model,the basis functions are usually chosen as Gaussian and its number is fixed, based on the properties of the input data. The weights of the hidden layer are adjusted using some approach like LMS algorithm. The limitation"with this approach is that it is not suitable for sequential learning and also results in too many hidden units"(Yingwei et al., 1998). To overcome these limitations, Platt (1991) "developed an algorithm that adds hidden units to the network based on the 'novelty' of the input data". Further according to him "learning with a fixed size network is a NP-complete problem and by allocating new resources, learning could be achieved in polynomial time". The architecture of RAN is similar to that of RBFNN. Each hidden unit has two parameters, a center x_j and width σ_j. The output of each hidden unit is multiplied by the connecting weights w_{kj} between hidden and output layer and summed to generate the model output, which is given by $O_k = \Sigma_j w_{kj} V_j$, $j = 1....n$, are the hidden units and

V_j where V_j is the response of the jth hidden unit. "The learning phase of RAN involves adding of new hidden units and modification of the free parameters. Initially the network has no hidden neurons and generates the same as it receives the input-output data". "The decision whether to add a new hidden unit or not depends on the novelty of the data, based on the two conditions:

Table 10. Sample testing results for use of Batch fuzzy-c means algorithm

Pattern No.	Desired output (mm)	Network output (mm)	Classification error
Training data			
1	0.09	0.110032	0.000201
2	0.20	0.181281	0.000175
3	0.30	0.355636	0.001548
4	0.41	0.43981	0.000444
5	0.50	0.504449	9.897484×10^{-6}
6	0.57	0.690509	0.007261
7	0.65	0.58248	0.002279
8	0.73	0.656774	0.002681
9	0.18	0.279994	0.004999
10	0.59	0.429393	0.012897
Test data			
1	0.22	0.235852	0.000126
2	0.25	0.241403	3.695146×10^{-5}
3	0.28	0.315637	0.000635
4	0.31	0.318367	3.500285×10^{-5}
5	0.34	0.353487	9.094973×10^{-5}

(i)   d $=x_j - \xi_i > \delta$ and (ii) e $= \zeta_k - O_k > e_{min}$, δ and e_{min} are thresholds to be fixed based upon the data".

"The initial condition is $\delta = \delta_{max}$, where δ_{max} is chosen as the maximum domain of interest in the input space. The distance δ is decayed exponentially as $\delta = max(\delta_{max} e^{-\frac{t}{\tau}}, \delta_{min})$. This reduction of the distance leads to fewer units with large widths initially and as the number of data increases, more basis functions with smaller widths are added to better the final result. The parameters corresponding to the new hidden units are: $w_{kj}^{new} = e$, $x_j^{new} = x_j$ and $\sigma_j^{new} = \underset{\sim}{K} x_j - \xi_i$, where $\underset{\sim}{K}$ is an overlap factor that determines the quantum of overlay of the responses of the hidden units in the input space. As $\underset{\sim}{K}$ grows larger, there is more overlay of responses". When a data pair (ξ_i, ζ_k) does not qualify the novelty criteria, a hidden unit is not added, but the network parameters are modified to adapt to the data(Platt, 1991) (Yingwei et al., 1998). The detailed RAN algorithm is available in (Nagabhushana, 1996)

Model Development: Results and Discussion

Several trials were carried out to fix the optimal values for the simulation parameters namely δ_{max}, $\underset{\sim}{K}$ and learning rate α. It was found that δ_{max} has the maximum influence on the behavior of the model, particularly the learning time and this was followed by overlap factor and learning rate. Variation of decay constant had no much influence on the results of the network. The optimal value of the simulation parameters is as given in Table 11.

Table 11. Simulation parameters

e_{min}	0.00005
δ_{max}	0.1
δ_{min}	0.01
$\underset{\sim}{K}$	0.2
τ	700
α	0.1
No. of Epochs	16
No. of RBF units	69

Figure 4.

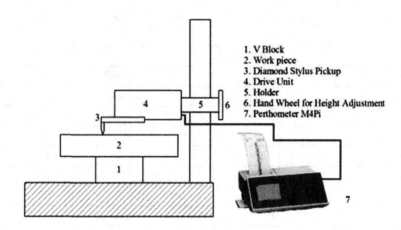

1. V Block
2. Work piece
3. Diamond Stylus Pickup
4. Drive Unit
5. Holder
6. Hand Wheel for Height Adjustment
7. Perthometer M4Pi

Figure 5.

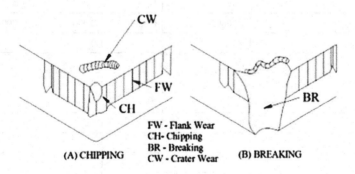

FW - Flank Wear
CH- Chipping
BR - Breaking
CW - Crater Wear

(A) CHIPPING   (B) BREAKING

Fig. 4 depicts the behavior of error as learning proceeds. The error reduces quickly initially and then the reduction is gradual. Fig. 5 shows the addition of RBF units as the network learns in sequence from the data. In the very first epoch, the model adds 65 hidden units and then the remaining 4 units are added in another two epochs and then it remains constant at 69 till 15 epochs are reached. Further to clearly understand the importance of different simulation parameters namely δ_{max}, $\underset{\sim}{K}$ and α, trials have been conducted. The results of testing on the training and test data set is as shown in Table 12.

Table 12. Performance of RAN network for different simulation parameters

e_{min}	0.00005	0.00005	0.00005	0.00005	0.00005
δ_{max}	0.8	0.6	0.4	0.2	0.1
δ_{min}	0.01	0.01	0.01	0.01	0.01
κ	0.6	0.6	0.6	0.6	0.6
τ	700	700	700	700	700
α	0.1	0.1	0.1	0.1	0.1
No. of Epochs	222	120	85	54	49
Accuracy on Training data	100%	100%	100%	100%	100%
Accuracy on Test data	93%	93%	80%	80%	73%
e_{min}	0.00005	0.00005	0.00005	0.00005	0.00005
δ_{max}	0.1	0.1	0.1	0.1	0.1
δ_{min}	0.01	0.01	0.01	0.01	0.01
κ	0.6	0.5	0.2	0.1	0.05
τ	700	700	700	700	700
α	0.1	0.1	0.1	0.1	0.1
No. of Epochs	49	54	16	18	18
Accuracy on Training data	100%	100%	100%	100%	100%
Accuracy on Test data	73%	80%	80%	80%	80%
e_{min}	0.00005	0.00005	0.00005	0.00005	
δ_{max}	0.1	0.1	0.1	0.1	
δ_{min}	0.01	0.01	0.01	0.01	
κ	0.2	0.2	0.2	0.2	
τ	700	700	700	700	
α	0.01	0.05	0.1	0.5	
No.of Epochs	6	16	16	11	
Accuracy on Training data	100%	100%	100%	100%	
Accuracy on Test data	13%	47%	80%	80%	

The training process begins with $\delta(t)=\delta_{max}$, which is the largest length scale of interest. It is generally the size of the complete input space of non-zero probability density. This distance then starts to decrease, until it reaches δ_{min}, which is the smallest length of scale [23]. From the table it is evident that δ_{max} and α have significant influence on the model behavior, especially on the test data. As δ_{max} decreases, the performance of the network deteriorates. As α increased, the performance improved till 0.1, beyond which there was no improvement, except for a decrease in the number of training epochs. The increase in κ caused an improvement in performance on the test data till 0.2, beyond which there was no improvement in performance, but the number of training epochs increased. As κ grows larger, there was more overlap among the responses of the hidden units (Platt, 1991). Fig. 6 shows the network output vs desired output for sample training and test data. The network is able to identify 100% of the training data and 80% of the test data.

Figure 6.

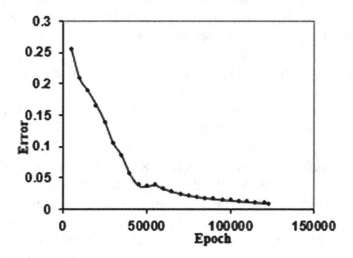

The RAN was also used to model data in type 3 format, which is the use of binary format for the output. The classification accuracy has been found to be 67% on the test data and required 80 training epochs. Thus, it is clear that the network not only performed poorly on the binary format of the data, but also required five time more training time compared to type 1 data requiring only 16 epochs.

Growing Cell Structures

This chapter discusses about the use of various neural network models for TCM applications. Each neural network type has its own advantages and disadvantages. With regard to MLP, there is a need to specify the optimal number of hidden neurons, it takes longer training time due to the possibility of the training getting stuck in local minima and its poor generalization ability. RBFNN also requires specifying of the number of RBF units again by trial and error, whichever may be the leaning strategy selected. This can be very time consuming and at times frustrating. RAN overcomes the limitation of both MLP and RBFNN in terms of specifying the number of hidden neurons and adds neurons based on the 'novelty' in presented input pattern. But it adds too many neurons, sometimes equal to the number of input patterns, resulting in a large network and memorizes the input patterns. This can affect its generalization performance.

To overcome all these limitations, Growing Cell Structures (GCS) was investigated in many of the real time problems and good results were obtained (Nagabhushana, 1996). In this work, results of applying GCS network to TCM applications has been presented to overcome the limitations of the networks already studied and interesting results have been obtained. The authors feel this is the first effort in using this network type for this kind of application.

GCS is an incremental neural network model, where the neurons in the hidden layer are added based on the input data and may vary locally. The architecture starts with two hidden units and adds a unit if certain conditions are violated and determines neurons that fail to perform desirably and removes them to fine tune the performance. It has several advantages over the other neural network models:

(i)   "The incremental nature of the model does not require to prespecify a network size.
(ii)   The growth process continues until a user-defined performance criterion or network size is met.
(iii) The network structure is automatically determined from the domain data to form the topology of the network.
(iv)   Its ability to insert and delete cells allows the accurate estimation of probability densities of input signals.
(v)   All parameters are constant over time in contrast to other models, which rely on decaying parameters" (Fritzke, 1994) (Azuaje et al., 2000).

A distinct GCS network has three layerssimilar to an RBF neural network. The hidden neurons have Gaussian activation functions with center xj and width σ_j. "The width is defined as the mean length of all edges emanating from the best matching unit. The hidden neurons are fully linked to the output layer nodes through weighted connections, w_{kj}, where k =1 and j =1, 2, …..c".

GCS is a learning algorithm based on radial basis functions, that adds resources, but uses a different approach to generate the network architecture. It combines both unsupervised and supervised stages of conventional learning algorithm, so that center adaptation and weight updation are performed for every presented pattern. The algorithm builds the network based on accumulated error information. The details of the algorithm are available in (Nagabhushana, 1996).

Model Development: Results And Discussion

The network architecture initially has two RBF units drawn from the input space and adds RBF units during the learning phase. Simulation parameters like α, A_{max}, β, η and the error for convergence need to be set.The behavior of the network has been analyzed by varying the simulation parameters. The objective is to develop a model with optimal number of hidden neurons, takes least training time and gives good prediction performance. Table 13 shows the performance of GCS network for different simulation parameters.

Table 13. Performance of GCS network for different simulation parameters

α	0.999	0.999	0.999	0.999	0.999	0.999	**0.999**
Amax	11	22	33	44	55	66	**77**
β	10	10	10	10	10	10	**10**
E_{min}	0.3	0.3	0.3	0.3	0.3	0.3	**0.3**
E_{tot}	0.2	0.2	0.2	0.2	0.2	0.2	**0.2**
η	0.05	0.05	0.05	0.05	0.05	0.05	**0.05**
Eps1	0.13	0.12	0.13	0.12	0.13	0.11	**0.12**
Eps2	0.000286	0.000207	0.000286	0.000207	0.000286	0.000146	**0.000207**
No. of Epochs	132	92	88	91	101	89	**90**
No. of RBF units	46	43	43	44	50	43	**25**

i) Varying the value of Amax

Table 14. Varying the value of β

α	0.999	0.999	0.999	0.999	0.999
Amax	77	77	77	77	77
β	10	20	30	40	50
E_{min}	0.3	0.3	0.3	0.3	0.3
E_{tot}	0.2	0.2	0.2	0.2	0.2
η	0.05	0.05	0.05	0.05	0.05
Eps1	0.12	0.11	0.12	0.13	0.13
Eps2	0.000207	0.000146	0.000207	0.000286	0.000286
No. of Epochs	90	95	121	122	280
No. of RBF units	25	45	46	46	84

Table 15. Varying the value of η

α	0.999	0.999	0.999	0.999	0.999
Amax	77	77	77	77	77
β	10	10	10	10	10
E_{min}	0.3	0.3	0.3	0.3	0.3
E_{tot}	0.2	0.2	0.2	0.2	0.2
η	0.01	0.05	0.1	0.2	0.3
Eps1	0.11	0.12	0.12	0.13	0.11
Eps2	0.000146	0.000207	0.000207	0.000286	0.000146
No. of Epochs	127	90	107	376	127
No. of RBF units	63	25	46	105	63

The increase in A_{max} increases decreases the training time. With the increase in the value of β, more number of RBF units are added and the number of epochs required for convergence is also found to increase. Similarly increase of learning rate η causes an increase in training time and the number of RBF units and varies between 25 to 105. The network uses constant adaptation parameters Eps 1 and Eps 2 for determining the optimal cluster centers, which are nothing but RBF centers. "For each input pattern presented, find the nearest localizing unit and call it the 'best matching unit' (BMU) and move the BMU Eps 1 times the current distance towards the input pattern and move all immediate neighbours of BMU, Eps 2 times the current distance towards the input pattern. This process is called 'center adaptation'. The values for Eps1 and Eps 2 have been determined by trial and error". Fig. 7 and 8 shows the behavior of error with epochs and addition of RBF units with epochs.

Figure 7.

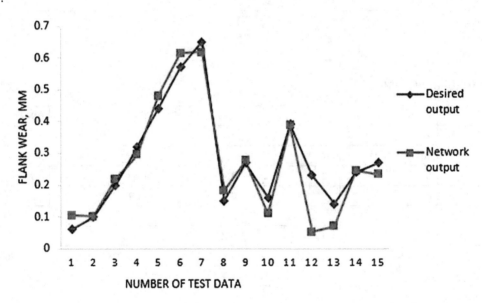

Figure 8.

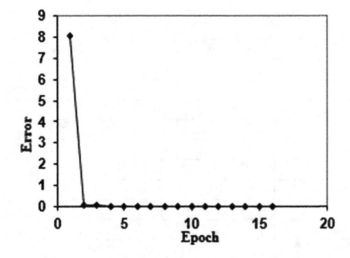

The error shows a gradual decrease, with some variations in between. The number of RBF units added is almost in a step like manner, till 25 units are added. Table 16 gives the testing results of the developed GCS network for sample training and test data.

Table 16. Sample Testing results for GCS network

Pattern No.	Actual output in mm	Model output in mm	Classification error
Training data			
1	0.09	0.1574	0.004549
2	0.20	0.1959	0.000017
3	0.30	0.3988	0.009770
4	0.41	0.4879	0.006071
5	0.50	0.4862	0.000191
6	0.57	0.4908	0.006274
7	0.65	0.6313	0.000350
8	0.73	0.6765	0.002860
9	0.18	0.3324	0.023217
10	0.59	0.5141	0.005762
Test data			
1	0.22	0.1850	0.001226
2	0.25	0.2411	0.000079
3	0.28	0.2870	0.000048
4	0.31	0.3408	0.000947
5	0.34	0.2875	0.002758

The developed GCS network has been able to provide a prediction accuracy of 96% on the training data and 93% on the test data. The network has a compact architecture with only 25 hidden neurons, as they get added automatically through a growth process, which can be stopped as soon as the network starts giving good prediction results. "Also, the positioning of the RBF units and the supervised training of the connection weights between the hidden and output layer happen in parallel, the current classification error can be used to determine the location of new RBF units.Also, the network generalizes well, as evident from the accuracies"(Fritzke, 1994b).

CONCLUSION

"Monitoring is an important requirement in manufacturing process control and management". Monitoring systems have seen lot of changes in the last several years, which are becoming intelligent (Oborski, 2014). Machining is an important component of any manufacturing process. The automation and optimization of the machining processes is influenced by the condition of the cutting tool. The tool condition influences product quality, increases downtime, increases costs and sometimes affects the machine tool and personnel. Tool Condition Monitoring (TCM) helps in detecting all the major problems related to the cutting tool during machining and helps to improve accuracy in machining and also the availability of machines. The developments in the field of TCM is due to developments in the field of methods, sensors, monitoring and supervision systems, acquisition of data, analysis and decision-making systems. The acquisition of data is related to direct and indirect measurement of signals, which can be either acquired offline after machining or online during machining. "This includes cutting forces, load drives, current, acoustic emission, sound, noise, vibration, vision etc". The data obtained needs to be analyzed using methods like ANN, fuzzy logic etc. The reliability and robustness of a monitoring system can be increased, if data based on several measurement signals are used (Oborski, 2014). This can lead to 'sensor fusion' or 'sensor integration'. This work basically focusses on using acoustic emission, which is an online monitored signal and surface roughness, which has been measured offline along with the cutting conditions to predict the tool wear, particularly flank wear in face milling operations carried out on En 8 steel using uncoated carbide inserts. Accordingly use of AE, surface roughness and cutting conditions has facilitated achieving sensor fusion.

Tool wear monitoring is a complex task and hence signals from two domain have been integrated using artificial neural networks. ANN can interpolate very effectively, even when the data is sparse and noisy. It can effectively model the input output relationships, without knowing the underlying distributions. The focus of this work is to suggest an ANN type, which can generate a compact and optimal architecture, which has good generalization ability, which is the ability to estimate tool wear and accordingly monitor the condition of the tool.

Some of the specific conclusions drawn from the study are as follows (Pai, 2004):

(i)   MLP is a widely used ANN type in tool condition monitoring applications. It performs well when the data is continuous in nature for both input and output. Though it is robust and accurate in estimating tool wear values, it requires longer training time, has problem of local minima and there is a need for several trials to establish the optimum number of hidden neurons.

(ii)   RBF neural networks another class of feed forward network has been explored in terms of learning strategies fixing the location of centers and the width of the hidden neurons. RBFNN using batch fuzzy c means algorithm performs well with good generalization ability. These networks do not get stuck in local minima as in case of MLPNN. But they suffer limitations in terms of fixing the number and location of centers and the widths of the RBF units. Also, the network architecture is not compact as in case of MLPNN.

(iii) RAN is a variant of RBF neural network, which uses a dynamic learning algorithm that builds the network architecture during training. It learns very fast when compared to other neural network models. Since it adds large number of hidden units, sometimes almost equal to the number of input patterns, it memorizes the data and hence generalizes poorly.

(iv)   GCS is a powerful learning algorithm based on RBF, that builds an optimal architecture. It is an incremental neural network model, wherein it adds and removes hidden units based on certain criteria. GCS network generates very compact network architecture. It trains faster and exhibits good generalization ability.

In this work, a compact ANN model of architecture 12-25-1 has been generated in least time (90 epochs) with good generalization performance in terms of 93% accuracy on tests data.

Thus, this chapter focusses on a systematic and detailed investigation in developing a compact and optimal neural network architecture, which can perform tool wear estimation effectively for TCM and can be easily applied offline in a practical shop floor environment.

ACKNOWLEDGMENT

This research received no specific grant from any funding agency in the public, commercial, or not-for-profit sectors.

Thanks are due to Dr. P.K. Ramakrishna Rao, Former Professor, Dept. of Mechanical Engg., SJCE, Mysuru for allowing the use of research facilities obtained from DST, New Delhi sponsored research project. The support of Dr. S.K. Padma, Professor, Dept. of Computer Science &Engg., SJCE, Mysuru, with regard to help in coding the algorithms used in this work is acknowledged.

REFERENCES

Azuaje, F., Dubitzky, W., Black, N., & Adamson, K. (2000). Discovering relevance knowledge in data: A Growing cell Structures approach. *IEEE Transactions on Systems, Man, and Cybernetics. Part B, Cybernetics*, *30*(3), 448–460. doi:10.1109/3477.846233 PMID:18252376

Balazinski, M., Czogala, E., Jemielniak, K., & Leski, J. (2002). Tool condition monitoring using artificial intelligence methods. *Engineering Applications of Artificial Intelligence*, *15*(1), 73–80. doi:10.1016/S0952-1976(02)00004-0

Chelladurai, H., Jain, V. K., & Vyas, N. S. (2008). Development of a cutting tool condition monitoring system for high speed turning operation by vibration and strain analysis. *International Journal of Advanced Manufacturing Technology*, *37*(5-6), 471–485. doi:10.100700170-007-0986-z

Chen, J. C., & Chen, J. C. (2005). An artificial-neural-networks-based in-process tool wear prediction system in milling operations. *International Journal of Advanced Manufacturing Technology*, *25*(5-6), 427–434. doi:10.100700170-003-1848-y

Cho, S., Binsaeid, S., & Asfour, S. (2010). Design of multisensor fusion-based tool condition monitoring system in end milling. *International Journal of Advanced Manufacturing Technology*, *46*(5-8), 681–694. doi:10.100700170-009-2110-z

Dimla, D. E. Jr, Lister, P. M., & Leighton, N. J. (1997). Neural Network solutions to the Tool Condition Monitoring Problem in Metal cutting – A critical review of methods. *International Journal of Machine Tools & Manufacture*, *37*(9), 1291–1241. doi:10.1016/S0890-6955(97)00020-5

Dornfeld, D. A. (1986). Acoustic Emission Monitoring for Untended Manufacturing. *Proceedings of Japan / USA Symposium on Flexible Automation*.

Elbestawi, M. A., & Dumitrescu, M. (2006). Tool Condition Monitoring in Machining – Neural Networks. In IFIP International Federation for Information Processing, Volume 220, Information Technology for Balanced manufacturing Systems(pp. 5-16). Boston: Springer.

Elbestawi, M. A., Dumitrescu, M., & Ng, E.-G. (2006). Tool Condition Monitoring in Machining. In *Condition Monitoring and Control for Intelligent Manufacturing* (pp 55-82). Springer-Verlag London Limited. doi:10.1007/1-84628-269-1_3

Fritzke, B. (1994). A Growing Neural Gas Network Learns Topologies. *Advances in Neural Information Processing Systems*, *6*, 625–632.

Fritzke, B. (1994). Growing Cell Structures – A Self organizing network for Unsupervised and Supervised learning. *Neural Networks*, *7*(9), 1441–1460. doi:10.1016/0893-6080(94)90091-4

Haykin, S. (1998). *Neural Networks – A Comprehensive Foundation*. New York: Macmillan College Publishing Company.

Jain, R. K. (2009). *Engineering Metrology*. New Delhi: Khanna Publishers.

Karayiannis, N. B. (1999). Reformulated Radial basis neural networks trained by Gradient descent. *IEEE Transactions on Neural Networks*, *10*(3), 657–671. doi:10.1109/72.761725 PMID:18252566

Kumar, S., Sharma, B., Sharma, V. K., & Poonia, R. C. (2018). Automated Soil prediction using bag-of-features and chaotic spider monkey optimization algorithm. *Evolutionary Intelligence*. doi:10.100712065-018-0186-9

Liang, S., & Dornfeld, D. A. (1989). Tool wear detection using time series analysis of acoustic emission. *ASME J. Eng. Ind. Trans.*, *111*(3), 199–205. doi:10.1115/1.3188750

Nagabhushana, T. N. (1996). *Fault diagnosis of AC and AC-DC systems using Constructive Learning RBF Neural Networks* (PhD Thesis). Dept. of High Voltage Engineering, IISc, Bangalore, India.

Oborski, P. (2014). Developments in integration of advanced monitoring systems. *International Journal of Advanced Manufacturing Technology*, *75*(9-12), 1613–1632. doi:10.100700170-014-6123-x

Ozel, T., & Karpat, Y. (2005). Predictive modeling of surface roughness and tool wear in hard turning using regression and neural networks. *International Journal of Machine Tools & Manufacture*, *45*(4-5), 467–479. doi:10.1016/j.ijmachtools.2004.09.007

Pai, P. S., Nagabhushana, T. N., & Rao, P. K. R. (2002). Flank wear estimation in Face milling based on Radial Basis Function Neural Networks. *International Journal of Advanced Manufacturing Technology*, *20*(4), 241–247. doi:10.1007001700200148

Pai, S. (2004). *Acoustic emission based Tool wear monitoring using Some Improved neural network methodologies* (PhD Thesis). Mysore University, Mysore, India.

Pai, S., Nagabhushana, T. N., & Rao, P. K. R. (2003) Tool wear monitoring in face milling using Fuzzy c means clustering techniques. In *Proceedings of National Conference on Advances in Manufacturing Technology, AMT 2003*. NSS Engineering College.

Panda, S. S., Chakraborty, D., & Pal, S. K. (2008). Flank wear prediction in Drilling using Back propagation neural network and Radial basis function network. *Applied Soft Computing*, *8*(2), 858–871. doi:10.1016/j.asoc.2007.07.003

Pandey, S., & Solanki, A. (2019). *Music Instrument Recognition using Deep Convolutional Neural Networks. International Journal of Information Technology.* doi:10.100741870-019-00285-y

Platt, J. (1991). A resource allocating network for function interpolation. *Neural Computation, 3*(2), 213–225. doi:10.1162/neco.1991.3.2.213 PMID:31167310

Rehorn, A. G., Jinag, J., & Orban, P. E. (2005). State-of-the-art methods and results in tool condition monitoring- A review. *International Journal of Advanced Manufacturing Technology, 26*(7-8), 693–710. doi:10.100700170-004-2038-2

Sharma, S., Sharma, B., Sharma, V.K., Sharma, H., & Bansal, J.C. (2018). Plant leaf disease identification using exponential spider monkey optimization. Sustainable Computing: Informatics and Systems. doi:10.1016/j.suscom.2018.10.004

Sick, B. (2002). On-line and Indirect tool wear monitoring in turning with artificial neural networks: A review of more than a decade of research. *Mechanical Systems and Signal Processing, 16*(4), 487–546. doi:10.1006/mssp.2001.1460

Xiaoli, L. (2002). A brief review: Acoustic emission method for tool wear monitoring during turning. *International Journal of Machine Tools & Manufacture, 42*(2), 157–165. doi:10.1016/S0890-6955(01)00108-0

Yingwei, L., Sundararajan, N., & Saratchandran, P. (1998). Performance evaluation of a Sequential Minimal Radial Basis Function (RBF) Neural network learning algorithm. *IEEE Transactions on Neural Networks, 9*(2), 308–318. doi:10.1109/72.661125 PMID:18252454

Zeng, W., Jiang, X., & Blunt, L. (2009). Surface characterization-based tool wear monitoring in peripheral milling. *International Journal of Advanced Manufacturing Technology, 40*(3-4), 226–233. doi:10.100700170-007-1352-x

ADDITIONAL READING

Zhou, Y., & Xue, W. (2018). Review of tool condition monitoring methods in milling processes. *International Journal of Advanced Manufacturing Technology, 96*(5-8), 2509–2523. doi:10.100700170-018-1768-5

KEY TERMS AND DEFINITIONS

ANN Architecture: The arrangement of neurons in different layers of a artificial neural network model for a given problem and after fixing the number of neurons in the hidden layer(s) based on the optimization strategy adopted.

ANN Model Development: It is a process of developing a model using artificial neural network type, which can represent the input-output relationships for a given problem.

Automation: It is a technology an activity can be performed with minimum human intervention.

Cutting Tool Failure: It is the inability of a cutting tool to perform its intended role in any machining operation and can occur in terms of wear, fracture or breakage.

Face Milling: It is a machining process, where in the surfaces are produced in a direction perpendicular to the axis of the cutter. It generally produces flat surfaces.

Incremental Neural Network: It is a method of developing an artificial neural network model, where the neurons in the hidden layer are added or removed based on certain criteria and the availability of the training data.

Sensor Fusion: It is a process of combining data from different sensors/sources such that uncertainty in information from one sensor is offset by that from other sensors and more information is available.

This research was previously published in the Handbook of Research on Emerging Trends and Applications of Machine Learning; pages 550-576, copyright year 2020 by Engineering Science Reference (an imprint of IGI Global).

Chapter 20
Role of Artificial Neural Network for Prediction of Gait Parameters and Patterns

Kamalpreet Sandhu

School of Design II, Product and Industrial Design, Lovely Professional University, India

Vikram Kumar Kamboj

School of Electronics and Electrical Engineering, Lovely Professional University, India

ABSTRACT

Walking is very important exercise. Walking is characterized by gait. Gait defines the bipedal and forward propulsion of center of gravity of the human body. This chapter describes the role of artificial neural network (ANN) for prediction of gait parameters and patterns for human locomotion. The artificial neural network is a mathematical model. It is computational system inspired by the structure, processing method, and learning ability of a biological brain. According to bio-mechanics perspective, the neural system is utilized to check the non-direct connections between datasets. Also, ANN model in gait application is more desired than bio-mechanics strategies or statistical methods. It produces models of gait patterns, predicts horizontal ground reactions forces (GRF), vertical GRF, recognizes examples of stand, and predicts incline speed and distance of walking.

INTRODUCTION

Ergonomics is the study of individuals at work. This field got its name in the mid-year of 1949 when a group of intrigued people gathered in Oxford, England to discuss human performance and its limits. Ergonomics comes from Greek word 'Ergo' and 'Nomics'. 'Ergo' implies work and 'Nomics' implies study. A few specialists define the objective of ergonomics and as designing machines to fit the human operator requirements. However, it is also necessary to fit operations to machine in the form of personnel channel selection and training. It is probably more accurate to describe this field as the study of human machine systems, with an emphasis on the human aspects. Ergonomists deals with the fact that people

DOI: 10.4018/978-1-6684-2408-7.ch020

come in different sizes and shapes, varying greatly in their strength, endurance and work capacity. A basic understanding of human anatomy, physiology and psychology can help ergonomists to find solutions that deal with these issues and help to prevent problems that can cause injury to workers. Scope of this problem, can be studied by considering some of the components system terms by the human body. Walking is very important exercise associated with human being. There are different types of walking i.e. Brisk walking, Treadmill waking, Interval walking, Water walking and Hill walking. Human want to walk for the purpose of the health benefits also. The human being has a stride length of 640.08 to 742mm, it take over 2000 steps to walk one mile. On an average a person covers 10,000 steps a day. Human foot movement is based on the gait cycle. Walking is characterized by Gait. Locomotion produced through the movement of human limbs. Gait defines the bipedal and forward propulsion of center of gravity (COG) of the human body. Natural gaits are of two types i.e. Walk and skip. The healthy person up to 6 years follows walking while under age of the 4 to 5 years called as skipping by children. The various stages of the gait cycle show in Figure1 are Heel contact, Flat foot, Mid-stance, Heel off and Toe off.

- **Heel Contact:** The starting of the stance phase is called the heel-strike because there is an impact between the heel and the ground.
- **Foot Flat:** After heel contact, the rest of the foot comes in contact with the ambulatory surface at foot flat. This generally occurs at about 8% of the gait cycle, just before toe off of the opposite leg. During the interval between heel strike and foot flat the GRF increase rapidly in magnitude.
- **Mid Stance:** The period of time between foot flat and heel off which occurs at about 30% of the gait cycle. At this point, the swing phase leg passes the stance phase leg.
- **Heel Off:** When the heel begins to lift from the walking surface. It occurs between 40-50% of the gait cycle.
- **Toe Off:** This occurs at about 60% of the gait cycle when the stance phase ends and swing phase begins. This phase is also commonly called the push off phase.
- **Mid Swing:** This is the opposite of mid-stance as the mid-swing on one leg corresponds to the mid-stance of the other. It is the time when the swinging leg passes the stance leg.

Figure 1. Various stages of the gait cycles (Marco, Augusto, Fabio, Giovanni, Carlo, Stefano, & Antonella, 2013)

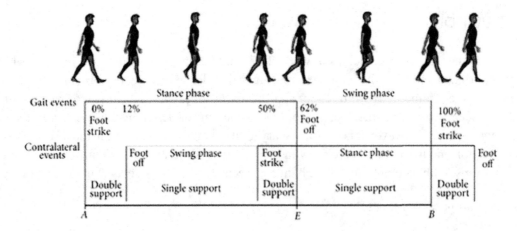

Methods of Measuring Gait

Different types of methods used to measure the gait analysis. The current technologies used for measure gait are: Motion capture camera, Force plates, Electromyography, Inertial measurement systems, Foot scan insole/Plantar pressure distribution insoles.

- **Motion Capture Camera:** The motion capture camera is basically used for measuring motion of objects or peoples. This system consider as gold standardize system and it require heavy equipment's and tight clothes for placement which may cause patients. Although wearing of heavy equipment's effect in natural gait of the human being. In addition this system is good for measuring the joint motions of lower extremity. The possibility of use this instrument in only laboratory and hard to use in daily living.
- **Force Plate:** The first commercial force plate discovered in 1969 (R Baker, 2007). Force plate consists of piezoelectric sensors mounted between two plates. The task of force plate is basically to calculate the ground reaction forces. Force plate is also used along with the motion capture camera. The disadvantage of force plate is basically it can be used in the laboratory.
- **Electromyography:** Electromyography in gait analysis used to measure the electrical activity of the muscle during contraction. Sensors are placed on the skin or the fine wire inserted into the muscle of interest.
- **Foot Scan Insole:** Foot scan insole is also known as plantar pressure distribution instrument. Basically used to measure the pressure on feet at different pressure points i.e. forefoot, mid-foot, hind-foot, heel, lateral, medial and overall foot. This system consists of thousands of pressure sensors which gives the pressure applied by the foot.
- **Sensor Based Insole:** It consists of different types of sensors. The typically used sensors are force sensitive resistors, PVDF, air pressure sensors, bi-directional sensors, bend sensor, flex sensors and electric field height sensors. This type of insole embeds into the shoes to collect pressure.

Figure 2. Current Gait measurement technologies

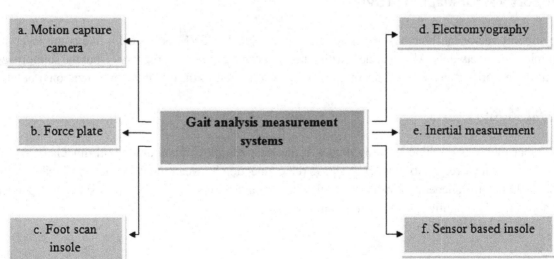

BACKGROUND

It is the use of man-made reasoning using for predicting the exact outcomes. It can get input information and used statistical analysis to predict the output value within an acceptable range.

Prediction using Machine Learning Models

Machine Learning comprises of two types supervised and unsupervised. Learning has different models: decision tree, random forest, ada boost, support vector machine, linear model and artificial neural network.

Random Forest

Random Forest is a machine learning method mainly used in regression and classification problems. After training, it generates multiple numbers of decision trees. Random forest work when different subset of training data are selected and with replacement to train each tree. The remaining data used for error calculations and importance of variables. Numbers of votes from the entire tree select the class alignment.

Decision Tree

Decision tree is a machine learning method using a tree like graph of decision. It used a set of binary rules and calculates the target values. It can be used as classification as well as regression problems. To determine the best node different types of algorithm was used.

Ada Boost

Ada boost is the machine learning method plays a good rule in linear classification problems. This type of method basically used in combination with many classification algorithms for improve the performance of the model.

Support Vector Machine (SVM)

The support vector machine is supervised learning model. The SVM is basically like a one layer and multiple neural networks. All machine learning method working on linear regression but the support vector machine working on the Non-linear regression problems. It uses the quadratic optimization problems.

Linear Model

The linear model is machine learning model, it the least complex model among all models. It will be nearer to the linear regression model. It shows the connection between the dependent and independent variable. Only one independent variable, it called as a simple regression model. At least two independent variables, it called multiple linear regression models.

Artificial Neural Networks

Artificial neural networks used in supervised, unsupervised and reinforced learning. This model looks like a neurons working in the mind. Neurons passed signal to another signal till the output is given by the body. The fundamental condition of the neural systems is given beneath:

Input $= W_1I_1 + W_2I_2 + \ldots\ldots\ldots W_nI_n + b$ 1.1
W= Weights
I= Inputs
b= bias
Output = f(WI+b) 1.2

It has been observed that force plate was expected to give us the GRF step by step (Winter, 1990) yet a few specialists express that the current strategies don't precisely reflect individual physical activity levels, and further techniques does not precisely respond individual physical action levels, and further strategies advancement of physical movement apparatuses should be high need of research (Goran, M.I, Sun, M, 1998). It has been discovered that the utilization of ANN model in gait application is more desired than biomechanics strategies or different methods (Sepulveda, F., Wells, D.M, Vaughan, C.L, 1993). Various researchers observed that ANN is good model for discovering complex connections between examples of various signals (Sepulveda, F., Wells, D.M, Vaughan, C.L, 1993), (Breit, G.A., Whalen, R.T., 1997). For a human locomotion, the ANN can be utilized to predict gait parameters (Su, F.C., Wu, W.L., 2000). And gait patterns [Sepulveda, F., Wells, D.M, Vaughan, C.L, 1993), (Srinivasan, S, Gander, R.E., Wood, H.C, 1992). It produces models of gait patterns (Savelberg, H.H.C.M, de Lange, A.L.H, 1999) predicts horizontal GRF (Gioftsos, G, Grieve, D.W., 1996), vertically GRF, recognizes examples of stand (Aminian, K, Robert, P, Jequier, E, Schutz, Y, 1995) and predicts incline speed and distance of walking (Crowe, A, Samson, M.M, Hoitsma, M.J, van Ginkel, A.A, 1996). GRF has been utilized to decide the walking pattern (Goran, M.I, Sun, M, 1998), (Bertani, A, Cappello, A, Benedetti, M.G, Simoncini, L, Catani, F, 1999), (Giakas, G, Baltzopoulos, V, 1997) and balance of gait and posture (Bertani, A, Cappello, A, Benedetti, M.G, Simoncini, L, Catani, F, 1999), (Andriacchi, T.P, Ogle, J.A, Galante, J.O, 1977). A study demonstrated relationship between the variety of walk forces parameters, speed, and power, which vary with foot ground contact time (Cavagna, G.A, Kaneko, M, 1977), (Cavanagh, P.R, Lafortune, M.A, 1980), (Grasso, R, Bianchi, L, Lacquaniti, F, 1998), (Munro, C.F, Miller, D.I, Fuglevand, A.J, 1987). When human being increase the walking speed results in higher vertically force, horizontal force and decrease in the foot ground contact time (Keller, T.S., Weisberger, A.M., Ray, J.L, Hassan, S.S, Shiavi, R.G,Spengler, D.M,1996). The Pictorial view of the ANN model.

The Objective of this chapter is to describe the role and importance of ANN for predicting the gait parameters and patterns.

Figure 3. Pictorial view of ANN

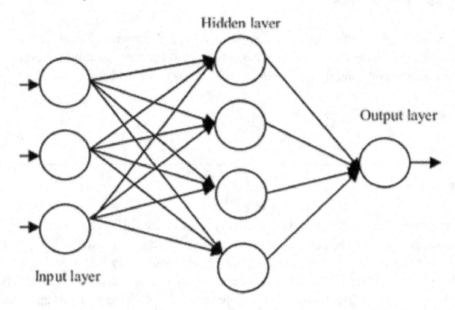

MAIN FOCUS AREA OF CHAPTER

The focus area of this chapter is to describe the role, importance and utilization of ANN for predicting the gait parameters and patterns by different researchers. Wang *et.al* (Wang, C.S, Wang, C.C. and Chang, T.R, 2013) researched the fitting of the human foot in various shoe insoles. Grey relational approach was utilized to evaluate the foot shapes and shoe insoles. ANN (Back propagation neural networks) was utilized to predict the most proper insoles for the foot. Results from plantar pressure experiment were analyzed with grey relational calculations and found the best insole for the human foot. Joo *et.al* (Joo, S.B, Oh, S.E, Sim, T, Kim, H, Choi, C.H, Koo, H. and Mun, J.H, 2014) predicted gait speed in stance and swing stage in reference to foot scan insole data gained by the plantar pressure measuring device. Information was gathered from 20 adults (10 guys and 10 females) having age 24.5±.3years and height 1.68±0.08m. The data collection was filtered with cut off frequency of 100 Hz. ANN was utilized to predict the gait speed. 99 weight sensors were used to create input information for the model. Robustness of models was checked by five k-fold validation. The model was evaluated for gait speed in three unique conditions normal walking, slow walking and fast walking. The correlation coefficient (r) was calculated and found 0.963 for normal walking, 0.998 for slow walking and 0.95 for fast walking.

Favre *el.al* (Favre, J, Hayoz, M, Erhart-Hledik, J.C. and Andriacchi, T.P, 2012) used ANN to predict knee adduction moments during walking based on the Ground Reaction Forces (GRF) and Anthropometric measurements. Force plate was used to measure forces and human link locomotion was capture by motion capture camera. The model was evaluated by using a correlation coefficients and mean absolute error. Correlation coefficients(r) were calculated for slow speed (mid-stance peak-0.74, terminal stance peak-0.55, mid stance angular impulse-0.78 and terminal stance angular impulse-0.63), normal speed (mid-stance peak-0.76, terminal stance peak-0.64, mid stance angular impulse-0.77 and terminal stance angular impulse-0.74) and fast speed (mid-stance peak-0.78, terminal stance peak-0.64, mid stance angular impulse-0.76 and terminal stance angular impulse-0.69).

Figure 4. Pictorial view of the joo et.al (Joo, S.B, Oh, S.E, Sim, T, Kim, H, Choi, C.H, Koo, H. and Mun, J.H, 2014) research efforts

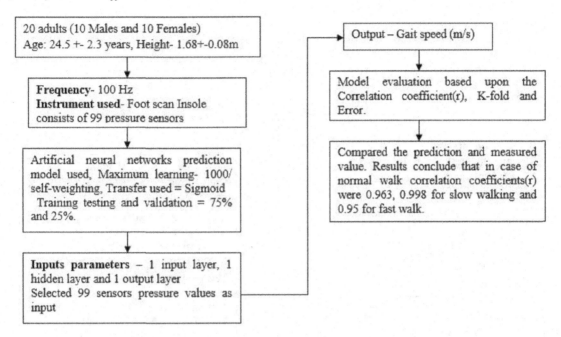

Figure 5. ANN architecture selected as prediction model (Joo, S.B, Oh, S.E, Sim, T, Kim, H, Choi, C.H, Koo, H. and Mun, J.H, 2014)

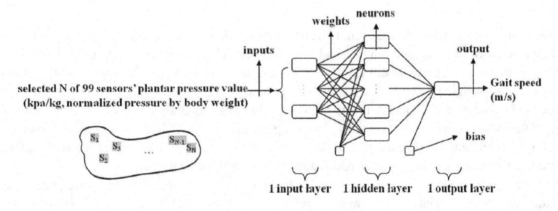

Zhang *et.al* (Zhang, K., Sun, M., Lester, D.K, Pi-Sunyer, F.X., Boozer, C.N. and Longman, R.W, 2005) suggested new method for measuring human locomotion. Portable insole system was used to measure the GRF. Data from 40 participated was collected in different conditions i.e. walking, running, ascending and descending stairs in slow, normal and fast speed. ANN was used to predict the type of walking and identify the human gait patterns. The model was evaluated on the basis of accuracy. Accuracy recorded 98.77%, 98.3% for 97.3% and 97.2% for walking, running, ascending and descending respectively.

Figure 6. Pictorial view of the Favre et.al (Favre, J, Hayoz, M, Erhart-Hledik, J.C. and Andriacchi, T.P, 2012) research efforts

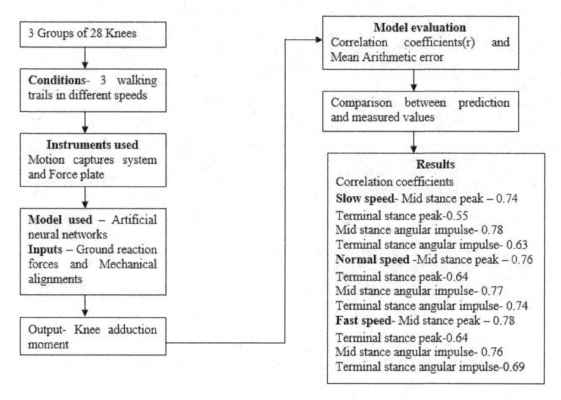

OH *el.al* (Oh, S.E, Choi, A. and Mun, J.H, 2013) described the prediction of Ground Reaction Forces during gait, based on kinematics. In this study Newtonian mechanics and ANN was used. The data was filtered with the cut off frequency of 120 Hz and walking time of 10 minute. The characteristics of ANN used were self-weighting and bipolar sigmoid. The input of the model was gait cycle and output was forces and moments in X, Y and Z directions. Ten k-fold cross validation was used to check the robustness of the model. The model was evaluated by using correlation coefficient and root mean square error (RMSE). Correlation coefficients(r) found for forces in X, Y and Z directions were 0.91, 0.98 and 0.99. A recorded value of moments in X, Y and Z directions were 0.98, 0.89 and 0.86.

Toso *el.al* (Toso, M.A. and Gomes, H.M, 2014) calculated vertical force (Fz) on force plate system. It calibrated using artificial neural networks to reduce uncertainties. Math-works (2011) was used in this work. Model was runs on default settings. Each cell data calculated from force plate was used as input for the ANN. ANN model predicted force (Fz) accurately. Ruperez *et.al* (Rupérez, M.J, Martín-Guerrero, J.D, Monserrat, C. and Alcañiz, M, 2012) predicted of pressure on the foot surface using artificial neural networks model using Multilayer perception. Inputs used for ANN model was characteristics of materials and data obtained from 14 sensors. The prediction values were compared with the measured values. The value of correlation coefficients(r) was found to be close to 0.9.

Figure 7. Pictorial view of the Zhang et.al (Zhang, K., Sun, M., Lester, D.K., Pi-Sunyer, F.X., Boozer, C.N. and Longman, R.W, 2005) research efforts

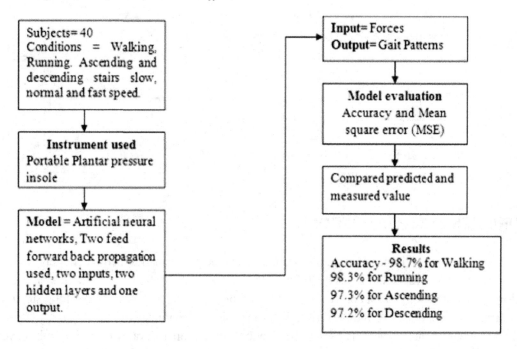

Figure 8. Pictorial view of the OH et.al (Oh, S.E, Choi, A. and Mun, J.H, 2013) research efforts

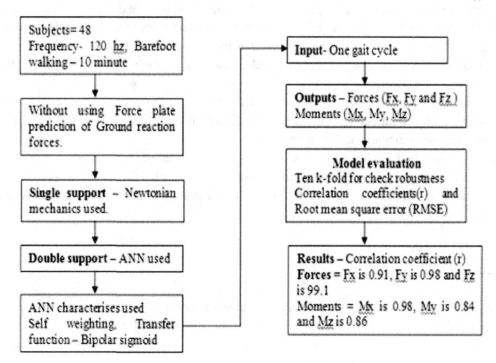

Figure 9. Process of predicting the GRF (Oh, S.E., Choi, A. and Mun, J.H., 2013)

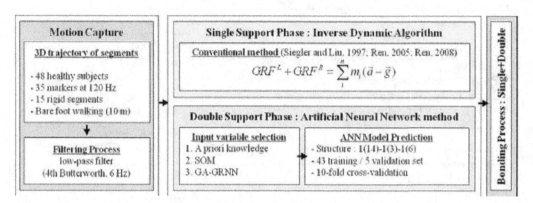

FUTURE RESEARCH DIRECTIONS

- Experiments with a larger domain of parameters can be performed to achieve better results.
- From the Literature survey it has been found that most of research efforts are made on short duration of time and single foot consider. For future scope of work, it may consider long step duration of time two foot consider and perform ANN to predict gait parameters.
- Technique with muscle activity as intrinsic feedback to obtain accurate end-point limb movements could form the basis of neural prosthesis interface for allowing people with SB and other paralyzed patients to independently control voluntary movements of prosthetic limbs. Looking ahead, we will develop a self-organizing adaptive controller with low-power and high-performance computing technology for neural prostheses to enhance independent movement for people with disability.
- Also, in Literature survey it has been found that mostly predicting of the gait parameters by using insole sensors but for future scope consider human age, height, weight for predict force and plantar pressure between the foot.
- In the future it will be necessary to develop a model that can Predict gait speed for abnormal gait by using patients' data and to study a new prediction method to overcome the problems of the training process in artificial neural networks.
- Since the gait speed prediction method through ANN suggested in this study is not affected by the limitation of experiment location and procedure, it is expected to contribute to the future studies of related research by being used as basic material in studies that require data on both plantar pressure and gait speed.

CONCLUSION

In this chapter effort has been made on role of artificial neural network for prediction of Gait parameters and patterns. It has been found that lot of research are pending in predicting the gait parameters and patterns. This chapter include that outcomes of previous research were tested with further subjects and results were found to be in close proximity.

REFERENCES

Aminian, K., Robert, P., Jéquier, E., & Schutz, Y. (1995). Incline, speed, and distance assessment during unconstrained walking. *Medicine and Science in Sports and Exercise, 27*(2), 226–234. doi:10.1249/00005768-199502000-00012 PMID:7723646

Andriacchi, T. P., Ogle, J. A., & Galante, J. O. (1977). Walking speed as a basis for normal and abnormal gait measurements. *Journal of Biomechanics, 10*(4), 261–268. doi:10.1016/0021-9290(77)90049-5 PMID:858732

Baker, R. (2007). The history of gait analysis before the advent of modern computers. *Gait & Posture, 26*(3), 331–342. doi:10.1016/j.gaitpost.2006.10.014 PMID:17306979

Bertani, A., Cappello, A., Benedetti, M. G., Simoncini, L., & Catani, F. (1999). Flat foot functional evaluation using pattern recognition of ground reaction data. *Clinical Biomechanics (Bristol, Avon), 14*(7), 484–493. doi:10.1016/S0268-0033(98)90099-7 PMID:10521632

Breit, G. A., & Whalen, R. T. (1997). Prediction of human gait parameters from temporal measures of foot-ground contact. *Medicine and Science in Sports and Exercise, 29*(4), 540–547. doi:10.1097/00005768-199704000-00017 PMID:9107638

Cavagna, G. A., & Kaneko, M. (1977). Mechanical work and efficiency in level walking and running. *The Journal of Physiology, 268*(2), 467–481. doi:10.1113/jphysiol.1977.sp011866 PMID:874922

Cavanagh, P. R., & Lafortune, M. A. (1980). Ground reaction forces in distance running. *Journal of Biomechanics, 13*(5), 397–406. doi:10.1016/0021-9290(80)90033-0 PMID:7400169

Crowe, A., Samson, M. M., Hoitsma, M. J., & van Ginkel, A. A. (1996). The influence of walking speed on parameters of gait symmetry determined from ground reaction forces. *Human Movement Science, 15*(3), 347–367. doi:10.1016/0167-9457(96)00005-X

Favre, J., Hayoz, M., Erhart-Hledik, J. C., & Andriacchi, T. P. (2012). A neural network model to predict knee adduction moment during walking based on ground reaction force and anthropometric measurements. *Journal of Biomechanics, 45*(4), 692–698. doi:10.1016/j.jbiomech.2011.11.057 PMID:22257888

Giakas, G., & Baltzopoulos, V. (1997). Time and frequency domain analysis of ground reaction forces during walking: An investigation of variability and symmetry. *Gait & Posture, 5*(3), 189–197. doi:10.1016/S0966-6362(96)01083-1

Gioftsos, G., & Grieve, D. W. (1996). The use of artificial neural networks to identify patients with chronic low-back pain conditions from patterns of sit-to-stand manoeuvres. *Clinical Biomechanics (Bristol, Avon), 11*(5), 275–280. doi:10.1016/0268-0033(96)00013-7 PMID:11415632

Goran, M. I., & Sun, M. (1998). Total energy expenditure and physical activity in prepubertal children: Recent advances based on the application of the doubly labeled water method. *The American Journal of Clinical Nutrition, 68*(4), 944S–949S. doi:10.1093/ajcn/68.4.944S PMID:9771877

Grasso, R., Bianchi, L., & Lacquaniti, F. (1998). Motor patterns for human gait: Backward versus forward locomotion. *Journal of Neurophysiology*, *80*(4), 1868–1885. doi:10.1152/jn.1998.80.4.1868 PMID:9772246

Joo, S. B., Oh, S. E., Sim, T., Kim, H., Choi, C. H., Koo, H., & Mun, J. H. (2014). Prediction of gait speed from plantar pressure using artificial neural networks. *Expert Systems with Applications*, *41*(16), 7398–7405. doi:10.1016/j.eswa.2014.06.002

Keller, T. S., Weisberger, A. M., Ray, J. L., Hasan, S. S., Shiavi, R. G., & Spengler, D. M. (1996). Relationship between vertical ground reaction force and speed during walking, slow jogging, and running. *Clinical Biomechanics (Bristol, Avon)*, *11*(5), 253–259. doi:10.1016/0268-0033(95)00068-2 PMID:11415629

Kram, R., & Taylor, C. R. (1990). Energetics of running: A new perspective. *Nature*, *346*(6281), 265–267. doi:10.1038/346265a0 PMID:2374590

McMahon, T. A., Valiant, G., & Frederick, E. C. (1987). Groucho running. *Journal of Applied Physiology*, *62*(6), 2326–2337. doi:10.1152/jappl.1987.62.6.2326 PMID:3610929

Munro, C. F., Miller, D. I., & Fuglevand, A. J. (1987). Ground reaction forces in running: A reexamination. *Journal of Biomechanics*, *20*(2), 147–155. doi:10.1016/0021-9290(87)90306-X PMID:3571295

Oh, S. E., Choi, A., & Mun, J. H. (2013). Prediction of ground reaction forces during gait based on kinematics and a neural network model. *Journal of Biomechanics*, *46*(14), 2372–2380. doi:10.1016/j.jbiomech.2013.07.036 PMID:23962528

ResearchGate. (n.d.). Retrieved from https://www.researchgate.net/figure/The-gait-cycle-A-schematic-representation-of-gait-cycle-with-stance-red-and-swing_fig1_249968026

Rupérez, M. J., Martín-Guerrero, J. D., Monserrat, C., & Alcañiz, M. (2012). Artificial neural networks for predicting dorsal pressures on the foot surface while walking. *Expert Systems with Applications*, *39*(5), 5349–5357. doi:10.1016/j.eswa.2011.11.050

Savelberg, H. H. C. M., & De Lange, A. L. H. (1999). Assessment of the horizontal, fore-aft component of the ground reaction force from insole pressure patterns by using artificial neural networks. *Clinical Biomechanics (Bristol, Avon)*, *14*(8), 585–592. doi:10.1016/S0268-0033(99)00036-4 PMID:10521642

Sepulveda, F., Wells, D. M., & Vaughan, C. L. (1993). A neural network representation of electromyography and joint dynamics in human gait. *Journal of Biomechanics*, *26*(2), 101–109. doi:10.1016/0021-9290(93)90041-C PMID:8429053

Srinivasan, S., Gander, R. E., & Wood, H. C. (1992). A movement pattern generator model using artificial neural networks. *IEEE Transactions on Biomedical Engineering*, *39*(7), 716–722. doi:10.1109/10.142646 PMID:1516938

Su, F. C., & Wu, W. L. (2000). Design and testing of a genetic algorithm neural network in the assessment of gait patterns. *Medical Engineering & Physics*, *22*(1), 67–74. doi:10.1016/S1350-4533(00)00011-4 PMID:10817950

Toso, M. A., & Gomes, H. M. (2014). Vertical force calibration of smart force platform using artificial neural networks. *Revista Brasileira de Engenharia Biomédica*, *30*(4), 406–411. doi:10.1590/1517-3151.0569

Wang, C. S., Wang, C. C., & Chang, T. R. (2013, July). Neural network evaluation for shoe insoles fitness. In *2013 Ninth International Conference on Natural Computation (ICNC)* (pp. 157-162). IEEE. 10.1109/ICNC.2013.6817962

Winter, D. A. (1990). Biomechanics and motor control of human movement Wiley. New York: Academic Press.

Zhang, K., Sun, M., Lester, D. K., Pi-Sunyer, F. X., Boozer, C. N., & Longman, R. W. (2005). Assessment of human locomotion by using an insole measurement system and artificial neural networks. *Journal of Biomechanics*, *38*(11), 2276–2287. doi:10.1016/j.jbiomech.2004.07.036 PMID:16154415

This research was previously published in AI Techniques for Reliability Prediction for Electronic Components; pages 124-135, copyright year 2020 by Engineering Science Reference (an imprint of IGI Global).

Chapter 21
Artificial Neural Network for PWM Rectifier Direct Power Control and DC Voltage Control

Arezki Fekik
Akli Mohand Oulhadj University, Bouira, Algeria

Hakim Denoun
University Mouloud Mammeri of Tizi-Ouzou, Algeria

Ahmad Taher Azar
ⓘ https://orcid.org/0000-0002-7869-6373
Benha University, Egypt & Nile University, Egypt

Mustapha Zaouia
University Mouloud Mammeri of Tizi-Ouzou, Algeria

Nabil Benyahia
University Mouloud Mammeri of Tizi-Ouzou, Algeria

Mohamed Lamine Hamida
University Mouloud Mammeri of Tizi-Ouzou, Algeria

Nacereddine Benamrouche
University of Tizi Ouzou, Algeria

Sundarapandian Vaidyanathan
Vel Tech University, India

ABSTRACT

In this chapter, a new technique has been proposed for reducing the harmonic content of a three-phase PWM rectifier connected to the networks with a unit power factor and also providing decoupled control of the active and reactive instantaneous power. This technique called direct power control (DPC) is based on artificial neural network (ANN) controller, without line voltage sensors. The control technique is based on well-known direct torque control (DTC) ideas for the induction motor, which is applied to eliminate the harmonic of the line current and compensate for the reactive power. The main idea of this control is based on active and reactive power control loops. The DC voltage capacitor is regulated by the ANN controller to keep it constant and also provides a stable active power exchange. The simulation results are very satisfactory in the terms of stability and total harmonic distortion (THD) of the line current and the unit power factor.

DOI: 10.4018/978-1-6684-2408-7.ch021

1. INTRODUCTION

Recently, different control approaches have been proposed for designing nonlinear systems for many practical applications, such as optimal control, nonlinear feedback control, adaptive control, sliding mode control, nonlinear dynamics, chaos control, chaos synchronization control, fuzzy logic control, fuzzy adaptive control, fractional order control, and robust control and their integrations (Azar & Vaidyanathan, 2015a,b,c, 2016; Azar & Zhu, 2015; Azar & Serrano, 2015a,b,c,d, 2016a,b, 2017; Boulkroune et al, 2016a,b; Ghoudelbourk et al., 2016; Meghni et al, 2017a,b,c; Azar et al., 2017a,b,c,d; Azar 2010a,b, 2012; Mekki et al., 2015; Vaidyanathan & Azar, 2015a,b,c,d, 2016a,b,c,d,e,f,g, 2017a,b,c; Zhu & Azar, 2015; Grassi et al., 2017; Ouannas et al., 2016a,b, 2017a,b,c,d,e,f,g,h,I,j; Singh et al., 2017; Vaidyanathan et al, 2015a,b,c; Wang et al., 2017; Soliman et al., 2017; Tolba et al., 2017).

The increasing use of electronically powered and controllable systems in the industrial sector, motivated by improved performance, has led to a proliferation of static converters. Today, the number of these devices connected to electricity grids is constantly increasing. The switching operation of the semiconductor components constituting these converters is the reason why their behavior with respect to the power source is non-linear. Indeed, they take non-sinusoidal currents and for the most part consume reactive power, which poses serious problems for electrical networks. Static converters have become the most important sources of harmonics on the network. The uncontrolled diode and controlled thyristor rectifier is the most polluting and widespread static converter in both industry and domestic appliances. Under certain operating conditions, it can introduce a harmonic distortion rate (THDi) of current greater than 30%. For this reason, some recent adapted international standards, such as IEEE Standard 519, IEC 61000 and EN 50160, impose limits on the THD of currents and voltages within the supply network (5% for currents and 3% for voltages). In view of this state of affairs, and in order to limit the harmonic disturbance caused by the power electronics systems connected to the network, it is necessary to develop curative devices such as active filtering on one side and the other to design preventive actions such as non-polluting converters, equipped with a control device making the current drawn on the network as sinusoidal as possible.

In this context and over the past few years, high-power static converters have started to appear on the market mainly concerning AC / DC conversion. Indeed, changes have been made on conventional bridge rectifiers modifying their structure or their control system in order to reduce their injection of harmonic currents into the network. These new AC / DC converters are distinguished by their structure and how to handle the currents absorbed. They can be divided into three classes: diode rectifier with power factor correction (PFC), rectifier with current injection and PWM-rectifier with voltage or current structure. Among these most popular and attractive structures are the voltage PWM-rectifier. It is characterized by a quasi-resistive behavior with respect to the supply network. In addition to its ability to control the currents absorbed and to operate with a power factor close to one unit, the voltage Pulse Width Modulation (PWM) rectifier can also operate in two modes: rectification and regeneration. Thus, it controls the flow of active and reactive power in both directions. This advantage enables it to be used in a wide range of applications, particularly in regeneration mode and bidirectional power flow control (variable speed drives). This converter currently a key research theme for specialists in the field. The research is carried out mainly on so-called advanced strategies (predictive, fuzzy, Neurons, etc.) as well as on the selection and sizing of the input filter. To solve this problem, several research works have been done on PWM rectifiers due to some of their important advantage such as power regeneration capabilities, control of DC-bus voltage, low harmonic distortion of input currents, and high-power factor (Bouafia

& Krim, 2008; Sanjuan, 2010; Escobar et al., 2003; Malinowski et al., 2004; Malinowski et al., 2003; Cichowlas et al., 2005). Various control strategies have being proposed in recent works on this type of PWM rectifier. A well know method of indirect active and reactive power control is Voltage Oriented Control (VOC) (Sanjuan, 2010; Fekik et al., 2015a). Voltage Oriented Control guarantees high dynamic and static performance via internal current control loop (Fekik et al., 2015b), however, the final configuration and performance of the VOC system largely depends on the quality of the applied current control strategy (Bouafia & Krim, 2008; Sanjuan, 2010).

Another less known method based on instantaneous direct active and reactive power control is called direct power control (DPC) (Escobar et al., 2003; Malinowski et al., 2004; Cichowlas et al., 2005). In this method, there are no internal current control loops and no PWM modulator block because the converter switching states are appropriately selected by a switching table based on the instantaneous errors between the commanded and estimated values of active and reactive power. This method requires a good estimate of the active and reactive powers (Bouafia & Krim, 2008; Fekik et al., 2015a,b; Lamterkati et al., 2014a,b; Fekik et al., 2016). In Bouafia et al. (2009), the selection of the control vectors is based on the fuzzy logic, whose switching table is replaced by a fuzzy controller and in this structure, there are no hysteresis regulators. Recently, predictive control model theories have grown (Antoniewicz & Kazmierkowski, 2008; Vazquez et al., 2014, 2008; Vazquez & Salmeron, 2003; Karamanakos et al., 2014; Geyer & Quevedo, 2015) and have been introduced for direct power control in order to improve system performance (Hu et al., 2013; Zhang, et al., 2013; Fischer et al., 2014; Song et al., 2016). Based on the predictive control theory of the model, another type of direct power controllers called predictive control of direct power control has been proposed (Larrinaga et al., 2007). During its implementation process, a sequence of voltage vectors must first be selected. The corresponding application time for these vectors is then determined by minimizing the cost function, which is constructed as a function of predicted values and power references. In most cases, excellent control performance can be achieved when the predictive direct power control strategy is adopted. Fekik et al. (2015a) presented a VOC for the control of the PWM-rectifier, and for the control of the DC bus voltage and it's compared with conventional PI regulator and Fuzzy logic controller. On the other hand, the researchers are interested in the application of the different DC bus voltage regulators (e.g. Fuzzy Sliding mode control) of the PWM-rectifier control by direct power control (Jiang, 2010).

In this chapter, a new control method called direct power control (DPC) of three phase PWM rectifier is proposed based on the artificial neural network (ANN) controller; which makes it possible to achieve unity power factor operation by directly controlling its instantaneous active and reactive power, without any power source voltage captor. The DC-voltage is controlled by ANN-controller which provides active power reference P_{ref}, while the reactive power reference Q_{ref} is set to zero to achieve unity power factor operation. The simulation results show the feasibility and efficiency of neural networks and voltage regulation under transient or steady state with a nearly sinusoidal current source and side THD standards-compliant standards.

This chapter is organized as follows: In section 2 modeling of a PWM rectifier is introduced. In section 3, direct power control (DPC) is described. In section 4, brief overview of neural network principle is presented. In section 5, DC-voltage regulation based on neural network controller is shown. Results and simulation are shown in section 6. Finally in section 7, concluding remarks with future directions are given.

2. MODELING OF A PWM RECTIFIER

The power circuit of the PWM rectifier contains a bridge of six power transistors with anti-parallel diodes, which is used to carry out the PWM generation as well as the power bidirectional conversion, the general diagram of the PWM rectifier is shown in Figure 1. The converter is supplied by a voltage source in series with an inductance and a resistance, which models the network. Generally, the network inductance is insufficient (Bouafia & Krim, 2008; Sanjuan, 2010; Fekik et al., 2017) to eliminate all the harmonics present in the current and voltage waveforms. To attenuate the ripples due to the switching operation of the PWM rectifier, a series filter having a more significant inductance is needed. A load and a capacitor are connected simultaneously at the output of the converter. The capacitor is used as a voltage source and allows the rectifier to also operate as an inverter (Escobar et al., 2003; Malinowski et al., 2004; Cichowlas et al., 2005; Fekik et al., 2015a,b, 2016, 2017):

Figure 1. General diagram of the PWM rectifier

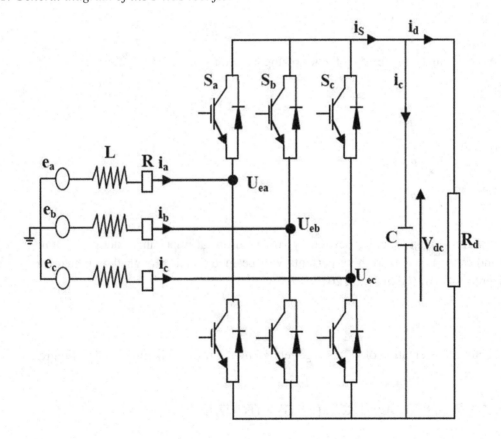

The logical states impose the rectifier input voltages, are given as (Fekik et al., 2016, 2017)

$$
\begin{aligned}
u_{ea} &= S_a.V_{dc} \\
u_{eb} &= S_b.V_{dc} \, , \\
u_{ec} &= S_c.V_{dc}
\end{aligned}
\tag{1}
$$

Thus, the operation principle of the rectifier is illustrated by the following matrix system (Fekik et al., 2016, 2017):

$$
\begin{bmatrix} u_{ea} \\ u_{eb} \\ u_{ec} \end{bmatrix} = V_{dc} \begin{pmatrix} \dfrac{2}{3} & -\dfrac{1}{3} & -\dfrac{1}{3} \\ -\dfrac{1}{3} & \dfrac{2}{3} & -\dfrac{1}{3} \\ -\dfrac{1}{3} & -\dfrac{1}{3} & \dfrac{2}{3} \end{pmatrix} \begin{pmatrix} S_a \\ S_b \\ S_c \end{pmatrix},
\tag{2}
$$

The AC side can be modeled by the following equations (Fekik et al., 2016, 2017)

$$
\begin{cases}
u_{ea} = e_a - Ri_a - L\dfrac{di_a}{dt} \\[2mm]
u_{eb} = e_b - Ri_b - L\dfrac{di_b}{dt}, \\[2mm]
u_{ec} = e_c - Ri_c - L\dfrac{di_c}{dt}
\end{cases}
\tag{3}
$$

AC currents i_a, i_b and i_c are generated by voltage drops at impedances network boundaries (e_a-u_{ea}), (e_b-u_{eb}) and (e_c-u_{ec}), and then these currents will be modulated through the switches to provide the D.C.current i_s such as (Fekik et al., 2016, 2017):

$$
i_s = S_a i_a + S_b i_b + S_c i_c,
\tag{4}
$$

The vector representation of voltages generated by the rectifier is illustrated in Figure 2.

3. DIRECT POWER CONTROL (DPC) STRATEGY

Direct Power Control (DPC) of PWM rectifiers can be generally classified into two types of estimation (Bouafia & Krim, 2008; Sanjuan, 2010):

- Voltage estimation,
- Virtual flux estimation,

Figure 2. Voltage vectors generated by the rectifier

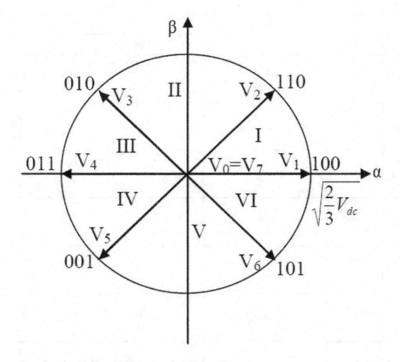

Different control strategies of a PWM rectifier are shown in Figure 3.

The main idea of DPC is similar to the well-known Direct Torque Control (DTC) for induction motors. It is based on instantaneous active and reactive power control loops (Bouafia & Krim, 2008; Sanjuan, 2010; Fekik et al., 2016, 2017). In DPC there are no internal current control loops and no PWM modulator block because the converter switching states are selected by a switching table based on the instantaneous errors between the reference and estimated values of active and reactive power as shown in Table 1.

Figure3. Different control strategies of a PWM rectifier

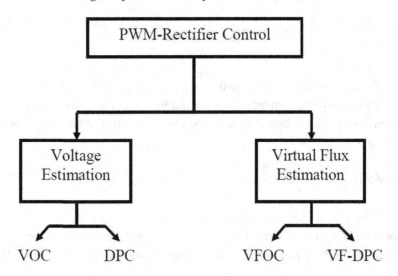

Table 1. Different switches configurations and the corresponding voltage vectors

S_a	S_b	S_c	U_{ea}	U_{eb}	U_{ec}	V_i
0	0	0	0	0	0	V_0
0	0	1	$-\dfrac{V_{dc}}{3}$	$-\dfrac{V_{dc}}{3}$	$\dfrac{2V_{dc}}{3}$	V_5
0	1	0	$-\dfrac{V_{dc}}{3}$	$\dfrac{2V_{dc}}{3}$	$-\dfrac{V_{dc}}{3}$	V_3
0	1	1	$-\dfrac{2V_{dc}}{3}$	$\dfrac{V_{dc}}{3}$	$\dfrac{V_{dc}}{3}$	V_4
1	0	0	$\dfrac{2V_{dc}}{3}$	$\dfrac{V_{dc}}{3}$	$\dfrac{V_{dc}}{3}$	V_1
1	0	1	$\dfrac{V_{dc}}{3}$	$-\dfrac{2V_{dc}}{3}$	$\dfrac{V_{dc}}{3}$	V_6
1	1	0	$\dfrac{V_{dc}}{3}$	$\dfrac{V_{dc}}{3}$	$-\dfrac{2V_{dc}}{3}$	V_2
1	1	1	0	0	0	V_7

3.1 DPC Based on Voltage Estimation

In order to remove the sensors from the alternating voltage, an instantaneous active and reactive power estimator has been made as a function of the switching states and the DC voltage as indicated by (Bouchakour, 2005; Fekik et al., 2016, 2017):

$$\hat{P} = L(\frac{di_a}{dt} + \frac{di_b}{dt} + \frac{di_C}{dt}) + V_{dc}(S_a i_a + S_b i_b + S_c i_c)$$

$$\hat{Q} = \frac{1}{\sqrt{3}}[L(\frac{di_a}{dt}i_c - \frac{di_c}{dt}i_a) + V_{dc}(S_a(i_b - i_c) + S_b(i_c - i_a) + S_c(i_a - i_b))] \tag{5}$$

The first parts of the two expressions shown above show the power in the line inductors. It's noted that the internal resistances of these inductances are negligible because the active power dissipated in these resistors is much lower in comparison with the power involved. Other parts represent the power in the converter (Bouchakour, 2005).

3.2 Estimated Voltage

The working area of the line voltage is required to determine the commands. Moreover, it is important to estimate the line voltage correctly, even with the existence of harmonics to achieve high power factor. The voltage drop across the inductor can be calculated by deriving the current. Thus, the voltage can be calculated by summing the reference voltage at the input of the converter with the voltage drop already calculated (Escobar et al., 2003; Malinowski et al., 2004; Cichowlas et al., 2005; Bouchakour, 2005; Fekik et al., 2016, 2017). On the other hand, this approach has a disadvantage which is the derivative of the current, where the noise is amplified. To avoid this drawback, a voltage estimator based on the power calculation can be applied. The following expression (6) gives the line currents i_a, i_b, i_c in the stationary coordinates a_β:

$$\begin{bmatrix} i_\alpha \\ i_\beta \end{bmatrix} = \sqrt{\frac{2}{3}} \begin{bmatrix} 1 & \dfrac{-1}{2} & \dfrac{-1}{2} \\ 0 & \dfrac{\sqrt{3}}{2} & \dfrac{-\sqrt{3}}{2} \end{bmatrix} \begin{bmatrix} i_a \\ i_b \\ i_c \end{bmatrix} \tag{6}$$

The expressions of the active and reactive powers can be written as:

$$\hat{p} = v_\alpha i_\alpha + v_\beta i_\beta$$
$$\hat{p} = v_\alpha i_\beta - v_\beta i_\alpha \tag{7}$$

The matrix writing of the preceding expressions is given as:

$$\begin{bmatrix} \hat{p} \\ \hat{q} \end{bmatrix} = \begin{bmatrix} v_\alpha & v_\beta \\ -v_\beta & v_\alpha \end{bmatrix} \begin{bmatrix} i_\alpha \\ i_\beta \end{bmatrix} \tag{8}$$

The matrix equation (8) can be rewritten as a function of the line current (measured) and the (estimated) power as follows:

$$\begin{bmatrix} \hat{v}_\alpha \\ \hat{v}_\beta \end{bmatrix} = \frac{1}{i_\alpha^2 + i_\beta^2} \begin{bmatrix} i_\alpha & -i_\beta \\ i_\beta & i_\alpha \end{bmatrix} \begin{bmatrix} \hat{P} \\ \hat{Q} \end{bmatrix} \tag{9}$$

Concordia's inverse transform of line tensions is written as:

$$\begin{bmatrix} \hat{v}_a \\ \hat{v}_b \\ \hat{v}_c \end{bmatrix} = \sqrt{\frac{2}{3}} \cdot \begin{bmatrix} 1 & 0 \\ -\dfrac{1}{2} & \dfrac{\sqrt{3}}{2} \\ -\dfrac{1}{2} & \dfrac{\sqrt{3}}{2} \end{bmatrix} \cdot \begin{bmatrix} \hat{v}_\alpha \\ \hat{v}_\beta \end{bmatrix} \tag{10}$$

3.3 Number of Sectors

The area of the voltage vector can be divided into twelve or six sectors, as shown in Figure 2. These sectors can be expressed numerically as follows (Bouchakour, 2005; Fekik et al., 2016, 2017):

$$(n-2)\frac{\pi}{6} < \theta_n < (n-1)\frac{\pi}{6} \tag{11}$$

where n=1,2,3...12 and indicates the sector number. It is instantaneously given by the voltage vector position and is computed as follows:

$$\theta_n = arct(\frac{v_\beta}{v_\alpha}) \tag{12}$$

where n is the number of all pass filters. It is clearly noted that by changing the value of resistor R, the amount of delay can vary and as the result the resolution of the delay block can be controlled easily.

3.4 Hysteresis Regulator

The great simplicity of the implementation of this control approach is also an important element in the choice of the two-level comparator. Moreover, the energy considerations on the converter impose a limited number of commutations. However, for the same control hysteresis width, the two-level comparator requires a smaller number of commutations (Chapuis, 1996; Escobar et al., 2003; Malinowski et al., 2004; Cichowlas et al., 2005). The width of the hysteresis regulators band has a considerable effect on the performance of the converter, particularly the current distortion, the average switching frequency of the converter and the pulsation of the power. In addition, the losses are strongly affected by the hysteresis band. The controller proposed in the DPC is the two-stage controller for active and reactive power. The regulator hysteresis at three levels can be considered for more improvement (Noguchi et al., 1998). The output of the hysteresis regulators given by the Boolean variables S_p and S_q, indicates the upper or lower amplitude exceedances of the powers according to the following expressions:

$$\begin{aligned}
\hat{q} &\prec q_{ref} - h_q \Rightarrow S_q = 1 \\
\hat{q} &\succ q_{ref} - h_q \Rightarrow S_q = 0 \\
\hat{p} &\prec p_{ref} - h_p \Rightarrow S_p = 1 \\
\hat{p} &\succ p_{ref} - h_p \Rightarrow S_p = 0
\end{aligned} \tag{13}$$

3.5 Switching Table

As shown in Figure 4, the instantaneous active and reactive powers depend on the position of the voltage vector Us because the voltage vector Us allows the phase and amplitude (linear) indirect control of the line current (Malinowski et al., 2001; Bouchakour, 2005). Figure 4 presents the four different situations, which illustrate the variations in instantaneous power. Point M shows the reference value of the active and reactive powers. The four possible situations of the instantaneous powers are schematized, in the case where the voltage vector is in the third sector (Bouchakour, 2005). The line current is ahead of the voltage U_L for the first two cases (a) and (b). However, its amplitude is greater in (a) and lower in (b) than in the reference current. In the last two cases (c) and (d), the current is lagging behind the voltage U_L, with a lower amplitude in (c) and greater in (d) (Malinowski & Kazmierkowski, 2000). The selection of the control vector must be chosen so that the error between the estimate and the reference is restricted in a hysteresis band. When the estimated voltage vector is close to the boundaries of a sector, two out of six possibilities are bad. These vectors can guarantee only the control of the instantaneous active power without being able to make correction on the error of the reactive power.

Figure 4. Variation of instantaneous powers

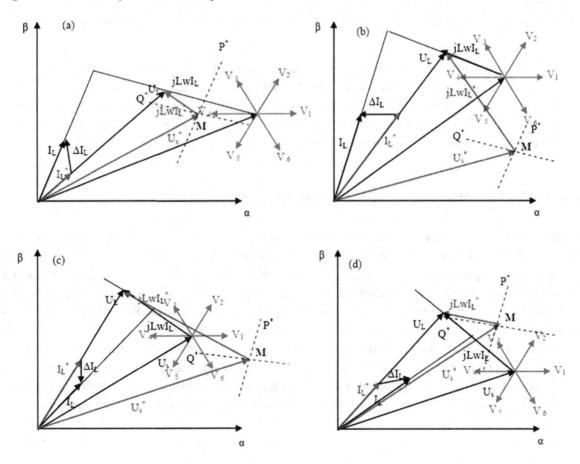

Some methods to improve the behavior of DPC within the boundaries of a sector are well known. One of them is to increase the number of sectors or to use comparators with hysteresis at several levels (Chen & Joos, 2001, 2008; Bouchakour, 2005). Generally, the switching table is constructed taking into account the number of sectors, dynamic performance and two or three stage hysteresis regulators. Table 2 gives the switchboard of the direct power control. The digitized errors S_p, S_q and the working sector θ_n are the inputs of this table, where the switching states S_a, S_b and S_c of the converter are stored. The optimum switching state of the converter is chosen in each switching state according to the combination of the digital signals S_p, S_q and number of sector. Thus, the choice is made so that the error of the active power can be restricted in a band with hysteresis of width $2\Delta h_p$ and the same for the error of the reactive power with a Band of width $2\Delta h_q$.

Table 2. Logical states of the rectifier switches are generated basing on the switching table

S_p	S_q	θ_1	θ_2	θ_3	θ_4	θ_5	θ_6	θ_7	θ_8	θ_9	θ_{10}	θ_{11}	θ_{12}
0	0	101	100	100	110	110	010	010	011	011	001	001	101
0	1	100	110	110	010	010	011	011	001	001	101	101	100
1	0	001	001	101	101	100	100	110	110	010	010	011	011
1	1	010	010	011	011	001	001	101	101	100	100	110	110

Figure 5 shows the configuration of direct instantaneous active and reactive power control based on neural network controller for three-phase PWM rectifier (Fekik et al., 2017). The controller is relay control of the active and reactive power by using hysteresis comparators and a switching table. In this configuration, the DC-voltage is regulated by controlling the active power using neural network controller, and the unity power factor operation is achieved by controlling the reactive power to be zero.

4. PRINCIPLE AND DEFINITION OF NEURAL NETWORKS

Neural networks form a set of nonlinear functions, allowing to build, by learning, a large family of models and nonlinear correctors (Mondal et al., 2002) A network of neurons is a system of interconnected nonlinear operators, receiving signals from the outside through its inputs, and delivering output signals, which are in fact the activities of certain neurons (Azar, 2013; Azar & El-Said, 2013; Hassanien et al., 2014). The formal neuron model presented here, from Mac Culloch and Pitts (Baghli, 1999), is a very simple mathematical model derived from an analysis of biological reality. It begins with a simple summation of the signals arriving at the neuron. These signals are commonly referred to as the neuron inputs (see Figure 6) (Mezache & Betto, 1997). The sum obtained is then compared with a threshold and the output of the neuron is deduced from the comparison. More formally, it is sufficient to obtain this behavior to subtract the threshold considered to the sum of the inputs (Mezache & Betto, 1997), and to pass the result by the transfer function of the neuron. The result after transfer function is the output of the neuron. This "summation" and then "nonlinearity" sequence finally represents the "physical" properties of the neuron.

Figure 5.DPC configuration

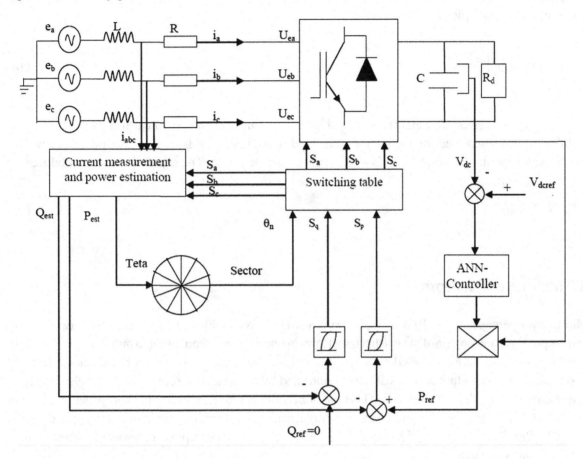

Figure 6. The formal neuron of MacCulloch and Pitts

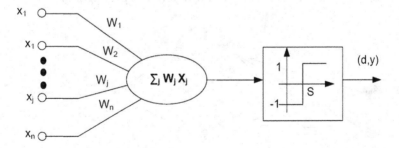

4.1 General Modeling of a Neuron

From a mathematical point of view, a formal neuron is a processing element having n inputs x_1, x_2, ..., x_n (are the external inputs or outputs of the other neurons), and an output. Signals are passed between neurons over connection links. Each connection link has an associated weight, which, in a typical neural net, multiplies the signal transmitted. Each neuron applies an activation function f (usually nonlinear) to its net input (sum of weighted input signals) to determine its output signal y (Baghli, 1999; Constant, 2000; Bimal & Bos, 1994).

$$y_i = f\left(\sum_{i=1}^{m} w_{ij}x_i\right) \qquad (14)$$

where W_{ij} is the weight (or weight) associated with the ith input of the neuron j. Sometimes there is an additional term b_j representing the internal threshold of the neuron, this term is considered as a weight W_{0j} associated with a constant input (Baghli, 1999; Constant, 2000). The expression can be modified to:

$$y_i = f\left(\sum_{i=1}^{m} w_{ij}x_i - b_j\right) \qquad (15)$$

4.2 Multilayer Perceptron

Multi-Layer perceptron (MLP) is a feedforward neural network with one or more layers between input and output layer. Feedforward means that data flows in one direction from input to output layer (forward). The hidden neurons are controlled by the inputs and are distributed in one layer but are not connected to one another; The output neurons are only controlled by the hidden neurons (Baghli, 1999). Figure 7 is an example of a 3-layer perceptron. This type of network is trained with the backpropagation learning algorithm. MLPs are widely used for pattern classification, recognition, prediction and approximation (Azar & Zhu, 2015; Azar & Vaidyanathan, 2015b). Multi-Layer Perceptron can solve problems which are not linearly separable.

Figure 7. Structure of a multilayer neural network with forward propagation

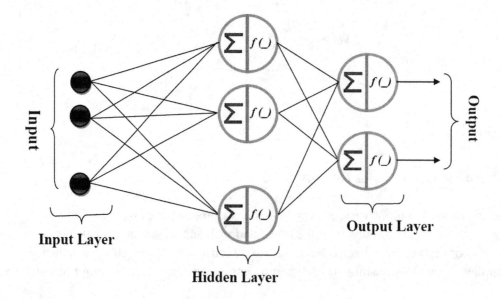

4.3 Learning by Error Retro-Propagation

The efficient function optimization algorithms generally use the differential of the function considered (i.e. its gradient because it has real values). When the transfer functions used in neurons are differentiable, and when the distance function is also differentiable, the error committed by a MLP is a differentiable function of the network synaptic coefficients (Baghli, 1999). The retro-propagation algorithm makes it possible to calculate the gradient of this error efficiently. The number of operations (multiplications and additions) to be made is indeed proportional to the number of connections of the network, as in the case of calculating the output of this one. This algorithm makes it possible to learn A MLP (Baghli, 1999).

Let the vector W contain the synaptic weights, m the number of outputs of the network, y_k and d_k the respective components of Y and D on the output k. The quadratic error committed in Example i is therefore:

$$E_w(i) = \frac{1}{2} \sum_{K=1}^{m} \left| y_k - d_k \right|^2 \tag{16}$$

On the learning set, we have:

$$E_w(i) = \frac{1}{2} \sum_{i=1}^{m} E_w(i) \tag{17}$$

The retrograde propagation is a gradient descent, which therefore modifies the weights by an amount proportional to the opposite of the gradient:

$$\Delta w_{ij} = -h \frac{\partial E}{\partial w_{ij}} \tag{18}$$

Where h is the learning step.

The algorithm consists of calculating an error term ε and makes the weight changes from the top layers to the lower layers. This method of learning is the most used in the training of neural networks, because of its simplicity. However, it has the disadvantage of having a very slow convergence (Baghli, 1999; Bose, 2001)

5. DC-VOLTAGE REGULATION BASED ON NEURAL NETWORK CONTROLLER

In this chapter, the neuron DC voltage regulation system is proposed. The PWM rectifier used in the work is designed around a Multi-Layer Perceptron (MLP) which can replace the conventional PI controller. The regulator is used to control the terminal voltage of the condenser C in order to keep it constant around a value of $V_{dcref} = 300V$. The architecture adopted for this network is a MLP which has three layers: an input layer corresponding to an error between V_{dc} and V_{dcref}, and an output layer corresponding to the identified output. The number of neurons in the hidden layer can be selected by performing several learning tests. In this study, six neurons are used and the LOG-sigmoid learning function of the network is realized with the Levenberg-Marquardt back-propagation algorithm (Bose, 2001). Other optimization methods like genetic algorithms can be used to determine neuron numbers. Figure 8 shows a block diagram of the ANN controller (Artificial Neural Network) used for DC voltage adjustment:

Figure 8. The external block of ANN-controller

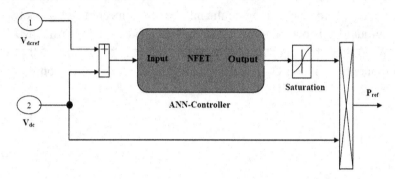

6. RESULTS AND SIMULATION

To validate the effectiveness of the control strategy studied in this paper, a digital simulation was carried out under MATLAB/SIMULINK environment. The system parameters studied in this chapter are given in Table 3.

Table 3. System parameters

R	0.25 Ω
L	0.016 H
C	0.0047 F
R_{load}	100 Ω
Peak amplitude of line voltage	120 V
Source voltage frequency	50 Hz
DC-Voltage V_{dcref}	300 V

6.1 Test Variation of DC-Voltage

The DC voltage control system is tested as well as the DPC using the ANN controller method following a DC voltage variation at t = 0.5 s from 300V to 380V. DC control of DC voltage is shown in Figure 9.

Figure 9 shows that the response of the system is fast (t <0.1s) and follows its reference without overflow according to the proposed controller based on neural networks.

Figure 9. Control system step response

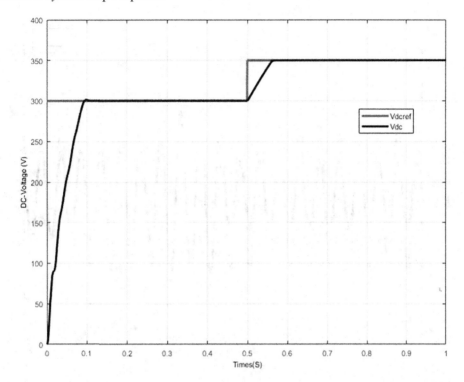

It is noted that the system has become stable and robust. The system response is acceptable and does not exceed. Figure 10 shows that when the DC voltage reaches the new reference value, the line current increases. In this case, the power increase is limited, which avoids dangerous risks for the operation of the system.

It is observed from Figure 10 that the current and the voltage of phase (a) are in phase, which guarantees a unit power factor.

Figure 11 shows that the DPC technique responds very quickly with respect to the variation of power reference according to to the regulator proposed in this work.

It's noted that the estimated active voltage follows its reference correctly based on the neuro-controller.

It can be observed from Figure 12 that the reactive power flow is low, which is very beneficial for the performance of the system.

It can be noted that the estimated reactive power imposed reference equal to zero, even in the case of a change in the reference DC voltage (the active power) (see Figures 9 and 11) Which guarantees a decoupled control of the instantaneous power.

The waveform of the line current is very close to the sinusoid and hence THD (total harmonic distortion) has been reduced to 3.47% (see Figure 13). Which guarantees a non-polluting system and therefore a very good quality of electrical energy. In order to keep the DC bus loaded, the DC voltage variation involves a reference variation in the instantaneous active power.

Figure 14 shows the estimated voltage V_{aest} and the detected voltage V_a. It can be observed that the estimated voltage follows the voltage captured on the side of the AC source. This is useful for estimating the two control variables accurately (active and reactive power).

Figure 10. Line voltage and line current

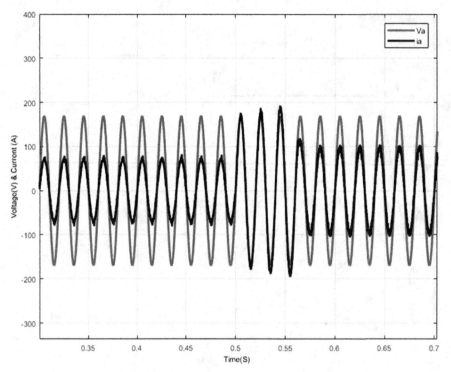

Figure 11. Reference and estimation active power

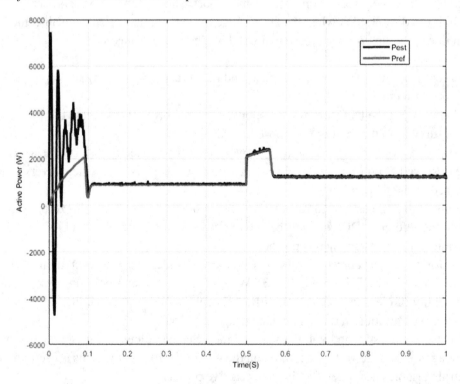

Figure 12. Estimated and reference instantaneous reactive power

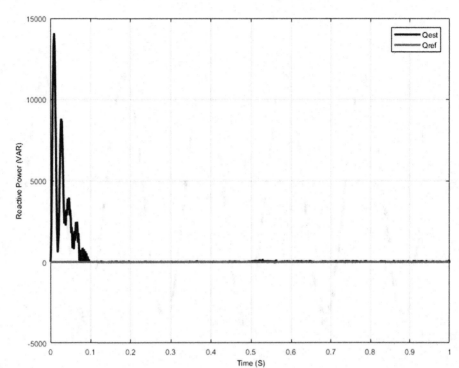

Figure 13. Harmonic spectrum and THD of the current with an ANN-controller

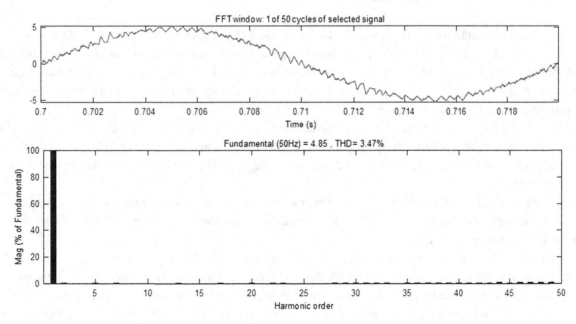

Figure 14. estimation voltage and voltage network

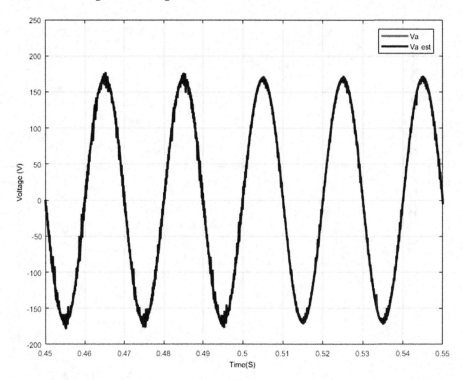

6.2 Test Variation of the Load Resistance

To test the performance of the regulator, the load resistance (R_d) varies from 100 Ω to 150 Ω at time t = 0.5 s. Figure 15 illustrates the results of the simulation after a sudden change in load (t = 0.5 s) and the DC bus voltage during the load variation. It can be observed that the voltage follows the reference signal with a very good precision even at the moment of the abrupt change of the load which demonstrates the robustness of the proposed regulator.

Figure 16 illustrates the voltage and the current of the phase (a) during the variation of the load. It is found that the current remains always in phase with the voltage and that the current decreases with the decrease of the load to ensure a continuous voltage at the desired reference by agitation on the active reference power.

Figure 17 illustrates the reference active power and the estimated power. During the variation of the load, it can be noted that the power reference is reduced when the load is demined with a very good result of the estimated value.

Figure 18 illustrates the reference and estimated reactive power. During the variation of the load, it can be seen that the reactive power follows its imposed reference equal to zero, which allows us to obtain a decoupled control of the two-instantaneous power which reveals the good regulation of the DC voltage.

The reactive power estimated remains always at its imposed value (equal to zero), so a unit power factor is achieved successfully. This regulator also guarantees a low current THD even in case of load variation as shown in Figure 19 (THDi = 4.36%).

Figure 15. Control system step response

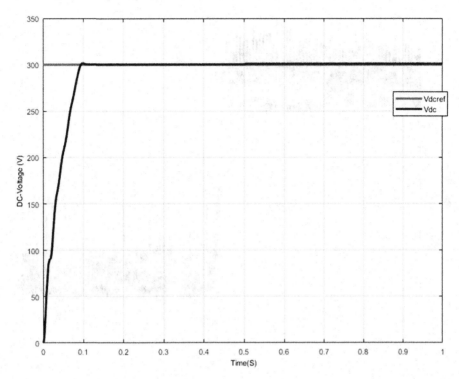

Figure 16. Line voltage and line current

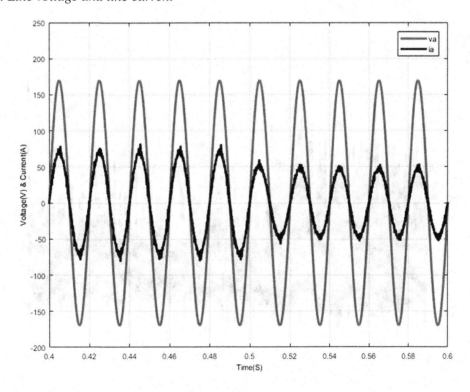

Figure 17. Reference and estimation active power

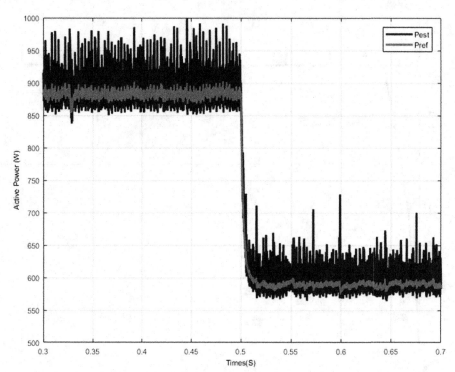

Figure 18. Estimated and reference instantaneous reactive power

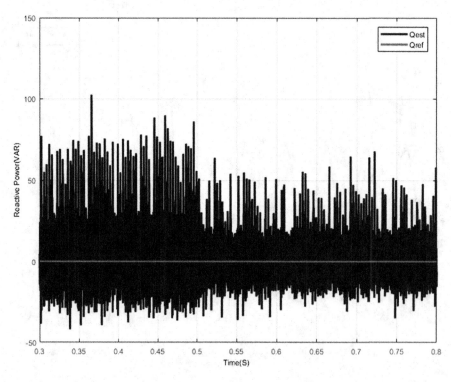

Figure 19. Harmonic spectrum and THD of the current with an ANN-controller

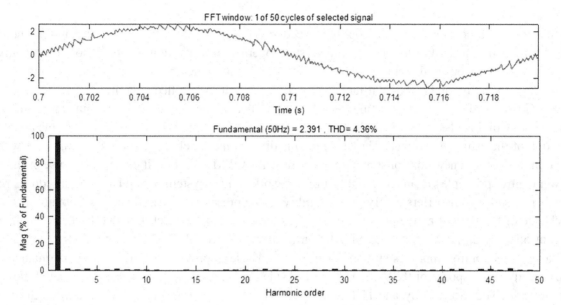

Figure 20. shows the estimated voltage V_{aest} and the voltage V_a during the variation of the load R_d. It can be observed that the estimated voltage follows the voltage captured on the side of the AC source; this confirms a control without sensor voltage in side grid.

Figure 20. Estimation voltage and voltage network

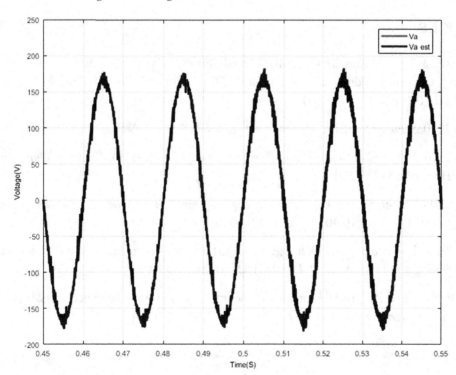

7. CONCLUSION

In this chapter, a new technique is proposed for controlling PWM-three-phase rectifier and harmonic content reduction to ensure a non-polluting system operates under a unit power factor. This control technique is analogous to direct torque control of the induction machine (DTC). Instead of torque and stator flux, the active and reactive instantaneous powers are the controlled quantities. This is known as Direct Control of Power. It consists in selecting a control vector according to a switching table and it's based on the digitized error S_p, S_q of the instantaneous active and reactive power, as well as the angular position of the estimated voltage. The plane ($\alpha\beta$) is divided into twelve sectors to determine the work area. In this work, a new control strategy is presented for PWM Rectifier. It concerns the use of direct power control principle via an Artificial Neural Network control system on the DC side; it reduces the number of sensors and offers a very good stability in the presence of disturbance. To obtain a stable exchange of the flow of active power between the converter and the electric network, the DC voltage is controlled by an ANN controller. Simulation results show that the technique combined with DPC voltage, ANN control improves system performance. These improvements affect the performance of the stability and response of the system on the DC side (and exceeded the response time), a unit power factor is achieved successfully, and THD is reduced to the lower line currents. For future work, the conventional switching table can be replaced by a multilayer neural network (MLP) for the selection of the optimum control vector. The inputs of the neuro-controller can be selected as the digitized errors of the active power S_p, reactive S_q and the angular position of the voltage θ_n. The output of neuro-controller can represent the pulses allowing the control of the switches of the rectifier (S_a, S_b, S_c). The adaptation of the PWM-rectifier parameters (inductance and resistance of the network) is also suggested using an ADALINE type neural network

REFERENCES

Antoniewicz, P., & Kazmierkowski, P. (2008). Virtual-flux-based predictive direct power control of AC/DC converters with online inductance estimation. *IEEE Transactions on Industrial Electronics*, *55*(12), 4381–4390. doi:10.1109/TIE.2008.2007519

Azar, A. T. (2010a). *Fuzzy Systems*. Vienna, Austria: IN-TECH.

Azar, A. T. (2010b). Adaptive Neuro-Fuzzy Systems. In A. T. Azar (Ed.), *Fuzzy Systems*. Vienna, Austria: IN-TECH. doi:10.5772/7220

Azar, A. T. (2012). Overview of Type-2 Fuzzy logic systems. *International Journal of Fuzzy System Applications*, *2*(4), 1–28. doi:10.4018/ijfsa.2012100101

Azar, A.T. (2013). Fast neural network learning algorithms for medical applications. *Neural Computing and Applications, 23*(3-4), 1019-1034. Doi:10.100700521-012-1026-y

Azar, A.T., & El-Said, S.A. (2013). Probabilistic neural network for breast cancer classification. *Neural Computing and Applications, 23*(6), 1737-1751. Doi:10.100700521-012-1134-8

Azar, A.T., & Serrano, F.E. (2014). Robust IMC-PID tuning for cascade control systems with gain and phase margin specifications. *Neural Computing and Applications, 25*(5), 983-995. DOI doi:10.100700521-014-1560-x

Azar, A. T., & Serrano, F. E. (2015a). Stabilization and Control of Mechanical Systems with Backlash. In Advanced Intelligent Control Engineering and Automation. IGI Global. doi:10.4018/978-1-4666-7248-2.ch001

Azar, A. T., & Serrano, F. E. (2015b). Design and Modeling of Anti Wind Up PID Controllers. In Complex system modelling and control through intelligent soft computations. Springer-Verlag. . 1. doi:10.1007/978-3-319-12883-2_1

Azar, A. T., & Serrano, F. E. (2015c). Adaptive Sliding mode control of the Furuta pendulum. In Advances and Applications in Sliding Mode Control systems. Springer-Verlag GmbH Berlin/Heidelberg. doi:10.1007/978-3-319-11173-5_1

Azar, A. T., & Serrano, F. E. (2015d). Deadbeat Control for Multivariable Systems with Time Varying Delays. In Chaos Modeling and Control Systems Design. Springer-Verlag GmbH Berlin/Heidelberg. DOI doi:10.1007/978-3-319-13132-0_6

Azar, A. T., & Serrano, F. E. (2016a). Robust control for asynchronous switched nonlinear systems with time varying delays. *Proceedings of the International Conference on Advanced Intelligent Systems and Informatics 2016, 533*, 891-899. 10.1007/978-3-319-48308-5_85

Azar, A. T., & Serrano, F. E. (2016b). Stabilization of Mechanical Systems with Backlash by PI Loop Shaping. *International Journal of System Dynamics Applications, 5*(3), 20–47. doi:10.4018/IJSDA.2016070102

Azar, A. T., & Serrano, F. E. (2017). Passivity Based Decoupling of Lagrangian Systems. *Proceedings of the International Conference on Advanced Intelligent Systems and Informatics 2016, 533*, 891-899. 10.1007/978-3-319-48308-5_85

Azar, A. T., & Vaidyanathan, S. (2015a). Handbook of Research on Advanced Intelligent Control Engineering and Automation. IGI Global. doi:10.4018/978-1-4666-7248-2

Azar, A. T., & Vaidyanathan, S. (2015b). *Computational Intelligence applications in Modeling and Control. Studies in Computational Intelligence* (Vol. 575). Springer-Verlag.

Azar, A. T., & Vaidyanathan, S. (2015c). *Chaos Modeling and Control Systems Design, Studies in Computational Intelligence* (Vol. 581). Springer-Verlag.

Azar, A. T., & Vaidyanathan, S. (2016). *Advances in Chaos Theory and Intelligent Control. Studies in Fuzziness and Soft Computing* (Vol. 337). Springer-Verlag. doi:10.1007/978-3-319-30340-6

Azar, A. T., Vaidyanathan, S., & Ouannas, A. (2017a). *Fractional Order Control and Synchronization of Chaotic Systems. Studies in Computational Intelligence* (Vol. 688). Springer-Verlag. doi:10.1007/978-3-319-50249-6

Azar, A.T., Volos, C., Gerodimos, N.A., Tombras, G.S., Pham, V.T., Radwan, A.G., … Munoz-Pacheco, J.M. (2017b). A novel chaotic system without equilibrium: Dynamics, synchronization and circuit realization. *Complexity*. doi:10.1155/2017/7871467

Azar, A. T., Ouannas, A., & Singh, S. (2017c). Control of New Type of Fractional Chaos Synchronization. *Proceedings of the International Conference on Advanced Intelligent Systems and Informatics 2017, 639,* 47-56.

Azar, A. T., Kumar, J., Kumar, V., & Rana, K. P. S. (2017d). Control of a Two Link Planar Electrically-Driven Rigid Robotic Manipulator Using Fractional Order SOFC. *Proceedings of the International Conference on Advanced Intelligent Systems and Informatics 2017, 639,* 47-56.

Azar, A. T., & Zhu, Q. (2015). *Advances and Applications in Sliding Mode Control systems. Studies in Computational Intelligence* (Vol. 576). Springer-Verlag.

Baghli, L. (1999). *Contribution à la Commande de la Machine Asynchrone, Utilisation de la Logique Floue, des Réseaux de Neurones et des Algorithmes Génétiques* (Thèse de Doctorat). Département de Génie Electrique Université Henri Poincaré, Nancy-I.

Bimal, & Bos, K. (1994). Expert system, fuzzy logic, and neural network applications in power electronics and motion control. *Proceedings of the IEEE, 82*(8), 1303 – 1323.

Bose, B. (2001). *Artificial neural network applications in power electronics.* The 27th Annual Conférence of the IEEE Industrial Electronics Society, Denver, CO. 10.1109/IECON.2001.975533

Bouchakour, S. (2005). *Commande Directe de Puissance d'un Convertisseur AC/DC Triphasé Sans Capteurs de Tension.* Memory of Magister Ecole Militaire Polytechnique Algeria.

Bouafia, A., & Krim, F. (2008). A fuzzy-Logic-Based Controller for Three-Phase PWM Rectifier with Unity Power Factor Operation. J. *Electrical Systems, 4*(1), 36–50.

Bouafia, A., Krim, F., & Gaubert, J. P. (2009). Fuzzy-Logic-Based Switching State Selection for Direct Power Control of Three-Phase PWM Rectifier. *IEEE Transactions on Industrial Electronics, 56*(6), 1984–1992. doi:10.1109/TIE.2009.2014746

Boulkroune, A., Bouzeriba, A., Bouden, T., & Azar, A. T. (2016a). Fuzzy Adaptive Synchronization of Uncertain Fractional-order Chaotic Systems. In A. T. Azar & S. Vaidyanathan (Eds.), *Advances in Chaos Theory and Intelligent Control. Studies in Fuzziness and Soft Computing* (Vol. 337). Springer-Verlag. doi:10.1007/978-3-319-30340-6_28

Boulkroune, A., Hamel, S., & Azar, A. T. (2016b). *Fuzzy control-based function synchronization of unknown chaotic systems with dead-zone input. Advances in Chaos Theory and Intelligent Control. Studies in Fuzziness and Soft Computing* (Vol. 337). Springer-Verlag.

Cichowlas, M., Malinowski, M., Kazmierkowski, P., Sobczuk, D., & Pou, J. (2005). Active filtering function of three-phase PWM boost rectifier under different line voltage conditions. *IEEE Transactions on Industrial Electronics, 52*(2), 410–419. doi:10.1109/TIE.2005.843915

Chapuis, Y. A. (1996). *Contrôle directe du couple d'une machine asynchrone par l'orientation de son flux statorique* (Doctoral thesis). INP-Grenoble, France.

Chen, B., & Joos, G. (2008). Direct power control of active filters with averaged switching frequency regulation. *IEEE Transactions on Power Electronics, 23*(6), 2729–2737. doi:10.1109/TPEL.2008.2004958

Chen, S., & Joos, G. (2001) Direct Power Control of Three Active filer with Minimum Energy Storage Components. *APEC 2001. Sixteenth Annual IEEE Applied Power Electronics Conference and Exposition*. DOI: 10.1109/APEC.2001.911703

Constant, L. (2000). *Modélisation de Dispositifs Electriques par Réseaux de Neurones en Vue de L'émulation Temps Réel* (Thesis Doctorate). Toulouse, France.

Escobar, G., Stankovic, A., Carrasco, M., Galvan, E., & Ortega, R. (2003). Analysis and design of direct power control (DPC) for a three phase synchronous rectifier via output regulation subspaces. *IEEE Transactions on Power Electronics*, *18*(3), 823–830. doi:10.1109/TPEL.2003.810862

Fekik, A., Denoun, H., Benamrouche, N., Benyahia, N., Zaouia, M., & Haddad, S. (2015a) Comparative study of PI and FUZZY DC- voltage control for Voltage Oriented Control-PWM rectifier. *The 14th International Conference on Circuits, Systems, Electronics, Control & Signal Processing 2015*.

Fekik, A., Denoun, H., Benamrouche, N., Benyahia, N., & Zaouia, M. (2015b). A Fuzzy Logic Based Controller For Three Phase PWM Rectifier With Voltage Oriented Control Strategy. *International Journal of Circuits, Systems and Signal Processing*, *9*, 412–419.

Fekik, A., Denoun, H., Benamrouche, N., Benyahia, N., Badji, A., & Zaouia, M. (2016*)* Comparative Analysis of Direct Power Control and Direct power control with space vector modulation of PWM rectifier. 4th IEEE *International Conference on Control Engineering & Information Technology (CEIT-2016)*. 10.1109/CEIT.2016.7929058

Fekik, A., Denoun, H., Benamrouche, N., Benyahia, N., Zaouia, M., Badji, A., & Vaidyanathan, S. (2017). Improvement of the Performances of the Direct Power Control Using Space Vector Modulation of Three Phases PWM-Rectifier. *International Journal of Control Theory and Applications*, *10*, 125–137.

Fischer, J. R., González, S. A., Carugat, I., Herrán, M. A., Judewicz, M. G., & Carrica, D. O. (2014). Robust predictive control of grid-tied converters based on direct power control. *IEEE Transactions on Power Electronics*, *29*(10), 5634–5643. doi:10.1109/TPEL.2013.2294919

Geyer, T., & Quevedo, E. (2015). Performance of multistep finite control set model predictive control for power electronics. *IEEE Transactions on Power Electronics*, *30*(3), 1633–1644. doi:10.1109/TPEL.2014.2316173

Ghoudelbourk, S., Dib, D., Omeiri, A., & Azar, A. T. (2016). MPPT Control in wind energy conversion systems and the application of fractional control (PIα) in pitch wind turbine. International Journal of Modelling *Identification and Control*, *26*(2), 140–151. doi:10.1504/IJMIC.2016.078329

Grassi, G., Ouannas, A., Azar, A. T., Radwan, A. G., Volos, C., Pham, V. T., . . . Stouboulos, I. N. (2017). *Chaos Synchronisation Of Continuous Systems Via Scalar Signal*. The 6th International Conference on Modern Circuits and Systems Technologies (MOCAST), Thessaloniki, Greece. 10.1109/MOCAST.2017.7937629

Hassanien, A.E., Moftah, H.M., Azar, A.T., & Shoman, M. (2014). MRI Breast cancer diagnosis hybrid approach using adaptive Ant-based segmentation and Multilayer Perceptron neural networks classifier. *Applied Soft computing, 14*(Part A), 62-71.

Hu, J., Zhu, J., Zhang, Y., Platt, G., Ma, Q., & Dorrell, D. G. (2013). Predictive direct virtual torque and power control of doubly fed induction generators for fast and smooth grid synchronization and flexible power regulation. *IEEE Transactions on Power Electronics*, *28*(7), 3182–3194. doi:10.1109/TPEL.2012.2219321

Jiang, W. (2010) Sliding-mode Control of Single-phase PWM Rectifier for DC Microgrid Applications. *International Conference on Computer and Electrical Engineering*, 53, 82-90. DOI: 10.7763/IPCSIT.2012.V53.No.1.82

Karamanakos, P., Geyer, T., Oikonomou, N., Kieferndorf, F., & Manias, S. (2014). Direct model predictive control: A review of strategies that achieve long prediction intervals for power electronics. *IEEE Industrial Electronics Magazine*, *8*(1), 32–43. doi:10.1109/MIE.2013.2290474

Lamterkati, J., Khafallah, M., & Ouboubker, L. (2014a). A New DPC for Three-phase PWM rectifier with unity power factor operation. *International Journal of Advanced Research in Electrical Electronics and Instrumentation Engineering*, *3*(4), 8273–8285.

Lamterkati, J., Khafallah, M., & Ouboubker, L. (2014b). Comparison of PI and Fuzzy logic DC-Link Voltage Controller for DPC PWM-Rectifier. *International Journal of Enhanced Research in Science Technology & Engineering*, *3*(4), 321–332.

Larrinaga, S. A., Vidal, M. A. R., Oyarbide, E., & Apraiz, J. R. T. (2007). Predictive control strategy for DC/AC converters based on direct power control. *IEEE Transactions on Industrial Electronics*, *54*(3), 1261–1271. doi:10.1109/TIE.2007.893162

Larrinaga, S., Vidal, M., Oyarbide, E., & Apraiz, J. (2007). Predictive control strategy of DC/AC converters based on direct power control. *IEEE Transactions on Industrial Electronics*, *54*(3), 1261–1271. doi:10.1109/TIE.2007.893162

Malinowski, M., Kazmierkowski, M. P., & Trzynadlowski, A. M. (2003). A Comparative Study of Control Techniques for PWM Rectifiers in AC Adjustable Speed Drives. *IEEE Transactions on Power Electronics*, *18*(6), 1390–1396. doi:10.1109/TPEL.2003.818871

Malinowski, M., Jasinski, M., & Kazmierkowski, P. (2004). Simple Direct power control of three phase PWM rectifier using space vector modulation (DPC-SVM). *IEEE Transactions on Industrial Electronics*, *51*(2), 447–454. doi:10.1109/TIE.2004.825278

Malinowski, M., Kaz'mierkowski, M. P., Hansen, S., Blaabjerg, F., & Marques, G. D. (2001). Virtual flux based direct power control of three-phase PWM rectifiers. *IEEE Transactions on Industry Applications*, *37*(4), 1019–1027. doi:10.1109/28.936392

Malinowski, M., & Kazmierkowski, M.P. (2000). *Simulation Study of Virtual Flux Based Direct Power Control for Three-Phase PWM Rectifiers*. 26th Annual Confjerence of the IEEE Industrial Electronics Society, Nagoya, Japan. Doi:10.1109/IECON.2000.972411

Meghni, B., Dib, D., Azar, A. T., Ghoudelbourk, S., & Saadoun, A. (2017a). *Robust Adaptive Supervisory Fractional order Controller For optimal Energy Management in Wind Turbine with Battery Storage*. *Studies in Computational Intelligence* (Vol. 688). Springer-Verlag.

Meghni, B., Dib, D., Azar, A. T., & Saadoun, A. (2017b). *Effective Supervisory Controller to Extend Optimal Energy Management in Hybrid Wind Turbine under Energy and Reliability Constraints. International Journal of Dynamics and Control.* Springer. doi:10.100740435-016-0296-0

Meghni, B., Dib, D., & Azar, A. T. (2017c). A Second-order sliding mode and fuzzy logic control to Optimal Energy Management in PMSG Wind Turbine with Battery Storage. *Neural Computing & Applications, 28*(6), 1417–1434. doi:10.100700521-015-2161-z

Mekki, H., Boukhetala, D., & Azar, A. T. (2015). Sliding Modes for Fault Tolerant Control. In Advances and Applications in Sliding Mode Control systems. Springer-Verlag GmbH Berlin/Heidelberg. doi:10.1007/978-3-319-11173-5_15

Mondal, S. K., Pinto, J. O. P., & Bose, B. K. (2002). A Neural-Network-Based Space-Vector PWM Controller for a three-Level Voltage-Fed Inverter Induction Motor Drive. *Industry Applications. IEEE Transactions on., 38*(3), 660–669.

Mezache, A., & Betto, K. (1997). *Estimation et Commande d'un Réacteur de Fabrication de Pâte a Papier par les Réseaux de Neurones Flous. Memory of Engineer.* University of Constantine.

Noguchi, T., Tomiki, H., Kondo, S., & Takahashi, I. (1998). Direct power control of PWM converter without power-source voltage sensors. *IEEE Transactions on Industry Applications, 34*(3), 473–479. doi:10.1109/28.673716

Ouannas, A., Azar, A. T., & Abu-Saris, R. (2016a). A new type of hybrid synchronization between arbitrary hyperchaotic maps. *International Journal of Machine Learning and Cybernetics.* doi:10.100713042-016-0566-3

Ouannas, A., Azar, A. T., & Radwan, A. G. (2016b). *On Inverse Problem of Generalized Synchronization Between Different Dimensional Integer-Order and Fractional-Order Chaotic Systems.* The 28th International Conference on Microelectronics, Cairo, Egypt. 10.1109/ICM.2016.7847942

Ouannas, A., Azar, A. T., Ziar, T., & Vaidyanathan, S. (2017a). *On New Fractional Inverse Matrix Projective Synchronization Schemes. Studies in Computational Intelligence* (Vol. 688). Springer-Verlag.

Ouannas, A., Azar, A. T., Ziar, T., & Vaidyanathan, S. (2017b). *Fractional Inverse Generalized Chaos Synchronization Between Different Dimensional Systems. Studies in Computational Intelligence* (Vol. 688). Springer-Verlag.

Ouannas, A., Azar, A. T., Ziar, T., & Vaidyanathan, S. (2017c). *A New Method To Synchronize Fractional Chaotic Systems With Different Dimensions. Studies in Computational Intelligence* (Vol. 688). Springer-Verlag.

Ouannas, A., Azar, A. T., Ziar, T., & Radwan, A. G. (2017d). *Study On Coexistence of Different Types of Synchronization Between Different dimensional Fractional Chaotic Systems. Studies in Computational Intelligence* (Vol. 688). Springer-Verlag.

Ouannas, A., Azar, A. T., Ziar, T., & Radwan, A. G. (2017e). *Generalized Synchronization of Different Dimensional Integer-order and Fractional Order Chaotic Systems. Studies in Computational Intelligence* (Vol. 688). Springer-Verlag.

Ouannas, A., Azar, A. T., & Vaidyanathan, S. (2017f). On A Simple Approach for Q-S Synchronization of Chaotic Dynamical Systems in Continuous-Time. *Int. J. Computing Science and Mathematics, 8*(1), 20–27.

Ouannas, A., Azar, A. T., & Vaidyanathan, S. (2017g). New Hybrid Synchronization Schemes Based on Coexistence of Various Types of Synchronization Between Master-Slave Hyperchaotic Systems. *International Journal of Computer Applications in Technology, 55*(2), 112–120. doi:10.1504/IJCAT.2017.082868

Ouannas, A., Azar, A. T., & Ziar, T. (2017h). *On Inverse Full State Hybrid Function Projective Synchronization for Continuous-time Chaotic Dynamical Systems with Arbitrary Dimensions*. Differential Equations and Dynamical Systems; doi:10.100712591-017-0362-x

Ouannas, A., Azar, A. T., & Vaidyanathan, S. (2017i). A Robust Method for New Fractional Hybrid Chaos Synchronization. *Mathematical Methods in the Applied Sciences, 40*(5), 1804–1812. doi:10.1002/mma.4099

Ouannas, A., Grassi, G., Azar, A. T., Radwan, A. G., Volos, C., Pham, V. T., . . . Stouboulos, I. N. (2017j). *Dead-Beat Synchronization Control in Discrete-Time Chaotic Systems*. The 6th International Conference on Modern Circuits and Systems Technologies (MOCAST), Thessaloniki, Greece. 10.1109/MOCAST.2017.7937628

Sanjuan, S. (2010). Voltage Oriented Control of Three-Phase Boost PWM Converters Design, simulation and implementation of a 3-phase boost battery Charger. Chalmers University of Technologie.

Singh, S., Azar, A. T., Ouannas, A., Zhu, Q., Zhang, W., & Na, J. (2017). *Sliding Mode Control Technique for Multi-switching Synchronization of Chaotic Systems. 9th International Conference on Modelling, Identification and Control (ICMIC 2017)*, Kunming, China.

Soliman, N. S., Said, L. A., Azar, A. T., Madian, A. H., Radwan, A. G., & Ouannas, A. (2017). *Fractional Controllable Multi-Scroll V-Shape Attractor with Parameters Effect*. The 6th International Conference on Modern Circuits and Systems Technologies (MOCAST), Thessaloniki, Greece.

Song, Z., Tian, Y., Chen, W., Zou, Z., & Chen, Z. (2016). Predictive duty cycle control of three-phase active-front-end rectifier. *IEEE Transactions on Power Electronics, 31*(1), 698–710. doi:10.1109/TPEL.2015.2398872

Tolba, M. F., AbdelAty, A. M., Soliman, N. S., Said, L. A., Madian, A. H., Azar, A. T., & Radwan, A. G. (2017). FPGA implementation of two fractional order chaotic systems. *International Journal of Electronics and Communications, 28*, 162–172. doi:10.1016/j.aeue.2017.04.028

Vaidyanathan, S., Sampath, S., & Azar, A. T. (2015a). Global chaos synchronisation of identical chaotic systems via novel sliding mode control method and its application to Zhu system. International Journal of Modelling *Identification and Control, 23*(1), 92–100. doi:10.1504/IJMIC.2015.067495

Vaidyanathan, S., Azar, A. T., Rajagopal, K., & Alexander, P. (2015b). Design and SPICE implementation of a 12-term novel hyperchaotic system and its synchronization via active control (2015). International Journal of Modelling *Identification and Control, 23*(3), 267–277. doi:10.1504/IJMIC.2015.069936

Vaidyanathan, S., Idowu, B. A., & Azar, A. T. (2015c). Backstepping Controller Design for the Global Chaos Synchronization of Sprott's Jerk Systems. In Chaos Modeling and Control Systems Design. Springer-Verlag GmbH Berlin/Heidelberg. doi:10.1007/978-3-319-13132-0_3

Vaidyanathan, S., & Azar, A. T. (2015a). Anti-Synchronization of Identical Chaotic Systems using Sliding Mode Control and an Application to Vaidyanathan-Madhavan Chaotic Systems. In Advances and Applications in Sliding Mode Control systems. Springer-Verlag GmbH Berlin/Heidelberg. doi:10.1007/978-3-319-11173-5_19

Vaidyanathan, S., & Azar, A. T. (2015b). Hybrid Synchronization of Identical Chaotic Systems using Sliding Mode Control and an Application to Vaidyanathan Chaotic Systems. In Advances and Applications in Sliding Mode Control system. Springer-Verlag GmbH Berlin/Heidelberg. doi:10.1007/978-3-319-11173-5_20

Vaidyanathan, S., & Azar, A. T. (2015c). Analysis, Control and Synchronization of a Nine-Term 3-D Novel Chaotic System. In Chaos Modeling and Control Systems Design. Springer-Verlag GmbH Berlin/Heidelberg. DOI doi:10.1007/978-3-319-13132-0_1

Vaidyanathan, S., & Azar, A. T. (2015d). Analysis and Control of a 4-D Novel Hyperchaotic System. In Chaos Modeling and Control Systems Design. Springer-Verlag GmbH Berlin/Heidelberg. DOI doi:10.1007/978-3-319-13132-0_2

Vaidyanathan, S., & Azar, A. T. (2016a). Takagi-Sugeno Fuzzy Logic Controller for Liu-Chen Four-Scroll Chaotic System. *International Journal of Intelligent Engineering Informatics*, 4(2), 135–150. doi:10.1504/IJIEI.2016.076699

Vaidyanathan, S., & Azar, A. T. (2016b). *Dynamic Analysis, Adaptive Feedback Control and Synchronization of an Eight-Term 3-D Novel Chaotic System with Three Quadratic Nonlinearities. Studies in Fuzziness and Soft Computing* (Vol. 337). Springer-Verlag.

Vaidyanathan, S., & Azar, A. T. (2016c). *Qualitative Study and Adaptive Control of a Novel 4-D Hyperchaotic System with Three Quadratic Nonlinearities. Studies in Fuzziness and Soft Computing* (Vol. 337). Springer-Verlag.

Vaidyanathan, S., & Azar, A. T. (2016d). *A Novel 4-D Four-Wing Chaotic System with Four Quadratic Nonlinearities and its Synchronization via Adaptive Control Method. Advances in Chaos Theory and Intelligent Control. Studies in Fuzziness and Soft Computing* (Vol. 337). Springer-Verlag.

Vaidyanathan, S., & Azar, A. T. (2016e). *Adaptive Control and Synchronization of Halvorsen Circulant Chaotic Systems. Advances in Chaos Theory and Intelligent Control. Studies in Fuzziness and Soft Computing* (Vol. 337). Springer-Verlag.

Vaidyanathan, S., & Azar, A. T. (2016f). *Adaptive Backstepping Control and Synchronization of a Novel 3-D Jerk System with an Exponential Nonlinearity. Advances in Chaos Theory and Intelligent Control. Studies in Fuzziness and Soft Computing* (Vol. 337). Springer-Verlag.

Vaidyanathan, S., & Azar, A. T. (2016g). *Generalized Projective Synchronization of a Novel Hyperchaotic Four-Wing System via Adaptive Control Method. Advances in Chaos Theory and Intelligent Control. Studies in Fuzziness and Soft Computing* (Vol. 337). Springer-Verlag.

Vaidyanathan, S., Azar, A. T., & Ouannas, A. (2017a). *An Eight-Term 3-D Novel Chaotic System with Three Quadratic Nonlinearities, its Adaptive Feedback Control and Synchronization. Studies in Computational Intelligence* (Vol. 688). Springer-Verlag.

Vaidyanathan, S., Zhu, Q., & Azar, A. T. (2017b). *Adaptive Control of a Novel Nonlinear Double Convection Chaotic System. Studies in Computational Intelligence* (Vol. 688). Springer-Verlag.

Vaidyanathan, S., Azar, A. T., & Ouannas, A. (2017c). *Hyperchaos and Adaptive Control of a Novel Hyperchaotic System with Two Quadratic Nonlinearities. Studies in Computational Intelligence* (Vol. 688). Springer-Verlag.

Vazquez, S., Sanchez, J., Carrasco, J., Leon, J., & Galvan, E. (2008). A model-based direct power control for three-phase power converters. *IEEE Transactions on Industrial Electronics*, *55*(4), 1647–11657. doi:10.1109/TIE.2008.917113

Vazquez, S., Leon, J. I., Franquelo, L. G., Rodriguez, J., Young, H., Marquez, A., & Zanchetta, P. (2014). Model predictive control: A review of its applications in power electronics. *IEEE Industrial Electronics Magazine*, *8*(1), 16–31. doi:10.1109/MIE.2013.2290138

Vazquez, J., & Salmeron, P. (2003). Active power filter control using neural network technologies. *IEE Proceedings. Electric Power Applications*, *150*(2), 139–145. doi:10.1049/ip-epa:20030009

Wang, Z., Volos, C., Kingni, S.T., Azar, A.T., & Pham, V.T. (2017). Four-wing attractors in a novel chaotic system with hyperbolic sine nonlinearity. *Optik - International Journal for Light and Electron Optics, 131*(2017), 1071-1078.

Zhang, Y., Xie, W., Li, Z., & Zhang, Y. (2013). Model predictive direct power control of a PWM rectifier with duty cycle optimization. *IEEE Transactions on Power Electronics*, *28*(11), 5343–5351. doi:10.1109/TPEL.2013.2243846

Zhu, Q., & Azar, A. T. (2015). *Complex system modelling and control through intelligent soft computations. Studies in Fuzziness and Soft Computing* (Vol. 319). Springer-Verlag.

This research was previously published in Advances in System Dynamics and Control; pages 286-316, copyright year 2018 by Engineering Science Reference (an imprint of IGI Global).

Chapter 22
Adaptive Power–Saving Mechanism for VoIP Over WiMAX Based on Artificial Neural Network

Tamer Emara
Shenzhen University, China

ABSTRACT

The IEEE 802.16 system offers power-saving class type II as a power-saving algorithm for real-time services such as voice over internet protocol (VoIP) service. However, it doesn't take into account the silent periods of VoIP conversation. This chapter proposes a power conservation algorithm based on artificial neural network (ANN-VPSM) that can be applied to VoIP service over WiMAX systems. Artificial intelligent model using feed forward neural network with a single hidden layer has been developed to predict the mutual silent period that used to determine the sleep period for power saving class mode in IEEE 802.16. From the implication of the findings, ANN-VPSM reduces the power consumption during VoIP calls with respect to the quality of services (QoS). Experimental results depict the significant advantages of ANN-VPSM in terms of power saving and quality-of-service (QoS). It shows the power consumed in the mobile station can be reduced up to 3.7% with respect to VoIP quality.

INTRODUCTION

Recently, Voice over Internet Protocol (VoIP) has increasingly become a common service for wireless networks such as worldwide interoperability for microwave access (WiMAX). As the VoIP technology offers Mobile WiMAX clients the ability to use voice services with lower expenses compared with Public Switched Telephone Network (PSTN). Skype has earned more and more popularity since it is seen as the best VoIP software (Adami, Callegari, Giordano, Pagano, & Pepe, 2012). For VoIP calls, packets are required to be sent constantly. Considering the real-time nature of voice, the radio cannot easily save

DOI: 10.4018/978-1-6684-2408-7.ch022

power. As it is difficult to transition to sleep state while sending inter-packets intervals (Zubair, Fisal, Abazeed, Salihu, & Khan, 2015).

A mobile station (MS) usually depends on a portable power source like batteries. These batteries have limited lifetime. Thus, all wireless systems offer power-saving classes (PSCs), such as in IEEE 802.16e (IEEE, 2006), to save the power consumed in MSs through sleep and active mode (Ghosh, Wolter, Andrews, & Chen, 2005).

Regarding IEEE 802.16e, an MS operates alternately between awake and sleep mode. It wakes up to exchange data with a base station (BS) in a listening period. The sleep mode includes sleep and listening periods. In sleep periods, BS buffers incoming packets to the MS, and BS sends it to the MS when MS switches to listen periods. To fit services and applications properties, three PSCs are offered by the IEEE 802.16e for different types of traffic for the purposes of power saving. Thus, MS can associate the sleep parameters for the suitable PSC when connected to a BS. The sleep parameters comprise the starting of sleep time, initial sleep period, final sleep period and the listen period. Clearly, the parameters of each class should be carefully determined to minimize the power consumed in the MS with restriction to the quality-of-service (QoS) requirements of that connection.

This chapter focuses on power saving in short latency periods included in active time which is sufficient for VoIP services. This chapter considers two states of VoIP conversation: mutual silent state and talk-spurt state. In mutual silent periods, there are not any packets transmitted between MS and BS. Therefore, the sleep period in mutual silence can be increased more than in the talk-spurt period to reduce the power consumption. Hence to increase energy-efficient, it is necessary to design a new algorithm that can place its sleep intervals flexibly in mutual silence periods.

In this chapter, a power conservation algorithm is proposed based on artificial neural network (ANN-VPSM). The proposed algorithm can be applied to VoIP service over WiMAX systems. Artificial Intelligent model using feed forward neural network with a single hidden layer has been developed to predict the mutual silent period that used to determine the sleep period for power saving class mode in IEEE 802.16. Artificial Neural Networks (ANNs) is a simulation of the biological nervous system in the human brain. That network can regulate neurons and learn through experience. The development of ANN using computer programs to identify patterns of data sets using training data through supervised learning. ANNs has a flexible learning system and adaptive ability allow them to learn from linear and non-linear function (Haykin, 2007).

An overview of previous attempts in power saving for VoIP services is addressed in the next section. Then the proposed prediction mechanism is presented. The simulation results of the proposed mechanism with discussion are introduced in experiment and results. Finally, the conclusion is discussed.

BACKGROUND AND RELATED WORK

WiMAX (IEEE 802.16e) introduces three types of PSCs suitable to several applications that produce different traffic characteristics (IEEE, 2006). There are various QoS requirements, for various types of connections between MS and BS. Subsequently, various connections are classified into varied PSCs to achieve their requirements of QoS.

1. **The Power Saving Class Type I (PSC-I):** Starts with initial sleep window (S_{min}), then this sleep window is doubled, if MS doesn't receive any message about the existence of data packets during

its listening window. This process is repeated consistently till reaching the maximum sleep window period (S_{max}), after that, the next keeps the same.

2. **The Power Saving Class Type II (PSC-II):** Has a sleep window (S_T) with the same size that is repeated consistently.

3. **The Power Saving Class Type III (PSC-III):** Has a sleep cycle with one predefined sleep interval (S_M) and without listening interval.

In Power Saving Mode (PSM), a trade-off exists between the performance of QoS for transmitting packets and conserving power of an MS (Nga, Kim, & Kang, 2007). In VoIP service, that trade-off occurs in accordance with the length of the sleep periods. To satisfy VoIP QoS, the sleep period can be equal to the time that is needed to generate packets of the VoIP codec, which is in a short period of 10 to 30 ms (Cox & Kroon, 1996), but it is not easy to get enough power conservation because of the comparatively short sleep period. On the contrary, if the sleep period's length is increased, certainly, more power will be saved, however, it leads to an additional delay to VoIP traffic which breaks up VoIP QoS. Thus, to estimate the exact length of the sleep periods, it should be considered the performance of PSM within the requirements of QoS.

There have been recent works that support VoIP service in the environment of WiMAX. In (Choi & Cho, 2007; Choi, Lee, & Cho, 2007; J. R. Lee, 2007; J. R. Lee & Cho, 2009; Lin, Liu, Wang, & Kwok, 2011), the authors introduce many power saving mechanisms, which mainly depend on applying PSC-II in a talk-spurt periods, however for saving more power, they applied PSC-I during silence periods. Emara (2016) applies PSC-III at mutual silence state, while authors in (Emara, Saleh, & Arafat, 2014) combine between PSC-III and PSC-I in mutual silence to increase power saving.

In (J. Lee & Cho, 2008), the authors discuss the methodology to choose the optimal sleep periods of the PSC-II, that have the most efficient energy. In (Choi, Lee, & Cho, 2009), the VoIP hybrid power saving mechanism (HPSM) performance had been estimated, according to the model of network delay. In (Namboodiri & Gao, 2010), an algorithm is presented for emerging dual-mode mobiles in order to save power by computing sleep/wake-up schedules, making the radio remain in the lower power sleep mode for curtail periods throughout a phone call.

Many scheduling algorithms are proposed in (Chen, Deng, Hsu, & Wang, 2012; Cheng, Wu, Yang, & Leu, 2014; Kao & Chuang, 2012; Ke, Chen, & Fang, 2014; Teixeira & Guardieiro, 2013), the packets are categorized according to the characteristics of their traffic. The objective of these algorithms is to transmit the packets in appropriate transmission time with the appropriate sleep-mode operation. These algorithms try to schedule packets for minimizing listening intervals and maximizing sleep intervals within the QoS requirement. In (Liao & Yen, 2009) the authors proposed a scheduling algorithm which considered the QoS jitter and delay types should be synchronized.

In case that the delay limit is less stringent and the traffic load is light, the authors in (Jin, Chen, Qiao, & Choi, 2011) examine sleep mode management suitable for IEEE802.16m that gains good performance. The authors (Kalle et al., 2010) introduce procedures of sub-frame sleep, variable listening interval, and discrete listening window extension to enhance VoIP traffic power saving in IEEE 802.16m. The analysis of power consumed in Transmission Control Protocol (TCP) data transfer was in (Hashimoto, Hasegawa, & Murata, 2015).

Problem Definition and Plane of Solution

The most famous standard speech codecs utilized in VoIP applications are G.723.1A (ITU-T, 2006), G.729B (ITU-T, 2012) and AMR (Abreu-Sernandez & Garcia-Mateo, 2000). These standards use the function of silence suppression. Silence suppression function does not permit the speech codec to generate VoIP packets in silent periods, so as to save system bandwidth. Anyway, considering the speech model suggested by ITU (ITU-T, 1993), human speech comprises interchanging silent periods and talk-spurt, Brady (Brady, 1969) concluded that about 60 percent of the total VoIP conversation duration is occupied by the silent periods. Therefore, it is not efficient to use PSC-II only, as PSC-II does not deal with the silent periods, its sleep interval has fixed length. To increase energy-efficient, it is necessary to design a new algorithm that can place its sleep intervals flexibly in mutual silence periods.

If each terminal uses the speech codec with silence suppression functionality, the codec generates VoIP packets at specific times continuously during talking periods, while the packets are not generated during silent periods. Instead of not generating packets in silent periods, it produces a Silent Insertion Descriptor (SID) frame (Estepa, Estepa, & Vozmediano, 2004). The SID packet is a small packet, in comparison with the voice packet. It contains only background noise information, which can help the receiving side's decoder to generate artificial noise during the silent period. SID is generated at the beginning of the silent period and sent only once. And so on, the SID frames receipt of both parts A and B could confirm the starting time of alternating silent. When SID frame is transmitted only at the starting of the mutual silence, bandwidth utilization increases (Hussain, Marimuthu, & Habib, 2014) and thus the network traffic is reduced.

Brady (Brady, 1969) shows that about 60% of the total VoIP conversation duration is occupied by the silent periods and about 19% for mutual silent periods and the mutual silence duration average is approximately 306 ms. Therefore, for saving more energy, MS can sleep during these mutual silence periods, yet the standard PSC-II has nothing to do with the VoIP traffic silent periods. Thus, MS must be activated at specific times continuously during those periods even if it doesn't receive any voice packets. Consequently, the main focus of the proposed mechanism (ANN-VPSM) is to apply another PSM depending on each side's voice activity. As shown in Figure 1, PSC-II is used during talk-spurt periods. Throughout the mutual silent intervals, PSC-III with S_M period is predicted using Artificial Neural Networks (ANNs) techniques. All the notations used in this chapter are described in Table 1.

Figure 1. An example of the proposed ANN_VPSM mechanism operation

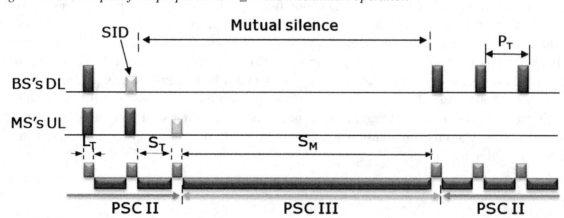

Table 1. Table of notations

Notation	Explanation
P_T	Packet interval
1 frame	One frame duration
L_T	Listen interval
S_T	Sleep interval for PSC-II
S_M	Sleep interval for PSC-III
S_{min}	Minimum sleep interval for PSC-I
S_{max}	Maximum sleep interval for PSC-I
X	Distribution of the mutual silent length
λ	Arrival rate
p_i	The probability of arriving the first voice packet after the mutual silent state started in the i-th sleep cycle
B_f	Buffering delay
E_1	Consumed energy per unit time in PSC-I
E_3	Consumed energy per unit time in PSC-III
E_m	Consumed energy per unit time during mutual silent periods
E_S	Consumed energy per unit time during sleep periods
E_L	Consumed energy per unit time during listen periods
S_i	Length of i-th sleep period in the i-th sleep cycle

PROPOSED POWER SAVING MECHANISM

ANN_VPSM Proposed Approach

In recent times, ANN technology has developed to make it possible to solve most complicated non-linear systems with variable parameters. ANN simulates a human nervous system that is working as the human brain. It is built with artificial neurons meanwhile; the interconnections are similar to the nervous system (Haykin, 2007). ANN has been effectively used to predict the mutual silence in a VoIP conversation.

This work utilizes a neural network to predict the mutual silent periods, which determines the value of the sleep cycle for PSC-III to achieve the maximum power saving. At the moment that ANN is built, it becomes ready to train. Since these initial weights are chosen randomly (Simoes & Bose, 1995). The proposed ANN-VPSM algorithm consists of two modes: the first is training mode; while the ANN trained, VPSM (Emara et al., 2014) mechanism is executed. The second mode is prediction mode; after ANN training finished, it is ready to predict the sleep cycle for PSC-III. ANN has the two inputs, last voice duration's time and last mutual silent duration's time and has one output, optimum sleep cycle for PSC-III.

In this study, the used ANN structure is Multilayer Perceptron (MLP); feeding input data to the neural layer for producing the desired output. The learning method is back-propagation method which feeds the output's error data to the input. The ANN constructs three layers with on hidden layer. The nodes numbers or Processing Elements (PEs) are chosen based on the complexity of the data and studies.

Training Mode

After constructing ANN, it needs to be trained. So, the training mode starts firstly. While the conversation is running, the needed data for training are collected. To save more power in training mode our previous work VPSM (Emara et al., 2014) is chosen.

The main aim of adopting the VPSM is using the PSC-II during talk-spurt intervals with a fixed sleep interval's length. While, throughout the mutual silent intervals, PSC-III with S_M less than 300 ms is launched at the outset, then PSC-I is applied till the end of mutual silence. Figure 3 illustrates the procedures of VPSM. Algorithm 1 is the proposed algorithm for training mode. It works on the frames which received or sent.

Sent Data

At the moment of the speech coder encode current data, the Voice Activity Detection (VAD) (ITU-T, 2012) is operated. The VAD result could be 1 or 0 depending on whether the voice activity is presented or absence respectively. The current encoded frame becomes SID if VAD result was equal to 0, while VAD result was equal to 1 if the current encoded frame is a voice.

The PSC-II has requested if the current encoded frame is active voice. However, to start the mutual silent state, the two sides confirm it by generating SID frame at the beginning of the silent period for each side. Therefore, if the current encoded frame is SID, the last received frame from the other side must be checked. If it is SID, the mutual silent state starts, otherwise, PSC-II is requested.

Received Data

When the frame is received, the G.729 decoder is used to decode the received packets. In case VAD result was 1, the active voice frames are reconstructed. Else, the comfort noise generator (CNG) module (ITU-T, 2012) reproduces the non-active voice frames.

The PSC-II is requested when the frame is for active voice. However, if the received frame is SID, current MS state must be in silence to start the mutual silent state. Thus, MS state must be checked, whether it is on silent or not. In case MS is in talking activity, then it is not the mutual silent state. Therefore, the PSC-II is launched. On the contrary, the mutual silent state is initialized if the last encoded frame for the current MS is SID.

Thus, we can summarize the work of this algorithm to the following points:

1. Mutual silence occurs when both sides in silence (i.e. current VAD = 0 and last received frame was SID)
2. Mutual silent sleep mode is initialized by launching PSC-III in case the current PSM is PSC-II.
3. If no frames sent or received during the sleep cycle of PSC-III, The PSC-I has launched after PSC-III termination.
4. The silent mode is over when a voice frame is received or encoded.

After finishing the mutual silent state, the network is being trained. By the end of this test for the current frame, it will be repeated for the coming frame (received or sent) to the call end.

Figure 2. An example of VPSM operation (Emara et al., 2014)

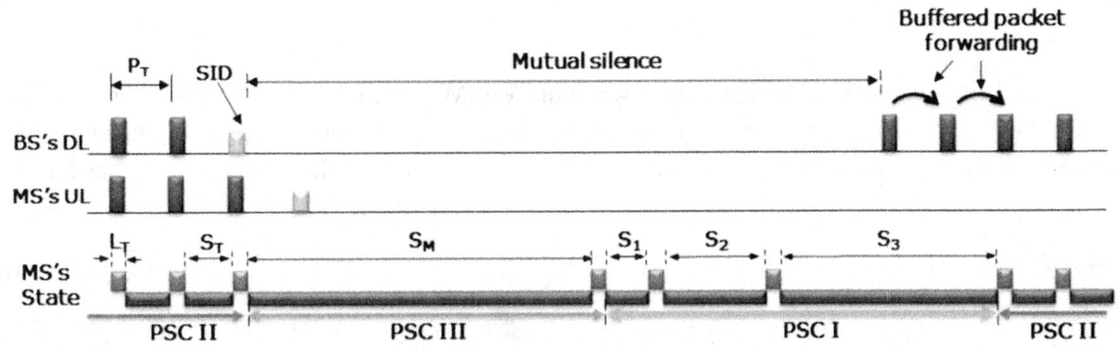

VPSM Numerical Analysis

For analyzing the VPSM during the mutual silent interval, there are two cases. Case 1 discusses the analysis of receiving active voice packets during S_M period, while case 2 discusses the receiving of active voice packets during any sleep cycle of PSC-I.

Case 1: For any active voice packet sent or received, PSC-II is applied. i.e., the MS sleeps with fixed S_T size and wakes up with fixed L_T size. While, the mutual silent state is started by launching PSC-III with S_M period. If there is any voice packet transmitted on uplink or downlink throughout the listen period of PSC-III, it backs again to PSC-II.

Let X be the distribution of a mutual silent length. According to Brady model, the cumulative distribution function of X is defined by:

$$F_X\left(t\right) = 1 - e^{-\lambda t} \tag{1}$$

λ is the arrival rate. Let p_i be the probability of arriving the first voice packet after starting the mutual silent state at the i-th sleep cycle.

$$p_i = P\{X \in [0, S_M]\} = F_X(S_M) \tag{2}$$

$$p_i = 1 - e^{-\lambda\left(S_M + L_T\right)} \tag{3}$$

Hence, the average duration of PSC-III, $E[S_M]$ is calculated by

$$E[S_M] = (S_M + L_T) \tag{4}$$

Assume that all voice packets that are buffered through the sleep period S_M will be transmitted immediately in the following listen period, the buffering delay is obtained by $Bf = S_M - X$, therefore, the average buffering delay becomes

$$E[Bf] = E[S_M] - E[X] = (S_M + L_T) - \frac{1}{\lambda} \qquad (5)$$

For calculating the total consumed energy when the VPSM is used as a mutual silent sleep mode in this case. Let E_S and E_L represent the energies consumed per unit time during sleep and listening periods, respectively. Therefore, the consumed energy per unit time in PSC-III, E_3, is calculated as follows:

$$E_3 = \frac{(S_M E_S + L_T E_L)}{S_M} \qquad (6)$$

Consequently, the energy consumption throughout mutual silent periods per unit time, E_m, is defined as follows:

$$E_m = E_3 \qquad (7)$$

Algorithm 1. The proposed algorithm in training mode

```
1:   Start Call
2:   for each frame do
3:       if Data sent then
4:           Coding data using voice coder
5:           if VAD=0 then
6:               Check last received frame
7:               if last received frame = SID then
8:                   Call Mutual_Silent_Case
9:               end if
10:          else
11:              Call Talking_Case
12:          end if
13:      else if Data received then
14:          Decode received frame using voice coder
15:          if received frame = SID then
16:              Check VAD for last sent frame
17:              if VAD=0 then
18:                  Call Mutual_Silent_Case
19:              end if
20:          else
21:              Call Talking_Case
22:          end if
23:      end if
24:  end for
25: End Call
```

```
26:
27: procedure Mutual_Silent_Case
28:     Check current PSC
29:     if current PSC = PSC-II then
30:         Request PSC-III
31:     else if current PSC= PSC-III then
32:         Request PSC-I
33:     end if
34: end procedure
35:
36: procedure Talking_Case
37:     Check current PSC
38:     if current PSC = PSC-III or current PSC = PSC-I then
39:         Request PSC-II
40:         Calculate silence period
41:         Train ANN
42:     end if
43:         end procedure
```

Case 2: if the sleep cycle of PSC-III finished without receiving or generating any active voice packet, the MS applies PSC-I directly. Considering S_i be the length of i-th sleep period in PSC-I, the length of the i-th sleep cycle, $S_i + L_T$, increases exponentially as follows:

$$S_i + L_T = \begin{cases} 2^{i-1} \cdot P_T, & if \ 1 \leq i < N \\ S_{max}, & if \ i \geq N \end{cases} \tag{8}$$

where the maximum sleep period is $[S_{max} = 2^N S_1]$, N is the number of doubled sleep window till the sleep window size reaches S_{max}.

VPSM mechanism is ended according to the arrival of a voice packet at the i-th sleep cycle. Let X be the distribution of the length of a mutual silent period. According to Brady model, the cumulative distribution function of X is defined by

$$F_X(t) = 1 - e^{-\lambda t} \tag{9}$$

where λ is arrival rate. Let p_i be the probability of arriving at the first voice packet after the beginning of mutual silence period in the i-th sleep cycle.

$$p_i = P\{X \in [L_{i-1}, L_i]\} = F_X(L_i) - F_X(L_{i-1}) \tag{10}$$

$$= e^{-\lambda L_{i-1}} \left(1 - e^{-\lambda \left(S_i + L_T \right)} \right) \tag{11}$$

where $L_i = \sum_{j=1}^{i}(S_j + L_T)$ then, the average duration of PSC-I, $E[L]$, will be;

$$E\left[L\right] = \sum_{i=1}^{\infty} p_i . L_i = \sum_{i=1}^{\infty} p_i \sum_{j=1}^{i}(S_j + L_T) \tag{12}$$

Assume that all voice packets that are buffered through the sleep period S_i will be transmitted instantly throughout the following listen period. The buffering delay is $Bf_i = L_i - X$. Consequently, the average buffering delay is calculated by

$$E\left[Bf\right] = E\left[L\right] - E\left[X\right] = \sum_{i=1}^{\infty} p_i \sum_{j=1}^{i}\left(S_j + L_T\right) - \frac{1}{\lambda} \tag{13}$$

The total consumed energy for VPSM during this case is an aggregate of the consumed energy in PSC-III and in PSC-I. Let E_S and E_L indicate the consumed energies per unit time in the sleep and listening periods, respectively. Then, the consumed energy per unit time in PSC-III, E_3, is obtained as follows:

$$E_3 = \frac{\left(S_M E_S + L_T E_L\right)}{S_M} \tag{14}$$

And the consumed energy per unit time in PSC-I, E_1, is obtained as follows:

$$E_1 = \frac{\sum_{i=1}^{\infty} p_i \sum_{j=1}^{i}\left(S_j E_S + L_T E_L\right)}{E\left[L\right]} \tag{15}$$

Therefore, the consumed energy during mutual silent periods per unit time, E_m, will be:

$$E_m = E_1 + E_3 \tag{16}$$

Prediction Mode

After finishing the training, the network is ready to run. A flowchart of the predicted mode is shown in Figure 3. The mechanism works on the frames which are received or sent.

Sent Data

VAD (ITU-T, 2012) is checked after the speech codec encoded the current frame. If its result was 0, it means the current frame is SID. While the current frame is active voice, in case the result was 1. When the current frame is active voice, the PSC-II is demanded. However, the mutual silence starts when the two sides generate SID frames at the beginning of the silent periods on each side to confirm the mutual silent state. Thus, if the current frame is SID, it doesn't mean this case is mutual silence without checking the last received frame. Therefore, if the last received frame from the other side was a voice that indicates this case is not mutual silence, as a result, the PSC-II is demanded. However, the mutual silent state starts when the last received frame was SID, therefore mutual silent sleep mode is initialized by launching PSC-III with sleep interval is predicted using the ANN.

Figure 3. Flowchart of ANN-VPSM in predicting mode

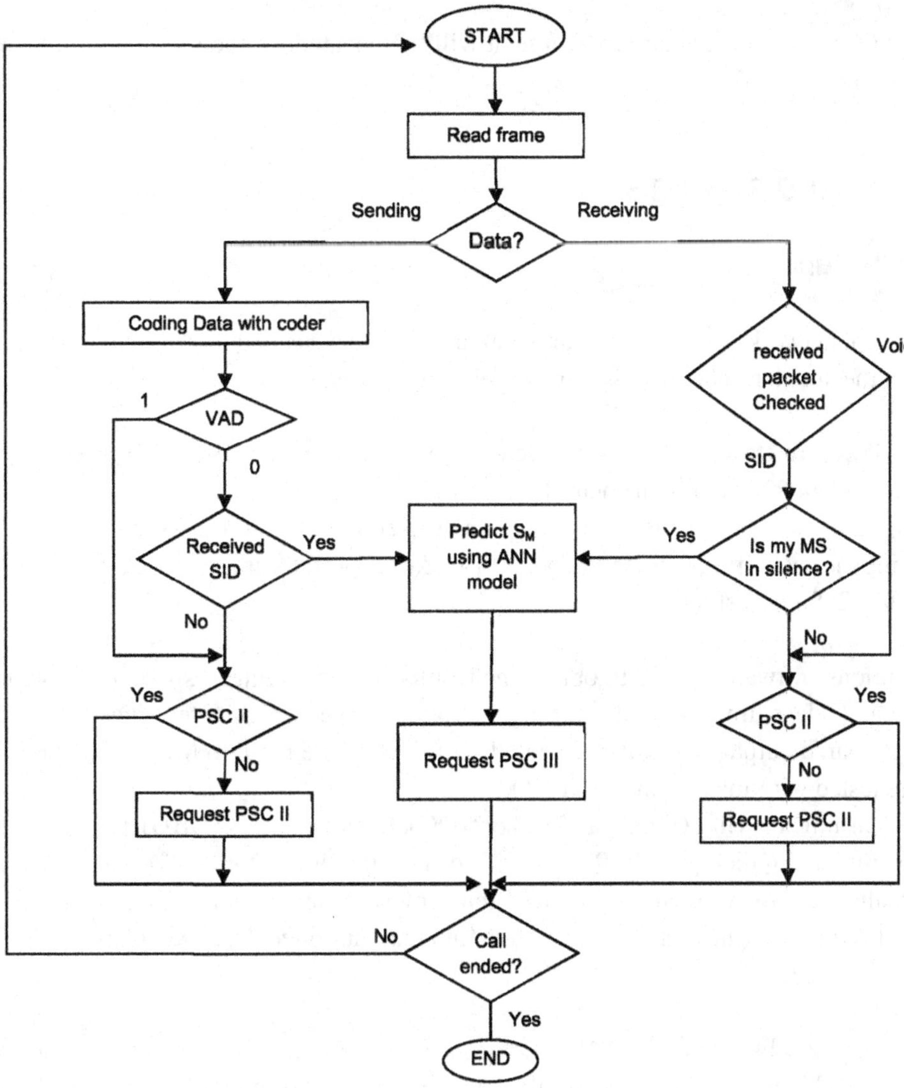

Received Data

Once the frame is received, the VAD is checked as the first step to decode it by G.729 decoder. In case that its value is equal 1, active voice frames will be reconstructed. But, if its value is equal 0, the non-active voice frames will be reproduced by CNG module (ITU-T, 2012).

If the received frame is active voice frame, the PSC-II is requested. However, if it is SID, the current MS state must be silent to start the mutual silent state. Thus, MS state must be checked, whether it is on silent or not. In case that MS state was active talk, it indicates the case is not mutual silence, as a result, the PSC-II is demanded. In contrast, if MS state was silent that shows this case is mutual silence. Consequently, the mutual silent sleep mode is initialized by launching PSC-III with sleep interval which is predicted using ANN.

By the end of this test for the current frame, it will be repeated for the following frame received or sent until the end of the call.

EXPERIMENT AND RESULTS

Simulation Setup

To design a neural network, a sufficiently large amount of data is needed for training, testing, and cross-validation. So, the simulation algorithm consists of three stages:

1. **Getting Training Data:** A program coded with C++ language and G.729B speech codec to get the required data for training the neural network.
2. **Building ANN:** The training is automated with the Neuro Solution (version 5) which trains the network using the back-propagation method. 60% of data is used for training, 15% for cross-validation and the last 25% for testing.

Neuro Solutions software is used to obtain the results and accordingly, simulations are carried out on voice time and silent time as inputs and next mutual silence, which determines the sleep cycle of PSC-III as the desired output. The voice time and silent time were input to MLP with one hidden layer of MLPs were tested with maximum epoch 1000.

Numerous learning rules like Conjugate Gradient (CG), Delta Bar Delta (DBD), Levenberg Marquardt (LM), momentum, and Quick prop (QP) are used for training and better performance parameters are observed. Results are observed while using different Transfer Functions like Tanh Axon, Linear Tanh Axon, Sigmoid Axon, and Linear Sigmoid Axon to find that minimize the power consumed in MS while still guaranteeing VoIP QoS.

3. **Performance Evaluation:** The ANN performance is validated by simulation coded with C++ language and G.729B speech codec to calculate the power consumption for the mutual silent period and mean opinion score (MOS). The MOS score has a scale of 1-5 with 1 representing the worst quality and 5 the best quality.

ITU-T G.729B (ITU-T, 2012) codec is considered as of being frequently used in VoIP applications for its low bandwidth requirements. The packet, P_T, is generated every 40ms. Therefore, the MS should wake up every 40 ms. So, $L_T=1$*frame* was decided. Since the VoIP packet size is very small (8kbps in G.729B) in comparison with the 802.16 bandwidth (about 30Mbps), L_T for 1 frame (10ms) is enough to receive the buffered VoIP packets. So, S_T, becomes 3 frames (30ms) because $P_T=S_T+L_T$. Table 2 summarizes the initial values for simulation factors.

Table 2. Initial values of simulation's factors

Parameter	Description	Value
P_T	Packet interval	40 ms
1 frame	One frame duration	10 ms
L_T	Listen interval	10 ms
S_T	Sleep interval for PSC-II	30 ms
S_M	Sleep interval for PSC-III	

RESULTS AND DISCUSSION

Using transfer function Tanh Axon to build the neural network. After constructing the neural network, training begins by changing learning rules. To see more clearly the effects of the neural network with a transfer function Tanh Axon throughout a call time, Figure 4-a plots the power consumed every 30s, Figure 4-b plots MOS every 30s. From these figures, the best performance made when using learning rule Momentum, less power is consumed with MOS greater than 3.8. Simulation results, when using learning rule Momentum, show that the power consumed in MS can be reduced up to 3.74%.

Using transfer function Sigmoid Axon to build the neural network. After constructing the neural network, training begins by changing learning rules. To see more clearly the effects of the neural network with a transfer function sigmoid axon throughout a call time, Figure 5-a plots the power consumed every 30s, Figure 5-b plots MOS every 30s. From these figures, the best performance made when using learning rule Quickprop. Simulation results, when using learning rule Quickprop, show that the power consumed in MS can be reduced up to 3.73% with MOS more than 3.8.

Using transfer function Linear Tanh Axon to build the neural network. After constructing the neural network, training begins by changing learning rules. To see more clearly the effects of the neural network with a transfer function Linear Tanh axon throughout a call time, Figure 6-a plots the power consumed every 30s, Figure 6-b plots MOS every 30s. From these figures, the best performance made when using learning rule Quickprop or Momentum. Simulation results show that the power consumed in MS can be reduced up to 3.76% with MOS more than 3.8.

Using transfer function Linear Sigmoid Axon to build the neural network. After constructing the neural network, training begins by changing learning rules. To see more clearly the effects of the neural network with a transfer function Linear Sigmoid axon throughout a call time, Figure 7-a plots the power consumed every 30s, Figure 7-b plots MOS every 30s. Simulation results indicate that the power consumed in MS can be reduced up to 3.75% with MOS more than 3.8.

Figure 4. Transfer function Tanh Axon a) Power consumption b) MOS

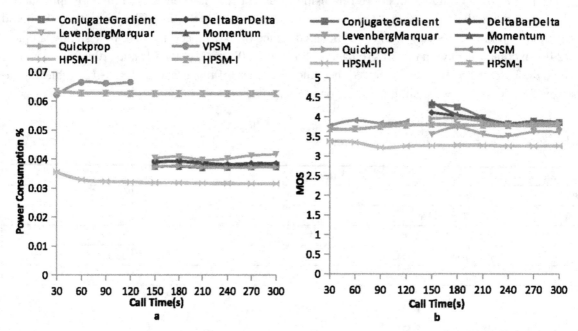

Figure 5. Transfer function Sigmoid Axon a) Power consumption b) MOS

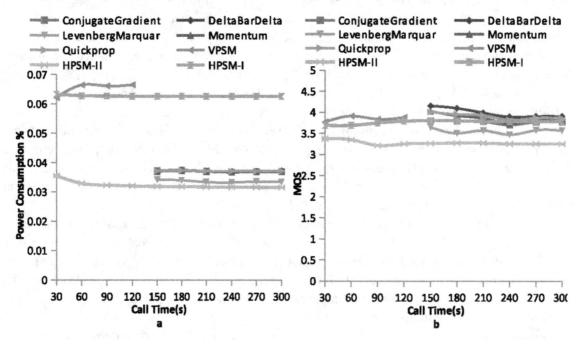

Figure 6. Transfer function Linear Tanh Axon a) Power consumption b) MOS

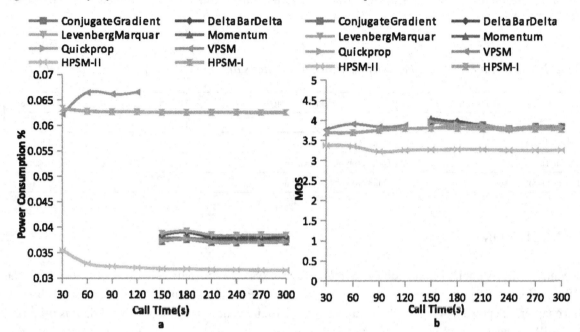

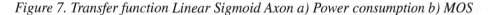

Figure 7. Transfer function Linear Sigmoid Axon a) Power consumption b) MOS

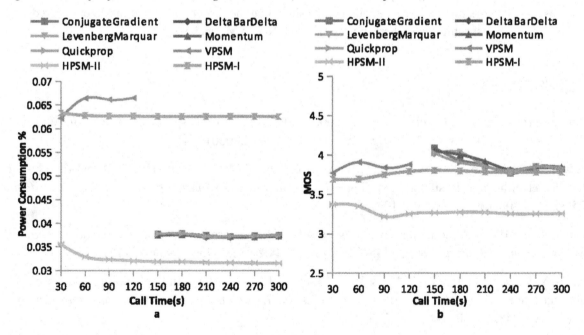

Table 3 summarizes the result achieved when various transfer functions are applied for the proposed ANN-VPSM.

Table 3. The result achieved when various transfer functions are applied for the proposed ANN-VPSM

Transfer Function	Best Learning Rule	Power Consumption	MOS
Tanh axon	Momentum	3.7%	3.8:4.2
Sigmoid axon	Quickprop	3.7%	3.8:4
Linear Tanh axon	Quickprop or Momentum	3.6%:3.7%	3.7:3.9
Linear Sigmoid axon	Quickprop or Momentum	3.7%	3.8:4

CONCLUSION

Recently, VoIP is applied in broadband wireless access systems for their voice services, therefore, the MS requires an effective power saving mechanism for VoIP services to increase its battery lifetime. In this chapter, the power saving mechanism based on artificial neural network (ANN-VPSM) is proposed for VoIP services over WiMAX systems. The proposed ANN-VPSM mechanism can maintain more power in mutual silent periods. The experimental findings indicate that ANN-VPSM can minimize the power consumed in MS efficiently. Furthermore, it can increase the utilization of the bandwidth and decrease the network traffic. Experimental results show that the power consumed in MS can be reduced up to 3.7% with respect to QoS when applying the ANN-VPSM mechanism.

REFERENCES

Abreu-Sernandez, V., & Garcia-Mateo, C. (2000). Adaptive multi-rate speech coder for VoIP transmission. *Electronics Letters*, *36*(23), 1978–1980. doi:10.1049/el:20001344

Adami, D., Callegari, C., Giordano, S., Pagano, M., & Pepe, T. (2012). Skype-Hunter: A real-time system for the detection and classification of Skype traffic. *International Journal of Communication Systems*, *25*(3), 386–403. doi:10.1002/dac.1247

Brady, P. T. (1969). A model for generating on-off speech patterns in two-way conversation. *The Bell System Technical Journal*, *48*(7), 2445–2472. doi:10.1002/j.1538-7305.1969.tb01181.x

Chen, Y. S., Deng, D. J., Hsu, Y. M., & Wang, S. D. (2012). Efficient uplink scheduling policy for variable bit rate traffic in IEEE 802.16 BWA systems. *International Journal of Communication Systems*, *25*(6), 734–748. doi:10.1002/dac.1206

Cheng, T. K., Wu, J. L. C., Yang, F. M., & Leu, J. S. (2014). IEEE 802.16e/m energy-efficient sleep-mode operation with delay limitation in multibroadcast services. *International Journal of Communication Systems*, *27*(1), 45–67. doi:10.1002/dac.2342

Choi, H. H., & Cho, D. H. (2007). Hybrid energy-saving algorithm considering silent periods of VoIP traffic for mobile WiMAX. *2007 IEEE International Conference on Communications*, 1-14, 5951-5956. 10.1109/ICC.2007.986

Choi, H. H., Lee, J. R., & Cho, D. H. (2007). Hybrid power saving mechanism for VoIP services with silence suppression in IEEE 802.16e systems. *IEEE Communications Letters*, *11*(5), 455–457. doi:10.1109/LCOMM.2007.070035

Choi, H. H., Lee, J. R., & Cho, D. H. (2009). On the Use of a Power-Saving Mode for Mobile VoIP Devices and Its Performance Evaluation. *IEEE Transactions on Consumer Electronics*, *55*(3), 1537–1545. doi:10.1109/TCE.2009.5278024

Cox, R. V., & Kroon, P. (1996). Low bit-rate speech coders for multimedia communication. *IEEE Communications Magazine*, *34*(12), 34–41. doi:10.1109/35.556484

Emara, T. Z. (2016). Maximizing Power Saving for VoIP over WiMAX Systems. *International Journal of Mobile Computing and Multimedia Communications*, *7*(1), 32–40. doi:10.4018/IJMCMC.2016010103

Emara, T. Z., Saleh, A. I., & Arafat, H. (2014). Power saving mechanism for VoIP services over WiMAX systems. *Wireless Networks*, *20*(5), 975–985. doi:10.100711276-013-0650-5

Estepa, A., Estepa, R., & Vozmediano, J. (2004). A new approach for VoIP traffic characterization. *IEEE Communications Letters*, *8*(10), 644–646. doi:10.1109/LCOMM.2004.835318

Ghosh, A., Wolter, D. R., Andrews, J. G., & Chen, R. H. (2005). Broadband wireless access with WiMax/802.16: Current performance benchmarks and future potential. *IEEE Communications Magazine*, *43*(2), 129–136. doi:10.1109/MCOM.2005.1391513

Hashimoto, M., Hasegawa, G., & Murata, M. (2015). An analysis of energy consumption for TCP data transfer with burst transmission over a wireless LAN. *International Journal of Communication Systems*, *28*(14), 1965–1986. doi:10.1002/dac.2832

Haykin, S. (2007). *Neural Networks: A Comprehensive Foundation* (3rd ed.). Prentice-Hall, Inc.

Hussain, T. H., Marimuthu, P. N., & Habib, S. J. (2014). Supporting multimedia applications through network redesign. *International Journal of Communication Systems*, *27*(3), 430–448. doi:10.1002/dac.2371

IEEE. (2006). IEEE Standard for Local and Metropolitan Area Networks Part 16: Air Interface for Fixed and Mobile Broadband Wireless Access Systems Amendment 2: Physical and Medium Access Control Layers for Combined Fixed and Mobile Operation in Licensed Bands and Corrigendum 1. In IEEE Std 802.16e-2005 and IEEE Std 802.16-2004/Cor 1-2005 (Amendment and Corrigendum to IEEE Std 802.16-2004) (pp. 0_1-822).

ITU-T. (1993). P.59: Artificial conversational speech. In ITU-T P.59 (03/93).

ITU-T. (2006). G.723.1: Dual rate speech coder for multimedia communications transmitting at 5.3 and 6.3 kbit/s. In ITU-T G.723.1 (05/06).

ITU-T. (2012). Coding of speech at 8 kbit/s using conjugate-structure algebraic-code-excited linear prediction (CS-ACELP). In ITU-T G.729

Jin, S., Chen, X., Qiao, D. J., & Choi, S. (2011). Adaptive sleep mode management in IEEE 802.16m wireless metropolitan area networks. *Computer Networks*, *55*(16), 3774–3783. doi:10.1016/j.comnet.2011.03.002

Kalle, R. K., Gupta, M., Bergman, A., Levy, E., Mohanty, S., Venkatachalam, M., & Das, D. (2010). Advanced Mechanisms for Sleep Mode Optimization of VoIP Traffic over IEEE 802.16m. *2010 IEEE Global Telecommunications Conference Globecom 2010*. 10.1109/GLOCOM.2010.5683895

Kao, S. J., & Chuang, C. C. (2012). Using GI-G-1 queuing model for rtPS performance evaluation in 802.16 networks. *International Journal of Communication Systems*, *25*(3), 314–327. doi:10.1002/dac.1242

Ke, S. C., Chen, Y. W., & Fang, H. A. (2014). An energy-saving-centric downlink scheduling scheme for WiMAX networks. *International Journal of Communication Systems*, *27*(11), 2518–2535. doi:10.1002/dac.2486

Lee, J., & Cho, D. (2008). An optimal power-saving class II for VoIP traffic and its performance evaluations in IEEE 802.16e. *Computer Communications*, *31*(14), 3204–3208. doi:10.1016/j.comcom.2008.04.029

Lee, J. R. (2007). A hybrid energy saving mechanism for VoIP traffic with silence suppression. *Network Control and Optimization. Proceedings*, *4465*, 296–304.

Lee, J. R., & Cho, D. H. (2009). Dual power-saving modes for voice over IP traffic supporting voice activity detection. *IET Communications*, *3*(7), 1239–1249. doi:10.1049/iet-com.2008.0300

Liao, W. H., & Yen, W. M. (2009). Power-saving scheduling with a QoS guarantee in a mobile WiMAX system. *Journal of Network and Computer Applications*, *32*(6), 1144–1152. doi:10.1016/j.jnca.2009.06.002

Lin, X. H., Liu, L., Wang, H., & Kwok, Y. K. (2011). On Exploiting the On-Off Characteristics of Human Speech to Conserve Energy for the Downlink VoIP in WiMAX Systems. *2011 7th International Wireless Communications and Mobile Computing Conference (Iwcmc)*, 337-342.

Namboodiri, V., & Gao, L. X. (2010). Energy-Efficient VoIP over Wireless LANs. *IEEE Transactions on Mobile Computing*, *9*(4), 566–581. doi:10.1109/TMC.2009.150

Nga, D. T. T., Kim, M. G., & Kang, M. (2007). Delay-guaranteed energy saving algorithm for the delay-sensitive applications in IEEE 802.16e systems 1339. *IEEE Transactions on Consumer Electronics*, *53*(4), 1339–1347. doi:10.1109/TCE.2007.4429222

Simoes, M. G., & Bose, B. K. (1995). Neural-Network-Based Estimation of Feedback Signals for a Vector Controlled Induction-Motor Drive. *IEEE Transactions on Industry Applications*, *31*(3), 620–629. doi:10.1109/28.382124

Teixeira, M. A., & Guardieiro, P. R. (2013). Adaptive packet scheduling for the uplink traffic in IEEE 802.16e networks. *International Journal of Communication Systems*, *26*(8), 1038–1053. doi:10.1002/dac.1390

Zubair, S., Fisal, N., Abazeed, M. B., Salihu, B. A., & Khan, A. S. (2015). Lightweight distributed geographical: A lightweight distributed protocol for virtual clustering in geographical forwarding cognitive radio sensor networks. *International Journal of Communication Systems*, *28*(1), 1–18. doi:10.1002/dac.2635

KEY TERMS AND DEFINITIONS

Base Station (BS): A BS is informed of the MS capabilities, security parameters, service flows, and full MAC context information. The MS transmits/receives data to/from the BS.

Mobile Station (MS): A station in the mobile service intended to be used while in motion or during halts at unspecified points. An MS is usually a subscriber station (SS).

Mutual Silence: The both sides of a conversation are in silence at the same moment.

Silent Insertion Descriptor (SID): For a VoIP conversation, if each side uses the speech codec with silence suppression functionality, the codec generates VoIP packets at specific times continuously during talking periods, while the packets are not generated during silent periods. Instead of that, it produces a SID packet. The SID is a small packet, in comparison with the voice packet. It contains only background noise information, which can help the receiving side's decoder to generate artificial noise during the silent period.

Speech Codec: An algorithm is designed to operate with a digital signal obtained by first performing telephone bandwidth filtering of the analog input signal, then sampling it.

Talk-Spurt: For at least one side of a conversation is talking at a moment.

Voice Over Internet Protocol: (VoIP): A service that allows users to communicate with each other through the internet. It has a lower expense compared with public switched telephone network (PSTN).

This research was previously published in Algorithms, Methods, and Applications in Mobile Computing and Communications; pages 158-177, copyright year 2019 by Engineering Science Reference (an imprint of IGI Global).

Chapter 23
Artificial Neural Network in Operation Management Regarding Communication Issue

Ayan Chatterjee
S. P. Jain Institute of Management and Research (SPJIMR), India

Susmita Sarkar
Bangabasi Evening College, India

Mahendra Rong
Bangabasi Evening College, India

Debmallya Chatterjee
 https://orcid.org/0000-0002-3395-691X
S. P. Jain Institute of Management and Research (SPJIMR), India

ABSTRACT

Communication issue in operation management is important concern in the age of 21st century. In opera-tion, communication can be described based on major three wings- Travelling Salesman Problem (TSP), Vehicle Routing Problem (VRP) and Transportation Problem (TP). Artificial Neural Network (ANN) is an important tool to handle these systems. In this chapter, different ANN based models are discussed in a comprehensive way. This chapter deals with how various approaches of ANN help to design the optimal communication network. This comprehensive study is important to the decision makers for the analytical consideration. Although there is a lot of development in this particular domain from a long time ago; but only the revolutionary contributed models are taken into account. Another motivation of this chapter is understanding the importance of ANN in the operation management area.

DOI: 10.4018/978-1-6684-2408-7.ch023

INTRODUCTION

Communication through a proper and optimal network by meeting demand in satisfactory level is an important part of decision-making in operation management. Proper and optimal network can be defined in a significant way. The term 'optimal' refers to optimization of cost, use of resources, like fuel, manpower etc. 'Proper' signifies congestion handling. More specifically, the term 'proper' follows the research question "How is congestion reduced in a specific network?" Considering these facts with different motivations and contexts, various decision-making models were developed in this area. Among all these models, ANN based models play a significant role for decision-making. In this chapter, a set of ANN based models are taken into account for analysing the efficacy of ANN as a tool. All the developed ANN based models are not taken as consideration. The specific models are selected based on three following criterion:

- Revolutionary change in goal over earlier models
- Revolutionary change in technical outcome
- Introducing a real scenario in modelling

Before going to the detail of the modelling analysis, a small outline of three major wings- Travelling Sales Problem (TSP), Vehicle Routing Problem (VRP) and Transportation Problem (TP) is given in the following:

Travelling Salesman Problem (TSP)

Travelling Salesman Problem is a combinatorial optimization problem as well as it is NP hard in nature. It is equally important in the area of operation research and operation management. The basic objective of this problem is to identify an optimal path for a traveller among a set of cities/nodes. Optimality of network can be described in terms of cost, time, distance etc. But in generally, optimization of cost is taken into account. The crucial assumption of this problem is that each city should be covered once only. Mathematical structure of TSP model is,

$$\text{Minimize } Z = \sum_i \sum_j c_{ij} X_{ij} \tag{1}$$

Subject to

$$\sum_i X_{ij} = 1 \; \forall j \tag{2}$$

$$\sum_j X_{ij} = 1 \; \forall i \tag{3}$$

$$X_{ij} \in \{0,1\} \tag{4}$$

The list notations and corresponding significance is given below:

c_{ij}: Cost of travelling through the edge (i,j)

$$X_{ij} = \begin{cases} 1, & \text{if the edge } (i, j) \text{ is considered in optimal network} \\ 0, & \text{otherwise} \end{cases}$$

Equation (1) denotes the objective function of TSP and that is minimization of total cost. Equations (2) and (3) ensure that each city is visited exactly once. Equation (4) represents that the only decision variable X_{ij} is binary in nature.

Transportation Problem (TP)

Transportation Problem (TP) is an optimization based problem. It is very much useful to connect the phases of supply chain. Also, it is useful to each phase of supply chain, i.e. in the cases of multiple production units, multiple retailing units, multiple warehouses etc. It is equally important to the critical issues of operation research. The objective of the problem is to minimize the transportation costs to ship goods from 'm' number of origins to 'n' number of destinations. Here, the transportation costs of goods from origins to destinations are given through a cost matrix. But there should be a balance between demand and supply of products. The LP structure of Transportation Problem is,

$$\text{Minimize } Z = \sum_i \sum_j d_{ij} X_{ij} \tag{5}$$

Subject to

$$\sum_j X_{ij} \leq S_i \ \forall i \tag{6}$$

$$\sum_i X_{ij} = d_j \ \forall j \tag{7}$$

$$X_{ij} \geq 0 \tag{8}$$

Here, d_{ij} represents cost of transportation of goods from *i-th* origin to *j-th* destination. Only decision variable X_{ij} is amount of goods to be transferred from *i-th* source to *j-th* destination. Objective (5) represents the minimization of cost. Constraints (6) and (7) represent the fulfillment of supply and demand of products respectively. Constraint (8) maintains feasibility condition of decision variable(s).

Vehicle Routing Problem (VRP)

Vehicle routing is also combinatorial optimization problem. It is very much realistic as well as it has wild range applications in present decade with different conditions and criterions. The objective of this problem is finding optimal set of ways for a finite set of vehicles to deliver a set of products to the customers properly. This is basically an extension of TSP. More particularly, objective function and constraints of TSP are same in VRP. Other assumptions of VRP are (i) balance between number of incoming and outgoing vehicles and (ii) capacities of vehicles must be greater than demand on each route. The particular NP hard problem is critical to handle in reality. The LP formulation of VRP is,

$$\text{Minimize } Z = \sum_i \sum_j d_{ij} X_{ij} \tag{9}$$

Subject to

$$\sum_i X_{ij} = 1 \ \forall j \tag{10}$$

$$\sum_j X_{ij} = 1 \ \forall i \tag{11}$$

$$\sum_i X_{i0} = K \tag{12}$$

$$\sum_j X_{0j} = K \tag{13}$$

$$\sum_i \sum_j X_{ij} \geq r(P) \tag{14}$$

$$X_{ij} \in \{0,1\} \tag{15}$$

Here, d_{ij} is cost of travelling by a single vehicle from *i-th* node to *j-th* node and the decision variable. X_{ij} determines that a particular edge is selected or not. Objective (9) represents minimization of vehicle traveling cost. Constraints (10) and (11) maintain the condition that each node is visited exactly once. Constraints (12) and (13) ensure that number of incoming and outgoing vehicles is same. Constraint (14) handles the condition that vehicle capacity on a particular path must be greater or equal to the demand of that route.

Artificial Neural Network (ANN) is a popular optimization tool in now a day. Actually different structures of Neural Network enhance the convergence of optimality in different ways. Also, in the area of operation management, decision makers can use the ANN based models for configuring the communication network corresponding to a particular firm. Among the techniques of ANN; Hopfield Network, co-adaptive network, Kohonen's network and Boltzman machines are popular most. The objective of the chapter is to develop a comprehensive analysis about the utilities of these specific neural network approaches with respect to the mentioned three fields.

Remaining parts of the chapter are maintained as follows: In the next section, a literature survey is developed on previous review articles of this field. After that different models are described with proper classification and analysis. At the end of the chapter, a conclusion is drawn with future direction of research in the field of communication management.

BACKGROUND

In the review article of artificial neural network based TSP models (Potvin, 1993), a comparative study is developed depending on three major architectures of neural network. These are elastic net, Hopfield Tank network and self-organizing map. TSP models are divided into two categories according to their implementation and performance. These are exact algorithms and heuristic algorithms. The major concern of this paper is to analyse the application of ANN in heuristic based themes. A thorough analysis of this paper says that Hopfield Tank network is not very much suitable to develop TSP models. But elastic net and self-organizing maps are better than that to find shortest way for a large number of cities.

Another important review (Daniel Graupe, 2001) is developed on TSP models using continuous Hopfield network. The objective of this paper is to develop a comparative study between Hopfield network and Kohonen self-organizing map in view of TSP models. In this development, it is shown that Hopfield network is better than Kohonen self-organizing map. This conclusion is drawn based on number of iterations to solve TSP models.

But these two previously mentioned reviews were developed in 1993 and 2001 respectively. After that some highly efficient TSP models are built up using ANN till today. In the proposed chapter, all such type of models are considered to analyse efficacy of ANN in TSP. But previously reviewed models are not excluded.

Another important field of communication management is Vehicle Routing Problem (VRP). A taxonomic review (Burak Eksioglu, 2009) was developed in the field of vehicle routing irrespective of tools and solution approaches. The main concern of this paper is how different solution approaches improve VRP. According to different application areas of VRP, the models are classified into some categories. The main attraction of the specific contribution is the synthesis of gradually improvement of VRP models using several approaches. But efficacy of neural network in this particular field was not analysed properly in this specific review article.

An excellent survey (M. Monica Subashini, 2014) was developed in the field neural network structure. In this particular contribution, different models of ANN are considered in comparative nature. These techniques are tested in the field Image processing. This particular paper is taken into account for choosing the required ANN models.

In the next section, the proposed discussion on communication management models is developed with suitable categorization.

Decision Making Models

In this section, different ANN based TSP, VRP and TP models are discussed with their corresponding unique efficiencies. For this purpose, 45 decision making models are collected from 29 different journals including conference proceedings. These models are selected based on technical efficiencies and consideration of significant realistic conditions. Among these, 8 are TSP models, 32 are VRP models, 1 is TP model and 4 are hybrid models. This categorization of models is listed in Table 1.

Table 1. Categorization of the communication management models wings wise

Models	TSP	VRP	TP
(Beasley, 2003)	✓		
(Hassan Ghaziri, 2003)	✓		
(Hui-Dong Jin, 2004)	✓		
(Junying Zhang, 2012)	✓		
(F. Jolai, 2010)	✓		
(Bert F. J. La Maire, 2012)	✓		
(Emile H.L. AARTS, 1989)	✓		
(Ricardo Insa Franco, 2016)		✓	
(Pedro M. Talavan, 2002)	✓		
(JEAN-YVES POTVIN, 1992)		✓	
(Jean-Yves Potvin, 1995)		✓	
(Linsen Chong, 2013)		✓	
(Xiaolei Ma, 2015)		✓	
(Weiliang Zeng, 2016)			✓
(Sina Dabiri, 2018)		✓	
(Jian Zheng, 2014)		✓	
(Peng, 2015)		✓	
(Abdolhamid Torki, 1997)		✓	
(Fabio Rafael Segundo, 2016)		✓	
(Koichi Maekawa, 2018)		✓	
(Georgios P. Mazarakis, 2007)		✓	
(Jae-Gon Kim, 2018)		✓	
(Nur E. Ozdemirel, 2000)		✓	
(Ke Song, 2018)		✓	
(Subramanya P. Nageshrao, 2017)		✓	
(Zhang Yi, 2016)	✓	✓	
(Jiaqiu Wang, 2016)	✓	✓	✓
(Irena Ištoka Otkovic, 2013)		✓	
(Aleksandar D. Jovanovic, 2014)		✓	
(Dragan Pamucar, 2014)		✓	
(Juan de Oña, 2014)		✓	
(Yajie Zou, 2018)		✓	
(Jian Zhang, 2018)		✓	

continues on following page

Table 1. Continued

Models	TSP	VRP	TP
(Nuno Coutinho, 2015)		✓	
(Zhang Lei, 2014)		✓	
(Douglas K.Swift, 2018)		✓	
(Hong Qu, 2012)		✓	✓
(LORENZO Mussone, 2013)		✓	✓
(Xiaogang Ruan, 2012)		✓	
(Zhongyi Zuo, 2014)		✓	
(Jittima Varagul, 2016)		✓	
(José S. C. Martini, 2017)		✓	
(Van-Suong Nguyen, 2018)		✓	
(Yang Zhao, 2016)		✓	
(Carl Goves, 2015)		✓	

TSP Models Using Artificial Neural Network

An important approach (Beasley, 2003) of TSP was developed considering the Euclidean distance among the pair of nodes. This particular model takes Co-Adaptive Net architecture of ANN. The speciality of this dignified approach is less time complexity with a huge number of nodes considerations. Actually, to find the shortest path by maintain all the principles of TSP with a huge number of cities, this particular model is developed. Experimentally, it is observed that this specific model is well suited up to consideration of 85,900 cities with less time and space requirement. Ultimately, this efficacy is much better in view of large data set handling in computation.

Another technique (Hassan Ghaziri, 2003) of TSP was developed by considering a backhaul condition. More specifically, all the visited customers are partitioned into two categories using Kohonen mapping network. Beginning side of the neurons represents line haul customers and the end side of neuron represents back haul customers. Uniqueness of this approach is development of two separate chains of neurons based new network architecture. In this particular case, four type interactions are considered. These are interaction of line haul customers in the first chain, interaction of backhaul customers in the second chain, interaction of the two chains together at the tails and interaction with the depot with the heads of two chains. As a result, it can be easily decided that the number of revisited customers in the next iteration. This chaining system enhances the procedure of finding two clusters easily iteration wise. Experimental analysis shows that it provides very good result up to 1000 customers' problem. This particular approach is developed based on SOFM (Self Organizing Feature Maps) 2 opt strategy. The limitation of this particular approach is failure of addressing non-Euclidean instances.

To reduce this problem, a TSP technique (Hui-Dong Jin, 2004) is developed using extended SOFM. This extension is dependent on two important properties of Operation Research (OR): neighbourhood preserving and the convex-hull properties. Specification of this approach is the closing property of excited neurons to input city and pushing these towards cooperative convex hull of the cities iteration wise. Efficiency of the scheme is analysed through both of theoretical and experimental ways. Experimentation is developed using standard data sets with various number of cities, ranging from 50 to 2400. This typical approach ensures that it is more efficient than some popular approaches, like- Budinich approach, KNIES algorithms and convex elastic net techniques. The complexity of this approach is very much less as well as it is sophisticated heuristic approach to handle a large amount of data set easily. Actually implicit property of convex hull with ESOM is implemented here to acquire topological neighbourhood among the preserved and inspected nodes of cities. As a result, it is tried to assure the necessary and sufficient conditions of optimal routes. So, it is observed that the particular approach is efficient logically; but it is not compared with some popular complicated heuristics approaches.

A particular methodology (Junying Zhang, 2012) of solving TSP is developed for symmetric Euclidean matrices. This novel approach is designed by combining two selective rules- overall and regional competition. These two competition methods are used to separate less competitive and more competitive neurons. More specifically, overall competition method is used to locate less competitive neurons and regional method is implemented to find more competitive neurons. After preparing the neurons priority wise, three important properties of operation research- preservation, convex hull and infiltration are used to find the optimal tour. The utility of infiltration is easily handling of complex TSP (both of symmetric and asymmetric cost matrices). Computational complexity of this approach is $O(N^3)$; N is the number of cities in a particular network.

Another efficient TSP technique (F. Jolai, 2010) is developed merging Hopfield network and data transformation. More specifically, logarithmic and z-score approaches are used as data transformations to enhance the efficacy of TSP over only using the Hopfield Network. Actually in Hopfield Network, only local optimum value is obtained. But inclusion of data transformation enhances the result to global optimum. This particular technique is tested with 10 cities and comparative analysis with other approaches shows the effectiveness of this particular scheme.

An innovative concept (Emile H.L. AARTS, 1989) is developed in the field of TSP with Boltzman machines. The idea of binary variable is introduced here to develop the decision making model. This is very much suitable to select a particular edge easily. The speciality of Boltzman structure is handling of the discrete models easily. Also, in the case of continuous problems, both of linear and quadratic forms are handled easily. The particular TSP model is developed on the basis of two consecutive approaches- (1) A Boltzman structure is selected in such a way that a particular TSP instance is directly mapped to the combinatorial structure and (2) the strength of connections are chosen in a specific manner such that cost function is represented with consensus function.

An important TSP model (Pedro M. Talavan, 2002) is developed by new types of parameter settings in Hopfield continuous network. Normally the drawback of Hopfield continuous network is occurrence of non-feasible solutions. More specifically, the trial-and-error approach brings a lot of non-feasible solutions in the optimal scenario. Here, some new parameters are introduced to ensure that an equilibrium point distinguishes an optimal feasible path. The particular enhancement is analysed through a set of 'n' cities, in both of using only CHN (Continuous Hopfield Network) and this extended model.

An important analytical review (Bert F. J. La Maire, 2012) is developed regarding Neural Network based TSP models. This particular analysis develops a comparative analysis of efficacy among Genetic Algorithm (GA), Hopfield Network and Kohonen Self Organizing Map. These three are basically taken into account due to soft computing efficiencies. Also, TSP is considered as NP complete in now a day. So, it is a good problem for analysing the efficacy of these three approaches. Ultimately, through various experiments it is observed that Self Organizing Map is efficient more among these three approaches.

VRP Models Using Artificial Neural Network

The vehicle routing problem (or demand responsive dial-a-ride problem) is concerned with the allocation of vehicles to service the customers properly. Decision making regarding dispatching of vehicles and corresponding crews is still dependent on manually expertise. From experience, it seems very difficult to develop model explicitly that expertise via a symbolic approach.

An alternative neural network model (JEAN-YVES POTVIN, 1992) is proposed as a sub-symbolic and empirical alternative for modelling the decision process of expert dispatchers. Preliminary results about the ability of the network to reproduce various decision rules are reported. This paper focuses on the problem: the dynamic dispatching of vehicles and crews. Utility of the neural network approach in this particular case is solved of dial-a-ride problems dynamically and feasibility of the dispatcher system. The flexibility of the neural network approach is very attractive in this context, because it can be trained in several dispatching platforms, and adapts them dynamically at the time of training phase.

A competitive neural network model (Jean-Yves Potvin, 1995) is developed to enhance the VRP with time windows. Basically, seed customers are identified over the whole distributed network properly. Here, ANN converges towards the centroid of clusters if such clusters are present. Here, the use of a competitive neural network during the initialization phase of an insertion heuristic for the Vehicle Routing Problem with Time Windows (VRPTW) is described. First, the neural network initialization is based on spatial considerations only. Better results are achieved by considering both spatial and temporal issues during the initialization phase. In this case, a third input unit relating to the time window at each customer would be added to the neural network. This specific approach of neural network is considered as ART network. Solomon's standard set is used for testing purpose.

A rule-based neural network model (Linsen Chong, 2013) is proposed to simulate driver behaviour in terms of lateral and longitudinal actions in two situations, car-following and safety critical events. The main attraction of this contribution is consideration of fuzzy for developing the rule based network. An approach of machine learning is introduced to mimic behaviour of individual driver. This particular method is equally applicable in both of homogeneous and heterogeneous data sets. Here, the importance of fuzzy logic is to divide reinforcement learning method and traffic state variables. The major extensions in this approach are inclusion of driver merging and lane changing behaviour.

Another model (Xiaolei Ma, 2015) on speed prediction is developed using a special type of neural network. This particular long short-term network is used to confine traffic dynamically in non-linear structure. The novelty of this model is automatic determination of optimal time lags with removing the error of back propagation.

In now a day, green vehicle routing is one of the most important research topics worldwide. A model (Sina Dabiri, 2018) is developed regarding this using convolution neural network. Here, this particular architecture is prepared with GPS trajectories. A channel is developed with four attributes (speed, acceleration, bearing and jerk). Then the large population segment is divided into small terms and it is prepared according to the model requirement of CNN. These small segments are handled individually and merging these solutions, ultimate path is obtained. The speciality of this methodology is obtaining more optimal result due to use of multiple layers iteration wise. The result is near about 84.8% accurate to the actual position. Another specification of this approach is removing the exposure to traffic and consideration of environmental conditions.

A great contribution (Jian Zheng, 2014) is developed for prediction of track changing decision of drivers using neural network architecture. The importance of this development are behavioural analysis of changing left and right track of the path. Also, path changing decision is considered in quantitative nature. This particular model is developed as multinomial model and the utility of this are estimation of model and validation checking. This is an initial enhancement in this particular field. So, the outcome of the model is not very well. Different experiments show that only 13.25% left track and 3.33% right track can be extracted correctly using this model.

To improve the accuracy of the particular model, another model (Peng, 2015) is developed with various criterions and different parameters. One of the most important parameter in this particular is time window and that is introduced here. Other considered parameters are visual search nature of drivers, vehicle operation, speed and condition of driving. The concept of back propagation together with neural network is used for predicting track changing behavior.

A self-organization Neural Network based VRP model (Abdolhamid Torki, 1997) is introduced in this paper for handling a group of Vehicle Routing Problems. Motivated by the outstanding performance of adaptive Neural Network approach in the Traveling Salesman Problem, an algorithm is devised to extend the domain of applicability of this approach to more complex problems. In this research, a new algorithm is designed based on SOFM for solving a class of routing problems. The simulation results demonstrate the capability of the algorithm to yield favourable solutions. Speciality of this particular model is that it is equally applicable to other type routing problems by a self-effacing modification.

A multi-copy routing strategy (Fabio Rafael Segundo, 2016) for a DTN built on the top of an Urban Bus Transportation System (UBTS) is presented with high efficiency. Using the buses as nodes, the contact history of nodes is used to improve the DTN communication. Depending on a journey predictor, a multi graph is built up in this formulation. The uniqueness of this approach is introducing minimal delay factor. Implementation of copy control algorithm enhances the concert of the system. In the UBTS context, the proposed multi-copy routing strategy outperforms the Max Prop strategy in terms of delivered messages, delivery rate, delivery delay, network load and cost of network messages per delivered message. The results indicate potential advantages of the ANN strategy over other ones in a real scenario.

A multi-scale simulation model with the pseudo-cracking method (Koichi Maekawa, 2018) is developed to estimate fatigue life of real RC bridge decks with a wide variety. An artificial neural network model is used for quick diagnosis for the remaining fatigue life at the site. The particular ANN model aims at quick but sound judgment equivalent to the pseudo-cracking method at the site.

In the model (Georgios P. Mazarakis, 2007) of signal processing work, the use of a time-domain encoding and feature extraction method is investigated to produce simple, fixed size matrices from complex acoustic and seismic signatures of vehicles for classification purposes. Classification is accomplished using an artificial Neural Network and a basic, L1 distance, archetype classifier and 8 bit microcontroller based sensor node. The TESPAR/FANN method provided high recognition rates between two types of vehicles using their acoustic and seismic signature. Different encoding alphabets have been tested and the effect on performance has been discussed. Classification performance is comparable with existing methods while computational cost is greatly reduced. A hardware implementation on a prototype wireless sensor node showed the effectiveness of that method to the vehicle classification task.

Another study (Jae-Gon Kim, 2018) proposes a neural network based predictive control (NNPC) approach that finds suitable weights for multiple factors dynamically so that the best performance of the intelligent parking guidance system can be achieved. This model enhances the efficiency of parking guidance system through dynamic control by selecting the parking lot in the best manner. Considering the fact that finding the best performance under public policy requires extensive processing time, the relatively low processing burden makes the proposed NNPC more applicable to real-time environments. Moreover, NNPC can adjust weight configurations in response to diverse parking environments.

A unique model (Nur E. Ozdemirel, 2000) of Automated Guided Vehicle routing is developed using the concept of artificial neural network. The main objective of this development is to find the shortest path for a single and free-ranging AGV that carry out more than one pick and deliver requests. This is NP hard in nature. Kohonen's self-organizing feature maps is developed to solve the problem. The developed algorithm outperforms the nearest neighbour rule for all request patterns and problem sizes in terms of the solution quality. But the nearest neighbour rule is always superior in computation time. A general result of these comparisons is that the algorithm provides good solutions within reasonable computation time for certain request patterns. The solution qualities for other patterns are acceptable but not as good. The main reason for this, is the unstable behaviour and that is considered as a major drawback also.

A learning vector quantization (LVQ) based neural network model (Ke Song, 2018) is developed for designing the driving patterns depending on the driving information of a vehicle. This multi-mode strategy shows the efficacy and it can automatically switch to the genetic algorithm under particular driving conditions depending on recognition results. The results show that the multi-mode energy management strategy can satisfy the needs of vehicle dynamic performance. And the energy management strategy can transform into a more suitable one based on driving conditions and produce a more economic performance than the thermostat strategy under the same dynamic conditions. In addition, a complex driving cycle is designed to verify the actual effect of this strategy MM_LVQ under complex driving conditions. The results show the efficacy under specific driving conditions. At the same time, the condition recognition effect helped the multi-mode strategy to adapt to real driving conditions.

An offline optimal charging strategic model (M. Gholami, 2013) is developed by taking the objective with minimizing the energy cost. This is done by exploiting the periodicity and predictable operation of the city buses. In this particular case, the actual demand of the energy of electric bus should be known and it has an important priority. A predictor is designed for addressing and the neural network model is capable to indicate the estimation of the energy demand of the next day. Three different optimal charging strategies are implemented using this. This shows considerable cost minimization i.e., capacity of charging the full battery at each available opportunity. A cost optimization between 32%− 54% is obtained at the time of comparing with the non-optimal strategy.

Another ANN based architecture (Douglas K.Swift, 2018) is developed to model and predict the traffic network. Application on the Connexion by Boeings (CBB) global broadband network was evaluated to establish feasibility. Exact classification and prediction regarding traffic network is very much essential for sizing network resource and for real-time network management. The purpose of this study was to examine whether or not network traffic on a large-scale broadband network could be modelled by adaptive, artificial intelligence, and computing techniques. The experimental results demonstrated that ANNs could indeed be used for network traffic modelling and have the potential for significant increases in accuracy and increased capability for adaptation.

A micro simulation based traffic model (Irena Ištoka Otkovic, 2013) represents the results of research on the applicability of neural networks in the process of computer calibration. VISSIM micro simulation model is used for calibration done at roundabouts in an urban area. It is developed on prediction of neural network for the traveling time between measuring points. Besides this, the process involves a comparison between the modelled and measured queue parameters at the initial level. The process of validation includes an analysis of traveling time and queue parameters on new sets of data gathered both at the modelled and at a new round about.

A neuro fuzzy approach (Aleksandar D. Jovanovic, 2014) is developed for authorities of local city with a serious effort to expand the number of low-greenhouse gas vehicles (green vehicles) at home. A system has been developed to optimize the green capacity in urban green vehicle routing. The objective of this paper is to propose a green vehicle distribution model in a public transportation network. The problem has been defined as a problem of non-linear optimization with dispersed input parameters, requiring neuro-fuzzy logic. An adaptive neural network was developed, taking into account the costs to be borne by operators and users, and the environmental parameters along the observed vehicle route. One of the advantages of this model is consideration of uncertainties in predicting the operator/passenger costs and environmental parameters. Besides, the model allows for planning the vehicle routes with the maximum of positive environmental effects, including reduced greenhouse gas emissions, and a better air quality in most densely populated areas.

Another model (Dragan Pamucar, 2014) of neuro fuzzy is built up for the routing of light delivery vehicles by logistics operators. The model takes into account the fact that logistics operators have a limited number of environmental friendly vehicles (EFV) available to them. At the time of defining a route, EFV vehicles and environmental unfriendly vehicles (EUV) are considered separately. For routing the particular model, an adaptive neural network is used to train by a simulated annealing algorithm. In this model, the input parameters are logistics operating costs, exhaust emissions and noise for the given vehicle route. This model has been developed to minimize air pollution, noise level and logistics operating costs. Although the benefits of using EFV are well-known, their introduction is gradual, and their optimal allocation on routes is very important, which gives the model presented here great practical significance. The practical value of this algorithm lies in the fact that the collected experience of a number of experts is incorporated into the model, thus avoiding a situation in which the routing of EFV is limited to the knowledge of individuals who find themselves in a position where they have to solve these problems alone.

A model (Juan de Oña, 2014) on service quality of public transportation is carried out using ANN. Here the service quality perceived by the passengers is analysed. The ANN is proposed in this research because of its numerous advantages over more traditional parametric models (such as regression models, structural equation models or logit/probit models), and other non-parametric models, such as decision trees. ANN allows to mitigate the inherent instability of ANN models, which is an important improvement in the ield of ''black-boxes'' techniques, to which ANN belong, since until now there is no consensus about what method of relative importance must be used for determining the variables relative importance.

A lane changing predictor based on Adaptive Fuzzy Neural Network (AFNN) model (Yajie Zou, 2018) is proposed to predict steering angles. The prediction model includes two parts: fuzzy neural network based on Takagi–Sugeno fuzzy inference, in which an improved Least Squares Estimator (LSE) is adopted to optimize parameters; and adaptive learning algorithm to update membership functions and rule base. The prediction results indicate effectiveness and stability of this model.

A neural network model (Jian Zhang, 2018) is employed with carefully selected traffic trajectory data. The virtual vehicle production is organized by a unique structure. The mobility model comes from the observed real-world traffic data, and is learnt by using a neural network. Differs from prediction in macro-level, detailed behaviours of vehicles is considered. Since the traffic flow is complicated and sensible may be faced in some unknown traffic situations, the mobility model is more reliable and produces more realistic traffic data than using a conventional car-following mode. A way is proposed on managing and organizing the vehicles that makes the proposed model to be executed efficiently. Finally, the presentation is implemented by employing the SUMO simulator.

An autonomous Quality of Experience management approach (Nuno Coutinho, 2015) is proposed for multiservice wireless mesh networks, where individual mesh nodes apply reinforcement learning methods to dynamically adjust their routing strategies. Within the forwarding nodes, a novel packet dropping strategy is developed that takes into account the impact on QoE. A novel source rate adaptation mechanism is considered here with the available network capacity. The introduction of source rate control improves further the QoE of each service types and for different WMN topologies. In addition, this approach exhibits a significantly smaller control traffic overhead.

A residual capacity estimation model (Zhang Lei, 2014) is built up based on an ANN. Both of charging and discharging current together with temperature are taken into account. This model comprises of three inputs (temperature, current and voltage) and one output (residual charge). The result shows that the proposed model can provide an accurate prediction of residual charge while maintaining good generalization capability. The established model can be used to precisely monitor the state of charge of the ultra-capacitors in ESS, and lays a reliable foundation for control strategy implementation and operation safety.

A method (Xiaogang Ruan, 2012) of realizing vehicle's photo taxis and negative photo taxis through a neural network is developed. A randomly generated network is used for computation purpose. During training only weights of the output units are changed during training.

An approach (Zhongyi Zuo, 2014) combining historical data and real-time situation information is developed to forecast the bus arrival time. This includes two phases: Radial Basis Function Neural Networks (RBFNN) model and an online oriented method. RBFNN is used to learn and to approximate the nonlinear relationship in historical data and online oriented method is introduced to adjust the actual situation. Ultimately, the system designing outline is given to summarize the structure and components of the system.

An algorithm (Jittima Varagul, 2016) is simulated for detecting object for Automated Guide Vehicle (AGV) guidance problem to avoid obstacle. This system is designed in security of internal transportation system to prevent collision. Depending on classification of obstacles, the system is designed. The obstacles recognition system using ANN with back-propagation learning algorithm by learning HOG features, 100% accuracy is achieved.

An adaptive biologically-inspired neural network model (José S. C. Martini, 2017) is made to receive the system state and is able to change the behaviour of the control scheme and order of semaphore phases. This particular adaptive control is evaluated on a single intersection scenario. The performance evaluation ensures that the model has higher adaptability and capacity than the previous traffic responsive control method, which is mainly attributed to its flexible and constant system monitoring and acting possibility.

A novel ANN controller (Van-Suong Nguyen, 2018) by using the head-up coordinate system is proposed to control automatically the ship into the berth in different ports without retraining the ANN structure. Numerical simulations are performed for two ports which verified the effectiveness of the proposed model.

A novel descriptor (Yang Zhao, 2016) is developed with road occupancy rate, for measuring campus trafdic congestion level and it is statistically proved to be the most effective descriptor among other descriptors. Markov model and back propagation neural network (BPNN), are combined with the proposed descriptors. Experimental results show that the proposed methods can achieve desirable performance for detecting trafdic congestion in campus, while the BPNN based method obtains more stable performance.

The results also point towards the importance of the proposed method for traffic congestion detection in campus.

By using Artificial Neural Networks (ANN), an excellent model (Carl Goves, 2015) is developed that 90% of the time predicts future traffic density 15 minutes into the future within 2.6 veh/km/lane of accuracy.

An energy consumption based ANN model (Ricardo Insa Franco, 2016) is developed to calculate the energy consumption of electric trains. It shows a good agreement with the target data. Output is compared with another subset of measured data and it provided a good estimation of the energy consumption with slight underestimation of negative energy peaks.

Transportation Model Using Artificial Neural Network

An ANN based transportation model (Weiliang Zeng, 2016) depending on theory of vehicle dynamics is developed to predict the vehicle CO_2 emission per kilometer and determine an eco-friendly path that results in minimum CO_2 emissions while satisfying travel time budget. The importance of this approach are-

(1) The relative importance analysis indicates that the average speed and average acceleration occupy 85.6% relative importance to the CO_2 emission model.

(2) Eco-friendly path offers significantly reduced CO_2 emissions at little cost in terms of increased travel time and the tours. On average, an eco-friendly path can reduce CO_2 emissions by 6.98%, 5.15%, and 10.17% relative to the observed path, the shortest distance path, and the least travel time path respectively.

(3) Compared to the observed path as selected empirically by the driver, the eco - friendly path offers significant advantage in terms of travel time(reducedby16.95%) and CO_2 emissions (reduced by 6.98%) though the travel distance is slightly longer (by 0.3 km).

(4) In an eco-routing experiment using all the observed OD pairs, it is found that the percentage of trips in which CO_2 emissions are reduced increases as the travel time buffer increases. Interestingly, when the travel time buffer reaches 10%, a certain degree of CO_2 emissions reduction is achieved for almost all trips.

(5) The average reduction in CO_2 emissions achieved by the eco-friendly path reaches a maximum of around 11% for trip OD distances between 6 km and 9 km and when the travel time buffer is around 10%. This indicates that setting a travel time buffer of 10% is appropriate for this eco-routing model, because this results in the greatest reduction in CO_2 emissions for the least cost in terms of travel time.

Hybrid Models Using Artificial Neural Network

A pulse coupled neural network model (Zhang Yi, 2016) is developed to find a single pair shortest path. A unique structure (on-forward/off-backward) is introduced to reduce the search space. In this mechanism, neighbourhood forward region is excited and backward region is inhibited at the time of firing a neuron. As a result, shortest path can be obtained quickly with less time complexity. Also, shortest path is involved in both of TSP and VRP. Therefore, it is considered in both these fields.

A space time delay network model (Jiaqiu Wang, 2016) is developed for merging temporal and spatial auto correlation of a network through both of local and dynamic approach. The concept of dynamic approach enhances the prediction of travel time efficiently.

Another modified continued pulse coupled network model (Hong Qu, 2012) was developed for large scale nonlinear shortest path computation. The idea of tree structure is used to handle the nonlinear structure. The specialty of the model is lateral connection among neurons through wave propagation. An approach (LORENZO Mussone, 2013) of multilayer forward network is developed to estimate Origin Destination (O-D) matrix of traffic. Here, the speciality is dynamic computation and due to that reason efficiency of the scheme is enhanced. Ultimately, missing data can be taken into account in this model for decision making.

CONCLUSION

In this critical review and discussion, three important categories (TSP, VRP and TP) of communication management are described shortly. Trends of research of these three particulars in last few years are realized properly. Moreover new policy enhancement, like- environment issue, zero carbon emission issue etc. are taken into consideration. From another view, the utility of artificial neural network can be comprehended properly in this particular research and development area. In the analysis of Potvin (Potvin, 1993), it was shown that ANN is not a sufficient approach in the area of communication management. But huge improvement ANN methodologies in last few years improve the decision making models with new policies efficiently.

FUTURE DIRECTION

Artificial Neural Network (ANN) is an important tool in the area of pattern recognition. In now a day, quantitative management research is using machine learning as a tool in different interdisciplinary fields, like- marketing, finance, human resource etc. Artificial Neural Network is also a part of machine learning. So, future researchers will be benefited by knowing about the different approaches of artificial neural network from this chapter. In view of optimization, researchers will be benefited from two sides- methods and applications. First, different methods of ANN that are discussed in this paper will give an overview about ANN regarding optimization. Second, the different application areas of optimization, like- VRP, TP and TSP can be enhanced in future by considering a lot of other real factors with other optimization models. That will also help to the researchers in the area of operation research and operation management.

REFERENCES

Abdolhamid Torki, S. S. (1997). A Competitive Neural Network Algorithm for Solving vehicle. *Computers & Industrial Engineering*, *33*(3-4), 473–476. doi:10.1016/S0360-8352(97)00171-X

Beasley, E. C. (2003). The co-adaptive neural network approach to the Euclidean Travelling Salesman Problem. *Neural Networks*, 1499–1525. PMID:14622879

Bert, F. J., & La Maire, V. M. (2012). Comparison of Neural Networks for Solving the. *11th Symposium on Neural Network Applications in Electrical Engineering* (pp. 21-24). Belgrade, Serbia: IEEE.

Coutinho, N., Matos, R., Marques, C., Reis, A., Sargento, S., Chakareski, J., & Kassler, A. (2015). Dynamic dual -reinforcement-learning routing strategies for quality of experience-aware wireless mesh networking. *Computer Networks*, *88*, 269–285. doi:10.1016/j.comnet.2015.06.016

Daniel Graupe, R. G. (2001). Implementation of traveling salesman's problem using neural network. *ECE 559 Neural Networks*.

de Oña, J. (2014). Neural networks for analyzing service quality in public transportation. *Expert Systems with Applications*, *41*(15), 6830–6838. doi:10.1016/j.eswa.2014.04.045

Eksioglu, B., Vural, A. V., & Reisman, A. (2009). The vehicle routing problem: A taxonomic review. *Computers & Industrial Engineering*, *57*(4), 1472–1483. doi:10.1016/j.cie.2009.05.009

Emile,, H. L., & Aarts, J. H. (1989). Boltzmann machines for travelling salesman problems. *European Journal of Operational Research*, 79–95.

Franco. (2016). Modelling electric trains energy consumption using Neural Networks. In *XII Conference on Transport Engineering, CIT, 7-9 June* (pp. 59 – 65). Valencia, Spain: Elsevier.

Gholami, M., Cai, N., & Brennan, R. W. (2013). An artificial neural network approach to the problem of wireless sensors. *Robotics and Computer-integrated Manufacturing*, *29*(1), 96–109. doi:10.1016/j.rcim.2012.07.006

Goves, C. (2015). Short term traffic prediction on the UK motorway network using neural networks. *European Transport Conference– from Sept-28 to Sept-30*, 184 – 195.

Hassan Ghaziri, I. H. (2003). A neural network algorithm for the traveling salesman problem with backhauls. *Computers & Industrial Engineering*, *44*(2), 267–281. doi:10.1016/S0360-8352(02)00179-1

Hui-Dong Jin, K.-S. L.-B. (2004). An expanding self-organizing neural network for the traveling salesman problem. *Neurocomputing*, 267–292.

Jean-Yves Potvin, C. R. (1995). Clustering for vehicle routing with a competitive neural network. *Neurocomputing*, *8*(2), 125–139. doi:10.1016/0925-2312(94)00012-H

Jian Zheng, K. S. (2014). Predicting driver's lane-changing decisions using a neural. *Simulation Modelling Practice and Theory*, *42*, 73–83. doi:10.1016/j.simpat.2013.12.007

Jolai, F., & Ghanbari, A. (2010). Integrating data transformation techniques with Hopfield neural networks for solving travelling salesman problem. *Expert Systems with Applications*, *37*(7), 5331–5335. doi:10.1016/j.eswa.2010.01.002

Jovanovic, A. D., Pamučar, D. S., & Pejčić-Tarle, S. (2014). Green vehicle routing in urban zones – A neuro-fuzzy approach. *Expert Systems with Applications*, *41*(7), 3189–3203. doi:10.1016/j.eswa.2013.11.015

Junying Zhang, X. B. (2012). An overall-regiona lcompetitive self-organizing map neural network for the Euclidean traveling salesman problem. *Neurocomputing*, *89*, 1–11. doi:10.1016/j.neucom.2011.11.024

Kim, J.-G. (2018). Dynamic control of intelligent parking guidance using neural network. *Computers & Industrial Engineering, 120*, 15–30. doi:10.1016/j.cie.2018.04.023

Lei, Z., W. Z. (2014). Residual Capacity Estimation for Ultracapacitors in Electric Vehicles Using Artificial Neural Network. *Proceedings of the 19th World Congress* (3899-3904). Cape Town, South Africa: The International Federation of Automatic Control. 10.3182/20140824-6-ZA-1003.00657

Linsen Chong, M. M. (2013). A rule-based neural network approach to model driver. *Transportation Research Part C, Emerging Technologies, 32*, 207–223. doi:10.1016/j.trc.2012.09.011

Maekawa, K. (2018). Remaining fatigue life assessment of in-service road bridge decks based. *Engineering Structures*, 602–616.

Martini. (2017). Adaptive traffic signal control based on bio-neural network. In *International Workshop on Adaptive Technology* (pp. 1182-1187). Elsevier.

Mazarakis, G. P., & Avaritsiotis, J. N. (2007). Vehicle classification in Sensor Networks using time-domain. *Microprocessors and Microsystems, 31*(6), 381–392. doi:10.1016/j.micpro.2007.02.005

Monica Subashini, M., & Sahoo, S. K. (2014). Pulse coupled neural networks and its applications. *Expert Systems with Applications, 41*(8), 3965–3974. doi:10.1016/j.eswa.2013.12.027

Mussone, L. (2013). OD Matrices Network Estimation from Link Counts by Neural Networks. *Journal of Transportation Systems Engineering and Information Technology, 13*(4), 84–93. doi:10.1016/S1570-6672(13)60117-8

Nguyen, V.-S. (2018). Artificial neural network controller for automatic ship berthing using head-up coordinate system. *International Journal of Naval Architecture and Ocean Engineering, 10*(3), 235–249. doi:10.1016/j.ijnaoe.2017.08.003

Otkovic, I. I. (2013). Calibration of microsimulation traffic model using neural network. *Expert Systems with Applications, 40*(15), 5965–5974. doi:10.1016/j.eswa.2013.05.003

Ozdemirel, N. E. (2000). A self-organizing neural network approach for the single AGV. *European Journal of Operational Research, 121*(1), 124–137. doi:10.1016/S0377-2217(99)00032-6

Pamucar, D. (2014). Green logistic vehicle routing problem: Routing light delivery vehicles in urban areas using a neuro-fuzzy model. *Expert Systems with Applications, 41*(9), 4245–4258. doi:10.1016/j.eswa.2014.01.005

Pedro, M., & Talavan, J. Y. (2002). Parameter setting of the Hopfield Network applied to TSP. *Neural Networks*, 363–373. PMID:12125891

Peng, J., Guo, Y., Fu, R., Yuan, W., & Wang, C. (2015). Multi-parameter prediction of drivers' lane-changing behaviour with. *Applied Ergonomics, 50*, 207–217. doi:10.1016/j.apergo.2015.03.017 PMID:25959336

Potvin, Y. S.-M. (1992). Neural networks for automated vehicle dispatching. *Computers Ops Res.*, 267-276.

Potvin, J.-Y. (1993). The Traveling Salesman Problem:A Neural Network Perspective. *ORSA Journal on Computing*, 1–60.

Qu, H., Yang, S. X., Yi, Z., & Wang, X. (2012). A novel neural network method for shortest path tree computation. *Applied Soft Computing, 12*(10), 3246–3259. doi:10.1016/j.asoc.2012.05.007

Ruan, X. L. D. (2012). Vehicle Study with Neural Networks. Physics Procedia, 25, 814 – 821.

Segundo, F. R. (2016). A DTN routing strategy based on neura lnetworks fo rurban bus. *Journal of Network and Computer Applications*, 216–228. doi:10.1016/j.jnca.2016.02.002

Sina Dabiri, K. H. (2018). Inferring transportation modes from GPS trajectories using a. *Transportation Research Part C, Emerging Technologies, 86*, 360–371. doi:10.1016/j.trc.2017.11.021

Song, K., Li, F., Hu, X., He, L., Niu, W., Lu, S., & Zhang, T. (2018). Multi-mode energy management strategy for fuel cell electric vehicles based. *Journal of Power Sources, 389*, 230–239. doi:10.1016/j.jpowsour.2018.04.024

Subramanya, P., & Nageshrao, J. J. (2017). *Charging cost optimization for EV buses. In International Federation of Automatic Control.* Elsevier.

Swift, D. K., & Dagli, C. H. (2018). A study on the network traffic of Connexion by Boeing:Modeling with artificial neural networks. *Engineering Applications of Artificial Intelligence, 21*(8), 1113–1129. doi:10.1016/j.engappai.2008.04.019

Varagul, J. (2016). Simulation of Detecting Function object for AGV using Computer Vision with Neural Network. In *20th International Conference on Knowledge Based and Intelligent Information and Engineering Systems* (pp. 159 – 168). Elsevier. 10.1016/j.procs.2016.08.122

Wang, J., Tsapakis, I., & Zhong, C. (2016). A space–time delay neural network model for travel time prediction. *Engineering Applications of Artificial Intelligence, 52*, 145–160. doi:10.1016/j.engappai.2016.02.012

Weiliang Zeng, T. M. (2016). Prediction of vehicle CO2 emission and its application. *Transportation Research Part C, Emerging Technologies, 68*, 194–214. doi:10.1016/j.trc.2016.04.007

Xiaolei Ma, Z. T. (2015). Long short-term memory neural network for traffic speed. *Transportation Research Part C, Emerging Technologies*, 187–197.

Yi, Z. (2016). Shortest path computation using pulse-coupled neural networks with restricted autowave. *Knowledge-Based Systems*, 1–11.

Zhang, J., & El Kamel, A. (2018). Virtual traffic simulation with neural network learned mobility model. *Advances in Engineering Software, 115*, 103–111. doi:10.1016/j.advengsoft.2017.09.002

Zhao. (2016). Research on campus traffic congestion detection using BP neural network and Markov model. *Journal of Information Security and Applications, 31*, 54-60.

Zou, Y. (2018). Lane-changes prediction based on adaptive fuzzy neural network. *Expert Systems with Applications, 91*, 452–463. doi:10.1016/j.eswa.2017.09.025

Zuo, Z. (2014). Bus Arrival Time Prediction Using RBF Neural Networks Adjusted by Online Data. In *The 9th International Conference on Traffic & Transportation Studies (ICTTS'2014)* (pp. 67 – 75). Elsevier.

KEY TERMS AND DEFINITIONS

Artificial Neural Network: A framework for handling machine learning procedures critically. More specifically, it is one of the best ways to realize a certain pattern automatically.

Communication Management: Organization of communication through vehicles properly with meeting the demand in an optimal way.

Transportation Problem: TP is management of production unit to retailing market in an optimal way such that cost is minimized and maximum amount of resources can be utilized.

Travelling Salesman Problem: TSP is a NP hard problem to find the shortest path in a particular network with covering all the nodes.

Vehicle Routing Problem: VRP is an extension of TSP. It is basically routing/scheduling of a set of different type vehicles in a specific network.

This research was previously published in the Encyclopedia of Organizational Knowledge, Administration, and Technology; pages 2303-2320, copyright year 2021 by Business Science Reference (an imprint of IGI Global).

Index

A

P

Paced 933, 939, 1249

Pancreatic Cyst 867, 876

pancreatic cystadenocarcinomas 868

parameter free surrogate 749, 752-753, 761-762, 767, 772, 776

Parameter Optimization 166-167, 194, 840, 1171, 1311

Particle Swarm Optimization (PSO) Algorithm 30, 167, 170, 195-198, 206, 227-228, 239-240, 703, 724-726, 728-729, 744, 804-805, 807-808, 817, 820-821, 823, 827-828, 833, 838, 850, 863, 915, 931, 951, 953, 967, 1059, 1121, 1171, 1301-1303, 1306-1307, 1310-1312, 1424, 1428, 1447, 1477, 1556

Pattern finding 669

Pattern Recognition 34, 38, 64, 70, 79, 137, 166, 203-204, 223, 281, 304, 325, 350, 356, 359-361, 371-373, 437, 504, 630, 637, 646-647, 654, 669, 672-673, 682-683, 685-686, 698-701, 781, 789, 800, 839, 849, 853, 876, 882, 886, 916, 932, 947, 967, 1010, 1040, 1156, 1268, 1291, 1314, 1362, 1420, 1455, 1507, 1511, 1520-1521, 1572, 1574

Payload 1522, 1528-1529

PCA 103, 189, 326, 543, 612, 614, 620-625, 628, 681, 685, 705, 1416

Peak Signal-To-Noise Ratio (PSNR) 922, 1157, 1168, 1522-1523, 1528, 1531

Peak-Current 824, 827-828, 833, 838

Pearsons's Correlation Coefficient 1130

Performance Evaluation 189, 220, 223, 425, 482, 487-488, 502, 606, 619, 706, 717, 947, 1075, 1105, 1142, 1154-1155, 1254, 1259, 1297-1298, 1449-1452, 1455-1457, 1461, 1467, 1537

photocatalysis 1313-1314, 1316-1318, 1320, 1322, 1329, 1332

Piece-Wise Linear Approximation 283

Polynomial Regression 1052, 1057, 1063, 1071, 1074, 1325, 1327, 1329

Pooling Layer 7, 100, 890, 896, 902, 1495, 1565, 1575

portfolio inflows 1427-1430, 1435, 1437-1438, 1440, 1442-1445, 1448

POTENTIAL CONFLICT SITUATION 1334, 1338

Power Consumption 471-472, 482, 484-485, 821, 1479, 1488, 1510-1511, 1517

power factor 440-442, 446, 450, 455, 458, 462, 464, 466

power saving 471-473, 475, 486-487

precipitation estimation 242, 245, 261, 264

Precipitation Sliding Window Period 242, 244, 249

Precision 29, 186, 207, 266-267, 269, 271-280, 330, 357, 370, 458, 599, 619, 675, 677, 708, 717-718,

720-721, 723, 754, 804-806, 825, 840-841, 934, 968, 1016, 1019-1020, 1022, 1030, 1284, 1422, 1428, 1431, 1465, 1471, 1473, 1502, 1510, 1514, 1516-1517, 1520

precursor 867-868, 874

Prediction 1, 3, 27, 46, 63-64, 68, 70-72, 74-77, 82-83, 89-90, 102, 109, 137-139, 151, 156-157, 160, 163-164, 166, 168, 173-176, 178-180, 184, 186, 188-189, 194-199, 204, 207, 223, 266-268, 277, 280-281, 283, 287, 295, 305, 308-309, 318, 329, 338-339, 353, 372-373, 377, 379, 381-382, 394, 402-404, 418, 421, 423-424, 427, 430, 433-434, 436-439, 452, 466, 472, 475, 480, 487, 498-502, 504-507, 512-513, 515, 517-519, 528, 531, 534, 538, 545, 555, 573-574, 582, 589, 596, 597-600, 602-611, 630-631, 635, 647-648, 651, 654, 664, 667, 677, 688, 692, 743, 749, 752-754, 761-762, 777, 780-782, 805, 808, 820, 834, 838-839, 850, 863, 865-866, 868-870, 872-875, 877-878, 882, 885, 888, 895, 898, 900, 902, 909, 912, 914, 932, 936, 952, 958, 967-973, 975, 980, 984-986, 988-990, 994, 1003-1005, 1009-1010, 1019-1020, 1022-1023, 1028-1029, 1049, 1055-1057, 1063, 1065, 1071-1080, 1084-1085, 1088-1096, 1115, 1118-1119, 1122, 1126-1128, 1130, 1132, 1134-1136, 1139, 1141, 1143-1145, 1171-1172, 1174, 1176-1181, 1188-1193, 1197-1198, 1202, 1207, 1210-1216, 1223, 1240-1241, 1251, 1257, 1259, 1261, 1271, 1283-1284, 1287-1289, 1291, 1296-1298, 1300, 1302, 1328, 1330-1331, 1337, 1362-1364, 1366-1367, 1377-1381, 1404, 1414-1418, 1420, 1422, 1424-1425, 1429, 1446-1447, 1457, 1459, 1467, 1469, 1488-1489, 1494-1495, 1498, 1500-1502, 1504-1506, 1508, 1510-1511, 1513, 1517, 1520-1521, 1532-1535, 1537, 1540-1542, 1546, 1550-1552, 1555-1558, 1563

Preventricular Contraction (PVC) 939

Process Parameters 330, 405, 699, 806, 808-809, 812, 820-821, 824, 827, 830, 834, 838-841, 846, 849-850, 855-858, 864, 866

prognostic 1132, 1491, 1496, 1498, 1509

Project Management 328, 509-510, 512, 514-515, 527, 530-540, 1115, 1242, 1244

Pros and Cons of ANN 31, 37

pull factors 1427, 1443, 1445

Pulse Off time 824, 826-828, 833, 838

Pulse-On Time 824-825, 828, 833, 838

push factor 1427, 1442, 1445

PWM-rectifier 441-442, 462, 465-466

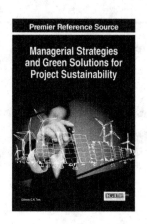

www.igi-global.com

Publisher of Peer-Reviewed, Timely, and
Innovative Academic Research Since 1988

IGI Global's Transformative Open Access (OA) Model:
How to Turn Your University Library's Database Acquisitions Into a Source of OA Funding

Well in advance of Plan S, IGI Global unveiled their OA Fee Waiver (Read & Publish) Initiative. Under this initiative, librarians who invest in IGI Global's InfoSci-Books and/or InfoSci-Journals databases will be able to subsidize their patrons' OA article processing charges (APCs) when their work is submitted and accepted (after the peer review process) into an IGI Global journal.

How Does it Work?

Step 1: **Library Invests in the InfoSci-Databases:** A library perpetually purchases or subscribes to the InfoSci-Books, InfoSci-Journals, or discipline/subject databases.

Step 2: **IGI Global Matches the Library Investment with OA Subsidies Fund:** IGI Global provides a fund to go towards subsidizing the OA APCs for the library's patrons.

Step 3: **Patron of the Library is Accepted into IGI Global Journal (After Peer Review):** When a patron's paper is accepted into an IGI Global journal, they option to have their paper published under a traditional publishing model or as OA.

Step 4: **IGI Global Will Deduct APC Cost from OA Subsidies Fund:** If the author decides to publish under OA, the OA APC fee will be deducted from the OA subsidies fund.

Step 5: **Author's Work Becomes Freely Available:** The patron's work will be freely available under CC BY copyright license, enabling them to share it freely with the academic community.

Note: *This fund will be offered on an annual basis and will renew as the subscription is renewed for each year thereafter. IGI Global will manage the fund and award the APC waivers unless the librarian has a preference as to how the funds should be managed.*

Hear From the Experts on This Initiative:

"I'm very happy to have been able to make one of my recent research contributions *freely available* along with having access to the *valuable resources* found within IGI Global's InfoSci-Journals database."

– Prof. Stuart Palmer,
Deakin University, Australia

"Receiving the support from IGI Global's OA Fee Waiver Initiative *encourages me to continue my research work without any hesitation*."

– Prof. Wenlong Liu, College of Economics and Management at Nanjing University of Aeronautics & Astronautics, China

For More Information, Scan the QR Code or Contact:
IGI Global's Digital Resources Team at eresources@igi-global.com.

Printed in the United States
by Baker & Taylor Publisher Services